THE THEATRE
AND ITS DRAMA

THE THEATRE AND ITS DRAMA

Principles and Practices

Ralph Borden Culp

University of Texas at El Paso

WM. C. BROWN COMPANY PUBLISHERS
Dubuque, Iowa

Contents

Prologue   vii

1 The Theatrical Image   1

2 The Theatre and Human Affairs   93

3 Playhouses and People   165

4 Mountebanks and Players   183

5 Playwrights and Playwriting   285

6 Directors and Producers   347

7 Designers and Managers   371

8 Children's Theatre and Creative Dramatics   403

9 Reviewers and Critics   417

Epilogue   429

Glossary   433

Index   441

FOR BETTY

This book is for people who like to play. It presumes that one man in his time plays many parts and that the most important of these is the act of playing itself. He performs this act because he must imitate the world he sees, impose his sense of order upon it, and dramatize his life-long struggle to survive in a hostile environment. Basically he is an actor performing the dreams in his head, but he is also playwright, director, scene designer, and audience. He is his own reviewer and critic, too.

This book is also for students and teachers who like to examine the ways in which people use the theatre to portray their dreams. The ideas in the book are not especially new, but they bear repeating in this day of "happenings" and "mixed-media" techniques that seem so revolutionary to the adolescents who are touting them. What is really exciting about *Laugh-In, Hair, Oh! Calcutta!*, or *The Persecution and Assassination of Jean-Paul Marat as Performed by the Inmates of the Asylum at Charenton Under the Direction of the Marquis de Sade* is not their techniques—which are at least as old as Thespis—but the rebirth of theatre as the heart of a community which these and other audience-participation, story-less, and mind-blowing theatrical experiences may possibly signify. If so, then once again the children shall lead us.

To say the *au courant* ideas of total theatre, living theatre, and orgi-astic theatre are ancient and honorable practices is not thereby to attack them. The establishment—whatever that is, in art or life—can always find reason enough to destroy ideas that seem to break with tradition. Yet the fact remains that what is now praised in theatrical capitals of the world —and also blamed—is nothing less than a return to the first principles and practices of theatre. Sophocles on the Aegean knew them well, and so did Shakespeare and Jean-Baptiste Poquelin. All that is being changed is the dominant motif of the last hundred years or so—the slice-of-life theatre. The so-called theatre of the absurd, theatre of cruelty, and theatre of participation signify principally a return to the concept of theatre as *symbol* rather than *life*. That is to say, nothing is being changed except our way of approaching and talking about the art of theatre.

A study of this complicated art in one book can be only an "introduction." The aim of this book is to discover principles through the study of practices that have worked in live situations. The procedures and approaches that are shown to a drama or a production are necessarily personal rather than general. They are meant to show *a* method, not *the* method, and thereby exemplify the principle being discussed. The reader is made to play many parts as he goes through the book: audience, historian, architect, actor, playwright, director, and so forth. The parts may be taken in any order, and the ideas studied in any sequence, but the present arrangement has proved itself through many semesters of teaching.

Although theatre is a unitary art with many interlocking elements, it is also a composite of many artistic contributions. The work of each contributor is studied in a separate chapter. There are nine of these, an epilogue, and a glossary. First the basic elements of theatre are considered. Then the theatre is examined as a participant in human affairs. After this, a series of chapters deals with the principles and techniques of creating theatre. These chapters focus collectively on "how a play means." All the artists, that is, share a common esthetic but from a slightly different technical point of view. Next the ever-new and newly exciting world of children's theatre and creative dramatics is examined in a chapter. And finally the reviewers and critics who so often determine not only what is going on in a play—their legitimate function—but also what it is and how the audience should react to it are treated in a brusque but fair analysis of their role in the human affair called theatre.

Some chapters have a play accompanying them to represent the particular aspect of drama and theatre being studied in that chapter. Other chapters, for obvious reasons, do not require a playscript to develop their subjects fully. At the close, there is an epilogue which restates the main ideas from all the chapters. The terms and points of view necessary for such an introduction to theatre are defined in a glossary.

Such a book, like the man who prepares it, is the result of many people's work and love. First of all there are the teachers, artists, and critics who shaped the man who now creates a book in their honor. It is only fair, in a day when teachers must strike to receive their just rewards, to mention Nell Miles, Willy Robertson, and Clinton Cone—among others who made school a pleasure and learning a delight, and who did not think it terrible to profess man and his theatre. The ideas in this book came from all of them, but especially from The Reverend Gilbert V. Hartke, O. P., and H. Darkes Albright, from Edyth Renshaw and George A. McCalmon, and from Milton Lyon. It is hoped their views are presented with some of the style and grace they themselves revealed.

The ideas have always been with us. Understanding came through the *Poetics* and the *Rhetoric* of Aristotle, and particularly through the guidance of Lane Cooper, Harry Caplan, Francis Fergusson, and Alan

Downer. The work of these men informs many of the pages which follow. They, and many others unnamed here, are cited in the lists of suggested readings at the close of each chapter. Let the bare titles represent my homage to them.

There are also the personal sources of this book to be acknowledged. There is Betty O'Bannon Culp, who more than anyone else encouraged the writing, and there are the children—Helen, Elizabeth, Richard, and Jeffrey—who made *not* writing a pleasure, but who allowed enough free time to finish the manuscript. And there are Harry and Martha Culp, and Shirley Buckingham—grandparents extraordinary—and Bertram and Jo Borden Culp, a father and a mother who were first of all my friends. And there are Dick Crews, an editor and a half, and Judith Wallis, whose illustrations brighten many dark corners in the book and whose comments helped more than she knew, and David Weiss, whose thoughtful review of the manuscript caused the book to be a good deal better than it might have been.

And finally there are my students, and their friends, who have been willing to die in battle for the rest of us. And most especially there is First Lieutenant Richard Corey King, who said of an impossible mission, "Hell, I'll take it. Someone has to do it," and who died "By Order of the Commander."

What there is that may be called good in this book these people made: "God send me to see suche a company together agayne when need is."

The drama's laws the drama's patrons give.

SAMUEL JOHNSON

Chapter 1

The Theatrical Image

When was the last time you went to a play? Can you recall what happened? Were you thrilled or bored? More important, perhaps, can you recall why you went? If you are a student, the chances are you were required to attend. It is a sad fact that, on the whole, you and your friends do not have the playgoing habit. The movie habit, yes; television, yes. But plays, no. Football games, basketball games, almost any spectator sport—most assuredly. Theatre games—not if you can help it.

Thus, given a choice, you may avoid drama and theatre. If you make this negation, however, you cut yourself off from man's oldest and most thrilling artistic experience. Properly attended—meaning you go because you want to—and properly presented, theatre offers the only honest-to-God multi-dimensional experience of your true self—and the world you live in—that you can find. All other arts, regardless of their virtues, are pale copies of theatre.

Yet if you have kicked the habit of centuries—the pleasure of drama and theatre—who is to blame? A little reading, or a talk with your teacher, would uncover a number of villains: the real estate magnate who owns a theatre building, the ticket brokers, the craft unions, Hollywood, or the decay of urban culture. Perhaps even the people who would like to earn their living in the theatre or through textbooks that tell you what it is—perhaps even these devotees are at fault.

No doubt theatre artists and teachers of drama will resist seeing themselves as contributors to the present unpopularity of theatre. Yet, to cite one example, a play was nearly stopped recently because a baby was crying in the audience. One of the actors was heard to remark, "They don't know how to behave at a play in this town." At another production, a children's play being watched by 1500 raucous sub-teenagers who were behaving much as they would at a circus or a basketball game, the play's director threw up his hands and exclaimed, "I'll never do another play

1

for these barbarians." Mothers and fathers in the audience also objected to the rowdy atmosphere, and several actors were incensed that their work was not met with reverent silence broken by loud but polite applause "at the proper places."

Teachers often discourage playgoing by excessive concern with "scholarship." If you were required to attend that last play you saw, no doubt you were tested on it when you returned to class. The test probably contained questions like "What kind of person is Rosalind?" or "In what ways is Jacques representative of the Elizabethan idea of melancholia?" Following these questions, the test might have asked "To what extent can *Othello* be considered 'tragic farce' rather than 'tragedy'?" or "In what ways is *Death of a Salesman* Aristotelian tragedy?" Perhaps there was even a question like "How did the setting help develop the playwright's central idea?"

And so it goes. From the very beginning of theatre as we know it, certain people have insisted that plays must contain moral doctrine or must in some way perform socially useful work. Even when plays have been viewed as responsible for some kind of healthy catharsis, the ideas or the subjects portrayed have been thought to cause the desired reaction. According to this theory, the central idea of *Oedipus the King* makes it a better drama than *Barefoot in the Park*.

As a result, fewer and fewer people have gone to plays willingly and joyously. Theatre artists who view drama as a means of achieving social prominence have found themselves without a livelihood. Teachers who for the most part love drama more than anything else in the world have had to force students to attend plays. Theatre-going has become a chore, a social obligation, a cultural function undergone for reasons alien to enjoyment. If the liveliness and the excitement—the wonder—of theatre disappear, the theatre itself will follow.

This book focuses on the wonder of theatre. No attempt is made to establish that theatre-going is a ritual, a religious experience, or a cultural advantage no sophisticated community should be without. There is no desire to make you behave and dress formally, sit quietly and be enlightened, or recognize the "art of theatre" and support it with your money and time.

Rather, this book asserts that theatre should be a game people play because they have fun doing it. All human activities are ritualistic, the game of theatre as much as anything else. This game can have religious or psychological significance, or deal with important subjects, but there is no law that says it has to. The game is its own reason for being.

The theatre is nevertheless a peculiar sort of game. With the help of a special kind of space—though any space will do—a group of spectators makes "imaginary puissance"—to borrow Shakespeare's comely phrase. The audience joins with a company of players to become "ciphers in this great accompt." What is accomplished is an image of the world and all that dwell therein. This image is metaphorical, or figurative, rather than literal or factual. It is nonlogical. It can only be felt while experiencing the play that expresses the image.

There are five elements in this experience: the audience, the dramatic construct, the *dramatis personae*, the language, and the dramatic environment. Many persons collaborate to perform this alchemy of wonder, but chiefly it is the audience whose thoughts must dress the stage.

The Audience

Whatever else is necessary for a play to happen, the audience is the primary element of theatre. Although it is possible to consider one person an audience, usually the term signifies a sizeable number of people gathered in some way about a space for performers.

Imagine yourself in just such a group. You and your friends are facing a stage on which a talented cast is performing *Othello*. The play is exciting, and you are hanging breathlessly on every moment. At the point of greatest suspense, however, the Beatles start one of their numbers behind you in the theatre. Everyone in the audience turns around to watch and listen, and maybe begins to dance. What then has happened to *Othello*? Does the Noble Moor who "loved not wisely but too well" and "in Aleppo once, where a malignant and a turbaned Turk beat a Venetian and traduced the state, took by the throat the circumcised dog and smote him—thus" exist any longer? Without you the audience, can there be a play at all?

Perhaps you believe your importance to a play is so obvious we need not discuss it. Yet many teachers, students, and even producers of drama and theatre seem to behave as if the public did not exist at all—or at best consisted of unenlightened fools who must be patronized and educated.

The opposite view informs this book. As Samuel Johnson phrased it, "the drama's laws the drama's patrons give." A play is created not by the performers onstage but by the spectators surrounding the stage, though of course both groups must always be present. Two broad principles seem to be at work here. Theatre is a game people play, and they employ a number of psychological processes to achieve their theatrical games.

People play games, of course, for several reasons. First of all, they are fun. They give pleasure. They provide refreshment after toil. More than this, or perhaps an important reason for the pleasure, they allow people to imitate the world around them, to impose their sense of order upon it, and to explore vicariously all the wild and impossible dreams in their heads. People play games to dramatize their lifelong struggle with a hostile environment.

They attend the theatre, when not coerced, for much the same reasons. From the comfort of their seats they let their imaginations loose.

They identify with the activities onstage, project their deepest feelings upon these impossible happenings, and imitate all manner of beasts.

This game of theatre involves at least seven of these psychological processes: attention, impersonation, identification, rationalization, projection, distancing, and imitation. The *process of attention* has been variously described, but the following is an acceptable definition:

> *Attention* is a neuromuscular process in which the total sensory and associative apparatus of an individual is focused on a single stimulus out of the many stimuli impinging on him at a given moment.

The process may be voluntary or involuntary, conscious or unconscious—or, in each instance, both simultaneously. What seems to happen in ordinary situations is that you and I carry into every situation both a capacity to respond objectively to it as a "perceiving apparatus" and a unique set of human preconceptions about it. Any stimulus either so forceful or so different from preceding or surrounding stimuli as to impose itself upon us will excite our senses whether we want it to or not. For us to perceive the stimulus, however, it must match our preconceptions. The vibration or the feel of the stimulus, that is, sets in motion a complicated series of electrochemical activities in our nervous systems. *If* our preconceptions about the situation are met, *if* the data we receive can be made to relate to our needs, attitudes, or frames of reference, *and if* we are inclined to accept the stimulus at that moment—*then* it will become imprinted on our nervous system.

We may work very hard at this perceiving, or we may find it happening automatically. Further, we may attend to many stimuli at once, but on several levels of willfulness and consciousness.

Assuming we do perceive a given stimulus or group of stimuli, we may go on to perform a further action. We may comprehend various things about the source of our perception. Planes and levels of "meaning" may flood over us, both engulfing the stimulus and giving it perspective. We may interpret or evaluate the experience; we may reason or rationalize from and about it. As a result of our perception, in fact, we may alter our behavior substantially. Once the perception is assimilated, however this occurs, it becomes part of the preconceptions which we take to the next situation.

Applied to the theatrical experience, this process seems to operate by means of two complex factors. When we attend a theatrical performance we have willfully chosen to be there. We work at paying attention, and we ourselves help create the stimulus situation. By virtue of our desire to participate imaginatively in the action onstage, we concentrate fully on the playing space. From this collective focusing comes an energy which is difficult to describe but which gives life to the images and symbols provided by actor, playwright, director, designer, and technicians.

Such focusing of attention is difficult for an individual alone in a theatre, easy for the same person in a crowd. The activities of others around us seem to multiply whatever energy we are feeling or expending. Our effort to pay attention is echoed, supported, and reinforced by the efforts of the crowd.

This crowd effect, moreover, is not just a subjective feeling we have when caught up in it. Observed from the stage, the mob of spectators does seem to communicate with the performers. Energy seems to flow in waves from the crowd of attentive onlookers.

This energy, though no means has been found to measure it, probably results from more than the willful focusing of attention. We have already noted six other processes that seem to be working when an audience attends a play. One of these six is the *process of impersonation*. A major part of playing both in the theatre and in daily life is assuming the roles of others. The life of a human being involves role-playing to such an extent that it is possible to define "self" or "personality" as a montage of roles. That is, we *play the role* of male or female, businessman or politician, leader or follower, father or mother—and so on—rather than actually *being* any of these creatures. What we individually *are* is a unique arrangement of such roles.

That "all the world's a stage, and all the men and women merely players," is a well-spoken commonplace of thought. In the theatre, two impersonations occur. One is that of the actor, whose craft and art we will examine in Chapter 4.

The other impersonation in a theatre is that carried out by the spectator—by you and me sitting or standing in a crowd around the performing-area. In life, besides playing all the social roles we must learn to survive as human beings, when we are alone we often pretend we are someone we could never be. We assume a role no one including ourselves would allow us to play in life. We are doctor, lawyer, Indian chief—hero and villain—larger than life. We play the boss, the lover, the astronaut, and no one is the wiser. Such impersonations both give us recreation and allow us to work out problems that beset us around the clock.

Out in the world, self-conscious about our roles, we must play only those we have been assigned. In the theatre, however, caught up in the crowd, we can lose self-consciousness and impersonate any character we can imagine.

Yet even here there are limits. Though it is not mandatory, usually we must use the imaginary materials provided onstage. The actor, the playwright, the other artists, and the drama they portray give us cues for controlling and directing our impersonations. Both the characters in the drama and the personalities of the actors playing them direct and control our role-playing. They somehow become creatures of *our* imaginations. Our impersonating force—our playacting—is focused by the activities we witness.

Nevertheless, *we* are the ones who do the ultimate pretending. We accomplish the pretense by means of three psychological processes that depend on the attention process but that function more or less independently to activate the impersonation process: identification, rationalization, and projection. The first of these—*identification*—is a process whereby we constantly and without thinking seem to become each experience we have and each person we meet or imagine as we go about our daily lives. Whether negatively or affirmatively, we tend to "identify with" the people and events that we experience. This activity seems as mysterious as it is inherent in the human psyche. It appears to be wholly unconscious; it is something that just happens. By going through an experience we take on its characteristics. We become Cornellians, for example, by going to Cornell; we are Navy men, Air Force men, Army men by virtue of service pleasant or unpleasant in one of these branches of the armed forces.

The second psychological activity that contributes to the theatrical experience is *rationalization*. Most of the time—some say all of the time—we act first and find reasons later. Or we plan to act and find reasons ahead of time to justify what we plan to do. We are essentially emotion-driven creatures, and one of our primary drives is to find moral or rational reasons for each action we perform. Even the most authentic ratiocination—mathematical and scientific analysis—appears to at least one observer primarily an expression of esthetic drives that are non-rational.[1]

Close to rationalization in the way it operates, though basically different, is *projection*. We have already noted our human tendency to pay attention only to what is already in our heads. Projection is the means whereby we find our own desires, thoughts, and characteristics outside ourselves. If we are angry, we see anger in others. If we expect impoliteness, we find everyone is impolite to us. The folk phrase "to borrow trouble" describes this process whereby we see ourselves in others. One form projection takes—actually finding human shapes or attributes in non-human things—is called anthropomorphism. In children's cartoons, in advertisements, we observe animals behaving like people and then we pretend they *are* people (see Chapter 8). It is sometimes a wrench to discover animals are not human when we meet them face to face.

In everyday situations, these three processes—identification, rationalization, projection—operate constantly, both consciously and unconsciously, and either independently or jointly. The same holds true in the theatre. We identify with the situations and behaviors onstage; they serve to rationalize our feelings and our views; and we project our dreams upon the dramatic activities.

These activities—the performance, the production, the play—serve as guidelines for our involvement in the drama. They are like the toys in Robert Louis Stevenson's "The Land of Counterpane":

---

1. For a careful statement of this point of view, see J. W. N. Sullivan, *The Limitations of Science*, copyright 1933, The Viking Press.

> And sometimes for an hour or so
> I watched my leaden soldiers go,
> With different uniforms and drills,
> Among the bed-clothes, through the hills;
>
> And sometimes sent my ships in fleets
> All up and down among the sheets;
> Or brought my trees and houses out,
> And planted cities all about.

The dreams we project may become larger, more sophisticated, or more various as we go from "Counterpane" to *Othello*. These changes, however, are principally matters of degree. The theatre is simply a larger and more complex "Land of Counterpane."

This analogy may be continued as we examine another psychological process important to the game of theatre—*distancing*. The idea here, sometimes called "esthetic distance," is less complicated than the terms make it seem. If we are going to participate freely in the drama onstage, we must realize always that the entire activity is a game. "Awareness of playing" would be another way to say it. Othello cannot actually murder Desdemona, for example, and we cannot truly be facing death at the moment we experience the journey of Everyman. We can only behave *as if* it were so. We must become totally involved in the drama while at the same time we feel completely alien to it. The simultaneity of these two states of mind is what is important, though the relative percentage of control each exerts may vary from play to play or from moment to moment in a given play. Historically, attempts to create one or the other of these states alone (see Chapter 2) have failed. A play's success, that is, usually results from the skillful combination of involvement and distance rather than the elimination of one or the other.

The sum of these psychological processes—attention, impersonation, identification, rationalization, projection, and distancing—is the spectator's playing of the drama. A final process—*imitation*—has long been considered the goal or purpose of dramatic activity. Aristotle, in the *Poetics*, stated that man's natural habit of imitation and his pleasure in the products thereof were the two causes of "poetry" (of which, to Aristotle, drama was a species).[2] In the prologue to our introduction to theatre, we accepted the Aristotelian view of imitation as part of the reason men play the game of theatre. The drive to imitate may cause men to engage in dramatic activity, but the goal of this activity includes more than just this one drive. In the same way, imitation is simply one of the processes involved in our enjoyment of drama. Though we cannot help seeking to imitate, we make a distinct effort to encourage the process. The result and the means of achieving it join to cause our pleasure.

To sum up all we have been saying about the participation of the audience in playmaking, we can use a familiar analogy. At a circus or

2. See Lane Cooper, *Aristotle on the Art of Poetry* (Ithaca, N. Y.: Cornell University Press, 1947).

a football game, we expect thrills from feats of derring-do and from grace under pressure. As we watch, we wish we could fly through the air with the greatest of ease. We fancy ourselves facing down the Bengal tigers. Yet even though we make-believe we can do the wonderful things we are seeing, we do not pretend the acrobat or the animal trainer is impersonating *us*. In no meaning of the word are the circus performers *players* (except sometimes for the clowns). They are real people who perform various feats with great skill, but they are not Prince Hamlet and they were never meant to be.

More important, we the spectators are not playing out a drama. We are not pretending that our experiences are being impersonated. We do not concentrate on the performing-space so that we may find ourselves mirrored by the activities in the center ring.

This analogy applies in another way. The circus performance is an end in itself. The presentation of a drama, on the other hand, seeks to create something outside the immediate pyrotechnics of the theatrical artists. That something else is a dramatic construct that results from interaction among characteristic human behavior patterns. The construct and the interaction are presented by means of verbal, aural, and visual images or symbols that are framed in a particular scenic environment.

The Dramatic Construct

Though we have stressed the importance of a group of spectators to the drama, quite obviously there must be something onstage for the audience to work with. Chief among the materials with which we play our dreams is a *dramatic construct*—that is, an amalgam of carefully plotted human experiences which organizes the psychological processes we have just described.

The heart of the dramatic construct is *life in action*. This behavior-in-process, when observed outside the theatre, is confusingly on the move. Temporally, spatially, biologically, and psychologically, this confusion buzzes around us. Our tendency aways is to create order out of chaos. The first step is to capture the human action in words—for example, "wit struggling with witchcraft in and for the soul of Othello." This phrase simply stands for the thoughts, feelings, decisions, and responses being presented in the drama we call *Othello*. To say the phrase requires two seconds. Yet two or three hours are needed to play the action the phrase symbolizes. The dramatic construct is therefore temporal; it exists only in a time-space continuum. That is, the action is played at a particular place, at a particular time, over a particular span of time. Each unit of time-space shows only a portion of the action. As a rule these units are called *incidents* or *episodes*.

We must remember, of course, that these incidents are in no way actual events. What we participate in is only an image of human struggle.

Moreover, the image is seen through a creative eye. The dramatic construct may be a "mirror up to nature," as Hamlet puts it, but the mirror gives us not ourselves but an artistic composition of ourselves seen by an evaluating consciousness. The result is not a distortion, as from a mirror in a funhouse, but an interpretation. We see ourselves as others see us.

The others who see us, and show us what they have found, are a motley crew. Each incident onstage, therefore, is a synthesis of many representations.

That a human experience in process can be wrought in such a way that a company of men can play the dreams in their heads with truth that is more than accuracy seems miraculous. There is magic in the web of it, and he is no student of theatre who will tell you otherwise.

The magic in the dramatic construct comes primarily from the forming principle that causes the units of the action to coalesce into a single dramatic event. The incidents do not happen at random. They are selected and arranged according to a rationale. Often this rationale is described as *purpose*. The drama seeks "to represent" or "to argue," or some combination of these goals. Within this overall strategic objective a number of purposes may be achieved—to show death affecting a mother, to tell the story of a dear father murdered, and so forth.

Just as often, however, the scheme that controls the flow of episodes is a *story*—that is, a series of events in time that are connected causally: "this happens, and then as a result this happens, and then three other things happen." The desire for a story is deep-seated in human beings, and many observers believe drama is merely a story that is performed onstage.

But the incidents in a drama may flash before the audience without being structured through a matrix of cause and effect. Imagine yourself in total darkness. Things are happening, but you are insulated from them. You can neither see nor hear the action. Suddenly lights pop on and off; with each flash of light, sound floods over you momentarily. In each moment of awareness you experience the action, and in each moment of darkness you are cut off from it again. What you see and hear may be threaded together with a story, but such interconnection is not inherently necessary. While you may impose a story on the proceedings—projection is one of the games we play in a theatre—all you have to do is live the moments of light and sound as fully as possible. The moments of impersonation, however, must delineate the *central idea*.

Another way to say this is to demand that the theatrical experience create a *commanding image*. This figurative vision becomes a metaphor of the action. A story, a race or a contest, a rhythm of nature, a courtroom, a melody—almost any human activity stands for the action and serves to articulate it. One production of *As You Like It*, for example, was presented as "Stop the Forest, I Want to Get Off."

Still another way to construct a drama is with *argumentation*. That is, the incidents are selected and arranged as a process of discourse in which a proposition is demonstrated by a series of premises leading to a logical conclusion. The drama does not argue for the proposition, but autonomously represents it. Two examples of this approach to structure are *Everyman,* the sample play at the end of Chapter 2, and *Major Barbara,* which is discussed in Chapter 7.

Whichever of these schemes—or whatever combination of them—controls a particular drama, the term most used to describe them is *plot.* If the action of the drama is "what happens," then the plot is "why it happens." We may think of the action as a gerund, the plot as an infinitive.

Yet the dramatic construct involves still more than *action being revealed through purposes.* "What and why" must have a "where." That is, actions and motives exist only in a *dramatic situation.* The construct must "make the scene," as it were.

What lies at the heart of any play, then, is a *dramatic construct* that incorporates *action* (a human experience in process), *purpose* (of each incident and of the total experience), and *situation* (the place where the drama happens). The construct *is* the drama. When all else is gone, or before anything else appears, there is the image of *someone doing something somewhere.* What this image is must be arrived at in a theatre with an audience. As the drama unfolds, the audience grasps the construct without thinking about it.

Let us take *Othello* as an extended example. The action seems to be "love-of-self (wit) struggling with love (witchcraft) in and for the soul of Othello." Among the many purposes at work are the following: to justify Othello's marriage to Desdemona, to defeat Othello's growth of love, to destroy Othello and Desdemona, and to sanctify the murder of Desdemona. These purposes—and many others—are controlled by the tuneless music of Iago's intrigue. Both the action and the purposes that delineate it, however, can exist only in a situation of complicated and hectic time-warping. In the spinning world of the dramatic construct, only love can survive. Unfortunately for Othello and Desdemona, the farcical pace of time prevents the Moor from ever achieving the love he needs.

Several sentences may be necessary to phrase this dramatic construct, and several decades of study to understand how it works, but in the theatre this meaning is available immediately and without predication.

The Dramatis Personae

Only with great difficulty can we imagine a drama that exists without people. Even Bugs Bunny is thought of as a person. Men "like us" must live the action or we simply cannot believe it. In fact, to think of great dramas is usually to remember great characters. It is legitimate, therefore, if somewhat inaccurate and misleading, to think of drama as character in action.

Yet there is no reason to claim the characters in a play are in fact people, as this word is usually defined. Etymologically the term *dramatis personae* means *masks of the drama*. That is, what we see onstage are characteristic patterns of behavior. A collection of human motivations is presented as a unique specimen of humanity. This *persona* moves himself about his business in such a way that the audience can become involved in what he does. In fact, a drama is often principally concerned with the ways in which one character's business contrasts or conflicts with the desires and activities of another character.

There are two aspects of characterization to be considered. Some of the individuals in a drama appear relatively autonomous and indeed may be thought of as people. Other individuals, and sometimes groups of individuals, serve primarily or only to enunciate ideas that set the scene, establish atmosphere, give exposition, develop a philosophy, or accomplish anything the dramatist wants. The traditional name for such a person or group is *chorus* or *choral character*. In some dramas the term used is *raissoneur*. This means of directly controlling audience reaction has long since proved its usefulness.

The individualized *personae* can be examined on two planes which are separate but related. The first plane ranges from absolute unreality—a character having life only in performance of the drama—to complete psychological reality in which the character is presented so that the audience feels he could be met on the street at any time. The hallmark of theatrical existence is selection and perhaps heightening of details; psychological existence requires full clinical details. It is rare to attempt such reality because it is unnecessary for success in characterization. A person in a drama needs to be understandable and believable *only while on the stage*.

As a matter of fact, most dramas are concerned with types of people, or with stereotypes. Just as in life, there is not time in a drama to focus on the infinite possibilities in every human being the drama portrays. We prefer to deal with people in categories. So and so is a teacher or a student, we say, or a drama major or a businessman. While the accuracy of such classifications is always questionable, it is true that people tend to behave in similar ways when governed by similar occupations, backgrounds, physical types, and so on. The drama usually needs only a kind of person, not the person himself.

When a type has been done to death, or is totally divorced from reality, the word often applied is *stereotype*. The term comes from the world of printing and means literally a packet of type already set. In psychology the word refers to pictures in the head which ordinarily have been formulated through symbol experience rather than actuality.

Type and stereotype come together in the *stock character*—a particular personage that has proved its theatrical effectiveness and hence is used over and over in dramas. Examples are the mother-in-law, the braggart soldier, the dirty redskin, the lone frontiersman, and the pure young man seeking identity and freedom in a crass world (as in the film *The Graduate*). Such characters originate or become popular with a given audience, which seemingly can never get enough of them.

The second plane on which a dramatic character exists is one involving dimensionality. Whether theatrical or real, a *persona* may be shown with any number of facets. A completely real character may be unidimensional; a stock character—Falstaff, let us say—may be multidimensional. High school teachers used to say that the most wonderful thing about Shakespeare was his capacity to make even one-line characters "people." Though this view is no longer fashionable, Shakespeare does seem to go to a good deal of trouble to give minor characters like Montano, the Governor of Cyprus in *Othello*, more than one dimension.

In *Death of a Salesman*, all the characters are types; some are generalized even to the point of being stereotypes. Yet there is considerable variation in the dimensionality of the characters. The protagonist, Willy Loman, despite all that happens to him, is required to lack depth if the dramatic construct of this play—"American citizen seeking, living, and dying for the false dreams of the modern business world"—is to be realized. A distinctly choral character, Bernard, besides being a stock "good guy," is also shown on just one plane of existence; he personifies and enunciates "the right way to behave." In contrast, Biff, the elder son of Willy, is portrayed in several dimensions as *he* struggles with the morality of Willy Loman and the world of salesmanship. Since Biff, unlike all the other characters, who are mostly choral, must understand what goes on, he must be shown capable of enlightenment. (In fact, it is entirely plausible to consider the "salesman" in the title to be Biff.)

As we just noted, even a chorus or a choral character may range from theatrical to actual, and may exhibit one or many dimensions, but usually his personality is relatively undeveloped.

The main thing about *dramatis personae*, however, is their believability —their workability—in the context of a given drama. The playgoer of today, for example, tends to expect characters to behave in accordance with the precepts of modern psychology. Audiences of other times have cared less about motivation and more about the excitement of the dramatic action. Does it really matter *why* Iago does what he does, though Shakespeare takes pains to give him a number of plausible motives? As we will note in Chapter 8, one of the most exciting modes of drama today is that which we call "children's theatre." Among its hallmarks is the acceptance of any kind of characterization so long as the dramatic action is furthered. To take another example, some of the puzzlement caused by *Waiting for Godot* probably stems from the difficulty in identifying with the two main characters. Yet the plays of Edward Albee— whose characters are easy to identify with—all portray the same persons more or less. If a spectator closes his eyes, or forgets for a moment where he is, he finds it difficult to say which Albee play he is witnessing. Under the spell of Albee's dramaturgy, however, it is also difficult to avoid the feeling that "Mommy" and "Daddy" are a particular set of parents—one's own.

Thus, the *dramatis personae* are people in places doing things that reveal—that are—the dramatic construct. We cannot think of *Othello* or *As You Like It* without thinking of a person like Othello or Rosalind living and talking the action of the drama. Dramatic actions and people are inseparable. The shadows seen onstage are not *people,* however, but revealed actions that people have been known to take, done in a manner that makes sense to an audience. Making sense depends as much on audience involvement with the character's words and activities as on the words and activities themselves.

Yet, however the *personae* are arrived at or perceived, the theatrical image cannot exist without them. Drama is people. Where people reside, there drama is.

The Language

But these people must talk and laugh and sing. They must share ideas and images, and they must move and dance. How can there be a drama without some expression of it?

In many ways a drama is a *language* at once verbal, oral, gestural, and pictorial. Usually but not necessarily the chief characteristic of this language is the fact that it is a series of exchanges—*dialogue.* The people onstage talk with each other, and both they and the total drama address themselves to the audience. The ways in which this conversation is achieved are examined in Chapter 2 for the ideas a drama expresses; in Chapter 3 for the playhouse; in Chapter 4 for the actor; in Chapter 6 for the director, and in Chapter 7 for the designer and the technical director.

Language is generally defined as an organized body of symbols that are used for communication of feelings and thought. Any work of art is principally ideas and images arranged to communicate a single *commanding image* or *central idea.* A drama is a symbol system, not reality. The means of expressing the symbol system move one step further from literalness. The language exhibits patterns of imagery that create the dramatic construct through a number of figurative comparisons. Metaphors come not in single spies, but in battalions.

The use of words in this way has always been called poetry. When dramas ceased to use poetry and took up prose, much was lost. The drama gave up one of its chief weapons—verbal wizardry—and sought to depend on merely the poetry of dramatic effect, what many commentators refer to as poetry of the theatre. The concatenation of theatrical activities experienced by the audience is unquestionably poetic, but we only have to compare the words of Shakespeare to those of Shaw, who gave us modern prose at its theatrical best, to find the loss of "Marlowe's mighty line" all too apparent.

The expression of a drama also includes rhythm and music over and above the way the words and scenes fit and work together. It is the rule rather than the exception to find dramas filled with music and song. *As You Like It,* for example, seems unthinkable without "Under the Greenwood Tree," and *Othello* without "Willow." Even where music is not directly provided by the drama, a director may insist on having an overture, *entr'actes,* and mood music within the scenes.

The *language of Dionysus,* then, is a complex system of spoken, sung, gestured, and pictured symbols. How they work their wonder will be seen in later chapters.

The Dramatic Environment

As we talk about *environment,* picture yourself with Tom Sawyer and Huckleberry Finn as they begin their incantation in the graveyard. Darkness lies upon you and the eerie noises of the night envelop you. The dead are walking and you are with them. You are overcome by dread as you cower among the gravestones and listen to the moaning of a wind, the breathy flutter of wings, the distant howling of a dog or two, and—suddenly—the ghastly mutter of voices coming closer and closer. Surely your end is near.

Now picture yourself the director of this scene in a production of *Mark Twain's The Adventures of Tom Sawyer,* which accompanies Chapter 4. Somehow you must make a graveyard scene incarnate fear and dread; you must create darkness that is alive and can be felt. At the same time you must provide enough light for the audience to see the actors. Imagine further that the lighting design is such that you seem forced to choose between total darkness and a scene without proper atmosphere. No setting on the rheostats is low enough to serve your purpose; yet below a certain reading, nothing is visible. Must you rely solely on the imagination of actors and audience?

Just as you are reaching that conclusion, the properties crew finishes the gravestones. They turn out to be huge—two feet by four feet by six inches, and white with a pebbled finish. Once more you try the scene, and suddenly it works. Though not painted to be phosphorescent, the gravestones' brilliant whiteness reflects enough light when the rheostats are at the lowest reading both to illuminate the actors and to give the scene an unearthly glow that satisfies the need for an atmosphere of frightfulness.

Once again you would notice the impact of a drama's environment as realized through scenic devices. Many critics of drama and theatre, perhaps taking their cue from Aristotle's *Poetics,* have dismissed the scenery of a play as "merely spectacle." Playgoers, on the other hand, have usually gone to the opposite extreme—the more spectacle the better.

Neither extreme is satisfactory. Every drama must exist in a "scene" of some kind. Whether or not this "environment" is employed as a separate force, without regard to the rest of the drama's elements, the place in which the play is occurring cannot be escaped. Moreover, the environment of a drama can serve—perhaps it should serve—to unite all the other dramatic forces. It can symbolize the total community as well, and sum up or collect the drama's images and ideas. Thus, in the duel at the close of *Hamlet*, the physical clash with real swords between Hamlet and Laertes serves as a replica of the total drama—being versus non-being, Hamlet versus Claudius, revenge versus forgiveness, action versus contemplation, to name only a few of the conflicts that constitute the drama. Again, the marriage bed that is supposed to serve as a symbol of union through love in *Othello* is distorted into a shrine upon which the Moor sacrifices Desdemona to his blind and prideful self-love. Or, as we note below, the magnificent symbolic foray into the byways of love that Shakespeare called *As You Like It* seems enhanced by a vast and empty playing area, perhaps artfully highlighted to encourage the wildest fancies of the audience to take wing with Rosalind's singing words. Whether naked stage dressed with words or detailed natural environment, the scene in which the drama takes place *is* the play.

Sample Play: AS YOU LIKE IT

Introduction

Every drama becomes a play only when audience and actors come together in a playhouse. This event happens uniquely each time. What is given us to read—the playscript—is but an echo or, more accurately, a ghostly prediction of things to come.

In the case of the finest dramas, however, what an echo it is! *As You Like It*, perhaps more than any drama in our heritage, exemplifies what we have been saying thus far in this chapter. The dramatic construct is a game called "Love in Never-Never-Land," in which the protagonist—Rosalind—experiments with several of the common and foolish byways of love—love as melancholy, love as barnyard sex, love as flirtation, and so forth—but arrives full-circle back at the happy center: *marriage-type love.*

The construct is plotted to allow Rosalind's exposure to many aspects of love as she seeks the correct means of achieving happiness through romance. Each of her dallyings is dramatized through an encounter with some person who embodies the given aspect and who, except for Jacques and Duke Frederick, accompanies Rosalind back from the byway to the main road of marriage. The plot is articulated chiefly by three intrigues—*first,* the ongoing struggle between the usurper, Duke Frederick, and the rightful ruler, Duke Senior, now living banished in the Forest of Arden; *second,* the ongoing quarrel between the brothers Oliver and Orlando over the latter's rightful share of their father's inheritance; *third,* the disguise of Rosalind as the young man Ganymede and of Celia as his sister Aliena, and their encounter in the forest wtih the love-struck Orlando, whom Ganymede teases by pretending to teach him how to woo, with the peasant girl Phoebe, who falls in love with Ganymede, and with Oliver, who comes to love Celia. The articulation also includes a comparative balancing of urban life (the court and Orlando's home, where only evil can exist) and pastoral life (the forest, where only good occurs), and a constant but always gentle satire on the pastoral ideals and conventions that provide the framework for the drama.

These ideals and conventions—that country life is better than city life, that simple folk are more admirable than complicated civilized people, and that any problem can be solved if taken out into the fresh air— were prominent in Elizabethan England. Indeed, in one way or another they have been a dominant mode of thought since men began to live in cities. In *As You Like It,* all who come to the Forest of Arden are changed for the better.

The story used in the drama was taken from Thomas Lodge's novel *Rosalynde.* Since the story is well-known, we have only to note that Shakespeare changed the novel very little: no battle scenes are shown; Orlando is wounded by a lioness and not by kidnappers; Touchstone, William, Audrey, and Jacques are added; and all the characters, rather than only the "good ones," enjoy a happy fate.

The situation involved in the dramatic construct is also well-known. There are three locales—the estate of Orlando and Oliver, the court, and the forest. The drama begins at the de Boys estate, then moves to the court, and finally arrives at the forest. In a series of short scenes, the action jumps around among the three locales. These scenes show Rosalind and Celia, Orlando, and finally Oliver having to head for the forest. There the paths of the fugitives, the pursuer (Oliver), the banished duke, and the denizens of the forest are skillfully intertwined as Rosalind seeks her father, plays at love with Orlando, and mixes in the problems of the peasants. All paths come together finally in a grand ceremony of marriage and forgiveness.

Many critics have noted that for the audience this construct is "as you like it." The same observation fits the *dramatis personae.* Rosalind is the central character, and a brighter, gayer, wittier, more delightful, more talkative young lady was never invented for the stage. She is presented in all possible moods, and whichever state she is in at a given moment, she explores its every facet in a brilliant shower of metaphor and wit. Yet her primary trait is her wholesomeness. Celia, her comrade, is equally bright but is more down-to-earth and less given to flights of fancy. Though principally Rosalind's foil, Celia is also her mentor. The two of them are full-blown persons. The rest of the characters, save perhaps Orlando, are carefully-delineated stock characters—the witty fool, the wise peasant, the good father, the bad father, the melancholy wit, and so forth. Yet we should note how each of these types, a symbol of some form of "love," is given his or her special identity. Orlando, also perhaps the stock young suitor, is yet a difficult character to believe. He is almost too handsome, too heroic, too much a patsy for Rosalind. Since he must carry an important part of the dramatic action, and above all must seem a worthy partner for Rosalind, his general shallowness tends to make the drama unbalanced. The scales can be righted only through the skill of the actor who plays Orlando.

The language of *As You Like It* is predominantly prose—yet what prose! It is stretched to the limits of English, and the flash of image and symbol is like a shower of broken glass. Perhaps to balance the large amount of prose, Shakespeare has included more songs than in any of his other plays. These lovely musical numbers seem part of the fantastic atmosphere of Arden.

That atmosphere, which pervades the entire drama, is strangely one of "the mind's eye." *As You Like It* has the romantic imagination for its environment. It is the land of Rosalind's scintillating wit. Somehow the dramatic setting must suggest this "over the rainbow" quality. The acting must be down-to-earth and human, though brilliantly theatrical. Costumes, sets, and lights must be as open as the sky, as fragile as gossamer. We might even say as fragile as love, for that is the heart of the play.

As You Like It

Dramatis Personae

DUKE SENIOR, the rightful Duke, living in banishment

DUKE FREDERICK, his brother, usurper of his dominions

AMIENS lord attending the banished Duke

JAQUES, lord attending on the banished Duke

LE BEAU, a courtier attending upon Frederick

CHARLES, wrestler to Frederick

OLIVER, eldest son of Sir Rowland de Boys

JAQUES, second son of Sir Rowland de Boys

ORLANDO, youngest son of Sir Rowland de Boys

ADAM, old servant to Oliver and Orlando

DENNIS, young servant to Oliver and Orlando

TOUCHSTONE, a clown

SIR OLIVER MARTEXT, a vicar

CORIN, an old shepherd

SILVIUS, a young shepherd

WILLIAM, a country bumpkin

ROSALIND, daughter to the banished Duke

CELIA, daughter to Frederick

PHEBE, a shepherdess

AUDREY, a country wench

HYMEN, goddess of marriage

LORDS, PAGES, ATTENDANTS, etc.

Reprinted from the Pelican Shakespeare Series, Alfred Harbage, editor, by permission of Penguin Books, Inc.

As You Like It

Orlando. As I remember, Adam, it was upon this fashion
bequeathed me by will but poor a thousand crowns, and,
as thou say'st, charged my brother on his blessing to
breed me well: and there begins my sadness. My brother
Jaques he keeps at school, and report speaks goldenly of   5
his profit. For my part, he keeps me rustically at home
or, to speak more properly, stays me here at home un-
kept: for call you that keeping for a gentleman of my
birth that differs not from the stalling of an ox? His horses
are bred better, for, besides that they are fair with their   10
feeding, they are taught their manage, and to that end
riders dearly hired; but I, his brother, gain nothing under
him but growth, for the which his animals on his dung-
hills are as much bound to him as I. Besides this nothing
that he so plentifully gives me, the something that nature   15
gave me his countenance seems to take from me: he lets
me feed with his hinds, bars me the place of a brother,
and as much as in him lies, mines my gentility with my
education. This is it, Adam, that grieves me; and the spirit
of my father, which I think is within me, begins to mu-   20
tiny against this servitude. I will no longer endure it,
though yet I know no wise remedy how to avoid it.

Enter Oliver.

Adam. Yonder comes my master, your brother.
Orlando. Go apart, Adam, and thou shalt hear how he will
    shake me up.   25
Oliver. Now, sir, what make you here?
Orlando. Nothing. I am not taught to make anything.
Oliver. What mar you then, sir?
Orlando. Marry, sir, I am helping you to mar that which
    God made, a poor unworthy brother of yours, with   30
    idleness.
Oliver. Marry, sir, be better employed, and be naught
    awhile.

I i, 2 *but poor* merely 6 *profit* progress *keeps* maintains 7 *stays* detains 11 *manage* actions
and paces 16 *countenance* attitude 17 *hinds* farm hands 18 *mines* undermines 26 *make* do
(but Orlando pretends to take it in another sense) 29 *Marry* why, indeed (originally an oath
by the Virgin Mary) 32-33 *be naught awhile* i.e. go to the devil

Orlando. Shall I keep your hogs and eat husks with them?
What prodigal portion have I spent that I should come   35
to such penury?

Oliver. Know you where you are, sir?

Orlando. O, sir, very well: here in your orchard.

Oliver. Know you before whom sir?

Orlando. Ay, better than him I am before knows me. I   40
know you are my eldest brother, and in the gentle condition of blood you should so know me. The courtesy
of nations allows you my better in that you are the first
born, but the same tradition takes not away my blood
were twenty brothers betwixt us. I have as much of my   45
father in me as you, albeit I confess your coming before
me is nearer to his reverence.

Oliver. What, boy!   *[Strikes him.]*

Orlando. Come, come, elder brother, you are too young
in this.   *[Seizes him.]*   50

Oliver. Wilt thou lay hands on me, villain?

Orlando. I am no villain. I am the youngest son of Sir
Rowland de Boys; he was my father, and he is thrice a
villain that says such a father begot villains. Wert thou
not my brother, I would not take this hand from thy   55
throat till this other had pulled out thy tongue for saying
so. Thou hast railed on thyself.

Adam. Sweet masters, be patient: for your father's remembrance, be at accord.

Oliver. Let me go, I say.   60

Orlando. I will not till I please. You shall hear me. My
father charged you in his will to give me good education:
you have trained me like a peasant, obscuring and hiding
from me all gentlemanlike qualities. The spirit of my
father grows strong in me, and I will no longer endure   65
it: therefore allow me such exercises as may become a
gentleman, or give me the poor allottery my father left
me by testament; with that I will go buy my fortunes.
                                                          [Releases him.]

Oliver. And what wilt thou do? beg when that is spent?
Well, sir, get you in. I will not long be troubled with   70
you. You shall have some part of your will. I pray you
leave me.

34-35 *eat husks... prodigal portion* (alluding to the Prodigal Son, who wasted his patri-
mony and then had to eat with the swine; see Luke 15:11-32) 38 *orchard* garden 41-42
gentle... blood bond of family loyalty 42-43 *courtesy of nations* recognized custom (of
primogeniture) 47 *reverence* revered rank 52 *villain* serf (Orlando quibbles on the two
meanings of *villain*) 57 *railed on* reviled 64 *qualities* accomplishments 67 *allottery* portion

Orlando. I will no further offend you than becomes me
    for my good.
Oliver. Get you with him you old dog.   75
Adam. Is 'old dog' my reward? Most true, I have lost my
    teeth in your service. God be with my old master; he
    would not have spoke such a word.

                                    Exeunt Orlando, Adam.
Oliver. Is it even so? Begin you to grow upon me? I will
    physic your rankness and yet give no thousand crowns   80
    neither. Holla, Dennis!

                    Enter Dennis.

Dennis. Calls your worship?
Oliver. Was not Charles the Duke's wrestler here to speak
    with me?
Dennis. So please you, he is here at the door and impor-   85
    tunes access to you.
Oliver. Call him in. *[Exit Dennis.]* 'Twill be a good way;
    and to-morrow the wrestling is.

                    Enter Charles.

Charles. Good morrow to your worship.
Oliver. Good Monsieur Charles, what's the new news at   90
    the new court?
Charles. There's no news at the court, sir, but the old news:
    that is, the old Duke is banished by his younger brother
    the new Duke, and three or four loving lords have put
    themselves into voluntary exile with him, whose lands   95
    and revenues enrich the new Duke; therefore he gives
    them good leave to wander.
Oliver. Can you tell if Rosalind, the Duke's daughter, be
    banished with her father?
Charles. O, no; for the Duke's daughter her cousin so loves   100
    her, being ever from their cradles bred together, that she
    would have followed her exile, or have died to stay be-
    hind her. She is at the court, and no less beloved of her
    uncle than his own daughter, and never two ladies loved
    as they do.   105
Oliver. Where will the old Duke live?

---

79 *grow upon me* i.e. encroach on my place 80 *physic* cure *rankness* exuberant growth (cf. l.
79)

Charles. They say he is already in the Forest of Arden, and
    a many merry men with him; and there they live like
    the old Robin Hood of England. They say many young
    gentlemen flock to him every day, and fleet the time   110
    carelessly as they did in the golden world.
Oliver. What, you wrestle to-morrow before the new
    Duke?
Charles. Marry do I, sir; and I came to acquaint you with
    a matter. I am given, sir, secretly to understand that your   115
    younger brother, Orlando, hath a disposition to come
    in disguised against me to try a fall. To-morrow, sir, I
    wrestle for my credit, and he that escapes me without
    some broken limb shall acquit him well. Your brother is
    but young and tender, and for your love I would be   120
    loath to foil him, as I must for my own honor if he come
    in: therefore, out of my love to you, I came hither to
    acquaint you withal, that either you might stay him from
    his intendment, or brook such disgrace well as he shall
    run into, in that it is a thing of his own search and alto-   125
    gether against my will.
Oliver. Charles, I thank thee for thy love to me, which
    thou shalt find I will most kindly requite. I had myself
    notice of my brother's purpose herein and have by under-
    hand means labored to dissuade him from it; but he is   130
    resolute. I'll tell thee, Charles, it is the stubbornest young
    fellow of France; full of ambition, an envious emulator
    of every man's good parts, a secret and villainous con-
    triver against me his natural brother: therefore use thy
    discretion. I had as lief thou didst break his neck as his   135
    finger. And thou wert best look to't; for if thou dost
    him any slight disgrace, or if he do not mightily grace
    himself on thee, he will practise against thee by poison,
    entrap thee by some treacherous device, and never leave
    thee till he hath ta'en thy life by some indirect means or   140
    other; for I assure thee, and almost with tears I speak it,
    there is not one so young and so villainous this day living.
    I speak but brotherly of him, but should I anatomize him
    to thee as he is, I must blush and weep, and thou must
    look pale and wonder.   145

---

110 *fleet* pass 111 *the golden world* (described by Ovid in *Metamorphoses,* Book I; here
men were innocent and food was plentiful) 117 *fall* bout 118 *credit* reputation 121 *foil*
throw 125 *search* seeking 129-30 *underhand* indirect 137-38 *grace himself on thee* gain
credit at your expense 138 *practise* plot 143 *anatomize* dissect, describe

Charles. I am heartily glad I came hither to you. If he come
to-morrow, I'll give him his payment. If ever he go
alone again, I'll never wrestle for prize more. And so
God keep your worship.

Oliver. Farewell, good Charles. *Exit [Charles].* Now will   150
I stir this gamester. I hope I shall see an end of him; for
my soul, yet I know not why, hates nothing more than
he. Yet he's gentle, never schooled and yet learned, full
of noble device, of all sorts enchantingly beloved; and
indeed so much in the heart of the world, and especially   155
of my own people, who best know him, that I am altogether misprised. But it shall not be so long; this wrestler
shall clear all. Nothing remains but that I kindle the boy
thither, which now I'll go about.   *Exit.*

Enter Rosalind and Celia.   I,ii

Celia. I pray thee, Rosalind, sweet my coz, be merry.

Rosalind. Dear Celia, I show more mirth than I am mistress
of, and would you yet I were merrier? Unless you could
teach me to forget a banished father, you must not learn
me how to remember any extraordinary pleasure.   5

Celia. Herein I see thou lov'st me not with the full weight
that I love thee. If my uncle, thy banished father, had
banished thy uncle, the Duke my father, so thou hadst
been still with me, I could have taught my love to take
thy father for mine. So wouldst thou, if the truth of thy   10
love to me were so righteously tempered as mine is to
thee.

Rosalind. Well, I will forget the condition of my estate to
rejoice in yours.

Celia. You know my father hath no child but I, nor none   15
is like to have; and truly, when he dies, thou shalt be his
heir; for what he hath taken away from thy father perforce, I will render thee again in affection. By mine
honor, I will, and when I break that oath, let me turn
monster. Therefore, my sweet Rose, my dear Rose, be   20
merry.

Rosalind. From henceforth I will, coz, and devise sports.
Let me see, what think you of falling in love?

Celia. Marry I prithee do, to make sport withal; but love
no man in good earnest, nor no further in sport neither   25

147-48 *go alone* walk without help 153 *gentle* possessed of the qualities of a gentleman 154
device designs *enchantingly* as by enchantment 157 *misprised* scorned I, ii, 1 *coz* cousin 4
learn teach 11 *righteously tempered* properly composed 17-18 *perforce* forcibly

than with safety of a pure blush thou mayst in honor
come off again.

Rosalind. What shall be our sport then?

Celia. Let us sit and mock the good housewife Fortune
    from her wheel, that her gifts may henceforth be be-   30
    stowed equally.

Rosalind. I would we could do so, for her benefits are
    mightily misplaced, and the bountiful blind woman doth
    most mistake in her gifts to women.

Celia. 'Tis true, for those that she makes fair she scarce   35
    makes honest, and those that she makes honest she makes
    very ill-favoredly.

Rosalind. Nay, now thou goest from Fortune's office to
    Nature's. Fortune reigns in gifts of the world, not in the
    lineaments of Nature.   40

Enter [Touchstone, the] Clown.

Celia. No; when Nature hath made a fair creature, may
    she not by Fortune fall into the fire? Though Nature
    hath given us wit to flout at Fortune, hath not Fortune
    sent in this fool to cut off the argument?

Rosalind. Indeed, there is Fortune too hard for Nature   45
    when Fortune makes Nature's natural the cutter-off of
    Nature's wit.

Celia. Peradventure this is not Fortune's work neither, but
    Nature's, who perceiveth our natural wits too dull to
    reason of such goddesses and hath sent this natural for   50
    our whetstone, for always the dullness of the fool is the
    whetstone of the wits. How now, wit; whither wander
    you?

Touchstone. Mistress, you must come away to your father.

Celia. Were you made the messenger?   55

Touchstone. No, by mine honor, but I was bid to come for
    you.

Rosalind. Where learned you that oath, fool?

Touchstone. Of a certain knight that swore by his honor
    they were good pancakes, and swore by his honor the   60
    mustard was naught. Now I'll stand to it, the pancakes
    were naught, and the mustard was good, and yet was
    not the knight forsworn.

---

26 *pure* innocent 27 *come off* get away 29 *good housewife* i.e. one who spins 30 *her wheel* (which carried some up, others down) 36 *honest* chaste 40 S.D. *Touchstone* (his name means a kind of flint used to test for gold and silver) 46 *natural* born fool 50 *and* (omitted in folio) 63 *forsworn* falsely sworn

Celia. How prove you that in the great heap of your
    knowledge?   65
Rosalind. Ay, marry, now unmuzzle your wisdom.
Touchstone. Stand you both forth now. Stroke your chins,
    and swear by your beards that I am a knave.
Celia. By our beards, if we had them, thou art.
Touchstone. By my knavery, if I had it, then I were; but if   70
    you swear by that that is not, you are not forsworn; no
    more was this knight, swearing by his honor, for he
    never had any; or if he had, he had sworn it away before
    ever he saw those pancakes or that mustard.
Celia. Prithee, who is't that thou mean'st?   75
Touchstone. One that old Frederick, your father, loves.
Celia. My father's love is enough to honor him enough:
    speak no more of him; you'll be whipped for taxation
    one of these days.
Touchstone. The more pity that fools may not speak wisely   80
    what wise men do foolishly.
Celia. By my troth, thou sayest true, for since the little wit
    that fools have was silenced, the little foolery that wise
    men have makes a great show. Here comes Monsieur
    Le Beau.   85

Enter Le Beau.

Rosalind. With his mouth full of news.
Celia. Which he will put on us as pigeons feed their young.
Rosalind. Then shall we be news-crammed.
Celia. All the better; we shall be the more marketable.
    Bon jour, Monsieur Le Beau, what's the news?   90
Le Beau. Fair princess, you have lost much good sport.
Celia. Sport; of what color?
Le Beau. What color, madam? How shall I answer you?
Rosalind. As wit and fortune will.
Touchstone. Or as the destinies decree.   95
Celia. Well said; that was laid on with a trowel.
Touchstone. Nay, if I keep not my rank—
Rosalind. Thou losest thy old smell.
Le Beau. You amaze me, ladies. I would have told you of
    good wrestling, which you have lost the sight of.   100
Rosalind. Yet tell us the manner of the wrestling.
Le Beau. I will tell you the beginning; and if it please your
    ladyships, you may see the end, for the best is yet to do,
    and here, where you are, they are coming to perform it.

78 *taxation* slander 87 *put on* force upon 92 *color* sort 96 *with a trowel* i.e. slapped on
thickly 97 *my rank* i.e. my rating as a witty person 99 *amaze* confuse

Celia. Well, the beginning that is dead and buried.   105

Le Beau. There comes an old man and his three sons.

Celia. I could match this beginning with an old tale.

Le Beau. Three proper young men, of excellent growth and
presence.

Rosalind. With bills on their necks, 'Be it known unto all   110
men by these presents.'

Le Beau. The eldest of the three wrestled with Charles,
the Duke's wrestler; which Charles in a moment threw
him and broke three of his ribs, that there is little hope
of life in him. So he served the second, and so the third.   115
Yonder they lie, the poor man, their father, making
such pitiful dole over them that all the beholders take his
part with weeping.

Rosalind. Alas!

Touchstone. But what is the sport, monsieur, that the ladies   120
have lost?

Le Beau. Why, this that I speak of.

Touchstone. Thus men may grow wiser every day. It is the
first time that ever I heard breaking of ribs was sport for
ladies.   125

Celia. Or I, I promise thee.

Rosalind. But is there any else longs to see this broken
music in his sides? Is there yet another dotes upon rib-
breaking? Shall we see this wrestling, cousin?

Le Beau. You must, if you stay here, for here is the place   130
appointed for the wrestling, and they are ready to perform it.

Celia. Yonder sure they are coming. Let us now stay and
see it.

> *Flourish. Enter Duke [Frederick], Lords, Orlando,*
> *Charles, and Attendants.*

Duke Frederick. Come on. Since the youth will not be   135
entreated, his own peril on his forwardness.

Rosalind. Is yonder the man?

Le Beau. Even he, madam.

Celia. Alas, he is too young; yet he looks successfully.

Duke Frederick. How now, daughter and cousin; are you   140
crept hither to see the wrestling?

Rosalind. Ay, my liege, so please you give us leave.

Duke Frederick. You will take little delight in it, I can tell
you, there is such odds in the man. In pity of the chal-

110 *bills* notices 117 *dole* lament 127-28 *broken music* wrong arrangement of parts 136
forwardness rashness 139 *successfully* likely to succeed 144 *odds* superiority

lenger's youth I would fain dissuade him, but he will not   145
be entreated. Speak to him, ladies; see if you can move
him.

Celia. Call him hither, good Monsieur Le Beau.

Duke Frederick. Do so. I'll not be by.   *[Steps aside.]*

Le Beau. Monsieur the challenger, the princess calls for you.   150

Orlando. I attend them with all respect and duty.

Rosalind. Young man, have you challenged Charles the
wrestler?

Orlando. No, fair princess. He is the general challenger; I
come but in as others do, to try with him the strength of   155
my youth.

Celia. Young gentleman, your spirits are too bold for your
years. You have seen cruel proof of this man's strength;
if you saw yourself with your eyes or knew yourself with
your judgment, the fear of your adventure would counsel   160
you to a more equal enterprise. We pray you for your
own sake to embrace your own safety and give over this
attempt.

Rosalind. Do, young sir. Your reputation shall not therefore be misprised; we will make it our suit to the Duke   165
that the wrestling might not go forward.

Orlando. I beseech you, punish me not with your hard
thoughts, wherein I confess me much guilty to deny so
fair and excellent ladies anything. But let your fair eyes
and gentle wishes go with me to my trial; wherein if I be   170
foiled, there is but one shamed that was never gracious;
if killed, but one dead that is willing to be so. I shall do
my friends no wrong, for I have none to lament me; the
world no injury, for in it I have nothing. Only in the
world I fill up a place, which may be better supplied   175
when I have made it empty.

Rosalind. The little strength that I have, I would it were
with you.

Celia. And mine to eke out hers.

Rosalind. Fare you well. Pray heaven I be deceived in you!   180

Celia. Your heart's desires be with you!

Charles. Come, where is this young gallant that is so desir-
ous to lie with his mother earth?

Orlando. Ready, sir; but his will hath in it a more modest
working.   185

Duke Frederick. You shall try but one fall.

---

150 *princess* (taken as plural by Orlando) 165 *misprised* undervalued 171 *gracious* graced by
fortune 180 *deceived in you* mistaken in my view of your abilities 185 *working* undertaking

Charles. No, I warrant your Grace you shall not entreat
    him to a second that have so mightily persuaded him
    from a first.
Orlando. You mean to mock me after. You should not   190
    have mocked me before. But come your ways.
Rosalind. Now Hercules be thy speed, young man!
Celia. I would I were invisible, to catch the strong fellow
    by the leg.   *Wrestle.*
Rosalind. O excellent young man!   195
Celia. If I had a thunderbolt in mine eye, I can tell who
    should down.   *[Charles is thrown.] Shout.*
Duke Frederick. No more, no more.
Orlando. Yes, I beseech your Grace; I am not yet well
    breathed.   200
Duke Frederick. How dost thou, Charles?
Le Beau.   He cannot speak, my lord.
Duke Frederick. Bear him away.   *[Charles is borne out.]*
                       What is thy name, young man?
Orlando. Orlando, my liege, the youngest son of Sir
    Rowland de Boys.
Duke Frederick. I would thou hadst been son to some man
    else.   205
    The world esteemed thy father honorable,
    But I did find him still mine enemy.
    Thou shouldst have better pleased me with this deed
    Hadst thou descended from another house.
    But fare thee well; thou art a gallant youth;   210
    I would thou hadst told me of another father.
                        Exit Duke, [with Train].
Celia. Were I my father, coz, would I do this?
Orlando. I am more proud to be Sir Rowland's son,
    His youngest son, and would not change that calling
    To be adopted heir to Frederick.   215
Rosalind. My father loved Sir Rowland as his soul,
    And all the world was of my father's mind.
    Had I before known this young man his son,
    I should have given him tears unto entreaties
    Ere he should thus have ventured.
Celia. Gentle cousin,   220
    Let us go thank him and encourage him.
    My father's rough and envious disposition
    Sticks me at heart. Sir, you have well deserved;

---

191 *come your ways* come on 192 *Hercules* (symbol of strength) *be thy speed* favor you
196 *If . . . eye* if I could cast a thunderbolt with my eyes 199-200 *well breathed* warmed up
207 *still* constantly 214 *calling* title 223 *Sticks* stabs

If you do keep your promise in love
But justly as you have exceeded all promise,   225
Your mistress shall be happy.
Rosalind.   Gentleman, *[Gives chain.]*
Wear this for me, one out of suits with fortune,
That could give more but that her hand lacks means.
Shall we go, coz?
Celia.   Ay. Fare you well, fair gentleman.
Orlando. Can I not say 'I thank you'? My better parts   230
Are all thrown down, and that which here stands up
Is but a quintain, a mere lifeless block.
Rosalind. He calls us back. My pride fell with my fortunes;
I'll ask him what he would. Did you call, sir?
Sir, you have wrestled well, and overthrown   235
More than your enemies.
Celia.   Will you go, coz?
Rosalind. Have with you. Fare you well.
                                            Exit [with Celia].

Orlando. What passion hangs these weights upon my
        tongue?
I cannot speak to her, yet she urged conference.

                        Enter Le Beau.

O poor Orlando, thou art overthrown!   240
Or Charles or something weaker masters thee.
Le Beau. Good sir, I do in friendship counsel you
To leave this place. Albeit you have deserved
High commendation, true applause, and love,
Yet such is now the Duke's condition   245
That he misconsters all that you have done.
The Duke is humorous. What he is, indeed,
More suits you to conceive than I to speak of.
Orlando. I thank you, sir; and pray you tell me this:
Which of the two was daughter of the Duke,   250
That here was at the wrestling?
Le Beau. Neither his daughter, if we judge by manners,
But yet indeed the taller is his daughter,
The other is daughter to the banished Duke,
And here detained by her usurping uncle   255

---

226 S.D. *chain* (see III, ii, 172) 227 *suits* favor 230 *better parts* i.e. composure and manners
232 *quintain* post with crossbars for tilting 237 *Have with you* come on 239 *urged conference* invited conversation 245 *condition* dispostion 246 *misconsters* misconstrues 247 *humorous* subject to emotional disturbances 253 *taller* (either Le Beau or Shakespeare is here
confused; Rosalind, not Celia, is later shown to be the taller)

To keep his daughter company, whose loves
Are dearer than the natural bond of sisters.
But I can tell you that of late this Duke
Hath ta'en displeasure 'gainst his gentle niece,
Grounded upon no other argument   260
But that the people praise her for her virtues
And pity her for her good father's sake;
And on my life, his malice 'gainst the lady
Will suddenly break forth. Sir, fare you well.
Hereafter, in a better world than this,   265
I shall desire more love and knowledge of you.
Orlando. I rest much bounden to you. Fare you well.

                                         [Exit Le Beau.]

Thus must I from the smoke into the smother,
From tyrant Duke unto a tyrant brother.
But heavenly Rosalind!   *Exit.* 270

                Enter Celia and Rosalind.   I,iii

Celia. Why, cousin, why, Rosalind! Cupid have mercy,
    not a word?
Rosalind. Not one to throw at a dog.
Celia. No, thy words are too precious to be cast away
    upon curs; throw some of them at me; come, lame me   5
    with reasons.
Rosalind. Then there were two cousins laid up, when the
    one should be lamed with reasons and the other mad
    without any.
Celia. But is all this for your father?   10
Rosalind. No, some of it is for my child's father. O, how
    full of briers is this working-day world!
Celia. They are but burrs, cousin, thrown upon thee in
    holiday foolery; if we walk not in the trodden paths,
    our very petticoats will catch them.   15
Rosalind. I could shake them off my coat; these burrs are
    in my heart.
Celia. Hem them away.
Rosalind. I would try, if I could cry 'hem,' and have him.
Celia. Come, come, wrestle with thy affections.   20
Rosalind. O, they take the part of a better wrestler than
    myself!
Celia. O, a good wish upon you! You will try in time, in
    despite of a fall. But turning these jests out of service,
    let us talk in good earnest. Is it possible on such a sudden 25

260 *argument* reason 265 *world* state of affairs 268 *smother* suffocation I, iii, 5-6 *lame me*
with reasons injure me with explanations 18 *Hem* tuck 19 *cry 'hem'* clear the throat 23 *try*
make trial (as 'wrestler'?) 24 *fall* (a quibble on this word)

you should fall into so strong a liking with old Sir Row-
land's youngest son?
Rosalind. The Duke my father loved his father dearly.
Celia. Doth it therefore ensue that you should love his son
    dearly? By this kind of chase, I should hate him, for my   30
    father hated his father dearly; yet I hate not Orlando.
Rosalind. No, faith, hate him not, for my sake.
Celia. Why should I not? Doth he not deserve well?

           Enter Duke [Frederick], with Lords.

Rosalind. Let me love him for that, and do you love him
    because I do. Look, here comes the Duke.   35
Celia. With his eyes full of anger.
Duke Frederick. Mistress, dispatch you with your safest haste
    And get you from our court.
Rosalind.   Me, uncle?
Duke Frederick.   You, cousin.
    Within these ten days if that thou beest found
    So near our public court as twenty miles,   40
    Thou diest for it.
Rosalind.   I do beseech your Grace
    Let me the knowledge of my fault bear with me.
    If with myself I hold intelligence
    Or have acquaintance with mine own desires,
    If that I do not dream or be not frantic,   45
    As I do trust I am not; then, dear uncle,
    Never so much as in a thought unborn
    Did I offend your Highness.
Duke Frederick.   Thus do all traitors.
    If their purgation did consist in words,
    They are as innocent as grace itself.   50
    Let it suffice thee that I trust thee not.
Rosalind. Yet your mistrust cannot make me a traitor.
    Tell me whereon the likelihoods depends.
Duke Frederick. Thou art thy father's daughter, there's
      enough.
Rosalind. So was I when your Highness took his dukedom;   55
    So was I when your Highness banished him.
    Treason is not inherited, my lord,
    Or if we did derive it from our friends,
    What's that to me? My father was no traitor.

---

30 *chase* argument 33 *deserve well* i.e. to be hated (but Rosalind ignores the implied conclusion) 37 *safest haste* i.e. the hastier the safer 43 *hold intelligence* am in communication
45 *frantic* insane 49 *purgation* exoneration 50 *grace* virtue 53 *likelihoods* i.e. suspicion
58 *friends* kin

Then, good my liege, mistake me not so much   60
  To think my poverty is treacherous.
Celia. Dear sovereign, hear me speak.
Duke Frederick. Ay, Celia. We stayed her for your sake,
  Else had she with her father ranged along.
Celia. I did not then entreat to have her stay;   65
  It was your pleasure and your own remorse.
  I was too young that time to value her,
  But now I know her. If she be a traitor,
  Why, so am I. We still have slept together,
  Rose at an instant, learned, played, eat together;   70
  And wheresoe'er we went, like Juno's swans,
  Still we went coupled and inseparable.
Duke Frederick. She is too subtile for thee; and her smooth-
    ness,
  Her very silence and her patience,
  Speak to the people, and they pity her.   75
  Thou art a fool. She robs thee of thy name,
  And thou wilt show more bright and seem more virtuous
  When she is gone. Then open not thy lips.
  Firm and irrevocable is my doom
  Which I have passed upon her; she is banished.   80
Celia. Pronounce that sentence then o me, my liege;
  I cannot live out of her company.
Duke Frederick. You are a fool. You, niece, provide your-
    self;
  If you outstay the time, upon mine honor,
  And in the greatness of my word, you die.   85

                                    Exit Duke, &c.

Celia. O my poor Rosalind, whither wilt thou go?
  Wilt thou change fathers? I will give thee mine.
  I charge thee be not thou more grieved than I am.
Rosalind. I have more cause.
Celia.   Thou hast not, cousin.
  Prithee be cheerful. Know'st thou not the Duke   90
  Hath banished me, his daughter?
Rosalind.   That he hath not.
Celia. No? hath not? Rosalind lacks then the love
  Which teacheth thee that thou and I am one.
  Shall we be sund'red, shall we part, sweet girl?
  No, let my father seek another heir.   95
  Therefore devise with me how we may fly,

---

66 *remorse* compunction 71 *Juno's swans* (according to Ovid it was Venus who was drawn through the air by a pair of swans) 73 *subtile* crafty 77 *virtuous* possessed of good qualities 85 *greatness* authority 96 *devise* plan

Whither to go, and what to bear with us;
And do not seek to take your change upon you,
To bear your griefs yourself and leave me out;
For, by this heaven, now at our sorrows pale,   100
Say what thou canst, I'll go along with thee.
Rosalind. Why, whither shall we go?
Celia. To seek my uncle in the Forest of Arden.
Rosalind. Alas, what danger will it be to us,
Maids as we are, to travel forth so far!   105
Beauty provoketh thieves sooner than gold.
Celia. I'll put myself in poor and mean attire
And with a kind of umber smirch my face;
The like do you; so shall we pass along
And never stir assailants.
Rosalind.   Were it not better,   110
Because that I am more than common tall,
That I did suit me all points like a man?
A gallant curtle-axe upon my thigh,
A boar-spear in my hand; and, in my heart
Lie there what hidden woman's fear there will,   115
We'll have a swashing and a martial outside,
As many other mannish cowards have
That do outface it with their semblances.
Celia. What shall I call thee when thou art a man?
Rosalind. I'll have no worse a name than Jove's own page,   120
And therefore look you call me Ganymede.
But what will you be called?
Celia. Something that hath a reference to my state:
No longer Celia, but Aliena.
Rosalind. But, cousin, what if we assayed to steal   125
The clownish fool out of your father's court;
Would he not be a comfort to our travel?
Celia. He'll go along o'er the wide world with me;
Leave me alone to woo him. Let's away
And get our jewels and our wealth together,   130
Devise the fittest time and safest way
To hide us from pursuit that will be made
After my flight. Now go in we content
To liberty, and not to banishment.   *Exeunt.*

---

98 *change* i.e. of fortunes 108 *umber* brown earth 112 *suit me all points* dress completely
113 *curtle-axe* curved sword 116 *swashing* blustering 117 *mannish* i.e. pretending manliness
118 *outface it* bluff 121 *Ganymede* (who for his beauty was made cupbearer to Jove)
124 *Aliena* i.e. estranged 125 *assayed* undertook 129 *woo* coax

----

Enter Duke Senior, Amiens, and two or three Lords,   II,i
like Foresters.

Duke Senior. Now, my co-mates and brothers in exile,
      Hath not old custom made this life more sweet
      Than that of painted pomp? Are not these woods
      More free from peril than the envious court?
      Here feel we not the penalty of Adam;   5
      The seasons' difference, as the icy fang
      And churlish chiding of the winter's wind,
      Which, when it bites and blows upon my body
      Even till I shrink with cold, I smile and say
      'This is no flattery'; these are counsellors   10
      That feelingly persuade me what I am.
      Sweet are the uses of adversity,
      Which, like the toad, ugly and venomous,
      Wears yet a precious jewel in his head;
      And this our life, exempt from public haunt,   15
      Finds tongues in trees, books in the running brooks,
      Sermons in stones, and good in everything.
Amiens. I would not change it; happy is your Grace
      That can translate the stubbornness of fortune
      Into so quiet and so sweet a style.   20
Duke Senior. Come, shall we go and kill us venison?
      And yet it irks me the poor dappled fools,
      Being native burghers of this desert city,
      Should, in their own confines, with forkèd heads
      Have their round haunches gored.
1. Lord.   Indeed, my lord,   25
      The melancholy Jaques grieves at that,
      And in that kind swears you do more usurp
      Than doth your brother that hath banished you.
      To-day my Lord of Amiens and myself
      Did steal behind him as he lay along   30
      Under an oak, whose antique root peeps out
      Upon the brook that brawls along this wood,
      To the which place a poor sequest'red stag
      That from the hunter's aim had ta'en a hurt
      Did come to languish; and indeed, my lord,   35

II, i, 5 *not* (frequently emended to *but*) *penalty of Adam* loss of innocence, expulsion from Garden of Eden (see Genesis 3) 6 *as* for example 7 *churlish* rough 13-14 *toad . . . head* ('The foul toad hath a fair stone in his head.'—Lyly, *Euphues*) 15 *haunt* society 19 *stubborness* hardness 22 *fools* pitiable creatures 23 *desert* uninhabited (rather than devoid of vegetation) 24 *confines* territory *forkèd heads* barbed arrowheads 27 *kind* way 32 *brawls* makes noisy sounds 33 *sequest'red* separated

The wretched animal heaved forth such groans
That their discharge did stretch his leathern coat
Almost to bursting, and the big round tears
Coursed one another down his innocent nose
In piteous chase; and thus the hairy fool,   40
Much markèd of the melancholy Jaques,
Stood on th' extremest verge of the swift brook,
Augmenting it with tears.
Duke Senior.   But what said Jaques?
Did he not moralize this spectacle?
1. Lord. O, yes, into a thousand similes.   45
First, for his weeping into the needless stream:
'Poor deer,' quoth he, 'thou mak'st a testament
As worldings do, giving thy sum of more
To that which had too much.' Then, being there alone,
Left and abandoned of his velvet friend: 50
''Tis right,' quoth he, 'thus misery doth part
The flux of company.' Anon a careless herd,
Full of the pasture, jumps along by him
And never stays to greet him; 'Ay,' quoth Jaques,
Sweep on, you fat and greasy citizens,   55
'Tis just the fashion; wherefore do you look
Upon that poor and broken bankrupt there?'
Thus most invectively he pierceth through
The body of the country, city, court,
Yea, and of this our life, swearing that we   60
Are mere usurpers, tyrants, and what's worse,
To fright the animals and to kill them up
In their assigned and native dwelling place.
Duke Senior. And did you leave him in this contemplation?
2. Lord. We did, my lord, weeping and commenting   65
Upon the sobbing deer.
Duke Senior.   Show me the place.
I love to cope him in these sullen fits,
For then he's full of matter.
1. Lord. I'll bring you to him straight.   *Exeunt.*

Enter Duke [Frederick], with Lords.   II,ii

Duke Frederick. Can it be possible that no man saw them?
It cannot be; some villains of my court
Are of consent and sufferance in this.

---

38 *tears* (wounded deer were commonly supposed to shed tears) 44 *moralize* draw a moral
from 46 *needless* needing no more water 50 *velvet* in the 'velvet' stage 52 *flux* confluence
62 *up* off 63 *assigned* i.e. in the natural order 67 *cope* cope with II, ii, 3 *of consent and
sufferance* in connivance

1. Lord. I cannot hear of any that did see her.
   The ladies her attendants of her chamber   5
   Saw her abed, and in the morning early
   They found the bed untreasured of their mistress.
2. Lord. My lord, the roynish clown at whom so oft
   Your Grace was wont to laugh is also missing.
   Hisperia, the princess' gentlewoman,   10
   Confesses that she secretly o'erheard
   Your daughter and her cousin much commend
   The parts and graces of the wrestler
   That did but lately foil the sinewy Charles,
   And she believes, wherever they are gone,   15
   That youth is surely in their company.
Duke Frederick. Send to his brother, fetch that gallant
     hither;
   If he be absent, bring his brother to me;
   I'll make him find him Do this suddenly,
   And let not search and inquisition quail   20
   To bring again these foolish runaways.   *Exeunt.*

Enter Orlando and Adam   II,iii

Orlando. Who's there?
Adam. What, my young master, O my gentle master,
   O my sweet master, O you memory
   Of old Sir Rowland, why, what make you here?
   Why are you virtuous? Why do people love you?   5
   And wherefore are you gentle, strong, and valiant?
   Why would you be so fond to overcome
   The bonny prizer of the humorous Duke?
   Your praise is come too swiftly home before you.
   Know you not, master, to some kind of men   10
   Their graces serve them but as enemies?
   No more do yours. Your virtues, gentle master,
   Are sanctified and holy traitors to you.
   O, what a world is this, when what is comely
   Envenoms him that bears it!   15
Orlando. Why, what's the matter?
Adam.   O unhappy youth,
   Come not within these doors; within this roof
   The enemy of all your graces lives.

8 *roynish* scurvy 13 *parts* good qualities 19 *suddenly* at once 20 *inquisition quail* enquiry
falter II, iii, 3 *memory* living memorial 7 *fond* foolish 8 *bonny prizer* sturdy prize-fighter
humorous temperamental, capricious 12 *No more* no better 12-13 *Your virtues . . . to you*
i.e. Orlando's virtues, although worthy of religious approval, have only worked against him
in the mind of his brother

Your brother, no, no brother, yet the son
(Yet not the son, I will not call him son)   20
Of him I was about to call his father,
Hath heard your praises, and this night he means
To burn the lodging where you use to lie
And you within it. If he fail of that,
He will have other means to cut you off.   25
I overheard him, and his practices;
This is no place, this house is but a butchery;
Abhor it, fear it, do not enter it!
Orlando. Why, whither, Adam, wouldst thou have me go?
Adam. No matter whither, so you come not here.   30
Orlando. What, wouldst thou have me go and beg my food,
  Or with a base and boist'rous sword enforce
  A thievish living on the common road?
  This I must do, or know not what to do;
  Yet this I will not do, do how I can.   35
  I rather will subject me to the malice
  Of a diverted blood and bloody brother.
Adam But do not so. I have five hundred crowns,
  The thrifty hire I saved under your father,
  Which I did store to be my foster nurse   40
  When service should in my old limbs lie lame
  And unregarded age in corners thrown.
  Take that, and he that doth the ravens feed,
  Yea, providently caters for the sparrow,
  Be comfort to my age. Here is the gold,   45
  All this I give you. Let me be your servant;
  Though I look old, yet I am strong and lusty,
  For in my youth I never did apply
  Hot and rebellious liquors in my blood,
  Nor did not with unbashful forehead woo   50
  The means of weakness and debility;
  Therefore my age is as a lusty winter,
  Frosty, but kindly. Let me go with you;
  I'll do the service of a younger man
  In all your business and necessities.   55
Orlando. O good old man, how well in thee appears
  The constant service of the antique world,
  When service sweat for duty, not for meed!
  Thou art not for the fashion of these times,

23 *use* are accustomed 26 *practices* plots 37 *diverted* i.e. from natural affection 39 *thrifty hire I saved* wages I thriftily saved 41 *service . . . lame* ability to serve should be weakend by old age 43-44 *ravens . . . sparrow* (see Psalms 147:9; Luke 12:6) 49 *rebellious* causing rebellion against self-control 50 *unbashful forehead* shameless face 57 *constant* faithful 58 *meed* reward

Where none will sweat but for promotion,   60
And having that, do choke their service up
Even with the having; it is not so with thee.
But, poor old man, thou prun'st a rotten tree
That cannot so much as a blossom yield
In lieu of all thy pains and husbandry.   65
But come thy ways, we'll go along together,
And ere we have thy youthful wages spent,
We'll light upon some settled low content.
Adam. Master, go on, and I will follow thee
To the last gasp with truth and loyalty.   70
From seventeen years till now almost fourscore
Here livèd I, but now live here no more;
At seventeen years many their fortunes seek,
But at fourscore it is too late a week;
Yet fortune cannot recompense me better   75
Than to die well and not my master's debtor.   *Exeunt.*

———

Enter Rosalind for Ganymede, Celia for Aliena, and   II,iv
Clown, alias Touchstone.

Rosalind. O Jupiter, how merry are my spirits!
Touchstone. I care not for my spirits if my legs were not
    weary.
Rosalind. I could find in my heart to disgrace my man's
    apparel and to cry like a woman; but I must comfort the   5
    weaker vessel, as doublet and hose ought to show itself
    courageous to petticoat. Therefore, courage, good
    Aliena!
Celia. I pray you bear with me; I cannot go no further.
Touchstone. For my part, I had rather bear with you than   10
    bear you; yet I should bear no cross if I did bear you, for
    I think you have no money in your purse.
Rosalind. Well, this is the Forest of Arden.
Touchstone. Ay, now am I in Arden, the more fool I.
    When I was at home, I was in a better place, but travel-   15
    lers must be content.

Enter Corin and Silvius.

Rosalind. Ay, be so, good Touchstone. Look you, who
        comes here,
    A young man and an old in solemn talk.

61-62 *do choke... having* cease their service on gaining promotion 65 *In lieu of* in return
for 68 *low content* humble contentment 74 *week* time II, iv, 1 *merry* (presumably ironic;
often emended to *weary*) 6 *doublet and hose* jacket and breeches 11 *cross* (1) burden (2)
penny, which had a cross stamped on it (a stock pun)

Corin. That is the way to make her scorn you still.
Silvius. O Corin, that thou knew'st how I do love her!   20
Corin. I partly guess, for I have loved ere now.
Silvius. No, Corin, being old, thou canst not guess,
 Though in thy youth thou wast as true a lover
 As ever sighed upon a midnight pillow.
 But if thy love were ever like to mine,   25
 As sure I think did never man love so,
 How many actions most ridiculous
 Hast thou been drawn to by thy fantasy?
Corin. Into a thousand that I have forgotten.
Silvius. O, thou didst then never love so heartily!   30
 If thou rememb'rest not the slightest folly
 That ever love did make thee run into,
 Thou hast not loved.
 Or if thou hast not sat as I do now,
 Wearing thy hearer in thy mistress' praise,   35
 Thou hast not loved.
 Or if thou hast not broke from company
 Abruptly, as my passion now makes me,
 Thou hast not loved. O Phebe, Phebe, Phebe!   *Exit.*
Rosalind. Alas, poor shepherd! Searching of thy wound,   40
 I have by hard adventure found mine own.
Touchstone. And I mine. I remember, when I was in love
 I broke my sword upon a stone and bid him take that
 for coming a-night to Jane Smile; and I remember the
 kissing of her batler, and the cow's dugs that her pretty   45
 chopt hands had milked; and I remember the wooing
 of a peascod instead of her, from whom I took two cods,
 and giving her them again, said with weeping tears,
 'Wear these for my sake.' We that are true lovers run
 into strange capers; but as all is mortal in nature, so is   50
 all nature in love mortal in folly.
Rosalind. Thou speak'st wiser than thou art ware of.
Touchstone. Nay, I shall ne'er be ware of mine own wit till
 I break my shins against it.
Rosalind. Jove, Jove! this shepherd's passion   55
 Is much upon my fashion.
Touchstone. And mine, but it grows something stale with
 me.

---

28 *fantasy* (Corin's love is likened to a mere fancy) 35 *Wearing* wearying 40 *Searching* probing *thy wound* (folio reads *they would*) 45 *batler* bat used in washing clothes 46 *chopt* chapped 47 *peascod* pea pod (here used for whole plan) 51 *mortal in folly* i.e. by its foolishness shows its human nature, which is subject to mortality 52 *ware* aware

Celia. I pray you, one of you question yond man
    If he for gold will give us any food.   60
    I faint almost to death.
Touchstone.   Holla, you clown!
Rosalind. Peace, fool! he's not thy kinsman.
Corin. Who calls?
Touchstone.   Your betters, sir.
Corin.   Else are they very wretched.
Rosalind. Peace, I say! Good even to you, friend.
Corin. And to you, gentle sir, and to you all.   65
Rosalind. I prithee, shepherd, if that love or gold
    Can in this desert place buy entertainment,
    Bring us where we may rest ourselves and feed.
    Here's a young maid with travel much oppressed,
    And faints for succor.
Corin.   Fair sir, I pity her   70
    And wish, for her sake more than for mine own,
    My fortunes were more able to relieve her;
    But I am shepherd to another man
    And do not shear the fleeces that I graze.
    My master is of churlish disposition   75
    And little recks to find the way to heaven
    By doing deeds of hospitality.
    Besides, his cote, his flocks, and bounds of feed
    Are now on sale, and at our sheepcote now,
    By reason of his absence, there is nothing   80
    That you will feed on; but what is, come see,
    And in my voice most welcome shall you be.
Rosalind. What is he that shall buy his flock and pasture?
Corin. That young swain that you saw here but ere-
    while,
    That little cares for buying anything.   85
Rosalind. I pray thee, if it stand with honesty,
    Buy thou the cottage, pasture, and the flock,
    And thou shalt have to pay for it of us.
Celia. And we will mend thy wages. I like this place
    And willingly could waste my time in it.   90
Corin. Assuredly the thing is to be sold.
    Go with me; if you like upon report
    The soil, the profit, and this kind of life,
    I will your very faithful feeder be
    And buy it with your gold right suddenly.   *Exeunt.* 95

---

61 *clown* yokel 67 *desert* uninhabited *entertainment* food and lodging 76 *recks* reckons
78 *cote* cottage *bounds of feed* pastures 82 *in my voice* as far as I have any influence
86 *if . . . honesty* if it is consistent with honorable dealing 88 *have to pay* have the money to
pay 89 *mend* improve 90 *waste* spend 92 *report* further information 94 *feeder* servant

Enter Amiens, Jaques, and others.

Song.

[*Amiens.*] Under the greenwood tree
    Who loves to lie with me,
    And turn his merry note
      Unto the sweet bird's throat,
Come hither, come hither, come hither.   5
      Here shall he see no enemy
    But winter and rough weather.

Jaques. More, more, I prithee more!
Amiens. It will make you melancholy, Monsieur Jaques.
Jaques. I thank it. More, I prithee more! I can suck melan-   10
    choly out of a song as a weasel sucks eggs. More, I
    prithee more!
Amiens. My voice is ragged. I know I cannot please you.
Jaques. I do not desire you to please me; I do desire you to
    sing. Come, more, another stanzo! Call you 'em stanzos?   15
Amiens. What you will, Monsieur Jaques.
Jaques. Nay, I care not for their names; they owe me
    nothing. Will you sing?
Amiens. More at your request than to please myself.
Jaques. Well then, if ever I thank any man, I'll thank you.   20
    But that they call compliment is like th' encounter of
    two dog-apes, and when a man thanks me heartily,
    methinks I have given him a penny and he renders me the
    beggarly thanks. Come, sing; and you that will not, hold
    your tongues.   25
Amiens. Well, I'll end the song. Sirs, cover the while; the
    Duke will drink under this tree. He hath been all this day
    to look you.
Jaques. And I have been all this day to avoid him. He is
    too disputable for my company. I think of as many   30
    matters as he, but I give heaven thanks and make no
    boast of them Come, warble, come.

Song.

All together here.

Who doth ambition shun
    And loves to live i' th' sun,
    Seeking the food he eats,   35
      And pleased with what he gets,

II, v, 3 *turn* attune 21 *compliment* politeness 21-22 *th' encounter . . . dog-apes* i.e. a mutual
mockery (*dog-apes*=baboons) 24 *beggarly* effusive, like a beggar's 26 *cover the while* meanwhile set the cloth for a meal 28 *to look* looking for

                    Come hither, come hither, come hither.
                        Here shall he see no enemy
                        But winter and rough weather.

Jaques. I'll give you a verse to this note that I made yester-   40
    day in despite of my invention.
Amiens. And I'll sing it.
Jaques. Thus it goes.   *[Gives paper.]*
Amiens.   If it do come to pass
                    That any man turn ass,   45
                    Leaving his wealth and ease
                    A stubborn will to please,
                    Ducdame, ducdame, ducdame.
                    Here shall he see gross fools as he,
                    An if he will come to me.   50

    What's that 'ducdame'?
Jaques. 'Tis a Greek invocation to call fools into a circle.
    I'll go sleep, if I can; if I cannot, I'll rail against all the
    first-born of Egypt.
Amiens. And I'll go seek the Duke. His banquet is prepared.   55

                                                            Exeunt.

                              ————

                    Enter Orlando and Adam.   II,vi

Adam. Dear master, I can go no further. O, I die for food.
    Here lie I down and measure out my grave. Farewell,
    kind master.
Orlando. Why, how now, Adam? no greater heart in thee?
    Live a little, comfort a little, cheer thyself a little. If this   5
    uncouth forest yield anything savage, I will either be
    food for it or bring it for food to thee. Thy conceit is
    nearer death than thy powers. For my sake be comfort-
    able; hold death awhile at the arm's end. I will here be
    with thee presently, and if I bring thee not something   10
    to eat, I will give thee leave to die; but if thou diest
    before I come, thou art a mocker of my labor. Well said;
    thou look'st cheerily, and I'll be with thee quickly. Yet
    thou liest in the bleak air. Come, I will bear thee to some

---

38-39 *no enemy . . . weather* (expanded from &c. in folio) 40 *note* tune 41 *in . . . invention*
although I lack imagination 44 *Amiens* (song sung by Jaques in Second Folio and most
modern editions) 48 *Ducdame* (trisyllabic; variously explained as deriving from gypsy 'dukrā
mē,' a fortuneteller's cry to the gullible; from Welsh 'dewch 'da mi,' meaning 'come with
me'; etc.) 54 *first-born of Egypt* (whose death finally resulted in sending the Israelites into
the wilderness; see Exodus 11, 12) II, vi, 6 *uncouth* uncivilized 7 *conceit* thought 8-9 *comfortable* cheerful

shelter, and thou shalt not die for lack of a dinner if   15
there live anything in this desert. Cheerily, good Adam.

                                                      Exeunt.

          Enter Duke Senior, and Lords, like Outlaws.   II,vii

Duke Senior. I think he be transformed into a beast,
  For I can nowhere find him like a man.
1. Lord. My lord, he is but even now gone hence;
  Here was he merry, hearing of a song.
Duke Senior. If he, compact of jars, grow musical,   5
  We shall have shortly discord in the spheres.
  Go seek him; tell him I would speak with him.

                Enter Jaques.

1. Lord. He saves my labor by his own approach.
Duke Senior. Why, how now, monsieur, what a life is this,
  That your poor friends must woo your company?   10
  What, you look merrily.
Jaques. A fool, a fool! I met a fool i' th' forest,
  A motley fool! a miserable world!
  As I do live by food, I met a fool
  Who laid him down and basked him in the sun   15
  And railed on Lady Fortune in good terms,
  In good set terms, and yet a motley fool.
  'Good morrow, fool,' quoth I. 'No, sir,' quoth he,
  'Call me not fool till heaven hath sent me fortune.
  And then he drew a dial from his poke,   20
  And looking on it with lack-lustre eye,
  Says very wisely, 'It is ten o'clock.
  Thus we may see,' quoth he, 'how the world wags.
  'Tis but an hour ago since it was nine,
  And after one hour more 'twill be eleven;   25
  And so, from hour to hour, we ripe and ripe,
  And then, from hour to hour, we rot and rot;
  And thereby hangs a tale.' When I did hear
  The motley fool thus moral on the time,
  My lungs began to crow like chanticleer   30
  That fools should be so deep contemplative;
  And I did laugh sans intermission

II, vii, 5 *compact of jars* composed of discords 6 *spheres* (the harmonious crystal spheres in
which the planets were supposedly set) 13 *motley* wearing a costume of mixed colors, the
conventional dress of a professional jester 20 *dial* portable sundial *poke* pocket 26 *hour to
hour* (perhaps a homonymic pun on 'whore') 29 *moral* moralize 30 *crow like chanticleer*
exclaim triumphantly, like the crowing of the cock 32 *sans* without

An hour by his dial. O noble fool,
    A worthy fool! Motley's the only wear.
Duke Senior. What fool is this?   35
Jaques. O worthy fool! One that hath been a courtier,
    And says, if ladies be but young and fair,
    They have the gift to know it. And in his brain,
    Which is as dry as the remainder biscuit
    After a voyage, he hath strange places crammed   40
    With observation, the which he vents
    In mangled forms. O that I were a fool!
    I am ambitious for a motley coat.
Duke Senior. Thou shalt have one.
Jaques.   It is my only suit,
    Provided that you weed your better judgments   45
    Of all opinion that grows rank in them
    That I am wise. I must have liberty
    Withal, as large a charter as the wind,
    To blow on whom I please, for so fools have.
    And they that are most gallèd with my folly,   50
    They most must laugh. And why, sir, must they so?
    The why is plain as way to parish church:
    He that a fool doth very wisely hit
    Doth very foolishly, although he smart
    Within, seem senseless of the bob. If not,   55
    The wise man's folly is anatomized
    Even by the squand'ring glances of the fool.
    Invest me in my motley, give me leave
    To speak my mind, and I will through and through
    Cleanse the foul body of th' infected world,   60
    If they will patiently receive my medicine.
Duke Senior. Fie on thee! I can tell what thou wouldst do.
Jaques. What, for a counter, would I do but good?
Duke Senior. Most mischievous foul sin, in chiding sin.
    For thou thyself has been a libertine,   65
    As sensual as the brutish sting itself;
    And all th' embossèd sores and headed evils
    That thou with license of free foot hast caught,
    Wouldst thou disgorge into the general world.
Jaques. Why, who cries out on pride   70
    That can therein tax any private party?

---

34 *wear* costume 39 *dry* (a dry brain was supposedly retentive) 44 *suit* (1) costume (2)
request 48 *large a charter* broad license 50 *gallèd* rubbed on a sore spot 55 *Within* (not in
folio) *senseless of the bob* unaware of the taunt *If not* if he does not acknowledge the hit
56 *anatomized* revealed, as by dissection 57 *squand'ring glances* random hits 63 *counter*
worthless coin 66 *brutish sting* carnal appetite 67 *embossèd* swollen (the image here is from
venereal disease) 68 *license . . . foot* licentious freedom 71 *tax* censure

Doth it not flow as hugely as the sea
Till that the weary very means do ebb?
What woman in the city do I name
When that I say the city woman bears   75
The cost of princes on unworthy shoulders?
Who can come in and say that I mean her,
When such a one as she, such is her neighbor?
Or what is he of basest function
That says his bravery is not on my cost,   80
Thinking that I mean him, but therein suits
His folly to the mettle of my speech?
There then, how then, what then? Let me see wherein
My tongue hath wronged him. If it do him right,
Then he hath wronged himself. If he be free,   85
Why, then my taxing like a wild goose flies
Unclaimed of any man. But who comes here?

Enter Orlando [with his sword drawn].

Orlando. Forbear, and eat no more!
Jaques.   Why, I have eat none yet.
Orlando. Nor shalt not, till necessity be served.
Jaques. Of what kind should this cock come of?   90
Duke Senior. Art thou thus boldened, man, by thy distress,
   Or else a rude despair of good manners,
   That in civility thou seem'st so empty?
Orlando. You touched my vein at first. The thorny point
   Of bare distress hath ta'en from me the show   95
   Of smooth civility; yet am I inland bred
   And know some nurture. But forbear, I say!
   He dies that touches any of this fruit
   Till I and my affairs are answerèd.
Jaques. An you will not be answerèd with reason, I must   100
   die.
Duke Senior. What would you have? Your gentleness shall
      force
   More than your force move us to gentleness.
Orlando. I almost die for food, and let me have it!
Duke Senior. Sit down and feed, and welcome to our table.   105

---

73 *weary . . . ebb* i.e. ostentation subsides from exhaustion 79 *function* position in society
80 *says . . . cost* says his finery is not bought at my price, i.e. denies my criticism
81-82 *therein . . . speech* thus matches his folly with the substance of my remarks 85 *free*
i.e. from blame 94 *vein* condition 96 *inland bred* raised in civilized society 97 *nurture*
proper upbringing 99 *answerèd* given attention 100 *an* if *reason* (perhaps a homonytmic pun
on 'raisin,' i.e. grape, as Jaques takes fruit from the table)

Orlando. Speak you so gently? Pardon me, I pray you.
   I thought that all things had been savage here,
   And therefore put I on the countenance
   Of stern commandment. But whate'er you are
   That in this desert inaccessible,   110
   Under the shade of melancholy boughs,
   Lose and neglect the creeping hours of time;
   If ever you have looked on better days,
   If ever been where bells have knolled to church,
   If ever sat at any good man's feast,   115
   If ever from your eyelids wiped a tear
   And know what 'tis to pity and be pitied,
   Let gentleness my strong enforcement be;
   In the white hope I blush, and hide by sword.
Duke Senior. True is it that we have seen better days,   120
   And have with holy bell been knolled to church,
   And sat at good men's feasts, and wiped our eyes
   Of drops that sacred pity hath engend'red;
   And therefore sit you down in gentleness,
   And take upon command what help we have   125
   That to your wanting may be minist'red.
Orlando. Then but forbear your food a little while,
   Whiles, like a doe, I go to find my fawn
   And give it food. There is an old poor man
   Who after me hath many a weary step   130
   Limped in pure love. Till he be first sufficed,
   Oppressed with two weak evils, age and hunger,
   I will not touch a bit.
Duke Senior.   Go find him out,
   And we will nothing waste till you return.
Orlando. I thank ye, and be blest for your good comfort!   135
                                  [Exit.]

Duke Senior. Thou seest we are not all alone unhappy:
   This wide and universal theatre
   Presents more woeful pageants than the scene
   Wherein we play in.
Jaques.   All the world's a stage,
   And all the men and women merely players;   140
   They have their exits and their entrances,
   And one man in his time plays many parts,
   His acts being seven ages. At first, the infant,
     Mewling and puking in the nurse's arms.

108 *countenance* appearance 114 *knolled* called by chimes 118 *enforcement* inducement
119 *blush* (original sense=glow) 125 *upon command* for the asking 139 *All . . . stage* (a
stock metaphor in classical and Renaissance literature, here given fresh vividness)
144 *Mewling* crying *puking* vomiting

Then the whining schoolboy, with his satchel 145
And shining morning face, creeping like snail
Unwillingly to school. And then the lover,
Sighing like furnace, with a woeful ballad
Made to his mistress' eyebrow. Then a soldier,
Full of strange oaths and bearded like the pard, 150
Jealous in honor, sudden and quick in quarrel,
Seeking the bubble reputation
Even in the cannon's mouth. And then the justice,
In fair round belly with good capon lined,
With eyes severe and beard of formal cut, 155
Full of wise saws and modern instances;
And so he plays his part. The sixth age shifts
Into the lean and slippered pantaloon,
With spectacles on nose and pouch on side;
His youthful hose, well saved, a world too wide 160
For his shrunk shank, and his big manly voice,
Turning again toward childish treble, pipes
And whistles in his sound. Last scene of all,
That ends this strange eventful history,
Is second childishness and mere oblivion, 165
Sans teeth, sans eyes, sans taste, sans everything.

Enter Orlando, with Adam.

Duke Senior. Welcome. Set down your venerable burden
  And let him feed.
Orlando. I thank you most for him.
Adam.   So had you need.
  I scarce can speak to thank you for myself. 170
Duke Senior. Welcome, fall to. I will not trouble you
  As yet to question you about your fortunes.
  Give us some music; and, good cousin, sing.

Song.

[*Amiens.*] Blow, blow, thou winter wind,
    Thou art not so unkind 175
      As man's ingratitude:
      Thy tooth is not so keen,
      Because thou art not seen,

150 *pard* leopard 151 *Jealous in* zealous in seeking *sudden* rash 154 *capon* (alluding to the well-known Elizabethan practice of offering a gift of a capon to a judge, in hope of gaining his favor) 156 *saws* maxims *modern instances* everyday examples 158 *pantaloon* ridiculous old man (a figure in Italian comedy) 163 *his* its 166 S.D. *Enter . . . Adam* (see Introduction, p. 22) 178 *not seen* (hence, not personal)

> Although thy breath be rude.
> Heigh-ho, sing heigh-ho, unto the green holly.   180
> Most friendship is faining, most loving mere folly:
>   Then, heigh-ho, the holly.
>   This life is most jolly.
>
> Freeze, freeze, thou bitter sky
> That dost not bite so nigh   185
>   As benefits forgot:
> Though thou the waters warp,
> Thy sting is not so sharp
>   As friend rememb'red not.
> Heigh-ho, sing, &c.   190

Duke Senior. If that you were the good Sir Rowland's son,
  As you have whispered faithfully you were,
  And as mine eye doth his effigies witness
  Most truly limned and living in your face,
  Be truly welcome hither. I am the Duke   195
  That loved your father. The residue of your fortune
  Go to my cave and tell me. Good old man,
  Thou art right welcome, as thy master is.
  Support him by the arm. Give me your hand,
  And let me all your fortunes understand.   *Exeunt.*   200

Enter Duke [Frederick], Lords, and Oliver.   III,i

Duke Frederick. Not see him since? Sir, sir, that cannot be.
  But were I not the better part made mercy,
  I should not seek an absent argument
  Of my revenge, thou present. But look to it:
  Find out thy brother, wheresoe'er he is;   5
  Seek him with candle; bring him dead or living
  Within this twelvemonth, or turn thou no more
  To seek a living in our territory.
  Thy lands, and all things that thou dost call thine
  Worth seizure, do we seize into our hands   10
  Till thou canst quit thee by thy brother's mouth
  Of what we think against thee.
Oliver. O that your Highness knew my heart in this!
  I never loved my brother in my life.

---

181 *faining* longing, wishful thinking 187 *warp* freeze 193 *effigies* replica (accent on second syllable) 194 *limned* portrayed 197 *Go* walk III, i, 3 *argument* subject, i.e. Orlando 4 *thou present* you being present 7 *turn* return 11 *quit* acquit

Duke Frederick. More villain thou. Well, push him out of
    doors,   15
    And let my officers of such a nature
    Make an extent upon his house and lands.
    Do this expediently and turn him going.   *Exeunt.*

              Enter Orlando, [with a writing].   III,ii

Orlando. Hang there, my verse, in witness of my love;
    And thou, thrice-crownèd Queen of Night, survey
With thy chaste eye, from thy pale sphere above,
    Thy huntress' name that my full life doth sway.
O Rosalind! these trees shall be my books,   5
    And in their barks my thoughts I'll character,
That every eye which in this forest looks
    Shall see thy virtue witnessed everywhere.
Run, run, Orlando, carve on every tree
The fair, the chaste, and unexpressive she.   *Exit.*   10

     Enter Corin and [Touchstone the] Clown.

Corin. And how like you this shepherd's life, Master
    Touchstone?
Touchstone. Truly, shepherd, in respect of itself, it is a good
    life; but in respect that it is a shepherd's life, it is naught.
    In respect that it is solitary, I like it very well; but in   15
    respect that it is private, it is a very vile life. Now in
    respect it is in the fields, it pleaseth me well; but in
    respect it is not in the court, it is tedious. As it is a spare
    life, look you, it fits my humor well; but as there is no
    more plenty in it, it goes much against my stomach.   20
    Hast any philosophy in thee, shepherd?
Corin. No more but that I know the more one sickens the
    worse at ease he is; and that he that wants money, means,
    and content is without three good friends; that the
    property of rain is to wet and fire to burn; that good   25
    pasture makes fat sheep, and that a great cause of the
    night is lack of the sun; that he that hath learned no wit
    by nature nor art may complain of good breeding, or
    comes of a very dull kindred.

---

17 *Make . . . upon* seize by writ III, ii, 2 *thrice-crownèd . . . Night* the moon (the triple
crowning probably refers to the three goddesses associated with the moon: Cynthia, Diana,
Proserpina) 4 *Thy huntress' name* (Rosalind is conceived as a chaste huntress waiting on
Diana) 6 *character* inscribe 8 *virtue* excellence 10 *unexpressive* beyond expression 13 *in
respect of* considering 16 *private* lonely 19 *humor* state of mind 28 *complain of* decry the
lack of

Touchstone. Such a one is a natural philosopher. Wast ever   30
   in court, shepherd?
Corin. No, truly.
Touchstone. Then thou art damned.
Corin. Nay, I hope.
Touchstone. Truly thou art damned, like an ill-roasted egg,   35
   all on one side.
Corin. For not being at court? Your reason.
Touchstone. Why, if thou never wast at court, thou never
   saw'st good manners; if thou never saw'st good manners,
   then thy manners must be wicked; and wickedness is   40
   sin, and sin is damnation. Thou art in a parlous state,
   shepherd.
Corin. Not a whit, Touchstone. Those that are good manners at the court are as ridiculous in the country as the
   behavior of the country is most mockable at the court.   45
   You told me you salute not at the court but you kiss
   your hands. That courtesy would be uncleanly if courtiers were shepherds.
Touchstone. Instance, briefly. Come, instance.
Corin. Why, we are still handling our ewes, and their   50
   fells you know are greasy.
Touchstone. Why, do not your courtier's hands sweat? and
   is not the grease of a mutton as wholesome as the sweat
   of a man? Shallow, shallow. A better instance, I say.
   Come.   55
Corin. Besides, our hands are hard.
Touchstone. Your lips will feel them the sooner. Shallow
   again. A more sounder instance, come.
Corin. And they are often tarred over with the surgery of
   our sheep, and would you have us kiss tar? The courtier's   60
   hands are perfumed with civet.
Touchstone. Most shallow man! Thou worms' meat in
   respect of a good piece of flesh indeed! Learn of the wise,
   and perpend. Civet is of a baser birth than tar, the very
   uncleanly flux of a cat. Mend the instance, shepherd.   65
Corin. You have too courtly a wit for me; I'll rest.
Touchstone. Wilt thou rest damned? God help thee, shallow
   man! God make incision in thee! thou art raw.
Corin. Sir, I am a true laborer; I earn that I eat, get that I
   wear, owe no man hate, envy no man's happiness, glad   70

39 *manners* (Touchstone plays on the meanings 'etiquette' and 'morals') 41 *parlous* perilous
46 *but* unless 49 *Instance* proof 50 *still* continually 51 *fells* fleeces 59 *tarred . . . surgery*
covered with the tar used as ointment for sores 62 *worms' meat* food for worms, moribund
flesh 64 *perpend* consider 65 *flux* secretion 68 *make incision in* operate on *raw* crude (with
play on 'sore,' requiring operation)

of other men's good, content with my harm; and the
greatest of my pride is to see my ewes graze and my
lambs suck.

Touchstone. That is another simple sin in you: to bring the
ewes and the rams together and to offer to get your living   75
by the copulation of cattle, to be bawd to a bell-wether
and to betray a she-lamb of a twelvemonth to a crooked-
pated old cuckoldly ram, out of all reasonable match. If
thou beest not damned for this, the devil himself will have
no shepherds; I cannot see else how thou shouldst 'scape.   80

Corin. Here comes young Master Ganymede, my new
mistress's brother.

Enter Rosalind, [with a writing].

Rosalind. [reads]
    'From the east to western Inde,
    No jewel is like Rosalinde.
    Her worth, being mounted on the wind,   85
    Through all the world bears Rosalinde.
    All the pictures fairest lined
    Are but black to Rosalinde.
    Let no face be kept in mind
    But the fair of Rosalinde.'   90

Touchstone. I'll rhyme you so eight years together, dinners
and suppers and sleeping hours excepted. It is the right
butterwomen's rank to market.

Rosalind. Out, fool!

Touchstone. For a taste: 95
    If a hart do lack a hind,
    Let him seek out Rosalinde.
    If the cat will after kind,
    So be sure will Rosalinde.
    Wintred garments must be lined,   100
    So must slender Rosalinde.
    They that reap must sheaf and bind,
    Then to cart with Rosalinde.
    Sweetest nut hath sourest rind,
    Such a nut is Rosalinde.   105
    He that sweetest rose will find
    Must find love's prick, and Rosalinde.

77-78 *crooked-pated* with crooked horns 78 *cuckoldly* i.e. because he has horns 87 *lined*
outlined, drawn 92-93 *It is . . . market* i.e. the verses jog on monotonously like farm women
riding to market 100 *Wintred* prepared for winter 103 *to cart* (female delinquents were
publicly carted through the streets)

This is the very false gallop of verses. Why do you infect
yourself with them?

Rosalind. Peace, you dull fool! I found them on a tree.   110

Touchstone. Truly the tree yields bad fruit.

Rosalind. I'll graff it with you and then I shall graff it with
a medlar. Then it will be the earliest fruit i' th' country;
for you'll be rotten ere you be half ripe, and that's the
right virtue of the medlar.   115

Touchstone. You have said; but whether wisely or no, let
the forest judge.

Enter Celia, with a writing.

Rosalind. Peace! Here comes my sister reading; stand aside.

Celia. 'Why should this a desert be?
    For it is unpeopled? No.   120
Tongues I'll hang on every tree
    That shall civil sayings show:
Some, how brief the life of man
    Runs his erring pilgrimage,
That the stretching of a span   125
    Buckles in his sum of age;
Some, of violated vows
    'Twixt the souls of friend and friend;
But upon the fairest boughs,
    Or at every sentence end,   130
Will I "Rosalinda" write,
    Teaching all that read to know
The quintessence of every sprite
    Heaven would in little show.
Therefore heaven Nature charged   135
    That one body should be filled
With all graces wide-enlarged.
    Nature presently distilled
Helen's cheek, but not her heart,
    Cleopatra's majesty,   140
Atalanta's better part,
    Sad Lucretia's modesty.
Thus Rosalinde of many parts
    By heavenly synod was devised,

---

108 *false gallop* gallop starting on wrong foot 112 *graff* graft 113 *medlar* a kind of pear not
ready to eat until it starts to decay (with pun on 'meddler') 122 *civil sayings* civilized
comments 125 *stretching of a span* breadth of an open hand 126 *Buckles in* encompasses
133 *quintessence* pure essence (accent on first syllable) *sprite* spirit 134 *in little* i.e. in one
person, the microcosm 139 *cheek* beauty *heart* i.e. false heart 141 *Atalanta's better part* i.e.
her beauty and swiftness, as opposed to her cruelty

Of many faces, eyes, and hearts, 145
    To have the touches dearest prized.
Heaven would that she these gifts should have,
And I to live and die her slave.'
Rosalind. O most gentle Jupiter, what tedious homily of
    love have you wearied your parishioners withal, and 150
    never cried, 'Have patience, good people'!
Celia. How now? Back, friends. Shepherd, go off a little.
    Go with him, sirrah.
Touchstone. Come, shepherd, let us make an honorable
    retreat; though not with bag and baggage, yet with 155
    scrip and scrippage.   *Exit [with Corin].*
Celia. Didst thou hear these verses?
Rosalind. O, yes, I heard them all, and more too; for some
    of them had in them more feet than the verses would bear.
Celia. That's no matter. The feet might bear the verses. 160
Rosalind. Ay, but the feet were lame, and could not bear
    themselves without the verse, and therefore stood lamely
    in the verse.
Celia. But didst thou hear without wondering how thy
    name should be hanged and carved upon these trees? 165
Rosalind. I was seven of the nine days out of the wonder
    before you came; for look here what I found on a palm
    tree. I was never so berhymed since Pythagoras' time
    that I was an Irish rat, which I can hardly remember.
Celia. Trow you who hath done this? 170
Rosalind. Is it a man?
Celia. And a chain that you once wore, about his neck.
    Change you color?
Rosalind. I prithee who?
Celia. O Lord, Lord, it is a hard matter for friends to meet; 175
    but mountains may be removed with earthquakes, and
    so encounter.
Rosalind. Nay, but who is it?
Celia. Is it possible?
Rosalind. Nay, I prithee now with most petitionary vehe- 180
    mence, tell me who it is.

---

146 *touches* features 149 *Jupiter* (frequently emended to *pulpiter*) 152 *How . . . friends* (folio reads *How now back friends:*) 156 *scrip and scrippage* shepherd's pouch and its contents 166 *nine days* (a reference to the common expression 'a nine days' wonder') 167 *palm* (Lodge, in *Rosalynde,* mentions a palm tree in one of his euphuistic aphorisms) 168 *Pythagoras* (to whom was attributed the doctrine of transmigration of souls) 169 *Irish rat* (alluding to the belief that Irish sorcerers could kill animals by means of rhymed spells) 170 *Trow you* have you any idea 176 *removed with* moved by 177 *encounter* be brought together 180 *petitionary* suppliant

Celia. O wonderful, wonderful, and most wonderful won-
     derful, and yet again wonderful, and after that, out of
     all hooping!
Rosalind. Good my complexion! Dost thou think, though I   185
     am caparisoned like a man, I have a doublet and hose in
     my disposition? One inch of delay more is a South Sea
     of discovery. I prithee tell me who is it quickly, and
     speak apace. I would thou couldst stammer, that thou
     mightst pour this concealed man out of thy mouth as   190
     wine comes out of a narrow-mouthed bottle; either too
     much at once, or none at all. I prithee take the cork out
     of thy mouth, that I may drink thy tidings.
Celia. So you may put a man in your belly.
Rosalind. Is he of God's making? What manner of man?   195
     Is his head worth a hat? or his chin worth a beard?
Celia. Nay, he hath but a little beard.
Rosalind. Why, God will send more, if the man will be
     thankful. Let me stay the growth of his beard, if thou
     delay me not the knowledge of his chin.   200
Celia. It is young Orlando, that tripped up the wrestler's
     heels and your heart both in an instant.
Rosalind. Nay, but the devil take mocking! Speak sad
     brow and true maid.
Celia. I' faith, coz, 'tis he.   205
Rosalind. Orlando?
Celia. Orlando.
Rosalind. Alas the day! what shall I do with my doublet
     and hose? What did he when thou saw'st him? What
     said he? How looked he? Wherein went he? What   210
     makes he here? Did he ask for me? Where remains he?
     How parted he with thee? and when shalt thou see him
     again? Answer me in one word.
Celia. You must borrow me Gargantua's mouth first; 'tis
     a word too great for any mouth of this age's size. To say   215
     ay and no to these particulars is more than to answer in
     a catechism.
Rosalind. But doth he know that I am in this forest, and
     in man's apparel? Looks he as freshly as he did the day
     he wrestled?   220

183-84 *out of all hooping* beyond all measure 185 *Good my complexion* O my (feminine)
temperament 186 *caparisoned* bedecked (commonly used of horses) 187-88 *One . . . discovery* another minute of waiting will be as tedious as a journey to the South Seas for
exploration 195 *of God's making* i.e., a real man, of flesh and blood 203-4 *sad . . . maid*
seriously and truthfully 210 *Wherein went he* what did he wear 211 *makes* does 214 *Gargantua's mouth* (Rabelais' giant swallowed five pilgrims in a salad)

Celia. It is as easy to count atomies as to resolve the propositions of a lover; but take a taste of my finding him, and
relish it with good observance. I found him under a tree,
like a dropped acorn.

Rosalind. It may well be called Jove's tree when it drops   225
such fruit.

Celia. Give me audience, good madam.

Rosalind. Proceed.

Celia. There lay he stretched along like a wounded knight.

Rosalind. Though it be pity to see such a sight, it well   230
becomes the ground.

Celia. Cry 'holla' to thy tongue, I prithee; it curvets unsea-
sonably. He was furnished like a hunter.

Rosalind. O, ominous! he comes to kill my heart.

Celia. I would sing my song without a burden. Thou   235
bring'st me out of tune.

Rosalind. Do you not know I am a woman? When I think, I
must speak. Sweet, say on.

Enter Orlando and Jaques.

Celia. You bring me out. Soft. Comes he not here?

Rosalind. 'Tis he! Slink by, and note him.   240

Jaques. I thank you for your company; but, good faith, I
had as lief have been myself alone.

Orlando. And so had I; but yet for fashion sake I thank you
too for your society.

Jaques. God b' wi' you; let's meet as little as we can.   245

Orlando. I do desire we may be better strangers.

Jaques. I pray you mar no more trees with writing love
songs in their barks.

Orlando. I pray you mar no more of my verses with reading
them ill-favoredly.   250

Jaques. Rosalind is your love's name?

Orlando. Yes, just.

Jaques. I do not like her name.

Orlando. There was no thought of pleasing you when she
was christened.   255

Jaques. What stature is she of?

Orlando. Just as high as my heart.

Jaques. You are full of pretty answers. Have you not been
acquainted with goldsmiths' wives, and conned them
out of rings?   260

221 *atomies* motes 221-22 *resolve the propositions* answer the questions 223 *relish it*
heighten it with sauce *observance* attention 225 *Jove's tree* (the oak was sacred to Jupiter)
226 *such* (folio reads *forth*) 231 *becomes* adorns 232 *holla* halt *curvets* prances 234 *heart*
(quibble on 'hart') 235 *burden* undersong, refrain 249 *moe* more 250 *ill-favoredly* badly
259-60 *conned . . . rings* memorized them from the verses engraved in rings

Orlando. Not so; but I answer you right painted cloth,
from whence you have studied your questions.
Jaques. You have a nimble wit; I think 'twas made of Ata-
lanta's heels. Will you sit down with me? and we
two will rail against our mistress the world and all our   265
misery.
Orlando. I will chide no breather in the world but myself,
against whom I know most faults.
Jaques. The worst fault you have is to be in love.
Orlando. 'Tis a fault I will not change for your best virtue.   270
I am weary of you.
Jaques. By my troth, I was seeking for a fool when I found
you.
Orlando. He is drowned in the brook. Look but in and you
shall see him.   275
Jaques. There I shall see mine own figure.
Orlando. Which I take to be either a fool or a cipher.
Jaques. I'll tarry no longer with you. Farewell, good Signior
Love.
Orlando. I am glad of your departure. Adieu, good Mon-   280
sieur Melancholy.   *[Exit Jaques.]*
Rosalind. I will speak to him like a saucy lackey, and under
that habit play the knave with him. Do you hear,
forester?
Orlando. Very well. What would you?   285
Rosalind. I pray you, what is't o'clock?
Orlando. You should ask me, what time o'day. There's
no clock in the forest.
Rosalind. Then there is no true lover in the forest, else
sighing every minute and groaning every hour would   290
detect the lazy foot of Time as well as a clock.
Orlando. And why not the swift foot of Time? Had not that
been as proper?
Rosalind. By no means, sir. Time travels in divers paces
with divers persons. I'll tell you who Time ambles withal,   295
who Time trots withal, who Time gallops withal, and
who he stands still withal.
Orlando. I prithee, who doth he trot withal?
Rosalind. Marry, he trots hard with a young maid between
the contract of her marriage and the day it is solemnized.   300
If the interim be but a se'nnight, Time's pace is so hard
that it seems the length of seven year.

261 *right painted cloth* cheap substitute tapestries, with painted pictures and mottoes
263-64 *Atalanta's heels* (Atalanta was speedy enough to outrun her suitors) 267 *breather*
living creature 283 *habit* garb 291 *detect* call attention to 295 *withal* with 301 *se'nnight*
week

Orlando. Who ambles Time withal?
Rosalind. With a priest that lacks Latin and a rich man that
    hath not the gout; for the one sleeps easily because he   305
    cannot study, and the other lives merrily because he feels
    no pain; the one lacking the burden of lean and wasteful
    learning, the other knowing no burden of heavy tedious
    penury. These Time ambles withal.
Orlando. Who doth he gallop withal?   310
Rosalind. With a thief to the gallows; for though he go as
    softly as foot can fall, he thinks himself too soon there.
Orlando. Who stays it still withal?
Rosalind. With lawyers in the vacation; for they sleep be-
    tween term and term and then they perceive not how   315
    times moves.
Orlando. Where dwell you, pretty youth?
Rosalind. With this shepherdess, my sister; here in the
    skirts of the forest, like fringe upon a petticoat.
Orlando. Are you native of this place?   320
Rosalind. As the cony that you see dwell where she is
    kindled.
Orlando. Your accent is something finer than you could
    purchase in so removed a dwelling.
Rosalind. I have been told so of many. But indeed an old   325
    religious uncle of mine taught me to speak, who was in
    his youth an inland man; one that knew courtship too
    well, for there he fell in love. I have heard him read
    many lectures against it; and I thank God I am not a
    woman, to be touched with so many giddy offenses as he   330
    hath generally taxed their whole sex withal.
Orlando. Can you remember any of the principal evils that
    he laid to the charge of women?
Rosalind. There were none principal. They were all like
    one another as halfpence are, every one fault seeming   335
    monstrous till his fellow fault came to match it.
Orlando. I prithee recount some of them.
Rosalind. No, I will cast away my physic but on those
    that are sick. There is a man haunts the forest that abuses
    our young plants with carving 'Rosalind' on their barks,   340
    hangs odes upon hawthorns, and elegies on brambles;
    all, forsooth, deifying the name of Rosalind. If I could

---

307 *wasteful* causing one to waste away 312 *softly* slowly 315 *term* court session 321 *cony* rabbit 322 *kindled* born 324 *purchase* acquire *removed* remote 326 *religious* in holy orders 327 *inland* (see note on II, vii, 96) *courtship* (quibble on 'courtliness' and 'wooing') 330 *touched* tainted

meet that fancy-monger, I would give him some good
counsel, for he seems to have the quotidian of love upon
him.   345

Orlando. I am he that is so love-shaked. I pray you tell me
your remedy.

Rosalind. There is none of my uncle's marks upon you. He
taught me how to know a man in love; in which cage of
rushes I am sure you are not prisoner.   350

Orlando. What were his marks?

Rosalind. A lean cheek, which you have not; a blue eye and
sunken, which you have not; an unquestionable spirit,
which you have not; a beard neglected, which you have
not: but I pardon you for that, for simply your having   355
in beard is a younger brother's revenue. Then your hose
should be ungartered, your bonnet unbanded, your sleeve
unbuttoned, your shoe untied, and everything about you
demonstrating a careless desolation. But you are no such
man: you are rather point-device in your accoustre-   360
ments, as loving yourself than seeming the lover of any
other.

Orlando. Fair youth, I would I could make thee believe I
love.

Rosalind. Me believe it? You may as soon make her that   365
you love believe it, which I warrant she is apter to do
than to confess she does; that is one of the points in the
which woman still give the lie to their consciences. But
in good sooth, are you he that hangs the verses on the
trees wherein Rosalind is so admired?   370

Orlando. I swear to thee, youth, by the white hand of
Rosalind, I am that he, that unfortunate he.

Rosalind. But are you so much in love as your rhymes
speak?

Orlando. Neither rhyme nor reason can express how much.   375

Rosalind. Love is merely a madness, and, I tell you, deserves
as well a dark house and a whip as madmen do; and the
reason why they are not so punished and cured is that
the lunacy is so ordinary that the whippers are in love
too. Yet I profess curing it by counsel.   380

Orlando. Did you ever cure any so?

---

343 *fancy-monger* i.e. one who advertises his so-called love 344 *quotidian* daily fever
349-50 *cage of rushes* flimsy prison (with a glancing allusion to the 'rush rings' used for
mock marriages) 352 *blue eye* i.e. with dark circles 353 *unquestionable* unwilling to converse 355-56 *your having ... revenue* you have only a small portion of a beard
360-61 *point-device ... accoustrements* dressed with exactness 377 *a dark ... whip* (the
shock treatment by which the Elizabethans attempted to cure insanity)

Rosalind. Yes, one, and in this manner. He was to imagine
    me his love, his mistress; and I set him every day to woo
    me. At which time would I, being but a moonish youth,
    grieve, be effeminate, changeable, longing and liking,   385
    proud, fantastical, apish, shallow, inconstant, full of tears,
    full of smiles; for every passion something and for no
    passion truly anything, as boys and women are for the
    most part cattle of this color; would now like him, now
    loathe him; then entertain him; then forswear him; now   390
    weep for him, then spit at him that I drave my suitor
    from his mad humor of love to a living humor of mad-
    ness, which was, to forswear the full stream of the world
    and to live in a nook merely monastic. And thus I cured
    him; and this way will I take upon me to wash your   395
    liver as clean as a sound sheep's heart, that there shall
    not be one spot of love in't.
Orlando. I would not be cured, youth.
Rosalind. I would cure you, if you would but call me
    Rosalind and come every day to my cote and woo me.   400
Orlando. Now, by the faith of my love, I will. Tell me
    where it is.
Rosalind. Go with me to it, and I'll show it you; and by
    the way you shall tell me where in the forest you live.
    Will you go?   405
Orlando. With all my heart, good youth.
Rosalind. Nay, you must call me Rosalind. Come, sister,
    will you go?   *Exeunt.*

> *Enter [Touchstone the] Clown, Audrey; and Jaques*   III, iii
> *[apart].*

Touchstone. Come apace, good Audrey. I will fetch up
    your goats, Audrey. And how, Audrey, am I the man
    yet? Doth my simple feature content you?
Audrey. Your features, Lord warrant us! What features?
Touchstone. I am here with thee and thy goats, as the most   5
    capricious poet, honest Ovid, was among the Goths.
Jaques. [aside] O knowledge ill-inhabited, worse than Jove
    in a thatched house!

---

384 *moonish* fickle 392 *humor* state 396 *liver* (supposed to be the source of the passions,
especially love) 400 *cote* cottage III, iii, 3 *simple feature* plain appearance 4 *features* (Audrey evidently misunderstands Touchstone, but the nature of the joke is obscure)
5-6 *goats . . . Goths* (Ovid was exiled among the Goths, here pronounced 'goats.' Touchstone quibbles on *goats* and *capricious,* the latter deriving from Latin 'caper,' a male goat)
7 *ill-inhabited* poorly lodged 7-8 *Jove . . . house* (Jupiter, in human form, was once entertained by two peasants in their thatched cottage)

Touchstone. When a man's verses cannot be understood,
   nor a man's good wit seconded with the forward child,   10
   understanding, it strikes a man more dead than a great
   reckoning in a little room. Truly, I would the gods had
   made thee poetical.
Audrey. I do not know what poetical is. Is it honest in deed
   and word? Is it a true thing?   15
Touchstone. No, truly; for the truest poetry is the most
   faining, and lovers are given to poetry, and what they
   swear in poetry may be said, as lovers, they do feign.
Audrey. Do you wish then that the gods had made me
   poetical?   20
Touchstone. I do truly; for thou swear'st to me thou art
   honest. Now if thou wert a poet, I might have some hope
   thou didst feign.
Audrey. Would you not have me honest?
Touchstone. No, truly, unless thou wert hard-favored; for   25
   honesty coupled to beauty is to have honey a sauce to
   sugar.
Jaques. [aside] A material fool.
Audrey. Well, I am not fair, and therefore I pray the gods
   make me honest.   30
Touchstone. Truly, and to cast away honesty upon a foul
   slut were to put good meat into an unclean dish.
Audrey. I am not a slut, though I thank the gods I am foul.
Touchstone. Well, praised be the gods for thy foulness!
   Sluttishness may come hereafter. But be it as it may be,   35
   I will marry thee; and to that end I have been with Sir
   Oliver Mar-text, the vicar of the next village, who hath
   promised to meet me in this place of the forest and to
   couple us.
Jaques. [aside] I would fain see this meeting.   40
Audrey. Well, the gods give us joy!
Touchstone. Amen. A man may, if he were of a fearful
   heart, stagger in this attempt; for here we have no temple
   but the wood, no assembly but horn-beasts. But what
   though? Courage! As horns are odious, they are neces-   45
   sary. It is said, 'Many a man knows no end of his goods.'
   Right! Many a man has good horns and knows no end

9-11 *When . . . understanding* i.e. Audrey has failed to appreciate Touchstone's wit, just as the Goths failed to appreciate Ovid's poetry 11-12 *a great reckoning in* a large bill for 16-18 *truest poetry . . . feign* (a play on 'fain'=desire and 'feign'=pretend runs through the passage) 25 *hard-favored* ugly 26 *honesty* chastity (a meaning latent in Touchstone's earlier use of *honest*) 28 *material* making good sense 33 *foul* (Audrey interprets the word as 'ugly') 36 *Sir* (an old-fashioned designation for a clergyman) 44 *horn-beasts* (throughout this passage Touchstone plays on the old joke that cuckolds, i.e. men whose wives play them false, sprout horns)

of them. Well, that is the dowry of his wife; 'tis none
of his own getting. Horns. Even so, poor men alone. No,
no; the noblest deer hath them as huge as the rascal. Is   50
the single man therefore blessed? No; as a walled town
is more worthier than a village, so is the forehead of a
married man more honorable than the bare brow of a
bachelor; and by how much defense is better than no
skill, by so much is a horn more precious than to want.   55

Enter Sir Oliver Mar-text.

Here comes Sir Oliver. Sir Oliver Mar-text, you are
well met. Will you dispatch us here under this tree, or
shall we go with you to your chapel?
Oliver Mar-text. Is there none here to give the woman?
Touchstone. I will not take her on gift of any man.   60
Oliver Mar-text. Truly, she must be given, or the marriage
is not lawful.
Jaques. [comes forward] Proceed, proceed; I'll give her.
Touchstone. Good even, good Master What-ye-call't. How
do you sir? You are very well met. Goddild you for   65
your last company; I am very glad to see you. Even a
toy in hand here, sir. Nay, pray be covered.
Jaques. Will you be married, motley?
Touchstone. As the ox hath his bow, sir, the horse his curb,
and the falcon her bells, so man hath his desires; and as   70
pigeons bill, so wedlock would be nibbling.
Jaques. And will you, being a man of your breeding, be
married under a bush like a beggar? Get you to church,
and have a good priest that can tell you what marriage
is. This fellow will but join you together as they join   75
wainscot; then one of you will prove a shrunk panel,
and like green timber warp, warp.
Touchstone. [aside] I am not in the mind but I were better
to be married of him than of another; for he is not like
to marry me well; and not being well married, it will be   80
a good excuse for me hereafter to leave my wife.
Jaques. Go thou with me and let me counsel thee.

---

50 *rascal* inferior deer 54 *defense* i.e. the art of defending oneself, probably fencing 55 *to want* i.e. to lack horns 57 *dispatch us* finish off our business 64 *Master What-ye-call't* (Touchstone calls attention to Jaques' name, which suggests the Elizabethan word for a privy, 'jakes') 65 *Goddild* God yield, i.e. reward 67 *toy* trifle 69 *bow* collar of the yoke 73 *married . . . bush* (Oliver is a 'hedge-priest,' i.e. uneducated, unable to expound the obligations of marriage) 75-76 *as . . . wainscot* i.e. as they set panelling together, without mortising or joining securely

Touchstone. Come, sweet Audrey.
　　We must be married, or we must live in bawdry.
　　Farewell, good Master Oliver: not   85
　　　　O sweet Oliver,
　　　　O brave Oliver,
　　　Leave me not behind thee;
　　but
　　　　Wind away,   90
　　　　Be gone, I say;
　　　I will not to wedding with thee.
　　　　　　　　　　　Exeunt [Jaques, Touchstone, and Audrey].
Oliver Mar-text. 'Tis no matter. Ne'er a fantastical knave
　of them all shall flout me out of my calling.   *[Exit.]*

———

　　　　　　　　Enter Rosalind and Celia.   III, iv

Rosalind. Never talk to me; I will weep.
Celia. Do, I prithee; but yet have the grace to consider
　that tears do not become a man.
Rosalind. But have I not cause to weep?
Celia. As good cause as one would desire; therefore weep.   5
Rosalind. His very hair is of the dissembling color.
Celia. Something browner than Judas's. Marry, his kisses
　are Judas's own children.
Rosalind. I' faith, his hair is of a good color.
Celia. An excellent color. Your chestnut was ever the only   10
　color.
Rosalind. And his kissing is as full of sanctity as the touch
　of holy bread.
Celia. He hath bought a pair of cast lips of Diana. A nun
　of winter's sisterhood kisses not more religiously; the   15
　very ice of chastity is in them.
Rosalind. But why did he swear he would come this morn-
　ing, and comes not?
Celia. Nay, certainly there is no truth in him.
Rosalind. Do you think so?   20
Celia. Yes; I think he is not a pickpurse nor a horse-
　stealer, but for his verity in love, I do think him as
　concave as a covered goblet or a worm-eaten nut.
Rosalind. Not true in love?
Celia. Yes, when he is in, but I think he is not in.   25

84 *bawdry* immorality 86 ff. *O sweet Oliver...* (snatches from a current ballad) 93 *fantastical* affected III, iv, 6 *dissembling color* i.e. reddish, the traditional color of Judas's hair 8 *Judas's own children* i.e. offspring of a betrayer 14 *cast* (1) discarded (2) statuary; perhaps with a play on 'chaste' (Diana was the goddess of chastity) 15 *of winter's sisterhood* i.e. sworn to coldness 23 *concave* hollow

Rosalind. You have heard him swear downright he was.

Celia. 'Was' is not 'is.' Besides, the oath of a lover is no
stronger than the word of a tapster; they are both the
confirmer of false reckonings. He attends here in the
forest on the Duke your father. 30

Rosalind. I met the Duke yesterday and had much question
with him He asked me of what parentage I was. I told
him, of as good as he; so he laughed and let me go. But
what talk we of fathers when there is such a man as
Orlando? 35

Celia. O, that's a brave man; he writes brave verses, speaks
brave words, swears brave oaths, and breaks them
bravely, quite traverse, athwart the heart of his lover,
as a puisny tilter, that spurs his horse but on one side,
breaks his staff like a noble goose. But all's brave that 40
youth mounts and folly guides. Who comes here?

Enter Corin.

Corin. Mistress and master, you have oft enquired
After the shepherd that complained of love,
Who you saw sitting by me on the turf,
Praising the proud disdainful shepherdess 45
That was his mistress.

Celia.   Well, and what of him?

Corin. If you will see a pageant truly played
Between the pale complexion of true love
And the red glow of scorn and proud disdain,
Go hence a little, and I shall conduct you, 50
If you will mark it.

Rosalind.   O, come, let us remove:
The sight of lovers feedeth those in love.
Bring us to this sight, and you shall say
I'll prove a busy actor in their play.   *Exeunt.*

Enter Silvius and Phebe.   III,v

Silvius. Sweet Phebe, do not scorn me; do not, Phebe!
Say that you love me not, but say not so
In bitterness. The common executioner,
Whose heart th' accustomed sight of death makes hard,
Falls not the axe upon the humbled neck 5
But first begs pardon. Will you sterner be
Than he that dies and lives by bloody drops?

36 *brave* excellent 38 *traverse* (a term in tilting, for hitting an opponent sideways, awk-
wardly, instead of head-on) 39 *puisny* puny, i.e. inferior 40 *noble goose* grand fool 47 *pageant* performance III, v, 5 *Falls* lets fall 7 *dies and lives* makes his living

Enter [apart] Rosalind, Celia, and Corin

Phebe. I would not be thy executioner.
    I fly thee, for I would not injure thee.
    Thou tell'st me there is murder in mine eye: 10
    'Tis pretty, sure, and very probable
    That eyes, that are the frail'st and softest things,
    Who shut their coward gates on atomies,
    Should be called tyrants, butchers, murderers.
    Now I do frown on thee with all my heart,   15
    And if mine eyes can wound, now let them kill thee.
    Now counterfeit to swound; why, now fall down;
    Or if thou canst not, O, for shame, for shame,
    Lie not, to say mine eyes are murderers.
    Now show the wound mine eye hath made in thee;   20
    Scratch thee but with a pin, and there remains
    Some scar of it; lean upon a rush,
    The cicatrice and capable impressure
    Thy palm some moment keeps; but now mine eyes,
    Which I have darted at thee, hurt thee not,   25
    Nor I am sure there is no force in eyes
    That can do hurt.
Silvius.   O dear Phebe,
    If ever, as that ever may be near,
    You meet in some fresh cheek the power of fancy,
    Then shall you know the wounds invisible   30
    That love's keen arrows make.
Phebe.   But till that time
    Come thou not near me; and when that time comes,
    Afflict me with thy mocks, pity me not,
    As till that time I shall not pity thee.
Rosalind. And why, I pray you? Who might be your
        mother,   35
    That you insult, exult, and all at once,
    Over the wretched? What though you have no beauty
    (As, by my faith, I see no more in you
    Than without candle may go dark to bed)
    Must you be therefore proud and pitiless?   40
    Why, what means this? Why do you look on me?
    I see no more in you than in the ordinary
    Of nature's sale-work. 'Od's my little life,
    I think she means to tangle my eyes too!

13 *atomies* motes 17 *counterfeit to swound* pretend to swoon 23 *cicatrice* mark (literally, scar) *capable impressure* i.e. impression capable of being seen 29 *fancy* love 39 *may . . . bed* i.e. she does not have the beauty which (metaphorically) illuminates the dark 42 *ordinary* common run 43 *sale-work* ready-made products, not distinctive

No, faith, proud mistress, hope not after it;   45
'Tis not your inky brows, your black silk hair,
Your bugle eyeballs, nor your cheek of cream
That can entame my spirits to your worship.
You foolish shepherd, wherefore do you follow her,
Like foggy south, puffing with wind and rain?   50
You are a thousand times a properer man
Than she a woman. 'Tis such fools as you
That makes the world full of ill-favored children.
'Tis not her glass, but you, that flatters her,
And out of you she sees herself more proper   55
Than any of her lineaments can show her.
But mistress, know yourself. Down on your knees,
And thank heaven, fasting, for a good man's love;
For I must tell you friendly in your ear,
Sell when you can, you are not for all markets.   60
Cry the man mercy, love him, take his offer;
Foul is most foul, being foul to be a scoffer;
So take her to thee, shepherd. Fare you well.
Phebe. Sweet youth, I pray you chide a year together;
I had rather hear you chide than this man woo.   65
Rosalind. [aside] He's fall'n in love with your foulness, and
she'll fall in love with my anger. If it be so, as fast as she
answers thee with frowning looks, I'll sauce her with
bitter words. *[to Phebe]* Why look you so upon me?
Phebe. For no ill will I bear you.   70
Rosalind. I pray you do not fall in love with me,
For I am falser than vows made in wine.
Besides, I like you not. If you will know my house,
Tis at the tuft of olives, here hard by.
Will you go, sister? Shepherd, ply her hard.   75
Come, sister. Shepherdess, look on him better
And be not proud. Though all the world could see,
None could be so abused in sight as he.
Come, to our flock.   *Exit [with Celia and Corin].*
Phebe. Dead shepherd, now I find thy saw of might,   80
'Who ever loved that loved not at first sight?'
Silvius. Sweet Phebe.
Phebe.   Ha! what say'st thou, Silvius?
Silvius. Sweet Phebe, pity me.

---

47 *bugle* glassy, with black center 50 *south* south wind 51 *properer* more handsome
61 *Cry... mercy* beg the man's pardon 62 *Foul is most foul* ugliness is most repulsive
80 *Dead shepherd* Christopher Marlowe (here referred to as a pastoral poet), who was killed
in 1593 *saw* saying 81 *'Who... sight'* (Marlowe's *Hero and Leander* [pub. 1598], I, 175)

Phebe. Why, I am sorry for thee, gentle Silvius.
Silvius. Wherever sorrow is, relief would be.   85
    If you do sorrow at my grief in love,
    By giving love your sorrow and my grief
    Were both extermined.
Phebe. Thou hast my love. Is not that neighborly?
Silvius. I would have you.
Phebe.   Why, that were covetousness.   90
    Silvius, the time was that I hated thee;
    And yet it is not that I bear thee love,
    But since that thou canst talk of love so well,
    Thy company, which erst was irksome to me,
    I will endure; and I'll employ thee too;   95
    But do not look for further recompense
    Than thine own gladness that thou art employed.
Silvius. So holy and so perfect is my love,
    And I in such a poverty of grace,
    That I shall think it a most plenteous crop   100
    To glean the broken ears after the man
    That the main harvest reaps. Loose now and then
    A scatt'red smile, and that I'll live upon.
Phebe. Know'st thou the youth that spoke to me erewhile?
Silvius. Not very well, but I have met him oft,   105
    And he hath brought the cottage and the bounds
    That the old carlot once was master of.
Phebe. Think not I love him, though I ask for him;
    'Tis but a peevish boy; yet he talks well.
    But what care I for words? Yet words do well   110
    When he that speaks them pleases those that hear.
    It is a pretty youth; not very pretty;
    But sure he's proud; and yet his pride becomes him.
    He'll make a proper man. The best thing in him
    Is his complexion; and faster than his tongue   115
    Did make offense, his eye did heal it up.
    He is not very tall; yet for his years he's tall.
    His leg is but so so; and yet 'tis well.
    There was a pretty redness in his lip,
    A little riper and more lusty red   120
    Than that mixed in his cheek; 'twas just the difference
    Betwixt the constant red and mingled damask.
    There be some women, Silvius, had they marked him

---

88 *extermined* expunged 89 *neighborly* (possibly a reference to the commandment 'Thou shalt love thy neighbor as thyself') 92 *it is not* the time has not come 107 *carlot* countryman 122 *mingled damask* pink and white, the colors of damask roses

In parcels as I did, would have gone near
To fall in love with him; but, for my part,   125
I love him not nor hate him not; and yet
I have more cause to hate him than to love him;
For what had he to do to chide at me?
He said mine eyes were black and my hair black;
And, now I am rememb'red, scorned at me.   130
I marvel why I answered not again.
But that's all one: omittance is no quittance.
I'll write to him a very taunting letter,
And thou shalt bear it. Wilt thou, Silvius?
Silvius. Phebe, with all my heart.
Phebe.   I'll write it straight;   135
The matter's in my head and in my heart;
I will be bitter with him and passing short.
Go with me, Silvius.   *Exeunt.*

       Enter Rosalind and Celia and Jaques.   IV,i

Jaques. I prithee, pretty youth, let me be better acquainted
    with thee.
Rosalind. They say you are a melancholy fellow.
Jaques. I am so; I do love it better than laughing.
Rosalind. Those that are in extremity of either are abomi-   5
    nable fellows, and betray themselves to every modern
    censure worse than drunkards.
Jaques. Why, 'tis good to be sad and say nothing.
Rosalind. Why then, 'tis good to be a post.
Jaques. I have neither the scholar's melancholy, which is   10
    emulation; nor the musician's, which is fantastical; nor
    the courtier's, which is proud; nor the soldier's, which
    is ambitious; nor the lawyer's, which is politic; nor the
    lady's, which is nice; nor the lover's, which is all these:
    but it is a melancholy of mine own, compounded of   15
    many simples, extracted from many objects, and indeed
    the sundry contemplation of my travels, which, by often
    rumination, wraps me in a most humorous sadness.
Rosalind. A traveller! By my faith, you have great reason
    to be sad. I fear you have sold your own lands to see   20

---

124 *In parcels* part by part 130 *rememb'red* reminded 132 *omittance is no quittance* i.e.
failure to assert one's rights is not renunciation of them 135 *straight* straightway 137 *passing*
short extremely curt IV, i, 5 *are in extremity* go to extremes 6 *modern* common 11 *emula-*
tion envy *fantastical* absurdly elaborate 13 *politic* a matter of policy (to appear learned)
14 *nice* over-refined 16 *simples* ingredients 17 *sundry* collected 18 *humorous* moody

other men's. Then to have seen much and to have
nothing is to have rich eyes and poor hands.
Jaques. Yes, I have gained my experience.

Enter Orlando.

Rosalind. And your experience makes you sad. I had
rather have a fool to make me merry than experience   25
to make me sad: and to travel for it too.
Orlando. Good day and happiness, dear Rosalind.
Jaques. Nay then, God b' wi' you, an you talk in blank
verse.   *[Exit.]*
Rosalind. Farewell, Monsieur Traveller. Look you lisp and   30
wear strange suits, disable all the benefits of your own
country, be out of love with your nativity, and almost
chide God for making you that countenance you are;
or I will scarce think you have swam in a gundello.
Why, how now, Orlando, where have you been all this   35
while? You a lover? An you serve me such another
trick, never come in my sight more.
Orlando. My fair Rosalind, I come within an hour of my
promise.
Rosalind. Break an hour's promise in love? He that will di-   40
vide a minute into a thousand parts and break but a part
of the thousand part of a minute in the affairs of love, it
may be said of him that Cupid hath clapped him o' th'
shoulder, but I'll warrant him heart-whole.
Orlando. Pardon me, dear Rosalind.   45
Rosalind. Nay, an you be so tardy, come no more in my
sight. I had as lief be wooed of a snail.
Orlando. Of a snail?
Rosalind. Ay, of a snail; for though he comes slowly, he
carries his house on his head; a better jointure, I think,   50
than you make a woman. Besides, he brings his destiny
with him.
Orlando. What's that?
Rosalind. Why, horns; which such as you are fain to be
beholding to your wives for; but he comes armed in his   55
fortune and prevents the slander of his wife.
Orlando. Virtue is no horn-maker, and my Rosalind is
virtuous.
Rosalind. And I am your Rosalind.

26 *travel* (folio reads *travaile,* and a pun on 'travail,' i.e. labor, is indicated) 30 *lisp* i.e. use
foreign sounds 31 *disable* disparage 32 *nativity* birthplace 34 *swam in a gundello* i.e. been to
Venice, to ride in a gondola 43-44 *clapped him o' th' shoulder* accosted him 50 *jointure*
marriage settlement 56 *prevents* forestalls

Celia. It pleases him to call you so; but he hath a Rosalind   60
  of a better leer than you.
Rosalind. Come, woo me, woo me; for now I am in a holiday humor and like enough to consent. What would
  you say to me now, an I were your very very Rosalind?
Orlando. I would kiss before I spoke.   65
Rosalind. Nay, you were better speak first, and when you
  were gravelled for lack of matter, you might take occasion to kiss. Very good orators, when they are out, they
  will spit; and for lovers, lacking—God warn us!—
  matter, the cleanliest shift is to kiss.   70
Orlando. How if the kiss be denied?
Rosalind. Then she puts you to entreaty, and there begins
  new matter.
Orlando. Who could be out, being before his beloved
  mistress?   75
Rosalind. Marry, that should you, if I were your mistress,
  or I should think my honesty ranker than my wit.
Orlando. What, of my suit?
Rosalind. Not out of your apparel, and yet out of your suit.
  Am not I your Rosalind?   80
Orlando. I take some joy to say you are, because I would
  be talking of her.
Rosalind. Well, in her person, I say I will not have you.
Orlando. Then, in mine own person, I die.
Rosalind. No, faith, die by attorney. The poor world is   85
  almost six thousand years old, and in all this time there
  was not any man died in his own person, videlicet, in a
  love cause. Troilus had his brains dashed out with a
  Grecian club; yet he did what he could to die before,
  and he is one of the patterns of love. Leander, he would   90
  have lived many a fair year though Hero had turned
  nun, if it had not been for a hot midsummer night; for,
  good youth, he went but forth to wash him in the
  Hellespont, and being taken with the cramp, was
  drowned; and the foolish chroniclers of that age found   95
  it was 'Hero of Sestos.' But these are all lies. Men have

---

61 *leer* look 67 *gravelled* stuck 68 *out* out of matter 69 *warn* save 77 *honesty* chastity
ranker less pure 78 *suit* plea (but Rosalind in reply puns on the word) 85 *by attorney* by
proxy 87 *videlicet* namely 88 *Troilus* the faithful lover of the faithless Cressida in Chaucer's
Troilus and Criseyde and earlier legends 88-89 *brains . . . club* (Rosalind's fiction is a trav-
esty on Troilus) 90 *Leander* the faithful lover in classical myth and Marlowe's *Hero and
Leander* (whose death Rosalind also travesties) 95-96 *foolish chroniclers . . . Sestos* the dim-
witted storytellers decided he died for love of Hero, the lady of Sestos

died from time to time, and worms have eaten them,
but not for love.

Orlando. I would not have my right Rosalind of this
mind, for I protest her frown might kill me.   100

Rosalind. By this hand, it will not kill a fly. But come,
now I will be your Rosalind in a more coming-on
disposition; and ask me what you will, I will grant it.

Orlando. Then love me, Rosalind.

Rosalind. Yes, faith, will I, Fridays and Saturdays and all.   105

Orlando. And wilt thou have me?

Rosalind. Ay, and twenty such.

Orlando. What sayest thou?

Rosalind. Are you not good?

Orlando. I hope so.   110

Rosalind. Why then, can one desire too much of a good
thing? Come, sister, you shall be the priest and marry us.
Give me your hand, Orlando. What do you say, sister?

Orlando. Pray thee marry us.

Celia. I cannot say the words.   115

Rosalind. You must begin, 'Will you, Orlando'—

Celia. Go to. Will you, Orlando, have to wife this Rosalind?

Orlando. I will.

Rosalind. Ay, but when?   120

Orlando. Why now, as fast as she can marry us.

Rosalind. Then you must say, 'I take thee, Rosalind, for
wife.'

Orlando. I take thee, Rosalind, for wife.

Rosalind. I might ask you for your commission; but I do   125
take thee, Orlando, for my husband. There's a girl goes
before the priest, and certainly a woman's thought runs
before her actions.

Orlando. So do all thoughts; they are winged.

Rosalind. Now tell me how long you would have her   130
after you have possessed her.

Orlando. For ever and a day.

Rosalind. Say 'a day,' without the 'ever.' No, no, Orlando;
men are April when they woo, December when they
wed. Maids are May when they are maids, but the sky   135
changes when they are wives. I will be more jealous of
thee than a Barbary cock-pigeon over his hen, more

---

125 *commission* authority 126-27 *goes before* anticipates 137 *Barbary cock-pigeon* the
'Barb' pigion, which originally came from the north of Africa

clamorous than a parrot against rain, more newfangled
than an ape, more giddy in my desires than a monkey.
I will weep for nothing, like Diana in the fountain, and   140
I will do that when you are disposed to be merry; I will
laugh like a hyen, and that when thou art inclined to
sleep.

Orlando. But will my Rosalind do so?

Rosalind. By my life, she will do as I do.   145

Orlando. O, but she is wise.

Rosalind. Or else she could not have the wit to do this;
the wiser, the waywarder. Make the doors upon a
woman's wit, and it will out at the casement; shut that,
and 'twill out at the keyhole; stop that, 'twill fly with   150
the smoke out at the chimney.

Orlando. A man that had a wife with such a wit, he might
say, 'Wit, whither wilt?'

Rosalind. Nay, you might keep that check for it till you
met your wife's wit going to your neighbor's bed.   155

Orlando. And what wit could wit have to excuse that?

Rosalind. Marry, to say she came to seek you there. You
shall never take her without her answer unless you take
her without her tongue. O, that woman that cannot
make her fault her husband's occasion, let her never   160
nurse her child herself, for she will breed it like a
fool.

Orlando. For these two hours, Rosalind, I will leave thee.

Rosalind. Alas, dear love, I cannot lack thee two hours!

Orlando. I must attend the Duke at dinner. By two o'clock   165
I will be with thee again.

Rosalind. Ay, go your ways, go your ways; I knew what
you would prove. My friends told me as much, and I
thought no less. That flattering tongue of yours won
me. 'Tis but one cast away, and so, come death! Two   170
o'clock is your hour?

Orlando. Ay, sweet Rosalind.

Rosalind. By my troth, and in good earnest, and so God
mend me, and by all pretty oaths that are not dangerous,
if you break one jot of your promise or come one minute   175

---

138 *against* in anticipation of 140 *Diana in the fountain* (Stow, in his *Survay of London,*
1603, reported that in 1596 at 'the great Crosse in West Cheape' was 'set up . . . an Alablas-
ter Image of Diana, and water convayed from the Thames, prilling from her naked brest.'
Rosalind changes the figure to weeping) 148 *Make* make fast 153 *wilt* will you go
154 *check* retort 160 *make . . . occasion* make her husband the cause of her fault 161 *breed*
raise

behind your hour, I will think you the most pathetical
break-promise, and the most hollow lover, and the
most unworthy of her you call Rosalind, that may be
chosen out of the gross band of the unfaithful. There-
fore beware my censure and keep your promise.   180
Orlando. With no less religion than if thou wert indeed
   my Rosalind. So adieu.
Rosalind. Well, Time is the old justice that examines all
   such offenders, and let Time try. Adieu.   *Exit [Orlando].*
Celia. You have simply misused our sex in your love-prate.   185
   We must have your doublet and hose plucked over your
   head, and show the world what the bird hath done to
   her own nest.
Rosalind. O coz, coz, coz, my pretty little coz, that thou
   didst know how many fathom deep I am in love! But   190
   it cannot be sounded. My affection hath an unknown
   bottom like the Bay of Portugal.
Celia. Or rather, bottomless, that as fast as you pour
   affection in, it runs out.
Rosalind. No, that same wicked bastard of Venus that was   195
   begot of thought, conceived of spleen, and born of madness, that blind rascally boy that abuses every one's eyes
   because his own are out, let him be judge how deep I am
   in love. I'll tell thee, Aliena, I cannot be out of the sight
   of Orlando. I'll go find a shadow, and sigh till he come.   200
Celia. And I'll sleep.   *Exeunt.*

       Enter Jaques; and Lords, [as] Foresters.   IV,ii

Jaques. Which is he that killed the deer?
[1.] Lord. Sir, it was I.
Jaques. Let's present him to the Duke like a Roman con-
   queror; and it would do well to set the deer's horns
   upon his head for a branch of victory. Have you no   5
   song, forester, for this purpose?
[2.] Lord. Yes, sir.
Jaques. Sing it. 'Tis no matter how it be in tune, so it make
   noise enough.   *Music.*

---

176 *pathetical* pitiful 181 *With . . . religion* no less religiously 192 *Bay of Portugal* (the sea
off the coast of Portugal was unplumbed) 195 *bastard of Venus* Cupid 196 *thought* i.e.
fancy *spleen* impulse IV, ii, 7 *[2.] Lord* (speech sometimes assigned in modern editions to
Amiens the singer, who may have begun this song in which the others join as they bear off
the killer of the deer)

Song.

What shall he have that killed the deer?   10
His leather skin and horns to wear:
   Then sing him home. *(The rest shall bear this burden.)*
Take thou no scorn to wear the horn,
It was a crest ere thou wast born,
    Thy father's father wore it,   15
    And thy father bore it.
The horn, the horn, the lusty horn,
Is not a thing to laugh to scorn.   *Exeunt.*

Enter Rosalind and Celia.   IV,iii

Rosalind. How say you now, is it not past two o'clock?
  And here much Orlando!
Celia. I warrant you, with pure love and troubled brain,
  he hath ta'en his bow and arrows and is gone forth to
  sleep.   5

Enter Silvius.

  Look who comes here.
Silvius. My errand is to you, fair youth.
  My gentle Phebe bid me give you this.   *[Gives a letter.]*
  I know not the contents, but, as I guess
  By the stern brow and waspish action   10
  Which she did use as she was writing of it,
  It bears an angry tenor. Pardon me;
  I am but as a guiltless messenger.
Rosalind. Patience herself would startle at this letter
  And play the swaggerer. Bear this, bear all!   15
  She says I am not fair, that I lack manners;
  She calls me proud, and that she could not love me,
  Were man as rare as phoenix. 'Od's my will!
  Her love is not the hare that I do hunt.
  Why writes she so to me? Well, shepherd, well,   20
  This is a letter of your own device.
Silvius. No, I protest, I know not the contents.
  Phebe did write it.
Rosalind.   Come, come, you are a fool,
  And turned into the extremity of love.
  I saw her hand. She has a leathern hand,   25
  A freestone-colored hand. I verily did think

12 S.D. *The rest... burden* (folio prints these words, possibly correctly, as part of the song)
burden refrain IV, iii, 18 *phoenix* (there was supposed to be only one phoenix in the world
at a time) 26 *freestone* soft sandstone or limestone, yellowish brown

That her old gloves were on, but 'twas her hands.
She has a housewife's hand; but that's no matter:
I say she never did invent this letter;
This is a man's invention and his hand.   30
Silvius. Sure it is hers.
Rosalind. Why, 'tis a boisterous and a cruel style,
    A style for challengers. Why, she defies me
    Like Turk to Christian. Women's gentle brain
    Could not drop forth such giant-rude invention,   35
    Such Ethiop words, blacker in their effect
    Than in their countenance. Will you hear the letter?
Silvius. So please you, for I never heard it yet;
    Yet heard too much of Phebe's cruelty.
Rosalind. She Phebes me. Mark how the tyrant writes.   40
    (Read.) 'Art thou god, to shepherd turned,
        That a maiden's heart hath burned?'
    Can a woman rail thus?
Silvius. Call you this railing?
Rosalind.
    (Read.) 'Why, thy godhead laid apart,   45
        Warr'st thou with a woman's heart?'
    Did you ever hear such railing?
        'Whiles the eye of man did woo me,
        That could do no vengeance to me.'
    Meaning me a beast.   50
        'If the scorn of your bright eyne
        Have power to raise such love in mine,
        Alack, in me what strange effect
        Would they work in mild aspect!
        Whiles you chid me, I did love;   55
        How then might your prayers move!
        He that brings this love to thee
        Little knows this love in me;
        And by him seal up thy mind,
        Whether that thy youth and kind   60
        Will the faithful offer take
        Of me and all that I can make,
        Or else by him my love deny,
        And then I'll study how to die.'
Silvius. Call you this chiding?   65
Celia. Alas, poor shepherd!

---

40 *Phebes me* addresses me with her characteristic cruelty 45 *thy . . . apart* i.e. as a god who
has assumed human form 49 *vengeance* harm 54 *in mild aspect* i.e. if they looked on me
pleasantly 59 *seal . . . mind* enclose your thoughts in a letter 60 *youth and kind* youthful
nature

Rosalind. Do you pity him? No, he deserves no pity. Wilt
   thou love such a woman? What, to make thee an instrument, and play false strains upon thee? Not to be endured! Well, go your way to her, for I see love hath   70
   made thee a tame snake, and say this to her: that if she
   love me, I charge her to love thee; if she will not, I will
   never have her unless thou entreat for her. If you be a
   true lover, hence, and not a word; for here comes more
   company.   *Exit Silvius.*   75

Enter Oliver.

Oliver. Good morrow, fair ones. Pray you, if you know,
   Where in the purlieus of this forest stands
   A sheepcote, fenced about with olive trees?
Celia. West of this place, down in the neighbor bottom
   The rank of osiers by the murmuring stream   80
   Left on your right hand brings you to the place.
   But at this hour the house doth keep itself;
   There's none within.
Oliver. If that an eye may profit by a tongue,
   Then should I know you by description,   85
   Such garments and such years: 'The boy is fair,
   Of female favor, and bestows himself
   Like a ripe sister; the woman low
   And browner than her brother.' Are not you
   The owner of the house I did enquire for?   90
Celia. It is no boast, being asked, to say we are.
Oliver. Orlando doth commend him to you both,
   And to that youth he calls his Rosalind.
   He sends this bloody napkin. Are you he?
Rosalind. I am. What must we understand by this?   95
Oliver. Some of my shame, if you will know of me
   What man I am, and how and why and where
   This handkercher was stained.
Celia.   I pray you tell it.
Oliver. When last the young Orlando parted from you,
   He left a promise to return again   100
   Within an hour; and pacing through the forest,
   Chewing the food of sweet and bitter fancy,
   Lo, what befell! He threw his eye aside,
   And mark what object did present itself:

68-69 *make . . . upon thee* use you (with pun on *instrument*) and deceive you at the same
time 71 *snake* i.e. base creature 77 *in the purlieus* within the borders 79 *neighbor bottom*
nearby valley 80 *rank of osiers* row of willows 87 *favor* features *bestows* conducts 88 *ripe*
mature 94 *napkin* handkerchief

Under an old oak, whose boughs were mossed with age   105
And high top bald with dry antiquity,
A wretched ragged man, o'ergrown with hair,
Lay sleeping on his back; about his neck
A green and gilded snake had wreathed itself,
Who with her head, nimble in threats, approached   110
The opening of his mouth; but suddenly,
Seeing Orlando, it unlinked itself
And with indented glides did slip away
Into a bush, under which bush's shade
A lioness, with udders all drawn dry,   115
Lay couching, head on ground, with catlike watch
When that the sleeping man should stir; for 'tis
The royal disposition of that beast
To prey on nothing that doth seem as dead.
This seen, Orlando did approach the man   120
And found it was his brother, his elder brother.
Celia. O, I have heard him speak of that same brother,
And he did render him the most unnatural
That lived amongst men.
Oliver.   And well he might so do,
For well I know he was unnatural.   125
Rosalind. But, to Orlando: did he leave him there,
Food to the sucked and hungry lioness?
Oliver. Twice did he turn his back and purposed so;
But kindness, nobler ever than revenge,
And nature, stronger than his just occasion,   130
Made him give battle to the lioness,
Who quickly fell before him in which hurtling
From miserable slumber I awaked.
Celia. Are you his brother?
Rosalind.   Was it you he rescued?
Celia. Was't you that did so oft contrive to kill him?   135
Oliver. 'Twas I. But 'tis not I. I do not shame
To tell you what I was, since my conversion
So sweetly tastes, being the thing I am.
Rosalind. But, for the bloody napkin?
Oliver.   By and by.
When from the first to last, betwixt us two,   140
Tears our recountments had most kindly bathed,
As how I came into that desert place:
In brief, he led me to the gentle Duke,
Who gave me fresh array and entertainment,

113 *indented* sinuous 116 *couching* crouched 123 *render* describe 129 *kindness* affection in kinship 132 *hurtling* tumult 139 *By and by* presently 141 *recountments* accounts (of events since we separated)

Committing me unto my brother's love, 145
Who led me instantly unto his cave,
There stripped himself, and here upon his arm
The lioness had torn some flesh away,
Which all this while had bled; and now he fainted,
And cried, in fainting, upon Rosalind. 150
Brief, I recovered him, bound up his wound;
And after some small space, being strong at heart,
He sent me hither, stranger as I am,
To tell this story, that you might excuse
His broken promise, and to give this napkin, 155
Dyed in his blood, unto the shepherd youth
That he in sport doth call his Rosalind. *[Rosalind swoons.]*
Celia. Why, how now Ganymede, sweet Ganymede!
Oliver. Many will swoon when they do look on blood.
Celia. There is more in it. Cousin Ganymede! 160
Oliver. Look, he recovers.
Rosalind. I would I were at home.
Celia. We'll lead you thither.
    I pray you, will you take him by the arm?
Oliver. Be of good cheer, youth. You a man! You lack a
    man's heart. 165
Rosalind. I do so, I confess it. Ah, sirrah, a body would
    think this was well counterfeited. I pray you tell your
    brother how well I counterfeited. Heigh-ho!
Oliver. This was not counterfeit. There is too great testi-
    mony in your complexion that it was a passion of earnest. 170
Rosalind. Counterfeit, I assure you.
Oliver. Well then, take a good heart and counterfeit to be
    a man.
Rosalind. So I do; but, i' faith, I should have been a woman
    by right. 175
Celia. Come, you look paler and paler. Pray you draw
    homewards. Good sir, go with us.
Oliver. That will I, for I must bear answer back
    How you excuse my brother, Rosalind.
Rosalind. I shall devise somthing. But I pray you com- 180
    mend my counterfeiting to him. Will you go?   *Exeunt.*

Enter [Touchstone the] Clown and Audrey.   V,i

Touchstone. We shall find a time, Audrey. Patience, gentle
    Audrey.

151 *Brief* in brief *recovered* revived 167 *counterfeited* acted, pretended 170 *passion of earnest* display of genuine emotion

Audrey. Faith, the priest was good enough, for all the old
    gentleman's saying.

Touchstone. A most wicked Sir Oliver, Audrey, a most   5
    vile Mar-text. But, Audrey, there is a youth here in the
    forest lays claim to you.

Audrey. Ay, I know who 'tis. He hath no interest in me in
    the world. Here comes the man you mean.

Enter William.

Touchstone. It is meat and drink to me to see a clown; by   10
    my troth, we that have good wits have much to answer
    for. We shall be flouting; we cannot hold.

William. Good ev'n, Audrey.

Audrey. God ye good ev'n, William.

William. And good ev'n to you, sir.   15

Touchstone. Good ev'n, gentle friend. Cover thy head, cover
    thy head. Nay, prithee be covered. How old are you,
    friend?

William. Five-and-twenty, sir.

Touchstone. A ripe age. Is thy name William?   20

William. William, sir.

Touchstone. A fair name. Wast born i' th' forest here?

William. Ay, sir, I thank God.

Touchstone. 'Thank God.' A good answer. Art rich?

William. Faith, sir, so so.   25

Touchstone. 'So so' is good, very good, very excellent
    good; and yet it is not, it is but so so. Art thou wise?

William. Ay, sir, I have a pretty wit.

Touchstone. Why, thou say'st well. I do now remember a
    saying, 'The fool doth think he is wise, but the wise man   30
    knows himself to be a fool.' The heathen philosopher,
    when he had a desire to eat a grape, would open his lips
    when he put it into his mouth, meaning thereby that
    grapes were made to eat and lips to open. You do love
    this maid?   35

William. I do, sir.

Touchstone. Give me your hand. Art thou learned?

William. No, sir.

Touchstone. Then learn this of me: to have is to have; for
    it is a figure in rhetoric that drink, being poured out of   40
    a cup into a glass, by filling the one doth empty the

V, i, 10 *clown* yokel (with a play on Touchstone's own profession) 12 *flouting* mocking
hold i.e. hold our tongues 29-34 *I do ... to open* (in this and the following passages Touchstone is burlesquing the style of Lyly's *Euphues* and Lodge's *Rosalynde*)

other; for all your writers do consent that *ipse* is he. Now,
you are not *ipse,* for I am he.

William. Which he, sir?

Touchstone. He, sir, that must marry this woman. There- 45
fore, you clown, abandon (which is in the vulgar, leave)
the society (which in the boorish is, company) of this
female (which in the common is, woman); which together is, abandon the society of this female, or, clown,
thou perishest; or, to thy better understanding, diest; or, 50
to wit, I kill thee, make thee away, translate thy life into
death, thy liberty into bondage. I will deal in poison with
thee, or in bastinado, or in steel; I will bandy with thee
in faction; I will o'errun thee with policy; I will kill thee
a hundred and fifty ways. Therefore tremble and depart. 55

Audrey. Do, good William.

William. God rest you, merry sir.   *Exit.*

Enter Corin.

Corin. Our master and mistress seeks you. Come away,
away!

Touchstone. Trip, Audrey, trip, Audrey. I attend, I attend. 60

                                                    Exeunt.

Enter Orlando and Oliver.   V,ii

Orlando. Is't possible that on so little acquaintance you
should like her? that but seeing, you should love her?
and loving, woo? and wooing, she should grant? And
will you persever to enjoy her?

Oliver. Neither call the giddiness of it in question, the 5
poverty of her, the small acquaintance, my sudden wooing, nor her sudden consenting; but say with me, I love
Aliena; say with her that she loves me; consent with
both that we may enjoy each other. It shall be to your
good; for my father's house, and all the revenue that 10
was old Sir Rowland's, will I estate upon you, and here
live and die a shepherd.

---

42 *ipse is he* he is the man (*ipse* was a fashionable literary term; Touchstone doubtless
alludes to its use in *Euphues*) 53 *bastinado* beating with sticks 53-54 *bandy . . . faction*
engage in controversy with you 54 *o'errun . . . policy* overwhelm you with political cunning
V, ii, 5 *Neither . . . question* do not raise questions about the speed of it 11 *estate* settle

Enter Rosalind.

Orlando. You have my consent. Let your wedding be to-
morrow: thither will I invite the Duke and all's contented
followers. Go you and prepare Aliena; for look you,   15
here comes my Rosalind.
Rosalind. God save you, brother.
Oliver. And you, fair sister.   *[Exit.]*
Rosalind. O my dear Orlando, how it grieves me to see
thee wear thy heart in a scarf!   20
Orlando. It is my arm.
Rosalind. I thought thy heart had been wounded with the
claws of a lion.
Orlando. Wounded it is, but with the eyes of a lady.
Rosalind. Did your brother tell you how I counterfeited   25
to sound when he showed me your handkercher?
Orlando. Ay, and greater wonders than that.
Rosalind. O, I know where you are! Nay, 'tis true. There
was never anything so sudden but the fight of two rams
and Caesar's thrasonical brag of 'I came, saw, and over-   30
came'; for your brother and my sister no sooner met but
they looked; no sooner looked but they loved; no sooner
loved but they sighed; no sooner sighed but they asked
one another the reason; no sooner knew the reason but
they sought the remedy: and in these degrees have they   35
made a pair of stairs to marriage, which they will climb
incontinent, or else be incontinent before marriage: they
are in the very wrath of love, and they will together;
clubs cannot part them.
Orlando. They shall be married to-morrow, and I will bid   40
the Duke to the nuptial. But, O, how bitter a thing it is
to look into happiness through another man's eyes! By
so much the more shall I to-morrow be at the height of
heart-heaviness, by how much I shall think my brother
happy in having what he wishes for.   45
Rosalind. Why then, to-morrow I cannot serve your turn
for Rosalind?
Orlando. I can live no longer by thinking.

18 *fair sister* (although Rosalind is still dressed like a man, Oliver addresses her according to
the manner in which she has been described to him by Orlando; see IV, iii, 86-88) 26 *to
sound* swooning 30 *thrasonical* boastful (like the braggart soldier, Thraso, in Terence's comedy *Eunuchus*) 35 *degrees* (Touchstone puns on the literal meaning 'steps') 37 *incontinent . . . incontinent* immediately . . . unrestrained sexually 38 *wrath* passion 39 *clubs* (commonly used to part combatants)

Rosalind. I will weary you then no longer with idle talking.
Know of me then, for now I speak to some purpose, that 50
I know you are a gentleman of good conceit. I speak not
this that you should bear a good opinion of my knowledge, insomuch I say I know you are; neither do I labor
for a greater esteem than may in some little measure
draw a belief from you, to do yourself good, and not to 55
grace me. Believe then, if you please, that I can do
strange things. I have, since I was three year old, conversed with a magician, most profound in his art and yet
not damnable. If you do love Rosalind so near the heart
as your gesture cries it out, when your brother marries 60
Aliena shall you marry her. I know into what straits of
fortune she is driven; and it is not impossible to me, if it
appear not inconvenient to you, to set her before your
eyes to-morrow, human as she is, and without any
danger. 65
Orlando. Speak'st thou in sober meanings?
Rosalind. By my life, I do, which I tender dearly, though
I say I am a magician. Therefore put you in your best
array, bid your friends; for if you will be married to-
morrow you shall; and to Rosalind, if you will. 70

Enter Silvius and Phebe.

Look, here comes a lover of mine and a lover of hers.
Phebe. Youth, you have done me much ungentleness
To show the letter that I writ to you.
Rosalind. I care not if I have. It is my study
To seem despiteful and ungentle to you. 75
You are there followed by a faithful shepherd:
Look upon him, love him; he worships you.
Phebe. Good shepherd, tell this youth what 'tis to love.
Silvius. It is to be all made of sighs and tears;
And so am I for Phebe. 80
Phebe. And I for Ganymede.
Orlando. And I for Rosalind.
Rosalind. And I for no woman.
Silvius. It is to be all made of faith and service;
And so am I for Phebe. 85
Phebe. And I for Ganymede.

51 *conceit* intelligence 55 *belief* i.e., confidence in my ability 56 *grace me* bring favor on
myself 57-58 *conversed* had dealings 59 *not damnable* not practising black magic 60 *gesture . . . out* behavior proclaims 63 *inconvenient* inappropriate 67 *tender* value (the practice
of magic was a capital offense. Rosalind is slyly admitting that she is not truly a magician)
74 *study* conscious endeavor

Orlando. And I for Rosalind.

Rosalind. And I for no woman.

Silvius. It is to be all made of fantasy,
    All made of passion, and all made of wishes,   90
    All adoration, duty, and observance,
    All humbleness, all patience, and impatience,
    All purity, all trial, all observance;
    And so am I for Phebe.

Phebe. And so am I for Ganymede.   95

Orlando. And so am I for Rosalind.

Rosalind. And so am I for no woman.

Phebe. *[to Rosalind]* If this be so, why blame you me to
    love you?

Silvius. *[to Phebe]* If this be so, why blame you me to love
    you?

Orlando. If this be so, why blame you me to love you?   100

Rosalind. Why do you speak too, 'Why blame you me to
    love you?'

Orlando. To her that is not here, nor doth not hear.

Rosalind. Pray you, no more of this; 'tis like the howling
    of Irish wolves against the moon. *[to Silvius]* I will help
    you if I can. *[to Phebe]* I would love you if I could.   105
    To-morrow meet me all together. *[to Phebe]* I will
    marry you if ever I marry a woman, and I'll be married
    to-morrow. *[to Orlando]* I will satisfy you if ever I satis-
    fied man, and you shall be married to-morrow. *[to
    Silvius]* I will content you if what pleases you contents   110
    you, and you shall be married to-morrow. *[to Orlando]*
    As you love Rosalind, meet. *[to Silvius]* As you love
    Phebe, meet. And as I love no woman, I'll meet. So
    fare you well. I have left you commands.

Silvius. I'll not fail if I live.   115

Phebe. Nor I.

Orlando. Nor I.   *Exeunt.*

———

      Enter [Touchstone the] Clown and Audrey.   V,iii

Touchstone. To-morrow is the joyful day, Audrey; to-
    morrow will we be married.

89 *fantasy* fancy 91 *observance* devotion 93 *observance* (many editors, assuming a composi-
tor's error from two lines above, emend to *obedience*) 101 *Why . . . too* (often emended to
Who . . . to) 103-4 *like . . . moon* (corresponding simile in *Rosalynde* reads: 'thou barkest
with the wolves of Syria against the moon')

Audrey. I do desire it will all my heart; and I hope it is no
 dishonest desire to desire to be a woman of the world.
 Here come two of the banished Duke's pages.   5

Enter two Pages.

1. Page. Well met, honest gentleman.
Touchstone. By my troth, well met. Come, sit, sit, and a
 song!
2. Page. We are for you. Sit i' th' middle.
1. Page. Shall we clap into't roundly, without hawking or   10
 spitting or saying we are hoarse, which are the only
 prologues to a bad voice?
2. Page. I' faith, i' faith! and both in a tune, like two
 gypsies on a horse.

Song.

It was a lover and his lass,   15
 With a hey, and a ho, and a hey nonino,
That o'er the green cornfield did pass
 In springtime, the only pretty ringtime,
When birds do sing, hey ding a ding, ding.
Sweet lovers love the spring.   20

Between the acres of the rye,
 With a hey, and a ho, and a hey nonino,
These pretty country folks would lie
 In springtime, &c.

This carol they began that hour,   25
 With a hey, and a ho, and a hey nonino,
How that a life was but a flower
 In springtime, &c.

And therefore take the present time,
 With a hey, and a ho, and a hey nonino,   30
For love is crownèd with the prime
 In springtime, &c.

Touchstone. Truly, young gentlemen, though there was no
 great matter in the ditty, yet the note was very untuneable.   35

V, iii, 4 *dishonest* immodest *to be . . . world* to be married (and also to go beyond her present rustic station in life) 9 *for you* ready for you 10 *clap into't roundly* start right off 11 *only* common 17 *cornfield* wheatfield 18 *ringtime* wedding season 29-32 *And . . . springtime, &c.* (in folio these lines follow l. 20) 31 *prime* spring 34-35 *untuneable* untuneful

1. Page. You are deceived, sir. We kept time, we lost not
    our time.
Touchstone. By my troth, yes; I count it but time lost to
    hear such a foolish song. God b' wi' you, and God mend
    your voices. Come, Audrey.   *Exeunt.*   40

       Enter Duke Senior, Amiens, Jaques, Orlando, Oliver,   V,iv
                            Celia.

Duke Senior. Dost thou believe, Orlando, that the boy
    Can do all this that he hath promised?
Orlando. I sometimes do believe, and sometimes do not,
    As those that fear they hope, and know they fear.

         Enter Rosalind, Silvius, and Phebe.

Rosalind. Patience once more, whiles our compact is urged.   5
    You say, if I bring in your Rosalind,
    You will bestow her on Orlando here?
Duke Senior. That would I, had I kingdoms to give with
    her.
Rosalind. And you say you will have her when I bring
    her?
Orlando. That would I, were I of all kingdoms king.   10
Rosalind. You say you'll marry me, if I be willing?
Phebe. That will I, should I die the hour after.
Rosalind. But if you do refuse to marry me,
    You'll give yourself to this most faithful shepherd?
Phebe. So is the bargain.   15
Rosalind. You say that you'll have Phebe, if she will?
Silvius. Though to have her and death were both one thing.
Rosalind. I have promised to make all this matter even.
    Keep you your word, O Duke, to give your daughter;
    You yours, Orlando, to receive his daughter;   20
    Keep your word, Phebe, that you'll marry me,
    Or else, refusing me, to wed this shepherd;
    Keep your word, Silvius, that you'll marry her
    If she refuse me; and from hence I go,
    To make these doubts all even.   25
                 Exeunt Rosalind and Celia.
Duke Senior. I do remember in this shepherd boy
    Some lively touches of my daughter's favor.

V, iv, 4 *fear they hope* i.e. fear they only hope 5 *urged* stressed 18 *even* plain
25 *make . . . even* clear up your misgivings 27 *lively* lifelike *favor* features

Orlando. My lord, the first time that I ever saw him
　　Methought he was a brother to your daughter.
　　But, my good lord, this boy is forest-born,　　　　　　　　　　30
　　And hath been tutored in the rudiments
　　Of many desperate studies by his uncle,
　　Whom he reports to be a great magician,
　　Obscurèd in the circle of this forest.

　　　　　　Enter [Touchtone the] Clown and Audrey.

Jaques. There is, sure, another flood toward, and these　　　　35
　　couples are coming to the ark. Here comes a pair of very
　　strange beasts, which in all tongues are called fools.
Touchstone. Salutation and greeting to you all!
Jaques. Good my lord, bid him welcome. This is the
　　motley-minded gentleman that I have so often met in　　　40
　　the forest. He hath been a courtier, he swears.
Touchstone. If any man doubt that, let him put me to my
　　purgation. I have trod a measure; I have flattered a lady;
　　I have been politic with my friend, smooth with mine
　　enemy; I have undone three tailors; I have had four　　　45
　　quarrels, and like to have fought one.
Jaques. And how was that ta'en up?
Touchstone. Faith, we met, and found the quarrel was upon
　　the seventh cause.
Jaques. How seventh cause? Good my lord, like this fellow.　　50
Duke Senior. I like him very well.
Touchstone. God 'ild you, sir; I desire you of the like. I
　　press in here, sir, amongst the rest of the country copu-
　　latives, to swear and to forswear, according as marriage
　　binds and blood breaks. A poor virgin, sir, an ill-favored　　55
　　thing, sir, but mine own; a poor humor of mine, sir, to
　　take that that no man else will. Rich honesty dwells like
　　a miser, sir, in a poor house, as your pearl in your foul
　　oyster.
Duke Senior. By my faith, he is very swift and sententious.　　60
Touchstone. According to the fool's bolt, sir, and such
　　dulcet diseases.

---

32 *desperate* dangerous 34 *Obscurèd* hidden 35 *toward* approaching 35-36 *these cou-*
ples... ark (see Genesis 7:2, where only the 'unclean beasts' go into the ark by couples)
43 *purgation* trial, proof *measure* dance, with measured steps 44 *politic* prudent 45 *undone*
ruined 47 *ta'en up* settled 52 *'ild* reward *I desire... like* I wish you the same compliment
53-54 *copulatives* i.e. those about to couple 55 *blood* passion 56 *humor* eccentricity 57 *hon-*
esty chastity 60 *sententious* full of sense 61 *bolt* arrow (which is quickly shot) 62 *dulcet*
diseases pleasant afflictions

Jaques. But, for the seventh cause. How did you find the
    quarrel on the seventh cause?

Touchstone. Upon a lie seven times removed (bear your   65
    body more seeming, Audrey) as thus, sir. I did dislike
    the cut of a certain courtier's beard. He sent me word,
    if I said his beard was not cut well, he was in the mind
    it was: this is called the Retort Courteous. If I sent him
    word again it was not well cut, he would send me word   70
    he cut it to please himself: this is called the Quip Modest.
    If again, it was not well cut, he disabled my judgment:
    this is called the Reply Churlish. If again, it was not well
    cut, he would answer I spake not true: this is called the
    Reproof Valiant. If again, it was not well cut, he would   75
    say I lie: this is called the Countercheck Quarrelsome:
    and so to the Lie Circumstantial and the Lie Direct.

Jaques. And how oft did you say his beard was not well
    cut?

Touchstone. I durst go no further than the Lie Circumstan-   80
    tial, nor he durst not give me the Lie Direct; and so we
    measured swords and parted.

Jaques. Can you nominate in order now the degrees of the
    lie?

Touchstone. O sir, we quarrel in print, by the book, as you   85
    have books for good manners. I will name you the
    degrees. The first, the Retort Courteous; the second,
    the Quip Modest; the third, the Reply Churlish; the
    fourth, the Reproof Valiant; the fifth, the Countercheck
    Quarrelsome; the sixth, the Lie with Circumstance; the   90
    seventh, the Lie Direct. All these you may avoid but the
    Lie Direct, and you may avoid that too, with an If. I knew
    when seven justices could not take up a quarrel, but when
    the parties were met themselves, one of them thought but
    of an If: as, 'If you said so, then I said so'; and they   95
    shook hands and swore brothers. Your If is the only
    peacemaker. Much virtue in If.

Jaques. Is not this a rare fellow, my lord? He's as good at
    anything, and yet a fool.

Duke Senior. He uses his folly like a stalking horse, and   100
    under the presentation of that he shoots his wit.

---

66 *seeming* properly 71 *Modest* moderate 72 *disabled* disqualified 76 *Countercheck* contradiction 77 *Circumstantial* indirect 85 *by the book* according to the rules 90 *with Circum-*
stance i.e. only circumstantial, indirect 93 *take up* settle 100 *stalking horse* any object used
to hide a hunter stalking game 101 *under . . . that* i.e. while using the guise of his folly.

                    Enter Hymen, Rosalind, and Celia. Still music.

Hymen.   Then is there mirth in heaven
             When earthly things made even
                 Atone together.
             Good Duke, receive thy daughter;   105
             Hymen from heaven brought her,
                 Yea, brought her hither,
             That thou mightst join her hand with his
             Whose heart within his bosom is.
Rosalind. *[to Duke]* To you I give myself, for I am yours.   110
    [To Orlando] To you I give myself, for I am yours.
Duke Senior. If there be truth in sight, you are my daughter.
Orlando. If there be truth in sight, you are my Rosalind.
Phebe. If sight and shape be true,
             Why then, my love adieu!   115
Rosalind. *[to Duke]* I'll have no father, if you be not he.
    [To Orlando] I'll have no husband, if you be not he.
    [To Phebe] Nor ne'er wed woman, if you be not she.
Hymen.   Peace ho! I bar confusion:
             'Tis I must make conclusion   120
                 Of these most strange events.
             Here's eight that must take hands
             To join in Hymen's bands,
                 If truth holds true contents.
             [To Orlando and Rosalind]
             You and you no cross shall part.   125
             [To Oliver and Celia]
             You and you are heart in heart.
             [To Phebe]
             You to his love must accord,
             Or have a woman to your lord.
             [To Touchstone and Audrey]
             You and you are sure together
             As the winter to foul weather.   130
             [To all]
             Whiles a wedlock hymn we sing,
             Feed yourselves with questioning,
             That reason wonder may diminish
             How thus we met, and these things finish.

S.D. *Hymen* the god of marriage (figuring, as in several other plays, in a masque symbolizing
a wedding ceremony) *Still* soft 104 *Atone* are set at one, join 108 *her* (folio reads *his*) 112
If... sight i.e. if he is not again deceived by appearances 124 *If... contents* i.e. if the
discoveries made by the couples reveal their genuine affections 125 *cross* disagreement 127
accord assent 129 *sure together* securely united 132 *Feed* satisfy 133 *reason* understanding

Song.

> Wedding is great Juno's crown,   135
>   O blessed bond of board and bed!
> 'Tis Hymen peoples every town;
>   High wedlock then be honored.
> Honor, high honor, and renown
> To Hymen, god of every town!   140

Duke Senior. O my dear niece, welcome thou art to me,
  Even daughter, welcome, in no less degree!
Phebe. [*to Silvius*] I will not eat my word, now thou art
  mine;
  Thy faith my fancy to thee doth combine.

Enter Second Brother.

2. Brother. Let me have audience for a word or two.   145
  I am the second son of old Sir Rowland
  That bring these tidings to this fair assembly.
  Duke Frederick, hearing how that every day
  Men of great worth resorted to this forest,
  Addressed a mighty power, which were on foot   150
  In his own conduct, purposely to take
  His brother here and put him to the sword;
  And to the skirts of this wild wood he came,
  Where, meeting with an old religious man,
  After some question with him, was converted   155
  Both from his enterprise and from the world,
  His crown bequeathing to his banished brother,
  And all their lands restored to them again
  That were with him exiled. This to be true
  I do engage my life.
Duke Senior.   Welcome, young man.   160
  Thou offer'st fairly to thy brothers' wedding:
  To one, his lands withheld; and to the other,
  A land itself at large, a potent dukedom.
  First, in this forest let us do those ends
  That here were well begun and well begot;   165
  And after, every of this happy number
  That have endured shrewd days and nights with us

---

142 *Even daughter* just as if you were my daughter 143 *eat* swallow, i.e. take back 144 *combine* unite S.D. *Second Brother* i.e. Jaques de Boys 150 *Addressed* assembled *power* force (of troops) 151 *conduct* command 154 *religious man* (evidently an anchorite) 155 *question* discussion 160 *engage* pledge 161 *Thou . . . fairly* you bring handsome prospects 164 *do those ends* complete those purposes 167 *shrewd* sharp, hard

Shall share the good of our returnèd fortune,
According to the measure of their states.
Meantime forget this new-fall'n dignity   170
And fall into our rustic revelry.
Play, music, and you brides and bridegrooms all,
With measure heaped in joy, to th' measures fall.
Jaques. Sir, by your patience. If I heard you rightly,
The Duke hath put on a religious life   175
And thrown into neglect the pompous court.
2. Brother. He hath.
Jaques. To him will I. Out of these convertites
There is much matter to be heard and learned.
[To Duke] You to your former honor I bequeath;   180
Your patience and your virtue well deserves it.
[To Orlando] You to a love that your true faith doth
   merit;
[To Oliver] You to your land and love and great allies;
[To Silvius] You to a long and well-deservèd bed;
[To Touchstone] And you to wrangling, for thy loving
   voyage   185
Is but for two months victualled. So, to your pleasures:
I am for other than for dancing measures.
Duke Senior. Stay, Jaques, stay.
Jaques. To see no pastime I. What you would have
I'll stay to know at your abandoned cave.   *Exit.* 190
Duke Senior. Proceed, proceed. We will begin these rites,
As we do trust they'll end, in true delights.
                                        Exit [in the Dance].

———

[EPILOGUE]   Epi.

Rosalind. It is not the fashion to see the lady the epilogue,
   but it is no more unhandsome than to see the lord the
   prologue. If it be true that good wine needs no bush, 'tis
   true that a good play needs no epilogue; yet to good
   wine they do use good bushes, and good plays prove the   5
   better by the help of good epilogues. What a case am I
   in then, that am neither a good epilogue, nor cannot
   insinuate with you in the behalf of a good play! I am
   not furnished like a beggar; therefore to beg will not
   become me. My way is to conjure you, and I'll begin   10

---

169 *states* i.e. status 175 *put . . . life* adopted the life of a monk or hermit 178 *convertites* converts Epi., 2 *unhandsome* unbecoming 3 *bush* ivy bush (formerly the sign of a vintner) 6 *case* predicament 8 *insinuate* ingratiate myself 9 *furnished* equipped, i.e. with rags and cup 10 *conjure* adjure, i.e. charge, as if on oath

with the women. I charge you, O women, for the love
you bear to men, to like as much of this play as please
you; and I charge you, O men, for the love you bear to
women (as I perceive by your simp'ring none of you
hates them), that between you and the women the play   15
may please. If I were a woman, I would kiss as many
of you as had beards that pleased me, complexions that
liked me, and breaths that I defied not; and I am sure,
as many as have good beards, or good faces, or sweet
breaths, will, for my kind offer, when I make curtsy, bid   20
me farewell.   *Exit.*

---

12 *like* (a reminder of the play's title) *please* may please 16 *If . . . woman* (a reminder that
the actor was a boy) 18 *liked me* I liked *defied* rejected 20-21 *bid me farewell* i.e. with
applause

AS YOU LIKE IT: An Afterword

You have now experienced one of the world's most memorable dramas. Did you, in truth, "like it"? Or did you miss the multiple stage of Shakespeare, which we will examine in Chapter 2? No doubt you missed the actor, whose work we will study in Chapter 4, although *As You Like It*, with its dependence on words, can be lived in the imagination perhaps better than any other drama. Yet unless you came to the play well-prepared to do so, you probably found it difficult to experience all the flights of fancy that make up this story of virtue triumphant through love in Never-Never-Land. The magic of the encounters between Rosalind and Orlando, between each of these students of love and some practitioner of a single, and restrictive, view of love, and between certain of the practitioners themselves is diminished when we have no human actors to play the roles.

Despite the emphasis on poetic fantasy, *As You Like It* focuses primarily on down-to-earth, human love. There is a particular need of human beings to incarnate the poetry. The flights of fancy must have their physical representation if the dramatic construct is to be fully realized.

Furthermore, Shakespeare not only gives us love "as we like it," but also gently kids the ways in which we commonly express our preoccupation with love. He also ridicules the belief that a pastoral life automatically insures the best of all possible worlds. All the people who reside in Arden—whether artificial or real—must have the civilizing influence of Rosalind in order to achieve their happiness. And Rosalind, along with the other people from the court, needs a brief respite from the corruption of civilization if she herself is to build a good life.

How all these realms of fancy are achieved by the actor and the designer we will examine shortly. Despite its seeming to consist only of words, *As You Like It* particularly requires the players and their stage to make the fancy real and to show the civilizing force of human love.

Suggestions for Further Reading

Butcher, S. H. *Aristotle's Theory of Poetry and Fine Art: With a Critical Text and Translation of the Poetics.* 4th ed. New York: Dover Publications, 1951.

Centeno, Augusto, ed. *The Intent of the Artist.* Princeton, N. J.: Princeton University Press, 1941.

Dewey, John. *Art as Experience.* New York: Minton, Balch & Co., 1934.

Fergusson, Francis. *The Idea of a Theatre.* Princeton, N. J.: Princeton University Press, 1949.

Peacock, Ronald. *The Art of Drama.* New York: The Macmillan Co., 1957.

Young, Stark. *The Theatre.* New York: Hill and Wang, 1954.

Chapter 2

The Theatre and Human Affairs

"Yes, I have tricks in my pocket," announces Tom Wingfield, "I have things up my sleeve. But I am the opposite of a stage magician. He gives you illusion that has the appearance of truth. I give you truth in the pleasant guise of illusion."[1]

And so have they all—these players and playwrights, these directors and technicians—from the time that Thespis (allegedly) stepped in front of the dithyrambic chorus and created drama. In Chapter 1, we established the idea that people come to theatre for the purpose of playing. In subsequent chapters we will examine the ways in which the "illusion of life" is presented onstage. The upshot will be that we are all "stage magicians."

Yet we are all Tom Wingfields as well. One of the reasons we like to play our dreams is that we have trouble assimilating the truth in them. Playing helps us live with the truth we find ourselves in from day to day —the storms of our own and someone's creation.

Not every age has had its "idea of a theatre," its desire or chance to play. This chapter intends to examine briefly those eras in which the best of what we have been studying was manifest. The usual approach to man and his theatre is to declare that both progressed from the simple dances of primitive rituals through the highly-sophisticated dramatized myths of the Greeks, and those who came after, to the mature play-making of the late sixteenth and early seventeenth centuries in Europe, but then declined into the movies and television of the present day.

There is nothing wrong, nor wholly inaccurate, about this historical approach. Yet much can be gained by presuming that the theatre of each historical era is separate and unique, but at the same time exactly

1. Reprinted from *The Glass Menagerie*, by Tennessee Williams, in *Best Plays of the Modern American Theatre: Second Series*, ed. John Gassner, Copyright, 1947, Crown Publishers, Inc. Used by permission.

like all the other periods of theatre. That is, each time man has developed a theatre he has faced and solved the same esthetic problems. The influence of the past, as he knew it at the time, was always one of the problems. But rather than build on what had gone before, each age simply used what it found for its own purposes.

Thus we will examine the history of our theatre in a topical rather than a chronological manner. What will result is a brief history of acting, design, stagecraft, and so forth.

Before examining the theatres of the world, however, we must deal with a more basic phenomenon. The theatre and its drama never exist in a vacuum. They are part of human affairs. Not only do they show their audience's "form and fashion," but also they help playgoers crystallize their view of themselves. Drama and theatre play a part in the development and the reinforcement of human ideas.

Drama and Ideas

It is a truism that dramatic art must follow, not lead, its audience. Drama is an imitation, not a persuasion. Yet the distinction between these two possible aims is not clear. The experience of attitudes and frames of reference generally serves to crystallize such predispositions. If they are subconscious, or subsurface, the crystallization may in fact persuade the audience to take them up. During the American Revolution, for example, a point came when the radicals in America were advocating certain opinions and attitudes toward Great Britain: that she was a nation of corrupt politicians, dandified and immoral men, and loose women, and that simple country folk were far more virtuous than sophisticated city-dwellers.

Samuel Adams and the Sons of Liberty based their campaign for rebellion on the establishment or crystallization of these beliefs. What is not so widely known is that the dramas seen in the American Colonies between 1763 and 1776 presented these same attitudes over and over. The Great Britain onstage was exactly like the country of evil the propagandists sought to portray. Though no absolute proof is available, we may certainly assume that the effect of the propaganda was enhanced by the effect of the drama.

The same effect can be ascribed to plays in any historical period. The Athenians were undoubtedly persuaded toward an attitude about their recent conduct when they witnessed *The Trojan Women*. Nearly a century earlier, *Oresteia* had clearly dramatized the system of justice then developing. And our view of Richard III is no doubt based on Shakespeare's masterfully propagandistic view of this much-maligned enemy of the Tudors.

We cannot say that drama and theatre *cause* changes in attitude. Probably in most instances they cannot. But over a long period of time, nothing influences human ideas more strongly than dramatic experience of them (and here we must include motion pictures and television). Does the audience create a stock character or a stereotypical action, for example, and the dramatist or the actor merely employ it artistically? Which came first, our view of the Negro, the Indian, the comic foreigner, or the presentation of them in drama? And did this presentation help our view along? No one can say for sure, but probably if the Negro—to take just one example—had been portrayed as a first-class citizen in drama, films, and television from the beginning of these arts in the United States, he would not have required an edict of the Supreme Court to achieve his birthright. At the very least, the edict would not have met such widespread resistance.

When drama is the heart of a community, the heart is deemed to speak wisdom the head knows not of. Drama exists not only to help us *play* our dreams, but also to make us *know* them.

Whether we act upon the knowledge is beside the point. The political comedy of Aristophanes represented a minority view, and hence was fated not to succeed. The same can be said of *Everyman,* the morality play at the end of this chapter. Medieval man was no more inclined to act upon the knowledge crystallized in this drama than is modern man. But both versions of mankind learn from *Everyman,* though neither act according to its precepts.

Moreover, the modern playgoer is probably struck most by the tragedy of the morality's dramatic action. What once was seen purely as propaganda is now a more universal portrait of man. In the same way, it is the comedy of Aristophanes we experience today, not his politics. It is the characters of Menander and Plautus, metamorphosed into twentieth-century equivalents, that capture today's audience. The popularity of domestic over cosmic wrangling has always been notable in drama and theatre.

Yet the ubiquity of stock actions by audience stereotypes of political or social origin increases the likelihood that the view of a person or a group the stereotype expresses will be reinforced. Audience behavior toward the person or group is directed by formulation onstage. If action or character comes from folk or mythological sources, the deep-seated emotional need thereby dredged up and seen more or less clearly helps to allay fears growing out of the need. *Othello,* for example, dramatized a seventeenth-century English stereotype by having a "super-subtle Venetian" perform the villainy that brings about the Moor's downfall. Iago was thus highly believable *as a result* of the Jacobean view of Venice. This view became *more* believable when seen onstage.

This understanding of Iago is a commonplace of criticism. That Othello himself represents a wild, irrational part of ourselves—this chaos that comes again and again—is perhaps not so widely accepted. Yet we *know* the marriage of racial, social, and generational extremes will not work. Onstage, in this drama, such a marriage does not work. Shakespeare's crafting of time and space notwithstanding, we are *relieved* at the failure of

Othello and Desdemona—or, to put it another way, the success of Iago. *Our belief is reinforced: a black and a white, a barbarian (Christian though he may be) and a European, an old man and a young girl cannot wed with impunity.* It is so onstage because we know it, and we know it because we see it onstage.

Yet despite contemporary tragic importance, *Everyman* is completely the creature of its own age. The dialogue about salvation is couched in images and ideas of the fifteenth century. A more modern dialogue about the same subject is *Major Barbara.* Undershaft, Cusins, and Barbara, incarnate money, brains, and love—which Shaw represents as the stuff to make salvation out of. Like the author of *Everyman,* however, Shaw places heaven offstage beyond the viewing time limits of the play.

Today, 1970, we take our salvation straight—onstage where we wait for Godot or celebrate *le fin de partie.* Or we moo at our own death, like "George" in *The Killing of Sister George.* The old joke about "if I can't take it with me when I go, I won't go" no longer holds. There is no place to go, there is only the standing and the taking of the blows, even to the final one, with courage and *engagement.* This is the affair of the twentieth century, and it is no true drama that avoids playing it. Yet no idea is new, even this one, and we remember Lear's "such a poor, bare, forked animal as thou art," or think along with Sophocles: "Look upon Oedipus. This is the king who solved the famous riddle and towered up, most powerful of men. No mortal eyes but looked on him with envy. Yet in the end ruin swept over him."

A drama, then, is a human affair in which the ideas of its time clash and contrast, intermingle, and formulate the life of its audience. The ideas may appear in the action, the incidents, the characters, the language—in short, any of the dramatic elements, or all of them at once. That we give the ideas or their typical patterns a name and call *Lear* a tragedy, *As You Like It* a comedy, *Everyman* a morality play, and so forth, is beside the point and relatively unimportant. The ideas of our time interplay onstage and we experience them in no other way so completely.

This experience is a far cry from persuasion or preachment, from any kind of prescription for behavior no matter how subtle. For Aristotle, "ideas" meant *dianoia*—that is, intellectual behavior, often translated as "thought." Men interacted through their thoughts as well as through their deeds. Our view, based on this, would be that the thoughts themselves interact—or, more accurately, form themselves into a tesselation, a kind of ethical and intellectual sub-stratum which informs the drama. It is the drama's value system, or attitudinal pattern.

That the entire system of ideas may be couched symbolically or imagistically does not disguise the centricity of the ideas themselves. Only a few times in man's history have theatres of the world existed at the heart of his community. Thus the ideas of an era have only at rare intervals been the ideas in the theatre. For the Greeks of fifth-century

Athens, for Englishmen during the time of Elizabeth I and James I, for the Spanish of the Golden Age, for the French of Molière and Racine—perhaps for the villagers who attended the Medieval miracle and mystery plays— drama was a force in the affairs of the time. Attitudes and frames of reference could be crystallized and promulgated. Today our theatre and its ideas seem more like "photoflashes in the darkness" than idea and value systems comprehending the total life of twentieth-century man.

Theatres of the World

Whatever the origin of theatre as we know it—some believe it came from primitive ritual and some that it was invented separately from religious practices—all theatre requires the same collaborators and the same elements. The history of theatre is usually examined in terms of nine periods:

1. Classical Greece and Rome.
2. Middle Ages.
3. Italian Renaissance.
4. Spain and England, 1200-1650.
5. France and Italy, 1500-1750.
6. England, 1650-1750.
7. Europe and America, 1750-1850.
8. Oriental Theatre, 1400-1950.
9. Modern Theatre, 1850-Present.

From period to period, however, the essential questions remain the same:

1. What are the demands and the affairs of the audience?
2. What kind of playhouse is provided for the audience to satisfy its demands in?
3. What are the plays that result? In particular,
   a. How does the dramatist achieve meanings?
   b. How does the director achieve meanings?
   c. How does the actor achieve meanings?
   d. How does the designer or the technical director achieve meanings?

Though in each historical period the answers to these questions are unique, remarkable similarity exists from period to period. Let us take each of our questions and see how theatres of the world, yesterday and today, respond.

AUDIENCES, YESTERDAY AND TODAY

Despite presumed differences based on assumptions about the origin and development of drama—which may not be accurate—people who attend the theatre for religious exaltation; for participation in the affairs of their time (there being no newspapers and few readers); for intellectual, spiritual, or esthetic enlightenment; or for all of these reasons actually seek much the same experience. What they want, though perhaps from various points of attack, is the impersonation of themselves in an artistically controlled playing of their dreams.

Why human beings persist in such activities is a question for psychologist, psychiatrist, and philosopher. The human persistence in dramatic activities was explored briefly in Chapter 1. The fact is, people do seem to prefer playing games to all other activity. From time to time, formal theatre games have been among the most popular. We must use the term "formal" to indicate playmaking in public. Informal drama—playmaking in private—is probably the predominant human activity, but information about it is difficult to come by. Be that as it may, artists of theatre fashion plays out of human affairs, and then audiences participate in them. The audience of each era seeks its "form and pressure" from theatre.

The Athenians who cheered Sophocles were theatre-wise. They had known at least one hundred years of highly-sophisticated dramas. Historians now dispute whether drama in truth had a religious origin, but the presence of dramatic contests at the festivals of Dionysus from 534 B.C. cannot be denied. The city gave a prize to the best tragedy and, from 487 B.C., to the best comedy.

The festivals of Dionysus—four annually in Athens alone: the City Dionysia, the Lenaia, the Rural Dionysia, and the Anthesteria—were orgies marked by competition among the tribes of Attica. Before 442 B.C., only the City Dionysia had drama; the Anthesteria never did. Each tribe entered a playwright in the contests that were held. He produced three tragedies and, from about 501 B.C., a satyr-play.

The people of Athens thus came to the theatre in a celebrative mood. Eating, drinking, and fornicating were part of the fun. The spectators particularly expected dramas that reflected their own sense of well-being and joy of living. Small wonder the playwrights usually dealt with mythological or nationalistic actions. Whether showing the high tragedy of Oedipus, the changing concept of Athenian justice, or the satirical comedy of Cloud-Cuckoo-Land, the dramas impersonated the Greeks as they thought of themselves.

Comedy, especially, seems to have come from the improvisations of crowds of revellers who sang, danced, and mocked leading citizens. Farce situations thus became associated with satire, word-play with song and dance, and what is called "Old Greek Comedy" resulted. Apparently there was also a long history of village farces and mimes that dealt with domestic rather than social characters and situations. After the downfall of Athens, these farces became the basis for the "New Greek Comedy."

The audience for the Old Comedy was the same as for tragedy—wild, celebrative, somewhat religious. If we cannot prove that tragedy came from such celebrations, we know it was long a part of them. The village farces, on the other hand, were principally for spectators who sought entertainment as part of market day or some other festive occasion.

Whether audience standards or playwright's art declined first, the historical fact remains that Greek audiences after the fifth century preferred domestic farce, mimes, and melodrama to high tragedy. In the times of Philip and Alexander, when all things Greek were spread throughout the known world, drama became part of many festivals that had no religious basis. The old classics were performed, but only for entertainment, though prizes were frequently given for the best performances. The people were fond enough of drama, however, to give special status to actors. As the demand for serious drama was reduced, the popularity of all other forms seems to have increased.

That the Hellenistic theatre, such as it was, had a popular audience seems undisputed. As the Romans took over the Mediterranean world, they ingested theatre along with the rest of Greek and Hellenistic culture.

Historians have long noted that the Romans were Greeks gone respectable. Rome gave Greek genius order and decorum. The same farces and mimes, many of the same religious festivals, that prevailed in Greece before the fifth century also existed in Italy. But since native drama of a high order did not develop as it did in Greece, we must assume the Roman audience never sought a form and pressure beyond the domestic and the crude. Even when absorbing Greek theatre, the Romans desired only the sententious and the melodramatic in the tragedy, and the farcical in the comedy.

Roman order controlled the Mediterranean world for more than five hundred years. Perhaps the people were too busy establishing an empire to seek a drama that went beyond the trivial. Or perhaps the drama *did* show the Romans *as they were,* and we are faced with the paradox of a trivial people who yet created the social and political world we have lived in ever since. Thus, the drama of Rome—the bloody, aphoristic melodramas of Seneca and the domestic farces of Plautus and the village festivals—have exerted incredible and widespread influence on the work of playwrights and the taste of audiences ever since.

Only rarely in two thousand years of Roman culture has this taste sought the greatness of tragedy or satiric comedy. Most of the time playwrights have shown their audiences lighthearted or thrilling, but essentially unreal, human actions.

To say this, however, is not to imply a moribund audience or theatre. Where audiences are, whatever they demand, there drama and theatre exist.

It is customary among today's historians to find the dark ages in Europe (500-1200 A.D.) filled with light. Life was a good deal richer and more varied than the term "dark" implies. As far as we know, there were no official theatres. Though men were just as sensual and secular as in every age, the Church was the central institution and it opposed drama for nearly 500 years. Yet apparently there were players of a kind, and by implication, audiences. Many of the pagan festivals survived in a new form. These had all the elements of drama, though no one can say that dramatic performances occurred.

Perhaps the Church introduced drama into its ceremonies to combat the pagan celebrations. If so, the audience was again seeking its form and pressure. Whatever the state of religious faith, the age was sacerdotal in the extreme. What better way is there to strengthen one's beliefs than to see them enacted in drama?

Be that as it may, the basic theatrical condition existed always in the church services—the audience and the actor (priest) exchanging symbols. A natural step would have been to add characters and impersonation, complex imagery, a story of some kind, scenic elements, and finally a second actor to engage in dialogue with the first.

Thus, whether or not the demand for drama was met during the centuries for which we have no records, the drama eventually appeared at the heart of the Medieval community—the Church. Though the desire to see oneself as one *is* eventually brought about secularization and removal from the Church, liturgical plays not only revived but also fed the need for drama. How natural it must have been to find devils more exciting than angels and to insist on rough and bawdy portrayals of saints as human beings like one's neighbors.

The audience of the Middle Ages thus shaped the drama that it experienced. All that was left to occur was the advent of more sophisticated playwrights. Only an audience trained by centuries of drama as a primary means of communal ritual could have welcomed the great theatres of the Renaissance. The two extant dramas which represent the height of the Medieval period—*The Second Shepherd's Play* and *Everyman*—show the seeds of this greatness to come. At the same time, they are very nearly perfect as projections of the consciousness of the Medieval audience. In fact, these two plays aptly reveal the drama as central to human affairs.

The greater sophistication of the drama in Elizabethan and Jacobean England, Louis XIV France, and Golden Age Spain rested on the achievements of the Middle Ages. Italy developed the *commedia dell'arte* and was the original site for the return of classical drama. Actually there were four types of *commedia*: the *dell'arte* (professional players); the *all'improviso* (improvised); the *a soggetto* (with plot, theme, or subject); and the *erudita* (learned). The last type was performed by amateur actors at courts and academies, but the others were given by professionals who toured Italy and later the continent.

The public audience in Italy, France, Spain, and England was largely the source of the good health enjoyed by the theatre in each country after 1550. About this time as well, a more erudite audience of university-trained critics and playwrights joined the commoners in desiring drama. From the classical scholars, the university men, and those who aped them or used the materials they uncovered came more sophisicated plays. These were copies of classical models at first; local and nationalistic, as the playwrights developed their skills.

The most complete fusion of these two kinds of audience occurred in England. Perhaps it is not too much to assert that the greatness of the Elizabethan-Jacobean theatre came from this blending of intellectual and commoner. As we examine the audiences of Spain, then France, and then Italy, we see a lesser and lesser fusion of social classes each time. Spain was nearly like England; France, more inclined to separate the intellectual critic from the common audience; Italy, the most scholar-bound of all. Where the scholar predominates, two theatres arise: the theatre of the streets and the theatre of the closet. The first is alive and ignorant of any rules except those the drama's patrons give. The second is concerned about following scholarly instructions, and is generally dead.

Eventually the Italian mode triumphed throughout Europe. The neo-classical Renaissance theatre acquired social sanction; the rough and bawdy theatre of the people floundered into circus, music hall, Punch and Judy, and burlesque. It is not that one audience is more important than the other, nor that one is less precious and more vital, which is true; but that both types of playgoers are necessary to a healthy theatre. At least that is what the history of Western European theatre seems to teach us.

As the Renaissance ended, the middle-class audience came to dominate the theatre—newly-rich artisans and burghers, half-schooled businessmen, successful workingmen. In England, this audience demanded the sentimental drama; in France, the well-made play; in Italy, the opera. The upper class also had its theatres: neo-classic tragedy in France; Restoration comedy in England; and still the opera in Italy. Perhaps the total community joined for Molière's comedies, perhaps not.

What had happened was the fragmentation of the community, long before the rise of science, which usually receives the blame. The idea of no theatre at the heart of the community perhaps was a result of the fragmentation. Perhaps also the division of the audience was a result of the snobbery of the new intellectuals. If playwrights were forced to work in an unnatural picture-frame stage with an esthetic derived by pseudo-Aristotelian critics and not based on theatre practices, perhaps they could not function creatively. The same quietus might not have affected other theatre artists because so long as the theatre of the commoners was alive and healthy, collaborators other than the playwright did not feel the pinch.

All this is speculation. The fact of the theatre's decline is obvious, but the causes are obscure. No doubt there are many of them, but surely the most basic is the rejection of the commonness of theatre that occurred in the Renaissance. Once the theatre lost its audience—the whole community—it lost its reason for being. Unless everyone comes together willingly and joyfully to play out his dreams with a group, all the rest of theatre is wasted at best and an empty shell at worst.

Today there is almost no theatre because there is almost no audience. In isolated pockets 'where the audience resides—a community here, a community there—theatre is still healthy. Certainly audiences keep regrouping; *they* have not deserted. But three hundred years without a theatre in the Elizabethan sense, two hunderd years with sentimental drama, and one-hundred years of pretense that a drama should be "real life" have very nearly destroyed Western Man's foremost art-form. This is so even without considering the rise of motion pictures and television. Moreover, even these excellent arts seem to be undergoing the same malaise that theatre suffers.

The audience for the Oriental theatre paralleled that for the European theatre up to the point fragmentation occurred, picture-frame perspective developed, and insistence on realism became dominant. There were as many Oriental traditions as there were cultures or countries, but the primary theatres were those of India, China, and Japan. Indian and Chinese theatre practices were at least as ancient as those of the West; the theatre in Japan began about 600 A.D. In India, the drama was part of festivals. Fundamental moods of the audience were dramatized; mythological or historical characters and incidents provided the framework for the impersonation. The audience did not demand illusion in the European sense, but instead participated in complex conventions that allowed the actor, symbolic language, music, and costume to suggest place and action.

The audience for the classical drama came primarily from the court and the aristocracy. Every locale had its folk drama, however, with a wider audience but no less stylized conventions. For at least 300 years, a pantomimic drama called *kathakali* has played to a fairly general audience in the temples of South India.

In China, the audience always considered the drama a symbolic ritual but nevertheless a casual old friend to be enjoyed while eating, drinking, and conversing. The playgoers were grouped on three sides of a platform. In Western terms, audience and performance were truly a single event. What happened onstage involved a complex arrangement of symbols expressed through movement, speech, costume, make-up, properties, music, and song. The audience had to be totally familiar with the symbol system.

The theatre of Japan, which apparently began later in history than those of India and China, was nevertheless similar to them in the audience's use of highly stylized and symbolic conventions. There were three types of theatre: the *noh,* primarily for an aristocratic audience, the doll theatre, and the *kabuki.* The last two theatres had a more popular audience. Perhaps because of this fact, *kabuki* was less conventional than the *noh* theatre. Modern *kabuki* has adopted the proscenium arch and the use of elaborate scenery, plus Western-style seating, but the audience-performance relationship has changed little.

PLAYHOUSES THEN AND NOW

In Chapter 3, we will describe three possible playhouses and postulate an ideal structure that would incorporate the best features of each. At present we must ignore this esthetic ideal and examine what types of buildings men have actually used through the ages to create theatre.

Greek and Roman playhouses were similar. In fact, little is known of Greek playhouses in the Classical period except through Hellenistic and Roman ruins or plans. We can only guess at the theatres of fifth-century Athens. The most basic attribute was the *orchestra* circle, about 66 feet in diameter, around which the audiences stood or sat to watch choral and other performances. It is presumed the *orchestra* evolved from the threshing circle in which ritual dances had been performed.

Given the topography of Attica, the spectators must have been grouped up a hillside on at least three sides of the *orchestra*. Whether there were seats or not, and whether they were stone or wood, is debatable. In the center of the circle, however, was the *thymele,* or altar.

Beyond these meagre facts little is known about the theatre structure in Athens. The plays that survive seem to require a scenehouse of some kind on the fourth side of the *orchestra,* the audience being placed on the hillside around the other three sides. Since grooves may be seen in the retaining wall of the *orchestra,* many historians believe that timbers supporting a temporary scenehouse for each festival stood in the grooves. The term used for such a house, *skene,* means "hut" or "tent," and thus perhaps referred to temporary structures of ancient origin. What these or the more permanent wooden scenehouses looked like, if such existed, cannot be known.

The same lack of evidence accompanies the quarrel among commentators about the existence of a stage in the Theatre of Dionysus in Athens. Such a platform, if it were in existence, must have been constructed between the *skene* and the orchestra. Probably such a stage would have been three to five feet in height and would have extended the width of the stage house. Some of the extant dramas seem to require such a stage, some do not. Others need to have the actors and the chorus mingled; most of them keep the chorus separate from the actors. If there was such a stage, it no doubt had steps to the *orchestra.*

Whatever the architecture and appearance of the *skene,* it was separated from the place for the audience by two passageways called *paradoi.* Through these entered the chorus and perhaps the actors.

The result of Greek habit and practice was something like a combination of arena and proscenium (see Chapter 3). The chorus, principally, but also the actors, could have worked both within the audience and in front of the audience. If there was a stage with a scenehouse behind it, this would have emphasized the proscenium aspect.

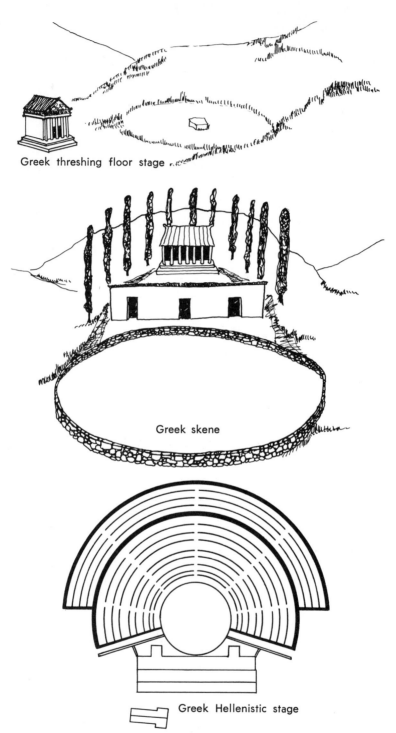

Greek threshing floor stage

Greek skene

Greek Hellenistic stage

FIGURE 2.1

About 325 B.C., the theatre in Athens became a permanent stone structure. This is the playhouse traditionally thought of as Greek and upon which conjecture about fifth-century practices is based. The layout is the same as that described above in the suppositions about the earlier structures. It, too, evolved into the Hellenistic theatre.

At Epidaurus, Greece, stand perhaps the best-known remains of a Hellenistic theatre like those which Alexander caused to be built throughout his brief empire. Except for a high stage and no *paraskenia* at either end of the *skene*, these theatres almost exactly resembled those we have been describing thus far. Stage height ranged from eight to thirteen feet, width was as long as the *skene,* and depth was also eight to thirteen feet. In some theatres, there were ramps at either end of the stage; in others, stairs led to the *orchestra*. The front edge of the stage rested on the *proskenion.* If there were two stories, the first was an open facade under the stage. The second story was placed along the back edge of the stage and was called the *episkenion.* Both stories were nearly equal in height. At Epidaurus, the *orchestra* was still a full circle. Elsewhere the *proskenion* extended several feet into the circle.

A question of later historical importance is the presence of doors in the *proskenion* and the *episkenion.* Theatre architects of the Renaissance placed three doors in their scenes, allegedly on the authority of the Classical Age. It is a matter of debate as to what the Athenian theatre had. There do seem to have been up to seven openings, or *thyromata,* in the *episkenion* of at least one Hellenistic theatre (at Eretria).

When the Romans began to build theatres, they apparently borrowed from all and sundry, including their own sports arenas. The first permanent theatre was erected in 55 B.C. Comments about theatres before that are based on it and later stone structures. What the earlier Romans actually had cannot be stated with accuracy.

In the theatres which are known, the audience occupied a stadium built around a half-circle. Seats and aisles were much like those in a modern football stadium. The other half of the orchestra circle was taken up with a stage about five feet high, twenty to forty feet in depth, and one to three hundred feet in width. The upstage wall was the *scaenae frons,* or facade of the stagehouse, which was called the *scaena.* The entire stagehouse was attached to the stadium, and the *scaenae frons* probably had niches and doors or deep alcoves with vestibules. The stage was roofed over, and there were doors in the walls at the ends of the stage. The whole was elaborately decorated, with statues in every niche, and a box for the emperor or the magistrates was placed just above the corridors into the orchestra and auditorium. Some theatres had a curtain, the *auleum,* at the front of the stage. The curtain was either lowered into the floor on telescoping poles or raised by ropes from overhead. Sometimes there was a curtain at the rear of the stage. This *siparium* could serve as a backdrop, and scenes could be painted on it. Entrances were made through slits in the curtain.

The Roman Empire collapsed from internal rot and outside pressure. All Roman institutions, including the playhouses, fell into disuse. During the so-called Middle Ages (500-1200 A.D.), if there were touring actors they played where they could. If there were local dramatic activities, the producers used whatever came to hand. A drama might have been performed in a village square, in a booth at a marketplace, or on a wagon with a platform. Performances given at court or in a baron's hall could have used the corner of a room or an alcove for a stage.

All this is guesswork until the rise of liturgical drama in the churches late in the 10th century. There the various alcoves and halls lent themselves to the evolution of a staging with two playing areas. In an alcove or separate from it, the players might erect a small scenic structure called a *mansion.* Next to this specialized space was a generalized area called the *place.* A *mansion* gave a scene a special locale; the *place* could be anywhere the drama required. The next step was to build a number of *mansions* adjacent to a *place,* set them up for their part of a scene, and then play from one to the other as the action shifted from one locale to another. Since each locale was set up permanently throughout the drama, *simultaneous staging* is the term we will use to describe this kind of theatre practice.

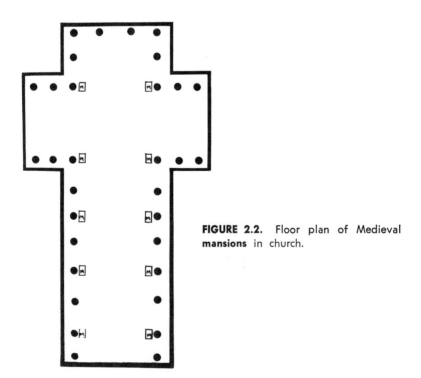

FIGURE 2.2. Floor plan of Medieval **mansions** in church.

When the drama was moved outside the church, the use of *mansions* continued. Now, however, they were sometimes placed on wagons grouped around an open space or in stationary but no more permanent stalls adjacent to the same space. There were also fixed stages on which all locales were placed. Platforms were often set against a building or a row of houses. Where the Roman theatres or amphitheatres were still available, these were used; sometimes the players built an open theatre similar in arrangement to the Roman ones. The size of the stages varied but was seldom less than 60 by 100 feet in area.

Whether in the church or out of it, indoors or out, the relation of the stage to the audience was usually intimate. The spectators normally stood or sat on three sides of the playing area, though full circles were not uncommon and there were some stages that were viewed from the front only. The effect was one of participation in the religious event being dramatized.

The theatres that developed in England, Spain, and France after 1500 thus had a local or national architectural tradition to work with. The concept of a playing area that was neutral but surrounded by settings that were localized and by the audience joined with the habit of playing in village squares and inn-yards to become the "wooden O" of Shakespeare and the *corrales* of Lope de Vega. The same evolution in France apparently was blocked by the prohibition of religious drama in 1548 and by the religious and political strife until after 1600. A further complication was the fact that the model for theatre structures was the tennis court. Moreover, the Italian theories of stage presentation reached France about the same time as the revival of the theatre.

The theatres of England possibly were developed from the innyards, the bull-baiting arenas, and pictures of a "Theatrum" that accompanied a 1493 edition of Terence's plays. The staging practices of Medieval times apparently served as the esthetic guide. The general layout of the Elizabethan and Jacobean public theatres, regardless of disputes about sources and precise accouterments, is well-known. Two or three galleries were constructed around a ground floor so that an open horseshoe would have been formed if the fourth wall were missing. That wall consisted of a two- or three-storied scenehouse. The facade of this house consisted of two doors and perhaps a central alcove or room on a level about five feet off the ground. The second story possibly repeated the doors and rooms, or had only the alcove or room. The third story had an open balcony where, perhaps, the musicians played. The whole was probably decorated symbolically to represent religious and mythological concepts of the populace.

At the first story, a stage extended into the "pit." The dimensions of only one—that at The Fortune—have survived. It was 27½ feet deep by 43 feet wide. Probably all the stages had a roof with an attic space and a floor with trapdoors to the space underneath. Most of the time the roof was supported by posts, but at one theatre the roof was cantilevered. The ceiling was usually decorated in the manner of the facade.

FIGURE 2.3. Globe Theatre with inner above and inner below.

A good deal of controversy exists about the English theatres, particularly insofar as the alcove or room between the doors in the facade of the scenehouse is concerned. Whether this "inner below" was a curtained room that was part of the architecture or a temporary pavilion, something seems to have been used for tableaux in that spot. Whether action occurred inside the room or flowed from it out on to the stage is also debated. Probably, given the impetus of Medieval practices, the tableaux were simply local color for actions played largely on the stage. What existed at the second story of the facade—gallery, room, or nothing— is unknown. Probably there were openings above the first-story doors and some kind of a playing space between them. Whether it was just space or was a curtained "inner above" is beyond knowing.

The total building was sometimes octagonal, sometimes circular, and sometimes square. Though the galleries and the stagehouse were roofed, the area over the yard was open. (We have already discussed the ceiling over the stage.) Some historians believe the galleries ran completely around the stage. If so, the plays would have been produced in an arena.

The patrons of the public theatres stood on the ground, or sat or stood in the galleries. In the galleries nearest the stage were private boxes—or lord's rooms. Admission during Elizabethan and Jacobean times was three-pence, twopence, and onepence, respectively, for box, gallery, and pit. Somewhere between 1500 and 2500 could attend at once, but probably the houses were half-filled at an ordinary performance. The plays began at 2 P.M. and were performed without intermission. Patrons could eat, drink, play cards, and smoke while the performance was in progress. By 1600, the practice of allowing a few spectators to sit on the stage had begun.

All this has pertained to the public theatres. Just as many, if not more, performances occurred indoors at various locations, but principally at Blackfriars and at Whitefriars. Between 1576 and 1642, however, there were at least six private theatres: three at Blackfriars (1576, 1596, 1614), one at Whitefriars (1606), The Phoenix (1616), and The Salisbury Court Theatre (1629). Until 1610, only boys' companies acted in the private theatres. Apparently preferred by the courtiers and aristocrats, these "Children of the Revels of the Queen" (to name but one company) competed successfully against the adult actors, who played in both the public and the private theatres.

The best estimate is that the private theatres were laid out much like the public theatres, except that there was no ceiling over the stage and the pit was filled with benches. The private theatres were roofed, were lit by candles, and were expensive—at least sixpence for the groundlings and up to 50 cents for the boxes.

Because of the long Moorish occupation and because of a desire to make Spain the most Catholic country in Europe, the theatre there developed later and with more emphasis on religious drama than in England. Early contacts with Italy ended about 1550 and from then until about 1680, Spain enjoyed an independent and nationalistic golden age of theatre.

Just when religious drama was losing force in the rest of Europe, it gained great importance in Spain. Associated with the church's sacraments, particularly with the feast of Corpus Christi, the plays were called *autos sacramentales*. Trade guilds at first, then professional companies, performed the *autos* three times a year until 1592, then four times a year until 1647, and finally twice a year until 1765.

Large, two-story wagons called *carros* and made of wooden frames covered with painted canvas were used to house actors and scenery. A portable stage on another wagon accompanied the *carros*, four for each play after 1647, two before that. After 1647, platforms were built at each playing place. The *carros* then were drawn up at the back and either end of the platforms. The acting area was 45 to 50 feet wide and about 36 feet deep.

Actors in the *autos* also performed dances and interludes, and a carnival spirit came to be associated with the presentations. Perhaps because of these secular, not to mention profane elements the plays were seldom produced in the churches. For about two hundred years the *autos* were exceedingly popular and easily rivaled the secular theatre.

This theatre was generally also performed in public—in the courtyards —from about 1568 onward. These *corrales* were built around a square,

FIGURE 2.4.   Medieval pageant wagon.

rectangular, or oval courtyard, or *patio*. Usually three in number, the galleries held males only except for the one at the end of the *patio*. There, above a tavern, was a gallery for women. Standing spectators occupied the *patio*, though a few benches were set up near the stage, which was constructed at the end of the *patio* opposite the female galleries.

Performances began at 2 P.M. in the fall and winter, and at 4 P.M. in the spring. The patrons gathered and faced the stage. This raised platform had no proscenium arch or front curtain. At the rear was the facade of the *corral*. Most of the facades had two pillars which divided a lower level into three openings. Those on the right and left were entrances. The upper level of the facade was also a gallery, but was used as scenery from time to time, or as a place for discoveries. The scenic conventions were approximately the same as in the public theatres of Elizabethan and Jacobean England.

Prior to 1625, the theatre in France more or less paralleled that of England and Spain. That is, mystery and miracle plays were performed with wagons and platforms in the villages. More so than in the other two countries, the *commedia dell'arte* was the popular fare. Even in Paris, at the *Hôtel de Bourgogne*, the second and most important of the permanent theatres (the first was the *Hôpital de la Trinité*, 1402), the platform stage with *mansions* was used. The first floor was a long pit, usually unoccupied. Along three walls were the galleries, which at one end formed a frame for a stage that was about 40 feet in width and up to 35 feet in depth (only about 25 feet of the width was visible). There was no proscenium arch, but the stage was raised. By the 1630's, though *mansions* were still in use, some of the backdrops were painted in perspective and the placement of the *mansions* had begun to imitate the Italian scenic practices.

Italy, as we have indicated, was the source of the Renaissance theatre and the new stagecraft. Beginning shortly after 1300, and reaching full momentum by the end of the 15th century, these new theatre practices

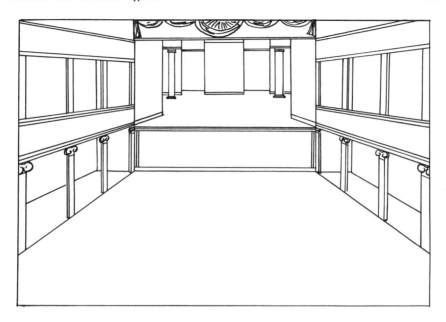

FIGURE 2.5. Hotel de Bourgogne.

were based on the classical treatises which came to light in the revival of learning. The principal source was Vitruvius' *De Architectura*, which was read as early as 1414 and printed by 1486. Another source for the new theatres was the development of perspective painting in which three-dimensions are achieved on a two-dimensional surface by drawing objects in an exact mathematical relationship with a fixed viewing-point.

Much experimentation over many years led to *Architettura*, by Sebastiano Serlio, in 1545. The stage was to lie within a frame and the first portion of the floor was to be on eye-level with the ruler in whose palace the stage was constructed. Back of this level front-portion, the stage was to slope upward at a sharp angle. Scenery took the form of right-angle wings (three on each side) and flat wings (one on each side), and a backdrop painted in perspective. The downstage wings were three-dimensional in many places, almost like houses, but none of the scenery could be moved. The setting for tragedy depicted the ceremonial part of a city; that for comedy, a more homely part; and that for pastoral drama, a wooded glen. Stadium seating around an orchestra, with the "king's seat" in the center of the horseshoe, completed the Serlio theatre.

The need to change the settings led to techniques for maneuvering wings and drops, as well as to the use of modified *periaktoi*. This ancient technique apparently was revived in 1543. Structures with from two to six sides were described in *Le Due Regola della Prospettiva Practica* (1583), but the fullest information about the new scenic practices was

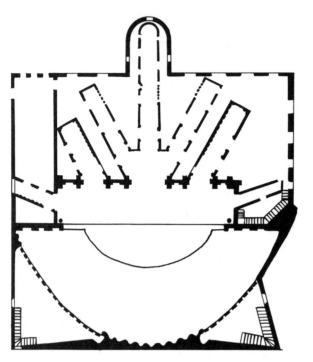

FIGURE 2.6.
Teatrico Olimpico.
Left, floor plan;
below, frontal view
of stage.

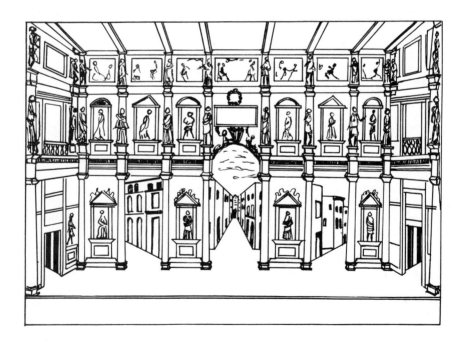

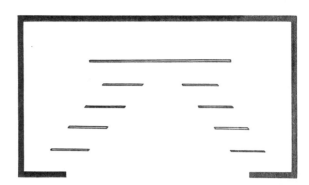

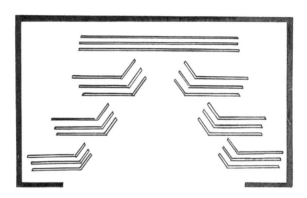

FIGURE 2.7. Methods of scene shifting used during the Italian Renaissance. Top to bottom: wing and drop, nesting, chariot and pole.

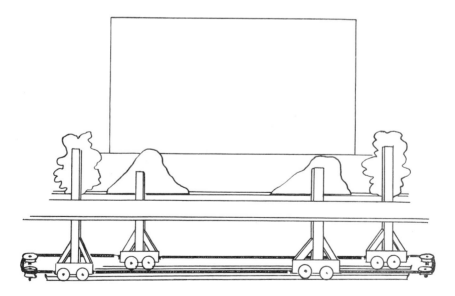

printed in Nicola Sabbatini's *Manual for Constructing Theatrical Scenes and Machines* (1638). The primary changes from Serlio were the replacement of three-dimensional detail with painting and the attempts to move the flats around or to change their painted coverings. The right-angle wings were a problem in maneuvering; the straight wings were simply moved in grooves placed in the floor.

Eventually just the straight wings were used. By 1650, the problem of painting in perspective on a series of flat wings was solved. Every setting could have side wings, overhead borders, and shutters (two flats that swung closed at center stage) or rolled cloths at the back. As machinery for flying came into use, the overhead borders could be changed as easily as the flats. The scene changes were accomplished with many stagehands, who shoved the flats through their grooves. Around 1645, however, the flats came to be attached to poles that were mounted on "chariots" below the floor. These moved on casters by means of an elaborate system of ropes, pulleys, and winches. A single winch was all that was necessary to shift scenery on the floor. The arrival of shifting and flying machinery led to frequent changes and grander settings. These required the painting of architectural features belonging to a single structure.

Theatre architecture in Italy had to keep pace with the new stage-craft. Elaborate machinery required more permanent theatres. Andrea Palladio, an architect, constructed a Roman theatre indoors for the *Teatro Olimpico*. The place for the audience was designed as part of an ellipse around an area similar to the Roman orchestra. The stage that rose above the orchestra was a rectangle measuring 70 feet by 18 feet. At the rear of the stage was a facade of pillars, three doors, places for statuary, and bas-reliefs. There were two doors at each end of the stage. When Palladio died during construction of this theatre, it was finished by Vincenzo Scamozzi. He constructed a view of city streets in forced perspective behind each of the five doors. Every spectator could see down at least one street, and all the streets appeared to open into a city square.

More important than the *Teatro Olimpico*, however, was another theatre built by Scamozzi at Sabbionetta in 1588, which had a single vista as wide as the proscenium opening and which used Serlio's plan for the stage itself. In 1618, the *Teatro Farnese* added the proscenium arch to the Serlio-Scamozzi plain stage with angled wings. The audience still stood or sat in a semi-circle around the orchestra. Where the proscenium arch came from is not known. Likely sources were the doorways of the Roman stage, the triumphal arches used for Medieval pageants, and the frames for perspective painting. The arch helped restrict the view of the audience and thus aided the illusion of reality while hiding the means of achieving it. A second or a third arch could be placed upstage of the proscenium opening and thereby increase the grandeur with more-highly-restricted, yet more breathtaking vistas. In the public theatres of

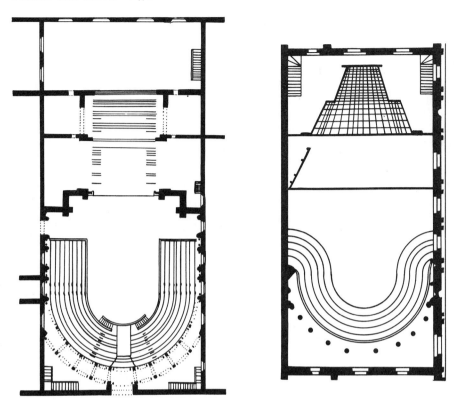

FIGURE 2.8. Floor plans of the Sabbionetta and Teatro Farnes in Parma.

Italy, which began about 1565 in Venice and which were showing opera by 1637, the new stages were adopted from the beginning. The auditorium, however, came to be arranged in tiers of boxes above the ground floor. The lower classes still stood on the floor. The first of these new houses was the *San Cassiano,* with five tiers and 31 boxes. By 1641, there were three other such theatres in Italy and the style was spreading thoughout Europe.

Thus, by way of a Roman architect, several Renaissance architects, and the growth of opera in Italy, the new stages came into being. In 1648, as we have seen, they spread to France. From about 1600 on, Inigo Jones was employing the new techniques in masques for the English court of James I. When the theatre returned to England in force after the Commonwealth, only the Italianate stage was used. That is, a play required the proscenium arch, elaborate machines, and perspective scenery. Some theatres used an apron in front of the proscenium arch, and these and others still had doors in the arch itself, but for all intents and purposes, the stage was a picture frame. A drama was a series of pictures viewed from a distance. The practice of letting everyone sit in the orchestra pit—or on the ground floor—and of eliminating most of the boxes, which came in during the nineteenth century, did not change the esthetic by which theatre existed. Nor did the withdrawal of the play into the proscenium opening—the creation of the "fourth wall" concept—change the esthetic in any important way.

This is the playhouse that dominates even the theatre of the twentieth century. Attempts to break out of the proscenium—the thrust stage, the runway, the forestage—are but the return of the apron which actors used until the middle of the nineteenth century. Between 1600 and 1900, only the means by which illusion was achieved came to be modified. The plays became more and more spectacular, then more and more realistic, and finally both realistic and spectacular. But the theatres seldom varied much from the Roman auditorium of Serlio, Sabbattini, Palladio, and Scamozzi—or from the spectacles of Parigi, Jones, and all who came after.

In the mid-twentieth century, attempts to change the traditional playhouse of Western drama focused primarily on creating a flexible theatre—

FIGURE 2.9. Floor plan of the never-constructed Staatliches Bauhaus in Weimar, Germany.

one in which stage and audience positions could be changed by mechanical or hydraulic means. The three configurations usually made a part of the system were the picture-frame stage, the arena stage, and the thrust stage. The principal source for the new trend in flexibility was the design of a "total theatre" in 1926 by Walter Gropius of the School of Fine Arts and Crafts at the *Staatliches Bauhaus* in Weimar, Germany. This design, which was never built, allowed for proscenium, thrust, arena, and audience staging (that is, playing areas within the audience), and for the projection of scenery onto screens around and over the audience.

Yet despite the construction of many new theatres throughout Europe and America along the lines of the *Bauhaus* or other concepts, the Renaissance theatre dominated the productions and the thinking of theatre people, and the "idea of a theatre" held by most spectators. Even the theatres of the Orient, though traditionally they have avoided illusionism and have kept their staging symbolic and part of the audience, have adopted the proscenium arch and the picture-frame concept. This is particularly true in Japan. In both China and Japan, however, the standard theatre consists of a platform with a roof, with the audience on three sides. The *noh* theatre in Japan also has a bridge from dressing rooms to the main stage; the bridge is used by the actors as a stage in itself.

Dramatists and Their Dramas

Except for Chapter 5, "Playwrights and Playwriting," our introduction to theatre will slight the dramatist. There are five reasons for this approach. First, despite the stress given the playscript in most literary studies, this least perishable of the theatrical elements is not necessarily the heart of the theatre. That it seems so is a result of both its relative permanence and the teachers who have persisted in focusing on dramatic literature rather than drama and theatre. Second, the proper study of drama requires detailed examination of every work of every dramatist, for each drama is a unique experience. Third, since a drama is only a "score," to treat the play without the players destroys the art-form. To treat both in detail would mean a book twice the size a publisher can afford. Fourth, such a book would be something other than an "introduction to theatre." Finally, if we know very little about many important periods of theatre—the Greek and Roman, for example—we know even less about the drama of these eras.

Yet each age gave us fine dramas that merit study. Of the perhaps 1500 dramas that existed during the 5th century B.C. in Greece, only 42 remain. Thirty-one of these are considered to be tragic—the works of Aeschylus, Sophocles, and Euripides—and eleven are comic works of Aristophanes. Whether these dramas were representative is moot; whether they were the best, likewise. Each play by each playwright is unique, but the characteristics of each dramatist inform all of his work. Seven plays by

Aeschylus have survived: *Persians* (472), *Seven Against Thebes* (467), *Oresteia*—a trilogy consisting of *Agamemnon, Libation Bearers,* and *Eumenides*—(458), *Suppliants* (after 468), and *Prometheus Bound* (after 468). Though there are differences (and we must remember that, except for *Oresteia*, every drama but *Persians* is all that remains of a trilogy), the plays of Aeschylus are similar in conception and technique. He deals with a tragic idea of cosmic proportions—for example, "the divine law of retribution *versus* justice" (*Oresteia*)—and his *personae* are lyrical or choral figures rather than people. Sometimes actor and chorus struggle together in a tragic situation, with the chorus also commenting; sometimes the actor is a single protagonist struggling with his own destiny or playing out an inner drama; sometimes the actor makes moral choices in the face of a changing tragic situation (enlarged by a second actor), while the chorus both participates and comments. In essence, the plots of Aeschylus lack movement forward incident by incident; the movement comes from an increasing sense of tragic inevitability. Everyone in the play recognizes the inevitability from the beginning, but the audience is in the dark. Awe is felt, but not pity. Since the tragic dilemmas may be resolved by a better idea, the happy ending is possible.

Such storyless, characterless dramaturgy quite obviously needs the full resources of theatrical spectacle. A chief characteristic of Aeschylean dramas is their monumental use of choruses, theatrical effects, and visual symbolism. Like all the Greek dramatists, of course, his poetry has been equaled but never surpassed.

In all but the quality of his poetry, Sophocles is almost the exact opposite of Aeschylus. Seven plays extant out of 120 reveal a tragic conception focused on complex human characters in conflict with the circumstances of the universe—chief among which are the character's motivations—and a technique to match. Sophoclean drama, though again we must note that each work is unique, shows subtle interplay among complex and well-motivated *personae* and between them and the chorus, which is not so much the commentator as the context for the dramatic action. (The chorus of elders *is* the city.) Thus motivated by character actions, the plots move forward through surprising twists and turns that reveal all necessary facets of the human psyches that are involved. Only the audience knows precisely how the plot will turn out; the *personae* are mystified until the end. (This is not to remove foreshadowing, at which Sophocles is a master.)

The dramas of Sophocles, then, concentrate on the tragedy of character wrenched awry by circumstances of which human motivations are a part. The seven plays that reveal this action in various ways are *Ajax* (450-440), *Antigone* (c. 441), *Oedipus Tyrannus* (c. 430-425), *Philoctetes* (409), *Electra* (c. 418-410), *Trachiniae* (c. 413), and *Oedipus at Colonus* (406).

Of the dramas of Euripides we have 18 out of about 90. These are *Alcestis* (438), *Medea* (431), *Hippolytus* (428), *Children of Heracles*

(n. d.), *Andromache* (n. d.), *Hecuba* (n. d.), *Heracles* (n. d.), *Suppliants* (n. d.), *Ion* (n. d.), *Trojan Women* (415), *Electra* (n. d.), *Iphigenia in Tauris* (n. d.), *Helen* (412), *Phoenician Women* (c. 409), *Orestes* (408), *Bacchae* (n. d.), *Iphigenia in Aulis* (n. d.), and *Cyclops* (a satyr-play; n. d.). The differences among the tragedies are even more marked than for the dramas of Aeschylus and Sophocles. Yet Euripides does seem to attempt a single kind of tragic conception and to evolve a characteristic technique to give it dramatic representation. His concept is that man is ruled by emotions that, kept in balance or focused on good ends, are not evil or harmful. Euripides dramatizes the running-amok of these same emotions. Woven into this concept is the view that traditional Greek values and myths—particularly the gods—are meaningless and irrational in themselves. The only proper world is one ruled by reason, but this is not the world Euripides sees.

His technique centers on embodying the terrifying emotions-run-amok in a figure such as Medea and in using or manipulating any incident, any theatrical device, that will serve his purpose. He is also noted for naturalistic characterization, language, and costuming. In a sense, Euripides' hallmark is the horror play—a kind of *Grand Guignol* with a tragic heart.

All three of these tragic dramatists use the same general structure—though of course with variation from drama to drama. Most widely used is the format that begins with a *prologue* followed by a *parados,* or entrance of the chorus, or sometimes with the *parados* alone. The *prologue* and the *parados* give exposition, set the mood or atmosphere, and establish the basic situation. Then comes a series of *episodes* in which the dramatic action is acted out. These are separated by choral *odes* that comment on the action, vocalize part of it, give further exposition, and reinforce the mood that has been set. The choral songs are called *stasima,* and are each divided into *strophe* and *antistrophe.*

Another format for Greek tragedy is employed principally by Aeschylus. The first *ode* establishes the tragic situation; then the actor enters to reveal his personal involvement; then a second *ode* increases the pressure on the actor; then a *kommos* or lamentation by chorus and actor enlarges the crisis; then a third *ode* comments on the crisis; then the actor faces the crisis and makes his tragic decision; then the fourth *ode* comments on the actor's decision; then the result of the decision is shown; and finally the drama ends with a choral *ode.*

Euripides, though he follows the general format, tries to stress the *episodes* by making the choral passages separate from the principal line of action. Moreover, the *episodes* are often merely forensic exchanges and at other times are unrelated causally.

The comedies of Aristophanes, all we have from the old greek comedy, are something else again. Eleven out of about 40 survive: *Acharnians* (425), *Knights* (424), *Clouds* (423), *Wasps* (422), *Peace* (421), *Birds* (414), *Lysistrata* (411), *Thesmophoriazusae* (411), *Frogs* (405), *Ecclesiazusae* (392-391), and *Plutus* (388). Each of these plays is built around the working out of an absurd idea that is usually an exaggeration of some commonplace activity or viewpoint in Athens. *Lysistrata*, for example, focuses on a sex strike as a means to end war. As the idea is worked out in each play, all manner of people and activities are satirized unmercifully. A *prologue* establishes the mood and sets forth the absurd idea. Then the chorus enters and there is a debate (*agon*) about the merits of the idea; the group decides to try it. Then the chorus sings the *parabasis*, an ode in which some social or political problem is examined. The *parabasis* divides the play in half. It is followed by a series of scenes that dramatize the results of adopting the initial idea. Finally, in the *kommos* or "revel-rout," the characters are reconciled and everyone exits to a feast.

The satiric drama and this powerful tragic experience were not to last. Even in Greece, tragedy became melodrama and Aristophanic satire became domestic farce. In Rome, the decline was continued. Today we remember the Roman dramatists for two things: the influence of Seneca on the drama of the Renaissance and the farces of Plautus that captured the comedy of later Greece and gave literary form to situations and characters from the ancient village farces. The *commedia dell'arte* troupes and the comedies of later centuries probably had their genesis in Plautine farce.

Let us take the comic influence first. As Athens lost its political freedom, the comedy turned from satire of the total community to farcical treatments of love, money, and family life. A *prologue* was followed by a series of scenes separated by choral passages that were largely incidental to the action. The influence of Euripides led to widespread use of mistaken identity, misunderstandings, revelations of lost information, and far-fetched coincidents. Sentimental and moral elements were often included, and language was that of everyday life—though still in verse. Of these plays, only Menander's *The Grumbler* remains intact. Noted for his fine and varied characterizations, natural style, use of sentimentality, and ingenious plots, Menander exerted great influence on the Romans.

The chief beneficiary of this influence was Plautus, who between 205 and 184 composed 21 farces based on the later Greek comedies: *The Comedy of Asses, The Merchant, The Braggart Warrior, The Casket, Pot of Gold, Stichus, Pseudolus, Curculio, Bacchides, Casina, Amphitryon, The Captives, Epidicus, The Menaechmi, The Haunted House, The Persian, The Carthaginian, Rope, Trinummus, Truculentus*, and *Vidularia*. Publius Terentius Afer (Terence) also composed farces based on Greek originals. Six of these survive: *Andria* (166), *Mother-in-Law* (165), *Self-Tormentor* (163), *Eunuch* (161), *Phormio* (161), and *The Brothers* (160). Plautus was noted for his dialogue, poetic variety, and farcical devices; Terence for his characterizations, complicated plots, and natural conversation. Both Plautus and Terence eliminated the chorus and stressed musical accompaniment for the dialogue.

Tragedy was also popular in Rome. Nine plays of Seneca have come down to us—*The Trojan Women, Medea, Oedipus, Phaedra, Thyestes, Hercules on Oeta, The Mad Hercules, The Phoenician Women,* and *Agamemnon*—but probably none were ever produced. Adapted from Greek originals, these closet dramas had great influence on the Renaissance through their five-act form, forensic speeches, moralizing by means of sensational deeds that illustrated the evils of unleashed emotion and *sententiae* about such behavior, scenes of violence and horror, use of the supernatural, characters with a single motivating force, and technical devices such as soliloquies, asides, and confidants. Senecan tragedy became the norm for the Renaissance.

During the Middle Ages, however, these dramas probably were not performed with any frequency. The *commedias,* if such existed, merely kept alive the tradition of dramatic performance. This tradition, as we have seen, encouraged the Church to use drama as a teaching tool. Out of these two sources there developed the mystery plays based on Biblical stories and events. From the mysteries it was a short move to the morality plays—dramas illustrating a philosophical or theological truth —of which *Everyman* at the end of this chapter is the principal example.

The recovery of classical learning led to attempts at playwriting in the universities, and when the new drama moved to the public at large the *commedias,* the mysteries, and the moralities had prepared the market.

The Renaissance was a phenomenon that began in Italy and spread throughout Europe. The discovery of classical manuscripts sparked a revival of learning and a complete cultural rebirth for Western Europe. The tragedies of Seneca, which had always been read for their philosophy, and the comedies of Plautus and Terence, which had been studied for their style, became important as guides to dramaturgy. The new playwrights built both on the classical and the medieval traditions. The result was high drama in England, France, Spain, and Italy. The Italian contribution, aside from initiating the cultural rebirth itself, was in the area of Latin comedy and the opera. We have already noted the *commedia* troupes that continued the village farce tradition and the stock characters of the *fabula Atellana.* The *commedia* had few dramas but many outlines of *lazzi,* or comic business.

The opera developed from more formal dramas. As the plays were presented, they had five acts. Between each pair of acts was a spectacle of some sort, which was called an *intermezzo.* By and large these *intermezzi* were allegorical tableaux with music and dance joined to scenic effects, and no dialogue. At first unconnected, the intermezzi came to have a story of their own. Soon they were more popular than the plays they interrupted.

While the *intermezzi* were thus gaining public approval, members of the Camerata of Florence began to perform plays with music similar to the Greek tragedies. The eventual result was a full-length work, *Dafne* (1597), which was the first opera. The form developed further until 1637, when an opera house in Venice made opera available to the general public. The new type of drama perfectly matched the desires that had been whetted by the *intermezzi,* which opera replaced.

In England, the drama developed in its own way—based on the discovery of classical works by the universities but also anchored firmly in the popular tradition of liturgical drama, rough farce, and principally the interludes. These were professional entertainments performed in courts and castles by itinerant actors. Classical myths, Biblical stories, historical events, English comedy scenes—all blended together in plays that were both comic and serious, that ranged widely over time and place, and that showed everything possible onstage. The school plays, on the other hand, strove to be more neatly classical—at least at first. Two outstanding farces illustrate the school comedies: Nicholas Udall's *Raph Roister Doister* (c. 1534-41) and *Gammer Gurton's Needle* (c. 1552-1563), by "Mr. S." Tragedy was represented by *Ferrex and Porrex, or Gorbuduc* (1561), by Thomas Sackville and Thomas Norton.

In the 1580's, four of the university dramatists—Thomas Kyd, John Lyly, Robert Greene, and Christopher Marlowe began to write for the public stage. Kyd, with *The Spanish Tragedy* (c. 1587), established all the Senecan devices and told a tale of murder and revenge that ranged freely over time and space. Lyly, who wrote primarily for boys' companies and aristocratic audiences, launched a tradition of pastoral, fairy-tale drama. Greene added love and adventure to the pastoral fairy tales.

Christopher Marlowe provided the finest dramas of this group and had the greatest influence on later practice in the Elizabethan and Jacobean drama. His chief works were *Tamburlaine, I and II* (1587-88), *The Tragical History of Doctor Faustus* (c. 1588), and *Edward II.* From Marlowe the emerging playwrights learned how to write blank verse in drama, how to create a chronicle play, how to make dramatic sense out of the Machiavellian hero and the "new men" that were assuming power in the Renaissance. The Faustian hero has been a hallmark of Western drama ever since.

Of William Shakespeare and Ben Jonson, Marlowe's greatest beneficiaries, we need say very little. For Shakespeare we do not even need to name his plays. They, and his contribution to dramatic literature, are too well-known. Suffice it to say that he was the complete dramatist: he did not innovate; he dramatized. There was no element of drama and theatre that he did not manage with consummate artistic skill. In his dramas he showed more, in his observation of human actions he saw more, than any dramatist who ever lived. In Western culture, perhaps only Homer—not a dramatist—equaled him. Working in all dramatic types, though not extensively with satiric farce, Shakespeare typically presented his action by means of several plot-lines that paralleled and echoed each other: a pavilion of sharply-etched *personae,* with the leading characters seen in many facets; an early attack on the story or stories; brilliant poetic dialogue and imagery; and masterful employment of the Elizabethan-Jacobean theatre facility.

Ben Jonson was not so far-ranging and versatile. The best of his dramas, however, his satiric farces, rank at the top of this dramatic category. Some have equaled, but no one has bettered *Every Man in His Humour* (1598), *Volpone* (1606), *The Alchemist* (1610), and *Bartholomew Fair* (1614). Contemporary, realistic but theatrical, full of wild and complicated plot twists and hilariously ribald (not to say filthy) language—Jonsonian farce held up his countrymen to complete ridicule for their shortcomings and foibles. Jonson also popularized the "comedy of humours," which focused on the idea that men are motivated by bodily humours—blood, phlegm, yellow bile, and black bile—and that human failings come from an imbalance among them. Another contribution of Jonson's was his deep concern with classical dramatic theory. He attempted to foster this theory in his dramas. His comedies succeeded but his tragedies—*Sejanus* (1603) and *Catiline* (1611)—failed. In his own time, and until at least the eighteenth century, Jonson was more highly regarded than Shakespeare.

A host of other dramatists—George Chapman, John Marston, Thomas Dekker, Thomas Heywood, Thomas Middleton, Cyril Tourneur, John Fletcher, Francis Beaumont (Beaumont and Fletcher were often collaborators.), William Rowley, Philip Massinger, John Webster, John Ford, and James Shirley—were popular with playgoers. Except that they were not so effective, the works of these dramatists paralleled Shakespeare and Jonson in dramaturgy. Increasingly as the 17th Century continued, however, the dramatists began to concern themselves with slickness and with melodramatic rather than tragic, comic rather than satiric, actions. Thrills and sentiment, wit and aristocratic manners, assumed greater importance than the significance of the dramatic actions. Moralizing replaced a moral sense.

Thus, as the theatres were closed in 1642, the drama and the dramatists were moving in the direction eventually taken during the Restoration and the Eighteenth Century—witty, sentimental comedy and melodramatic, sentimental tragedy.

In the meantime, theatres had been developing in Spain and France. Those in Spain between about 1500 and 1700 were uniquely productive, with some 30,000 dramas being written and performed. In Spain as in England, medieval practices merged with an awakening interest in classical learning to create a popular theatre. Not performed but widely-enough read to be influential was *The Comedy of Calisto and Melibea* (1499), presumably by Fernando de Rojas, in which naturalistic characters and dialogue set in earthy situations carried the drama. Other important playwrights of the time were Juan del Encina, Bartolemé de Torres Naharro, and Gil Vincente. These dramatists worked primarily for an aristocratic audience, but the later dramatists who served the public theatres learned much from the earlier group of playwrights.

As in England, until the dramatists began composing for the general public their work was not first-rate. The chief playwright in the early days of the professional theatre in Spain was Lope de Rueda, who composed earthy, picturesque farces in the medieval mold. Following Rueda were Juan de la Cueva, who combined classical subjects with scenes from everyday life and who was one of the first historical dramatists, and Miguel de Cervantes, who composed plays about historical subjects, adventures, and contemporary Spanish life.

Spanish drama came of age with the advent of Lope Félix de Vega Carpio. "Lope" apparently produced 1800 dramas, of which more than 450 survive today. Along with his contemporaries, de Vega evolved three-act dramas that were *capa y espada* (cape and sword)—that is, romantic adventures involving minor nobility or less-important gentlemen—or *teatro ruido* (or *cuerpo*)—that is, theatre of noise, or of corpse: rulers, nobles, saints, or mythological figures performed actions in remote places or periods. Other forms were the *entremése*, or interlude, and the *sainete*, which was a short farce.

Of Lope de Vega's hundreds of dramas—most of which involved suspenseful conflicts between love and honor, characters from all walks of life, naturalistic dialogue in a host of verse forms, but little penetration into the deeper meanings of human actions—the most appealing for today's audiences is *Fuente Ovejuna* (*The Sheep-Well*), which dates from about 1614. Villagers clash with a tyrannous feudal lord, kill him, refuse to confess under torture, and are saved by the intervention of the king. Though Lope was simply favoring the king over the feudal system, the drama seems peculiarly modern by virtue of its group-protagonist—"*Fuente Ovejuna.*"

There were many dramatists working in Spain along with de Vega. Chief among these were Guillen de Castro, who is remembered for the play that was later used by Corneille as a basis for *Le Cid* (see below), Tirso de Molina, whose *El Burlador de Sevilla* was the first dramatization of the Don Juan story, and Juan Ruiz de Alarcón, who was noted for his polished dramas of court life.

More or less following this group of dramatists in time were Pedro Calderón de la Barca, Rojas Zorilla, and Augustín Moreto. Of these three, the principal dramatist was Calderón. Noted for his stately and lyrical *autos*, he also composed a number of secular dramas that explored love intrigues and misunderstandings, jealousy and honor, and at least once— in *Life is a Dream* (c. 1636)—the mystery and meaning of human life.

In France, the drama paralleled that of England and Spain until religious struggles halted its development. That is, medieval mystery and morality plays combined with *commedia* troupes to enliven the public, and university men began about 1500 to compose dramas on the classical plan. Because of the interruption, however, French drama did not achieve greatness in its earlier, native period. That was reserved for the return of the drama after 1600, this time modeled on Italian neo-classical theories (see Chapter 9). Typical of this change in technique was Pierre Corneille, who wrote *Le Cid* as an extensive romantic tragedy about love versus honor. Chastised severely by French playwrights and critics for violating classical theories, Corneille withdrew from playwriting for a while, then returned with plays more in the neo-classical ideal. *Horace* (1640), *Cinna* (1640), and others dramatized the action of a strong-willed man who chooses death rather than dishonor. The protagonists were typically simple, and the plots complex. Corneille also produced a number of comedies that set the stage for the later work of Molière.

The finest examples of French neo-classical tragedy, however, came from Jean Racine. His dramas dealt with the psychological action that occurs within a noble character when he is forced to choose between reason (manifest as a sense of duty, or of social fitness) and emotion (uncontrollable passion, violent or savage deeds). The character talked out his action with a *confidant* at a point just before the decision must be made (the climax). The entire decision-making process occurred in one locale, within the time-span of the play, and was centered on one person and one dramatic action—thus preserving "the unities"—and was held together by *liaison*—a technique in which one character from a given scene remains onstage to participate in the next scene. Some of the finest poetry and clearest psychological insights—particularly with regard to women—gave these dramas tremendous impact despite what seems to an English theatregoer to be nothing but interminal verbiage. Racine's masterpiece was *Phèdre* (1677); other examples of his artfulness were *Andromaque* (1667), *Britannicus* (1669), *Bérénice* (1670), *Bejazet* (1672), *Mithridate* (1673), and *Iphigénie* (1674).

While Racine was creating the epitome of French neo-classical tragedy, Jean-Baptiste Poquelin—called Molière—was producing some of the finest satiric farces and comedies of character and manners the world has known. Working clearly within the neo-classical ideal of five acts, the unities, and comedy as a corrective for social excesses, Molière focused on a *persona* who typifies one or more social evils (greed, hypocrisy, misanthropy), dialogue, and social commentary, and held customs and social types up to ridicule. The problems in these plays either were resolved by some external force without the characters being changed or were left unresolved. Molière, that is, did not offer or imply a better society than he showed his audiences. He simply revealed the society of Louis XIV for what it was—and let it go at that.

Master of farce and of theatrical techniques—almost *commedia dell'arte* in his approach to drama—Molière's finest achievements were *The Doctor in Spite of Himself* (1666), *The School for Wives* (1662), *The Misanthrope* (1666), *The Miser* (1668), *Tartuffe* (1664, 1667, 1669), *The Would-Be Gentleman* (1670), and *The Imaginary Invalid* (1673). These and many other plays established a high-water mark in comedy for Western Europe.

Imported into England with the ascent of Charles II (1660), the French ideals of tragedy and comedy joined with the remnants of the drama before the Commonwealth. (1644 to 1660 was not a total blackout.) The Italianate staging had come to England for the masques at the court of James I. In 1656, William Davenant staged *The Siege of Rhodes* in the Italian manner for public performances. As theatre returned to prominence under Charles II, only the proscenium staging was used. Neo-classical tragedy was manifest as heroic drama—in which the ideal hero and heroine face a conflict between love and honor. Patently artificial— see John Dryden's *The Conquest of Granada* (1669-70) for an example— heroic plays soon gave way to blank verse tragedies that embodied neo-classicism in English drama. Chief examples were Dryden's *All for Love* (1677) and Thomas Otway's *Venice Preserv'd* (1682).

English opera also flourished during the Restoration. *The Tempest,* for example, was played only as opera. The new parts were by Thomas Shadwell.

Restoration comedy, however, was the hallmark of the age. At first the dramatists concentrated on comedies of intrigue and of humours. The French influence plus the ascendancy of a glorious high society led most supremely to the comedy of manners as it has never since been achieved in such abundance in English. The preoccupation of the upper classes with aristocratic pursuits, witty repartee, seduction, the latest fashions, arranged marriages—in short "the way of the world"—were brilliantly cap- tured in sparkling scenes, dialogue, and characterizations. This is not to say there were not both bad and good plays during the Restoration. There were, but the best were outstanding examples of the comedy of manners: John Dryden's *Marriage á la Mode* (1672); George Etherege's *The Man of Mode* (1676); William Wycherley's *The Country Wife* (1675) and *The Plain Dealer;* and William Congreve's *Love for Love* (1695) and *The Way of the World* (1700).

Yet so apt a portrayal of a particular segment of society could not last when that society was replaced—or at least had its sensibilities changed. Symbolic of this change, and also very influential, was Jeremy Collier's *A Short View of the Immorality and Profaneness of the English Stage* (1698). As the middle-class merchants began to assume greater im- portance in society, the drama changed to meet a new morality and a new "community." Brilliant revelation of amorality was replaced by sen- timental depiction of the trials and tribulations of noble and sympathetic characters who suffer for a while (tragedy), or are discomfitted for a while (comedy), but in the end are rescued from their problems and rewarded. That is, what we today would call melodrama, for the eighteenth century in England was sentimental comedy or tragedy.

There were a number of transitional plays. Chief among these were George Farquhar's *The Constant Couple* (1699), *The Recruiting Officer* (1706), and *The Beaux' Strategem* (1707).

Comedy in the new vein was best represented by Richard Steele's *The Conscious Lovers* (1722); tragedy, by Nicholas Rowe's *The Fair Peni- tent* (1703) and *The Tragedy of Jane Shore* (1714), and by Joseph

Addison's *Cato* (1713). These and others showed the distress of upper or upper-middle class heroes, and heroines, who nobly withstood trials and learned the virtues of being properly moral and sensible.

Probably the most significant of early eighteenth-century dramas in England was George Lillo's *The London Merchant* (1731). The hero was a lowly apprentice who was led astray by a prostitute. Because he had committed murder he was hanged despite his repentance.

Another important work of the time was John Gay's *The Beggar's Opera* (1728). This ballad opera combined music, lyrics, and dialogue to portray the lowlife of London and to satirize the political and social conditions of the time. The type did not prove permanent, however, and was replaced by comic operas and by satirical burlesques, of which the best was Henry Fielding's *Tom Thumb, or the Tragedy of Tragedies.* The Licensing Act of 1737, unfortunately, drove Fielding out of the theatre along with ballad and comic opera. What the drama lost, the novel gained.

Nor did comedies remain totally sentimental. In reaction to this mode were Oliver Goldsmith's *She Stoops to Conquer* (1773) and Richard Sheridan's *The Rivals* (1775) and *The School for Scandal* (1777). Goldsmith and Sheridan attempted satirical or "laughing" comedy once again and portrayed the manners of the new upper-middle class rather than the old aristocracy. "Comedy of manners" took on a broader meaning that it has held ever since. The lampooning was basically gentle, and morals were upheld. Plot movement, dialogue, and character portrayal were nevertheless in the high style of Molière and the Restoration dramatists.

From 1750 onward in Europe, with rare exceptions, the dramas became increasingly romantic and melodramatic. When America acquired a drama, essentially from England and Germany, the same modes were followed. Romanticism as a point of view in Western thought had existed at least since the Late Middle Ages. Perhaps as a reaction to neo-classicism, perhaps as an outgrowth of the new theories of democratic government, and perhaps as a formalizing of middle-class sentimentality, romanticism became a distinct philosophical and literary movement in the late eighteenth century. What it meant for drama was (1) a break with the neo-classical stress on the unities and on form and decorum; (2) an emphasis on the variable individual person and incident; (3) an interest in the bizarre, the grotesque, and the adventuresome; (4) a concern for emotion rather than reason; (5) a use of heroic (and nationalistic) rebels for protagonists; (6) an interest in spiritual matters and in the ideals toward which mankind was deemed to be striving; and (7) a preference for the natural, the rural, and the "unspoiled" over the products of civilization.

The earliest and best dramatists who are considered "romantic" were Gotthold Ephraim Lessing, Johann Wolfgang von Goethe and Friedrich Schiller—although Goethe and Schiller denied the association and thought of themselves as "classicists." Less important but more popular were August Wilhelm Iffland and August Friedrich von Kotzebue. Lessing, a noted critic (see Chapter 9) as well as a playwright, produced four dramas that set the standards for the romanticists to come: *Miss Sara Sampson* (1755), which transformed the Medea legend into sentimental middle-class tragedy by focusing on a young victim of Medea's fury; *Minna von Barnhelm* (1767), a love story that dramatized the current schism in Germany and resolved the difficulties through love; *Emilia Galotti* (1772), the story of Appius and Virginia transferred to eighteenth-century Germany as an attack on the nobility; *Nathan the Wise* (1779), a plea for religious tolerance. These works were transitional between neo-classical and romantic drama.

Even the *Sturm und Drang* ("Storm and Stress") dramatists, who openly revolted against the restrictions of neo-classicism, were concerned with classical forms and decorum. Goethe, for example, wrote *Goetz von Ber-lichingen* (1773) in 54 scenes and nearly as many plots filled with na-tionalistic fervor and high emotionalism. Yet he denied his break with classicism even while preparing *Faust, I and II*—the epitome of far-ranging romantic drama about man's search for perfection and his sal-vation through both romantic and divine love.

Schiller, who assisted Goethe in the Weimar Theatre, was more openly a romantic dramatist in his attempts to portray vast portions of mankind in a struggle with philosophical, historical, and moral problems. A trilogy on the Thirty Years' War—*Mary Stuart* (1800), *The Maid of Orleans* (1801), and *Wilhelm Tell* (1804)—treated major historical events with passion and theatrical spendor.

It remained for Iffland and Kotzebue, however, to establish German drama throughout Europe and America. The tenets and scenes of ro-manticism were boiled down to sentimental and highly melodramatic domestic dramas. These plays, now happily forgotten, provided audiences of the middle and lower classes with thrills and spills attached to just enough romantic idealism to satisfy the desire for morality in drama while titillating with shocking and sensational spectacles. At the turn of the nineteenth century. Kotzebue was the most popular dramatist in the world.

For at least half of the nineteenth century, the melodrama that Kotze-bue helped establish was the primary type of drama in Europe and America. Even today, sometimes comic and sometimes serious melodrama dominates the professional theatre. Certain playwrights composed drama outside this mainstream, however, and these are worth noting. Georg Buchner, for example, wrote *Danton's Death* (1835), *Leonce and Lena* (1836) and *Woyzeck* (1836). The first and the last of these were es-pecially notable—*Danton's Death* as an excellent dramatization of the plight of the idealist who questioned even his own motives and in the end despaired of all ideals; *Woyzeck* as a protonaturalistic study of a man trapped and degraded by his heredity and environment, the whole pre-sented by means of what later were called expressionistic techniques.

Another playwright ahead of his time was Friedrich Hebbel, whose *Maria Magdalena* (1844) presented a realistic heroine from ordinary circumstances who was destroyed by society. Hebbel was particularly concerned with the conflict between social values and changing moral consciousness.

Romantic drama was barely established in France by Victor Hugo's *Hernani* (1830) when the taste of playwrights and audiences began to shift in the direction of greater and greater realism. Concern for social problems which the romanticists seemed unable to solve led dramatists to experiment with the presentation of these problems onstage in a manner calculated to bring about solutions. A thesis or proposition was to be proved by the illusion in the theatre. The chief practitioners were Alexandre Dumas *fils*, with *Camille* (1852), Émile Augier, Eugène Scribe and Victorien Sardou.

Scribe was especially successful with the "well-made play"—in which with careful exposition and foreshadowing a matrix of cause and effect built to a powerful climax based on withheld information, surprising reversals, and suddenly-important trivia. Using Scribe's formula, Sardou became one of the most popular playwrights of the nineteenth century.

English drama throughout the century merely repeated or reflected the work on the continent, and American drama followed the lead of England, though with certain notable exceptions—the development of distinctly native stock characters like the Yankee; the Horatio Alger hero; the Rip Van Winkle character; the wisecracking city boy; the Western hero; and the noble or ignoble redskin, the comic Negro, and other ethnic or racial stereotypes. Of all the dramatists at work in the theatre, perhaps Dion Boucicault was most notable in both England and America because he helped the dramatist achieve control of his drama through stringent copyright laws. Boucicault also raised the melodrama to its highest possible level of perfection.

After 1850, however, what we now call "modern drama" took the stage. Often viewed as an attempt first to establish naturalism onstage and then to combat naturalism with greater and greater theatricality—sometimes thought of as a series of movements promulgating shifts and changes in dramaturgy and themes—the period of 1850-1950 in Western European and American drama actually is best described as "eclecticism." That is, while the theatre came to be less and less the heart of the community, a number of gifted dramatists persisted in creating works calculated to show the limited audience a total view of modern man. That view was primarily existential, absurd (the tragic made laughable), and formalistic. The presentation of the view was largely didactic or journalistic. Dramatists strove to make the theatre an effective agent in twentieth-century human affairs.

The first and most preeminent of these great moderns was Henrik Ibsen. At first inclined toward romantic historical dramas, he later composed in nearly every mode the present-day theatre has seen. Two long plays, *Brand* (1866) and *Peer Gynt* (1867) dealt with the central concern of modern drama: the nature of man and his world, his responsibility to his moral vision, and the problems in knowing clearly what that vision is. In *Brand,* an idealist sacrificed everything to his personal ideals; in *Peer Gynt,* a man sacrificed everything to avoid choosing, facing, or living up to any ideas. The latter drama was especially significant as a repository of all the dramatic techniques that later became "movements" in modern drama. After these two monumental works, Ibsen composed a series of thesis dramas that were more than merely didactic and explored both naturalistic and theatrical techniques for structuring his dramatic vision. Whatever modern drama has become, the source was largely Ibsen.

A contemporary of his, August Strindberg, was also important in the development of modern drama. In *Miss Julie* (1888) and other similar works, Strindberg created the epitome of naturalistic and particularly psychological dramas. Other of his works, similar to *The Ghost Sonata* (1907), were models for the technique called "expressionism" (see Chapter 9). Most modern dramatists tended to copy either Ibsen or Strindberg— or both.

George Bernard Shaw, an English comic dramatist often considered second only to Shakespeare, was particularly influenced by Ibsen's realism and didacticism. Shaw wanted primarily to correct society's ills—to impose his ideas—through drama. His genius was comedy, however, and even though he structured his most important dramas as arguments, the comic impact of his ideas, his stock characters, and particularly the manner in which he caused the people and ideas to interact made such plays as *Arms and the Man* (1894), *Candida* (1895), *The Devil's Disciple* (1897), *Man and Superman* (1903), *Major Barbara* (1906), and *Saint Joan* (1924) the most important English dramas of modern times. Shaw was rebelling principally against the social and economic practices of Victorian England. Studied closely, his comedies show not only the rotten core of that society but the results that are still with us today.

In Italy during the 1920's, Luigi Pirandello turned from the novel to the drama, and in *Six Characters in Search of an Author* (1921) and *Henri IV* (1922), among others, created the pivotal plays of the twentieth century. Pirandello was interested in the nature of reality, perception, and the roles people play as they go through life. This concern has informed nearly every major drama since Pirandello.

Shaw's didactic comedy was a precursor of Bertold Brecht's "epic theatre"—a conscious attempt to create a drama without illusion, in fact to break illusion whenever possible. Yet in such dramas as *Mother Courage and Her Children* (1937), Brecht employed a wide range of theatrical devices to make the audience experience the play as if it were real life in which the spectator was actually participating. Brecht stated he wanted to "alienate" his audience; he succeeded in capturing them with much the same theatricality as the pre-illusionistic drama.

In America, one playwright stood out. Eugene O'Neill attempted all the modes of contemporary drama except perhaps epic theatre. Haltingly, yet greatly, he strove to present the essential alienation of modern man. Whatever his faults, the dramas he created were a powerful delineation of man's deepest feelings. Probably his most effective works were *Desire Under the Elms* (1924), *The Great God Brown* (1926), *Strange Interlude* (1928), *Mourning Becomes Electra* (1931), *Ah, Wilderness!* (1933), and *A Long Day's Journey Into Night* (1957).

After 1950, but with roots going back to the 1890's, the "theatre of the absurd" dominated the drama of Western Europe and America. The absurdists concentrated on the irrationality of human existence and used structures without cause and effect but with incongruous incidents and language subordinate to nonverbal behavior—that is, theatrical chaos—to represent the meaningless chaos of the universe. The best of this group were Eugène Ionesco, Samuel Beckett, and Jean Genet.

In the 1960's, Western drama turned increasingly toward what is called "total theatre"—a desire to immerse the audience in an experience, a "happening." Shaw's dialectic, Brecht's epic theatre, Pirandello's ambiguity, and Strindberg's expressionism—in effect *Peer Gynt*—merged in Peter Weiss' *The Persecution and Assassination of Jean-Paul Marat as Performed by the Inmates of the Asylum of Charenton under the Direction of the Marquis de Sade* (1959). The idea of anarchy clashed with the idea of social order, and the conflict was plotted as a performance of a play in which each moment contained all its causes and effects. The collision was made to occur on the deepest level of the psyche. Reality as experienced was shown with great irony. By the end of the play, the audience seemed insane and the inmates simply manifestations of each spectator's most horrible fears and urges. What was significant was the attempt at total participation, perhaps the most important current trend in Western drama.

PLAYMAKING THROUGH THE AGES

The drama cannot exist unless actors perform it in a scenic environment of some kind. In each period of theatre, the audience and the players shared a set of conventions that allowed the drama to be performed *as if the events onstage were real.* That is, the production elements were symbols of illusion. Theatrical realism was thus achieved. Until the modern era there was no attempt to go beyond such symbolism to actual environments. Audiences and performers were content to share an imaginary moment that was made as "real" as necessary but above all as spectacular as possible.

Fifth-century Greece, for which we have little evidence but much speculation, was a case in point. Actors wore masks and conventional costumes, and declaimed their roles. Since there were probably only three actors at the most, one man performed several roles. All females were portrayed by men. Actors had to speak, recite, sing, and dance well. Tragedy had simple but dignified movements and gestures; comedy exaggerated everyday actions. Though the characterizations were in no sense actual, in the way we use this term, they were completely real to the audiences of the time.

The formal chorus was an important convention. For tragedy, the size of the chorus cannot be determined; for Aristophanes' comedies, the chorus had 24 members. In all plays, however, the chorus could serve as an agent in the dramatic action, establish the social or ethical framework for the action, observe the events as an ideal spectator, set the mood and heighten theatrical effects, create pauses in the action, and perform songs and dances.

Whoever did the performing, music and dance were an integral part of the drama. We know next to nothing about either, however, though apparently flutes and lyres were used for music. The dances were mimetic and extremely varied as to steps, rhythms, and styles.

Even our knowledge of scenic practices is inadequate. There seems to have been a movement toward greater and greater naturalism in costume, though many authorities believe tragedy and comedy each had a standard dress. We have pictures of actors in tunics, short cloaks, and long cloaks—with comic ones exaggeratedly short or tight—but no one knows for sure. The comic actor wore a phallus. All performers wore masks of linen, cork, or wood. In tragedy, the actors' masks were varied, but the chorus members all looked alike. Comic masks were exaggerated and as a rule highly individualized.

In later Greek times, the actors used a good deal of scenic machinery. We cannot prove the existence of these devices in the fifth century, though we may assume them. Chief staging devices were the *ekkyklema,* a wagon or a platform on wheels that was used to show tableaux; the *mechane,* a basket suspended from a crane and used to fly characters through the air; *pinakes,* flat panels that were painted to represent a given scene and were changed as needed; *periaktoi,* three-sided prisms with a different scene painted on each side so the scene could be changed by spinning the prism; and whatever properties that were needed (couches, chariots, weapons), though undoubtedly the properties were as simple, as few, and as symbolic as possible.

The producer and the director in fifth-century Athens were, respectively, the *choregus*—a wealthy citizen who produced the drama as a civic duty—and the playwright, who may have acted in his play as well. All the city provided was the theatre and the prizes which were shared by author and *choregus.*

Throughout later Greek times, and in the Hellenistic period, scenic practices continued to increase in sophistication and complexity. Tragic actors were given padded boots (the *cothurnus*), a high headdress (the *onkos*), and large exaggerated masks. Apparently there were 28 basic masks, and the actor's appearance was conventionalized and distorted. Comedians were dressed in more ordinary fashion, however, and the masks—some 44 in all—were for the most part realistic.

The staging made use of the devices we have already described. The chorus gradually fell into disuse, and hence all action took place onstage.

After 307, an elected official called the *agonothetes* produced the plays with a state appropriation. Authors, actors, and other theatre artists became highly professionalized. They formed a guild, the Artists of Dionysus, and provided a city or a festival with all that was needed to produce a play.

It was this popular theatre that Rome used as a model for its own practices. To what extent the Romans had always known a primitive theatre, and thus the extent of their borrowing from the Greeks, is not fully known. Probably the farces were native and all else came from Greece. Plays were produced at festivals by a magistrate with a grant who contracted with managers of professional troupes. The actors were masked—presumably the masks of the Hellenistic theatre—and apparently declaimed rather than acted their roles. Costumes were based on the Greek, and along with masks became both highly stylized and individualized to a character-type—particularly in comedy. The types in the farces seem to have had considerable influence on the *commedias* that developed in the late Middle Ages, though the relationship is largely conjectural.

Roman scenery was similar to the Greek in layout, but the *scaenae frons* assumed greater importance in the Roman theatre. This was a facade with doors, porticoes, alcoves, and so forth. The different doors represented different houses or different entrances to the same building, and scene changes were made largely with *periaktoi*.

With the passing of Rome, all these methods of play production were lost to sight for some 500 years. When drama appeared definitely again —about the 10th century—scenic practices peculiar to the medieval experience came with it. However the mysteries and moralities were performed—in church alcoves, on pageant wagons, in stalls around the village square—the principle of theatrical realism still governed. Quite obviously the dramas were highly symbolic, with conventionalized actions and characters in largely unlocalized settings. Yet many of the scenes called for naturalistic detail that went far beyond the need for symbolism.

Production was at first the responsibility of the Church, then later was assigned to the trade guilds or to lay groups somewhat like fraternities. Often a town itself assumed the responsibility for production. When the guilds produced plays, the dramas probably were assigned on the basis of the guild's trade: Noah to the shipwrights, the Last Supper to the bakers, and so forth. In many instances, there was a single director for an entire cycle of plays. This man was responsible for all theatrical details.

At times, besides scenic problems, the director might have as many as 300 actors, although many of the dramas required only five or ten at the most. These performers were largely amateurs, yet not necessarily unskillful. No doubt a man would play a part for many years and thus become well-versed in it. Most of the roles demanded only the achievement of a proper emotional state—such as joy or grief—and subtlety was not required.

The ultimate success of the plays depended on the staging—and that was principally special effects. The actors were rehearsed briefly, and they sat onstage until their cues. Their costumes were everyday dress, unless they were playing some special part, like God, who was dressed like a Pope, or Satan and his minions, who were portrayed as monsters of various kinds. The stages were the *mansions* we have already mentioned, one grand one to represent heaven usually, and a horrible hell mouth to occupy the opposite side of the stage. Other places had plain houses to represent them. Most impressive of all stage activity were special things like flying, executions, floods, and Biblical "miracles." The directors and their technical assistants sought spectacular and realistic means of depicting the events in the dramas. Though both secular and religious music were part of the productions, we know little more than that there were choirs, solos, and instrumental selections both during and between the scenes.

What the medieval audience enjoyed, then, despite what seem to be exceedingly simple dramas barren of spectacle, was full-fledged theatre in which the whole community could participate. The spectator's ideas of earth, heaven, and hell—his view of myths and Biblical stories—were presented in such a way that he could believe in their reality onstage. He could play out his beliefs, well aware he was experiencing "theatre" but also convinced of the reality of the symbols he played with.

This concept of total theatre that is thoroughly real *during the play* was carried forward into the Renaissance. Whether or not the theatre "advanced"—and indeed the plays were considerably more sophisticated than in the medieval period—the great drama of England, Spain, France, Germany, and Italy was based firmly on medieval concepts of theatre. This was even more so for staging practices. The Italian Renaissance stage may have begun in adoration of classical practices and as an extension of the painters' perspective techniques, but the stage succeeded largely because it was better suited to spectacle than other types of stages throughout Europe. That by the eighteenth century theatrical effects had come to overshadow other elements of drama should not disguise the fact that such effects were demanded by their audiences. From the moving wings and shutters of Serlio to the construction of an actual Childs Restaurant onstage by David Belasco to the East River waterfront complete with a river for swimming (Sidney Kingsley's *Dead End,* 1936) was a straight line. Whether we call such effects "real" or "theatrical," and accept one type but not the other, the fact remains that the audience considers all effects real in the context of a given play.

Even after the Renaissance, Italy was the source of scenic innovations. Whole families were engaged in stage construction—notably the Bibienas, who developed angle perspective (two or more vanishing points), means of increasing the apparent size of the setting (divorcing it from the theatre, that is), excessive ornamentation, and the practice of dividing the stage into a foreground for actors and a background for perspective scenery; Filippo Juvarra, who experimented with curvilinear and unit settings; and Gian Battista Piranesi, who led the painters to use light and shadow to stress atmosphere rather than clarity of detail.

All this is not to say the other theatres avoided scenic splendor. Though at least one authority's reconstruction of the Elizabethan theatre shows it plain and unadorned, many other historians deny such a view and insist that painting and sculpting were an important part of Shakespeare's "wooden O." Probably the truth is that there was enough scenic adornment to satisfy the audiences but that the emphasis lay on grandeur of properties, costumes, and special effects. Certainly a stage placed in the middle of the audience cannot achieve the visual effects of the picture-frame stage. What can be achieved, however, are three-dimensional spectacles like battles with the audience virtually a part of the scene. Though properties were more symbolic than illusionistic, they were nevertheless considered real when used.

The Italianate stage came to England by way of the court masques. Inigo Jones, the principal designer, gradually incorporated the Italian techniques into his designs. The public theatres, recognizing a trend, also began to employ the new scenic practices. As we have noted, when drama returned with the Restoration, the picture-frame stage was the only type used. Both English and French staging, however, continued to use the forestage until the nineteenth century, when for the sake of realism, the actors were pulled back into the proscenium opening. Though scenery was still largely painted, the trend was toward more accurate portrayal of "real life." The next step was to attempt three-dimensional settings within the picture-frame—to make the setting an environment rather than a backdrop. The aim of both approaches, however, was an illusion of reality. The audience was asked less and less to participate imaginatively in the making of this reality.

Acting during the centuries from 1500 to 1800 seems to have approximated the work of the scenic artists. In the medieval period, actors were skillful amateurs and their work was probably more declamation than portrayal. During the Renaissance, acting became once again a profession (assuming it had ever been anything else). The actors of note (Richard Burbage in England, for example, or Montfleury in France) seem to have concentrated on *presenting* their characters rather than *representing* them. The difference is perhaps subtle, and not one between theatricality and reality, for presentation focuses on making the drama's symbols clear and impactful. The audience then supplies the reality by means of imaginative absorption of the presented symbols. In each period of theatre, however, the trend of acting was toward more and more accurate representation of persons, less and less presentation of conventions and symbols.

This cycle of alternation between presentation and representation may be seen in each country. In Germany, for example, Goethe devoted much of his energy from 1798 onward to creating a theatre group at Weimar in which the actors trained as an ensemble under a single director (Goethe himself). The actors worked hard to create not an illusion of reality but an illusion of ideal beauty. All elements of the production—the actors being only the central element—were joined harmoniously. In England, John Philip Kemble aimed at much the same effects in the acting of his troupe. Kemble, however, stressed the individual actor rather than the ensemble.

Such apparently was the approach throughout the sixteenth, seventeenth, and eighteenth centuries. Acting of individuals may have moved from declaiming to realism, but the effect of the ensemble was largely neglected until Goethe. When declamatory acting came to be replaced in the early nineteenth century—that is, when representation of details to create illusion of reality was dominant—there was little concern with the ensemble at first. What was sought was realism of the emotions, not of total effect, and emphasis lay on the individual actor and the way he achieved his characterization.

The increasing desire for historical accuracy in the nineteenth century, however, led inevitably to the attempt to make all the actors artistic parts of the entire production. Again the lead came from Germany. In the Duchy of Saxe-Meinengen—as in several places—pictorial illusion and historical accuracy were carried to their logical conclusions. More important, the company of actors were included in the attempted illusion. To the trends that had begun with the scenery of Renaissance Italy was now added the idea of realistic ensemble acting. What was important was the total effect. The goal differed from that of Goethe only in that what was seen onstage was to be real, not ideal.

The actor's use of costumes from 1500 to 1800 usually was the exact opposite of realism. As a rule, contemporary clothes were worn. There were, however, conventional costumes in each period that stood for another era. "Romans" might wear drapery of one kind or another, for example, or Hamlet might always be dressed in black. Whatever the period, sumptiousness of costuming was stressed. From the middle of the eighteenth century, concern for historical accuracy appeared sporadically. This demand increased as the nineteenth century progressed. By 1850, accurate portrayal of historical periods was the norm everywhere and was the supreme hallmark of the Meinengen players.

Besides insistence on historicity, the nineteenth century added two scenic elements to the production. One—the box set, in which three or more walls close in the playing area and the only opening is the "fourth wall" in the proscenium—had never been used previously.

The second addition was improved lighting. Until the late Renaissance, theatre had been most often played either outdoors or under an open roof. When dramas were given indoors, candles were used unless daylight through windows was available. Candles and chandeliers were the norm indoors, however, until a calcium light was invented by Thomas Drummond in 1816. Compressed oxygen and hydrogen were directed against a column of lime, causing it to glow. If the "limelight" were placed inside a box and fitted with a lens and a reflector, an effective "spotlight" resulted. The carbon arc lamp, in which an electrical pole was attached to each end of a stick of carbon, in turn replaced the limelight when electrical power became available toward the end of the century. Finally, Edison's incandescent lamp replaced them both. The addition of dependable sources of light led to better means of controlling brightness and color. Henry Irving, the English actor-manager, along with Saxe-Meinengen, began careful and creative use of brightness and hue. Lighting came to seem as important as scenery—if not more so—in the presentation of illusion.

The work of Richard Wagner—playwright-composer—and his disciple Adolph Appia was a case in point. Wagner refused to accept the idea that a theatrical production should create historically accurate illusion. He believed that drama and theatre were *purely* symbolic and should therefore represent only the ideal world. Among other things, he rejected dialogue in favor of singing. In fact, music was the element he chose to unify his onstage illusion. The author-composer was to control everything in the production.

Adolph Appia, an admirer of Wagner's theories about music-dramas, also sought complete unity in the production. His means focused principally on light, which he believed was the visual counterpart of music. He also stressed that all scenery should be three-dimensional and the actor should be primarily a dancer who uses rhythmical movements to create the visual presentation. Appia joined Wagner in asserting the importance of the single theatre artist, but left him on the point of historical illusion. Appia sought to create principally feeling and mood of a dramatic action, rather than the action itself. Yet even though he sought to stylize them, Appia emphasized both actor and text.

Edward Gordon Craig, an English designer, continued Appia's ideas about visual effects but sought to eliminate actor and drama. Only the director was important in the theatre, Craig felt, and all else was his working material. Like Appia, Craig stressed feeling as opposed to actuality.

The theatre of the twentieth century, for which Appia and Craig were the principal theorists, contributed three elements to what went on before. The first was complete technical proficiency in the use of scenes and machines advocated and employed since the beginning of theatre but particularly since 1500. The second was total eclecticism in production; anything that worked for an audience was considered good theatre. And the third was the dominance of the director. While these additions were being made, drama and theatre were declining throughout the Western world. Whether the slight renaissance after 1955 indicated an upswing is certainly debatable. Nonetheless, the twentieth century saw decline coupled with high artistic achievement. Fewer and fewer people went to the theatre, but perhaps they saw better and better productions.

If so, it would seem that the rise of the director was the chief cause of the improvement. We have already noted that in the great periods of Western theatre, a single artist seems to have controlled the production of a given drama. The Greek tragedians, Shakespeare, Molière—all directed their own works. Presumably they were directors and actors before they were playwrights. Ibsen and Shaw were trained as directors, though they seldom staged their own dramas. Just prior to the modern period, as we have seen, Goethe achieved artistic control of the productions at Weimar. The Meinengen players, along with other groups in the mid-nineteenth century, initiated the modern era with just such control.

The only possible basis for effective theatre today, when each artist is highly professional, unionized, and individualistic, is the concept of the single controlling theatre artist. In educational theatre—meaning theatre in schools and perhaps the nonprofessional community theatres—where most of the artists are in effect students, the director is the key to success.

Success, in theatre terms, ought to mean more and better dramatic productions for more and more people, and higher and higher artistic achievement with all elements of the production. The ultimate success, once such universality and such quality have been achieved, is for the theatre to assume once again its place at the heart of the community. The theatre and human affairs ought to be bound together. Technical proficiency, professional artistry, sublime vision—these have one aim today as they had one achievement in the great periods of the past. That aim is to help each member of the audience play out the storms he lives in. Not to change them, not to recommend policies or actions, not to teach or even to delight—though all of these activities may occur— but to show the form and pressure, the style and grace, of the twentieth century: that is the place of the theatre in human affairs.

Sample Play: EVERYMAN

The great plays of every era have been uniquely part of that era *and* uniquely part of all the years of mankind. In a very special way, playgoers have to grow up to their playwrights. *We* find more in Shakespeare when we are sixty, for example, than when we are twenty. The change is in us, not in *Shakespeare*. The same holds true for all the plays that stand the test of time.

Such a play is *Everyman*. Though there are perhaps finer dramas available for study, there are none which are so apt an expression of their age but at the same time fit every age, and particularly the mid-twentieth century. At heart, all philosophies revolve around "salvation"— what is the purpose of life, what ought a man consider good and true and beautiful, what are his available moral choices and how ought he to make them? The center of every age—the driving force that makes it go—is the answer it gives to these central questions.

Everyman, being a morality play from the very late Middle Ages, expects the audience to draw a definite conclusion: "Perform ye good deeds throughout life if ye expect God to receive you." Yet the play transcends its form. The sense of tragic wonder at "unaccommodated man" making his moral choice—at his having the capacity of choice and the willingness to choose—makes the play not only universal but also high tragic drama.

*Everyman**

Characters

GOD

MESSENGER	KNOWLEDGE
DEATH	CONFESSION
EVERYMAN	BEAUTY
FELLOWSHIP	STRENGTH
KINDRED	DISCRETION
COUSIN	FIVE WITS
GOODS	ANGEL
GOOD DEEDS	DOCTOR

Here Beginneth a Treatise how the High Father of Heaven Sendeth Death to Summon Every Creature to Come and Give Account of their Lives in this World, and is in Manner of a Moral Play.

MESSENGER: I pray you all give your audience,
    And hear this matter with reverence,
    By figure[1] a moral play:
    The *Summoning of Everyman* called it is,
    That of our lives and ending shows
    How transitory we be all day.
    This matter is wondrous precious,
    But the intent of it is more gracious,
    And sweet to bear away.
    The story saith: Man, in the beginning
    Look well, and take good heed to the ending,
    Be you never so gay!
    Ye think sin in the beginning full sweet,
    Which in the end causeth the soul to weep,
    When the body lieth in clay.
    Here shall you see how Fellowship and Jollity,
    Both Strength, Pleasure, and Beauty,
    Will fade from thee as flower in May;
    For ye shall hear how our Heaven King
    Calleth Everyman to a general reckoning:
    Give audience, and hear what he doth say.   *(Exit.)*

Reprinted from *Everyman and Mediaeval Miracle Plays,* edited by A.C. Cawley, a Dutton Everyman Paperback, by permission of E.P. Dutton & Co., Inc. Canadian rights granted by J.M. Dent & Sons, Ltd.
[1] form

(GOD *speaketh:*)

GOD: I perceive, here in my majesty,
How that all creatures be to me unkind,
Living without dread in worldly prosperity:
Of ghostly[2] sight the people be so blind,
Drowned in sin, they know me not for their God;
In worldly riches is all their mind,
They fear not my righteousness, the sharp rod.
My law that I showed, when I for them died,
They forget clean,[3] and shedding of my blood red;
I hanged between two, it cannot be denied;
To get them life I suffered[4] to be dead;
I healed their feet, with thorns hurt was my head.
I could do no more than I did, truly;
And now I see the people do clean forsake me:
They use the seven deadly sins damnable,
As pride, covetise, wrath, and lechery
Now in the world be made commendable;
And thus they leave of angels the heavenly company.
Every man liveth so after his own pleasure,
And yet of their life they be nothing[5] sure:
I see the more that I them forbear
The worse they be from year to year.
All that liveth appaireth[6] fast;
Therefore I will, in all the haste,
Have a reckoning of every man's person;
For, and[7] I leave the people thus alone
In their life and wicked tempests,
Verily they will become much worse than beasts;
For now one would by envy another up eat;
Charity they do all clean forget.
I hoped well that every man
In my glory should make his mansion,
And thereto I had them all elect;
But now I see, like traitors deject,
They thank me not for the pleasure that I to them meant,
Nor yet for their being I them have lent.
I proffered the people great multitude of mercy,
And few there be that asketh it heartily.
They be so cumbered with worldly riches
That needs on them I must do justice,
On every man living without fear.
Where art thou, Death, though mighty messenger?

---

[2]spiritual [3]completely, altogether [4]allowed myself [5]not at all [6]becomes worse [7]if

(*Enter* DEATH.)

DEATH: Almighty God, I am here at your will,
  Your commandment to fulfil.
GOD: Go thou to Everyman,
  And show him, in my name,
  A pilgrimage he must on him take,
  Which he in no wise[8] may escape;
  And that he bring with him a sure reckoning
  Without delay or any tarrying.   (GOD *withdraws.*)
DEATH: Lord, I will in the world go run overall,[9]
  And cruelly outsearch both great and small;
  Every man will I beset that liveth beastly
  Out of God's laws, and dreadeth not folly.
  He that loveth riches I will strike with my dart,
  His sight to blind, and from heaven to depart[10]—
  Except that alms be his good friend—
  In hell for to dwell, world without end.
  Lo, yonder I see Everyman walking.
  Full little he thinketh on my coming;
  His mind is on fleshly lusts and his treasure,
  And great pain it shall cause him to endure
  Before the Lord, Heaven King.

(*Enter* EVERYMAN.)

  Everyman, stand still! Whither art thou going
  Thus gaily? Hast thou thy Maker forget?
EVERYMAN: Why askest thou?
  Wouldest thou wit?[11]
DEATH: Yea, sir; I will show you:
  In great haste I am sent to thee
  From God out of his majesty.
EVERYMAN: What, sent to me?
DEATH: Yea, certainly.
  Though thou have forget him here,
  He thinketh on thee in the heavenly sphere,
  As, ere we depart, thou shalt know.
EVERYMAN: What desireth God of me?
DEATH: That shall I show thee:
  A reckoning he will needs have
  Without any longer respite.
EVERYMAN: To give a reckoning longer leisure I crave;
  This blind[12] matter troubleth my wit.
DEATH: On thee thou must take a long journey;
  Therefore thy book of count[13] with thee thou bring,

---

[8]manner   [9]everywhere   [10]separate   [11]know   [12]obscure   [13]account

For turn again thou cannot by no way.
And look thou be sure of thy reckoning,
For before God thou shalt answer, and show
Thy many bad deeds, and good but a few;
How thou hast spent thy life, and in what wise,
Before the chief Lord of paradise.
Have ado[14] that we were in that way,[15]
For, wit thou well, thou shalt make none[16] attorney.
EVERYMAN: Full unready I am such reckoning to give.
I know thee not. What messenger art thou?
DEATH: I am Death, that no man dreadeth,[17]
For every man I rest,[18] and no man spareth;
For it is God's commandment
That all to me shall be obedient.
EVERYMAN: O Death, thou comest when I had thee least in mind!
In thy power it lieth me to save;
Yet of my good will I give thee, if thou will be kind:
Yea, a thousand pound shalt thou have,
And defer this matter till another day.
DEATH: Everyman, it may not be, by no way.
I set not by[19] gold, silver, nor riches,
Ne by pope, emperor, king, duke, ne princes;
For, and I would receive gifts great,
All the world I might get;
But my custom is clean contrary.
I give thee no respite. Come hence, and not tarry.
EVERYMAN: Alas, shall I have no longer respite?
I may say Death giveth no warning!
To think on thee, it maketh my heart sick,
For all unready is my book of reckoning.
But twelve year and I might have abiding,
My counting-book I would make so clear
That my reckoning I should not need to fear.
Wherefore, Death, I pray thee, for God's mercy,
Spare me till I be provided of remedy.
DEATH: Thee availeth not to cry, weep, and pray;
But haste thee lightly[20] that thou were gone that journey,
And prove thy friends if thou can;
For, wit thou well, the tide abideth no man,
And in the world each living creature
For Adam's sin must die of nature.[21]
EVERYMAN: Death, if I should this pilgrimage take,
And my reckoning surely make,

---

[14]see to it   [15]on that journey   [16]have no   [17]dreads no man   [18]arrest   [19]do not care for
[20]quickly   [21]as a natural thing

Show me, for[22] saint charity,
Should I not come again shortly?
DEATH: No, Everyman; and thou be once there,
Thou mayst never more come here,
Trust me verily.
EVERYMAN: O gracious God in the high seat celestial,
Have mercy on me in this most need!
Shall I have no company from this vale terrestrial
Of mine acquaintance, that way me to lead?
DEATH: Yea, if any be so hardy
That would go with thee and bear thee company.
Hie[23] thee that thou were gone to God's magnificence,
Thy reckoning to give before his presence.
What, weenest[24] thou thy life is given thee,
And thy worldly goods also?
EVERYMAN: I had wend[25] so, verily.
DEATH: Nay, nay; it was but lent thee;
For as soon as thou art go,
Another a while shall have it, and then go therefro,[26]
Even as thou hast done.
Everyman, thou art mad! Thou hast thy wits five,
And here on earth will not amend thy life;
For suddenly I do come.
EVERYMAN: O wretched caitiff, whither shall I flee,
That I might scape this endless sorrow?
Now, gentle Death, spare me till to-morrow,
That I may amend me
With good advisement.[27]
DEATH: Nay, thereto I will not consent,
Nor no man will I respite;
But to the heart suddenly I shall smite
Without any advisement.
And now out of thy sight I will me hie;
See thou make thee ready shortly,
For thou mayst say this is the day
That no man living may scape away.   (*Exit* DEATH.)
EVERYMAN: Alas, I may well weep with sighs deep!
Now have I no manner of company
To help me in my journey, and me to keep;
And also my writing is full unready.
How shall I do now for to excuse me?
I would to God I had never be get![28]
To my soul a full great profit it had be;
For now I fear pains huge and great.

---

[22]in the name of [23]hurry [24]think [25]thought [26]from it [27]reflection [28]been born

The time passeth. Lord, help, that all wrought!
For though I mourn it availeth nought.
The day passeth, and is almost ago;[29]
I wot not well what for to do.
To whom were I best my complaint to make?
What and I to Fellowship thereof spake,
And showed him of this sudden chance?
For in him is all mine affiance;[30]
We have in the world so many a day
Be good friends in sport and play.
I see him yonder, certainly.
I trust that he will bear me company;
Therefore to him will I speak to ease my sorrow.
Well met, good Fellowship, and good morrow!

(FELLOWSHIP *speaketh:*)

FELLOWSHIP: Everyman, good morrow, by this day!
    Sir, why lookest thou so piteously?
    If any thing be amiss, I pray thee me say,
    That I may help to remedy.
EVERYMAN: Yea, good Fellowship, yea;
    I am in great jeopardy.
FELLOWSHIP: My true friend, show to me your mind;
    I will not forsake thee to my life's end,
    In the way of good company.
EVERYMAN: That was well spoken, and lovingly.
FELLOWSHIP: Sir, I must needs know your heaviness;[31]
    I have pity to see you in any distress.
    If any have you wronged, ye shall revenged be,
    Though I on the ground be slain for thee—
    Though that I know before that I should die.
EVERYMAN: Verily, Fellowship, gramercy.
FELLOWSHIP: Tush! by thy thanks I set not a straw.
    Show me your grief, and say no more.
EVERYMAN: If I my heart should to you break,[32]
    And then you to turn your mind from me,
    And would not me comfort when ye hear me speak,
    Then should I ten times sorrier be.
FELLOWSHIP: Sir, I say as I will do indeed.
EVERYMAN: Then be you a good friend at need:
    I have found you true herebefore.
FELLOWSHIP: And so ye shall evermore;
    For, in faith, and thou go to hell,
    I will not forsake thee by the way.

[29] gone   [30] trust   [31] sorrow   [32] open

EVERYMAN: Ye speak like a good friend; I believe you well.
  I shall deserve it, and I may.
FELLOWSHIP: I speak of no deserving, by this day!
  For he that will say, and nothing do,
  Is not worthy with good company to go;
  Therefore show me the grief of your mind,
  As to your friend most loving and kind.
EVERYMAN: I shall show you how it is:
  Commanded I am to go a journey,
  A long way, hard and dangerous,
  And give a strait count, without delay,
  Before the high Judge, Adonai.[33]
  Wherefore, I pray you, bear me company,
  As ye have promised, in this journey.
FELLOWSHIP: That is matter indeed. Promise is duty;
  But, and I should take such a voyage on me,
  I know it well, it should be to my pain;
  Also it maketh me afeard, certain.
  But let us take counsel here as well as we can,
  For your words would fear[34] a strong man.
EVERYMAN: Why, ye said if I had need
  Ye would me never forsake, quick[35] ne dead,
  Though it were to hell, truly.
FELLOWSHIP: So I said, certainly,
  But such pleasures be set aside, the sooth to say;
  And also, if we took such a journey,
  When should we come again?
EVERYMAN: Nay, never again, till the day of doom.
FELLOWSHIP: In faith, then will not I come there!
  Who hath you these tidings brought?
EVERYMAN: Indeed, Death was with me here.
FELLOWSHIP: Now, by God that all hath bought,
  If Death were the messenger,
  For no man that is living to-day
  I will not go that loath journey—
  Not for the father that begat me!
EVERYMAN: Ye promised otherwise, pardie.[36]
FELLOWSHIP: I wot well I said so, truly;
  And yet if thou wilt eat, and drink, and make good cheer,
  Or haunt to women the lusty company,[37]
  I would not forsake you while the day is clear,[38]
  Trust me verily.
EVERYMAN: Yea, thereto ye would be ready!
  To go to mirth, solace, and play,

[33]Hebrew name for God   [34]frighten   [35]alive   [36]by God   [37]frequent the pleasant company
of women   [38]until daybreak

Your mind will sooner apply,
Than to bear me company in my long journey.
FELLOWSHIP: Now, in good faith, I will not that way.
But and thou will murder, or any man kill,
In that I will help thee with a good will.
EVERYMAN: O, that is a simple advice indeed.
Gentle fellow, help me in my necessity!
We have loved long, and now I need;
And now, gentle Fellowship, remember me.
FELLOWSHIP: Whether ye have loved me or no,
By Saint John, I will not with thee go.
EVERYMAN: Yet, I pray thee, take the labour, and do so much for me
To bring me forward,[39] for saint charity,
And comfort me till I come without the town.
FELLOWSHIP: Nay, and thou would give me a new gown,
I will not a foot with thee go;
But, and thou had tarried, I would not have left thee so.
And as now God speed thee in thy journey,
For from thee I will depart as fast as I may.
EVERYMAN: Whither away, Fellowship? Will thou forsake me?
FELLOWSHIP: Yea, by my fay![40] To God I betake[41] thee.
EVERYMAN: Farewell, good Fellowship; for thee my heart is sore.
Adieu for ever! I shall see thee no more.
FELLOWSHIP: In faith, Everyman, farewell now at the ending;
For you I will remember that parting is mourning.

(*Exit* FELLOWSHIP.)

EVERYMAN: Alack! shall we thus depart indeed—
Ah, Lady, help!—without any more comfort?
Lo, Fellowship forsaketh me in my most need.
For help in this world whither shall I resort?
Fellowship herebefore with me would merry make,
And now little sorrow for me doth he take.
It is said, 'In prosperity men friends may find,
Which in adversity be full unkind.'
Now whither for succour shall I flee,
Sith that[42] Fellowship hath forsaken me?
To my kinsmen I will, truly,
Praying them to help me in my necessity;
I believe that they will do so,
For kind[43] will creep where it may not go.
I will go say, for yonder I see them.
Where be ye now, my friends and kinsmen?

---

[39]escort me [40]faith [41]commend [42]since [43]kinship, family

(*Enter* KINDRED *and* COUSIN.)

KINDRED: Here be we now at your commandment.
  Cousin, I pray you show us your intent
  In any wise, and do not spare.[44]
COUSIN: Yea, Everyman, and to us declare
  If ye be disposed to go anywhither;
  For, wit you well, we will live and die together.
KINDRED: In wealth and woe we will with you hold,
  For over his kin a man may be bold.[45]
EVERYMAN: Gramercy, my friends and kinsmen kind.
  Now shall I show you the grief of my mind:
  I was commanded by a messenger,
  That is a high king's chief officer;
  He bade me go a pilgrimage, to my pain,
  And I know well I shall never come again;
  Also I must give a reckoning strait,
  For I have a great enemy[46] that hath me in wait,
  Which intendeth me for to hinder.
KINDRED: What account is that which ye must render?
  That would I know.
EVERYMAN: Of all my works I must show
  How I have lived and my days spent;
  Also of ill deeds that I have used[47]
  In my time, sith life was me lent;
  And of all virtues that I have refused.
  Therefore, I pray you, go thither with me
  To help to make mine account, for saint charity.
COUSIN: What, to go thither? Is that the matter?
  Nay, Everyman, I had liefer[48] fast[49] bread and water
  All this five year and more.
EVERYMAN: Alas, that ever I was bore![50]
  For now shall I never be merry,
  If that you forsake me.
KINDRED: Ah, sir, what ye be a merry man!
  Take good heart to you, and make no moan.
  But one thing I warn you, by Saint Anne—
  As for me, ye shall go alone.
EVERYMAN: My Cousin, will you not with me go?
COUSIN: No, by our Lady! I have the cramp in my toe.
  Trust not to me, for, so God me speed,
  I will deceive you in your most need.
KINDRED: It availeth not us to tice.[51]
  Ye shall have my maid with all my heart;

---

[44]hold back [45]a man may freely command the services of his family [46]*i.e.*, the Devil [47]practiced [48]rather [49]have nothing but [50]born [51]entice

She loveth to go to feasts, there to be nice,[52]
And to dance, and abroad to start:[53]
I will give her leave to help you in that journey,
If that you and she may agree.
EVERYMAN: Now show me the very effect of your mind:
   Will you go with me, or abide behind?
KINDRED: Abide behind? Yea, that will I, and I may!
   Therefore farewell till another day.   (*Exit* KINDRED.)
EVERYMAN: How should I be merry or glad?
   For fair promises men to me make,
   But when I have most need they me forsake.
   I am deceived; that maketh me sad.
COUSIN: Cousin Everyman, farewell now,
   For verily I will not go with you.
   Also of mine own an unready reckoning
   I have to account; therefore I make tarrying.
   Now God keep thee, for now I go.   (*Exit* COUSIN.)
EVERYMAN: Ah, Jesus, is all come hereto?
   Lo, fair words maketh fools fain;[54]
   They promise, and nothing will do, certain.
   My kinsmen promised me faithfully
   For to abide with me steadfastly,
   And now fast away do they flee:
   Even so Fellowship promised me.
   What friend were best me of to provide?[55]
   I lose my time here longer to abide.
   Yet in my mind a thing there is:
   All my life I have loved riches;
   If that my Good[56] now help me might,
   He would make my heart full light.
   I will speak to him in this distress—
   Where art thou, my Goods and riches?

(GOODS *speaks from a corner:*)

GOODS: Who calleth me? Everyman? What! hast thou haste?
   I lie here in corners, trussed and piled so high,
   And in chests I am locked so fast,
   Also sacked in bags. Thou mayst see with thine eye
   I cannot stir; in packs low I lie.
   What would ye have? Lightly me say.
EVERYMAN: Come hither, Good, in all the haste thou may,
   For of counsel I must desire thee.
GOODS: Sir, and ye in the world have sorrow or adversity,
   That can I help you to remedy shortly.

[52]wanton [53]rush [54]glad [55]to provide me with [56]goods, possessions

EVERYMAN: It is another disease that grieveth me;
    In this world it is not, I tell thee so.
    I am sent for, another way to go,
    To give a strait count general
    Before the highest Jupiter of all;
    And all my life I have had joy and pleasure in thee,
    Therefore, I pray thee, go with me;
    For, peradventure, thou mayst before God Almighty
    My reckoning help to clean and purify;
    For it is said ever among[57]
    That money maketh all right that is wrong.
GOODS: Nay, Everyman, I sing another song.
    I follow no man in such voyages;
    For, and I went with thee,
    Thou shouldst fare much the worse for me;
    For because on me thou did set thy mind,
    Thy reckoning I have made blotted and blind,
    That thine account thou cannot make truly;
    And that has thou for the love of me.
EVERYMAN: That would grieve me full sore,
    When I should come to that fearful answer.
    Up, let us go thither together.
GOODS: Nay, not so! I am too brittle, I may not endure;
    I will follow no man one foot, be ye sure.
EVERYMAN: Alas, I have thee loved, and had great pleasure
    All my life-days on good and treasure.
GOODS: That is to thy damnation, without leasing,
    For my love is contrary to the love everlasting;
    But if thou had me loved moderately during,
    As to the poor to give part of me,
    Then shouldst thou not in this dolour be,
    Nor in this great sorrow and care.
EVERYMAN: Lo, now was I deceived ere I was ware,
    And all I may wite[58] misspending of time.
GOODS: What, weenest thou that I am thine?
EVERYMAN: I had wend so.
GOODS: Nay, Everyman, I say no.
    As for a while I was lent thee;
    A season thou hast had me in prosperity.
    My condition is man's soul to kill;
    If I save one, a thousand I do spill.
    Weenest thou that I will follow thee?
    Nay, not from this world, verily.
EVERYMAN: I had wend otherwise.

---

[57]at times   [58]blame on

GOODS: Therefore to thy soul Good is a thief;
    For when thou art dead, this is my guise[59]—
    Another to deceive in this same wise
    As I have done thee, and all to his soul's reprief.[60]
EVERYMAN: O false Good, cursed may thou be,
    Thou traitor to God, that has deceived me
    And caught me in thy snare!
GOODS: Marry, thou brought thyself in care,
    Whereof I am glad;
    I must needs laugh, I cannot be sad.
EVERYMAN: Ah, Good, thou hast had long my heartly love;
    I gave thee that which should be the Lord's above.
    But wilt thou not go with me indeed?
    I pray thee truth to say.
GOODS: No, so God me speed!
    Therefore farewell, and have good day.   (*Exit* GOODS.)
EVERYMAN: O, to whom shall I make my moan
    For to go with me in that heavy journey?
    First Fellowship said he would with me gone;
    His words were very pleasant and gay,
    But afterward he left me alone.
    Then spake I to my kinsmen, all in despair,
    And also they gave me words fair;
    They lacked no fair speaking,
    But all forsook me in the ending.
    Then went I to my Goods, that I loved best,
    In hope to have comfort, but there had I least;
    For my Goods sharply did me tell
    That he bringeth many into hell.
    Then of myself I was ashamed,
    And so I am worthy to be blamed;
    Thus may I well myself hate.
    Of whom shall I now counsel take?
    I think that I shall never speed
    Till that I go to my Good Deed.
    But, alas, she is so weak
    That she can neither go nor speak;
    Yet will I venture on her now.
    My Good Deeds, where be you?

(GOOD DEEDS *speaks from the ground:*)

GOOD DEEDS: Here I lie, cold in the ground;
    Thy sins hath me sore bound,
    That I cannot stir.

---

[59]practice   [60]shame

EVERYMAN: O Good Deeds, I stand in fear!
  I must you pray of counsel,
  For help now should come right well.
GOOD DEEDS: Everyman, I have understanding
  That ye be summoned account to make
  Before Messias, of Jerusalem King;
  And you do by me,[61] that journey with you will I take.
EVERYMAN: Therefore I come to you, my moan to make;
  I pray you that ye will go with me.
GOOD DEEDS: I would full fain, but I cannot stand, verily.
EVERYMAN: Why, is there anything on you fall?
GOOD DEEDS: Yea, sir, I may thank you of[62] all;
  If ye had perfectly cheered me,
  Your book of count full ready had be.
  Look, the books of your works and deeds eke![63]
  Behold how they lie under the feet,
  To your soul's heaviness.
EVERYMAN: Our Lord Jesus help me!
  For one letter here I cannot see.
GOOD DEEDS: There is a blind reckoning in time of distress.
EVERYMAN: Good Deeds, I pray you help me in this need,
  Or else I am for ever damned indeed;
  Therefore help me to make reckoning
  Before the Redeemer of all thing,
  That King is, and was, and ever shall.
GOOD DEEDS: Everyman, I am sorry of your fall,
  And fain would I help you, and I were able.
EVERYMAN: Good Deeds, your counsel I pray you give me.
GOOD DEEDS: That shall I do verily;
  Though that on my feet I may not go,
  I have a sister that shall with you also,
  Called Knowledge, which shall with you abide,
  To help you to make that dreadful reckoning.

(*Enter* KNOWLEDGE.)

KNOWLEDGE: Everyman, I will go with thee, and be thy guide,
  In thy most need to go by thy side.
EVERYMAN: In good condition I am now in every thing,
  And am wholly content with this good thing,
  Thanked be God my creator.
GOOD DEEDS: And when she hath brought you there
  Where thou shalt heal thee of thy smart,[64]
  Then go you with your reckoning and your Good Deeds together,

---

[61]as I advise   [62]for   [63]also   [64]pain

For to make you joyful at heart
Before the blessed Trinity.
EVERYMAN: My Good Deeds, gramercy!
I am well content, certainly,
With your words sweet.
KNOWLEDGE: Now go we together lovingly
To Confession, that cleansing river.
EVERYMAN: For joy I weep; I would we were there!
But, I pray you, give me cognition
Where dwelleth that holy man, Confession.
KNOWLEDGE: In the house of salvation:
We shall find him in that place,
That shall us comfort, by God's grace.

(KNOWLEDGE *takes* EVERYMAN *to* CONFESSION.)

Lo, this is Confession. Kneel down and ask mercy,
For he is in good conceit[65] with God Almighty.
EVERYMAN: O glorious fountain, that all uncleanness doth clarify,
Wash from me the spots of vice unclean,
That on me no sin may be seen.
I come with Knowledge for my redemption,
Redempt with heart and full contrition;
For I am commanded a pilgrimage to take,
And great accounts before God to make.
Now I pray you, Shrift,[66] mother of salvation,
Help my Good Deeds for my piteous exclamation.
CONFESSION: I know your sorrow well, Everyman.
Because with Knowledge ye come to me,
I will you comfort as well as I can,
And a precious jewel I will give thee,
Called penance, voider of adversity;
Therewith shall your body chastised be,
With abstinence and perserverance in God's service.
Here shall you receive that scourge of me,
Which is penance strong that ye must endure,
To remember thy Saviour was scourged for thee
With sharp scourges, and suffered it patiently;
So must thou, ere thou scape that painful pilgrimage.
Knowledge, keep him in this voyage,
And by that time Good Deeds will be with thee.
But in any wise be siker[67] of mercy,
For your time draweth fast; and ye will saved be,
Ask God mercy, and he will grant truly.
When with the scourge of penance man doth him[68] bind,
The oil of forgiveness then shall he find.

[65]esteem   [66]confession   [67]sure   [68]himself

EVERYMAN: Thanked be God for his gracious work!
 For now I will my penance begin;
 This hath rejoiced and lighted my heart,
 Though the knots be painful and hard within.
KNOWLEDGE: Everyman, look your penance that ye fulfil,
 What pain that ever it to you be;
 And Knowledge shall give you counsel at will
 How your account ye shall make clearly.
EVERYMAN: O eternal God, O heavenly figure,
 O way of righteousness, O goodly vision,
 Which descended down in a virgin pure
 Because he would every man redeem,
 Which Adam forfeited by his disobedience:
 O blessed Godhead, elect and high divine,
 Forgive my grievous offence;
 Here I cry thee mercy in this presence.
 O ghostly treasure, O ransomer and redeemer,
 Of all the world hope and conductor,[69]
 Mirror of joy, and founder of mercy,
 Which enlumineth heaven and earth thereby,[70]
 Hear my clamorous complaint, though it late be;
 Receive my prayers, of thy benignity;
 Though I be a sinner most abominable,
 Yet let my name be written in Moses' table.
 O Mary, pray to the Maker of all thing,
 Me for to help at my ending;
 And save me from the power of my enemy,
 For Death assaileth me strongly.
 And, Lady, that I may by mean of thy prayer
 Of your Son's glory to be[71] partner,
 By the means of his passion, I it crave;
 I beseech you help my soul to save.
 Knowledge, give me the scourge of penance;
 My flesh therewith shall give acquittance:[72]
 I will now begin, if God give me grace.
KNOWLEDGE: Everyman, God give you time and space!
 Thus I bequeath you in the hands of our Saviour;
 Now may you make your reckoning sure.
EVERYMAN: In the name of the Holy Trinity,
 My body sore punished shall be:
 Take this, body, for the sin of the flesh!   *(Scourges himself.)*
 Also thou delightest to go gay and fresh,
 And in the way of damnation thou did me bring.
 Therefore suffer now strokes and punishing.

[69]guide [70]besides [71]be [72]atonement

Now of penance I will wade the water clear,
To save me from purgatory, that sharp fire.

(GOOD DEEDS *rises from the ground.*)

GOOD DEEDS: I thank God, now I can walk and go,
And am delivered of my sickness and woe.
Therefore with Everyman I will go, and not spare;
His good works I will help him to declare.
KNOWLEDGE: Now, Everyman, be merry and glad!
Your Good Deeds cometh now; ye may not be sad.
Now is your Good Deeds whole and sound,
Going upright upon the ground.
EVERYMAN: My heart is light, and shall be evermore;
Now will I smite faster than I did before.
GOOD DEEDS: Everyman, pilgrim, my special friend,
Blessed be thou without end;
For thee is preparate the eternal glory.
Ye have me made whole and sound,
Therefore I will bide by thee in every stound.[73]
EVERYMAN: Welcome, my Good Deeds; now I hear thy voice,
I weep for very sweetness of love.
KNOWLEDGE: Be no more sad, but ever rejoice;
God seeth thy living in his throne above.
Put on this garment to thy behoof,[74]
Which is wet with your tears,
Or else before God you may it miss,
When ye to your journey's end come shall.
EVERYMAN: Gentle Knowledge, what do ye it call?
KNOWLEDGE: It is a garment of sorrow:
From pain it will you borrow;[75]
Contrition it is,
That geteth forgiveness;
It pleaseth God passing well.
GOOD DEEDS: Everyman, will you wear it for your heal?
EVERYMAN: Now blessed be Jesu, Mary's Son,
For now have I on true contrition
And let us go now without tarrying;
Good Deeds, have we clear our reckoning?
GOOD DEEDS: Yea, indeed, I have it here.
EVERYMAN: Then I trust we need not fear;
Now, friends, let us not part in twain.
KNOWLEDGE: Nay, Everyman, that will we not, certain.
GOOD DEEDS: Yet must thou lead with thee
Three persons of great might.

---

[73] always (or: in every attack) [74] advantage [75] take

EVERYMAN: Who should they be?
GOOD DEEDS: Discretion and Strength they hight,[76]
  And thy Beauty may not abide behind.
KNOWLEGE: Also ye must call to mind
  Your Five Wits as for your counsellors.
GOOD DEEDS: You must have them ready at all hours.
EVERYMAN: How shall I get them hither?
KNOWLEDGE: You must call them all together,
  And they will hear you incontinent.[77]
EVERYMAN: My friends, come hither and be present,
  Discretion, Strength, my Five Wits,[78] and Beauty.

(*Enter* BEAUTY, STRENGTH, DISCRETION, *and* FIVE WITS.)

BEAUTY: Here at your will we be all ready.
  What will ye that we should do?
GOOD DEEDS: That ye would with Everyman go,
  And help him in his pilgrimage.
  Advise you, will ye with him or not in that voyage?
STRENGTH: We will bring him all thither,
  To his help and comfort, ye may believe me.
DISCRETION: So will we go with him all together.
EVERYMAN: Almighty God, lofed[79] may thou be!
  I give thee laud that I have hither brought
  Strength, Discretion, Beauty, and Five Wits. Lack I nought.
  And my Good Deeds, with Knowledge clear,
  All be in my company at my will here;
  I desire no more to[80] my business.
STRENGTH: And I, Strength, will by you stand in distress,
  Though thou would in battle fight on the ground.
FIVE WITS: And though it were through the world round,
  We will not depart for sweet ne sour.
BEAUTY: No more will I unto death's hour,
  Whatsoever thereof befall.
DISCRETION: Everyman, advise you first of all;
  Go with a good advisement and deliberation.
  We all give you virtuous monition
  That all shall be well.
EVERYMAN: My friends, harken what I will tell:
  I pray God reward you in his heavenly sphere.
  Now harken, all that be here,
  For I will make my testament
  Here before you all present:
  In alms half my good I will give with my hands twain
  In the way of charity, with good intent,

[76] are called   [77] immediately   [78] senses   [79] praised   [80] for

And the other half still shall remain
In queth,[81] to be returned there[82] it ought to be.
This I do in despite of the fiend of hell,
To go quit out of his peril
Ever after and this day.
KNOWLEDGE: Everyman, harken what I say:
　Go to priesthood, I you advise,
　And receive of him in any wise
　The holy sacrament and ointment together.
　Then shortly see ye turn again hither;
　We will all abide you here.
FIVE WITS: Yea, Everyman, hie you that ye ready were.
　There is no emperor, king, duke, ne baron,
　That of God hath commission
　As hath the least priest in the world being;
　For of the blessed sacraments pure and benign
　He beareth the keys, and thereof hath the cure[83]
　For man's redemption—it is ever sure—
　Which God for our soul's medicine
　Gave us out of his heart with great pine.
　Here in this transitory life, for thee and me,
　The blessed sacraments seven there be:
　Baptism, confirmation, with priesthood good,
　And the sacrament of God's precious flesh and blood,
　Marriage, the holy extreme unction, and penance;
　These seven be good to have in remembrance,
　Gracious sacraments of high divinity.
EVERYMAN: Fain would I receive that holy body,
　And meekly to my ghostly father I will go.
FIVE WITS: Everyman, that is the best that ye can do.
　God will you to salvation bring.
　For priesthood exceedeth all other thing:
　To us Holy Scripture they do teach,
　And converteth man from sin heaven to reach;
　God hath to them more power given
　Than to any angel that is in heaven.
　With five words[84] he may consecrate,
　God's body in flesh and blood to make,
　And handleth his Maker between his hands.
　The priest bindeth and unbindeth all bands,
　Both in earth and in heaven.
　Thou ministers[85] all the sacraments seven;
　Though we kissed thy feet, thou were worthy;
　Thou art surgeon that cureth sin deadly:

---

[81] bequest [82] where [83] charge [84] *i.e., Hoc est enim corpus meum* (For this is my body); from the sacrament of the Eucharist [85] administer

No remedy we find under God
But all only[86] priesthood.
Everyman, God gave priests that dignity,
And setteth them in his stead among us to be;
Thus be they above angels in degree.

(EVERYMAN *goes to the priest to receive the last sacraments.*)

KNOWLEDGE: If priests be good, it is so,[87] surely.
    But when Jesus hanged on the cross with great smart,
    There he gave out of his blessed heart
    The same sacrament in great torment:
    He sold them not to us, that Lord omnipotent.
    Therefore Saint Peter the apostle doth say
    That Jesu's curse hath all they
    Which God their Saviour do buy or sell,
    Or they for any money do take or tell.[88]
    Sinful priests giveth the sinners example bad;
    Their children sitteth by other men's fires, I have heard;
    And some haunteth women's company
    With unclean life, as lusts of lechery:
    These be with sin made blind.
FIVE WITS: I trust to God no such may we find;
    Therefore let us priesthood honour,
    And follow their doctrine for our souls' succour.
    We be their sheep, and they shepherds be
    By whom we all be kept in surety.
    Peace, for yonder I see Everyman come,
    Which hath made true satisfaction.
GOOD DEEDS: Methink it is he indeed.

(*Re-enter* EVERYMAN.)

EVERYMAN: Now Jesu be your alder speed![89]
    I have received the sacrament for my redemption,
    And then mine extreme unction:
    Blessed by all they that counselled me to take it!
    And now, friends, let us go without longer respite;
    I thank God that ye have tarried so long.
    Now set each of you on this rood[90] your hand,
    And shortly follow me:
    I go before there I would be; God be our guide!
STRENGTH: Everyman, we will not from you go
    Till ye have done this voyage long.
DISCRETION: I, Discretion, will bide by you also.

---

[86]except [87]*i.e.,* "above angels in degree" [88]count [89]help to all of you [90]cross

KNOWLEDGE: And though this pilgrimage be never so strong,[91]
    I will never part you fro.
STRENGTH: Everyman, I will be as sure by thee
    As ever I did by Judas Maccabee.[92]

(EVERYMAN *comes to his grave.*)

EVERYMAN: Alas, I am so faint I may not stand;
    My limbs under me doth fold.
    Friends, let us not turn again to this land,
    Not for all the world's gold;
    For into this cave must I creep
    And turn to earth, and there to sleep.
BEAUTY: What, into this grave? Alas!
EVERYMAN: Yea, there shall ye consume, more and less.[93]
BEAUTY: And what, should I smother here?
EVERYMAN: Yea, by my faith, and never more appear.
    In this world live no more we shall,
    But in heaven before the highest Lord of all.
BEAUTY: I cross out all this; adieu, by Saint John!
    I take my cap in my lap, and am gone.
EVERYMAN: What, Beauty, whither will ye?
BEAUTY: Peace, I am deaf; I look not behind me,
    Not and thou wouldest give me all the gold in thy chest.   (*Exit* BEAUTY.)
EVERYMAN: Alas, whereto may I trust?
    Beauty goeth fast away from me;
    She promised with me to live and die.
STRENGTH: Everyman, I will thee also forsake and deny;
    Thy game liketh me not at all.
EVERYMAN: Why, then, ye will forsake me all?
    Sweet Strength, tarry a little space.
STRENGTH: Nay, sir, by the rood of grace!
    I will hie me from thee fast,
    Though thou weep till thy heart to-brast.[94]
EVERYMAN: Ye would ever bide by me, ye said.
STRENGTH: Yea, I have you far enough conveyed.
    Ye be old enough, I understand,
    Your pilgrimage to take on hand;
    I repent me that I hither came.
EVERYMAN: Strength, you to displease I am to blame;
    Yet promise is debt, this ye well wot.
STRENGTH: In faith, I care not.
    Thou art but a fool to complain;

---

[91]hard, difficult [92]Jewish religious and national leader against Syria in the 2nd century B.C.
He told his men that "the success of war is not in the multitude: but strength cometh from
heaven." (Apocrypha, I Maccabees, 3:19) [93]high and low [94]broke to pieces

You spend your speech and waste your brain.
Go thrust thee into the ground!   (*Exit* STRENGTH.)
EVERYMAN: I had wend surer I should you have found.
He that trusteth in his Strength
She him deceiveth at the length.
Both Strength and Beauty forsaketh me;
Yet they promised me fair and lovingly.
DISCRETION: Everyman, I will after Strength be gone;
As for me, I will leave you alone.
EVERYMAN: Why, Discretion, will ye forsake me?
DISCRETION: Yea, in faith, I will go from thee,
For when Strength goeth before
I follow after evermore.
EVERYMAN: Yet, I pray thee, for the love of the Trinity,
Look in my grave once piteously.
DISCRETION: Nay, so nigh will I not come;
Farewell, every one!   (*Exit* DISCRETION.)
EVERYMAN: O, all thing faileth, save God alone—
Beauty, Strength, and Discretion;
For when Death bloweth his blast,
They all run from me full fast.
FIVE WITS: Everyman, my leave now of thee I take;
I will follow the other, for here I thee forsake.
EVERYMAN: Alas, then may I wail and weep,
For I took you for my best friend.
FIVE WITS: I will no longer thee keep;
Now farewell, and there an end.   (*Exit* FIVE WITS.)
EVERYMAN: O Jesu, help! All hath forsaken me.
GOOD DEEDS: Nay, Everyman; I will bide with thee.
I will not forsake thee indeed;
Thou shalt find me a good friend at need.
EVERYMAN: Gramercy, Good Deeds! Now may I true friends see.
They have forsaken me, every one;
I loved them better than my Good Deeds alone.
Knowledge, will ye forsake me also?
KNOWLEDGE: Yea, Everyman, when ye to Death shall go;
But not yet, for no manner of danger.
EVERYMAN: Gramercy, Knowledge, with all my heart.
KNOWLEDGE: Nay, yet I will not from hence depart
Till I see where ye shall become.
EVERYMAN: Methink, alas, that I must be gone
To make my reckoning and my debts pay,
For I see my time is nigh spent away.
Take example, all ye that this do hear or see,
How they that I loved best do forsake me,
Except my Good Deeds that bideth truly.

GOOD DEEDS: All earthly things is but vanity:
    Beauty, Strength, and Discretion do man forsake,
    Foolish friends, and kinsmen, that fair spake—
    All fleeth save Good Deeds, and that am I.
EVERYMAN: Have mercy on me, God most mighty;
    And stand by me, thou mother and maid, holy Mary.
GOOD DEEDS: Fear not; I will speak for thee.
EVERYMAN: Here I cry God mercy.
GOOD DEEDS: Short[95] our end, and minish our pain;
    Let us go and never come again.
EVERYMAN: Into thy hands, Lord, my soul I commend;
    Receive it, Lord, that it be not lost.
    As thou me boughtest, so me defend,
    And save me from the fiend's boast,
    That I may appear with that blessed host
    That shall be saved at the day of doom.
    In manus tuas, of mights most
    For ever, *commendo spiritum meum.* [96]   *(He sinks into his grave.)*
KNOWLEDGE: Now hath he suffered that we all shall endure;
    The Good Deeds shall make all sure.
    Now hath he made ending;
    Methinketh that I hear angels sing,
    And make great joy and melody
    Where Everyman's soul received shall be.
ANGEL: Come, excellent elect spouse, to Jesu!
    Hereabove thou shalt go
    Because of thy singular virtue.
    Now the soul is taken the body fro,
    Thy reckoning is crystal-clear.
    Now shalt thou into the heavenly sphere,
    Unto the which all ye shall come
    That liveth well before the day of doom.

(Enter DOCTOR*)*

DOCTOR: This moral men may have in mind.
    Ye hearers, take it of worth,[97] old and young,
    And forsake Pride, for he deceiveth you in the end;
    And remember Beauty, Five Wits, Strength, and Discretion,
    They all at the last do every man forsake,
    Save[98] his Good Deeds there doth he take.
    But beware, for and they be small
    Before God, he hath no help at all;
    None excuse may be there for every man.

---

[95] shorten   [96] into they hands I commend my spirit (Luke, 23:46)   [97] value it   [98] unless

Alas, how shall he do then?
For after death amends may no man make,
For then mercy and pity doth him forsake.
If his reckoning be not clear when he doth come,
God will say: *'Ite, maledicti, in ignem eternum.'*[99]
And he that hath his account whole and sound,
High in heaven he shall be crowned;
Unto which place God bring us all thither,
That we may live body and soul together.
Thereto help the Trinity!
Amen, say ye, for saint charity.

Thus Endeth this Moral Play of EVERYMAN.

---

[99] depart, ye cursed, into everlasting fire (Matthew, 25:41)

SUGGESTIONS FOR FURTHER READING

APPIA, ADOLPHE. *The Work of Living Art and Man Is the Measure of All Things.* Coral Gables, Fla.: University of Miami Press, 1960.

BEARE, WILLIAM. *The Roman Stage: A Short History of Latin Drama in the Time of the Republic.* 2nd ed. London: Methuen and Co., 1955.

BIEBER, MARGARETE. *The History of the Greek and Roman Theatre.* 2nd ed. Princeton: Princeton University Press, 1961.

BROCKETT, OSCAR G. *History of the Theatre.* Boston: Allyn and Bacon, 1968.

CHAMBERS, E. K. *The Medieval Stage.* 2 vols. London: Oxford University Press, 1903.

————. *The Elizabethan Stage.* 4 vols. London: Oxford University Press, 1923.

ESSLIN, MARTIN. *The Theatre of the Absurd.* Garden City, N. Y.: Doubleday & Company, Inc., 1961.

HARTNOLL, PHYLLIS, ed. *The Oxford Companion to the Theatre.* 2nd ed. London: Oxford University Press, 1957.

HAVEMEYER, LOOMIS. *The Drama of Savage Peoples.* New Haven: Yale University Press, 1916.

HEWITT, BERNARD. *Theatre USA, 1668-1957.* New York: McGraw-Hill Book Co., 1959.

KERNODLE, GEORGE. *From Art to Theatre: Form and Convention in the Renaissance.* Chicago: University of Chicago Press, 1943.

KITTO, H. D. F. *Greek Tragedy: A Literary Study.* Garden City, N. Y.: Doubleday & Co., 1954.

MACGOWAN, KENNETH, and WILLIAM MELNITZ. *The Living Stage: A History of World Theatre.* Englewood Cliffs, N. J.: Prentice-Hall, Inc., 1955.

NICOLL, ALLARDYCE. *The Development of the Theatre.* 5th ed. London: Harrap & Co., Ltd., 1966.

ROBERTS, VERA MOWRY. *On Stage: A History of Theatre.* New York: Harper & Row, 1962.

Chapter 3

Playhouses and People

This is the church, goes the old rhyme, and this is the steeple; open the doors and see all the people. But what do the people see? Despite occasional modernity, the chances are they see a relic of the Middle Ages.

The same applies to most theatres. Except for those on a few college campuses or in a few fine arts centers, what the people see is a relic of what some Italian Renaissance painters and architects thought they found in the writings of a Roman architect named Vitruvius. *He* thought he was describing what the Greeks had done in Athens some five hundred years before *his* day.

As we noted in Chapter 2, the Renaissance painters and architects decided that a play is a picture, beautifully drawn to the laws of perspective and designed to be viewed from far away. The proscenium opening is a frame for this picture. Everything that happens within the frame is controlled by the scenic artist. The play becomes a *tableau vivant,* and the audience is expected simply to marvel at the wonders. The place for the audience fans out from the stage or the pit that usually separates stage from audience. Since the Renaissance painters and architects were usually supported by a single wealthy patron, one seat in the auditorium was perfect and the others were largely ignored. Theatres in this style today attempt to make all the seats worthwhile. By and large, however, most proscenium theatres contain more bad seats than good.

Yet most towns and most campuses have at least one theatre. Despite obvious problems in the esthetic experience, many people attend these theatres. Frequently they are enriched by the experience. The point we must continue to note, however, is that more people would participate in the theatre and its drama and the enrichment would probably be far greater if architects could invent a building which accomplished all the conflicting ideals that should control the theatrical experience.

Many new theatres have experimented with just this problem, particularly on university campuses. Taken in the abstract, there are three modes of organizing people in a playhouse. We will examine these modes in some detail, then describe the standard theatre, and finally delineate the principles that inform an ideal playhouse.

Arena Staging[1]

Picture yourself in a crowd of people. No one notices anyone else. Suddenly there is a quarrel that quickly escalates into a fight. Two men begin wrestling on the floor. Probably the remaining people will group themselves into a circle with the fighting area at the center.

Or, to be less violent, suppose you are at a dance. Many couples are sharing the dance floor. As the dancing becomes more and more frenetic, one or two couples really get carried away. Their gyrations become so noticeable and perhaps so artistic that the other dancers stop to observe. Once again the crowd probably forms itself into a circle with the performers at the center.

These not so far-fetched examples show how easy and natural it is to develop an arena stage. Whatever happens in the arena, the crowd is perhaps best situated if it sits around the performing area. If the spectators are arranged in tiers, each row of people will be able to see easily. If the farthest row is within easy earshot, hearing will be no problem. Probably audience involvement in the drama will occur with considerable ease.

Distancing, however, is difficult to achieve in arena staging. Since the theatre is usually small, the audience tends to participate in the action onstage without being particularly aware that a game is occurring. The classic example of the spectator who stepped into the arena to light an actor's cigaret when the performer's lighter failed reveals the tendency to merge the theatre game with one's own life. Even the obvious presence of spectators on the other sides of the arena does not seem to aid distancing particularly. Apparently the sight of other people concentrating on the arena, though it may cause some distancing, actually increases one's own sense of involvement. On the other hand, the sight of empty seats across the arena probably reduces the feeling of involvement.

Moreover, though size of the house is not automatically controlled by the desire to group people about an arena, the tendency is to keep such a theatre small. One of the finest professional repertory theatres in the United States, *Theatre '48* in Dallas, Texas, failed to take hold of the

1. The terms used in this chapter to describe various kinds of theatre space are derived from two textbooks: H. D. Albright, W. P. Halstead, and Lee Mitchell, *Principles of Theatre Art* (2nd ed. Boston: Houghton Mifflin Co., 1968), p. 146, and Alan H. Downer, *The Art of the Play: An Anthology of Nine Plays* (New York: Holt, Rinehart and Winston, 1955), pp. 56-125. Both these textbooks define the terms somewhat differently, however, and focus primarily on the appearance of the theatre styles in history.

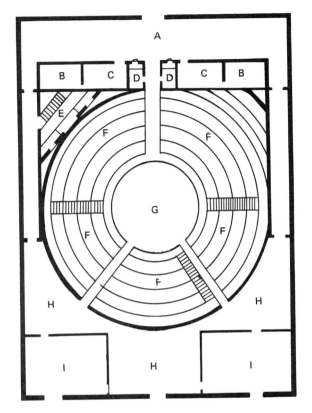

A. Lobby.
B. Restrooms.
C. Lounges.
D. Boxoffices.
E. Light and sound booth.
F. Audience seating on
   raised levels.
G. Acting area.
H. Construction and back-
   stage work area.
I. Dressing rooms.

FIGURE 3.1. Floor plan of an arena theatre.

city despite excellent productions. One of the reasons may have been the small size of the theatre. Laying aside considerations of comfort, there were only so many seats to be filled. When every seat was occupied, there was still no *crowd*. The individual spectator felt lonely and shut-in, rather than expanded and fulfilled. This problem may be concomitant with size, but it also may be inherent in arena staging. After all, a person on one side of the audience is in fact part of only one-fourth of the group. The impact of the crowd is diminished by more than half.

Awareness of the crowd—of being part of something larger than one-self—suffers from the same problem of division. The lateral interaction among the spectators is weakened even when all the seats on a given side of the arena are occupied. If only a few people are present, there is apt to be no crowd effect at all. At a recent arena production of *Little Mary Sunshine*, for example, I sat with eight scattered patrons on one side of a square arena. The seats on the side to my left were all occupied. At some of the funniest moments in the production, when spectators in the filled side were laughing uproariously, the eight of us on the empty East Side merely sat glumly silent. In two-and-one-half hours, I laughed four or five times at the most.

Even when the audience is a full house and the spectators merge easily together and focus their attention on the arena, there is still the problem of symbolizing the community. A few properties, perhaps a low set piece or two, and the scenic possibilities of the arena stage are exhausted. Although successful companies perform all types of plays in the arena, a drama that depends heavily on an elaborate scenic apparatus and hundreds of properties—for instance, *Major Barbara*—is difficult to realize as its playwright intended it to be shown. The audience cannot easily be presented with evidence of its belonging to a community.

Furthermore, all members of this community are not seeing the same play. Those seated on a given circle of the three or four concentric ones may possibly share the same involvement and the same distancing, but as the spectator-area fans out, each concentric group experiences something a little different. Experiments have been made with less regular arrangements in the hope of avoiding this problem. For example, a seven-eighths arena with the stage shaped like a keyhole, and with entrances from every compass point and the audience seated along the whole periphery worked fairly well for a recent production of *Huckleberry Finn*. Practically every spectator saw the same play as every other spectator.

None of these experiments, however, dealt properly with the problem of audience concentration. Although arena staging contains a high degree of involvement, the intensity of concentration varies more obviously than in other types of theatre. Only one place onstage—the exact center— feels the full force of the audience. All other parts of the stage are farther from some spectators than from others. When the actors are on my side of the arena, for example, I have stronger ties with them than when they are on the other side. The direction they are facing receives *their* fullest concentration. Also, patterns of movement may be severely limited by the necessity for having the actor keep his face moving. It is thus too easy for groupings without dramaturgic or symbolic significance to occur over and over in arena staging.

Proscenium Staging

Perhaps because we are used to the idea, or perhaps because it is just as natural as "forming a circle," crowds can collect in such a way that the wrestlers or the dancers we mentioned earlier occupy a space on one side of a dividing line while the spectators are grouped on the other. Because of the difficulty in seeing if both remain on one level, it is also natural to raise the stage or the spectators, or both.

The important difference from arena staging lies in the separation of actors and audience into two distinct groups. The spectators all face in one direction and the actors play in front of them. The proscenium stage, with or without its framing arch, functions always as a tableau—a kind of live motion picture. The players are *there*, and the spectators are *here*, and it is somewhat like a gigantic art museum.

One of the prime characteristics of the proscenium stage, in fact, is the importance of painting—whether with pigment or with light. If three-dimensional construction is called for, moreover, the carpenter becomes as important as the painter or the lighting technician. These craftsmen can provide any kind of locale, in any kind of style, that a drama may call for.

The use of locale provides a handy method for describing three types of proscenium staging. First the locale may remain the same for the entire drama. It is "Outside the Palace of Oedipus" for the whole performance. The actors perform in front of this facade. While the use of the scenery and the equipment which is part of it may vary from play to play, the *formal setting* remains throughout and serves to collect and unite the various human actions being presented.

The second type of proscenium staging is a natural variation of the first. Very little imagination is required to desire the facade to change from scene to scene. While the overall structure may remain the same, key changes occur to indicate "Another Part of the Forest." Pieces of scenery fly in, roll in, spin, rise, or descend. The actors have as many ways of entering as the scenery, but they perform always in front of it. Walls, doors, pictures, or whatever serve merely as the background for the performers. The scenic devices may achieve quite spectacular effects, but the actor is as much a spectator as the audience. Or sometimes he is simply part of the scenery—frozen into a tableau.

The term we will use for this kind of staging—in which the scenery may represent any aspect of the community and may be quite localized—is *theatrical setting*. A third type of setting is called *actualistic*. The scenery is just as localized, just as changeable, as for the theatrical stage, but the actors use the setting as environment rather than as backdrop. Instead of playing in front of the setting, the actor lives *in* it.

All three variations—formal, theatrical, and actualistic—contain the virtues and flaws inherent in proscenium staging. One virtue, outside the range of our criteria, is the proscenium theatre's ubiquity. In its present form this theatre has been standard in Western Civilization since at least 1600, and one can make a case for its appearance several thousand years before that. Few people today can even think of another arrangement for spectators and their drama.

Popular as it is, the proscenium stage unfortunately encourages the idea that a play is something to view from afar, to be distanced from, to examine coldly as one does a picture or a tableau in a museum. Seeing and hearing properly depends on the size and acoustics of the building.

Hearing, in particular, need be no problem if the engineers know what they are doing, regardless of the theatre's size. Even with artificial amplification, though hearing may no longer be related to size, acoustics can still prove bothersome. Seeing the play well, however, does depend on the size of the auditorium. No matter how many seats are provided, the key factor is distance from a given spectator to the stage. A play viewed through the wrong end of a telescope is no play at all.

The point to be made is not architectural but esthetic. If a play *is* a picture to be viewed from afar, then it does not matter where the viewer sits, so long as he can see the entire picture. Anything that distracts him from the viewing is harmful, much like small boys wrestling on the floor near where one contemplates a Van Gogh. On the other hand, if theatre is a game people play with the help of actors and other artists, and it is necessary for the spectators as well as the actors to be *players,* then the proscenium stage may easily be detrimental to this involvement. Two psychological elements in this activity—identification and projection—depend a great deal on perception. If actor and spectator are separated enough for perception to be interfered with, participation on the part of the audience may require extreme psychic effort that may not be forthcoming.

Yet who can predict the activity of innate psychological processes or the amount of effort a spectator may bring to a play? Some involvement may always occur, and size may be the controlling factor. At a performance of *A Funny Thing Happened on the Way to the Forum,* I found nothing funny from the last row of the top balcony. Zero Mostel appeared to be about the size of Mickey Rooney, and much of the drama's comic business was wasted. From one performance of *The Boy Friend,* I can remember only moving heads and arms seen from a balcony seat almost directly above the stage. Another time, I saw the musical from a balcony about fifty yards from the stage. The actors were mere shadows against the scenery. Admittedly, however, I have never had an involvement problem in the several proscenium theatres I know of in which the farthest any spectator is from the stage is fifty feet.

As you may have guessed from the foregoing discussion, any proscenium staging is particularly helpful with distancing. The spectator cannot help being aware that he is in a theatre. Even with actualistic staging in which the proscenium opening is supposedly a fourth wall of someone's house, the signs of a theatre are as impelling as the action onstage. The architecture tells the spectator point-blank that he cannot be Othello because the Moor is *there* and the spectator is *here.* In fact, a great deal of the actor's technique and energy is spent overcoming the distance between drama and spectator.

If esthetic distance is necessary for enjoyment of a play, the proscenium theatre scores one hundred per cent in this category. The need for a crowd is usually well-met, too. One reason this type of theatre building is popular lies in its capacity for large audiences. If the patrons can be attracted, the return on the promoter's investment is extremely good when the auditorium is oversized. Consequently, most proscenium theatres are made to hold a great many people. If the seats are filled, or are filled from the front, the impact of the crowd is almost always overwhelming.

Awareness of the crowd is seldom a problem, either. True, the spectator can *see* only those in front of him or to the side. But he can *feel* the others because the group is acting as a unit and because, as a rule, the seats are close together. He literally touches those around him. This massive reaction in a single direction, toward a single stimulus, appears to swallow up the individual playgoer. He feels expanded and enlarged by the presence of so many others behaving as he does.

Probably the most helpful aspect of proscenium staging, however, is its ability to symbolize the community the drama is representing. We have already noted the importance of painters and lighting technicians in this type of theatre. Whatever its style, the setting reinforces the drama by stating totally and visually the central idea, or any subsidiary ideas, and by collecting and uniting all the separate dramatic actions and all the artistic contributions into a single theatrical image. The stage itself can become the world of the spectator.

Unfortunately this world may be different as one moves from place to place in the auditorium. The desire to provide equality of experience for each spectator cannot possibly be met when the audience is fanned out from a line or a space that separates playgoer from player. Examined logically or geometrically, of course, the fan-shaped auditorium would seem ideally suited for giving all the people seated in a particular transverse row the same experience of the stage. If so, there would be a gradual but slight diminuendo of experience as the spectator moved to the rear of the auditorium. Rarely, however, does this seem to be the case. Whole sections of seats are excellent—and bring top prices—and other sections are terrible. The effect of the last row in the balcony of a New York theatre has already been noted. In many "Broadway" theatres, the very best seats are in the first balcony. The orchestra seats are below the stage level, and the other balconies soar steeply into the stratosphere.

Yet the desire for evenness in the distribution of the energy resulting from audience concentration is usually encouraged by proscenium staging. On a given plane running across the stage there is relatively little difference in the effect of a given position. Downstage areas are generally considered to have more impact than upstage areas, but there seems to be very little change as an actor crosses from left to right or from right to left. The cross itself may vary in forcefulness—left to right being stronger than right to left (from the audience's point of view) because of Occidental reading habits—but even this assertion is largely hypothetical or personal.

Panoramic Staging

There seems to be no reason plays cannot occur both within and in front of their audiences. The advantages of arena and proscenium staging can be combined. One authority has called this stage the *focused playhouse,* referring to Ancient Greece, and the *panoramic playhouse* referring to Europe in the Middle Ages and the time of Elizabeth I and James I in England. Another commentator prefers to use *formal staging* when describing the Greeks; *simultaneous staging* when dealing with the medieval period; and *multiple staging* when writing about the Elizabethan theatre.[2]

As we examine the possibilities of combining the effects of arena and proscenium staging, we can borrow these terms and put them to our own uses. *Panoramic* describes a theatre in which the action of a drama may or may not change locales but the performance occurs sometimes in front of and sometimes within the audience. When the locales do not change with the movement of the actors, the setting is *formal* or *focused.* When different places on the stage represent different locales which are set up permanently but which do not figure in the action until the actors move into them, the setting may be called *simultaneous.* Finally, when separate parts of the stage represent separate locales which are *not* set up permanently but which the actor can both activate and change ("How sweet the moonlight sleeps upon this bank!"), the staging is *multiple.*

Quite obviously, simultaneous or multiple effects can be achieved in the proscenium theatre alone and in the arena theatre alone, though the latter is less obvious. But if we assume the panoramic playhouse already described, what do we find? Seeing and hearing the drama—and becoming involved in it—depends on the size and the layout of the theatre. If each locale is truly a separate *stage,* with the audience passing by as at a carnival midway, the milling about will probably decrease the involvement of the audience. Should all the locales be in performance simultaneously, one may distract the audience from another. Performing the locale in a church alcove, a stall, or a wagon may reduce the involvement to that of the proscenium stage unless there is a platform thrust out into the audience.

These same observations apply to the multiple setting unless part of the playing area lies within the audience and unless the spectators are somehow permanently grouped around the stage. If these two conditions exist, and the patrons are close to the players, involvement in the action will be as strong as in arena staging.

The phantasmagoria of human actions may inhibit audience involvement in simultaneous or multiple staging, but not in formal or focused staging as we have defined it. If all the locales are collected in a single

---

2. See note, p. 166

area, the architecture will encourage unity and singleness of effect. As a rule, moreover, a play's dramatic construct will provide unity of action among the multiplicity of effects. The theatrical experience may be "The Old Testament" or "Man's Journey Through Life," or it may be *The Tragedy of Othello, The Moor of Venice*. There is no reason, that is, for a drama to be limited in scope if the action being portrayed is singular. As a matter of fact, increasing the scope may make the drama more lifelike in that it recreates the "circus of human actions" that comprise "experience."

If the architecture permits, therefore, involvement in a panorama of events is probably no more difficult than involvement in a single event. Coalescing the separate locales into a single playing area, whether they are structured permanently or created momentarily, undoubtedly will enhance distancing. If each locale on stage is set up permanently, each will impinge on the audience at all times regardless of which one is being used at a given moment. Even if each part of the stage is neutral and changes locale at the actor's whim, the space and whatever structures there are will remind the audience that everyone is playing. Moreover, there is no reason for the structure itself to be bare or empty. Any decoration is permissible, so long as it is unlocalized.

Nothing inherent in the panoramic playhouse works against having audiences large enough to be called a crowd. The focused theatre of the Greeks contained more than fifteen thousand people, the multiple stage of the Elizabethans around two thousand, and the simultaneous stages of the Medieval Period a random number but perhaps the entire population of a village. The problem is not crowd size but division into pockets of attention. Simultaneous stages not coalesced tend to break their audiences into small groups that cannot function as a crowd. We have already noted this effect in the arena theatre. The audience must be grouped so that the drama is surrounded without separation between parts of the audience.

Awareness of the crowd is also affected by the amorphous quality of an audience witnessing several stages simultaneously and by the problem of dividing the audience into several groups that fail to interact. The architecture of the panoramic theatre must coalesce the audience as well as the many stages into one artistic whole.

The playing area itself, though part of it may be an arena or a forestage, seems amply equipped to provide symbols of the community or any portion of it. The concepts which were applied to the proscenium stage, also fit the panoramic playhouse. Sometimes the setting is background, changing or unchanging, and sometimes it is environment. The degree of actualism may vary from pure theatre ("Well, this is the forest of Arden," says Rosalind in the midst of a bare stage.) to a scene that must be actual ("Desdemona asleep in her bed. Enter Othello with a light."). Historically, in fact, it was naturalism as much as anything else that forced the medieval plays out of the churches. On the other hand, despite the capacity for employing environment when necessary, the Elizabethan playhouse was capable of symbolizing the Elizabethan world-view through a structured joining of hell, earth, and heaven. The mulitple actions were thus played within man's view of the universe. The degree of actualism or the use made of conventions from painting and sculpture in the panoramic playhouse may be debatable, but the *possibility* of symbolizing the community of playgoers is not.

Of special importance to this symbolizing is the inherent flexibility of the panoramic stage, particularly when multiple settings are used. Nearly all the techniques of the motion picture are available—with the added attraction of being *alive*. Long shots, close-ups, dissolves, split-screens, montages, even with lighting fade-outs and fade-ins—these and other filmic devices are the rule rather than the exception in dramas conceived for the panoramic stage. Moreover, elaborate scenic effects can be accomplished by preparing tableaux behind draperies which are drawn across one or more of the separate areas. The stage thus may symbolize not only the total community but any of its parts or aspects.

Like the arena theatre and the proscenium theatre, however, the panoramic playhouse has trouble establishing an equality of theatrical experience for all spectators. Each person in the audience takes up a certain amount of space. If each space is organized into a pattern (rows of seats, aisles, and so forth), some people are bound to see a different play than others. The multiple stage at Stratford, Canada, for example, works beautifully for the actors. The audience, however, is spread out so far from the playing area few spectators have any feeling of sharing the same drama with their cohorts. Spreading simultaneous stages over a wide area—with audiences partaking of each stage at will—probably works against equality of experience.

A partial solution lies in the staging, but the complete answer must somehow be derived from the premise underlying the panoramic theatre. The staging answer is like that for arena: keep the actors moving, make use of all areas and all possible devices to hold and involve the audience, and stress the total experience rather than any of its parts. The danger here lies in activity or artistic gambits used for their own sake.

The premise controlling panoramic theatre is that playgoers and players are *both* participants in the drama. There is no real separation between audience and stage. Taken to its logical conclusion, this premise means that all playgoers will share the drama equally because they are playing it in unison with the actors. Unfortunately, few playhouses seek this ideal through their architecture. Most depend on the individual playwright or director to solve the esthetic problems of space for actors and audience to play a drama.

The problem of audience concentration may be studied in this same manner. Proper staging for the panoramic playhouse uses all areas and all techniques that are available. But staging for its own sake is often the result. And the presence of other stages than the one being used at a given moment works to dissipate the intensity of audience concentration. The question must be "To what extent does this dissipation counteract the sense of total theatre—of being swept up into the drama of human life portrayed as it is normally lived—a wild and spinning phantasmagoria?" Once again the answer should come from architect or audience, rather than playwright and director.

The Standard Theatre

Regardless of architectural style, the standard theatre calls for several structures that are more or less universal. They may be listed as follows:

1. *Lobby area*, with ticket booth, rest rooms, food counter.
2. *Audience area*, arranged so all may see and hear as well as possible given the size.
3. *Orchestra pit*, below and in front of the stage.
4. *Apron*, in front of the stage proper.
5. *Proscenium arch and opening*, with up to three curtains hanging just upstage and opening at will.
6. *Teaser and tormentor curtain strips*, masking the backstage area when the main curtains are open.
7. *Battens*, on which lights and special curtains are hung.
8. *Stage floor.*
9. *Fly loft*, the space above the stage higher than the top of the proscenium arch.
10. *Gridiron*, near the ceiling.
11. *Counterweight system and pinrail.*
12. *Scene dock.*
13. *Sky dome or cyclorama.*
14. *Trapdoors* in the stage floor.
15. *Loading facilities.*
16. *Lighting and sound control boards.*
17. *Shop.*
18. *Dressing Rooms, Greenroom, Rehearsal Room.*

Designer, technical director, crew chiefs, and crews will seldom have anything to say about the building. If there is a choice, however, they must first make sure the audience can see and hear the actors with ease and some comfort. Access to the seats should be as simple as possible, and there must be easy exit in case of fire. There should be ample facilities for meeting the spectators' bodily needs. The playing area should be large enough for any type of scene. Whatever equipment it requires must be provided. The actors need a place to stay when not on stage; make-up can be applied and removed there as well. Lights and sound ought to have a control board, or at least a place where control can be exercised. If scenery is to be constructed in the building, a shop is necessary. If scenery is to be stored, a scene dock is required.

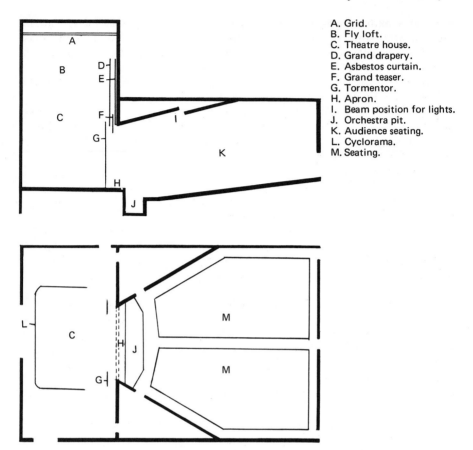

A. Grid.
B. Fly loft.
C. Theatre house.
D. Grand drapery.
E. Asbestos curtain.
F. Grand teaser.
G. Tormentor.
H. Apron.
I. Beam position for lights.
J. Orchestra pit.
K. Audience seating.
L. Cyclorama.
M. Seating.

FIGURE 3.2. Cross section and floor plan of a proscenium theatre.

It is fashionable these days to put several different types of theatres into a single building. Sometimes the differences are only in size, however. Another popular gambit is to create a building that allows change from one kind of theatre to another within the same space. Placement of seats is altered while the stage is shifted from one position to another. Often the only change possible in such a *flexible theatre* is the replacement of orchestra pit with platforms that create a thrust stage.

Wherever the stage is, whatever its structure, the audience must be placed so that a maximum number of people can be collected together. Usually aisles run through the spectators, or past the ends of rows, or both. Though no esthetic reason exists to require seating, it is normal to seat the spectators. The seats may be comfortable or uncomfortable, and a case can be made for each state. What is called *continental seating*— in which aisles are eliminated and sufficient space is provided between rows so a seated person does not have to rise to let others pass—can be used. It accommodates nearly as many spectators as grouping with aisles, but fire laws often demand the construction of aisles from which no seat is more than six places distant.

Groups of seats can be on one or more floors. The first row in the balcony can be boxes for special (or wealthy) spectators, and in many commercial theatres the boxes extend from the balcony along both sides of the auditorium to the edge of the proscenium arch. Even where boxes no longer appear in balconies, they are retained as decoration at the sides of the proscenium.

The problem, as we noted earlier, is to let the patrons see and hear the actors. Though this is a problem in all theatre styles, it is particularly acute in proscenium theatres. Let us take seeing first. Most buildings seek to compromise among the three possibilities: square, elliptical or oval and fan-shaped. The square arrangement is the easiest to construct in a rectangular building, but it provides neither good seeing nor good hearing. The elliptical or oval auditorium provides good hearing but bad seeing. The fan-shaped grouping can offer the best combination of good seeing and good hearing.

It has been estimated that six hundred is the maximum number of spectators a theatre can have if all of them are to see well enough to obtain a nearly uniform impression of the stage and its action.[3] Most proscenium theatres double or triple this number and thus presumably allow only a third or a half of their audiences to see the drama properly. The larger auditoriums seem to be tunnels, or telescopes, through which the drama is viewed from far-off. The telescope seems turned around, and the stage action looks to be "some other where."

To help reduce this effect, the side walls may be curved slightly, or broken with exits, or both. A large auditorium may be twice as wide as the proscenium opening, but a small one cannot spread this much. Even in a small auditorium, it is difficult to arrange things so every spectator can see all of the action on the stage. Psychologically, the seats in the back always seem farther from the stage than they are—which in most proscenium theatres is far enough.

To aid visibility, many theatres have raked floors. That is, seats more distant from the stage are elevated in relation to those nearer the stage. Fire laws require ramped aisles with no steps, so the rake usually is much too shallow to do much good. When the slope is straight, the tunnel effect is increased. A better approach is to dish the floor—rake it increasingly toward the back. Increased distance is compensated for by having the back spectators on a better level with the stage than the patrons down front. As a rule, however, because of the fire laws, the

---

3. See Kenneth MacGowan, "Architecture for the Audience," in "Papers Presented at the Eighth Ann Arbor Conference: The Theatre" (University of Michigan College of Architecture and Design, 1950), p. 9. (Mimeographed.) Cited in Albright, Halstead, and Mitchell, p. 174.

dish is too shallow to help much. Another approach is the stadium slope, in which the seats are arranged in the manner of a football stadium. This provides good sight lines and good acoustics, but is seldom used. What is most usual in proscenium theatres is a slightly raked orchestra floor accompanied by one or more steeply raked balconies. Though this arrangement provides maximum seating capacity, the worst features of straight and shallow-dished slopes are combined to make a theatre in which only a small percentage of the spectators can see anything much at all on the stage.

The foregoing discussion of "sight lines" has often mentioned the problem of hearing. If the actors are heard clearly and with force, they seem to grow in stature. An actor the audience can hear seems to be seen more fully as well. It is unfortunate, therefore, that in many proscenium theatres hearing is next to impossible except in a few of the seats. The problem is less acute in a small theatre than in a large one, but acoustics are not inherently related to size. Sound reflects in a straight line from hard surfaces, just as light does, but is absorbed by soft or porous surfaces. In a small space, unlike light, sound can be amplified. Since the amplification may distort the quality of the sound, this is not necessarily helpful. Both to the listener and to the reflecting surfaces, the sound moves in a straight line. After leaving the reflector, the sound must be diffused or it will become an echo. Thus, to construct an auditorium in which every spectator hears the same play at the same time without distortion of any kind is probably more difficult than to provide acceptable sight lines.

Other things being equal, seeing and hearing the play affect the spectator's sense of comfort. Absorbed in the drama, he forgets hard and badly-shaped seats, poor ventilation, uneven temperature, and other problems. But since most theatres of the modern world do not allow for proper seeing and hearing, the spectator usually is given as much comfort as possible—well-shaped and well-spaced seats, good heating and cooling, acceptable ventilation, and so forth. Another aspect of comfort is the decor. Furnishings and decoration in the lobby and the auditorium should contribute to the festive mood of the spectator—help him enjoy the play, that is.

Comfort also resides in safety. A theatre building must be constructed so that fire and panic cannot occur, can be controlled with ease, or can have as little effect on the audience as possible. Most fire codes require an asbestos curtain between audience and stage, with a mechanism that lowers the curtain automatically in case of fire; an adequate number of clearly-designated fire exits; open passages for escape; and adequate flame-proofing of all scenery. Obviously, no smoking can be allowed in the auditorium or backstage.

Having the audience comfortable and in a position to see and hear is only a small part of the problem with the theatre building. Whether proscenium theatre or some other type, there must be space for actors in view of the spectators and for actors and technicians out of sight of the audience. The stagehouse ought to have at least the same amount of space as the auditorium, though the shape is vertical rather than horizontal.

Much of the time the acting area, whether arena or proscenium, is rather small. Also most of the time, unfortunately, the backstage area is severely restricted. What is needed is vertical and horizontal room to store scenery, equipment, and actors: ideally sixty to ninety feet in width, forty-five to sixty feet in depth, and seventy-five to ninety feet in height. Where the proscenium is thirty feet wide and eighteen feet high—the ordinary, though not standard, dimensions—the backstage would contain 357 to 881 cubic feet for each square foot of proscenium opening. The height of the proscenium is usually three-fifths of its width.

Almost as important as total space backstage is the placing of equipment. There should be as much wall space as possible. Necessary items of equipment should be grouped together, preferably in corners. There should be working space above the gridiron, which is a framework of steel beams near the top of the stagehouse in a proscenium theatre and which is used to support the rigging needed for flying scenery.

Close to or part of the proscenium arch are a number of curtains. From the proscenium to upstage, there is first the fire curtain. This is supposed to keep backstage fires, if such occur, from reaching the audience. Immediately upstage from the fire curtain is the grand drapery, an elaborate valance that dresses the proscenium arch. Not all theatres have a grand drapery, since it is decorative only and since it fits only period-style auditoriums. Next is the act curtain that is used to close off the scenes in a play. Some theatres have tableau and contour curtains as well, although these are not ordinarily needed. As a rule, directly upstage of the act curtain is the teaser—a horizontal frame usually covered with black velour. It should be possible to raise and lower the teaser, which should be at least four feet wider than the proscenium arch. Right and left of the scene are masking frames, usually covered in black velour, called tormentors. They should be as tall as the proscenium height and should be capable of being moved on and off stage.

In the space over the stage and below the gridiron—called rigging loft, fly loft, or flies—there may be hung a series of steel pipes several feet longer than the arch is wide and hanging in rows from downstage to upstage. From these pipes—called battens—are hung scenery, lights, or anything else that needs to be raised out of sight and lowered into the scene.

The battens are usually hung by ropes or wires tied into a counterweight system with a pinrail. The lines pass through the gridiron pulleys, or loft blocks, over the gridiron and toward a side wall, where the lines go through a head block containing a sheave for each line. The lines have counterweights tied into them and are fastened to the pinrail. The lines are controlled at the rail, and enough weights are placed on each line so the object flown is slightly heavier than the weights. The pinrail and the tieoff rail may be on the floor or just below the gridiron.

The back wall of a stage sometimes must serve as part of the scene. Some theatres have this wall plastered and curved so as to seem to be a sky. It is more efficient to have a cloth cyclorama, or sky drop, that curves around the upper portion of the stage. When used, it can give beautiful sky effects; when not needed, the drop can be flown out of sight. Though it limits backstage space, entrances, and the use of light projections, the cyclorama is capable of producing an illusion of great distance.

The stage floor itself—the playing area for all types of theatre—is the single most important part of the stage house. It is made of soft wood that is unvarnished. Downstage is toward the audience; upstage, away from the audience. At one time these two terms were literal; the upstage portion of the floor was higher than the downstage portion. Right and left are measured facing the audience, and as a rule the floor is thought of as having areas: Down Left, Down Center, Down Right; Up Left, Up Center, and Up Right. One side of the stage—the right in the United States, the left in England—is the prompt side. Here are usually found controls for lights and sound, if there is no booth at the rear of the auditorium, the pinrail, the curtain-pull, and a place for the stage manager. The other side of the stage is known as the opposite prompt, or O. P., side. All offstage space is called the wings.

It is helpful if the floor has trapdoors that allow entrances and exits from the sub-floor area. Further help is obtained when some kind of elevator is part of the trap.

Moving stages have been used in many plays and constructed for many theatres. Often all or a part of the floor revolves and/or descends into the basement—and sometimes both movements are possible simultaneously. The problem with such stages, however, is the amount of space and expensive machinery they require. A reasonable substitute for moving floors are wagons or platforms that move across the floor and are temporarily constructed for a given drama. The moving portions may revolve, slide from left to right or right to left, or swing into the proscenium like a jackknife.

The playing area may extend beyond the proscenium opening into what is called the apron or, when it extends far enough, the forestage. If there is an orchestra pit, platforms may be constructed that cover it with a floor at stage level. Sometimes the floor of the pit itself can be raised to the level of the stage floor. All parts of the floor often are, and probably should be covered. This ground cloth is usually heavy brown canvas, though carpeting and even linoleum may be used.

In the non-professional theatre at least, the building ought to contain a place for scene construction and storage. A well-equipped shop either near the stage or connected to it by elevator, and a place to build and paint scenery, are necessities. Whether or not the construction facilities are in the same building as the stage, the theatre should have adequate facilities for loading—a door and a platform both at stage level and at truck-bed level when the truck is backed up to the door. Needless to say, the door should accommodate the largest scenery.

Offstage there must be places for actors to dress, to make up, and to rest before and during the performance. Traditionally the gathering place for actors is the greenroom. The dressing rooms, which may be combined with or separate from the greenroom, require mirrors, lights, tables, and chairs. Lockers are also helpful. As a rule there are different rooms for each sex, with adequate toilet and washing facilities in both dressing rooms.

Finally, a space that most theatres need but few have is a rehearsal room. It is axiomatic that a theatre will usually be required to do double duty. Even if this is avoided, the theatrical season may contain so many plays or so many long runs that rehearsal time onstage may be short. Hence a room in the dimensions of the stage and perhaps equipped with lights and other paraphernalia should be a permanent part of the theatre.

The Ideal Playhouse

This book is for college students. Talking with students, particularly freshmen, is seldom so difficult as talking with architects, building committees, and even other theatre professors about the ideal playhouse. Everyone agrees that it is something we would like to have, someday, somewhere, but that reconciling differences among the concepts of what is ideal seems impossible. Recently, for example, two hours were spent in a meeting with a fine arts building committee trying to get the word "auditorium" changed to "theatre" in the committee's proposal. And when theatre was defined as a playhouse in the literal sense of "a place to play," even several of the theatre faculty stopped listening.

Most of us are conditioned by four hundred years of exposure to the Renaissance theatre—what some Italian painters thought a Roman architect reported that the Ancient Greeks had used. Today many school boards compound this error by constructing *cafetoriums* and *gymnatoriums*. These structures may serve for eating lunch or playing basketball; they are practically worthless as theatres.

If agreement on *this* point seems to be widespread, probably the unanimity comes from agreement about what facilities every theatre should have. There is also a fair amount of consensus on the need to consider more than one method of organizing the audience-actor relationship. Theatre artists no doubt prefer having the capability to play their dramas at will in any of the three staging possibilities: *within* the audience (arena), *in front of* the audience (proscenium), and *both within and in front of the audience at the same time* (panoramic).

Such flexibility may well be the only ideal theatre that is truly possible. Whether this goal is sought, or whether the attempt is made to create the ideal in a single playhouse—regardless of what the structure looks like as a *building*—there are seven principles that should govern the arrangement of theatre space. Whatever its design, and assuming it contains the proper facilities, any playhouse must conform to the following principles:

1. The audience must be in a position to see and hear the players easily, so that involvement—that is identification, projection, rationalization, and impersonation—may occur as spontaneously as possible. *The spectators should feel they are part of the action onstage.*
2. The audience must also feel separated from the stage. Such distancing may be psychological rather than architectural, so long as *the spectators realize they are playing in a theatre.*
3. Because theatre is a crowd experience, there must be room for a large number of people where the audience is placed. The precise number is debatable. *The spectator must be able to lose his individuality by joining the crowd.*
4. *Each member of the audience should be aware of the group as a whole.* Group awareness aids involvement by reducing inhibitions while helping create esthetic distance through knowledge of the crowd of spectators.
5. Without undue separation between audience and actor, the stage must be designed to symbolize *either* the audience's community as a whole *or* some part of it, *or both.* Moreover, the stage must be capable of being transformed into a setting that may range from pure symbolism to complete actuality. *The stage and the drama must stand for the world of the spectator.*
6. *Each member of the audience should have approximately the same theatrical experience as every other member.*
7. Since the drama exists onstage largely because the audience "wills it," *the audience must be positioned so that the entire playing area receives the full impact of audience concentration.*

All the other problems inherent in building a theatre—backstage space, lobby space, aisles and seating, rest rooms, and the like—may be structured in any suitable manner. If the playhouse is esthetically right for the *game of theatre,* all the rest will follow.

Suggestions for Further Reading

Albright, H. D., William P. Halstead, and Lee Mitchell. *Principles of Theatre Art.* 2nd ed. Boston: Houghton Mifflin Co., 1968.

Burris-Meyer, Harold, and Edward C. Cole. *Theatres and Auditoriums.* New York: Reinhold, 1948.

Downer, Alan H. *The Art of the Play: An Anthology of Nine Plays.* New York: Holt, Rinehart and Winston, 1955.

Isaacs, Edith J. R. *Architecture for the New Theatre.* New York: Theatre Arts, Inc., 1935.

Macgowan, Kenneth. *The Theatre of Tomorrow.* New York: Boni & Liveright, 1921.

Chapter 4

Mountebanks and Players

Is it not monstrous, says Hamlet, that a player in a dream of passion can with his voice and body create all the aspects of Hecuba weeping for her lost children and city, while *he* can do and say nothing to avenge a father murdered? Though we do not share Hamlet's personal problem, we can still wonder how it is an actor works his will with us. We *know* he is pretending—in a theatre we are all pretending—but we are moved to tears and laughter nonetheless.

This pretense is the place to start our analysis of acting. Who has not imagined a brave new world peopled with creatures like himself, in which he may triumph gloriously or fail miserably, but live more fully regardless? Only a child may do it overtly, unashamed, but it is the human condition to live in dreams. Except for the most creative among us, however, these dreams are truncated unless someone lives them with us. If I am a "cowboy," I must have an "Indian." We do not play "Cops," but "Cops and Robbers." Our next step is to have them both in our dream, but separate from us, so we may vicariously assume both roles simultaneously. That way we can double our participation and therefore our fun.

This is where the actor comes in: he incarnates our dreams. First, we must be present in a crowd. Then we must concentrate all the psychic energy of our dreams on the stage. The area we concentrate on, whether as large as the total stage or as small as the space occupied by a single actor, becomes a "magic circle." Finally, the actor assumes a place in the circle. With energy and skill he focuses so strongly on the imaginary circumstances of the drama that all of us come to believe it.

If the dramatic circumstances and the character who is involved in it were *real*, what would he *do* and *how would he go about it?* This is the question answered by the actor with his mind and body. Acting, that is, means doing what the drama and the audience require.

As a rule, the stage is peopled with more than one character. If two or more are on the stage at the same time, then our dream must have more than one actor. Though we still must imagine the drama, much more complicated actions are possible. Our imagination delightfully moves from a one-character, small-scale dream to a multi-character extravaganza. As a matter of fact, most dramas begin with at least two people, and then enlarge the cast as soon as possible.

For us as we watch, the drama *is* the actors. From what they do and say to each other, and about each other, we learn the behavior of the *dramatis personae*. We then pretend we are seeing *people*. All we really experience, however, is the answer a craftsman provides for the question "What kind of person is this, how would he behave in the imagined circumstances, and what would I do if I were he?"

Once upon a time the actors all were priests. Even today, as we are caught up in their magic circle, we may well inquire into the nature of playing. *Our* question becomes "What manner of man is this craftsman of Dionysus, and how does he work his will with us?"

The Craftsman of Dionysus

In the beginning, we are told by the anthropologists, a god created the actor to lead the rites celebrating his religion. This the actor did by impersonating the god. Whether or not this is accurate, and there are several points of view, two facts about human behavior are apparent and are germane to our study. It is obvious that human beings play-act all the time. Each person consciously and unconsciously assumes roles that seem to fit society's requirements of him and to match his conception of himself in that society.

Yet this psychological fact about role-playing does little to explain what makes an actor in the theatre. In creative dramatics, which is the subject of Chapter 8, the basic premise is that every child is a natural actor. A film like *The Bicycle Thief*—where the actors are the ordinary people of Rome—seems to extend this generalization to adults as well. Perhaps any person can be an actor.

From long years of working with actors, most of them non-professional, I would agree that any adult can act in a drama. To do so, however, he must have the desire to act—to be an actor. Those adults who succeed as "Craftsmen of Dionysus" seem to possess seven qualities in greater abundance than those who fail at this demanding craft.

1. The actor feels alive only when he is pretending to be someone he is not, when he is dramatizing himself, and particularly when he is performing in front of an audience. An actor is inspired rather than cowed by public attention. This *histrionic urge* is what drives a person to be an actor in a theatre before an audience.

2. Yet the desire to perform in public is only a beginning. The actor must have a strong *histrionic capability*. This capability—trainable but essentially inherent and unlearned—involves perceiving the world in terms of a single person's psychophysical "action." Along with this *seeing* goes an instant *doing* with voice and body. An actor is instantly *mimetic*.

3. The urge to perform and the capability to sense and mimic the world through action are wasted, however, unless a third quality is present. This quality is *imagination*—what Constantine Stanislavsky, the Russian actor and director whose system has dominated professional actors for nearly fifty years, called the "magic if." The actor must be capable of throwing himself into a set of imagined circumstances and then behaving *as if the magic world existed and he were a certain kind of person in that world*. As a rule he sees the larger action of the total drama only in terms of that person.

4. Yet it is possible to want to perform, to sense the world in terms of action, and to be able to imagine all possible worlds without being an actor. A fourth ability that seems necessary is the ability to concentrate. To some extent inborn, but highly susceptible to training, *concentration* involves shutting out everything but the imagined circumstances of the drama being portrayed. The resultant focusing of the actor's energy has been described as a "circle of light" or a "circle of character."

5. The use of these attributes to create a drama on stage demands *a trained instrument*. The actor's voice and body must present instantly and accurately what his imagination demands. Whatever the mechanics of achieving it, the performance must seem intuitive.

6. The person who has the five attributes described above may well be an actor. In most of the theatres he will work in, a sixth quality is important. The actor's personality—and his assumed *persona*—must grow in size under public scrutiny. When this happens, the result is called *presence*, or *stage presence*. Most people tend to shrink in public; the actor expands.

7. The seventh quality necessary to be an actor is *projection*. The actor must project his performance out to the audience. Loudness, clarity of diction, grandeur of movement and gesture, intensity of concentration, and level of energy—all these are important to projection, but the chief ingredient is a feeling of communion with the audience. The actor must believe he is engaged in a dialogue with every member of the audience, no matter how far away he is.

No doubt you and I, and everyone we know, has these seven attributes in *some* measure. If you have them in *great* measure, you are well on your way to being an actor. What is it you will *do*, however, when you "act"?

The Craft of Acting

The trouble with intellectualizing and systematizing the craft of acting is that the activity is not made much clearer thereby. The same holds true of most acting classes. People who *can* act learn how. People who cannot act never seem to learn. However we describe acting, and we can imagine a physiologist being extraordinarily accurate about the behavior of neurons in the brain, we have no way of doing the acting in our description. The best we can manage is a delineation of approaches to a role. We can say what acting seems to be, and how many fine actors have gone about their business, but *you* must prove them *yourself*.

Let us assume, therefore, that you are going to play Othello—or Iago, if you prefer, or perhaps Orlando or Touchstone. How are you going to go about it? Well, first let us announce what you should *not* do. You should not assume that acting is showing off or selling yourself. Your desire and your skill is "to perform the role of another"—quite a different thing. You are not a mountebank, that is, a charlatan or a trickster selling treats, but a player. We do not need to call you "priest" to emphasize the seriousness and the difficulty of your task. The theatre is not a religion—and perhaps it never was—but your approach to your craft must contain all the dedication of the priest or you will never succeed. Nor do you need to be pretentious about your devotion. Pomposity and artiness have nothing to do with dedication; serious striving and mastery of infinite detail do.

As you go about this task, what you are interested in are *actions*, not *emotions*. We have already observed that a drama is a collection of people doing things. Your job is to find out what your *persona* does in the drama. As a rule, you will find that what a character does in a drama consists of one central action—called the *spine*, the *through line of action*, the *purpose*, or the *intention*—and many subsidiary and tributary actions. What you call your action is irrelevant, so long as you find it.

No doubt there are as many ways of searching as there are actors. Three of these seem to dominate most actors, however, and probably you will prefer to create your own out of them. One group of actors may approach the drama primarily through its *expression*, principally the style of the speeches his character pronounces, but also the actions indicated in scene directions. Although the words are central to this approach, those who use it first attempt to express the images in the words through pantomime. Parts of the body, then the entire body, then the ground and air immediately around the actor are brought into play. Without words, the actor expresses the movement and rhythms exhibited by the pattern of words and images.

If this seems difficult to imagine, much less to accomplish, it is. Try it, however, before you ridicule it. Once the movement of a speech is communicable through bodily activity alone, sighs and groans—great open-throated but meaningless sounds—are brought into the interpretation. Often, as you go through the pantomime stage, you will find yourself breaking into sound that seems to fit the emotional rhythm you are expressing.

Once the speech is expressable through physical actions and elongated moans and growls, the actor begins to use the words themselves. What he has discovered is the deepseated motives and actions which underlie the speech—and hence of the character himself.

In this approach to acting, then, the character's expression of himself *is* the character. The modes of expression are an *interpretation* of the character action. Properly realized by the actor, this interpretation presents the audience with the through line of action, and all tributary actions, without perhaps ever verbalizing or otherwise consciously describing these actions.

A second approach to finding the action of a *persona* focuses on what we might call the *external manifestation* of the character. If you observe this actor at work, you find him searching for a way of standing or walking, a vocal mannerism, a stage property or costume, or perhaps a real tool or weapon or article of clothing. Sometimes he searches for a real or imagined person or animal that metaphorically stands for the character being portrayed. Often this actor applies his own personality to the character, which then becomes "Actor X as Othello," for example. Once this key to the character action is found, and physically and vocally performed, the character's actions are manifest on stage. "My action is like that of my dog Sam chasing a rabbit," the actor may say, and when he presents Sam chasing the rabbit, the *persona* in the given drama suddenly comes to life. You may find this as hard to believe as I do, but I have seen actors do it time and time again.

The third approach to a character's actions insists on dealing with his *inner goals*. Although the goal is viewed as psychological, it is described in physical terms. Othello's through line of action, for example, might be "to reconstruct the world in his own image"; Iago's, "to destroy Othello"; and Desdemona's, "to create a marriage with Othello." The important thing is to phrase the goal actively—that is, as an *active infinitive*. Carrying out the physical activity necessary to reach the goal will cause the psychological concomitants of the physical life to occur. The mind will follow the body, as it were, and the character will be realized. At no time in this process should the actor *be* anything; he must only *do* things.

Assuming you understand these three approaches to the action of a character, which should you use to create Othello? The answer is, use whatever suits you. Simply reading Othello's lines aloud will help you to understand what he is doing in the drama. Interpreting them with your total body, and your full repertory of sounds, as well as with the words themselves, should lead you to the actions of Othello. Perhaps along the way you will hit upon a stance or a movement that will help. The actor of this role in a recent production conceived of Othello as "the crucified Christ." The position of Christ on the Cross began to appear in his interpretation. Subtly, almost without the actor realizing it, the position became that of a puppet on a string. The moment this image was manifest in the playing, the production took on an inner glow that lit up every rehearsal and performance from then on. The reason perhaps was that Othello is largely a puppet, and the manipulator of the strings is not Iago but Othello's view of himself—the "savior of the world." A man at the mercy of his messiah complex is indeed a "puppet on a string."

There is no reason, however, that the actor could not have found the puppet image via an understanding of Othello as "to remake the world in his own image." Careful study of the Moor's inner life might well reveal this through line of action. For certain plays no other approach would work so well. But for *Othello,* and no doubt for much of poetic drama, the stylistic approach may prove just as helpful.

Let us say, therefore, that through some combination of miracles you know the actions of Othello—or Iago, or Orlando, or what have you—*in your bones.* Have you reached your artistic goal? Not yet, for a given character does not exist in a vacuum. Each drama has its own set of "given circumstances": a particular dramatic construct, a collection of characters, modes of expression, a dramatic environment. You must find out what is going on in the drama and how your *persona* is involved in the proceedings.

At this point, you may decide to leave well enough alone. Up till now you have achieved an understanding of the way a particular kind of person behaves while experiencing a particular set of circumstances. What there is of value in *Othello* you have made your own. You are not in any way committed to playing the drama in a theatre before an audience.

Let us assume, however, that you *do* wish to portray what you have found out about Othello. To do so, you must take yourself through a three-stage personal orientation to the role. First you must place yourself in the drama by asking, What would *I* do *if* there were such a situation as *Othello, if* there were such a person as Othello, *and if I* were that person? "What would *I do*" means "how would *I* carry out the *physical life* of Othello?" You imagine what Othello would do in the playwright's given circumstances, *if he and they were real,* and then you simply *do* those things.

Assuming that you find a physical life that is true to Othello *if you were he,* then the next stage in your orientation to the role involves making yourself *believe* in the truth you have found. Achieving *believability* is your goal. Although the drama is certainly imaginary, and in certain types of drama you must take pains to indicate that you are pretending, you yourself must believe the drama is *real.* If you can do this, your audience will accept whatever you show them.

"Believing" is easier said than done. Your detailed study of the play *with your whole body* will help. The accouterments of production, as you go through rehearsal after rehearsal with your fellow actor-characters, will certainly increase your capacity to believe. But the last mile you must go alone. There can be no halfway measures. At some point, hopefully early in the preparation of the role, *you simply must believe Othello is true*.

Given your belief, you must then commit all your energy and enthusiasm to it. You must concentrate all your attention on what Othello is doing, on what the other characters are doing, and on what both you and the others are saying and thinking. We have already observed that this *intensity of concentration* is what more than anything else makes the drama happen on the stage. The audience and all the collaborating artists help, but it is the actor who *wills the drama into being*. You must act and react, listen and respond, as if you were truly Othello and as if all that happens to him is not only real but is happening for the first and only time. When that occurs, and not before or after, there will be a play called *Othello*.

When you have achieved Othello in such a way that your audience can believe him as strongly as you do, you have only one more task. *You must relax*. "It is only art that conceals art," someone has said. Your audience will tend to disbelieve your portrayal if you seem to be trying too hard. Paradoxical as it may seem, intensity of concentration should not result in physical tension or nervousness. Quite the opposite, for total involvement in the true life of your character should lead to greater relaxation. The next time you find yourself totally absorbed in some activity, observe yourself for a few moments. If you know precisely what you are doing, you will note how smoothly your body goes about its business. When you were learning it—in rehearsals—you may have felt a great deal of nervousness. Now you have been trained, and your body works at maximum efficiency. The same holds true in the theatre.

If you would be an actor, then, the suggestions in the foregoing paragraphs may help you. They do not tell you how to do it. They set goals for you to aim at as you play many parts. Only through such playing— through constant practice in as many different roles as possible—will you achieve whatever goals you set. You are the painter and the brush; all life is your palette. You must live your life as fully as possible, and you must notice details in everything you experience. When you prepare a role, your experiences that relate to it are the source of your reactions. You will have to find some concomitant experience that matches the drama being presented. The connection may be purely figurative— "What's it like?" is a key question—or directly literal. All that is important is that your body remember the similar experience mimetically.

So the actor experiences life through *mimesis*, and then plays on stage those portions of his experience that fit the character and the drama he is portraying. The drama contains the circumstances; the actor incarnates them. A dream of passion becomes for a moment the passion itself. Actor and audience play the world of the drama.

Sample Play: OTHELLO

INTRODUCTION

What had always seemed an ordinary Shakespearean tragedy, more concentrated than most, but more powerful thereby, became a nightmare of crosscurrents battering the very heart of the production. The stage was simple enough: a simulated Elizabethan facade at the proscenium opening, with an "inner below" the size of a curtained alcove, a balcony above it, doors at ground level to the left and right of the curtained alcove, windows above these doors, platforms extending the stage some fifteen feet into the auditorium, with a false ceiling high above it. For decoration, the ceiling was painted with a zodiac in the Elizabethan manner.

The preparation of the play was also straightforward enough: a year's concentrated study of the script, its sources, and all commentary on it, with now the addition of a cast that fit every role and that had studied the script together for two months prior to the first rehearsal. By that time, characterizations were nearly learned and the general staging was written in the production book.

The ax fell at first rehearsal. As the detailed staging was prepared on the modified "stage of Shakespeare," a new *Othello* began to emerge. Moment after moment, scene after scene, began to twist and turn, and hurtle pell-mell through time and logic. The drama was suddenly a Marx Brothers movie, a *Laugh-In*, a *Hair*. What was emerging from the first rehearsals was a *commedia dell'arte* farce, with spinning, rapid-fire incidents, characters at the mercy of plot or story, sudden switches and reversals of direction, pratfalls, and even comic melodrama.

The director, being a purist when it comes to Shakespeare and having started with the avowed intention of producing *Othello* "as the Jacobean audience must have seen it," was horrified. What, he thought, will happen to the "tragic Moor"? Will this farcical approach to the tragedy destroy *Othello*? If so, the director had three choices: stop the production, stop the changes being made at rehearsals, or follow the lead of the spontaneous creation that was occurring.

Before choosing the third option, the director rephrased his questions. Can *Othello* be considered "tragic farce," he asked, and what values are inherent in such a view? The answer was a production of *Othello* as if it were *commedia dell'arte*. The bare Elizabethan stage, with its highly-stylized zodiac, was kept. Costumes were from the Renaissance, but except for those of Othello and Desdemona, were given the color and style of *commedia* costumes-sans-mask. Every dramatic unit in the play except Othello's scenes were staged in farce style and, where possible, were made as broad and as slapstick as possible. Iago remained a villain, but became an evil Harlequin—the quick-witted and unscrupulous servant. Brabantio was Pantallone; Roderigo the gull, a farcical parallel to Othello. Cassio was Pierrot, and Desdemona was Pierrette—both naive, innocent, and tragically destroyed, though Cassio is left alive at the end of the drama. In the *commedia*, the character of Columbine had several variants. One was the innocent young lover, named above as "Pierrette" to distinguish her from the earlier versions. These were vulgar servant girls and women of the streets—represented in this production by Emilia and Bianca.

In the midst of this whirling *commedia* stood the magnificent Othello—simple, soldierly, honorable, but essentially blind to the nuances of behavior in Venice, and given to dramatic posturing and to oratorical flourishes because they protected or enhanced his romantic vision of himself. We have already described the situation in which the Moor finds his vision confused and blocked by Venetian intrigue. At first he stands supremely in command above the petty confusions that symbolize Venice. He has married into this strange new world, but before he can be soiled, he is removed to Cyprus and the war. There his soldierly virtues should continue to triumph.

Yet we all know they do not, for the conflict ends and Iago sets down the tune that brings "Venice" to Cyprus. If we miss the point, the Clown and the Musicians remind us. He sings off-key through his nose, and they play out-of-tune. Iago banters his way from villainy to villainy, and the farce becomes as swift and improbable as the fanciful gyrations of Groucho Marx.

Yet the cumulative effect is one of horror. In the world of Iago, Brabantio, the absurd Senators—the world of pretenses and intrigue rather than substance—Othello is foredoomed. *He is capable of love, but he does not have time to make his marriage work.* The chaos triumphs before he can truly love Desdemona—before, that is, he can substitute her needs for his own. He becomes more and more grotesque under the influence of Iago and Iago's world. Othello comes to behave in the manner of Pulcinnello, or Punch, the vulgar and villainous clown. As Gratiano sums it up, "All that's spoke is marred."

Othello

Dramatis Personae

OTHELLO, the noble moor

BRABANTIO, a Venetian senator, father to Desdemona

CASSIO, an honorable lieutenant to Othello

IAGO, Othello's ancient, a villain

RODERIGO, a gulled gentleman

DUKE OF VENICE

SENATORS OF VENICE

MONTANO, governor of Cyprus

LODOVICO, kinsman to Brabantio, a noble Venetian

GRATIANO, kinsman to Brabantio, a noble Venetian

SAILORS

CLOWN

DESDEMONA, wife to Othello

EMILIA, wife to Iago

BIANCA, a courtesan

MESSENGER, HERALD, OFFICERS, VENETIAN GENTLEMEN, MUSICIANS, ATTENDANTS

Scene

Venice and Cyprus

Reprinted from the Pelican Shakespeare Series, Alfred Harbage, editor, by permission of Penguin Books, Inc.

Othello

Enter Roderigo and Iago.

Roderigo. Tush, never tell me! I take it much unkindly
    That thou, Iago, who hast had my purse
    As if the strings were thine, shouldst know of this.
Iago. 'Sblood, but you will not hear me!
    If ever I did dream of such a matter,   5
    Abhor me.
Roderigo. Thou told'st me thou didst hold him in thy hate.
Iago. Despise me if I do not. Three great ones of the city,
    In personal suit to make me his lieutenant,
    Off-capped to him; and, by the faith of man,   10
    I know my price; I am worth no worse a place.
    But he, as loving his own pride and purposes,
    Evades them with a bombast circumstance.
    Horribly stuffed with epithets of war;
    [And, in conclusion,]   15
    Nonsuits my mediators; for, 'Certes,' says he,
    'I have already chose my officer.'
    And what was he?
    Forsooth, a great arithmetician,
    One Michael Cassio, a Florentine   20
    (A fellow almost damned in a fair wife)
    That never set a squadron in the field,
    Nor the division of a battle knows
    More than a spinster; unless the bookish theoric,
    Wherein the togèd consuls can propose   25
    As masterly as he. Mere prattle without practice
    Is all his soldiership. But he, sir, had th' election;
    And I (of whom his eyes had seen the proof
    At Rhodes, at Cyprus, and on other grounds
    Christian and heathen) must be belee'd and calmed   30
    By debitor and creditor; this counter-caster,
    He, in good time, must his lieutenant be,
    And I—God bless the mark!—his Moorship's ancient.
Roderigo. By heaven, I rather would have been his hangman.

I, i, 3 *this* i.e. Desdemona's elopement 4 *'Sblood* by God's blood 10 *him* i.e. Othello 13 *a bombast circumstance* pompous circumlocutions 16 *Nonsuits* rejects 19 *arithmetician* theoretician 21 *almost... wife* (an obscure allusion; Cassio is unmarried, but see IV, i, 123) 30 *belee'd and calmed* left in the lurch 31 *counter-caster* bookkeeper 33 *ancient* ensign

Iago. Why, there's no remedy; 'tis the curse of service.   35
    Preferment goes by letter and affection,
    And not by old gradation, where each second
    Stood heir to th' first. Now, sir, be judge yourself,
    Whether I in any just term am affined
    To love the Moor.
Roderigo.   I would not follow him then.   40
Iago. O, sir, content you;
    I follow him to serve my turn upon him.
    We cannot all be masters, nor all masters
    Cannot be truly followed. You shall mark
    Many a duteous and knee-crooking knave   45
    That, doting on his own obsequious bondage,
    Wears out his time, much like his master's ass,
    For naught but provender; and when he's old, cashiered.
    Whip me such honest knaves! Others there are
    Who, trimmed in forms and visages of duty,   50
    Keep yet their hearts attending on themselves;
    And, throwing but shows of service on their lords,
    Do well thrive by them, and when they have lined their
        coats,
    Do themselves homage. These fellows have some soul;
    And such a one do I profess myself. For, sir,   55
    It is as sure as you are Roderigo,
    Were I the Moor, I would not be Iago.
    In following him, I follow but myself;
    Heaven is my judge, not I for love and duty,
    But seeming so, for my peculiar end;   60
    For when my outward action doth demonstrate
    The native act and figure of my heart
    In compliment extern, 'tis not long after
    But I will wear my heart upon my sleeve
    For daws to peck at; I am not what I am.   65
Roderigo. What a full fortune does the thick-lips owe
    If he can carry't thus!
Iago.   Call up her father,
    Rouse him. Make after him, poison his delight,
    Proclaim him in the streets. Incense her kinsmen,
    And though he in a fertile climate dwell,   70
    Plague him with flies; though that his joy be joy,

---

36 *affection* favoritism 39 *affined* obliged 48 *cashiered* turned off 50 *trimmed* dressed up
62 *The ... heart* what I really believe and intend 63 *compliment extern* outward appearance
66 *thick-lips* (Elizabethans made no clear distinction between Moors and Negroes) *owe* own

Yet throw such changes of vexation on't
   As it may lose some color.
Roderigo. Here is her father's house. I'll call aloud.
Iago. Do, with like timorous accent and dire yell   75
   As when, by night and negligence, the fire
   Is spied in populous cities.
Roderigo. What, ho, Brabantio! Signior Brabantio, ho!
Iago. Awake! What, ho, Brabantio! Thieves! thieves!
   thieves!
   Look to your house, your daughter, and your bags!   80
   Thieves! thieves!

Brabantio at a window.

Brabantio. *(above)* What is the reason of this terrible sum-
   mons?
   What is the matter there?
Roderigo. Signior, is all your family within?
Iago. Are your doors locked?
Brabantio.   Why, wherefore ask you this?   85
Iago. Zounds, sir, y'are robbed! For shame, put on your
   gown!
   Your heart is burst; you have lost half your soul.
   Even now, now, very now, an old black ram
   Is tupping your white ewe. Arise, arise!
   Awake the snorting citizens with the bell,   90
   Or else the devil will make a grandsire of you.
   Arise, I say!
Brabantio.   What, have you lost your wits?
Roderigo. Most reverend signior, do you know my voice?
Brabantio. Not I. What are you?
Roderigo. My name is Roderigo.
Brabantio.   The worser welcome!   95
   I have charged thee not to haunt about my doors.
   In honest plainness thou hast heard me say
   My daughter is not for thee; and now, in madness,
   Being full of supper and distemp'ring draughts,
   Upon malicious bravery dost thou come   100
   To start my quiet.
Roderigo. Sir, sir, sir—
Brabantio.   But thou must needs be sure
   My spirit and my place have in them power
   To make this bitter to thee.
Roderigo.   Patience, good sir.

75 *timorous* terrifying 81 *S.D. Brabantio at a window* (added from quarto) 90 *snorting*
snoring 100 *bravery* defiance

Brabantio. What tell'st thou me of robbing? This is Venice;   105
    My house is not a grange.
Roderigo.   Most grave Brabantio,
    In simple and pure soul I come to you.
Iago. Zounds, sir, you are one of those that will not serve
    God if the devil bid you. Because we come to do you
    service, and you think we are ruffians, you'll have your   110
    daughter covered with a Barbary horse; you'll have your
    nephews neigh to you; you'll have coursers for cousins,
    and gennets for germans.
Brabantio. What profane wretch art thou?
Iago. I am one, sir, that comes to tell you your daughter and   115
    the Moor are now making the beast with two backs.
Brabantio. Thou art a villain.
Iago.   You are—a senator.
Brabantio. This thou shalt answer. I know thee, Roderigo.
Roderigo. Sir, I will answer anything. But I beseech you,
    If't be your pleasure and most wise consent,   120
    As partly I find it is, that your fair daughter,
    At this odd-even and dull watch o' th' night,
    Transported, with no worse nor better guard
    But with a knave of common hire, a gondolier,
    To the gross clasps of a lascivious Moor—   125
    If this be known to you, and your allowance,
    We then have done you bold and saucy wrongs;
    But if you know not this, my manners tell me
    We have your wrong rebuke. Do not believe
    That, from the sense of all civility,   130
    I thus would play and trifle with your reverence.
    Your daughter, if you have not given her leave,
    I say again, hath made a gross revolt,
    Tying her duty, beauty, wit, and fortunes
    In an extravagant and wheeling stranger   135
    Of here and everywhere. Straight satisfy yourself.
    If she be in her chamber, or your house,
    Let loose on me the justice of the state
    For thus deluding you.
Brabantio.   Strike on the tinder, ho!
    Give me a taper! Call up all my people!   140
    This accident is not unlike my dream.

---

106 *grange* isolated farmhouse 112 *nephews* i.e. grandsons 113 *gennets for germans* Spanish horses for near kinsmen 122 *odd-even* between night and morning 126 *allowance* approval 130 *from the sense* in violation 135 *extravagant and wheeling* expatriate and roving 141 *accident* occurrence

Belief of it oppresses me already.
Light, I say! light!   *Exit [above].*
Iago.   Farewell, for I must leave you.
It seems not meet, nor wholesome to my place,
To be produced—as, if I stay, I shall—   145
Against the Moor. For I do know the state,
However this may gall him with some check,
Cannot with safety cast him; for he's embarked
With such loud reason to the Cyprus wars,
Which even now stand in act, that for their souls   150
Another of his fathom they have none
To lead their business; in which regard,
Though I do hate him as I do hell-pains,
Yet, for necessity of present life,
I must show out a flag and sign of love,   155
Which is indeed but sign. That you shall surely find him,
Lead to the Sagittary the raisèd search;
And there will I be with him. So farewell.   *Exit.*

> *Enter, [below,] Brabantio in his nightgown, and Servants*
> *with torches.*

Brabantio. It is too true an evil. Gone she is;
And what's to come of my despisèd time   160
Is naught but bitterness. Now, Roderigo,
Where didst thou see her?—O unhappy girl!—
With the Moor, say'st thou?—Who would be a father?—
How didst thou know 'twas she?—O, she deceives me
Past thought!—What said she to you?—Get moe tapers!   165
Raise all my kindred!—Are they married, think you?
Roderigo. Truly I think they are.
Brabantio. O heaven! How got she out? O treason of the
      blood!
Fathers, from hence trust not your daughters' minds
By what you see them act. Is there not charms   170
By which the property of youth and maidhood
May be abused? Have you not read, Roderigo,
Of some such thing?
Roderigo.   Yes, sir, I have indeed.
Brabantio. Call up my brother.—O, would you had had
      her!—
Some one way, some another,—Do you know   175
Where we may apprehend her and the Moor?

---

147 *check* reprimand 148 *cast* discharge 150 *stand in act* are going on 151 *fathom* capacity
157 *Sagittary* an inn 158 S.D. *nightgown* dressing-gown 165 *moe* more 171 *property* nature

Roderigo. I think I can discover him, if you please
  To get good guard and go along with me.
Brabantio. Pray you lead on. At every house I'll call;
  I may command at most.—Get weapons, ho!   180
  And raise some special officers of night.—
  On, good Roderigo; I'll deserve your pains.   *Exeunt.*

            Enter Othello, Iago, and Attendants with torches.   I,ii

Iago. Though in the trade of war I have slain men,
  Yet do I hold it very stuff o' th' conscience
  To do no contrived murther. I lack iniquity
  Sometimes to do me service. Nine or ten times
  I had thought t' have yerked him here under the ribs.   5
Othello. 'Tis better as it is.
Iago.   Nay, but he prated,
  And spoke such scurvy and provoking terms
  Against your honor
  That with the little godliness I have
  I did full hard forbear him. But I pray you, sir,   10
  Are you fast married? Be assured of this,
  That the magnifico is much beloved,
  And hath in his effect a voice potential
  As double as the Duke's. He will divorce you,
  Or put upon you what restraint and grievance   15
  The law, with all his might to enforce it on,
  Will give him cable.
Othello.   Let him do his spite.
  My services which I have done the signiory
  Shall out-tongue his complaints. 'Tis yet to know—
  Which, when I know that boasting is an honor,   20
  I shall promulgate—I fetch my life and being
  From men of royal siege; and my demerits
  May speak unbonneted to as proud a fortune
  As this that I have reached. For know, Iago,
  But that I love the gentle Desdemona,   25
  I would not my unhousèd free condition
  Put into circumscription and confine
  For the sea's worth.

---

182 *deserve* show gratitude for I, ii, 5 *yerked* stabbed 11 *fast* securely 12 *magnifico* grandee
(Brabantio) 13 *potential* powerful 14 *double* doubly influential 18 *signiory* Venetian government 19 *yet to know* still not generally known 22 *siege* rank *demerits* deserts 23-24 *May
speak . . . reached* are equal, I modestly assert, to those of Desdemona's family 26 *unhousèd*
unrestrained

Enter Cassio, with torches, Officers.

But look, what lights come yond?
Iago. Those are the raisèd father and his friends.
　You were best go in.
Othello.　　Not I; I must be found.　　　　　　　　　　　30
　My parts, my title, and my perfect soul
　Shall manifest me rightly. Is it they?
Iago. By Janus, I think no.
Othello. The servants of the Duke, and my lieutenant.
　The goodness of the night upon you, friends!　　　　　35
　What is the news?
Cassio.　　The Duke does greet you, general;
　And he requires your haste-post-haste appearance
　Even on the instant.
Othello.　　What's the matter, think you?
Cassio. Something from Cyprus, as I may divine.
　It is a business of some heat. The galleys　　　　　　　40
　Have sent a dozen sequent messengers
　This very night at one another's heels,
　And many of the consuls, raised and met,
　Are at the Duke's already. You have been hotly called
　　for;
　When, being not at your lodging to be found,　　　　　45
　The Senate hath sent about three several quests
　To search you out.
Othello.　　'Tis well I am found by you.
　I will but spend a word here in the house,
　And go with you.　　　　　　　　　　　　　　　*[Exit.]*
Cassio.　　Ancient, what makes he here?
Iago. Faith, he to-night hath boarded a land carack.　　50
　If it prove lawful prize, he's made for ever.
Cassio. I do not understand.
Iago.　　He's married.
Cassio.　　　　To who?

[Enter Othello.]

Iago. Marry, to—Come, captain, will you go?
Othello.　　　　　　　　　　　Have with you.
Cassio. Here comes another troop to seek for you.

---

31 *perfect soul* stainless conscience　41 *sequent* consecutive　50 *carack* treasure ship

Enter Brabantio, Roderigo, and others with lights and
weapons.

Iago. It is Brabantio. General, be advised.   55
    He comes to bad intent.
Othello.   Holla! stand there!
Roderigo. Signior, it is the Moor.
Brabantio.   Down with him, thief!
                            [They draw on both sides.]
Iago. You, Roderigo! Come, sir, I am for you.
Othello. Keep up your bright swords, for the dew will
    rust them.
    Good signior, you shall more command with years   60
    Than with your weapons.
Brabantio. O thou foul thief, where has thou stowed my
    daughter?
    Damned as thou art, thou hast enchanted her!
    For I'll refer me to all things of sense,
    If she in chains of magic were not bound,   65
    Whether a maid so tender, fair, and happy,
    So opposite to marriage that she shunned
    The wealthy curlèd darlings of our nation,
    Would ever have, t' incur a general mock,
    Run from her guardage to the sooty bosom   70
    Of such a thing as thou—to fear, not to delight.
    Judge me the world if 'tis not gross in sense
    That thou hast practiced on her with foul charms,
    Abused her delicate youth with drugs or minerals
    That weaken motion. I'll have't disputed on;   75
    'Tis probable, and palpable to thinking.
    I therefore apprehend and do attach thee
    For an abuser of the world, a practicer
    Of arts inhibited and out of warrant.
    Lay hold upon him. If he do resist,   80
    Subdue him at his peril.
Othello.   Hold your hands,
    Both you of my inclining and the rest.
    Were it my cue to fight, I should have known it
    Without a prompter. Where will you that I go
    To answer this your charge?
Brabantio.   To prison, till fit time   85
    Of law and course of direct session
    Call thee to answer.

72 *gross in sense* obvious 75 *motion* perception 77 *attach* arrest

Othello.   What if I do obey?
  How may the Duke be therewith satisfied,
  Whose messengers are here about my side
  Upon some present business of the state   90
  To bring me to him?
Officer.   'Tis true, most worthy signior.
  The Duke's in council, and your noble self
  I am sure is sent for.
Brabantio.   How? The Duke in council?
  In this time of the night? Bring him away.
  Mine's not an idle cause. The Duke himself,   95
  Or any of my brothers of the state,
  Cannot but feel this wrong as 'twere their own;
  For if such actions may have passage free,
  Bondslaves and pagans shall our statesmen be.   *Exeunt.*

      Enter Duke and Senators, set at a table, with lights and   I,iii
                        Attendants.

Duke. There is no composition in these news
  That gives them credit.
1. Senator.   Indeed they are disproportioned.
  My letters say a hundred and seven galleys.
Duke. And mine a hundred forty.
2. Senator.   And mine two hundred.
  But though they jump not on a just account—   5
  As in these cases where the aim reports
  'Tis oft with difference—yet do they all confirm
  A Turkish fleet, and bearing up to Cyprus.
Duke. Nay, it is possible enough to judgment.
  I do not so secure me in the error   10
  But the main article I do approve
  In fearful sense.
Sailor. (within)   What, ho! what, ho! what, ho!
Officer. A messenger from the galleys.

                Enter Sailor.

Duke.   Now, what's the business?
Sailor. The Turkish preparation makes for Rhodes.
  So was I bid report here to the state   15
  By Signior Angelo.
Duke. How say you by this change?

---

95 *idle* trifling I, iii, 1 *composition* consistency 5 *jump* agree 6 *aim* conjecture 10 *so secure me* take such comfort 11 *article* substance *approve* accept

1. Senator.   This cannot be
   By no assay of reason. 'Tis a pageant
   To keep us in false gaze. When we consider
   Th' importancy of Cyprus to the Turk,   20
   And let ourselves again but understand
   That, as it more concerns the Turk than Rhodes,
   So may he with more facile question bear it,
   For that it stands not in such warlike brace,
   But altogether lacks th' abilities   25
   That Rhodes is dressed in—if we make thought of this,
   We must not think the Turk is so unskillful
   To leave that latest which concerns him first,
   Neglecting an attempt of ease and gain
   To wake and wage a danger profitless.   30
Duke. Nay, in all confidence he's not for Rhodes.
Officer. Here is more news.

Enter a Messenger.

Messenger. The Ottomites, reverend and gracious,
   Steering with due course toward the isle of Rhodes,
   Have there injointed them with an after fleet.   35
1. Senator. Ay, so I thought. How many, as you guess?
Messenger. Of thirty sail; and now they do restem
   Their backward course, bearing with frank appearance
   Their purposes toward Cyprus. Signior Montano,
   Your trusty and most valiant servitor,   40
   With his free duty recommends you thus,
   And prays you to believe him.
Duke. 'Tis certain then for Cyprus.
   Marcus Luccicos, is not he in town?
1. Senator. He's now in Florence.   45
Duke. Write from us to him; post, post-haste dispatch.

*Enter Brabantio, Othello, Cassio, Iago, Roderigo, and
Officers.*

1. Senator. Here comes Brabantio and the valiant Moor.
Duke. Valiant Othello, we must straight employ you
   Against the general Ottoman.
   [To Brabantio] I did not see you. Welcome, gentle
     signior.   50
   We lacked your counsel and your help to-night.

---

18 *assay* test 19 *in false gaze* looking the wrong way 23 *with . . . bear* more easily capture
24 *brace* posture of defense 30 *wake and wage* rouse and risk 37 *restem* steer again

Brabantio. So did I yours. Good your grace, pardon me.
   Neither my place, nor aught I heard of business,
   Hath raised me from my bed; nor doth the general care
   Take hold on me; for my particular grief   55
   Is of so floodgate and o'erbearing nature
   That it engluts and swallows other sorrows,
   And it is still itself.
Duke.   Why, what's the matter?
Brabantio. My daughter! O, my daughter!
All.   Dead?
Brabantio.   Ay, to me.
   She is abused, stol'n from me, and corrupted   60
   By spells and medicines bought of mountebanks;
   For nature so prepost'rously to err,
   Being not deficient, blind, or lame of sense,
   Sans witchcraft could not.
Duke. Whoe'er he be that in this foul proceeding   65
   Hath thus beguiled your daughter of herself,
   And you of her, the bloody book of law
   You shall yourself read in the bitter letter
   After your own sense; yea, though our proper son
   Stood in your action.
Brabantio.   Humbly I thank your grace.   70
   Here is the man—this Moor, whom now, it seems,
   Your special mandate for the state affairs
   Hath hither brought.
All.   We are very sorry for't.
Duke. [to Othello] What, in your own part, can you say to
   this?
Brabantio. Nothing, but this is so.   75
Othello. Most potent, grave, and reverend signiors,
   My very noble, and approved good masters,
   That I have ta'en away this old man's daughter,
   It is most true; true I have married her.
   The very head and front of my offending   80
   Hath this extent, no more. Rude am I in my speech,
   And little blessed with the soft phrase of peace;
   For since these arms of mine had seven years' pith
   Till now some nine moons wasted, they have used
   Their dearest action in the tented field;   85
   And little of this great world can I speak
   More than pertains to feats of broil and battle;

---

56 *floodgate* torrential 57 *engluts* devours 63 *deficient* feeble-minded 69 *our proper* my own 70 *Stood in your action* were accused by you 77 *approved* tested by experience 81 *Rude* unpolished 83 *pith* strength

And therefore little shall I grace my cause
In speaking for myself. Yet, by your gracious patience,
I will a round unvarnished tale deliver   90
Of my whole course of love—what drugs, what charms,
What conjuration, and what mighty magic
(For such proceeding am I charged withal)
I won his daughter.
Brabantio.   A maiden never bold;
Of spirit so still and quiet that her motion   95
Blushed at herself; and she—in spite of nature,
Of years, of country, credit, everything—
To fall in love with what she feared to look on!
It is a judgment maimed and most imperfect
That will confess perfection so could err   100
Against all rules of nature, and must be driven
To find out practices of cunning hell
Why this should be. I therefore vouch again
That with some mixtures pow'rful o'er the blood,
Or with some dram, conjured to this effect,   105
He wrought upon her.
Duke.   To vouch this is no proof,
Without more certain and more overt test
Than these thin habits and poor likelihoods
Of modern seeming do prefer against him.
1. Senator. But, Othello, speak.   110
Did you by indirect and forcèd courses
Subdue and poison this young maid's affections?
Or came it by request, and such fair question
As soul to soul affordeth?
Othello.   I do beseech you,
Send for the lady to the Sagittary   115
And let her speak of me before her father.
If you do find me foul in her report,
The trust, the office, I do hold of you
Not only take away, but let your sentence
Even fall upon my life.
Duke.   Fetch Desdemona hither.   120
Othello. Ancient, conduct them; you best know the place.
                    Exit [Iago, with] two or three [Attendants].
And till she come, as truly as to heaven
I do confess the vices of my blood,
So justly to your grave ears I'll present

---

90 *round* plain 95-96 *her motion Blushed* her own emotions caused her to blush 102 *practices* plots 103 *vouch* assert 104 *blood* passions 108 *thin habits* slight appearances 109 *modern seeming* everyday supposition 111 *forced* violent 113 *question* conversation

How I did thrive in this fair lady's love, 125
And she in mine.
Duke. Say it, Othello.
Othello. Her father loved me, oft invited me;
  Still questioned me the story of my life
  From year to year—the battles, sieges, fortunes 130
  That I have passed.
  I ran it through, even from my boyish days
  To th' very moment that he bade me tell it.
  Wherein I spake of most disastrous chances,
  Of moving accidents by flood and field; 135
  Of hairbreadth scapes i' th' imminent deadly breach;
  Of being taken by the insolent foe
  And sold to slavery; of my redemption thence
  And portance in my travel's history;
  Wherein of anters vast and deserts idle, 140
  Rough quarries, rocks, and hills whose heads touch
    heaven,
  It was my hint to speak—such was the process;
  And of the Cannibals that each other eat,
  The Anthropophagi, and men whose heads
  Do grow beneath their shoulders. This to hear 145
  Would Desdemona seriously incline;
  But still the house affairs would draw her thence;
  Which ever as she could with haste dispatch,
  She'ld come again, and with a greedy ear
  Devour up my discourse. Which I observing, 150
  Took once a pliant hour, and found good means
  To draw from her a prayer of earnest heart
  That I would all my pilgrimage dilate,
  Whereof by parcels she had something heard,
  But not intentively. I did consent, 155
  And often did beguile her of her tears
  When I did speak of some distressful stroke
  That my youth suffered. My story being done,
  She gave me for my pains a world of sighs.
  She swore, i' faith, 'twas strange, 'twas passing strange; 160
  'Twas pitiful, 'twas wondrous pitiful.
  She wished she had not heard it; yet she wished
  That heaven had made her such a man. She thanked me;
  And bade me, if I had a friend that loved her,
  I should but teach him how to tell my story, 165

---

129 *Still* continually 139 *portance* behavior 140 *anters* caves 142 *hint* occasion 144 *Anthropophagi* man-eaters 151 *pliant* propitious 153 *dilate* recount in full 154 *parcels* portions 155 *intentively* with full attention

And that would woo her. Upon this hint I spake.
She loved me for the dangers I had passed,
And I loved her that she did pity them.
This only is the witchcraft I have used.
Here comes the lady. Let her witness it.   170

Enter Desdemona, Iago, Attendants.

Duke. I think this tale would win my daughter too.
   Good Brabantio,
   Take up this mangled matter at the best.
   Men do their broken weapons rather use
   Than their bare hands.
Brabantio.   I pray you hear her speak.   175
   If she confess that she was half the wooer,
   Destruction on my head if my bad blame
   Light on the man! Come hither, gentle mistress.
   Do you perceive in all this noble company
   Where most you owe obedience?
Desdemona.   My noble father,   180
   I do perceive here a divided duty.
   To you I am bound for life and education;
   My life and education both do learn me
   How to respect you: you are the lord of duty;
   I am hitherto your daughter. But here's my husband;   185
   And so much duty as my mother showed
   To you, preferring you before her father,
   So much I challenge that I may profess
   Due to the Moor my lord.
Brabantio.   God b' wi' ye! I have done.
   Please it your grace, on to the state affairs.   190
   I had rather to adopt a child than get it.
   Come hither, Moor.
   I here do give thee that with all my heart
   Which, but thou hast already, with all my heart
   I would keep from thee. For your sake, jewel,   195
   I am glad at soul I have no other child;
   For thy escape would teach me tyranny,
   To hang clogs on them. I have done, my lord.
Duke. Let me speak like yourself and lay a sentence
   Which, as a grise or step, may help these lovers   200
   [Into your favor.]
   When remedies are past, the griefs are ended

166 *hint* opportunity 182 *education* upbringing 188 *challenge* claim the right 191 *get* beget
195 *For your sake* because of you 197 *escape* escapade 199 *like yourself* as you should
sentence maxim 200 *grise* step

By seeing the worst, which late on hopes depended.
To mourn a mischief that is past and gone
Is the next way to draw new mischief on.   205
What cannot be preserved when fortune takes,
Patience her injury a mock'ry makes.
The robbed that smiles steals something from the
    thief;
He robs himself that spends a bootless grief.
Brabantio. So let the Turk of Cyprus us beguile: 210
We lose it not so long as we can smile.
He bears the sentence well that nothing bears
But the free comfort which from thence he hears;
But he bears both the sentence and the sorrow
That to pay grief must of poor patience borrow.   215
These sentences, to sugar, or to gall,
Being strong on both sides, are equivocal.
But words are words. I never yet did hear
That the bruisèd heart was piecèd through the ear.
Beseech you, now to the affairs of state.   220
Duke. The Turk with a most mighty preparation makes
for Cyprus. Othello, the fortitude of the place is best
known to you; and though we have there a substitute
of most allowed sufficiency, yet opinion, a sovereign
mistress of effects, throws a more safer voice on you.   225
You must therefore be content to slubber the gloss of
your new fortunes with this more stubborn and boisterous
expedition.
Othello. The tyrant custom, most grave senators,
Hath made the flinty and steel couch of war   230
My thrice-driven bed of down. I do agnize
A natural and prompt alacrity
I find in hardness; and do undertake
These present wars against the Ottomites.
Most humbly, therefore, bending to your state,   235
I crave fit disposition for my wife,
Due reference of place, and exhibition,
With such accomodation and besort
As levels with her breeding.
Duke.   If you please,
Be't at her father's.
Brabantio.   I'll not have it so.   240
Othello. Nor I.

---

222 *fortitude* fortification 224 *allowed* acknowledged *opinion* public opinion 226 *slubber*
sully 231-33 *agnize . . . hardness* recognize in myself a natural and easy response to hardship
237 *exhibition* allowance of money 238 *besort* suitable company 239 *levels* corresponds

Desdemona.   Nor I. I would not there reside,
   To put my father in impatient thoughts
   By being in his eye. Most gracious Duke,
   To my unfolding lend your prosperous ear,
   And let me find a charter in your voice,   245
   To assist my simpleness.
Duke. What would you, Desdemona?
Desdemona. That I did love the Moor to live with
         him,
   My downright violence, and storm of fortunes,
   May trumpet to the world. My heart's subdued   250
   Even to the very quality of my lord.
   I saw Othello's visage in his mind,
   And to his honors and his valiant parts
   Did I my soul and fortunes consecrate.
   So that, dear lords, if I be left behind,   255
   A moth of peace, and he go to the war,
   The rites for which I love him are bereft me,
   And I a heavy interim shall support
   By his dear absence. Let me go with him.
Othello. Let her have your voices.   260
   Vouch with me, heaven, I therefore beg it not
   To please the palate of my appetite,
   Nor to comply with heat—the young affects
   In me defunct—and proper satisfaction;
   But to be free and bounteous to her mind;   265
   And heaven defend your good souls that you think
   I will your serious and great business scant
   For she is with me. No, when light-winged toys
   Of feathered Cupid seel with wanton dullness
   My speculative and officed instruments,   270
   That my disports corrupt and taint my business,
   Let housewives make a skillet of my helm,
   And all indign and base adversities
   Make head against my estimation!
Duke. Be it as you shall privately determine,   275
   Either for her stay or going. Th' affair cries haste,
   And speed must answer it. You must hence to-
         night.
[*Desdemona.* To-night, my lord?
Duke.   This night.]
Othello.   With all my heart.

244 *prosperous* favorable 246 *simpleness* lack of skill 263 *heat* passions *young affects* tend-
encies of youth 268 *For* because 269 *seel* blind 270 *My . . . instruments* my perceptive and
responsible faculties 271 *That* so that 273 *indign* unworthy 274 *estimation* reputation

Duke. At nine i' th' morning here we'll meet again.
   Othello, leave some officer behind,   280
   And he shall our commission bring to you,
   With such things else of quality and respect
   As doth import you.
Othello.   So please your grace, my ancient;
   A man he is of honesty and trust.
   To his conveyance I assign my wife,   285
   With what else needful your good grace shall think
   To be sent after me.
Duke.   Let it be so.
   Good night to every one. *[to Brabantio]* And, noble
     signior,
   If virtue no delighted beauty lack,
   Your son-in-law is far more fair than black.   290
1. Senator. Adieu, brave Moor. Use Desdemona well.
Brabantio. Look to her, Moor, if thou hast eyes to see:
   She has deceived her father, and may thee.
           Exeunt [Duke, Senators, Officers, &c.].
Othello. My life upon her faith!—Honest Iago,
   My Desdemona must I leave to thee.   295
   I prithee let thy wife attend on her,
   And bring them after in the best advantage.
   Come, Desdemona. I have but an hour
   Of love, of worldly matters and direction,
   To spend with thee. We must obey the time.   300
              Exit Moor and Desdemona.
Roderigo. Iago,—
Iago. What say'st thou, noble heart?
Roderigo. What will I do, think'st thou?
Iago. Why, go to bed and sleep.
Roderigo. I will incontinently drown myself.   305
Iago. If thou dost, I shall never love thee after. Why, thou
   silly gentleman!
Roderigo. It is silliness to live when to live is torment; and
   then have we a prescription to die when death is our
   physician.   310
Iago. O villainous! I have looked upon the world for four
   times seven years; and since I could distinguish betwixt
   a benefit and an injury, I never found man that knew
   how to love himself. Ere I would say I would drown
   myself for the love of a guinea hen, I would change my   315
   humanity with a baboon.

283 *import* concern 289 *delighted* delightful 297 *in the best advantage* at the best opportunity 305 *incontinently* forthwith

Roderigo. What should I do? I confess it is my shame to be
　　so fond, but it is not in my virtue to amend it.
Iago. Virtue? a fig! 'Tis in ourselves that we are thus or
　　thus. Our bodies are our gardens, to the which our wills   320
　　are gardeners; so that if we will plant nettles or sow
　　lettuce, set hyssop and weed up thyme, supply it with
　　one gender of herbs or distract it with many—either to
　　have it sterile with idleness or manured with industry—
　　why, the power and corrigible authority of this lies in   325
　　our wills. If the balance of our lives had not one scale
　　of reason to poise another of sensuality, the blood and
　　baseness of our natures would conduct us to most
　　preposterous conclusions. But we have reason to cool our
　　raging motions, our carnal stings, our unbitted lusts;   330
　　whereof I take this that you call love to be a sect or scion.
Roderigo. It cannot be.
Iago. It is merely a lust of the blood and a permission of
　　the will. Come, be a man! Drown thyself? Drown cats
　　and blind puppies! I have professed me thy friend, and I   335
　　confess me knit to thy deserving with cables of perdurable
　　toughness. I could never better stead thee than now. Put
　　money in thy purse. Follow these wars; defeat thy
　　favor with an usurped beard. I say, put money in thy
　　purse. It cannot be that Desdemona should long continue   340
　　her love to the Moor—put money in thy purse—nor he
　　his to her. It was a violent commencement, and thou
　　shalt see an answerable sequestration—put but money in
　　thy purse. These Moors are changeable in their wills—
　　fill thy purse with money. The food that to him now is   345
　　as luscious as locusts shall be to him shortly as bitter as
　　coloquintida. She must change for youth: when she is
　　sated with his body, she will find the error of her choice.
　　[She must have change, she must.] Therefore put money
　　in thy purse. If thou wilt needs damn thyself, do it a more   350
　　delicate way than drowning. Make all the money thou
　　canst. If sanctimony and a frail vow betwixt an erring
　　barbarian and a supersubtle Venetian be not too hard for
　　my wits and all the tribe of hell, thou shalt enjoy her.
　　Therefore make money. A pox of drowning! 'Tis clean   355
　　out of the way. Seek thou rather to be hanged in com-
　　passing thy joy than to be drowned and go without her.

323 *gender* species 325 *corrigible authority* corrective power 327 *poise* counterbalance
327-28 *blood and baseness* animal instincts 330 *motions* appetites *unbitted* uncontrolled
331 *sect or scion* offshoot, cutting 338-39 *defeat thy favor* spoil thy appearance 343 *sequestration* estrangement 347 *coloquintida* a medicine 351 *Make* raise 352 *erring* wandering

Roderigo. Wilt thou be fast to my hopes, if I depend on the
　　issue?

Iago. Thou art sure of me. Go, make money. I have told　　360
　　thee often, and I retell thee again and again, I hate the
　　Moor. My cause is hearted; thine hath no less reason.
　　Let us be conjunctive in our revenge against him. If thou
　　canst cuckold him, thou dost thyself a pleasure, me a
　　sport. There are many events in the womb of time, which　　365
　　will be delivered. Traverse, go, provide thy money!
　　We will have more of this to-morrow. Adieu.

Roderigo. Where shall we meet i' th' morning?

Iago. At my lodging.

Roderigo. I'll be with thee betimes.　　370

Iago. Go to, farewell.—Do you hear, Roderigo?

[*Roderigo.* What say you?

Iago. No more of drowning, do you hear?

Roderigo. I am changed.

Iago. Go to, farewell. Put money enough in your purse.]　　375

Roderigo. I'll sell all my land.　　　　　　　　　　　　*Exit.*

Iago. Thus do I ever make my fool my purse;
　　For I mine own gained knowledge should profane
　　If I would time expend with such a snipe
　　But for my sport and profit. I hate the Moor;　　380
　　And it is thought abroad that 'twixt my sheets
　　H'as done my office. I know not if't be true;
　　Yet I, for mere suspicion in that kind,
　　Will do as if for surety. He holds me well;
　　The better shall my purpose work on him.　　385
　　Cassio's a proper man. Let me see now:
　　To get his place, and to plume up my will
　　In double knavery—How, how?—Let's see:—
　　After some time, to abuse Othello's ear
　　That he is too familiar with his wife.　　390
　　He hath a person and a smooth dispose
　　To be suspected—framed to make women false.
　　The Moor is of a free and open nature
　　That thinks men honest that but seem to be so;
　　And will as tenderly be led by th' nose　　395
　　As asses are.
　　I have't! It is engendered! Hell and night
　　Must bring this monstrous birth to the world's light.

　　　　　　　　　　　　　　　　　　　　　　　　Exit.

---

362 *My cause is hearted* my heart is in it 366 *Traverse* forward march 379 *snipe* fool
384 *well* in high regard 387 *plume up* gratify 391 *dispose* manner 393 *free* frank

---

Enter Montano and two Gentlemen.

Montano. What from the cape can you discern at sea?

1. Gentleman. Nothing at all: it is a high-wrought flood.
    I cannot 'twixt the heaven and the main
    Descry a sail.

Montano. Methinks the wind hath spoke aloud at land;   5
    A fuller blast ne'er shook our battlements.
    If it hath ruffianed so upon the sea,
    What ribs of oak, when mountains melt on them,
    Can hold the mortise? What shall we hear of this?

2. Gentleman. A segregation of the Turkish fleet.   10
    For do but stand upon the foaming shore,
    The chidden billow seems to pelt the clouds;
    The wind-shaked surge, with high and monstrous mane,
    Seems to cast water on the burning Bear
    And quench the Guards of th' ever-fixèd pole.   15
    I never did like molestation view
    On the enchafèd flood.

Montano.   If that the Turkish fleet
    Be not ensheltered and embayed, they are drowned;
    It is impossible they bear it out.

Enter a third Gentleman.

3. Gentleman. News, lads! Our wars are done.   20
    The desperate tempest hath so banged the Turks
    That their designment halts. A noble ship of Venice
    Hath seen a grievous wrack and sufferance
    On most part of their fleet.

Montano. How? Is this true?

3. Gentleman.   The ship is here put in,   25
    A Veronesa; Michael Cassio,
    Lieutenant to the warlike Moor Othello,
    Is come on shore; the Moor himself at sea,
    And is in full commission here for Cyprus.

Montano. I am glad on't. 'Tis a worthy governor.   30

3. Gentleman. But this same Cassio, though he speak of
        comfort
    Touching the Turkish loss, yet he looks sadly
    And prays the Moor be safe, for they were parted
    With foul and violent tempest.

II, i, 9 *hold the mortise* hold their joints together 10 *segregation* scattering 15 *Guards* stars near the North Star *pole* polestar 16 *molestation* tumult 22 *designment halts* plan is crippled 23 *sufferance* disaster 26 *Veronesa* ship furnished by Verona

Montano.   Pray heaven he be;
  For I have served him, and the man commands   35
  Like a full soldier. Let's to the seaside, ho!
  As well to see the vessel that's come in
  As to throw out our eyes for brave Othello,
  Even till we make the main and th' aerial blue
  An indistinct regard.
3. Gentleman.   Come, let's do so;   40
  For every minute is expectancy
  Of more arrivance.

Enter Cassio.

Cassio. Thanks, you the valiant of this warlike isle,
  That so approve the Moor! O, let the heavens
  Give him defense against the elements,   45
  For I have lost him on a dangerous sea!
Montano. Is he well shipped?
Cassio. His bark is stoutly timbered, and his pilot
  Of very expert and approved allowance;
  Therefore my hopes, not surfeited to death,   50
  Stand in bold cure.   *(Within)* A sail, a sail, a sail!

Enter a Messenger.

Cassio. What noise?
Messenger. The town is empty; on the brow o' th' sea
  Stand ranks of people, and they cry 'A sail!'
Cassio. My hopes do shape him for the governor.   *A shot.*   55
2. Gentleman. They do discharge their shot of courtesy:
  Our friends at least.
Cassio.   I pray you, sir, go forth
  And give us truth who 'tis that is arrived.
2. Gentleman. I shall.   *Exit.*
Montano. But, good lieutenant, is your general wived?   60
Cassio. Most fortunately. He hath achieved a maid
  That paragons description and wild fame;
  One that excels the quirks of blazoning pens,
  And in th' essential vesture of creation
  Does tire the ingener.

Enter Second Gentleman.

How now? Who has put in?   65

40 *An indistinct regard* indistinguishable 50 *surfeited to death* overindulged 51 *in bold cure*
a good chance of fulfillment 62 *paragons* surpasses 63 *quirks* ingenuities *blazoning* describing 64-65 *And . . . ingener* merely to describe her as God made her exhausts her praiser

2. Gentleman. 'Tis one Iago, ancient to the general.
Cassio. H'as had most favorable and happy speed:
    Tempest themselves, high seas, and howling winds,
    The guttered rocks and congregated sands,
    Traitors ensteeped to clog the guiltless keel,   70
    As having sense of beauty, do omit
    Their mortal natures, letting go safely by
    The divine Desdemona.
Montano.   What is she?
Cassio. She that I spake of, our great captain's captain,
    Left in the conduct of the bold Iago,   75
    Whose footing here anticipates our thoughts
    A se'nnight's speed. Great Jove, Othello guard,
    And swell his sail with thine own pow'rful breath,
    That he may bless this bay with his tall ship,
    Make love's quick pants in Desdemona's arms,   80
    Give renewed fire to our extincted spirits,
    [And bring all Cyprus comfort!]

> *Enter Desdemona, Iago, Roderigo, and Emilia [with*
> *Attendants].*

    O, behold!
    The riches of the ship is come on shore!
    Ye men of Cyprus, let her have your knees.
    Hail to thee, lady! and the grace of heaven,   85
    Before, behind thee, and on every hand,
    Enwheel thee round!
Desdemona.   I thank you, valiant Cassio.
    What tidings can you tell me of my lord?
Cassio. He is not yet arrived; nor know I aught
    But that he's well and will be shortly here.   90
Desdemona. O but I fear! How lost you company?
Cassio. The great contention of the sea and skies
    Parted our fellowship.   *(Within)* A sail, a sail! *[A shot.]*
        But hark. A sail!
2. Gentleman. They give their greeting to the citadel;
    This likewise is a friend.
Cassio.   See for the news.   95

                                              [Exit Gentleman.]

    Good ancient, you are welcome. *[to Emilia]* Welcome,
        mistress.—
    Let it not gall your patience, good Iago,
    That I extend my manners. 'Tis my breeding
    That gives me this bold show of courtesy.   *[Kisses Emilia.]*

69 *guttered* jagged 70 *ensteeped* submerged 72 *mortal* deadly 76 *footing* landing 77 *se'n-night's* week's 99 S.D. *Kisses Emilia* (kissing was a common Elizabethan form of social courtesy)

Iago. Sir, would she give you so much of her lips   100
  As of her tongue she oft bestows on me,
  You would have enough.
Desdemona.   Alas, she has no speech!
Iago. In faith, too much.
  I find it still when I have list to sleep.
  Marry, before your ladyship, I grant,   105
  She puts her tongue a little in her heart
  And chides with thinking.
Emilia. You have little cause to say so.
Iago. Come on, come on! you are pictures out of
    doors,
  Bells in your parlors, wildcats in your kitchens,   110
  Saints in your injuries, devils being offended,
  Players in your housewifery, and housewives in your
    beds.
Desdemona. O, fie upon thee, slanderer!
Iago. Nay, it is true, or else I am a Turk:
  You rise to play, and go to bed to work.   115
Emilia. You shall not write my praise.
Iago.   No, let me not.
Desdemona. What wouldst thou write of me, if thou
    shouldst praise me?
Iago. O gentle lady, do not put me to't,
  For I am nothing if not critical.
Desdemona. Come on, assay.—There's one gone to the
    harbor?   120
Iago. Ay, madam.
Desdemona. I am not merry; but I do beguile
  The thing I am by seeming otherwise.—
  Come, how wouldst thou praise me?
Iago. I am about it; but indeed my invention   125
  Comes from my pate as birdlime does from frieze—
  It plucks out brains and all. But my Muse labors,
  And thus she is delivered:
  If she be fair and wise, fairness and wit—
  The one's for use, the other useth it.   130
Desdemona. Well praised! How if she be black and witty?
Iago. If she be black, and thereto have a wit,
  She'll find a white that shall her blackness fit.
Desdemona. Worse and worse!
Emilia. How if fair and foolish?   135
Iago. She never yet was foolish that was fair,
  For even her folly helped her to an heir.

112 *housewifery* housekeeping *housewives* hussies 120 *assay* try 126 *birdlime* a sticky paste
frieze rough cloth 131 *black* brunette 137 *folly* wantonness

Desdemona. These are old fond paradoxes to make fools
 laugh i' th' alehouse. What miserable praise hast thou
 for her that's foul and foolish?   140
Iago. There's none so foul, and foolish thereunto,
 But does foul pranks which fair and wise ones do.
Desdemona. O heavy ignorance! Thou praisest the worst
 best. But what praise couldst thou bestow on a deserving
 woman indeed—one that in the authority of her merit   145
 did justly put on the vouch of very malice itself?
Iago. She that was ever fair, and never proud;
 Had tongue at will, and yet was never loud;
 Never lacked gold, and yet went never gay;
 Fled from her wish, and yet said 'Now I may';   150
 She that, being angered, her revenge being nigh,
 Bade her wrong stay, and her displeasure fly;
 She that in wisdom never was so frail
 To change the cod's head for the salmon's tail;
 She that could think, and ne'er disclose her mind;   155
 See suitors following, and not look behind:
 She was a wight (if ever such wight were)—
Desdemona. To do what?
Iago. To suckle fools and chronicle small beer.
Desdemona. O most lame and impotent conclusion! Do   160
 not learn of him, Emilia, though he be thy husband.
 How say you, Cassio? Is he not a most profane and
 liberal counsellor?
Cassio. He speaks home, madam. You may relish him
 more in the soldier than in the scholar.   165
Iago. [*aside*] He takes her by the palm. Ay, well said,
 whisper! With as little a web as this will I ensnare as
 great a fly as Cassio. Ay, smile upon her, do! I will gyve
 thee in thine own courtship.—You say true; 'tis so, indeed!—If such tricks as these strip you out of your lieu- 170
 tenantry, it had been better you had not kissed your
 three fingers so oft—which now again you are most apt
 to play the sir in. Very good! well kissed! an excellent
 curtsy! 'Tis so, indeed. Yet again your fingers to your
 lips? Would they were clyster pipes for your sake!   175
 (*Trumpet within.*) The Moor! I know his trumpet.

---

138 *fond* foolish 140 *foul* ugly 146 *put on the vouch* compel the approval 154 *To . . . tail*
i.e. to exchange the good for the poor but expensive 159 *chronicle small beer* keep petty
household accounts 162-63 *profane and liberal* wordly and licentious 164 *home* bluntly
168-69 *gyve . . . courtship* manacle you by means of your courtly manners 173 *sir* courtly
gentleman 174 *curtsy* courtesy 175 *clyster pipes* syringes

Cassio. 'Tis truly so.
Desdemona. Let's meet him and receive him.
Cassio. Lo, where he comes.

Enter Othello and Attendants.

Othello. O my fair warrior!
Desdemona.　　　　My dear Othello!　　　　　　　　　　180
Othello. It gives me wonder great as my content
　　To see you here before me. O my soul's joy!
　　If after every tempest come such calms,
　　May the winds blow till they have wakened death!
　　And let the laboring bark climb hills of seas　　　185
　　Olympus-high, and duck again as low
　　As hell's from heaven! If it were now to die,
　　'Twere now to be most happy; for I fear
　　My soul hath her content so absolute
　　That not another comfort like to this　　　　　　190
　　Succeeds in unknown fate.
Desdemona.　　　　The heavens forbid
　　But that our loves and comforts should increase
　　Even as our days do grow.
Othello.　　　　　　　　　Amen to that, sweet powers!
　　I cannot speak enough of this content;
　　It stops me here; it is too much of joy.　　　　　195
　　And this, and this, the greatest discords be　　*They kiss.*
　　That e'er our hearts shall make!
Iago.　　　　　　　　　*[aside]* O, you are well tuned now!
　　But I'll set down the pegs that make this music,
　　As honest as I am.
Othello.　　Come, let us to the castle.
　　News, friends! Our wars are done; the Turks are
　　　　drowned.　　　　　　　　　　　　　　　200
　　How does my old acquaintance of this isle?—
　　Honey, you shall be well desired in Cyprus;
　　I have found great love amongst them. O my sweet,
　　I prattle out of fashion, and I dote
　　In mine own comforts. I prithee, good Iago,　　　205
　　Go to the bay and disembark my coffers.
　　Bring thou the master to the citadel;
　　He is a good one, and his worthiness
　　Does challenge much respect.—Come, Desdemona,
　　Once more well met at Cyprus.　　　　　　　　210
　　　　　　Exit Othello [with all but Iago and Roderigo].

198 *set down* loosen 202 *well desired* warmly welcomed 207 *master* ship captain 209 *challenge* deserve

Iago. *[to an Attendant, who goes out]* Do thou meet me
    presently at the harbor. *[to Roderigo]* Come hither. If thou
    be'st valiant (as they say base men being in love have
    then a nobility in their natures more than is native to
    them), list me. The lieutenant to-night watches on the   215
    court of guard. First, I must tell thee this: Desdemona
    is directly in love with him.
Roderigo. With him? Why, 'tis not possible.
Iago. Lay thy finger thus, and let thy soul be instructed.
    Mark me with what violence she first loved the Moor,   220
    but for bragging and telling her fantastical lies; and will
    she love him still for prating? Let not thy discreet heart
    think it. Her eye must be fed; and what delight shall she
    have to look on the devil? When the blood is made dull
    with the act of sport, there should be, again to inflame it   225
    and to give satiety a fresh appetite, loveliness in favor,
    sympathy in years, manners, and beauties; all which the
    Moor is defective in. Now for want of these required
    conveniences, her delicate tenderness will find itself
    abused, begin to heave the gorge, disrelish and abhor the   230
    Moor. Very nature will instruct her in it and compel her
    to some second choice. Now, sir, this granted—as it is a
    most pregnant and unforced position—who stands so
    eminent in the degree of this fortune as Cassio does? A
    knave very voluble; no further conscionable than in put-   235
    ting on the mere form of civil and humane seeming for
    the better compassing of his salt and most hidden loose
    affection? Why, none! why, none! A slipper and subtle
    knave; a finder-out of occasions; that has an eye can
    stamp and counterfeit advantages, though true advantage   240
    never present itself; a devilish knave! Besides, the knave
    is handsome, young, and hath all those requisites in him
    that folly and green minds look after. A pestilent com-
    plete knave! and the woman hath found him already.
Roderigo. I cannot believe that in her; she's full of most   245
    blessed condition.
Iago. Blessed fig's-end! The wine she drinks is made of
    grapes. If she had been blessed, she would never have
    loved the Moor. Blessed pudding! Didst thou not see her
    paddle with the palm of his hand? Didst not mark that?   250
Roderigo. Yes, that I did; but that was but courtesy.

---

216 *court of guard* headquarters 219 *thus* i.e. on your lips 229 *conveniences* compatibilities
230 *heave the gorge* be nauseated 233 *pregnant* evident 235 *conscionable* conscientious
236 *humane* polite 237 *salt* lecherous 238 *slipper* slippery 246 *condition* character

Iago. Lechery, by this hand! an index and obscure prologue
    to the history of lust and foul thoughts. They met so
    near with their lips that their breaths embraced together.
    Villainous thoughts, Roderigo! When these mutalities   255
    so marshal the way, hard at hand comes the master and
    main exercise, th' incorporate conclusion. Pish! But, sir,
    be you ruled by me: I have brought you from Venice.
    Watch you to-night; for the command, I'll lay't upon
    you. Cassio knows you not. I'll not be far from you: do   260
    you find some occasion to anger Cassio, either by speak-
    ing too loud, or tainting his discipline, or from what
    other course you please which the time shall more favor-
    ably minister.
Roderigo. Well.   265
Iago. Sir, he is rash and very sudden in choler, and haply
    with his truncheon may strike at you. Provoke him that
    he may; for even out of that will I cause these of Cyprus
    to mutiny; whose qualifications shall come into no true
    taste again but by the displanting of Cassio. So shall you   270
    have a shorter journey to your desires by the means I shall
    then have to prefer them; and the impediment most
    profitably removed without the which there were no
    expectation of our prosperity.
Roderigo. I will do this if you can bring it to any oppor-   275
    tunity.
Iago. I warrant thee. Meet me by and by at the citadel; I
    must fetch his necessaries ashore. Farewell.
Roderigo. Adieu.   *Exit.*
Iago. That Cassio loves her, I do well believe it;   280
    That she loves him, 'tis apt and of great credit.
    The Moor, howbeit that I endure him not,
    Is of a constant, loving, noble nature,
    And I dare think he'll prove to Desdemona
    A most dear husband. Now I do love her too;   285
    Not out of absolute lust, though peradventure
    I stand accountant for as great a sin,
    But partly led to diet my revenge,
    For that I do suspect the lusty Moor
    Hath leaped into my seat; the thought whereof   290
    Doth, like a poisonous mineral, gnaw my inwards;
    And nothing can or shall content my soul

---

255 *mutualities* exchanges 257 *incorporate* carnal 262 *tainting* discrediting 266 *sudden in choler* violent in anger 269 *qualification* appeasement 269-70 *true taste* satisfactory state 272 *prefer* advance 281 *apt* probable 287 *accountant* accountable 288 *diet* feed

Till I am evened with him, wife for wife:
Or failing so, yet that I put the Moor
At least into a jealousy so strong   295
That judgment cannot cure. Which thing to do,
If this poor trash of Venice, whom I trash
For his quick hunting, stand the putting on,
I'll have our Michael Cassio on the hip,
Abuse him to the Moor in the rank garb   300
(For I fear Cassio with my nightcap too),
Make the Moor thank me, love, and reward me
For making him egregiously an ass
And practicing upon his peace and quiet
Even to madness. 'Tis here, but yet confused: 305
Knavery's plain face is never seen till used.   *Exit.*

Enter Othello's Herald, with a proclamation.   II,ii

Herald. It is Othello's pleasure, our noble and valiant general, that, upon certain tidings now arrived, importing
the mere perdition of the Turkish fleet, every man put
himself into triumph; some to dance, some to make bon-
fires, each man to what sport and revels his addiction   5
leads him. For, besides these beneficial news, it is the celebration of his nuptial. So much was his pleasure should
be proclaimed. All offices are open, and there is full liberty of feasting from this present hour of five till the bell
have told eleven. Heaven bless the isle of Cyprus and our   10
noble general Othello!   *Exit.*

Enter Othello, Desdemona, Cassio, and Attendants.   II,iii

Othello. Good Michael, look you to the guard to-night.
Let's teach ourselves that honorable stop,
Not to outsport discretion.
Cassio. Iago hath direction what to do;
But not withstanding, with my personal eye   5
Will I look to't.
Othello.   Iago is most honest.
Michael, good night. To-morrow with your earliest
Let me have speech with you. *[to Desdemona]* Come, my
      dear love.

---

297 *I trash* I weight down (in order to keep under control) 298 *For* in order to develop
stand the putting on responds to my inciting 299 *on the hip* at my mercy 300 *rank garb*
gross manner 304 *practicing upon* plotting against II, ii, 3 *mere perdition* complete destruction 8 *offices* kitchens and storerooms

The purchase made, the fruits are to ensue;
That profit's yet to come 'tween me and you.— 10
Good night.

Exit [Othello with Desdemona and Attendants].

Enter Iago.

Cassio. Welcome, Iago. We must to the watch.
Iago. Not this hour, lieutenant; 'tis not yet ten o' th' clock.
   Our general cast us thus early for the love of his Desde-
   mona; who let us not therefore blame. He hath not yet 15
   made wanton the night with her, and she is sport for
   Jove.
Cassio. She's a most exquisite lady.
Iago. And, I'll warrant her, full of game.
Cassio. Indeed, she's a most fresh and delicate creature. 20
Iago. What an eye she has! Methinks it sounds a parley to
   provocation.
Cassio. An inviting eye; and yet methinks right modest.
Iago. And when she speaks, is it not an alarum to love?
Cassio. She is indeed perfection. 25
Iago. Well, happiness to their sheets! Come, lieutenant, I
   have a stoup of wine, and here without are a brace of
   Cyprus gallants that would fain have a measure to the
   health of black Othello.
Cassio. Not to-night, good Iago. I have very poor and un- 30
   happy brains for drinking; I could well wish courtesy
   would invent some other custom of entertainment.
Iago. O, they are our friends. But one cup! I'll drink for
   you.
Cassio. I have drunk but one cup to-night, and that was 35
   craftily qualified too; and behold what innovation it
   makes here. I am unfortunate in the infirmity and dare
   not task my weakness with any more.
Iago. What, man! 'Tis a night of revels: the gallants desire
   it. 40
Cassio. Where are they?
Iago. Here at the door; I pray you call them in.
Cassio. I'll do't, but it dislikes me.   *Exit.*
Iago. If I can fasten but one cup upon him
   With that which he hath drunk to-night already, 45
   He'll be as full of quarrel and offense
   As my young mistress' dog. Now my sick fool Roderigo,

II, iii, 14 *cast* dismissed 27 *stoup* two-quart tankard 36 *qualified* diluted *innovation* disturb-
ance

Whom love hath turned almost the wrong side out,
To Desdemona hath to-night caroused
Potations pottle-deep; and he's to watch.   50
Three lads of Cyprus—noble swelling spirits,
That hold their honors in a wary distance,
The very elements of this warlike isle—
Have I to-night flustered with flowing cups,
And they watch too. Now, 'mongst this flock of drunk-
    ards   55
Am I to put our Cassio in some action
That may offend the isle.

      Enter Cassio, Montano, and Gentlemen; [Servants fol-
               lowing with wine].

    But here they come.
 If consequence do but approve my dream,
 My boat sails freely, both with wind and stream.
Cassio. 'Fore God, they have given me a rouse al-   60
   ready.
Montano. Good faith, a little one; not past a pint, as I am a
   soldier.
Iago. Some wine, ho!
   [Sings] And let me the canakin clink, clink;   65
           And let me the canakin clink.
              A soldier's a man;
              A life's but a span,
            Why then, let a soldier drink.
 Some wine, boys!   70
Cassio. 'Fore God, an excellent song!
Iago. I learned it in England, where indeed they are most
   potent in potting. Your Dane, your German, and your
   swag-bellied Hollander—Drink, ho!—are nothing to
   your English.   75
Cassio. Is your Englishman so expert in his drinking?
Iago. Why, he drinks you with facility your Dane dead
   drunk; he sweats not to overthrow your Almain; he
   gives your Hollander a vomit ere the next pottle can be
   filled.   80
Cassio. To the health of our general!
Montano. I am for it, lieutenant, and I'll do you justice.

---

50 *pottle-deep* bottoms up 52 *That . . . distance* very sensitive about their honor 53 *very elements* true representatives 60 *rouse* bumper

Iago. O sweet England!

    [Sings] King Stephen was a worthy peer;   85
            His breeches cost him but a crown;
        He held 'em sixpence all too dear,
            With that he called the tailor lown.
        He was a wight of high renown,
            And thou art but of low degree.
        'Tis pride that pulls the country down;   90
            Then take thine auld cloak about thee.

    Some wine, ho!

Cassio. 'Fore God, this is a more exquisite song than the
    other.

Iago. Will you hear't again?   95

Cassio. No, for I hold him to be unworthy of his place that
    does those things. Well, God's above all; and there
    be souls must be saved, and there be souls must not be
    saved.

Iago. It's true, good lieutenant.   100

Cassio. For mine own part—no offense to the general, nor
    any man of quality—I hope to be saved.

Iago. And so do I too, lieutenant.

Cassio. Ay, but, by your leave, not before me. The lieu-
    tenant is to be saved before the ancient. Let's have no   105
    more of this; let's to our affairs.—God forgive us our
    sins!—Gentlemen, let's look to our business. Do not
    think, gentlemen, I am drunk. This is my ancient; this
    is my right hand, and this is my left. I am not drunk now.
    I can stand well enough, and speak well enough.   110

All. Excellent well!

Cassio. Why, very well then. You must not think then that
    I am drunk.   *Exit.*

Montano. To th' platform, masters. Come, let's set the
    watch.

Iago. You see this fellow that is gone before.   115
    He is a soldier fit to stand by Caesar
    And give direction; and do but see his vice.
    'Tis to his virtue a just equinox,
    The one as long as th' other. 'Tis pity of him.
    I fear the trust Othello puts him in,   120
    On some odd time of his infirmity,
    Will shake this island.

Montano.   But is he often thus?

---

87 *lown* rascal 118 *just equinox* exact equivalent

Iago. 'Tis evermore the prologue to his sleep:
　　He'll watch the horologe a double set
　　If drink rock not his cradle.
Montano.　　　　It were well   125
　　The general were put in mind of it.
　　Perhaps he sees it not, or his good nature
　　Prizes the virtue that appears in Cassio
　　And looks not on his evils. Is not this true?

　　　　　　　　　　Enter Roderigo.

Iago. [aside to him] How now, Roderigo?   130
　　I pray you after the lieutenant, go!　　　　*Exit Roderigo.*
Montano. And 'tis great pity that the noble Moor
　　Should hazard such a place as his own second
　　With one of an ingraft infirmity.
　　It were an honest action to say   135
　　So to the Moor.
Iago.　　Not I, for this fair island!
　　I do love Cassio well and would do much
　　To cure him of this evil.　　　　　　　*(Within)* Help! help!
　　　　But hark! What noise?

　　　　　　　Enter Cassio, driving in Roderigo.

Cassio. Zounds, you rogue! you rascal!
Montano. What's the matter, lieutenant?
Cassio.　　　　　　　　　　A knave teach me my duty?　140
　　I'll beat the knave into a twiggen bottle.
Roderigo. Beat me?
Cassio.　　Dost thou prate, rogue?　　　　　　*[Strikes him.]*
Montano.　　　　　　　　　　Nay, good lieutenant!
　　　　　　　　　　　　　　　　　[Stays him.]

　　Pray, sir, hold your hand.
Cassio.　　Let me go, sir,
　　Or I'll knock you o'er the mazzard.
Montano.　　　　　　　　Come, come, you're drunk!
Cassio. Drunk?　　　　　　　　　　*They fight.*　145
Iago. [aside to Roderigo] Away, I say! Go out and cry a
　　mutiny!　　　　　　　　　　*Exit Roderigo.*
　　Nay, good lieutenant. God's will, gentlemen!
　　Help, ho!—lieutenant—sir—Montano—sir—
　　Help, masters!—Here's a goodly watch indeed!

　　　　　　　　　　　　　　　A bell rung.

---

124 *watch . . . set* stay awake twice around the clock 141 *twiggen* wickercovered 144 *mazzard* head

Who's that which rings the bell? Diablo, ho!   150
The town will rise. God's will, lieutenant, hold!
You will be shamed for ever.

Enter Othello and Gentlemen with weapons.

Othello.   What is the matter here?
Montano. Zounds, I bleed still. I am hurt to the death.
   He dies!
Othello. Hold for your lives!   155
Iago. Hold, hold! Lieutenant—sir—Montano—gentle-
   men!
   Have you forgot all sense of place and duty?
   Hold! The general speaks to you. Hold, hold, for shame!
Othello. Why, how now, ho? From whence ariseth this?
   Are we turned Turks, and to ourselves do that   160
   Which heaven hath forbid the Ottomites?
   For Christian shame put by this barbarous brawl!
   He that stirs next to carve for his own rage
   Holds his soul light; he dies upon his motion.
   Silence that dreadful bell! It frights the isle   165
   From her propriety. What's the matter, masters?
   Honest Iago, that looks dead with grieving,
   Speak. Who began this? On thy love, I charge thee.
Iago. I do not know. Friends all but now, even now,
   In quarter, and in terms like bride and groom   170
   Devesting them for bed; and then, but now—
   As if some planet had unwitted men—
   Swords out, and tilting one at other's breast
   In opposition bloody. I cannot speak
   Any beginning to this peevish odds,   175
   And would in action glorious I had lost
   Those legs that brought me to a part of it!
Othello. How comes it, Michael, you are thus forgot?
Cassio. I pray you pardon me; I cannot speak.
Othello. Worthy Montano, you were wont be civil;   180
   The gravity and stillness of your youth
   The world hath noted, and your name is great
   In mouths of wisest censure. What's the matter
   That you unlace your reputation thus
   And spend your rich opinion for the name   185
   Of a night-brawler? Give me answer to't.

---

163 *carve for* indulge 166 *propriety* proper self 170 *quarter* friendliness 175 *peevish odds* childish quarrel 183 *censure* judgment 184 *unlace* undo 185 *rich opinion* high reputation

Montano. Worthy Othello, I am hurt to danger.
    Your officer, Iago, can inform you,
    While I spare speech, which something now offends
      me,
    Of all that I do know; nor know I aught   190
    By me that's said or done amiss this night,
    Unless self-charity be sometimes a vice,
    And to defend ourselves it be a sin
    When violence assails us.
Othello.   Now, by heaven,
    My blood begins my safer guides to rule,   195
    And passion, having my best judgment collied,
    Assays to lead the way. If I once stir
    Or do but lift this arm, the best of you
    Shall sink in my rebuke. Give me to know
    How this foul rout began, who set it on;   200
    And he that is approved in this offense,
    Though he had twinned with me, both at a birth,
    Shall lose me. What! in a town of war,
    Yet wild, the people's hearts brimful of fear,
    To manage private and domestic quarrel?   205
    In night, and on the court and guard of safety?
    'Tis monstrous. Iago, who began't?
Montano. If partially affined, or leagued in office,
    Thou dost deliver more or less than truth,
    Thou art no soldier.
Iago.   Touch me not so near.   210
    I had rather have this tongue cut from my mouth
    Than it should do offense to Michael Cassio;
    Yet I persuade myself, to speak the truth
    Shall nothing wrong him. Thus it is, general.
    Montano and myself being in speech,   215
    There comes a fellow crying out for help,
    And Cassio following him with determined sword
    To execute upon him. Sir, this gentleman
    Steps in to Cassio and entreats his pause.
    Myself the crying fellow did pursue,   220
    Lest by his clamor—as it so fell out—
    The town might fall in fright. He, swift of foot,
    Outran my purpose; and I returned the rather
    For that I heard the clink and fall of swords,
    And Cassio high in oath; which till to-night   225

189 *offends* pains 195 *blood* passion 196 *collied* darkened 197 *Assays* tries 201 *approved in* proved guilty of 205 *manage* carry on 208 *partially . . . office* prejudiced by comradeship or official relations 218 *execute* work his will

I ne'er might say before. When I came back—
For this was brief—I found them close together
At blow and thrust, even as again they were
When you yourself did part them.
More of this matter cannot I report;   230
But men are men; the best sometimes forget.
Though Cassio did some little wrong to him,
As men in rage strike those that wish them
    best,
Yet surely Cassio I believe received
From him that fled some strange indignity,   235
Which patience could not pass.
Othello.   I know, Iago,
Thy honesty and love doth mince this matter,
Making it light to Cassio. Cassio, I love thee;
But never more be officer of mine.

                Enter Desdemona, attended.

Look if my gentle love be not raised up!   240
I'll make thee an example.
Desdemona.   What's the matter?
Othello. All's well now, sweeting; come away to bed.
  [To Montano] Sir, for your hurts, myself will be your
    surgeon.
Lead him off.   *[Montano is led off.]*
Iago, look with care about the town   245
And silence those whom this vile brawl distracted.
Come, Desdemona: 'tis the soldiers' life
To have their balmy slumbers waked with strife.
               Exit [with all but Iago and Cassio].
Iago. What, are you hurt, lieutenant?
Cassio. Ay, past all surgery.   250
Iago. Marry, God forbid!
Cassio. Reputation, reputation, reputation! O, I have lost
  my reputation! I have lost the immortal part of myself,
  and what remains is bestial. My reputation, Iago, my
  reputation!   255
Iago. As I am an honest man, I thought you had received
  some bodily wound. There is more sense in that than in
  reputation. Reputation is an idle and most false imposi-
  tion; oft got without merit and lost without deserving.
  You have lost no reputation at all unless you repute your-   260
  self such a loser. What, man! there are ways to recover
  the general again. You are but now cast in his mood—a

261 *recover* regain favor with 262 *cast in his mood* dismissed because of his anger

punishment more in policy than in malice, even so as one
would beat his offenseless dog to affright an imperious
lion. Sue to him again, and he's yours.   265

Cassio. I will rather sue to be despised than to deceive so
good a commander with so slight, so drunken, and so
indiscreet an officer. Drunk! and speak parrot! and
squabble! swagger! swear! and discourse fustian with
one's own shadow! O thou invisible spirit of wine, if   270
thou has no name to be known by, let us call thee devil!

Iago. What was he that you followed with your sword?
What had he done to you?

Cassio. I know not.

Iago. Is't possible?   275

Cassio. I remember a mass of things, but nothing distinctly;
a quarrel, but nothing wherefore. O God, that men
should put an enemy in their mouths to steal away their
brains! that we should with joy, pleasance, revel, and
applause transform ourselves into beasts!   280

Iago. Why, but you are now well enough. How came you
thus recovered?

Cassio. It hath pleased the devil drunkenness to give place
to the devil wrath. One unperfectness shows me another,
to make me frankly despise myself.   285

Iago. Come, you are too severe a moraler. As the time, the
place, and the condition of this country stands, I could
heartily wish this had not so befall'n; but since it is as it is,
mend it for your own good.

Cassio. I will ask him for my place again: he shall tell me I   290
am a drunkard! Had I as many mouths as Hydra, such an
answer would stop them all. To be now a sensible man,
by and by a fool, and presently a beast! O strange! Every
inordinate cup is unblest, and the ingredient is a devil.

Iago. Come, come, good wine is a good familiar creature   295
if it be well used. Exclaim no more against it. And, good
lieutenant, I think you think I love you.

Cassio. I have well approved it, sir. I drunk!

Iago. You or any man living may be drunk at some time,
man. I'll tell you what you shall do. Our general's wife is   300
now the general. I may say so in this respect, for that he
hath devoted and given up himself to the contemplation,
mark, and denotement of her parts and graces. Confess
yourself freely to her; importune her help to put you in

---

268 *parrot* meaningless phrases 269 *fustian* bombastic nonsense 280 *applause* desire to
please 291 *Hydra* monster with many heads 294 *ingredient* contents 298 *approved* proved

your place again. She is of so free, so kind, so apt, so 305
blessed a disposition she holds it a vice in her goodness
not to do more than she is requested. This broken joint
between you and her husband entreat her to splinter; and
my fortunes against any lay worth naming, this crack
of your love shall grow stronger than 'twas before. 310
Cassio. You advise me well.
Iago. I protest, in the sincerity of love and honest kindness.
Cassio. I think it freely; and betimes in the morning will I
beseech the virtuous Desdemona to undertake for me. I
am desperate of my fortunes if they check me here. 315
Iago. You are in the right. Good night, lieutenant; I must
to the watch.
Cassio. Good night, honest Iago. *Exit Cassio.*
Iago. And what's he then that says I play the villain,
When this advice is free I give and honest, 320
Probal to thinking, and indeed the course
To win the Moor again? For 'tis most easy
Th' inclining Desdemona to subdue
In any honest suit; she's framed as fruitful
As the free elements. And then for her 325
To win the Moor—were't to renounce his baptism,
All seals and symbols of redeemed sin—
His soul is so enfettered to her love
That she may make, unmake, do what she list,
Even as her appetite shall play the god 330
With his weak function. How am I then a villain
To counsel Cassio to this parallel course,
Directly to his good? Divinity of hell!
When devils will the blackest sins put on,
They do suggest at first with heavenly shows, 335
As I do now. For whiles this honest fool
Plies Desdemona to repair his fortunes,
And she for him pleads strongly to the Moor,
I'll pour this pestilence into his ear,
That she repeals him for her body's lust; 340
And by how much she strives to do him good,
She shall undo her credit with the Moor.
So will I turn her virtue into pitch,
And out of her own goodness make the net
That shall enmesh them all.

---

305 *free* bounteous 308 *splinter* bind up with splints 309 *lay* wager 321 *Probal* probable
323 *subdue* persuade 332 *parallel* corresponding 333 *Divinity* theology 334 *put on* incite
340 *repeals him* seeks his recall

Enter Roderigo.

　　　　How, now, Roderigo?   345
Roderigo. I do follow here in the chase, not like a hound that
　　hunts, but one that fills up the cry. My money is almost
　　spent; I have been to-night exceedingly well cudgelled;
　　and I think the issue will be—I shall have so much ex-
　　perience for my pains; and so, with no money at all, and   350
　　a little more wit, return again to Venice.
Iago. How poor are they that have not patience!
　　What wound did ever heal but by degrees?
　　Thou know'st we work by wit, and not by witchcraft;
　　And wit depends on dilatory time.   355
　　Does't not go well? Cassio hath beaten thee,
　　And thou by that small hurt hast cashiered Cassio.
　　Though other things grow fair against the sun,
　　Yet fruits that blossom first will first be ripe.
　　Content thyself awhile. By the mass, 'tis morning!   360
　　Pleasure and action make the hours seem short.
　　Retire thee; go where thou are billeted.
　　Away, I say! Thou shalt know more hereafter.
　　Nay, get thee gone!   *Exit Roderigo.*
　　　　　　Two things are to be done:
　　My wife must move for Cassio to her mistress;   365
　　I'll set her on;
　　Myself the while to draw the Moor apart
　　And bring him jump when he may Cassio find
　　Soliciting his wife. Ay, that's the way!
　　Dull not device by coldness and delay.   *Exit.*   370

Enter Cassio, with Musicians.   III,i

Cassio. Masters, play here, I will content your pains:
　　Something that's brief; and bid 'Good morrow, general.'

　　　　　　　　　　　　　　　　　　[They play.]

Enter the Clown.

Clown. Why, masters, ha' your instruments been at
　　Naples, that they speak i' th' nose thus?
Musician. How, sir, how?   5
Clown. Are these, I pray, called wind instruments?
Musician. Ay, marry, are they, sir.

347 *cry* pack 357 *cashiered Cassio* maneuvered Cassio's discharge 368 *jump* at the exact
moment III, i, 1 *content* reward 4 *Naples* (notorious for its association with venereal disease)

Clown. O, thereby hangs a tail.

Musician. Whereby hangs a tale, sir?

Clown. Marry, sir, by many a wind instrument that I know.　10
　But, masters, here's money for you; and the general so
　likes your music that he desires you, for love's sake, to
　make no more noise with it.

Musician. Well, sir, we will not.

Clown. If you have any music that may not be heard, to't　15
　again: but, as they say, to hear music the general does
　not greatly care.

Musician. We have none such, sir.

Clown. Then put up your pipes in your bag, for I'll away.
　Go, vanish into air, away!　　*Exit Musician [with his fellows].*　20

Cassio. Dost thou hear, my honest friend?

Clown. No, I hear not your honest friend. I hear you.

Cassio. Prithee keep up thy quillets. There's a poor piece of
　gold for thee. If the gentlewoman that attends the gen-
　eral's wife be stirring, tell her there's one Cassio entreats　25
　her a little favor of speech. Wilt thou do this?

Clown. She is stirring, sir. If she will stir hither, I shall seem
　to notify unto her.

Cassio. [Do, good my friend.]　　*Exit Clown.*

　　　　　　Enter Iago.

　　　　In happy time, Iago.

Iago. You have not been abed then?　　30

Cassio. Why, no; the day had broke
　Before we parted. I have made bold, Iago,
　To send in to your wife: my suit to her
　Is that she will to virtuous Desdemona
　Procure me some access.

Iago.　　　　　　I'll send her to you presently;　35
　And I'll devise a mean to draw the Moor
　Out of the way, that your converse and business
　May be more free.

Cassio. I humbly thank you for't.　　*Exit [Iago].*
　　　　I never knew
　A Florentine more kind and honest.　　40

　　　　　　Enter Emilia.

Emilia. Good morrow, good lieutenant. I am sorry
　For your displeasure; but all will sure be well.

---

23 *quillets* quips 29 *In happy time* well met 40 *Florentine* i.e. even a Florentine (like Cassio; Iago was a Venetian)

The general and his wife are talking of it,
And she speaks for you stoutly. The Moor replies
That he you hurt is of great fame in Cyprus   45
And great affinity, and that in wholesome wisdom
He might not but refuse you; but he protests he loves
     you,
And needs no other suitor but his likings
To take the safest occasion by the front
To bring you in again.
Cassio.   Yet I beseech you,   50
If you think fit, or that it may be done,
Give me advantage of some brief discourse
With Desdemona alone.
Emilia.   Pray you come in.
I will bestow you where you shall have time
To speak your bosom freely.
Cassio.   I am much bound to you.   *Exeunt.*   55

Enter Othello, Iago, and Gentlemen.   III, ii

Othello. These letters give, Iago, to the pilot
And by him do my duties to the Senate.
That done, I will be walking on the works;
Repair there to me.
Iago.   Well, my good lord, I'll do't.
Othello. This fortification, gentlemen, shall we see't?   5
Gentlemen. We'll wait upon your lordship.   *Exeunt.*

Enter Desdemona, Cassio, and Emilia.   III, iii

Desdemona. Be thou assured, good Cassio, I will do
All my abilities in thy behalf.
Emilia. Good madam, do. I warrant it grieves my husband
As if the cause were his.
Desdemona. O, that's an honest fellow. Do not doubt,
     Cassio,   5
But I will have my lord and you again
As friendly as you were.
Cassio.   Bounteous madam,
Whatever shall become of Michael Cassio,
He's never anything but your true servant.
Desdemona. I know't; I thank you. You do love my lord;   10
You have known him long; and be you well assured

---

46 *affinity* family connections 49 *occasion* opportunity *front* forelock 55 *your bosom* your
inmost thoughts III, ii, 3 *works* fortifications

He shall in strangeness stand no farther off
Than in a politic distance.
Cassio.　　　　　　Ay, but, lady,
　That policy may either last so long,
　Or feed upon such nice and waterish diet,　　　　　　　　15
　Or breed itself so out of circumstance,
　That, I being absent, and my place supplied,
　My general will forget my love and service.
Desdemona. Do not doubt that; before Emilia here
　I give thee warrant of thy place. Assure thee,　　　　　　20
　If I do vow a friendship, I'll perform it
　To the last article. My lord shall never rest;
　I'll watch him tame and talk him out of patience;
　His bed shall seem a school, his board a shrift;
　I'll intermingle everything he does　　　　　　　　　　25
　With Cassio's suit. Therefore be merry, Cassio,
　For thy solicitor shall rather die
　Than give thy cause away.

Enter Othello and Iago [at a distance].

Emilia. Madam, here comes my lord.
Cassio. Madam, I'll take my leave.　　　　　　　　　　30
Desdemona. Why, stay, and hear me speak.
Cassio. Madam, not now: I am very ill at ease,
　Unfit for mine own purposes.
Desdemona. Well, do your discretion.　　　　*Exit Cassio.*
Iago. Ha! I like not that.
Othello.　　　　　　What dost thou say?　　　　　　35
Iago. Nothing, my lord; or if—I know not what.
Othello. Was not that Cassio parted from my wife?
Iago. Cassio, my lord? No, sure, I cannot think it,
　That he would steal away so guilty-like,
　Seeing you coming.
Othello.　　　　　　I do believe 'twas he.　　　　　　40
Desdemona. How now, my lord?
　I have been talking with a suitor here,
　A man that languishes in your displeasure.
Othello. Who is't you mean?
Desdemona. Why, your lieutenant, Cassio. Good my lord,　45
　If I have any grace or power to move you,
　His present reconciliation take;

III, iii, 12 *strangeness* aloofness 13 *Than ... distance* than wise policy requires
15 *Or ... diet* or be continued for such slight reasons 19 *doubt* fear 23 *watch him tame*
keep him awake until he gives in 24 *shrift* confessional 47 *present* immediate

For if he be not one that truly loves you,
That errs in ignorance, and not in cunning,
I have no judgment in an honest face.   50
I prithee call him back.
Othello.   Went he hence now?
Desdemona. Yes, faith; so humbled
  That he hath left part of his grief with me
  To suffer with him. Good love, call him back.
Othello. How now, sweet Desdemon; some other time.   55
Desdemona. But shall't be shortly?
Othello.   The sooner, sweet, for you.
Desdemona. Shall't be to-night at supper?
Othello.   No, not to-night.
Desdemona. To-morrow dinner then?
Othello.   I shall not dine at home;
  I meet the captains at the citadel.
Desdemona. Why then, to-morrow night, or Tuesday
    morn,   60
  On Tuesday noon or night, or Wednesday morn.
  I prithee name the time, but let it not
  Exceed three days. I' faith, he's penitent;
  And yet his trespass, in our common reason
  (Save that, they say, the wars must make examples   65
  Out of their best), is not almost a fault
  T' incur a private check. When shall he come?
  Tell me, Othello. I wonder in my soul
  What you could ask me that I should deny
  Or stand so mamm'ring on. What? Michael Cassio,   70
  That came a-wooing with you, and so many a time,
  When I have spoke of you dispraisingly,
  Hath ta'en your part—to have so much to do
  To bring him in? By'r Lady, I could do much—
Othello. Prithee no more. Let him come when he will!   75
  I will deny thee nothing.
Desdemona.   Why, this is not a boon;
  'Tis as I should entreat you wear your gloves,
  Or feed on nourishing dishes, or keep you warm,
  Or sue to you to do a peculiar profit
  To your own person. Nay, when I have a suit   80
  Wherein I mean to touch your love indeed,
  It shall be full of poise and difficult weight,
  And fearful to be granted.

---

66 *not almost* hardly 67 *a private check* even a private reprimand 70 *mamm'ring on* hesitating about

Othello.   I will deny thee nothing!
  Whereon I do beseech thee grant me this,
  To leave me but a little to myself.   85
Desdemona. Shall I deny you? No. Farewell, my lord.
Othello. Farewell, my Desdemon: I'll come to thee straight.
Desdemona. Emilia, come.—Be as your fancies teach you;
  Whate'er you be, I am obedient.   *Exit [with Emilia].*
Othello. Excellent wretch! Perdition catch my soul   90
  But I do love thee! and when I love thee not,
  Chaos is come again.
Iago. My noble lord—
Othello.   What dost thou say, Iago?
Iago. Did Michael Cassio, when you wooed my lady,
  Know of your love?   95
Othello. He did, from first to last. Why dost thou ask?
Iago. But for a satisfaction of my thought;
  No further harm.
Othello.   Why of thy thought, Iago?
Iago. I did not think he had been acquainted with her.
Othello. O, yes, and went between us very oft.   100
Iago. Indeed?
Othello. Indeed? Ay, indeed! Discern'st thou aught in that?
  Is he not honest?
Iago.   Honest, my lord?
Othello.   Honest. Ay, honest.
Iago. My lord, for aught I know.
Othello. What dost thou think?
Iago.   Think, my lord?
Othello.   Think, my lord? 105
  By heaven, he echoes me,
  As if there were some monster in his thought
  Too hideous to be shown. Thou dost mean something:
  I heard thee say but now, thou lik'st not that,
  When Cassio left my wife. What didst not like?   110
  And when I told thee he was of my counsel
  In my whole course of wooing, thou cried'st 'Indeed?'
  And didst contract and purse thy brow together,
  As if thou then hadst shut up in thy brain
  Some horrible conceit. If thou dost love me,   115
  Show me thy thought.
Iago. My lord, you know I love you.
Othello.   I think thou dost;
  And, for I know thou'rt full of love and honesty
  And weigh'st thy words before thou giv'st them breath,

90 *wretch* (a term of endearment) 115 *conceit* fancy

Therefore these stops of thine fright me the more;   120
For such things in a false disloyal knave
Are tricks of custom; but in a man that's just
They are close dilations, working from the heart
That passion cannot rule.
Iago.   For Michael Cassio,
I dare be sworn I think that he is honest.   125
Othello. I think so too.
Iago.   Men should be what they seem;
Or those that be not, would they might seem none!
Othello. Certain, men should be what they seem.
Iago. Why then, I think Cassio's an honest man.
Othello. Nay, yet there's more in this.   130
I prithee speak to me as to thy thinkings,
As thou dost ruminate, and give thy worst of thoughts
The worst of words.
Iago.   Good my lord, pardon me:
Though I am bound to every act of duty,
I am not bound to that all slaves are free to.   135
Utter my thoughts? Why, say they are vile and false,
As where's that palace whereinto foul things
Sometimes intrude not? Who has a breast so pure
But some uncleanly apprehensions
Keep leets and law days, and in session sit   140
With meditations lawful?
Othello. Thou dost conspire against thy friend, Iago,
If thou but think'st him wronged, and mak'st his ear
A stranger to thy thoughts.
Iago.   I do beseech you—
Though I perchance am vicious in my guess   145
(As I confess it is my nature's plague
To spy into abuses, and oft my jealousy
Shapes faults that are not), that your wisdom yet
From one that so imperfectly conjects
Would take no notice, nor build yourself a trouble   150
Out of his scattering and unsure observance.
It were not for your quiet nor your good,
Nor for my manhood, honesty, or wisdom,
To let you know my thoughts.
Othello.   What dost thou mean?

123-24 *close dilations ... rule* secret emotions which well up in spite of restraint 127 *seem
none* i.e. not pretend to be men when they are really monsters 135 *bound ... free to* bound
to tell that which even slaves are allowed to keep to themselves 140 *leets and law days*
sittings of the courts 147 *jealousy* suspicion 149 *conjects* conjectures

Iago. Good name in man and woman, dear my lord,   155
   Is the immediate jewel of their souls.
   Who steals my purse steals trash; 'tis something, nothing;
   'Twas mine, 'tis his, and has been slave to thousands;
   But he that filches from me my good name
   Robs me of that which not enriches him   160
   And makes me poor indeed.
Othello. By heaven, I'll know thy thoughts!
Iago. You cannot, if my heart were in your hand;
   Nor shall not whilst 'tis in my custody.
Othello. Ha!
Iago.   O, beware, my lord, of jealousy!   165
   It is the green-eyed monster, which doth mock
   The meat it feeds on. That cuckold lives in bliss
   Who, certain of his fate, loves not his wronger;
   But O, what damned minutes tells he o'er
   Who dotes, yet doubts—suspects, yet strongly loves!   170
Othello. O misery!
Iago. Poor and content is rich, and rich enough;
   But riches fineless is as poor as winter
   To him that ever fears he shall be poor.
   Good God, the souls of all my tribe defend   175
   From jealousy!
Othello.   Why, why is this?
   Think'st thou I'ld make a life of jealousy,
   To follow still the changes of the moon
   With fresh suspicions? No! To be once in doubt
   Is once to be resolved. Exchange me for a goat   180
   When I shall turn the business of my soul
   To such exsufflicate and blown surmises,
   Matching thy inference. 'Tis not to make me jealous
   To say my wife is fair, feeds well, loves company,
   Is free of speech, sings, plays, and dances well;   185
   Where virtue is, these are more virtuous.
   Nor from mine own weak merits will I draw
   The smallest fear or doubt of her revolt,
   For she had eyes, and chose me. No, Iago;
   I'll see before I doubt; when I doubt, prove;   190
   And on the proof there is no more but this—
   Away at once with love or jealousy!
Iago. I am glad of this; for now I shall have reason
   To show the love and duty that I bear you

---

156 *immediate* nearest the heart 166 *mock* play with, like a cat with a mouse 173 *fineless* unlimited 182 *exsufflicate and blown* spat out and flyblown 188 *revolt* unfaithfulness

With franker spirit. Therefore, as I am bound,   195
Receive it from me. I speak not yet of proof.
Look to your wife; observe her well with Cassio;
Wear your eye thus, not jealous nor secure:
I would not have your free and noble nature,
Out of self-bounty, be abused. Look to't.   200
I know our country disposition well:
In Venice they do let God see the pranks
They dare not show their husbands; their best conscience
Is not to leave't undone, but keep't unknown.
Othello. Dost thou say so?   205
Iago. She did deceive her father, marrying you;
   And when she seemed to shake and fear your looks,
   She loved them most.
Othello.   And so she did.
Iago.   Why, go to then!
   She that, so young, could give out such a seeming
   To seel her father's eyes up close as oak—   210
   He thought 'twas witchcraft—but I am much to blame.
   I humbly do beseech you of your pardon
   For too much loving you.
Othello.   I am bound to thee for ever.
Iago. I see this hath a little dashed your spirits.
Othello. Not a jot, not a jot.
Iago.   I' faith, I fear it has.   215
   I hope you will consider what is spoke
   Comes from my love. But I do see y' are moved.
   I am to pray you not to strain my speech
   To grosser issues nor to larger reach
   Than to suspicion.   220
Othello. I will not.
Iago.   Should you do so, my lord,
   My speech should fall into such vile success
   As my thoughts aim not at. Cassio's my worthy friend—
   My lord, I see y' are moved.
Othello.   No, not much moved:
   I do not think but Desdemona's honest.   225
Iago. Long live she so! and long live you to think so!
Othello. And yet, how nature erring from itself—
Iago. Ay, there's the point! as (to be bold with you)
   Not to affect many proposed matches
   Of her own clime, complexion, and degree,   230

---

198 *secure* overconfident 200 *self-bounty* natural goodness 210 *seel* close *oak* oak grain
219 *To grosser issues* to mean something more monstrous 222 *vile success* evil outcome
225 *honest* chaste

Whereto we see in all things nature tends—
Foh! one may smell in such a will most rank,
Foul disproportion, thoughts unnatural—
But pardon me—I do not in position
Distinctly speak of her; though I may fear   235
Her will, recoiling to her better judgment,
May fall to match you with her country forms,
And happily repent.
Othello.   Farewell, farewell!
If more thou dost perceive, let me know more.
Set on thy wife to observe. Leave me, Iago.   240
Iago. My lord, I take my leave.   *[Going.]*
Othello. Why did I marry? This honest creature doubtless
Sees and knows more, much more, than he unfolds.
Iago. [returns] My lord, I would I might entreat your
honor
To scan this thing no further: leave it to time.   245
Although 'tis fit that Cassio have his place,
For sure he fills it up with great ability,
Yet, if you please to hold him off awhile,
You shall by that perceive him and his means.
Note if your lady strain his entertainment   250
With any strong or vehement importunity;
Much will be seen in that. In the mean time
Let me be thought too busy in my fears
(As worthy cause I have to fear I am)
And hold her free, I do beseech your honor.   255
Othello. Fear not my government.
Iago. I once more take my leave.   *Exit.*
Othello. This fellow's of exceeding honesty,
And knows all qualities, with a learned spirit
Of human dealings. If I do prove her haggard,   260
Though that her jesses were my dear heartstrings,
I'd whistle her off and let her down the wind
To prey at fortune. Haply, for I am black
And have not those soft parts of conversation
That chamberers have, or for I am declined   265

234 *position* definite assertion 236 *recoiling* reverting 237 *fall to match* happen to compare 238 *happily* haply, perhaps 250 *strain his entertainment* urge his recall 253 *busy* meddlesome 255 *hold her free* consider her guiltless 256 *government* self-control 259 *qualities* natures 259-60 *learned spirit Of* mind informed about 260 *haggard* a wild hawk 261 *jesses* thongs for controlling a hawk 262-63 *whistle . . . fortune* turn her out and let her take care of herself 263 *for* because 264 *soft . . . conversation* ingratiating manners 265 *chamberers* courtiers

Into the vale of years—yet that's not much—
She's gone. I am abused, and my relief
Must be to loathe her. O curse of marriage,
That we can call these delicate creatures ours,
And not their appetites! I had rather be a toad   270
And live upon the vapor of a dungeon
Than keep a corner in the thing I love
For others' uses. Yet 'tis the plague of great ones;
Prerogatived are they less than the base.
'Tis destiny unshunnable, like death.   275
Even then this forkèd plague is fated to us
When we do quicken. Look where she comes.

Enter Desdemona and Emilia.

If she be false, O, then heaven mocks itself!
I'll not believe't.
Desdemona.   How now, my dear Othello?
Your dinner, and the generous islanders   280
By you invited, do attend your presence.
Othello. I am to blame.
Desdemona.   Why do you speak so faintly?
Are you not well?
Othello. I have a pain upon my forehead, here.
Desdemona. Faith, that's with watching; 'twill away again.   285
Let me but bind it hard, within this hour
It will be well.
Othello.   Your napkin is too little;
                    [*He pushes the handkerchief from him, and it falls
                                                        unnoticed.*]
Let it alone. Come, I'll go in with you.
Desdemona. I am very sorry that you are not well.
                                          Exit [with Othello].
Emilia. I am glad I have found this napkin;   290
This was her first remembrance from the Moor.
My wayward husband hath a hundred times
Wooed me to steal it; but she so loves the
    token
(For he conjured her she should ever keep it)
That she reserves it evermore about her   295
To kiss and talk to. I'll have the work ta'en out

---

273 *great ones* prominent men 274 *Prerogatived* privileged 276 *forkèd plague* i.e. horns of a
cuckold 277 *do quicken* are born 280 *generous* noble 285 *watching* working late 287 *napkin*
handkerchief 288 *it* i.e. his forehead 296 *work ta'en out* pattern copied

And give't Iago.
What he will do with it heaven knows, not I;
I nothing but to please his fantasy.

Enter Iago.

Iago. How now? What do you here alone?   300
Emilia. Do not you chide; I have a thing for you.
Iago. A thing for me? It is a common thing—
Emilia. Ha?
Iago. To have a foolish wife.
Emilia. O, is that all? What will you give me now   305
    For that same handkerchief?
Iago.   What handkerchief?
Emilia. What handkerchief!
    Why, that the Moor first gave to Desdemona;
    That which so often you did bid me steal.
Iago. Hast stol'n it from her?   310
Emilia. No, faith; she let it drop by negligence,
    And to th' advantage, I, being here, took't up.
    Look, here it is.
Iago.   A good wench! Give it me.
Emilia. What will you do with't, that you have been so
        earnest
    To have me filch it?
Iago.   Why, what's that to you?   *[Snatches it.]*   315
Emilia. If it be not for some purpose of import,
    Give't me again. Poor lady, she'll run mad
    When she shall lack it.
Iago. Be not acknown on't; I have use for it.
    Go, leave me.   *Exit Emilia.*   320
    I will in Cassio's lodging lose this napkin
    And let him find it. Trifles light as air
    Are to the jealous confirmations strong
    As proofs of holy writ. This may do something.
    The Moor already changes with my poison: 325
    Dangerous conceits are in their natures poisons,
    Which at the first are scarce found to distaste,
    But with a little act upon the blood
    Burn like the mines of sulphur.

Enter Othello.

        I did say so.
    Look where he comes! Not poppy nor mandragora,   330

---

299 *fantasy* whim 316 *import* importance 319 *Be . . . on't* do not acknowledge it 326 *conceits* ideas 330 *mandragora* a narcotic

Nor all the drowsy syrups of the world,
Shall ever med'cine thee to that sweet sleep
Which thou owedst yesterday.
Othello.   Ha! ha! false to me?
Iago. Why, how now, general? No more of that!
Othello. Avaunt! be gone! Thou has set me on the rack.   335
  I swear 'tis better to be much abused
  Than but to know't a little.
Iago.   How now, my lord?
Othello. What sense had I of her stol'n hours of lust?
  I saw't not, thought it not, it harmed not me;
  I slept the next night well, fed well, was free and merry;   340
  I found not Cassio's kisses on her lips.
  He that is robbed, not wanting what is stol'n,
  Let him not know't, and he's not robbed at all.
Iago. I am sorry to hear this.
Othello. I had been happy if the general camp,   345
  Pioners and all, had tasted her sweet body,
  So I had nothing known. O, now for ever
  Farewell the tranquil mind! farewell content!
  Farewell the plumèd troop, and the big wars
  That make ambition virtue! O, farewell!   350
  Farewell the neighing steed and the shrill trump,
  The spirit-stirring drum, th' ear-piercing fife,
  The royal banner, and all quality,
  Pride, pomp, and circumstance of glorious war!
  And O you mortal engines whose rude throats   355
  Th' immortal Jove's dread clamors counterfeit,
  Farewell! Othello's occupation's gone!
Iago. Is't possible, my lord?
Othello. Villain, be sure thou prove my love a whore!
  Be sure of it; give me the ocular proof;   360
  Or, by the worth of man's eternal soul,
  Thou hadst been better have been born a dog
  Than answer my waked wrath!
Iago.   Is't come to this?
Othello. Make me to see't; or at the least so prove it
  That the probation bear no hinge nor loop   365
  To hang a doubt on— or woe upon thy life!
Iago. My noble lord—
Othello. If thou dost slander her and torture me,
  Never pray more; abandon all remorse;

---

340 *free* carefree 342 *wanting* missing 364 *Pioners* sappers, laborers 349 *big* stately 354 *circumstance* pageantry 355 *mortal engines* deadly artillery 356 *counterfeit* imitate 365 *probation* proof

On horror's head horrors accumulate;   370
Do deeds to make heaven weep, all earth amazed;
For nothing canst thou to damnation add
Greater than that.
Iago.   O grace! O heaven forgive me!
Are you a man? Have you a soul or sense?—
God b' wi' you! take mine office. O wretched fool,   375
That liv'st to make thine honesty a vice!
O monstrous world! Take note, take note, O world,
To be direct and honest is not safe.
I thank you for this profit; and from hence
I'll love no friend, sith love breeds such offense.   380
Othello. Nay, stay. Thou shouldst be honest.
Iago. I should be wise; for honesty's a fool
And loses that it works for.
Othello.   By the world,
I think my wife be honest, and think she is not;
I think that thou art just, and think thou art not.   385
I'll have some proof. Her name, that was as fresh
As Dian's visage, is now begrimed and black
As mine own face. If there be cords, or knives,
Poison, or fire, or suffocating streams,
I'll not endure it. Would I were satisfied!   390
Iago. I see, sir, you are eaten up with passion:
I do repent me that I put it to you.
You would be satisfied?
Othello.   Would? Nay, I will.
Iago. And may; but how; how satisfied, my lord?
Would you, the supervisor, grossly gape on?   395
Behold her topped?
Othello.   Death and damnation! O!
Iago. It were a tedious difficulty, I think,
To bring them to that prospect. Damn them then,
If ever mortal eyes do see them bolster
More than their own! What then? How then?   400
What shall I say? Where's satisfaction?
It is impossible you should see this,
Were they as prime as goats, as hot as monkeys,
As salt as wolves in pride, and fools as gross
As ignorance made drunk. But yet, I say,   405
If imputation and strong circumstances
Which lead directly to the door of truth
Will give you satisfaction, you may have't.

---

379 *profit* profitable lesson   390 *satisfied* completely informed   395 *supervisor* spectator
399 *bolster* lie together   403 *prime* lustful   404 *salt* lecherous *pride* heat

Othello. Give me a living reason she's disloyal.
Iago. I do not like the office.   410
   But sith I am entered in this cause so far,
   Pricked to't by foolish honesty and love,
   I will go on. I lay with Cassio lately,
   And being troubled with a raging tooth,
   I could not sleep.   415
   There are a kind of men so loose of soul
   That in their sleeps will mutter their affairs.
   One of this kind is Cassio.
   In sleep I heard him say, 'Sweet Desdemona,
   Let us be wary, let us hide our loves!'   420
   And then, sir, would he gripe and wring my hand,
   Cry 'O sweet creature!' and then kiss me hard,
   As if he plucked up kisses by the roots
   That grew upon my lips; then laid his leg
   Over my thigh, and sighed, and kissed, and then   425
   Cried 'Cursèd fate that gave thee to the Moor!'
Othello. O monstrous! monstrous!
Iago.   Nay, this was but his dream.
Othello. But this denoted a foregone conclusion:
   'Tis a shrewd doubt, though it be but a dream.
Iago. And this may help to thicken other proofs   430
   That do demonstrate thinly.
Othello.   I'll tear her all to pieces!
Iago. Nay, but be wise. Yet we see nothing done;
   She may be honest yet. Tell me but this—
   Have you not sometimes seen a handkerchief
   Spotted with strawberries in your wife's hand?   435
Othello. I gave her such a one; 'twas my first gift.
Iago. I know not that; but such a handkerchief—
   I am sure it was your wife's— did I to-day
   See Cassio wipe his beard with.
Othello.   If't be that—
Iago. If it be that, or any that was hers,   440
   It speaks against her with the other proofs.
Othello. O, that the slave had forty thousand lives!
   One is too poor, too weak for my revenge.
   Now do I see 'tis true. Look here, Iago:
   All my fond love thus do I blow to heaven.   445
   'Tis gone.
   Arise, black vengeance, from the hollow hell!
   Yield up, O love, thy crown and hearted throne

---

428 *foregone conclusion* previous experience 429 *a shrewd doubt* cursedly suspicious

To tyrannous hate! Swell, bosom, with thy fraught,
For 'tis of aspics' tongues! 450
Iago.   Yet be content.
Othello. O, blood, blood, blood!
Iago. Patience, I say. Your mind perhaps may change.
Othello. Never, Iago. Like to the Pontic sea,
    Whose icy current and compulsive course
    Ne'er feels retiring ebb, but keeps due on 455
    To the Propontic and the Hellespont,
    Even so my bloody thoughts, with violent pace,
    Shall ne'er look back, ne'er ebb to humble love,
    Till that a capable and wide revenge
    Swallow them up. *(He kneels.)* Now, by yond marble
        heaven, 460
    In the due reverence of a sacred vow
    I here engage my words.
Iago.   Do not rise yet.   *Iago kneels.*
    Witness, you ever-burning lights above,
    You elements that clip us round about,
    Witness that here Iago doth give up 465
    The execution of his wit, hands, heart
    To wronged Othello's service! Let him command,
    And to obey shall be in me remorse,
    What bloody business ever.   *[They rise.]*
Othello.   I greet thy love,
    Not with vain thanks but with acceptance bounteous, 470
    And will upon the instant put thee to't.
    Within these three days let me hear thee say
    That Cassio's not alive.
Iago. My friend is dead; 'tis done at your request.
    But let her live.
Othello.   Damn her, lewd minx! O, damn her! 475
    Come, go with me apart. I will withdraw
    To furnish me with some swift means of death
    For the fair devil. Now art thou my lieutenant.
Iago. I am your own for ever.   *Exeunt.*

      Enter Desdemona, Emilia, and Clown.   III,iv

Desdemona. Do you know, sirrah, where Lieutenant Cassio
    lies?
Clown. I dare not say he lies anywhere.

---

449 *fraught* burden 450 *aspics* deadly poisonous snakes 453 *Pontic sea* Black Sea 459 *capa-*
ble all-embracing 464 *clip* encompass 466 *execution* activities *wit* mind 468 *remorse* pity
III, iv 2 *lies* lives, lodges

Desdemona. Why, man?

Clown. He's a soldier, and for me to say a soldier lies is   5
stabbing.

Desdemona. Go to. Where lodges he?

Clown. To tell you where he lodges is to tell you where I
lie.

Desdemona. Can anything be made of this?   10

Clown. I know not where he lodges; and for me to devise
a lodging, and say he lies here or he lies there, were to
lie in mine own throat.

Desdemona. Can you enquire him out, and be edified by
report?   15

Clown. I will catechize the world for him; that is, make
questions, and by them answer.

Desdemona. Seek him, bid him come hither. Tell him I
have moved my lord on his behalf and hope all will be
well.   20

Clown. To do this is within the compass of man's wit, and
therefore I'll attempt the doing of it.   *Exit.*

Desdemona. Where should I lose that handkerchief, Emilia?

Emilia. I know not, madam.

Desdemona. Believe me, I had rather have lost my purse   25
Full of crusadoes; and but my noble Moor
Is true of mind, and made of no such baseness
As jealous creatures are, it were enough
To put him to ill thinking.

Emilia.   Is he not jealous?

Desdemona. Who? he? I think the sun where he was born   30
Drew all such humors from him.

Enter Othello.

Emilia.   Look where he comes.

Desdemona. I will not leave him now till Cassio
Be called to him.—How is't with you, my lord?

Othello. Well, my good lady. *[aside]* O, hardness to dis-
semble!—
How do you, Desdemona?

Desdemona.   Well, my good lord.   35

Othello. Give me your hand. This hand is moist, my lady.

Desdemona. It yet hath felt no age nor known no sorrow.

Othello. This argues fruitfulness and liberal heart.
Hot, hot, and moist. This hand of yours requires
A sequester from liberty, fasting and prayer,   40

---

26 *crusadoes* Portuguese gold coins 31 *humors* inclinations 40 *sequester* removal

Much castigation, exercise devout;
For here's a young and sweating devil here
That commonly rebels. 'Tis a good hand,
A frank one.
Desdemona.   You may, indeed, say so;
  For 'twas that hand that gave away my heart.   45
Othello. A liberal hand! The hearts of old gave hands;
  But our new heraldry is hands, not hearts.
Desdemona. I cannot speak of this. Come now, your prom-
    ise!
Othello. What promise, chuck?
Desdemona. I have sent to bid Cassio come speak with you.   50
Othello. I have a salt and sorry rheum offends me.
  Lend me thy handkerchief.
Desdemona.   Here, my lord.
Othello. That which I gave you.
Desdemona.   I have it not about me.
Othello. Not?
Desdemona.   No, faith, my lord.
Othello.   That is a fault.
  That handkerchief   55
  Did an Egyptian to my mother give.
  She was a charmer, and could almost read
  The thoughts of people. She told her, while she kept it,
  'Twould make her amiable and subdue my father
  Entirely to her love; but if she lost it   60
  Or made a gift of it, my father's eye
  Should hold her loathly, and his spirits should hunt
  After new fancies. She, dying, gave it me,
  And bid me, when my fate would have me wive,
  To give it her. I did so; and take heed on't;   65
  Make it a darling like your precious eye.
  To lose't or give't away were such perdition
  As nothing else could match.
Desdemona.   Is't possible?
Othello. 'Tis true. There's magic in the web of it.
  A sibyl that had numbered in the world   70
  The sun to course two hundred compasses,
  In her prophetic fury sewed the work;
  The worms were hallowed that did breed the silk;
  And it was dyed in mummy which the skillful
  Conserved of maidens' hearts.

---

47 *heraldry* heraldic symbolism 51 *salt . . . rheum* distressing head-cold 56 *Egyptian* gypsy
57 *charmer* sorceress 59 *amiable* lovable 67 *perdition* disaster 71 *compasses* annual rounds
74 *mummy* a drug made from mummies

Desdemona.   I' faith? Is't true?   75
Othello. Most veritable. Therefore look to't well.
Desdemona. Then would to God that I had never seen't!
Othello. Ha! Wherefore?
Desdemona. Why do you speak so startingly and rash?
Othello. Is't lost? Is't gone? Speak, is it out o' th' way?   80
Desdemona. Heaven bless us!
Othello. Say you?
Desdemona. It is not lost. But what an if it were?
Othello. How?
Desdemona. I say it is not lost.
Othello.   Fetch't, let me see't!   85
Desdemona. Why, so I can, sir; but I will not now.
    This is a trick to put me from my suit:
    Pray you let Cassio be received again.
Othello. Fetch me the handkerchief! My mind misgives.
Desdemona. Come, come!   90
    You'll never meet a more sufficient man.
Othello. The handkerchief!
Desdemona.   I pray talk me of Cassio.
Othello. The handkerchief!
Desdemona.   A man that all his time
    Hath founded his good fortunes on your love,
    Shared dangers with you—   95
Othello. The handkerchief!
Desdemona. I'faith, you are to blame.
Othello. Zounds!   *Exit.*
Emilia. Is not this man jealous?
Desdemona. I ne'er saw this before.   100
    Sure there's some wonder in this handkerchief;
    I am most unhappy in the loss of it.
Emilia. 'Tis not a year or two shows us a man.
    They are all but stomachs, and we all but food;
    They eat us hungerly, and when they are full,   105
    They belch us.

                    Enter Iago and Cassio.

    Look you—Cassio and my husband!
Iago. There is no other way; 'tis she must do't.
    And lo the happiness! Go and importune her.
Desdemona. How now, good Cassio? What's the news
        with you?
Cassio. Madam, my former suit. I do beseech you   110
    That by your virtuous means I may again

108 *happiness* good luck

Exist, and be a member of his love
Whom I with all the office of my heart
Entirely honor. I would not be delayed.
If my offense be of such mortal kind   115
That neither service past, nor present sorrows,
Nor purposed merit in futurity,
Can ransom me into his love again,
But to know so must be my benefit.
So shall I clothe me in a forced content,   120
And shut myself up in some other course,
To fortune's alms.
Desdemona.   Alas, thrice-gentle Cassio!
My advocation is not now in tune.
My lord is not my lord; nor should I know him,
Were he in favor as in humor altered.   125
So help me every spirit sanctified
As I have spoken for you all my best
And stood within the blank of his displeasure
For my free speech! You must awhile be patient.
What I can do I will; and more I will   130
Than for myself I dare. Let that suffice you.
Iago. Is my lord angry?
Emilia.   He went hence but now,
And certainly in strange unquietness.
Iago. Can he be angry? I have seen the cannon
When it hath blown his ranks into the air   135
And, like the devil, from his very arm
Puffed his own brother—and can he be angry?
Something of moment then. I will go meet him.
There's matter in't indeed if he be angry.
Desdemona. I prithee do so.   *Exit [Iago].*
                    Something sure of state,   140
Either from Venice or some unhatched practice
Made demonstrable here in Cyprus to him,
Hath puddled his clear spirit; and in such cases
Men's natures wrangle with inferior things,
Though great ones are their object. 'Tis even so;   145
For let our finger ache, and it endues
Our other, healthful members even to that sense
Of pain. Nay, we must think men are not gods,
Nor of them look for such observancy

---

121 *shut myself up in* confine myself to 123 *advocation* advocacy 125 *favor* appearance
128 *blank* bull's-eye of the target 140 *state* public affairs 141 *unhatched practice* budding
plot 143 *puddled* muddied 146 *endues* brings

As fits the bridal. Beshrew me much, Emilia,   150
I was, unhandsome warrior as I am,
Arraigning his unkindness with my soul;
But now I find I had suborned the witness,
    And he's indicted falsely.
Emilia. Pray heaven it be state matters, as you think,   155
    And no conception nor no jealous toy
    Concerning you.
Desdemona. Alas the day! I never gave him cause.
Emilia. But jealous souls will not be answered so;
    They are not ever jealous for the cause,   160
    But jealous for they are jealous. 'Tis a monster
    Begot upon itself, born on itself.
Desdemona. Heaven keep that monster from Othello's
        mind!
Emilia. Lady, amen.
Desdemona. I will go seek him. Cassio, walk here about: 165
    If I do find him fit, I'll move your suit
    And seek to effect it to my uttermost.
Cassio. I humbly thank your ladyship.
                            Exeunt Desdemona and Emilia.

                        Enter Bianca.

Bianca. Save you, friend Cassio!
Cassio.   What make you from home?
    How is it with you, my most fair Bianca?   170
    I' faith, sweet love, I was coming to your house.
Bianca. And I was going to your lodging, Cassio.
    What, keep a week away? seven days and nights?
    Eightscore eight hours? and lovers' absent hours,
    More tedious than the dial eightscore times?   175
    O weary reck'ning!
Cassio.   Pardon me, Bianca:
    I have this while with leaden thoughts been pressed;
    But I shall in a more continuate time
    Strike off this score of absence. Sweet Bianca,
                    [Gives her Desdemona's handkerchief.]
    Take me this work out.
Bianca.   O Cassio, whence came this?   180
    This is some token from a newer friend.

---

151 *unhandsome warrior* inadequate soldier 152 *Arraigning . . . soul* indicting his unkindness before the bar of my soul 156 *toy* fancy 175 *dial* clock 178 *continuate* uninterrupted
180 *Take . . . out* copy this embroidery for me

To the felt absence now I feel a cause.
Is't come to this? Well, well.
Cassio.   Go to, woman!
  Throw your vile guesses in the devil's teeth,
  From whence you have them. You are jealous now   185
  That this is from some mistress, some remembrance.
  No, by my faith, Bianca.
Bianca.   Why, whose is it?
Cassio. I know not, sweet; I found it in my chamber.
  I like the work well; ere it be demanded,
  As like enough it will, I'd have it copied.   190
  Take it and do't, and leave me for this time.
Bianca. Leave you? Wherefore?
Cassio. I do attend here on the general
  And think it no addition, nor my wish,
  To have him see me womaned.
Bianca.   Why, I pray you?   195
Cassio. Not that I love you not.
Bianca.   But that you do not love me!
  I pray you bring me on the way a little,
  And say if I shall see you soon at night.
Cassio. 'Tis but a little way that I can bring you,
  For I attend here; but I'll see you soon.   200
Bianca. 'Tis very good. I must be circumstanced.

                                        Exeunt.

              —————

            Enter Othello and Iago.   IV,i

Iago. Will you think so?
Othello.   Think so, Iago?
Iago.   What,
  To kiss in private?
Othello.   An unauthorized kiss.
Iago. Or to be naked with her friend in bed
  An hour or more, not meaning any harm?
Othello. Naked in bed, Iago, and not mean harm?   5
  It is hypocrisy against the devil.
  They that mean virtuously, and yet do so,
  The devil their virtue tempts, and they tempt heaven.
Iago. So they do nothing, 'tis a venial slip.
  But if I give my wife a handkerchief—   10
Othello. What then?

---

201 *circumstanced* governed by circumstances IV, i, 6 *hypocrisy . . . devil* i.e. feigned sin
instead of feigned virtue

Iago. Why, then 'tis hers, my lord; and being hers,
   She may, I think, bestow't on any man.
Othello. She is protectress of her honor too;
   May she give that?   15
Iago. Her honor is an essence that's not seen;
   They have it very oft that have it not.
   But for the handkerchief—
Othello. By heaven, I would most gladly have forgot it!
   Thou said'st—O, it comes o'er my memory   20
   As doth the raven o'er the infected house,
   Boding to all!—he had my handkerchief.
Iago. Ay, what of that?
Othello.   That's not so good now.
Iago.   What
   If I had said I had seen him do you wrong?
   Or heard him say—as knaves be such abroad   25
   Who having, by their own importunate suit,
   Or voluntary dotage of some mistress,
   Convincèd or supplied them, cannot choose
   But they must blab—
Othello.   Hath he said anything?
Iago. He hath, my lord; but be you well assured,   30
   No more than he'll unswear.
Othello.   What hath he said?
Iago. Faith, that he did—I know not what he did.
Othello. What? what?
Iago. Lie—
Othello. With her?
Iago.   With her, on her; what you will.
Othello. Lie with her? lie on her?—We say lie on her when   35
   they belie her.—Lie with her! Zounds, that's fulsome.—
   Handkerchief—confessions—handkerchief!—To con-
   fess, and be hanged for his labor—first to be hanged, and
   then to confess! I tremble at it. Nature would not invest
   herself in such shadowing passion without some instruc-   40
   tion. It is not words that shakes me thus.—Pish! Noses,
   ears, and lips? Is't possible?—Confess?—Handkerchief?
   —O devil!   *Falls in a trance.*
Iago. Work on,
   My med'cine, work! Thus credulous fools are caught,   45
   And many worthy and chaste dames even thus,
   All guiltless, meet reproach.—What, ho! my lord!
   My lord, I say! Othello!

---

21 *infected* plague-stricken 28 *Convincèd or supplied* overcome or gratified 39-41 *Nature . . . instruction* my natural faculties would not be so overcome by passion without
reason

Enter Cassio.

         How now, Cassio?

Cassio. What's the matter?

Iago. My lord is fall'n into an epilepsy.   50
   This is his second fit; he had one yesterday.

Cassio. Rub him about the temples.

Iago.   No, forbear.
   The lethargy must have his quiet course.
   If not, he foams at mouth, and by and by
   Breaks out to savage madness. Look, he stirs.   55
   Do you withdraw yourself a little while.
   He will recover straight. When he is gone,
   I would on great occasion speak with you.

                            [Exit Cassio.]

   How is it, general? Have you not hurt your head?

Othello. Dost thou mock me?

Iago.   I mock you? No, by heaven.   60
   Would you would bear your fortune like a man!

Othello. A hornèd man's a monster and a beast.

Iago. There's many a beast then in a populous city,
   And many a civil monster.

Othello. Did he confess it?

Iago.   Good sir, be a man.   65
   Think every bearded fellow that's but yoked
   May draw with you. There's millions now alive
   That nightly lie in those unproper beds
   Which they dare swear peculiar: your case is better.
   O, 'tis the spite of hell, the fiend's arch-mock,   70
   To lip a wanton in a secure couch,
   And to suppose her chaste! No, let me know;
   And knowing what I am, I know what she shall be.

Othello. O, thou art wise! 'Tis certain.

Iago.   Stand you awhile apart;
   Confine yourself but in a patient list.   75
   Whilst you were here, o'erwhelmed with your grief—
   A passion most unsuiting such a man—
   Cassio came hither. I shifted him away
   And laid good 'scuse upon your ecstasy;
   Bade him anon return, and here speak with me;   80
   The which he promised. Do but encave yourself
   And mark the fleers, the gibes, and notable scorns

---

62 *hornèd man* cuckold 68 *unproper* not exclusively their own 69 *peculiar* exclusively their own 71 *secure* free from fear of rivalry 75 *in a patient list* within the limits of self-control 79 *ecstasy* trance 81 *encave* conceal

That dwell in every region of his face;
For I will make him tell the tale anew—
Where, how, how oft, how long ago, and when   85
He hath, and is again to cope your wife.
I say, but mark his gesture. Marry, patience!
Or shall I say you are all in all in spleen,
And nothing of a man.
Othello.   Dost thou hear, Iago?
I will be found most cunning in my patience;   90
But—dost thou hear?—most bloody.
Iago.   That's not amiss;
But yet keep time in all. Will you withdraw?

[Othello retires.]

Now will I question Cassio of Bianca,
A huswife that by selling her desires
Buys herself bread and clothes. It is a creature   95
That dotes on Cassio, as 'tis the strumpet's plague
To beguile many and be beguiled by one.
He, when he hears of her, cannot refrain
From the excess of laughter. Here he comes.

Enter Cassio.

As he shall smile, Othello shall go mad;   100
And his unbookish jealousy must conster
Poor Cassio's smiles, gestures, and light behavior
Quite in the wrong. How do you now, lieutenant?
Cassio. The worser that you give me the addition
Whose want even kills me.   105
Iago. Ply Desdemona well, and you are sure on't.
Now, if this suit lay in Bianca's power,
How quickly should you speed!
Cassio.   Alas, poor caitiff!
Othello. Look how he laughs already!
Iago. I never knew a woman love man so.   110
Cassio. Alas, poor rogue! I think, i' faith, she loves
        me.
Othello. Now he denies it faintly, and laughs it out.
Iago. Do you hear, Cassio?
Othello.   Now he importunes him
To tell it o'er. Go to! Well said, well said!
Iago. She gives it out that you shall marry her.   115
Do you intend it?

86 *cope* meet 88 *all in all in spleen* wholly overcome by your passion 94 *huswife* hussy
101 *unbookish* uninstructed *conster* construe, interpret 104 *addition* title 108 *caitiff* wretch

Cassio. Ha, ha, ha!

Othello. Do you triumph, Roman? Do you triumph?

Cassio. I marry her? What, a customer? Prithee bear
    some charity to my wit; do not think it so unwholesome.   120
    Ha, ha, ha!

Othello. So, so, so, so! They laugh that win!

Iago. Faith, the cry goes that you shall marry her.

Cassio. Prithee say true.

Iago. I am a very villain else.   125

Othello. Have you scored me? Well.

Cassio. This is the monkey's own giving out. She is per-
    suaded I will marry her out of her own love and flattery,
    not out of my promise.

Othello. Iago beckons me; now he begins the story.   130

Cassio. She was here even now; she haunts me in every
    place. I was t' other day talking on the sea bank with cer-
    tain Venetians, and thither comes the bauble, and, by this
    hand, she falls me thus about my neck—

Othello. Crying 'O dear Cassio!' as it were. His gesture   135
    imports it.

Cassio. So hangs, and lolls, and weeps upon me; so hales
    and pulls me! Ha, ha, ha!

Othello. Now he tells how she plucked him to my chamber.
    O, I see that nose of yours, but not that dog I shall throw't   140
    to.

Cassio. Well, I must leave her company.

Enter Bianca.

Iago. Before me! Look where she comes.

Cassio. 'Tis such another fitchew! marry, a perfumed one.
    What do you mean by this haunting of me?   145

Bianca. Let the devil and his dam haunt you! What did you
    mean by that same handkerchief you gave me even now?
    I was a fine fool to take it. I must take out the whole
    work? A likely piece of work that you should find it in
    your chamber and know not who left it there! This is   150
    some minx's token, and I must take out the work? There!
    Give it your hobby-horse. Wheresoever you had it, I'll
    take out no work on't.

Cassio. How now, my sweet Bianca? How now? how
    now?   155

---

119 *customer* prostitute 126 *scored me* settled my account (?) 130 *beckons* signals 133 *bauble* plaything 137 *hales* hauls 144 *fitchew* polecat (slang for whore) 152 *hobby-horse* harlot

Othello. By heaven, that should be my handkerchief!
Bianca. An you'll come to supper to-night, you may; an
    you will not, come when you are next prepared for.   *Exit.*
Iago. After her, after her!
Cassio. Faith, I must; she'll rail i' th' street else.   160
Iago. Will you sup there?
Cassio. Yes, I intend so.
Iago. Well, I may chance to see you; for I would very fain
    speak with you.
Cassio. Prithee come. Will you?   165
Iago. Go to! say no more.   *Exit Cassio.*
Othello. [*comes forward*] How shall I murder him, Iago?
Iago. Did you perceive how he laughed at his vice?
Othello. O Iago!
Iago. And did you see the handkerchief?   170
Othello. Was that mine?
Iago. Yours, by this hand! And to see how he prizes the
    foolish woman your wife! She gave it him, and he hath
    giv'n it his whore.
Othello. I would have him nine years a-killing!—A fine   175
    woman! a fair woman! a sweet woman!
Iago. Nay, you must forget that.
Othello. Ay, let her rot, and perish, and be damned to-
    night; for she shall not live. No, my heart is turned to
    stone; I strike it, and it hurts my hand. O, the world hath   180
    not a sweeter creature! She might lie by an emperor's
    side and command him tasks.
Iago. Nay, that's not your way.
Othello. Hang her! I do but say what she is. So delicate with
    her needle! an admirable musician! O, she will sing the   185
    savageness out of a bear! Of so high and plenteous wit
    and invention—
Iago. She's the worse for all this.
Othello. O, a thousand thousand times! And then, of so
    gentle a condition!   190
Iago. Ay, too gentle.
Othello. Nay, that's certain. But yet the pity of it, Iago! O
    Iago, the pity of it, Iago!
Iago. If you are so fond over her iniquity, give her patent to
    offend; for if it touch not you, it comes near nobody.   195
Othello. I will chop her into messes! Cuckold me!
Iago. O, 'tis foul in her.
Othello. With mine officer!
Iago. That's fouler.

190 *condition* disposition 194 *patent* license

Othello. Get me some poison, Iago, this night. I'll not ex-   200
 postulate with her, lest her body and beauty unprovide
 my mind again. This night, Iago!
Iago. Do it not with poison. Strangle her in her bed, even
 the bed she hath contaminated.
Othello. Good, good! The justice of it pleases. Very good!   205
Iago. And for Cassio, let me be his undertaker: you shall
 hear more by midnight.
Othello. Excellent good!   *A trumpet.*
     What trumpet is that same?
Iago. Something from Venice, sure.

    Enter Lodovico, Desdemona, and Attendants.

      'Tis Lodovico,
 Come from the Duke; and see, your wife is with him.   210
Lodovico. God save you, worthy general!
Othello.   With all my heart, sir.
Lodovico. The Duke and senators of Venice greet you.
             [Gives him a letter.]
Othello. I kiss the instrument of their pleasures.
          [Opens the letter and reads.]
Desdemona. And what's the news, good cousin Lodovico?
Iago. I am very glad to see you, signior.   215
 Welcome to Cyprus.
Lodovico. I thank you. How does Lieutenant Cassio?
Iago.   Lives, sir.
Desdemona. Cousin, there's fall'n between him and my lord
 An unkind breach; but you shall make all well.
Othello. Are you sure of that?   220
Desdemona. My lord?
Othello. [reads] 'This fail you not to do, as you will—'
Lodovico. He did not call; he's busy in the paper.
 Is there division 'twixt thy lord and Cassio?
Desdemona. A most unhappy one. I would do much   225
 T' atone them, for the love I bear to Cassio.
Othello. Fire and brimstone!
Desdemona.   My lord?
Othello.   Are you wise?
Desdemona. What, is he angry?
Lodovico.   May be the letter moved him;
 For, as I think, they do command him home,
 Deputing Cassio in his government.   230
Desdemona. By my troth, I am glad on't.

---

201 *unprovide* unsettle 206 *be his undertaker* undertake to deal with him 226 *atone* recon-
cile

Othello.   Indeed?
Desdemona.   My lord?
Othello. I am glad to see you mad.
Desdemona.   Why, sweet Othello—
Othello. Devil!   *[Strikes her.]*
Desdemona. I have not deserved this.
Lodovico. My lord, this would not be believed in Venice,   235
    Though I should swear I saw't. 'Tis very much.
    Make her amends; she weeps.
Othello.   O devil, devil!
    If that the earth could teem with woman's tears,
    Each drop she falls would prove a crocodile.
    Out of my sight!
Desdemona.   I will not stay to offend you.   *[Going.]*   240
Lodovico. Truly, an obedient lady.
    I do beseech your lordship call her back.
Othello. Mistress!
Desdemona.   My lord?
Othello.   What would you with her, sir?
Lodovico. Who? I, my lord?
Othello. Ay, You did wish that I would make her turn.   245
    Sir, she can turn, and turn, and yet go on
    And turn again; and she can weep, sir, weep;
    And she's obedient; as you say, obedient,
    Very obedient.—Proceed you in your tears.—
    Concerning this, sir—O well-painted passion!—   250
    I am commanded home.—Get you away;
    I'll send for you anon.—Sir, I obey the mandate
    And will return to Venice.—Hence, avaunt!
                                                    [Exit Desdemona.]
    Cassio shall have my place. And, sir, to-night
    I do entreat that we may sup together.   255
    You are welcome, sir, to Cyprus.—Goats and monkeys!
                                                            Exit.
Lodovico. Is this the noble Moor whom our full Senate
    Call all in all sufficient? Is this the nature
    Whom passion could not shake? whose solid virtue
    The shot of accident nor dart of chance   260
    Could neither graze nor pierce?
Iago.   He is much changed.
Lodovico. Are his wits safe? Is he not light of brain?

---

238 *teem* breed 239 *crocodile* (crocodiles were supposed to shed hypocritical tears to lure
men to destruction) 250 *passion* grief

Iago. He's that he is; I may not breathe my censure.
　What he might be—if what he might he is not—
　I would to heaven he were!
Lodovico. 　　　　What, strike his wife? 　　　　265
Iago. Faith, that was not so well; yet would I knew
　That stroke would prove the worst!
Lodovico. 　　　　Is it his use?
　Or did the letters work upon his blood
　And new-create this fault?
Iago. 　　　　Alas, alas!
　It is not honesty in me to speak 　　　　270
　What I have seen and known. You shall observe him,
　And his own courses will denote him so
　That I may save my speech. Do but go after
　And mark how he continues.
Lodovico. I am sorry that I am deceived in him. 　　*Exeunt.* 275

———

　　　　Enter Othello and Emilia. 　　　　IV,ii

Othello. You have seen nothing then?
Emilia. Nor ever heard, nor ever did suspect.
Othello. Yes, you have seen Cassio and she together.
Emilia. But then I saw no harm, and then I heard
　Each syllable that breath made up between them. 　　　　5
Othello. What, did they never whisper?
Emilia. 　　　　Never, my lord.
Othello. Nor send you out o' th' way?
Emilia. Never.
Othello. To fetch her fan, her gloves, her mask, nor
　nothing?
Emilia. Never, my lord. 　　　　10
Othello. That's strange.
Emilia. I durst, my lord, to wager she is honest,
　Lay down my soul at stake. If you think other,
　Remove your thought; it doth abuse your bosom.
　If any wretch have put this in your head, 　　　　15
　Let heaven requite it with the serpent's curse!
　For if she be not honest, chaste, and true,
　There's no man happy; the purest of their wives
　Is foul as slander.
Othello. 　　　　Bid her come hither. Go. 　　*Exit Emilia.*
　She says enough; yet she's a simple bawd 　　　　20
　That cannot say as much. This is a subtle whore,

267 *use* custom

A closet lock and key of villainous secrets;
And yet she'll kneel and pray; I have seen her do't.

Enter Desdemona and Emilia.

Desdemona. My lord, what is your will?
Othello.   Pray, chuck, come hither.
Desdemona. What is your pleasure?
Othello.   Let me see your eyes.   25
    Look in my face.
Desdemona.   What horrible fancy's this?
Othello. [to Emilia] Some of your function, mistress,
    Leave procreants alone and shut the door;
    Cough or cry hem if anybody come.
    Your mystery, your mystery! Nay, dispatch!   30

                                          Exit Emilia.

Desdemona. Upon my knees, what doth your speech im-
        port?
    I understand a fury in your words,
    [But not the words.]
Othello. Why, what art thou?
Desdemona.   Your wife, my lord; your true
    And loyal wife.
Othello.   Come, swear it, damn thyself;   35
    Lest, being like one of heaven, the devils themselves
    Should fear to seize thee. Therefore be double-damned—
    Swear thou art honest.
Desdemona.   Heaven doth truly know it.
Othello. Heaven truly knows that thou art false as hell.
Desdemona. To whom, my lord? With whom? How am I
        false?   40
Othello. Ah, Desdemon! away! away! away!
Desdemona. Alas the heavy day! Why do you weep?
    Am I the motive of these tears, my lord?
    If haply you my father do suspect
    An instrument of this your calling back,   45
    Lay not your blame on me. If you have lost him,
    Why, I have lost him too.
Othello.   Had it pleased heaven
    To try me with affliction, had they rained
    All kinds of sores and shames on my bare head,
    Steeped me in poverty to the very lips,   50
    Given to captivity me and my utmost hopes,
    I should have found in some place of my soul

IV, ii, 30 *mystery* trade, occupation 36 *being... heaven* looking like an angel 38 *honest* chaste 45 *An instrument* to be the cause

A drop of patience. But, alas, to make me
A fixed figure for the time of scorn
To point his slow unmoving finger at!   55
Yet could I bear that too; well, very well.
But there where I have garnered up my heart,
Where either I must live or bear no life,
The fountain from the which my current runs
Or else dries up—to be discarded thence,   60
Or keep it as a cistern for foul toads
To knot and gender in—turn thy complexion there,
Patience, thou young and rose-lipped cherubin!
Ay, there look grim as hell!
Desdemona. I hope my noble lord esteems me honest.   65
Othello. O, ay; as summer flies are in the shambles,
      That quicken even with blowing, O thou weed,
      Who art so lovely fair, and smell'st so sweet,
      That the sense aches at thee, would thou hadst ne'er been
            born!
Desdemona. Alas, what ignorant sin have I committed?   70
Othello. Was this fair paper, this most goodly book,
      Made to write 'whore' upon? What committed?
      Committed? O thou public commoner!
      I should make very forges of my cheeks
      That would to cinders burn up modesty,   75
      Did I but speak thy deeds. What committed?
      Heaven stops the nose at it, and the moon winks;
      The bawdy wind, that kisses all it meets,
      Is hushed within the hollow mine of earth
      And will not hear it. What committed?   80
      Impudent strumpet!
Desdemona.   By heaven, you do me wrong!
Othello. Are not you a strumpet?
Desdemona.   No, as I am a Christian!
      If to preserve this vessel for my lord
      From any other foul unlawful touch
      Be not to be a strumpet, I am none.   85
Othello. What, not a whore?
Desdemona.   No, as I shall be saved!
Othello. Is't possible?
Desdemona. O, heaven forgive us!
Othello.   I cry you mercy then.
      I took you for that cunning whore of Venice

---

54 *time of scorn* scornful world 62 *turn thy complexion there* change thy color at that
point 66 *shambles* slaughterhouse 67 *quicken* come to life 73 *commoner* harlot 77 *winks*
closes her eyes 88 *cry you mercy* beg your pardon

That married with Othello.—*[calling]* You, mistress,   90
That have the office opposite to Saint Peter
And keep the gate of hell!

Enter Emilia.

     You, you, ay, you!
We have done our course; there's money for your pains:
I pray you turn the key, and keep our counsel.   *Exit.*
Emilia. Alas, what does this gentleman conceive?   95
   How do you, madam? How do you, my good lady?
Desdemona. Faith, half asleep.
Emilia. Good madam, what's the matter with my lord?
Desdemona. With who?
Emilia. Why, with my lord, madam.   100
Desdemona. Who is thy lord?
Emilia.   He that is yours, sweet lady.
Desdemona. I have none. Do not talk to me, Emilia.
   I cannot weep; nor answer have I none
   But what should go by water. Prithee to-night
   Lay on my bed my wedding sheets, remember;   105
   And call thy husband hither.
Emilia.   Here's a change indeed!   *Exit.*
Desdemona. 'Tis meet I should be used so, very meet.
   How have I been behaved, that he might stick
   The small'st opinion on my least misuse?

Enter Iago and Emilia.

Iago. What is your pleasure, madam? How is't with you?   110
Desdemona. I cannot tell. Those that do teach young babes
   Do it with gentle means and easy tasks:
   He might have chid me so; for, in good faith,
   I am a child to chiding.
Iago.   What is the matter, lady?
Emilia. Alas, Iago, my lord hath so bewhored her,   115
   Thrown such despite and heavy terms upon her
   As true hearts cannot bear.
Desdemona. Am I that name, Iago?
Iago.   What name, fair lady?
Desdemona. Such as she says my lord did say I was.
Emilia. He called her whore. A beggar in his drink   120
   Could not have laid such terms upon his callet.
Iago. Why did he so?
Desdemona. I do not know; I am sure I am none such.

109 *small'st opinion* least suspicion *least misuse* slightest misconduct 121 *callet* whore

Iago. Do not weep, do not weep. Alas the day!

Emilia. Hath she forsook so many noble matches,   125
  Her father and her country, all her friends,
  To be called whore? Would it not make one weep?

Desdemona. It is my wretched fortune.

Iago.   Beshrew him for't!
  How comes this trick upon him?

Desdemona.   Nay, heaven doth know.

Emilia. I will be hanged if some eternal villain,   130
  Some busy and insinuating rogue,
  Some cogging, cozening slave, to get some office,
  Have not devised this slander. I'll be hanged else.

Iago. Fie, there is no such man! It is impossible.

Desdemona. If any such there be, heaven pardon him!   135

Emilia. A halter pardon him! and hell gnaw his bones!
  Why should he call her whore? Who keeps her com-
            pany?
  What place? what time? what form? what likelihood?
  The Moor's abused by some most villainous knave,
  Some base notorious knave, some scurvy fellow.   140
  O heaven, that such companions thou'dst unfold,
  And put in every honest hand a whip
  To lash the rascals naked through the world
  Even from the east to th' west!

Iago.   Speak within door.

Emilia. O, fie upon them! Some such squire he was   145
  That turned your wit the seamy side without
  And made you to suspect me with the Moor.

Iago. You are a fool. Go to.

Desdemona.   O good Iago,
  What shall I do to win my lord again?
  Good friend, go to him; for, by this light of heaven,   150
  I know not how I lost him. Here I kneel:
  If e'er my will did trespass 'gainst his love
  Either in discourse of thought or actual deed,
  Or that mine eyes, mine ears, or any sense
  Delighted them in any other form,   155
  Or that I do not yet, and ever did,
  And ever will (though he do shake me off
  To beggarly divorcement) love him dearly,
  Comfort forswear me! Unkindness may do much;
  And his unkindness may defeat my life,   160

---

129 *trick* freakish behavior 132 *cogging, cozening* cheating, defrauding 141 *companions*
rogues *unfold* expose 144 *within door* with restraint 153 *discourse* course 159 *Comfort
forswear* happiness forsake 160 *defeat* destroy

But never taint my love. I cannot say 'whore.'
It doth abhor me now I speak the word;
To do the act that might th' addition earn
Not the world's mass of vanity could make me.
Iago. I pray you be content. 'Tis but his humor.   165
    The business of the state does him offense,
    [And he does chide with you.]
Desdemona. If 'twere no other—
Iago.   'Tis but so, I warrant.

                                                        [Trumpets within.]
    Hark how these instruments summon you to supper.
    The messengers of Venice stay the meat: 170
    Go in, and weep not. All things shall be well.

                                    [Exeunt Desdemona and Emilia.]

                        Enter Roderigo.

    How now, Roderigo?
Roderigo. I do not find that thou deal'st justly with me.
Iago. What in the contrary?
Roderigo. Every day thou daff'st me with some device, Iago,   175
    and rather, as it seems to me now, keep'st from me all
    conveniency than suppliest me with the least advantage
    of hope. I will indeed no longer endure it; nor am I yet
    persuaded to put up in peace what already I have fool-
    ishly suffered.   180
Iago. Will you hear me, Roderigo?
Roderigo. Faith, I have heard too much; for your words and
    performance are no kin together.
Iago. You charge me most unjustly.
Roderigo. With naught but truth. I have wasted myself out   185
    of means. The jewels you have had from me to deliver to
    Desdemona would half have corrupted a votarist. You
    have told me she hath received them, and returned me
    expectations and comforts of sudden respect and ac-
    quaintance; but I find none.   190
Iago. Well, go to; very well.
Roderigo. Very well! go to! I cannot go to, man; nor 'tis
    not very well. By this hand, I say 'tis very scurvy, and
    begin to find myself fopped in it.
Iago. Very well.   195
Roderigo. I tell you 'tis not very well. I will make myself
    known to Desdemona. If she will return me my jewels,

---

175 *thou . . . device* you put me off with some trick 177 *conveniency* favorable opportu-
nities 187 *votarist* nun 189 *sudden respect* immediate notice 194 *fopped* duped

I will give over my suit and repent my unlawful solicita-
tion; if not, assure yourself I will seek satisfaction of you.
Iago. You have said now.   200
Roderigo. Ay, and said nothing but what I protest intend-
ment of doing.
Iago. Why, now I see there's mettle in thee; and even from
this instant do build on thee a better opinion than ever
before. Give me thy hand, Roderigo. Thou hast taken   205
against me a most just exception; but yet I protest I have
dealt most directly in thy affair.
Roderigo. It hath not appeared.
Iago. I grant indeed it hath not appeared, and your suspicion is not without wit and judgment. But, Roderigo, if   210
thou hast that in thee indeed which I have greater reason
to believe now than ever, I mean purpose, courage, and
valor, this night show it. If thou the next night following
enjoy not Desdemona, take me from this world with
treachery and devise engines for my life.   215
Roderigo. Well, what is it? Is it within reason and compass?
Iago. Sir, there is especial commission come from Venice to
depute Cassio in Othello's place.
Roderigo. Is that true? Why, then Othello and Desdemona
return again to Venice.   220
Iago. O, no; he goes into Mauritania and takes away with
him the fair Desdemona, unless his abode be lingered
here by some accident; wherein none can be so deter-
minate as the removing of Cassio.
Roderigo. How do you mean removing of him?   225
Iago. Why, by making him uncapable of Othello's place—
knocking out his brains.
Roderigo. And that you would have me to do?
Iago. Ay, if you dare do yourself a profit and a right. He
sups to-night with a harlotry, and thither will I go to him.   230
He knows not yet of his honorable fortune. If you will
watch his going thence, which I will fashion to fall out
between twelve and one, you may take him at your
pleasure. I will be near to second your attempt, and he
shall fall between us. Come, stand not amazed at it, but   235
go along with me. I will show you such a necessity in his
death that you shall think yourself bound to put it on
him. It is now high supper time, and the night grows to
waste. About it!
Roderigo. I will hear further reason for this.   240
Iago. And you shall be satisfied.   *Exeunt.*

215 *engines for* plots against 222-23 *abode . . . here* stay here be extended 223-24 *determi-
nate* effective

Enter Othello, Lodovico, Desdemona, Emilia, and   IV,iii
Attendants.

Lodovico. I do beseech you, sir, trouble yourself no further.
Othello. O, pardon me; 'twill do me good to walk.
Lodovico. Madam, good night. I humbly thank your lady-
    ship.
Desdemona. Your honor is most welcome.
Othello.   Will you walk, sir?
    O, Desdemona—   5
Desdemona. My lord?
Othello. Get you to bed on th' instant; I will be returned
    forthwith. Dismiss your attendant there. Look't be done.
Desdemona. I will, my lord.
                    Exit [Othello, with Lodovico and Attendants.]
Emilia. How goes it now? He looks gentler than he did.   10
Desdemona. He says he will return incontinent.
    He hath commanded me to go to bed,
    And bade me to dismiss you.
Emilia.   Dismiss me?
Desdemona. It was his bidding; therefore, good Emilia,
    Give me my nightly wearing, and adieu.   15
    We must not now displease him.
Emilia. I would you had never seen him!
Desdemona. So would not I. My love doth so approve him
    That even his stubbornness, his checks, his frowns—
    Prithee unpin me—have grace and favor in them.   20
Emilia. I have laid those sheets you bade me on the bed.
Desdemona. All's one. Good faith, how foolish are our
                minds!
    If I do die before thee, prithee shroud me
    In one of those same sheets.
Emilia.   Come, come! You talk.
Desdemona. My mother had a maid called Barbary.   25
    She was in love; and he she loved proved mad
    An did forsake her. She had a song of 'Willow';
    An old thing 'twas; but it expressed her fortune,
    And she died singing it. That song to-night
    Will not go from my mind; I have much to do   30
    But to go hang my head all at one side
    And sing it like poor Barbary. Prithee dispatch.
Emilia. Shall I go fetch your nightgown?
Desdemona.   No, unpin me here.
    This Lodovico is a proper man.

IV, iii, 11 *incontinent* at once 19 *stubbornness* roughness *checks* rebukes 26 *mad* wild,
faithless 33 *nightgown* dressing-gown

Emilia. A very handsome man.   35
Desdemona. He speaks well.
Emilia. I know a lady in Venice would have walked bare-
    foot to Palestine for a touch of his nether lip.
Desdemona. (sings)
        'The poor soul sat sighing by a sycamore tree,
           Sing all a green willow;   40
        Her hand on her bosom, her head on her knee,
           Sing willow, willow, willow.
        The fresh streams ran by her and murmured her
           moans;
           Sing willow, willow, willow;
        Her salt tears fell from her, and soft'ned the stones'—   45
  Lay by these.
           'Sing willow, willow, willow'—
  Prithee hie thee; he'll come anon.
        'Sing all a green willow must be my garland.
        Let nobody blame him; his scorn I approve'—   50
  Nay, that's not next. Hark! who is't that knocks?
Emilia. It is the wind.
Desdemona. [sings]
        'I called my love false love; but what said he then?
           Sing willow, willow, willow:
        If I court moe women, you'll couch with moe men.'   55
  So, get thee gone; good night. Mine eyes do itch.
  Doth that bode weeping?
Emilia.   'Tis neither here nor there.
Desdemona. I have heard it said so. O, these men, these men!
  Dost thou in conscience think—tell me, Emilia—
  That there be women do abuse their husbands   60
  In such gross kind?
Emilia.   There be some such, no question.
Desdemona. Wouldst thou do such a deed for all the world?
Emilia. Why, would not you?
Desdemona.   No, by this heavenly light!
Emilia. Nor I neither by this heavenly light.
  I might do't as well i' th' dark.   65
Desdemona. Wouldst thou do such a deed for all the world?
Emilia. The world's a huge thing; it is a great price for a
  small vice.
Desdemona. Good troth, I think thou wouldst not.
Emilia. By my troth, I think I should; and undo't when I   70
  had done it. Marry, I would not do such a thing for a

48 *hie thee* hurry

joint-ring, nor for measures of lawn, nor for gowns, petti-
coats, nor caps, nor any petty exhibition; but, for all the
whole world—'Ud's pity! who would not make her hus-
band a cuckold to make him a monarch? I should venture   75
purgatory for't.
Desdemona. Beshrew me if I would do such a wrong
    For the whole world.
Emilia. Why, the wrong is but a wrong i' th' world; and
    having the world for your labor, 'tis a wrong in your   80
    own world, and you might quickly make it right.
Desdemona. I do not think there is any such woman.
Emilia. Yes, a dozen; and as many to th' vantage as would
    store the world they played for.
    But I do think it is their husbands' faults   85
    If wives do fall. Say that they slack their duties
    And pour our treasures into foreign laps;
    Or else break out in peevish jealousies,
    Throwing restraint upon us; or say they strike us,
    Or scant our former having in despite—   90
    Why, we have galls; and though we have some grace,
    Yet have we some revenge. Let husbands know
    Their wives have sense like them. They see, and smell,
    And have their palates both for sweet and sour,
    As husbands have. What is it that they do   95
    When they change us for others? Is it sport?
    I think it is. And doth affection breed it?
    I think it doth. Is't frailty that thus errs?
    It is so too. And have not we affections,
    Desires for sport, and frailty, as men have?   100
    Then let them use us well; else let them know,
    The ills we do, their ills instruct us so.
Desdemona. Good night, good night. God me such usage
        send,
    Not to pick bad from bad, but by bad mend!   *Exeunt.*

          Enter Iago and Roderigo.   V,i

Iago. Here, stand behind this bulk; straight will he come.
    Wear thy good rapier bare, and put it home.
    Quick, quick! Fear nothing; I'll be at thy elbow.
    It makes us, or it mars us—think on that,
    And fix most firm thy resolution.   5

---

72 *joint-ring* ring made in separable halves 73 *exhibition* gift 83 *to th' vantage* besides
84 *store* populate 88 *peevish* senseless 90 *having* allowance 91 *galls* spirits to resent
103 *usage* habits V, i, 1 *bulk* projecting shop-front

Roderigo. Be near at hand; I may miscarry in't.
Iago. Here, at thy hand. Be bold, and take thy stand.

                                            [Stands aside.]

Roderigo. I have no great devotion to the deed,
    And yet he hath given me satisfying reasons.
    'Tis but a man gone. Forth my sword! He dies!   10
Iago. I have rubbed this young quat almost to the sense,
    And he grows angry. Now whether he kill Cassio,
    Or Cassio him, or each do kill the other,
    Every way makes my gain. Live Roderigo,
    He calls me to a restitution large   15
    Of gold and jewels that I bobbed from him
    As gifts to Desdemona.
    It must not be. If Cassio do remain,
    He hath a daily beauty in his life
    That makes me ugly; and besides, the Moor   20
    May unfold me to him; there stand I in much peril.
    No, he must die. Be't so! I hear him coming.

                      Enter Cassio.

Roderigo. I know his gait. 'Tis he. Villain, thou diest!

                        [Makes a pass at Cassio.]

Cassio. That thrust had been mine enemy indeed
    But that my coat is better than thou know'st.   25
    I will make proof of thine.   *[Draws, and wounds Roderigo.]*
Roderigo.   O, I am slain!
          *[Iago darts from concealment behind Cassio, wounds him
                            in the leg, and exit.]*
Cassio. I am maimed for ever. Help, ho! Murder! murder!

                                        [Falls.]

                      Enter Othello.

Othello. The voice of Cassio. Iago keeps his word.
Roderigo. O, villain that I am!
Othello.   It is even so.
Cassio. O, help, ho! light! a surgeon!   30
Othello. 'Tis he. O brave Iago, honest and just,
    That hast such noble sense of thy friend's wrong!
    Thou teachest me. Minion, your dear lies dead,
    And your unblest fate hies. Strumpet, I come.

---

11 *quat* pimple *sense* quick 16 *bobbed* swindled 25 *coat* under-shirt of mail 33 *Minion* mistress 34 *hies* hurries on

Forth of my heart those charms, thine eyes, are blotted.   35
Thy bed, lust-stained, shall with lust's blood be spotted.

Exit.

Enter Lodovico and Gratiano.

Cassio. What, ho? No watch? No passage? Murder! mur-
    der!
Gratiano. 'Tis some mischance. The cry is very direful.
Cassio. O, help!
Lodovico. Hark!   40
Roderigo. O wretched villain!
Lodovico. Two or three groan. It is a heavy night.
    These may be counterfeits. Let's think't unsafe
    To come in to the cry without more help.
Roderigo. Nobody come? Then shall I bleed to death.   45
Lodovico. Hark!

Enter Iago, with a light.

Gratiano. Here's one comes in his shirt, with light and
        weapons.
Iago. Who's there? Whose noise is this that cries on mur-
        der?
Lodovico. We do not know.
Iago.   Did not you hear a cry?
Cassio. Here, here! For heaven's sake, help me!
Iago.   What's the matter;   50
Gratiano. This is Othello's ancient, as I take it.
Lodovico. The same indeed, a very valiant fellow.
Iago. What are you here that cry so grievously?
Cassio. Iago? O, I am spoiled, undone by villains!
    Give me some help.   55
Iago. O me, lieutenant! What villains have done this?
Cassio. I think that one of them is hereabout
    And cannot make away.
Iago.   O treacherous villains!
    [To Lodovico and Gratiano] What are you there? Come
        in, and give some help.
Roderigo. O, help me here!   60
Cassio. That's one of them.
Iago.   O murd'rous slave! O villain!
                            [Stabs Roderigo.]

Roderigo. O damned Iago! O inhuman dog!
Iago. Kill men i' th' dark?—Where be these bloody
        thieves?—

37 *passage* passers-by 42 *heavy* cloudy, dark

How silent is this town!—Ho! murder! murder!—
What may you be? Are you of good or evil?　　　　65
Lodovico. As you shall prove us, praise us.
Iago. Signior Lodovico?
Lodovico. He, sir.
Iago. I cry you mercy. Here's Cassio hurt by villains.
Gratiano. Cassio?　　　　　　　　　　　　　70
Iago. How is it, brother?
Cassio. My leg is cut in two.
Iago.　　　　　　Marry, heaven forbid!
　Light, gentlemen. I'll bind it with my shirt.

Enter Bianca.

Bianca. What is the matter, ho? Who is't that cried?
Iago. Who is't that cried?　　　　　　　　　75
Bianca. O my dear Cassio! my sweet Cassio!
　O Cassio, Cassio, Cassio!
Iago. O notable strumpet!—Cassio, may you suspect
　Who they should be that thus have mangled you?
Cassio. No.　　　　　　　　　　　　　　80
Gratiano. I am sorry to find you thus. I have been to seek
　　　　you.
Iago. Lend me a garter. So. O for a chair
　To bear him easily hence!
Bianca. Alas, he faints! O Cassio, Cassio, Cassio!
Iago. Gentlemen all, I do suspect this trash　　　85
　To be a party in this injury.—
　Patience awhile, good Cassio.—Come, come!
　Lend me a light. Know we this face or no?
　Alas, my friend and my dear countryman
　Roderigo? No.—Yes, sure.—O heaven, Roderigo!　90
Gratiano. What, of Venice?
Iago. Even he, sir. Did you know him?
Gratiano.　　　　　　　　　　Know him? Ay.
Iago. Signior Gratiano? I cry you gentle pardon.
　These bloody accidents must excuse my manners
　That so neglected you.
Gratiano.　　　　I am glad to see you.　　　95
Iago. How do you, Cassio?—O, a chair, a chair!
Gratiano. Roderigo?
Iago. He, he, 'tis he! *[A chair brought in.]* O, that's well
　　　　said; the chair.
　Some good man bear him carefully from hence.

82 *chair* litter 98 *well said* well done

I'll fetch the general's surgeon. *[to Bianca]* For you, mis-
        tress,   100
Save you your labor.—He that lies slain here, Cassio,
Was my dear friend. What malice was between you?
Cassio. None in the world; nor do I know the man.
Iago. *[to Bianca]* What, look you pale?—O, bear him out
        o' th' air.   *[Cassio and Roderigo are borne off.]*
Stay you, good gentlemen.—Look you pale, mistress?—   105
Do you perceive the gastness of her eye?—
Nay, if you stare, we shall hear more anon.
Behold her well; I pray you look upon her.
Do you see, gentlemen? Nay, guiltiness will speak,
Though tongues were out of use.   110

Enter Emilia.

Emilia. 'Las, what's the matter? What's the matter, hus-
        band?
Iago. Cassio hath here been set on in the dark
By Roderigo, and fellows that are scaped.
He's almost slain, and Roderigo dead.
Emilia. Alas, good gentleman! alas, good Cassio!   115
Iago. This is the fruit of whoring. Prithee, Emilia,
Go know of Cassio where he supped to-night.
        [To Bianca] What, do you shake at that?
Bianca. He supped at my house; but I therefore shake not.
Iago. O, did he so? I charge you go with me.   120
Emilia. Fie, fie upon thee, strumpet!
Bianca. I am no strumpet, but of life as honest
As you that thus abuse me.
Emilia.   As I? Foh! fie upon thee!
Iago. Kind gentlemen, let's go see poor Cassio dressed.
        [To Bianca] Come, mistress, you must tell's another tale.   125
Emilia, run you to the citadel
And tell my lord and lady what hath happed.
                                                                      [Exit Emilia.]
Will you go on afore?   *Exeunt [all but Iago].*
        This is the night
That either makes me or fordoes me quite.   *[Exit.]*

————

Desdemona [asleep] in her bed. Enter Othello with a light.   V,ii

Othello. It is the cause, it is the cause, my soul.
Let me not name it to you, you chaste stars!
It is the cause. Yet I'll not shed her blood,

106 *gastness* terror 122 *honest* chaste 129 *fordoes* destroys V, ii, 1 *cause* cause of justice

Nor scar that whiter skin of hers than snow,
And smooth as monumental alabaster.   5
Yet she must die, else she'll betray more men.
Put out the light, and then put out the light.
If I quench thee, thou flaming minister,
I can again thy former light restore,
Should I repent me; but once put out thy light,   10
Thou cunning'st pattern of excelling nature,
I know not where is that Promethean heat
That can thy light relume. When I have plucked the rose,
I cannot give it vital growth again;
It needs must wither. I'll smell thee on the tree.   15

           He kisses her.

O balmy breath, that dost almost persuade
Justice to break her sword! One more, one more!
Be thus when thou art dead, and I will kill thee,
And love thee after. One more, and this the last!
So sweet was ne'er so fatal. I must weep,   20
But they are cruel tears. This sorrow's heavenly;
It strikes where it doth love. She wakes.
Desdemona. Who's there? Othello?
Othello.   Ay, Desdemona.
Desdemona. Will you come to bed, my lord?
Othello. Have you prayed to-night, Desdemon?
Desdemona.   Ay, my lord.   25
Othello. If you bethink yourself of any crime
Unreconciled as yet to heaven and grace,
Solicit for it straight.
Desdemona. Alack, my lord, what may you mean by that?
Othello. Well, do it, and be brief; I will walk by.   30
I would not kill thy unpreparèd spirit.
No, heaven forfend! I would not kill thy soul.
Desdemona. Talk you of killing?
Othello.   Ay, I do.
Desdemona.   Then heaven
Have mercy on me!
Othello.   Amen, with all my heart!
Desdemona. If you say so, I hope you will not kill me.   35
Othello. Hum!
Desdemona. And yet I fear you; for you are fatal then
When your eyes roll so. Why I should fear I know
        not,
Since guiltiness I know not; but yet I feel I fear.

8 *minister* servant 12 *Promethean heat* divine fire 13 *relume* relight 32 *forfend* forbid

Othello. Think on thy sins.
Desdemona.   They are loves I bear to you.   40
Othello. Ay, and for that thou diest.
Desdemona. That death's unnatural that kills for loving.
    Alas, why gnaw you so your nether lip?
    Some bloody passion shakes your very frame.
    These are portents; but yet I hope, I hope,   45
    They do not point on me.
Othello.   Peace and be still!
Desdemona. I will so. What's the matter?
Othello. That handkerchief which I so loved and gave thee
    Thou gav'st to Cassio.
Desdemona.   No, by my life and soul!
    Send for the man and ask him.
Othello.   Sweet soul, take heed,   50
    Take heed of perjury; thou art on thy deathbed.
Desdemona. Ay, but not yet to die.
Othello.   Yes, presently.
    Therefore confess thee freely of thy sin;
    For to deny each article with oath
    Cannot remove nor choke the strong conception   55
    That I do groan withal. Thou art to die.
Desdemona. Then Lord have mercy on me!
Othello.   I say amen.
Desdemona. And have you mercy too! I never did
    Offend you in my life; never loved Cassio
    But with such general warranty of heaven   60
    As I might love. I never gave him token.
Othello. By heaven, I saw my handkerchief in's hand!
    O perjured woman! thou dost stone my heart,
    And mak'st me call what I intend to do
    A murder, which I thought a sacrifice.   65
    I saw the handkerchief.
Desdemona.   He found it then.
    I never gave it him. Send for him hither.
    Let him confess a truth.
Othello.   He hath confessed.
Desdemona. What, my lord?
Othello. That he hath used thee.
Desdemona.   How? unlawfully?
Othello.   Ay.   70
Desdemona. He will not say so.
Othello.   No, his mouth is stopped.
    Honest Iago hath ta'en order for't.

52 *presently* at once 55 *conception* belief 59 *Offend* wrong 63 *stone my heart* turn my
heart to stone 72 *ta'en order* taken measures

Desdemona. O, my fear interprets. What, is he dead?
Othello. Had all his hairs been lives, my great revenge
    Had stomach for them all.   75
Desdemona. Alas, he is betrayed, and I undone!
Othello. Out, strumpet! Weep'st thou for him to my
             face?
Desdemona. O, banish me, my lord, but kill me not!
Othello. Down, strumpet!
Desdemona. Kill me to-morrow; let me live to-night!   80
Othello. Nay, an you strive—
Desdemona. But half an hour!
Othello.   Being done, there is no pause.
Desdemona. But while I say one prayer!
Othello.   It is too late.
                                    Smothers her.

[*Desdemona.* O Lord, Lord, Lord!]

Emilia at the door.

Emilia. (calls within) My lord, my lord! What, ho, my
    lord, my lord!   85
Othello. What noise is this? Not dead? not yet quite dead?
    I that am cruel am yet merciful;
    I would not have thee linger in thy pain.
    So, so.
Emilia. (within) What, ho! my lord, my lord!
Othello.   Who's there?   90
Emilia. [within] O, good my lord, I would speak a word
    with you!
Othello. Yes, 'tis Emilia.—By and by.—She's dead.—
    'Tis like she comes to speak of Cassio's death.
    The noise was here. Ha! no more moving?
    Still as the grave.—Shall she come in? Were't good?—   95
    I think she stirs again. No.—What's best to do?
    If she come in, she'll sure speak to my wife.
    My wife! my wife! what wife? I have no wife.
    O, insupportable! O heavy hour!
    Methinks it should be now a huge eclipse   100
    Of sun and moon, and that th' affrighted globe
    Should yawn at alteration.
Emilia.   *[within]* I do beseech you
    That I may speak with you, O good my lord!

102 *yawn* open, as in an earthquake

Othello. I had forgot thee. O, come in, Emilia.
    Soft, by and by.—Let me the curtains draw.—   105

                                  [Closes the bed-curtains.]
    Where art thou?   *[Opens the door.]*

               Enter Emilia.

    What's the matter with thee now?
Emilia. O my good lord, yonder's foul murder done!
Othello. What? Now?
Emilia. But now, my lord.
Othello. It is the very error of the moon.   110
    She comes more nearer earth than she was wont
    And makes men mad.
Emilia. Cassio, my lord, hath killed a young Venetian
    Called Roderigo.
Othello.   Roderigo killed?
    And Cassio killed?
Emilia.   No, Cassio is not killed.   115
Othello. Not Cassio killed? Then murder's out of tune,
    And sweet revenge grows harsh.
Desdemona. O, falsely, falsely murdered!
Emilia.   O Lord! what cry is that?
Othello. That? What?
Emilia. Out and alas! that was my lady's voice.   120
    Help! help, ho! help! O lady, speak again!
    Sweet Desdemona! O sweet mistress, speak!
Desdemona. A guiltless death I die.
Emilia. O, who hath done this deed?
Desdemona. Nobody—I myself. Farewell.   125
    Commend me to my kind lord. O, farewell!   *She dies.*
Othello. Why, how should she be murd'red?
Emilia.   Alas, who knows?
Othello. You heard her say herself, it was not I.
Emilia. She said so. I must needs report the truth.
Othello. She's like a liar gone to burning hell!   130
    'Twas I that killed her.
Emilia.   O, the more angel she,
    And you the blacker devil!
Othello. She turned to folly, and she was a whore.
Emilia. Thou dost belie her, and thou art a devil.
Othello. She was false as water.
Emilia.   Thou art rash as fire to say   135
    That she was false. O, she was heavenly true!

110 *error* straying off course

Othello. Cassio did top her. Ask thy husband else.
   O, I were damned beneath all depth in hell
   But that I did proceed upon just grounds
   To this extremity. Thy husband knew it all.   140
Emilia. My husband?
Othello. Thy husband.
Emilia. That she was false to wedlock?
Othello. Ay, with Cassio. Nay, had she been true,
   If heaven would make me such another world   145
   Of one entire and perfect chrysolite,
   I'ld not have sold her for it.
Emilia. My husband?
Othello.   Ay, 'twas he that told me first.
   An honest man he is, and hates the slime
   That sticks on filthy deeds.
Emilia.   My husband?   150
Othello. What needs this iterance? Woman, I say thy hus-
        band.
Emilia. O mistress, villainy hath made mocks with love!
   My husband say that she was false?
Othello.   He, woman.
   I say, thy husband. Dost understand the word?
   My friend, thy husband; honest, honest Iago.   155
Emilia. If he say so, may his pernicious soul
   Rot half a grain a day! he lies to th' heart.
   She was too fond of her most filthy bargain.
Othello. Ha!
Emilia. Do thy worst.   160
   This deed of thine is no more worthy heaven
   Than thou wast worthy her.
Othello.   Peace, you were best.
Emilia. Thou hast not half the power to do me harm
   As I have to be hurt. O gull! O dolt!
   As ignorant as dirt! thou has done a deed—   165
   I care not for thy sword; I'll make thee known,
   Though I lost twenty lives. Help! help! O, help!
   The Moor hath killed my mistress! Murder! murder!

Enter Montano, Gratiano, Iago, and others.

Montano. What is the matter? How now, general?
Emilia. O, are you come, Iago? You have done well,   170
   That men must lay their murders on your neck.
Gratiano. What is the matter?

151 *iterance* repetition 164 *to be hurt* to endure hurt

Emilia. Disprove this villain, if thou be'st a man.
　　He says thou told'st him that his wife was false.
　　I know thou didst not; thou'rt not such a villain.　　　　175
　　Speak, for my heart is full.
Iago. I told him what I thought, and told no more
　　Than what he found himself was apt and true.
Emilia. But did you ever tell him she was false?
Iago. I did.　　　　　　　　　　　　　　　　　　　180
Emilia. You told a lie, an odious damnèd lie!
　　Upon my soul, a lie! a wicked lie!
　　She false with Cassio? Did you say with Cassio?
Iago. With Cassio, mistress. Go to, charm your tongue.
Emilia. I will not charm my tongue; I am bound to speak:　　185
　　My mistress here lies murdered in her bed—
All. O heavens forfend!
Emilia. And your reports have set the murder on.
Othello. Nay, stare not, masters. It is true indeed.
Gratiano. 'Tis a strange truth.　　　　　　　　　　　190
Montano. O monstrous act!
Emilia.　　　　　　　　Villainy, villainy, villainy!
　　I think upon't—I think I smell't!—O villainy!
　　I thought so then.—I'll kill myself for grief.—
　　O villainy, villainy!
Iago. What, are you mad? I charge you get you home.　　195
Emilia. Good gentlemen, let me have leave to speak.
　　'Tis proper I obey him, but not now.
　　Perchance, Iago, I will ne'er go home.
Othello. O! O! O!　　　　　　　　　　*Falls on the bed.*
Emilia.　　　　　　Nay, lay thee down and roar!
　　For thou hast killed the sweetest innocent　　　　200
　　That e'er did lift up eye.
Othello.　　　　　　O, she was foul!　　　　　*[Rises.]*
　　I scarce did know you, uncle. There lies your niece,
　　Whose breath, indeed, these hands have newly stopped.
　　I know this act shows horrible and grim.
Gratiano. Poor Desdemon! I am glad thy father's dead.　　205
　　Thy match was mortal to him, and pure grief
　　Shore his old thread in twain. Did he live now,
　　This sight would make him do a desperate turn;
　　Yea, curse his better angel from his side,
　　And fall to reprobation.　　　　　　　　　210
Othello. 'Tis pitiful; but yet Iago knows
　　That she with Cassio hath the act of shame

---

184 *charm* cast a spell on 204 *shows* appears 208 *turn* act 210 *reprobation* rejection by
God, damnation

A thousand times committed. Cassio confessed it;
And she did gratify his amorous works
With that recognizance and pledge of love   215
Which I first gave her. I saw it in his hand.
It was a handkerchief, an antique token
My father gave my mother.
Emilia. O God! O heavenly God!
Iago. Zounds, hold your peace!
Emilia.   'Twill out, 'twill out! I peace?   220
No, I will speak as liberal as the north.
Let heaven and men and devils, let them all,
All, all, cry shame against me, yet I'll speak.
Iago. Be wise, and get you home.
Emilia.   I will not.

>   *[Iago draws and threatens Emilia.]*

Gratiano.   Fie!
Your sword upon a woman?   225
Emilia. O thou dull Moor, that handkerchief thou speak'st
              of
I found by fortune, and did give my husband;
For often with a solemn earnestness—
More than indeed belonged to such a trifle—
He begged of me to steal't.
Iago.   Villainous whore!   230
Emilia. She give it Cassio? No, alas, I found it,
And I did give't my husband.
Iago.   Filth, thou liest!
Emilia. By heaven, I do not, I do not, gentlemen.
O murd'rous coxcomb! what should such a fool
Do with so good a wife?
Othello.   Are there no stones in heaven   235
But what serves for the thunder? Precious villain!

>   *The Moor runs at Iago, [but is disarmed by Montano].*
>   *Iago kills his wife.*

Gratiano. The woman falls. Sure he hath killed his wife.
Emilia. Ay, ay. O, lay me by my mistress' side.   *Exit Iago.*
Gratiano. He's gone, but his wife's killed.
Montano. 'Tis a notorious villain. Take you this weapon,   240
Which I have here recovered from the Moor.
Come, guard the door without. Let him not pass,
But kill him rather. I'll after that same villain,
For 'tis a damnèd slave.

>   *Exit [Montano, with all but Othello and Emilia].*

---

214 *gratify* reward 215 *recognizance* token 221 *liberal as the north* unchecked as the north
wind blows 235 *stones* bolts like those used for thunderbolts 240 *notorious* notable

Othello.   I am not valiant neither;
   But every puny whipster gets my sword.   245
   But why should honor outlive honesty?
   Let it go all.
Emilia.   What did thy song bode, lady?
   Hark, canst thou hear me? I will play the swan,
   And die in music. *[Sings]* 'Willow, willow, willow.'
   Moor, she was chaste. She loved thee, cruel Moor: 250
   So come my soul to bliss as I speak true.
   So speaking as I think, I die, I die.   *She dies.*
Othello. I have another weapon in this chamber;
   It is a sword of Spain, the Isebrook's temper.
   O, here it is.—Uncle, I must come forth.   255
Gratiano. (within) If thou attempt it, it will cost thee dear.
   Thou hast no weapon, and perforce must suffer.
Othello. Look in upon me then and speak with me,
   Or, naked as I am, I will assault thee.

[Enter Gratiano.]

Gratiano. What is the matter?
Othello.   Behold, I have a weapon;   260
   A better never did itself sustain
   Upon a soldier's thigh. I have seen the day
   That with this little arm and this good sword
   I have made my way through more impediments
   Than twenty times your stop. But O vain boast!   265
   Who can control his fate? 'Tis not so now.
   Be not afraid, though you do see me weaponed.
   Here is my journey's end, here is my butt,
   And very seamark of my utmost sail.
   Do you go back dismayed? 'Tis a lost fear.   270
   Man but a rush against Othello's breast,
   And he retires. Where should Othello go?
   Now, how dost thou look now? O ill-starred wench!
   Pale as thy smock! When we shall meet at compt,
   This look of thine will hurl my soul from heaven,   275
   And fiends will snatch at it. Cold, cold, my girl?
   Even like thy chastity.
   O cursèd, cursèd slave! Whip me, ye devils,
   From the possession of this heavenly sight!

---

245 *puny whipster* top-whipping boy 254 *Isebrook's temper* i.e. tempered at Innsbruck, where the finest armorer's steel of the time was made 259 *naked* disarmed 265 *stop* power to stop 268 *butt* limit 269 *seamark* beacon, destination 270 *lost* wasted 271 *Man but a rush* wield only a reed 274 *compt* final accounting, Last Judgment

Blow me about in winds! roast me in sulphur!   280
Wash me in steep-down gulfs of liquid fire!
O Desdemona, Desdemona! dead!
O! O! O!

      Enter Lodovico, Montano, Iago [as prisoner,] and
           Officers; Cassio in a chair.

Lodovico. Where is this rash and most unfortunate man?
Othello. That's he that was Othello. Here I am.   285
Lodovico. Where is that viper? Bring the villain forth.
Othello. I look down towards his feet—but that's a fable.
   If that thou be'st a devil, I cannot kill thee.   *[Wounds Iago.]*
Lodovico. Wrench his sword from him.   *[Othello is disarmed.]*
Iago.   I bleed, sir, but not killed.
Othello. I am not sorry neither. I'ld have thee live;   290
   For in my sense, 'tis happiness to die.
Lodovico. O thou Othello that wert once so good,
   Fall'n in the practice of a damnèd slave,
   What shall be said to thee?
Othello.   Why, anything:
   An honorable murderer, if you will;   295
   For naught did I in hate, but all in honor.
Lodovico. This wretch hath part confessed his villainy.
   Did you and he consent in Cassio's death?
Othello. Ay.
Cassio. Dear general, I never gave you cause.   300
Othello. I do believe it, and I ask your pardon.
   Will you, I pray, demand that demi-devil
   Why he hath thus ensnared my soul and body?
Iago. Demand me nothing. What you know, you know.
   From this time forth I never will speak word.   305
Lodovico. What, not to pray?
Gratiano.   Torments will ope your lips.
Othello. Well, thou dost best.
Lodovico. Sir, you shall understand what hath befall'n,
   Which, as I think, you know not. Here is a letter
   Found in the pocket of the slain Roderigo;   310
   And here another. The one of them imports
   The death of Cassio to be undertook
   By Roderigo.
Othello. O villain!
Cassio.   Most heathenish and most gross!

---

287 *I . . . feet* i.e. to see if they are cloven, like the Devil's 293 *practice* plot 298 *consent in* agree upon

Lodovico. Now here's another discontented paper   315
    Found in his pocket too; and this, it seems,
    Roderigo meant t' have sent this damnèd villain;
    But that, belike, Iago in the nick
    Came in and satisfied him.
Othello.   O thou pernicious caitiff!—
    How came you, Cassio, by that handkerchief   320
    That was my wife's?
Cassio.   I found it in my chamber;
    And he himself confessed but even now
    That there he dropped it for a special purpose
    Which wrought to his desire.
Othello.   O fool! fool! fool!
Cassio. There is besides in Roderigo's letter,   325
    How he upbraids Iago that he made him
    Brave me upon the watch; whereon it came
    That I was cast; and even but now he spake,
    After long seeming dead—Iago hurt him,
    Iago set him on.   330
Lodovico. You must forsake this room and go with us.
    Your power and your command is taken off,
    And Cassio rules in Cyprus. For this slave,
    If there be any cunning cruelty
    That can torment him much and hold him long,   335
    It shall be his. You shall close prisoner rest
    Till that the nature of your fault be known
    To the Venetian state. Come, bring away.
Othello. Soft you! a word or two before you go.
    I have done the state some service, and they know't.   340
    No more of that. I pray you, in your letters,
    When you shall these unlucky deeds relate,
    Speak of me as I am. Nothing extenuate,
    Nor set down aught in malice. Then must you speak
    Of one that loved not wisely, but too well;   345
    Of one not easily jealous, but, being wrought,
    Perplexed in the extreme; of one whose hand,
    Like the base Judean, threw a pearl away
    Richer than all his tribe: of one whose subdued eyes,
    Albeit unusèd to the melting mood,   350
    Drop tears as fast as the Arabian trees
    Their med'cinable gum. Set you down this.
    And say besides that in Aleppo once,

318 *nick* nick of time   328 *cast* dismissed   347 *Perplexed* distracted   348 *Judean* Judas
Iscariot (?) (quarto reads 'Indian')   349 *subdued* i.e. conquered by grief

Where a malignant and a turbaned Turk
Beat a Venetian and traduced the state,   355
I took by th' throat the circumcisèd dog
And smote him—thus.   *He stabs himself.*
Lodovico. O bloody period!
Gratiano.   All that's spoke is marred.
Othello. I kissed thee ere I killed thee. No way but this,
Killing myself, to die upon a kiss.   360
                              He [falls upon the bed and] dies.
Cassio. This did I fear, but thought he had no weapon;
For he was great of heart.
Lodovico.   [*to Iago*] O Spartan dog,
More fell than anguish, hunger, or the sea!
Look on the tragic loading of this bed.
This is thy work. The object poisons sight;   365
Let it be hid. Gratiano, keep the house,
And seize upon the fortunes of the Moor,
For they succeed on you. To you, lord governor,
Remains the censure of this hellish villain,
The time, the place, the torture. O, enforce it!   370
Myself will straight aboard, and to the state
This heavy act with heavy heart relate.   *Exeunt.*

---

358 *period* ending 363 *fell* cruel 366 *Let it be hid* i.e. draw the bed curtains 367 *seize upon* take legal possession of 369 *censure* judicial sentence

Suggestions for Further Reading

ALBRIGHT, H. D. *Working up a Part*. Boston: Houghton Mifflin Co., 1947.

BENEDETTI, ROBERT. *The Actor at Work*. Englewood Cliffs, N. J.: Prentice-Hall, Inc., 1970.

BOLESLAVSKY, RICHARD. *Acting: The First Six Lessons*. New York: Theatre Arts, Inc., 1933.

COLE, TOBY, and HELEN KRITCH CHINOY. *Actors on Acting*. New York: Crown Publishers, 1949.

KJERBÜHL-PETERSEN, LORENZ. *Psychology of Acting*. Tr. Sarah T. Barrows. Boston: The Expression Co., 1935.

McGAW, CHARLES. *Acting Is Believing: A Basic Method*. 2nd ed. New York: Holt, Rinehart and Winston, 1966.

STANISLAVSKY, CONSTANTIN. *An Actor Prepares*. Tr. Elizabeth Reynolds Hapgood. New York: Theatre Arts, Inc., 1936.

————. *Building a Character*. Tr. Elizabeth Reynolds Hapgood. New York: Theatre Arts, Inc., 1949.

Chapter 5

Playwrights and Playwriting

Playmaking is like rainmaking. You get together all the participants and all the paraphernalia. Then you go through all the proven routines. Hard work, careful practice, and devotion are required for each attempt, but sometimes it rains and sometimes it does not.

In Chapter 1, we stated that a play was a unique combination of audience, actors, and a drama. Producing the drama usually demands the services of a playwright, a director, a designer, and a manager—not to mention a host of technicians. In the eyes of most people, however, the process of playmaking begins with a playwright.

Let us imagine, therefore, that you have given up acting for playmaking. Let us assume further that, having read Chapter 1, you have a pretty good idea what a play *is*. Where, then, should you begin? First and foremost, you cannot write a play. You do not necessarily begin by putting words on paper. Though no one can truly say how a given playwright should work, and though the written materials may well be the only part of the process that endures, you construct the play from its elements. You are a maker, not a writer.

Perhaps we should restate the elements of a drama. Your raw material consists of (1) a *dramatic construct* that includes action, plot, story, and situation; (2) *dramatis personae* who perform the action; (3) *modes of language* that symbolize the action; and (4) *a scenic environment* in which the action takes place.

The second thing you must realize is that you may start anywhere. No doubt your inspiration will come first from people, second from a situation, and then from the other elements in no particular order. On the other hand, you may overhear or imagine a snatch of dialogue, and the rest will follow. Another time, a story may catch your fancy and you will start there. It is conceivable, in fact, that you might begin with an artistic task such as "I would like to present *The Adventures of Tom Sawyer* in a two-hour play."

The Dramatic Construct

Wherever you start, sooner or later you must construct the drama. Let us say, for example, that you are dramatizing *Tom Sawyer*. Your intent is to capture the entire novel in two hours of playing, and you want to please both adults and children.

What is the *action* of this famous novel? A study of Mark Twain the man and the novelist reveals that a twin-headed energy informed his work: *naturalistic portrayal* of whatever subject he chose and gentle or not-so-gentle *mockery* of the scene being portrayed. Usually this scene was nineteenth-century America.

This observation, though certainly not new about Twain in general, may seem alien to your concept of *Tom Sawyer*. Twain himself states in his introduction that he intends to re-create events that actually happened. What results, however, is not so much a children's book as a book about children. Moreover, whether or not Tom's adventures really happened, they manage very well as dreams of what it would be fun to *have* happen. Who would not love to attend his own funeral, run away to a desert island with two boon companions, find a buried treasure and be set up for life, foil a dastardly villain, and save a maiden fair? Or, to look at the matter from Becky Thatcher's point of view, who would not want to *be* saved and to have a handsome young man take her beatings for her? Who, in fact, boy or girl, would not like to have a mammoth cave practically in the backyard, to use for picnics and to get lost in for a short while?

Thus it is obvious that in *Tom Sawyer* Twain has presented a kind of nineteenth-century Disneyland—the childhood all of us, young and old together, would have *liked* to have had. As you study the work, however, you discover this magic portrayal is simply a framework for a tongue-in-cheek amplification of "the American dream." The action goes something like this: By luck, mostly, and by pluck, but also by creative and original dramatizing of the events in his life—that is, by *lying*—Tom Sawyer becomes a hero and a success, American style.

In the novel, this action is portrayed through a series of adventures that are narrated by an adult storyteller. Each adventure is recalled accurately and vividly, but with just enough exaggeration to reveal the author's point of view. During and between the scenes themselves the narrator's commentary often—but not always—enhances both the incidents and the point of view. That the novel is arranged in story form is incidental, for the narrative is not the book's chief attraction. Nor are the characters important as *people*. Although they must seem believable as both agents of the story and participants in the events, their chief function is to serve as vehicles upon which the reader can project his dreams and wishes.

Dramatizing this *action* so that your audience will experience the total novel is your chosen task. If you had begun from scratch, you would have to invent the incidents and situations and characters. You may even have created the storyline. Eventually, however, you would have had to deal with the ways in which the action is to be communicated.

At that point you would begin plotting—a creative activity considerably more crucial for the drama than for the novel. From all possible manifestations of the action, you can select only enough to fill two hours clock time. Your plotting is thus a series of decisions that narrow and sharpen the focus of the dramatic vision. Each decision controls the decisions that follow. The moments of the action—the incidents and situations—which you choose must exhibit a special visual and/or verbal effectiveness before an audience. Each scene should also reveal as much as possible about the action, should be capable of exciting your audience instantly, should be a "happening" or a "doing," and should perform whatever dramaturgic tasks are necessary at the time the scene appears.

Our use of the word *scene* here may be confusing. Usually this term refers to a portion of the drama that is recognizable as a unit with its own beginning, middle, and end, and that to some extent can stand alone. *Incident* and *episode* are terms with a similar problem. Let us use these words interchangeably, however, to mean simply a moment in the drama in which a single goal or purpose controls the performance.

Your drama will consist of a series of such *units*. Your chief task as playwright is to weave them into a coherent whole. Besides those units which further the action, there are many *technical units* at your disposal. Usually, for example, you will need an *opening*—an episode in which the drama is launched in such a way as to quickly capture audience attention. Many plots require an *inciting incident* as well. This is a scene that provides an element of conflict with the situation in existence at the beginning of the drama. Resolving the conflict is the means of articulating the drama. As a rule, also, your audience must be informed about many things necessary to understanding the plot or to achieving the proper mood or emotional tone. The *exposition scene* narrates the facts, and the *atmosphere scene* sets the mood. Furthermore, since your action is performed by people, you may have to employ a *character development scene* to give detailed knowledge of one or more *personae*. At some point in your drama, you may need a *recognition scene* in which one or more of the people in the drama learn something about themselves or others in the situation. Many plots also contain a *climax* or high point of emotional or ideational impact—the *crisis* of the given situation. And where conflict or confusion is part of the plot, there is usually a scene in which all aspects of the drama are brought to a satisfactory conclusion—the *denouement*. And finally, you may have to invent scenes that provide *transition* between incidents—usually called a *bridge*—or that serve to articulate the plot.

Three ancient and honorable devices for accomplishing the technical necessities are the *chorus*, the *choral character*, and the *choral scene*. Often the chorus is embodied in a single *persona* and is called the *narrator* or (in modern drama) the *raissoneur*.

Your plotting, therefore, involves selecting the proper units and finding a ploy that organizes them so the action is instantly intelligible and so the audience pays attention throughout the two or three hours the drama takes. You will also want to encourage identification with the people and the incidents, and projection of needs and attitudes upon them—"instant participation," as it were.

Probably, if we take the broadest possible view, you have two choices. Most plotting for drama involves conflict of one kind or another: man against himself, man against man, man against nature or God, or some combination of these. Conflict, however, may simply be an extreme form of contrast and comparison between interacting people or goals. As a rule, such conflicts or contrasts are developed out of a matrix of cause and effect: "this happens and then *as a result* this happens, and so on." The incidents progress from opening to inciting event to complications to climax to denouement. There is a rising action to the climax; then a falling action till the end. Two high points may exist. One is ideational and usually around the middle of the drama; the other is emotional and somewhere near the denouement.

Another method of articulating the series of conflicts may be called *narrational*. Rather than the scenes themselves holding together inherently, one character tells the audience the drama from his "memory" while other characters act out the scenes. The standard cause-effect relationships may be used as well.

Your second plotting choice—one without conflict, story, or narration—may be called the "revue." Each scene is like a sketch or a number in a musical revue, and there is no necessary link between or among the scenes. *Mark Twain's The Adventures of Tom Sawyer,* was deliberately constructed in this manner. Another means of articulating the "sketches" in a drama constructed as a "revue" is to allow the audience to project its ideas and images in such a way that a coherent "story" results. Again, such linking is not necessary to the impact of the scenes or of the drama as a whole.

Nor does the pattern have to be causal. The human mind works largely by association, and there seems to be no reason why the scenes in a drama cannot progress in the same way. Each scene may be an independent unit, relevant only in that it is some aspect of the action, but there must be variety within a pattern leading to a crescendo. Variety and contrast may occur as to mood, activity, and duration. There may be singles, duets, trios and an occasional production number. Except for such vague notions as "You have to have a finale" and "The biggest number comes just before intermission," we know very little about the plotting of a revue. Each one is unique and exhibits a pattern and a rhythm suitable to it alone. Such was the case with *Tom Sawyer.*

As you structure your incidents, whatever your approach to plotting, you must be concerned with the development of a simple, a complex, or a compound sequence of events. A simple plot is one in which there is a single progression of incidents from one point in the action to another. You prepare your audience for a particular outcome, and then you provide it. The complex plot, on the other hand, involves a progression of events with an outcome different from the initial expectation. One or more unexpected shifts in direction—usually called reversals—prove to be more logical than the original expectation.

The compound plot is one with two or more progressions. Sometimes they are merely parallel presentations that balance each other; sometimes they are interrelated so that one depends on the other for its development. Each of the progressions may be either simple or complex. In causal dramaturgy, more than three progressions is rare because the audience is apt to become confused. The revue drama, however, may contain as many progressions as there are scenes—which may well account for the rarity of this kind of plotting.

Your choice, in fact, as you work with your dramatization of *Tom Sawyer,* is dictated by the nature of your material. Twain saw fit to provide an adventure storyline, and you may be hard put to do without it. The same problem would inhere if you were inventing all the materials. If the action were one of conflict, for example, or cause and effect, you probably could not change it to suit a theory of dramaturgy.

Since so many human actions do involve conflicts of one kind or another, perhaps we should examine this mode of dramaturgy in greater detail. Conflict—in which two outcomes of lines of action, two goals, or two motives are incompatible with each other—may be *direct* or *sequential.* In the first of these, one purpose lies immediately in opposition to the other. In the second type, one purpose overtakes another and supercedes it. Obviously you may combine these types in a given drama or scene.

One of the common methods of presenting conflicts is the "dilemma." You dramatize a choice between equally attractive or equally repellent alternatives, or you show no triumph of one outcome over another. This decision-making seems to be popular with audiences, and usually you must not leave the dilemma unresolved. Such plotting is not unknown, and may be effective in this age of indecision, but most theatregoers prefer to have the conflicts in a drama worked out before the final curtain.

In fact, one of the hardest concepts of plotting for you to grasp may be the need to let the audience in on the drama. You want to order your materials so that suspense and surprise occur, but you must remember that these two are not the same. When a decisive action is delayed, or when time is stretched between action and its consequence—all, that is, held in suspension—considerable excitement is possible. Sometimes the suspense is created by withholding information, but you must be highly selective in your concealment. "What happens next?" is a normal dramatic question. It is made possible, however, by letting the audience know what the possibilities are. The best suspense is that in which we wonder *how* the end will be reached, not *what* it is.

Yet striking revelation of the unexpected has always been part of play-making. Your audience enjoys surprise, particularly if the sudden turn of events seems more relevant to what has gone before than what had been expected. It also helps if the new outcome is not only more logical but also the exact opposite of the previously-considered possibilities.

What you must realize, however, is that *dramatic* suspense and surprise both depend primarily on your audience having full knowledge of the situation, the characters, and the possible outcomes if conflict is part of your dramaturgy. Though *narrative* suspense and surprise—what is called "a good story"—can be important in your plotting, to judge by the great dramas of the world these elements are among your least important tools. Even the original audiences for *Oedipus the King* and *Hamlet* knew the story by heart. What they wanted was to join with the actors in *playing* the story. As far as *Othello* and *As You Like It* are concerned, though the original audiences may not have been familiar with the stories which served as sources for Shakespeare, the playgoers knew well enough what *had* to happen when a man like Othello married a girl like Desdemona—particularly against her father's will—or when a group of lovers and villains left the court and journeyed to the Forest of Arden. The thrill lay principally in seeing one's expectations played out.

The Dramatis Personae

We have noted several times that where people are, drama exists. The reverse is also true. Working on your "Tom Sawyer," you have focused primarily on the action or the central idea of the novel, and the selection and arrangement of incidents to represent that action. You have been concerned with the *dramatic construct* of your play.

Yet each particular incident is shown as the characteristic actions of *people*. It is the interplay among a number of "characteristic modes of behavior" that usually constitutes a scene. Although you are a maker of plots that control patterns of action, you must usually focus on those patterns through a *protagonist*—a single, central character who carries out the action of the dramatic construct. If that construct involves conflict, you will probably need to employ an *antagonist* as well. And each scene in which one or both of these creations find themselves will need at least one and perhaps several less-important personages to support or challenge them.

In dramatizing *Tom Sawyer*, you have no problem discovering who your protagonist is. Another time, however, you may create a play in which two or more *personae* have equal importance to the action of the dramatic construct. *Major Barbara* is such a drama, and so is *A Streetcar Named Desire*.

Regardless of what your decision is on *this* matter, you will have to conceive your scenes in terms of character goals. To some extent you have to provide motives for the pursuit of these goals. If the goals themselves make sense and fit your dramatic construct, you do not have to reveal motivation. You simply have to show or employ a *persona* whom the audience can believe seeking the goal in question. Your audience mostly wants to get on with the action. Of course part of your action may be the interplay of motives. If handled dramatically, such a character study can be part of your play. You then must take care to probe the psychological motivation, the ethical motivation, or both types as they pertain to *personae* in your drama. As a rule, however, you reveal only those traits which help your audience focus on the character goals necessary for each scene.

You reveal these traits by what you show a *persona* doing, by what you have him say, by the appearance you give him, and by what you have others say of him. Your characters' activities are the most important source of knowledge about them. You must show your people in action. Anything they say about themselves will usually be accepted at face value unless it contradicts their actions. Such contradiction may itself be used as a character trait. Either way, your *personae* need to look like, or look unlike, they sound and behave. Appearance is generally considered a hallmark of character. Can we believe a small Othello, for example, or an ugly Rosalind? And finally, you must take care with what you have others say about a given person in your drama. Such clues help your audience immensely, and their dramatic worth is obvious. What Iago says of Othello, what the Moor reveals of himself, and what Cassio says of both men are vital to our accepting Othello's dramatic action. Even more important in this drama is the fact that no one except Othello believes Iago when he describes Desdemona as "false."

All these methods of character development may be used in various combinations. Though any behavior and any motivation that fits the dramatic action may be acceptable, you need to have your characters show a consistency that is rarely found in real life. Whatever mode of behavior you ask your audience to accept should be followed throughout the drama.

This is not to say a character cannot grow or change as we observe him in the fire of events. Such a metamorphosis, if within the bounds of what is shown about the character and of what your audience will accept as human nature, is always highly dramatic. Not to be mistaken for growth is simply greater knowledge of a dramatic personage at the end of the drama than at the beginning; that nearly always occurs. Nor do we mean acquisition of knowledge by a character. Othello, in particular, sees more clearly what he is when the drama is over than he did at its beginning; yet he cannot or does not change himself one iota. On the other hand, two of the three major characters in *Major Barbara*— Cusins and Barbara—must change or the play does not work.

Perhaps even more important than consistency, whether or not it involves growth or change, is stageworthiness. Although any person is theoretically "dramatic," you must choose those who are easily recognizable as "humans," who are interesting to watch, and who are capable of being presented by an actor in the short time allowed for a drama. This last quality may be the most important. Almost any actor can portray Murray, for example, whose eccentricity lies at the heart of *A Thousand Clowns,* but what about Arnold—Murray's vapid, ordinary brother? Although he is "the best possible Arnold Burns," as he says in one of the finest speeches in the drama, he is presented as so "average" that he is easily forgettable. Yet the actor who played him in the motion picture version received the award that year for "Best Supporting Actor."

The problem of stageworthiness is most easily surmountable if you give your *personae* life and vitality. Actors of presence and energy can lend vitality to any character—witness television soap operas—but you must discover characteristic behaviors that provide a special energy and intensity. In dramatizing *Tom Sawyer,* for example, you should have no trouble with the central character. He does and says so much that is inherently interesting; he cannot be silenced or weakened. But what about his sidekick, Huckleberry Finn? For that matter, what about Becky Thatcher? To present even a modicum of what Twain reveals about Tom, you must slight all the others. In fact, one reason you might have for keeping the scenes about the runaway or about Injun Joe's plot against the Widow is that these adventures develop the character of Huckleberry Finn. If you choose *not* to present these adventures, then what you do show of Huck must be as revealing as possible. The same applies to all the "supporting characters" for Tom's adventures.

Moreover, since your drama contains a large number of *personae*—as do many plays—you need to attempt characterizations that differ from, and contrast with, each other. A drama that focuses on conflict, in fact, often sets up disparate character goals. The resultant clash can be the entire drama—as between Barbara and Undershaft in *Major Barbara* —or it can symbolize the action of the drama, as does the contrast and clash between Hamlet and Laertes.

You may contrast your characters in personality and temperament, in motivation or in types of motivation (psychological versus ethical, for example), in goal or purpose, and in situation or actions to achieve a goal. Usually such conflicts involve two *groups* of people. *Othello,* for instance, contains the "Iago Force" and the "Desdemona Force." These "armies" struggle for the control of the Moor.

As you set out to apply these concepts to *Tom Sawyer,* you have Twain to help you. Not only has he accurately portrayed Tom and the other children, but he has surrounded them with a host of briefly-sketched, yet perfectly-drawn adults. Your chief task will be to concentrate this universe of *personae* into two hours of playing time. We have already mentioned that you must focus on Tom's development, to the exclusion of the others in the novel who are also many-faceted. Everyone else then becomes a choral character or, more accurately, part of an environment within which Tom goes through his adventures.

Once you have plotted your scenes to reveal as much as possible about Tom, you give some thought to the tributary characterizations in each scene. The most important of these throughout are the children. Your dramatic construct calls for some thirty children, who appear in all but two of your scenes. The group may be fairly evenly divided among boys and girls, and brief as may be number of lines each has, you must invent actions for them that establish individual differences. The leading children—Sid, Huck, Ben Rogers, for example, to name only the boys— have more lines and are developed more fully by Twain than the background children. Becky Thatcher is the only girl who must stand out, but the other girls must be sufficiently individualized to contrast different feminine actions.

The adults, taken as a group, are the enemy, though only Injun Joe is an out-and-out villain. His co-conspirators may be altered slightly to reduce their villainy. Doctor Robinson is killed, and Muff Potter is regenerated through Tom's action in court. If you present Muff as essentially a victim who is saved from his wicked ways by a child, you will have one of the favorite stock characters in the history of theatre. Huckleberry Finn also has something of this quality. But Huck is much more than a stock character, even in the truncated version your dramatic construct calls for. The other adults in the novel are essentially caricatures, and you need to be careful not to emphasize this through the reduction in particularization made necessary by dramatic concentration. Taken out of the context of Twain's narration, that is, the speeches of Judge Thatcher, the schoolmaster, the Sunday School superintendent, and even Aunt Polly may easily seem like over-exaggerations. This is a problem of characterization as well as of language, and you must find humanizing activities to counter the absurdity of their speeches.

Aunt Polly is the most warmly drawn adult in the novel. You must show her with special care. She is not to be taken as quite real, but she is a long way from ridiculous. This is still another reason for the additional dialogue with a neighbor which your dramatic construct calls for in the scene in which Tom's involvement with the jam and the swimming hole is discovered.

If you plan to show the trial in any detail, the characters whom Twain merely describes, but who are necessary to give substance to the courtroom, will have to be developed. What we have just noted about the other adults applies with full force. You will need a prosecutor and a defense counsel—who should be rather pompous and upright Tweedledum and Tweedledee—and whatever witnesses you require: the sheriff, at least one person to swear about the knife, and one to testify about Muff's being covered with blood. An interesting gambit with this last witness might be to make her a farmwoman of the "Ma Kettle" variety. She could have discovered Muff sleeping in a pool of blood in her barn, and she can relish the notoriety of testifying. The impact of such a character would enliven the courtroom scene with humor to balance the heavy melodrama of Injun Joe's threats and escape, and of Tom's theatrical disclosure.

Since the school and the Sunday School are variations of the same symbol—"The Authority of the Community"—you may find it helpful to combine the schoolmaster and the superintendent into a single personage. If you do this, you may use one of the names for both, or you may invent a new name. The mother of the boy Tom defeats in a fight—the woman in conversation with Aunt Polly in Scene III—you will have to flesh out from the description Twain gives of the boy's mother when she chases Tom away from their house. In the novel Twain is not so clear as he might have been about whether *this* sissy is the same Alfred Temple who, much to Tom's disgust, takes up with Becky after she has rejected Tom. You can certainly use the name "Temple," or you can invent a new name for both the boy and the mother. Since you have dispensed with the Alfred-Becky episode, a new name may be called for.

In view of the fact that you are preparing this play for an audience of modern children, you may want to take one liberty with Twain's concept of characterization. We have noted the presence of boys and girls, and in the book these are separate entities. You may find it helpful to add variety by creating a tomboy character. In 1840, boys were boys and girls were girls, and that was that. For an audience in 1970, the mixture of boyish activities with girlish body is a favorite stock character. It is not one of your more important decisions, but one you may give some thought to.

To sum up what we have noted about your playwright's way with *dramatis personae,* we need only reiterate that characterization is a means not an end. You create not characters but actions. Then you "shake scenes" that portray the action of your drama. Then, and only then, although observing or imagining a person may have gotten you started in the first place, you show *people in action.* Your scenes are the interplay of characteristic behavior patterns that human beings use in their pursuit of goals. The patterns are what count, and you reveal whatever motivation is necessary to make them believable.

The Language

The principal means of dramatic revelation is language at once vocal, verbal, gestural, and pictorial. Although your play must "speak" to your audience in many ways, here we are concerned with language other than scenic. The dramatic environment will be considered later in this chapter, and the work of the designer in Chapter 7.

Your dramatic construct is expressed through ideas and images that appear as vocal, verbal, and gestural symbols. These symbols are part of your tools. Though sound and body movements are inherent in vocalization, your principal focus lies on verbal symbols—or "words." Ideas and images can be conceived in a non-verbal manner, but it is difficult to think of them or to communicate them without words.

Each individual word is a collection of sounds that you and your audience have agreed to give a particular meaning to. This meaning may be direct and literal, or indirect, implied, and figurative. Words themselves are then combined into patterns which also possess specific denotation and connotation. Not only do the words and word-groups carry meaning, but also the interrelations among them, the tempo of their occurrence, and the rhythm of their recurrence.

Moreover, these configurations of symbols exist on at least two levels—the outer, or spoken, and the inner thoughts which are ordinarily unspoken. That is, these "inner symbols" may not find vocal or verbal expression at a given moment. Nevertheless, they are revealed in body attitude, in facial expression, or in gestures. As a rule, inner and outer languages are in harmony, unless disharmony is the aim.

At each moment in your drama, you need to be aware of these levels of expression and their various planes of meaning. Now a gesture, now a look, but usually a group of words will carry the burden of symbolizing your dramatic construct. Your verbal language may be prose or poetry—the difference between the two being primarily more formal rhythm patterns and more heightened use of imagery for poetry.

Your words always issue from a character or a chorus—who may be a single person or a group. The language may be directed to the audience or to other characters, or to both either separately or simultaneously. Addressing the audience through a single character is called the *soliloquy,* in which the character tells something of himself, the action, other characters, or the philosophy underlying the action. Sometimes you may want to give a character a one- or two-line *aside* to the audience. This brief address makes some comment on the proceedings, or reveals an emotion or point of view that the character holds. A more formal and usually longer address, sometimes to the audience and sometimes to other characters, is called the *set speech.* Usually this speech contains special ideas or a more rhetorical structure than the rest of your language in the scene.

Whether poetic or prosaic, however, dramatic verbalizing is generally in the form of *dialogue*—that is, conversational exchanges between or among characters. Indeed, many people think first of dialogue when they think of drama. If we enlarge the definition to include all the language spoken or unspoken in a drama, and allow that the actor may sometimes converse with the audience directly, then in a real sense drama *is* dialogue: actor with actor, actor with audience, actor with himself, or all of these at once.

The words that you use in your drama must first of all be *aural*—heard rather than seen for sense. Your audience must listen to sound and sense without strain, and indeed must take pleasure in the sound regardless of the sense. Nor must your actors strain to pronounce your words and phrases. They must be *oral*—composed so that an actor can speak them with ease and freedom. Unfortunately, the demands of the actor and the audience tend to contradict each other. Intelligible speaking requires well placed vowel sounds and careful framing without excessive use of consonants. English consonant clusters are difficult to articulate, and some of them give speech a harsh, grating quality. Moreover, you must allow the actor time to breathe.

For aural sense, many consonants are needed, with correspondingly fewer vowels, and phrasing can be longer than biological demands allow. Intelligibility, however, calls for short phrases; aural and oral demands coincide. Sense and pleasure are both enhanced by alliteration and assonance, particularly when these two qualities are in combination. The first is repetition of initial sounds, and the second is ordered repetition of vowels. Antithesis—repetitions that are similar in sound but opposite in sense—is especially effective.

Your phrasing exhibits rhythm, diction, and imagery. The first involves recurrence of emphasis; the second, choice of words and phrases; and the third, the use of words to create sensory pictures in the nervous system of your listeners. In addition, your words and phrases must seem to originate in the idiosyncrasies of a particular character in your drama. Though you need a richer and more vivid speech than is expected in everyday conversation, and though your *personae* necessarily must speak theatrically, you still need to make the dialogue seem to come from the actual people you are portraying.

Another problem with language is the relation between words and ideas. Though Aristotle and other critics have considered "thought" one of the basic elements of drama, we have altered this view somewhat. The study of ideas in drama was part of Chapter 2. This is not to mean a playwright's treating the action as if it were some philosophical idea about the nature of human existence and the universe in which it finds itself. So long as the idea is conceived *in action*, it can lie at the heart of your dramatic construct. It is also possible for you to plot a drama so that your argument for acceptance of a given idea controls the selection and movement of your incidents. Many people—Americans in particular—cannot find pleasure or satisfaction in a drama that does not argue for, or dramatize, a point of view about human behavior. "What does it mean?" is a common critical question in our theatre today.

Characterization may also delineate ideas about human behavior. What man *is*, in the opinion of the playwright, becomes clear through the kinds of men his drama shows, the choices they are allowed to make, and how they respond to stress or other things in their lives. Sometimes characters reveal a concept of what man *ought to be*. Either one or more characters portray this concept, or the ideal is implied or stated through a situation in which particular failings are revealed. Usually, in this approach, characterization is used to answer some combination of the following questions:

1. To what extent, if any, are men self-determined through conscious choices?
2. To what extent, if any, are men capable of change or growth in stature?
3. How many kinds or varieties of men are there in the world?

Whether offered straight or by means of the *dramatis personae*, profound or complex thoughts normally find apt expression in words and phrases. It is typical of drama that the ideas themselves are not especially fresh or brilliant, but their expression seems to say it best for all time. Moreover, you should attempt to make your word-arrangements and your patterns of imagery express the ideational heart of your drama— as the verbal conceits about love say "fun and games" in *As You Like It*, or the imagery of musical harmony forms a counterpoint to the action of *Othello*.

Your use of language in *Mark Twain's The Adventures of Tom Sawyer* is governed by all these factors. That it is an adaptation gives you the advantage of having pre-tested dialogue to choose speeches from, but even where you employ phrases direct from Twain you need to create the language afresh in the dramatic context.

When you study the novel, you discover that the narrated portions are in a colloquial style that is very similar to conversation. Though you have dispensed with the storyteller, you may find portions of his narration and description useful for other characters. The dialogue exchanges also have their good and bad points. Except for possible changes in slang, Twain's rendering of dialect can hardly be improved on. In fact, you should pattern any additional dialogue that you desire after his. The speeches are easily spoken and easily understood by the ear alone. Many of them, however, are much too long and involved for use on the stage. In most of the exchanges, although the scene is set up dramatically, the sequence and rhythm of even the short speeches are much too slow-paced for the theatre. Thus whatever Twain dialogue passages you employ will have to be cut. The best rule to follow is to remove any speeches that can be acted out or otherwise shown visually. Substitute the actor for the storyteller's leisurely narration.

Moreover, if you have altered the arrangement of the incidents, you may want to change the placement of many dialogue exchanges. Where you have invented a new scene or dramatized a piece of description, you must invent new dialogue as well. Passages from parts of the book not being shown may possibly serve your new scenes. If so, you gain the added advantage of suggesting portions you have been unable to represent on stage.

All of the language, yours and Twain's, must be scrutinized carefully for its dramatic aptness. Each scene must work *onstage*, and the language must be honed to that purpose. If the dramatic points are made, you may try for others as well. In an original play there would be no "other points," but since you have set your task as the realization of Twain's entire novel, you may have to ask your language to achieve other than dramatic effects. A favorite incident or comment, even a favorite piece of business, that has not been shown may now be presented by means of your language.

Your spoken, sung, and gestured symbols carry a major part of your dramaturgic load. In many ways, the language of your play *is* the play.

The Scenic Environment

Your play must talk in more ways than with words, music, and dance. Though you may have a talented designer who can turn your drama into a visual success, you should develop the basic concept of your scenic environment yourself. Some playwrights, of course, are no more concerned with scenery than Shakespeare. They are content to write something like "Here we are in Cyprus." Twain himself often dispenses with realistic details. Other playwrights, however, must fashion the entire scene in complete detail before constructing the rest of the play. Even Shakespeare uses scenic apparatus when he needs it, and presumably he had a locale in mind for each scene.

With regard to *Tom Sawyer,* your decision to create as filmic a drama as possible seems to point toward proscenium staging. Yet the involvement of your audience is so crucial that you may well sacrifice the quick changes possible in proscenium for the participation inherent in the arena.

Perhaps you will seek to compromise with an arrangement of space in which your audience sits on tiers around two or three sides of an area that can be built into a neutral structure useful for symbolizing the cave, the river, and other locales necessary for Tom's adventures. The arena portion of the stage can serve as the schoolyard, the village square, and the graveyard. Whatever platforms you have on the one open side can serve as the school, the church, and part of the cave. If you desire, scaffolding can be used to symbolize the forests around St. Petersburg, Missouri—the locale of the story—and to hold draw curtains which can become the walls of the cave when in use. Key pieces of scenery, such as the fence that Tom whitewashes, can be rolled or brought on stage, or can be constructed as permanent parts of the three-quarters arena stage.

Your dramatic construct calls for ten scenes and a total playing time of two hours. Probably you will dispense with actualistic scenery for the most part. To aid your audience's involvement, you may want benches where the first row of seats would be. These benches can be pews in the church and seats in the courtroom.

Since you will probably eliminate scenery other than that which we have just indicated, you will have to depend on lights, music, and sound to establish and maintain the "scenic environment." You may especially need music and sound effects to "create" the cave and the graveyard scenes. Probably you can simply describe the effect you want and rely on your director and designer to achieve it.

This much prescription, of course, is optional as you prepare a manuscript for the director and the designer. You may spell out as much as you want or as little as you want.

Sample Play

MARK TWAIN'S THE ADVENTURES OF TOM SAWYER[1]

Dramatized by Ralph Borden Culp

For George and Dorothy

Production Notes

MARK TWAIN'S THE ADVENTURES OF TOM SAWYER was first performed in El Paso, Texas, on July 25-28, 1968, by the American Children's Theatre Institute of The University of Texas at El Paso. The production was directed by George E. Stewart and Dorothy Pamelia, with the following cast:

TOM SAWYER	Greg Seale
BECKY THATCHER	Jeryl Zimmerman
HUCKLEBERRY FINN	Eric Peabody
SID SAWYER	Joe Antone
AUNT POLLY	Dorothy Keyser
CARRIE DAYTON	Rosemary O'Brennan
WILLIAM DAYTON	Barry Martin
BEN ROGERS	Ed Wenzer
BILLY FISHER	Lang Leslie
JOHNNY MILLER	Roger Martin
JACKIE MOORE	Merry Moreland
MR. DOBBIN	R. B. Fields
JUDGE THATCHER	Scott Saylors
MRS. THATCHER	Roberta Upton
JEFFREY THATCHER	Dominic Hradek
AMY LAWRENCE	Robin Drake
KATHY AUSTIN	Julie Cobb
SALLY MOORE	Sheri Moreland
SUSY HARPER	Rita Robbins
GRACIE MILLER	Ella Jane Oliver
JOE HARPER	Ronnie Roth
WIDOW DOUGLAS	Alicia Muñoz
DOCTOR ROBINSON	Charles Clay
MUFF POTTER	E. W. Gourd

---

1. This dramatization is intended for the reader only. Inquiries about production should be addressed to Dr. Ralph B. Culp, 325 Ridgemont Drive, El Paso, Texas, 79912.

INJUN JOE ....Steven Oliver
MR. PARRISH ....Pat Bowen
MR. MCBRIDE ....José Alvarez
MRS. MCBRIDE ....Cathie Poe
SHERIFF ....Jimmy Reyes
SARAH BROWN ....Star Hayner
SERENA HARPER ....Susie Hackett
RIVERBOAT CAPTAIN ....John Oliver

TOWNSPEOPLE ....Clairessa Cantrell, Janette Bradley,
                                            Richard Pence, Layloni Drake, Susan
                                            Evans, Yvette Valencia, Carol Himelstein,
                                            Star Stuart, Rhonda Robbins, Michael
                                            Steven Ginn

The production was designed by Albert C. Ronke, and the Technical
Director was Edward Houser. The Costumer was E. W. Gourd. The
production staff was as follows:

STAGE MANAGER ....Peggy Hackett
COSTUMES ....Ellen Stuart (Supervisor), Rosemary
                                            O'Brennan (Chief), Clairessa Cantrell,
                                            Juanita Stuart, Marina Minjares, Sheri
                                            Moreland, Pat Peterson

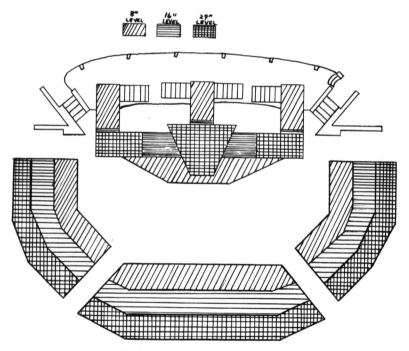

FIGURE 5.1. Floor plan for **Tom Sawyer.**

PROPERTIES ....Roy Evans (Chief), Roberta Upton, Charlotte Henry, Ed Wenzer, Merry Moreland
SOUND ....Bat'ya Podos
STAGE CREW ....Alicia Muñoz (Chief), Kathy Kuncel, Eric Peabody, Roger Martin, Barry Martin, Lang Leslie, Jimmy Reyes, Dorothy Keyser, Janette Bradley

Light Plot

Cue #1 House down; entire lights (floor and platform) up full slowly
Cue #2a Platform lights down
Cue #2b Platform lights back up
Cue #3 Blackout
Cue #4 Full lights up
Cue #4b Platform lights down
Cue #5 Blackout
Cue #6 Floor and Platform A lights up
Cue #7 Blackout
Cue #8 Floor and platform lights up
Cue #9 Blackout

Cue #10 Full lights up
Cue #11 Blackout
Cue #12 Blue Graveyard lights and Platforms B&C lights up to 3
Cue #13 Blackout
Cue #14 Full lights up to 7 – bleed up full when Judge enters and court rises
Cue #15 Fadeout
Cue #16 Floor area lights up
Cue #17 Floor lights dim down to 1
Cue #18 Floor lights back up

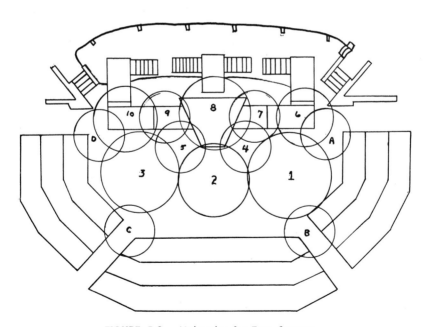

FIGURE 5.2. Light plot for **Tom Sawyer.**

Cue #19 Crossfade into green cave
lights
Cue #20 Green spot on Joe out
Cue #20b Crossfade back to picnic
area set at 5
Cue #21 Fadeout
Cue #22 Floor lights and Platform
A up to 7
Cue #23 Blackout

Cue #24 Green cave lights up and
Platform F up to 3
Cue #25 Platform F out when Tom
drops candle
Cue #26 Fadeout
Cue #27 Full lights up
Cue #28 Fadeout, then back up
for curtain call

Sound Plot

Cue #1 Introductory music—must
fadeout as lights up
Cue #2 Church bells begin in
blackout
Cue #3 Dogs howling and graveyard music begin in blackout
Cue #4 Boat music begins and
continues until picnic scene begins
Cue #5 Boat whistle and boat
music fading into picnic music
and sounds

Cue #6 Cave music and dripping
sounds
Cue #7 Church bells begin in
blackout.
Cue #8 Alarm bell rings furiously
on into blackout
Cue #9 Cave music and drips begin
Cue #10 Sad tolling church bells
begin in blackout
Cue #11 Boat whistles and gun-
shots
Cue #12 Finale and curtain call
music

Property Plot

Scene 1

Set Properties:
Stump—SR
Stool—SL
Schoolmaster's desk on Platform D

Hand Properties:
Books for Dobbin
Books and slates for
children
Apple for Sid
Whipping stick
for Dobbin
Dead cat for Huck
Bell for Dobbin

Scene 2

Set Properties:
Same

Hand Properties:
Slate and apple for Tom

Scene 3

Set Properties:
Stool—SL
Chair—porch

Hand Properties:
Bowl and pan of peas
for Polly
Knitting for Carrie
Switch for Polly

Scene 4

Set Properties:
Fence around acting area (yard); remains
stationary throughout play

Hand Properties:
Ball and stick for Sid
Bucket and brush for
Tom
Kite, mable, and Bible
school tickets
for Billy
Apple, marble, and
Bible school tickets
for Ben
Bell for Ben
Dead cat and Bible
school tickets for
Johnny
Bible school tickets
for Jackie

Scene 5

Set Properties:
Pews behind chancel rail (fence) remain
in place throughout play
Pulpit for Dobbin—center
Bench for Thatchers—Platform E.

Hand Properties:
Bible school tickets
for Tom
Fans for congregation
Covered Bibles for
Dobbin

Scene 6

Set Properties:
Coffin lid behind Platform C
Four tombstones on SL side of stage

Hand Properties:
Dead cats for Tom
and Huck
Lantern for Robinson
Knives for Joe and Muff
Shovels for Tom and
Muff
Bottle for Muff
Money pouches for Joe

Scene 7

Set Properties:
Judge's table and chair on Platform D
Clerk's chair on Platform F
Witness chair on Platform A
Table and chair for Parrish—SR
Table and chair for McBride on SL
Chair for sheriff and stool for Muff on
Platform B
Benches and court railing

Hand Properties:
Fans for jury
Books, fans, pens,
papers, etc. for
Judge, Parrish,
McBride
Handkerchief for
Sarah Brown
Badge for Sheriff
Arm manacles for Muff
Notebook and pencil
for Clerk
Gavel for Judge

Scene 8

Set Properties:
  Pews and chancel rail

Hand Properties:
  Table cloths and
    picnic baskets for
    McBrides and chil-
    dren
  Candle for Tom
  Lantern, bottle, and
    knife for Joe
  Treasure chest and
    money bags with
    gold coins for Tom
    and Muff

Scene One

The scene is a schoolyard, with the inside of a one-room schoolhouse visible through windows and a door. The children are gathering just prior to the start of school on a sunny morning in June. Boys are with boys, girls with girls, and all are engaged in activities and games. The girls mostly watch the boys, but turn away from them if noticed. Among other groups, there are a circle game, a hopscotch contest, a ball game, and a marbles competition. In the circle game are JACKIE, KATHY, BECKY, SALLY, SUSY, and one other girl. Playing hopscotch are GRACIE, AMY, and two other girls. The ball game enthralls SID, WILLIAM, and a third boy. Shooting marbles are JOHNNY, BILLY, BEN, TOM, JOE, and a fifth boy. Suddeny BECKY falls and goes crying to a stump, on which she sits. TOM sees her, and uses a stray marble as an excuse to go to her. He tries to make her laugh with a number of wild antics. JOHNNY, BILLY, and WILLIAM laugh when BECKY rejects TOM. She is cold and aloof, but amused. As TOM runs away, all the chidren laugh.

MR. DOBBIN calls school with a bell. After much scuffling, the children line up according to height, the girls in one line and the boys in another. The two lines march into the schoolhouse. SID hands DOBBIN an apple. HUCKLEBERRY FINN has sneaked to the end of the boys' line, but DOBBIN discovers him and sends him away.

As HUCKLEBERRY is leaving, DOBBIN calls the school to order and begins the first lesson. He and the children freeze in position, in darkness, as the scene continues.

TOM reappears and sees HUCK.

TOM: Huckleberry Finn! Hey, Huck!
HUCK: Hey yourself, Tom Sawyer. Don't shout so loud.
TOM: What's that you got?
HUCK: Dead cat.

TOM: Lemme see him. My, he's pretty stiff. Where'd you get him?

HUCK: Traded Ben Rogers a hoop-stick.

TOM: Guess you got the best of him. Say, what's a dead cat good for?

HUCK: Good for? Cure warts with, that's what.

TOM: Cure warts! How?

HUCK: Why, you take your cat and go and get in the graveyard at midnight, right after someone who was wicked has been buried. A devil, or maybe two or three, come at midnight to take the feller away. You can't hear'em or see'em usually, though sometimes there's a sound like the wind and sometimes they let you hear'em talk. When they take the dead feller away, you heave your dead cat after'em, and say: "Devil follow corpse, cat follow devil, warts follow cat, *I'm* done with ye! That'll fetch *any* wart.

TOM: Sounds right. When you gonna try it?

HUCK: Monday night. Reckon they'll come after old Hoss Williams then.

TOM: But they're buryin' him tomorrow. Won't the devils come tomorrow night?

HUCK: Heck, no! Tomorrow's Saturday, and their charms don't work till midnight. By then it's Sunday. Devils don't slosh around much of a Sunday.

TOM: I never thought of that. Can I go with you Monday night?

HUCK: Sure—if you ain't afeard.

TOM: Afeard! 'Tain't likely. Where'll we meet?

HUCK: Let's meet at the graveyard.

TOM: Will you meow?

HUCK: Yes. And you meow back right quick. We don't want to wake up no one else.

TOM: This old cat'll be ripe by then, sure enough. You better keep him.

HUCK: Okay. Him and me's gettin' to be friends. So long, Tom.

TOM: So long, Huck.

HUCK waves with the dead cat, and goes off. After watching him until he is out of sight, TOM starts for the schoolhouse. At the steps to the schoolhouse, TOM halts and starts to follow HUCK. At this moment, the lights come up inside the school.

WILLIAM: Mr. Dobbin, sir!

DOBBIN: Yes, William?

SID (Simultaneously with WILLIAM): Tom's missing!

WILLIAM (Simultaneously with SID): Tom's missing!

DOBBIN: What's that?

ALL THE CHILDREN: Tom's missing!

Startled, DOBBIN glances hurriedly around the room and then moves toward the front door of the school. When he reaches the porch, he spies

TOM about to leave the school grounds. The children are talking and gig-
gling.

DOBBIN: Thomas Sawyer!
TOM (Stopping and turning around): Sir?
DOBBIN: Come here. Now, sir, why are you late this time? The truth,
  now, or you'll be punished severely. There is a vacant place with the
  girls—next to Miss Thatcher.
TOM: I—I—I stopped to talk with Huckleberry Finn.

There is a loud explosion of voices in the schoolhouse. DOBBIN reacts
to the noise as much as to TOM.

DOBBIN: You children be quiet, now! (As silence ensues) Once again,
  young man, you—did what?
TOM (Shouting): Stopped to talk with Huckleberry Finn!
DOBBIN: Thomas Sawyer, this is the most astounding confession I have
  ever heard. No mere sitting with the girls will answer for this offense.
  Sid Sawyer, please bring me the punishment stick. You, Thomas, bend
  over.

SID brings out a four-foot stick and gives it to DOBBIN, then crosses to
the porch and stops to watch. The children crowd around the windows
and the door. As DOBBIN whips TOM, across the bottom, the children count
out loud: "One! Two! Three! Four! Five! Six!"
TOM bears the whipping stoically.

DOBBIN: There, sir! That should be a warning to you—and to everyone.
  And you will sit *with the girls* all morning.

DOBBIN takes TOM by the ear and leads him into the school. The children scurry to their places. DOBBIN places TOM with the girls, in a seat next
to BECKY. For a moment there is complete silence. Then the class explodes
into talking and laughing.

DOBBIN: Children, children!

                              Fadeout

Scene Two

  While the lights are down, the schoolbell rings for noon recess. When
the bell rings, the lights come up inside and outside the schoolhouse. As

the lights come up, the children rise and form a line of boys and a line of girls.

ALL THE CHILDREN: Good day, Mr. Dobbin!

The children file out through the front door, alternating boy-girl, boy-girl. Until they reach the porch, the children are very sedate. Once through the door, however, they explode into noise and action. TOM and BECKY pair up momentarily.

TOM: Give the girls some story, and then meet me back here. I'll do the same with the boys.

As BECKY nods her assent, TOM runs off with a crowd of boys. SUSY and SALLY come up to BECKY, and the three of them walk off a little way. As they walk, BECKY pantomimes an explanation. Eventually the girls go on without her, and she returns to the schoolyard and sits on the stoop. After a moment, TOM approaches her shyly. He is carrying a slate and an apple. When he offers her the apple, she turns away.

TOM: Please take it. I got more.
BECKY: All right.

BECKY takes the apple and turns her head to take a dainty bite. TOM sits beside her, but faces away from her. He begins drawing on the slate. Presently she tries to see what he is doing, but he will not show her the drawing.

BECKY (As TOM continues to work): Please let me see it. You let me see the house when we were inside. (TOM still refuses) Please, Tom.
TOM (With feigned reluctance): All right, here. Recognize it?
BECKY: No.
TOM: It's *your* house. And here, I'll make your father standing in front of the house.

TOM draws some more on the slate, then shows the result to BECKY. She reacts with pleasure.

BECKY: Oh, it's nice. It's a beautiful man. Now make me coming along.

TOM draws some more, and then shows the slate to BECKY. She claps her hands with glee.

BECKY: It's ever so nice. I wish I could draw.

TOM: It's easy. I'll learn you. (TOM takes BECKY's hand and guides it over the slate) And you must call me "Tom." Thomas is the name they lick me by.

BECKY: But I don't really know you that well.

TOM: We could talk here until you *do* know me.

BECKY: All right.

TOM: Let's talk about the things we like.

BECKY: I like picnics and parties and—

TOM: Do you like *rats*?

BECKY: No! I hate them!

TOM: Well, I do, too—*live* ones. But I mean *dead* ones, to swing around your head with a string.

BECKY: No, I don't care for rats much—alive *or* dead. What I *do* like, though, is chewing gum.

TOM: Me, too. Wish I had some.

BECKY: So do I!

TOM: I got some bully gum at the circus once. Was you ever at a circus?

BECKY: Yes, and papa's going to take me again sometime.

TOM: I been to the circus three or four times. Church ain't nothing to a circus for things going on. I'm gonna be a clown when I grow up.

BECKY: Oh, I love to see the clowns! They're so spotted up.

TOM: That's right. And they get slathers of money—most a dollar a day. Say, Becky, was you ever engaged?

BECKY: What's that?

TOM: Engaged to be married.

BECKY: No.

TOM: Would you like to be?

BECKY: I reckon so. I don't know. What's it like?

TOM: Why it ain't *like* anything. You only just tell a boy you won't ever marry anybody but him.

BECKY: I'll never love anybody but you, Tom, and I'll never marry anybody but you. And you ain't ever to marry anybody but me, either.

TOM: Of course. That's *part* of it. And when there ain't anyone looking, you're to walk with me. And at parties you choose me and I choose you, because that's the way you do when you're engaged.

BECKY: It's so nice. I never heard of it before.

TOM: Oh, it's wonderful! Why, me and Amy Lawrence—

BECKY: Amy Lawrence! Oh, Tom, I ain't the first you ever been engaged to!

TOM (As BECKY turns away and begins to weep): Please don't cry, Becky. I don't care for her anymore.

BECKY continues to weep and pushes TOM away from her. When he tries again to put his arms around her, she repulses him. He walks away several paces and waits, but still she weeps. Presently he turns back toward her.

TOM: I—I don't care for anybody but *you*! (No reply, but louder sobs) Becky, won't you *please* believe me?

BECKY (Turning on TOM in a fury): Oh, I hate you! I hate you, I hate you!

BECKY stomps on TOM's foot and then rushes off, still weeping. TOM makes a grand, pleading gesture as she leaves.

TOM: Come back, Becky! Please come back! Oh, bother! (He kicks at the stoop and hurts his foot again) Ouch! (He hops about on one foot) Darn Amy Lawrence, anyway! Why'd I have to mention *her*? (He sits dejectedly on the stoop) Now Becky'll never speak to me again. I wish I'd never seen her. I wish she'd *stayed* at the County Seat with her old man. I bet she's had *lots* of boys engaged to her. (He mimics BECKY) "It's so nice. I never heard of it before." (He leaps up) Oh, darn her, darn her. I wish I was dead. I wish I was lying quiet and nice, with grass and flowers over me. And no school to go to. And wouldn't she be sorry? After she treated me like a dog? She'd be sorry when I was dead and buried. And I'd just laugh at her tears. Oh, if I could only die just for a little while! Then she'd see how mean she treated me. (He ponders this idea for a moment) Maybe I could go away. I could become a clown and make everybody laugh, though my heart was broken. (He mimics BECKY) "Oh, I love to see the clowns. They're so spotted up." Boy, is that silly! (He thinks some more) I know, I'll be a soldier—or maybe an Injun. That's it! I'll be an Injun. Won't she feel funny when I come back and scalp all her friends? Won't they be jealous of my feathers and war paints? Boy! (He thinks some more) No, maybe I won't be an Injun. I'll be—a pirate! Yes, that's it! I'll sail the seven seas and rob all the ships I meet. And then, when all the navies in the world are looking for me, I'll come back and walk into church, and won't that be something! They'll all stare, and whisper, and shake in their seats. (As TOM begins to swagger about the stage, WILLIAM enters unseen by TOM and mimics his "pirate" gestures) They'll all cringe and whisper, "It's Tom Sawyer the Pirate! It's Tom Sawyer, The Black Avenger of the Spanish Main!

WILLIAM (Aping TOM): The Black Avenger of the Spanish Main!

TOM (Spinning about, and then stalking up to WILLIAM. The two boys circle each other belligerently): You think you're mighty smart, don't you? I could lick you with one hand tied behind my back, if I wanted to.

WILLIAM: Well, why don't you do it, Mr. Pirate? Mr. Black Avenger?

TOM: Any more of your sass, and I'll bounce a rock off'n your head.

TOM pushes at WILLIAM, who pushes back, as they continue to circle each other. The circling and the pushing increases in tempo.

WILLIAM: Go on, big mouth. I dare you!

TOM: You're a coward and a pup. I've got a brother that can lick you with his little finger. I'll make him do it, too.

WILLIAM: Think I care? *My* brother's bigger'n yours ever thought of being.

TOM (Leaping on WILLIAM): That's a lie!

TOM forces WILLIAM to the ground, where the two boys roll and tumble in the dirt. The fight is heated and vicious.

Blackout

Scene Three

The scene is the porch of AUNT POLLY's house, which fronts on a yard with a fence around it. As the lights come slowly up, AUNT POLLY is seated on the porch shelling peas. Sitting beside her is CARRIE DAYTON, and sprawled on the stoop is SID SAWYER. At the first moment the characters are visible, CARRIE is seen to be in the midst of a harangue. The speech is pantomimed until the lights are full up.

CARRIE (At the climax of her speech; almost a shout): I tell you, Polly, Tom is a bad, vicious child, and vulgar to boot.

POLLY: Now, Carrie, I admit I ain't doin' my duty by that boy. I can't hit him a lick. Spare the rod and spoil the child, as the Good Book says, and that's the Lord's truth. But laws-a-me, he's my own dead sister's boy, poor thing, and I won't have you callin' him bad nor vicious.

SID: He's awful mean to me, sometimes.

CARRIE: And Sid's his own half-brother, Polly.

POLLY: Now, Siddy, you know Tom don't never mean you no harm.

CARRIE: Harm! I wish you could have seen my William. Him and his clothes was torn up something fearful.

POLLY: Oh, don't worry. I'll punish Tom somehow.

CARRIE: If it was me, I'd whip him good.

POLLY: It ain't you, Carrie. I ain't got the heart to lash him.

SID: You could keep him home tomorrow, and make him work.

POLLY: That's so. He hates work more'n he hates a whippin'. Besides, it'll be awful for him if he misses his Saturday off from school.

SID: You could have him whitewash the fence.

POLLY: That fence does need a coat of whitewash. And I'll be doin' my duty by Tom as well.

CARRIE: Maybe you're right, Polly. But if you ask me—

POLLY: I ain't askin' you, Carrie Dayton.

At this moment TOM appears from inside the house. He is no longer mussed, and his hair is wet and brushed. He is busily licking his fingers. The door slams behind him and the others react to the sudden sound.

TOM (As he enters and the door is slamming; through his fingers): Evenin', Mrs. Dayton. How're you, Aunt Polly?

CARRIE: Good evening, Thomas.

POLLY (As TOM continues walking off the porch): You, Tom! Just a minute, young man. Stop right there.

TOM (Stopping): Yes'm?

POLLY: Tom, was you fightin' with Willie Dayton this noon?

TOM (Continuing to lick at his fingers): We was just playin', Aunt Polly.

CARRIE (Simultaneously with SID): Playing, my foot!

SID (Simultaneously with CARRIE): Some playing!

POLLY: Please, Carrie. You, too, Sid. Tom, you look mighty well-dressed for the end of a school day.

TOM: See? I couldn't have been *fightin'*.

SID: If I didn't know better, I'd say he wore his *blue* jacket this morning. That one's *yaller*!

POLLY: Why so it is. Tom, did you wear blue or yaller this mornin'?

TOM: Blue, Aunt Polly.

POLLY: Why did you change?

TOM: Uh—some of us pumped water on our heads. See, mine's still wet. My jacket got wet, too.

POLLY: I see. Tom, was it powerful warm in school today?

TOM: Yes'm. That's why I pumped—

POLLY: Didn't you want to play hookey and go a-swimmin'?

TOM: Yes'm, but I had to stay in school.

POLLY: You wasn't fightin', and you stayed in school, and you changed your jacket because you got it wet when you pumped water on your head. Is that right?

TOM: Yes'm.

POLLY: Did you undo your shirt collar where I sewed it? When you pumped the water, I mean.

As AUNT POLLY starts to move closer to him, TOM quickly unbuttons his jacket. The shirt is sewed at the collar.

TOM (Showing his collar): See, Aunt Polly? It's still sewed.

POLLY (As she inspects TOM's collar): Why so it is.

SID (Having followed POLLY; inspecting the collar): Well, now, Auntie, I would've sworn you sewed his collar with white thread, but it's black now.

POLLY (As she peers closely at TOM's collar): Why, it *is* black! And I did sew it with *white*!

TOM (Taking a swipe at SID, who ducks out of the way): Well, uh—

POLLY: And, Tom! What is that on your shirt?

TOM (Hastily wiping at his shirt, then at his fingers): I don't know what it is, Aunt Polly.

SID: If I didn't know you'd told him to leave it alone, Auntie, I'd *swear* it was jam.

POLLY (Scraping some off on her finger and tasting it): Why, it *is* jam. Thomas Sawyer, I've told you forty times to leave that jam alone. Oh, where is my switch?

SID (Quickly running into the house): I'll get it, Aunt Polly.

CARRIE (Settling down to enjoy the spectacle): I'd skin him if he was mine.

SID (Running from the house): Here it is, Aunt Polly.

SID gives the switch to POLLY, who motions TOM to come toward her. SID now stands beside his aunt, and CARRIE leans forward expectantly. TOM walks slowly toward his three executioners.

Suddenly, just as he nears them, TOM lets out a terrifying shriek, jumps in the air and backwards, and points toward a spot behind the threesome.

TOM (As he screams and points):   Look out behind you! There's a rattler!

SID and the two women jump, scream, and whirl about. On the instant, TOM scrambles through the yard and over the fence.

Blackout

Scene Four

The scene is still the porch, yard, and fence of AUNT POLLY's house. It is Saturday morning, early. As the lights come up slowly, SID appears from inside the house. He is eating an apple. Whistling and humming as he eats, he walks along the fence, his hand trailing along the top crossboard.

SID: Boy, will I be glad to see Tom a-workin' on this fence.

TOM appears around the corner of the house. He is carrying a long-handled brush and a large bucket of whitewash. SID's voice stops him.

SID: Hey, Tommy, wanta go for a swim?

TOM (Unconcernedly veering toward SID): Mornin', Sid. Guess what I'm gonna do with this brush?

TOM suddenly whips the brush into and out of the bucket and chases after SID, who runs screaming toward the house. Just as TOM is about to catch him, AUNT POLLY appears on the porch.

POLLY: You, Tom! You stop that! (TOM stops short, but waves the brush threateningly) You hear me?

TOM (Stopping his aggression): Yes, ma'm.

POLLY: And you, Sid. You go along inside and let Tom be.

SID: All right, Auntie. Goodbye, oh great painter—

POLLY: Inside, I said! (SID enters the house) Now, Tom, I want this fence whitewashed from one end to the other. And don't you run off when *you* think it's finished. You ask me, and *I'll* say if you can go or not.

POLLY marches TOM to the fence and sets him in place. Then she sweeps back toward the house. TOM raises the brush in a threatening gesture to her back. Just at that moment she turns around to look at him. He hastily transforms the threat into his first swipe at the fence. POLLY enters the house.

With great sighs of despair and resignation, TOM makes a few more sweeps of the fence. Then he stops and slowly walks from one end to the other. With each step he becomes more melancholy. At long last he returns to the bucket and feebly begins the job again. Almost immediately he halts to survey the task remaining. Then, even more discouraged, he starts again. For a while he alternately whitewashes a small portion and stops to examine the rest of the fence. Each time he starts whitewashing he becomes more downcast. Finally he goes to the porch and sits dejectedly. After a moment he hears a sound from offstage.

BEN (Offstage): Hey, there! Stop her, sir! Ting-a-ling-ling! Wheeeeeoooo!

At this sound, TOM perks up to listen. Suddenly he stiffens with inspiration. With slow, elaborate movements he rises from the stoop and walks slowly to the fence. Once there, he surveys the boards as if he were an artist. Then he begins whitewashing as if he were creating a brilliant work of art. His exaggerated "painting" absorbs all his attention. After several moments, the voice from offstage continues even louder than before.

BEN (Offstage): Chug, chug, chug, chug, chug! Wheeeeeoooo! (BEN appears in view, both his arms describing circles and his cheeks huffing and puffing) Wheeeeeoooo! Chug, chug, chug. Chow, chow! Ch-chow, chow, wow! Ahoy, there! We're coming in! Chow, chow! Stop her, sir! Ting-a-ling-ling! (His arms straighten and stiffen down his sides) Ship up to back! Ting-a-ling-ling! (His right hand describes a stately circle) Set her back on the stabboard! Ting-a-ling-ling! Chow! Ch-chow-wow! Chow!

With such appropriate noises of the boat and its bell, and with shouts of captain and crew, BEN majestically guides the steamboat he is impersonating into dock. TOM ignores the entire process, even when BEN "floats" between TOM and the fence. His interest caught, BEN steps back and watches TOM's artistic performance.

BEN (After staring for a while): Hey, you're up a stump, ain't you? (TOM continues whitewashing, but with more and more "artistry") Hey, Tom Sawyer! You got to work, hey?

TOM (Looking up suddenly): Why, Ben Rogers! Where'd *you* come from?

BEN: Why, from home. Didn't you *see* me or *hear* me?

TOM: Sorry, Ben. I warn't noticin'.

BEN: Say, I'm goin' swimmin'! Don't you wish you could?

TOM: Don't know as I do, Ben.

BEN: Huh! I suppose you'd druther *work*. Sure you would!

TOM (Contemplating BEN): Depends on what you call work.

BEN: Why, ain't *that* work?

TOM (Resuming his whitewashing): Well, maybe it is, and maybe it ain't. All I know is, it suits Tom Sawyer.

BEN: Fiddlesticks! You don't mean you *like* to whitewash?

TOM (Continuing to whitewash): Like it? Well, I don't see why I *shouldn't* like it. Does a boy get to whitewash a fence every day?

BEN: No, I don't reckon he does.

TOM: That's why it *suits Tom Sawyer.*

BEN (After watching TOM's "artistry" for several moments): Say, Tom, let *me* whitewash a little. (TOM considers, starts to hand over the brush, then goes back to doing the job himself) Please, Tom?

TOM (Continuing to whitewash): No, Ben, I reckon it wouldn't hardly do. Aunt Polly's awful particular about this fence. There ain't one boy in a thousand can do her the way she's got to be done.

BEN: How come?

TOM: Well, it's right here on the street. If it was the back fence, I wouldn't mind—and *she* wouldn't, either.

BEN: Aw, come on. Lemme just *try*. I'd let *you*, if you was me.

TOM: I'd like to, Ben. Honest Injun, I would. But don't you see how I'm fixed? If you was to tackle this fence and anythin' was to go wrong—

BEN: Shucks, I'll be just as careful as you are. Please. I'll give you this here apple.

TOM (Taking the apple and inspecting it): Well—

BEN: And this here taw.

TOM (Taking the marble and holding it up against the sun): Well, I don't know—

BEN (Emptying his pockets): I'll give you whatever you want from all this stuff.

TOM (Inspecting BEN's possessions): How about these here Bible tickets for Sunday School?

BEN (Making a gesture that surrenders everything he owns): Sure.

TOM (Pulling BEN into position and carefully placing the brush in his hand): Well—all right. But you be careful.

Gathering up his new wealth, TOM crosses to the porch and sits while BEN whitewashes. After a while, BILLY FISHER comes into the yard. He watches BEN in silence for a moment. BILLY has a kite tied to his belt.

BILLY (After several moments): What're *you* doin'?

BEN (Ignoring him): What does it look like? I'm whitewashin' this here fence. Not many boys get to do *that* you know.

BILLY: Can I do some?

BEN: I should say not!

BILLY (Trying to get the brush away from BEN): I can do it as well as you. Here, gimme!

BEN (Thrusting BILLY away): No! You'll have to ask Tom.

BILLY (Crossing to TOM): Hey, Tom! Can I help Ben whitewash your fence?

TOM: Well, I don't know—

BILLY: I'll give you my kite.

TOM (Examining the kite): It's broken, Billy. What'll I do with a broken kite?

BILLY: Muff Potter knows how to fix'em.

TOM: Sure, but that don't help *me*. What else you got to swap?

BILLY (Emptying his pockets): Just some darned old Bible tickets.

TOM: What color?

BILLY: Blue ones and red ones mostly. Couple of yaller ones.

TOM: Okay. You give me them tickets and this kite, and you can whitewash some.

BILLY: Oh, boy! Thanks!

BILLY crosses triumphantly to BEN and with great arrogance takes away the brush. BEN surrenders regretfully and after a moment of tantrum, stands aside to watch BILLY majestically whitewashing. BEN assumes the attitude of a "foreman." Soon the two boys are joined at the fence by JACKIE MOORE, a gangly, freckle-faced tomboy. She has a black eye.

JACKIE: What're you doin'?

BILLY: You blind in both eyes? I'm whitewashin' this here fence. You never seen many boys do *that,* I bet!

JACKIE: No, I ain't. Can I do some of it?

BILLY: Naw! This ain't no work for a *girl!*

JACKIE: I ain't a girl! Come on, let me do some!

BILLY: Go on, get out of here before I black your other eye!

JACKIE (Grappling with BILLY for the brush; BEN dancing in attendance): You think I can't do it as well as you? I can do it *better!* Give me that brush!

BEN (Pulling JACKIE away from BILLY, who continues to whitewash): Here, Jackie, stop that! You gotta ask Tom, anyway. It's his fence, and his whitewash.

JACKIE (Crossing to Tom): Tom, can I whitewash some?

TOM: Maybe. You got any firecrackers on you?

JACKIE: No. My maw won't let me carry'em.

TOM: Don't look to me like you're carryin' anythin'. If you want to whitewash, you got to trade somethin'.

JACKIE: Can I go home and get somethin'?

TOM: What can you get?

JACKIE: I've got lots of them Bible tickets.

TOM: All right. You go get'em.

JACKIE leaves just as JOHNNY MILLER enters the yard. He watches the whitewashing for a while and then tries to snatch the brush away. BILLY and BEN struggle with him.

JOHNNY: Hey, why can't I whitewash some?

BEN (Simultaneously with BILLY): You have to ask Tom!

BILLY (Simultaneously with BEN): You have to ask Tom!

JOHNNY (As BEN and BILLY heave him toward TOM): Hey, Tom, why can't I help whitewash your fence?

TOM: You can, if you got somethin' to trade.

JOHNNY: How about some firecrackers? And this here jackknife?

TOM (As JOHNNY shows his wares): Got any Bible tickets?

JOHNNY: A few.

TOM: Well, give me all them, and this knife, and these here crackers— and you can whitewash all you want!

JOHNNY: That seems like right much—

TOM: Take it or leave it.

JOHNNY: I'll take it! Billy, gimme that brush!

JOHNNY rushes over to the fence and wrestles the brush away from BILLY, and then chases the two other boys toward TOM. They crouch on the stoop, and JOHNNY returns to the fence. He begins whitewashing busily and artistically. After several moments, JACKIE returns carrying a double handful of yellow, red, and blue tickets. She marches proudly up to TOM and dumps the tickets into his lap.

JACKIE: Here, Tom!

TOM: Wow, Jackie!

JACKIE: Can I whitewash *now*?

TOM: You sure can! You can finish the whole fence, and then do it over if you want to!

JACKIE: Thanks, Tom! (She crosses to JOHNNY) Tom says I can white-wash the whole fence.

JOHNNY: Not while I'm here!

JACKIE (Grappling for the brush): You've got to let me!

JOHNNY (Struggling with her): The heck I do! Get out of here!

JACKIE: You toad, you!

JOHNNY (Pushing her away finally): Get out of here!

JACKIE is thrown sprawling. With great deliberation she gets up, stalks over to JOHNNY, picks up the whitewash bucket, and dumps it over his head.

Blackout

Scene Five

While the stage is still dark, a church bell tolls its solemn yet joyous "Come to meeting!" As the tolling continues, the lights come up to reveal the outside and inside of the village church. It is Sunday morning. Inside the church, arrangements have been made for the awards ceremony. On this day, those children who have memorized two thousand verses will receive a beautiful white Bible. Needless to say, the occasion is a rare one. The Sunday School Superintendent, who is MR. DOBBIN, has arranged for JUDGE THATCHER to present the Bibles.

As the lights come up, the townspeople are arriving in family groups. DOBBIN and his assistants are scurrying around getting things ready. The various families greet each other as they arrive, and converse as they enter the church. The children, of course, are as playful as possible: the girls mostly talk and primp, and sneak looks at the boys, who are mainly occupied with picking at each other.

On his way into the sanctuary, TOM meets JOE HARPER. They become a noticeable twosome amidst the general confusion.

TOM (Pulling JOE aside): Say, Joe Harper, you got any yaller tickets?

JOE: Sure, Tom. What about it?

TOM: What'll you take for'em?

JOE: What'll you give?

TOM: These here firecrackers, and this bully taw.

JOE (Looking at the marble): Hey, this is a grand one!

TOM: Can I have the tickets?

JOE (Still looking at the marble): Sure. Here.

TOM quickly takes the tickets and stuffs them into his pocket. He is walking away when JOE remembers the trade is not yet complete.

JOE (Grabbing TOM): Hey, where's the crackers?

TOM (Struggling): Ain't the marble enough, Joe?

JOE (Struggling with TOM): You said the marble *and* the crackers. Gimme!

The frenetic though small-scale fight continues until AUNT POLLY, on one side, grabs TOM. On the other side, SERENA HARPER clasps JOE at the same time.

POLLY (Simultaneously with SERENA): Young man, you stop that this instant—and come with me!

SERENA (Simultaneously with POLLY): Joe Harper, what *can* you be thinking of?

The two guardians march their charges into the church. There the noise and confusion, though muted, is still dominant. THATCHER and his family arrive. They are met by DOBBIN with much fawning, and are ushered to the platform at one end of the sanctuary. When he spies BECKY, TOM pulls a boy's hair; the boy takes vengeance on an innocent bystander. Then TOM sticks a pin in another boy, and is shaken by AUNT POLLY. As soon as DOBBIN has seated the Thatchers, he takes the podium.

DOBBIN (Tapping the lectern): Now, children. Children! I want you to sit as straight and pretty as you can, and give me all of your attention. Children, please! (There is relative silence) There—that is it. That is the way good little boys and girls should do. Oh, oh! I see one little girl who is looking out the window. I am afraid she thinks I am out there somewhere, perhaps up in the trees making a speech to the little birds. (A titter runs through the children, until their parents hush them) I want to tell you how good it makes me feel to see so many bright, clean little faces assembled in a place like this, learning to do right and be good. Today we will see the boys and girls who have been especially good receive their beautiful new Bibles. As you know, every child who memorizes two verses from the Bible receives a blue ticket. Your teachers have told me how fast you have been earning them. For ten blue tickets, each child receives one red ticket, and for ten red tickets, a yellow one. Today, those students who have ten *yellow* tickets will be awarded one of these Illustrated Bibles. Our own beloved County Judge, Mr. Orin Thatcher, has graciously consented to make the awards. Seated on the platform with him are the charming Mrs. Thatcher, his son Jeffrey, and his daughter Rebecca. Mrs. Thatcher designed and made the beautiful covers on our prizes. Young ladies and gentlemen, let us applaud our own Judge Thatcher!

Amid a light applause, THATCHER takes a position at the podium opposite DOBBIN. The judge acknowledges the applause with a nod. DOBBIN simply beams.

DOBBIN (Proudly): Will those children who have ten yellow tickets please come forward. (No response) John Miller!

JOHNNY (Rising, sheepish): Sir, I don't have enough yaller tickets.

DOBBIN: I do not understand, Master Miller. You showed them to me on Friday.

JOHNNY: Yes, sir. I mean I don't have them now, sir.

DOBBIN: Please be seated then. (JOHNNY sits) William Fisher!

BILLY (Rising): Sir, I don't have enough tickets.

DOBBIN: Sid Sawyer!

SID (Rising): Sir, I don't have enough tickets.

DOBBIN: William Dayton!

WILLIAM (Rising): Sir, I don't have enough tickets.

At this point, laughter and whispering break out in the audience.

DOBBIN: Children, good little boys and girls are not rude. (Quiet ensues) Judge Thatcher, I am sorry to report that—

TOM (Jumping up and waving his arms): Mr. Dobbin, sir! Mr. Dobbin!

DOBBIN: Yes—Thomas?

TOM: Sir, I have nine yellow tickets, nine red tickets, and ten blue ones.

DOBBIN: You—you have *what*?

TOM (Stepping into the aisle): I have nine yellow, nine red, and ten blue tickets!

DOBBIN: Why, uh—

THATCHER: Why, that is splendid, young man. Please come forward.

TOM struts proudly toward the platform, but trips on the first step. His handful of tickets goes flying, and he frantically tries to pick them up. Once on his feet again, he has noticeably lost confidence. The sight of BECKY pointedly ignoring him does not help his composure.

THATCHER: You are certainly a fine little man. May I ask your name?

TOM: Uh—my name—uh—is—

THATCHER: Come, now. A splendid young man who has learned two thousand verses from the Good Book surely must remember his own name.

TOM: Uh—sir—uh—it's Tom!

THATCHER: Oh, no, not Tom. It is—

TOM: Thomas.

THATCHER: Ah, that's it. That is a fine name. And I dare say you have another one. Will you tell me that one?

TOM: Tom—uh—Thomas—uh—

DOBBIN: Tell the gentleman your other name, Thomas. And say *sir*. We mustn't forget our manners.

TOM: Thomas Sawyer—sir.

THATCHER: That's it! That's a good boy. Fine boy. Fine, manly little fellow. You are just the kind of lad we like to see receive this splendid, elegant Bible.

THATCHER holds out the Bible, and TOM reaches for it. The judge, however, pulls it away. Throughout THATCHER's speech, TOM keeps trying to take the Bible. The judge will not let him have it.

THATCHER (Continuing his speech): Yes, we are proud of little boys who learn. Two thousand verses is a great many, but you will never be sorry for the trouble you took to learn them. Knowledge is worth more than anything in the whole world.

TOM makes one last grab for the Bible, but THATCHER snatches it away.

THATCHER (Continuing smoothly): Now, before I give you your beautiful reward, I dare say you would like to show us some of your learning. Why don't you tell us—I have it!—why don't you tell us about the twelve disciples. No doubt you know the names of all of them. Won't you tell us the first two?

TOM looks startled and for a moment seems about to run. Then he tugs at his clothes and looks sheepish.

DOBBIN (As TOM hesitates): Answer the gentleman, Thomas. Don't be afraid.

MRS. THATCHER (Rising): I know you'll tell *me*, Thomas. The names of the first two disciples were—

TOM (Shouting): David and Goliath!

The audience gasps and bursts into laughter. DOBBIN does a broad "take." THATCHER drops the Bible.

Blackout

Scene Six

The noise resulting from TOM's pronouncement about "David and Goliath" is overcome by the pregnant silence of a graveyard—reinforced possibly by eerie, ghostly music and by various "night noises": the moaning of a wind, the breathy flutter of wings, the distant howling of a dog or two. The scene is the village cemetery, shortly before midnight. Still in darkness, there are several sharp, whining "meows." Then silence again. Then further meowing. Possibly there might be muffled curses and the sound of something crashing against a wooden fence.

There is another "meow" as HUCK comes creeping into the graveyard. He pauses and listens a moment. From offstage comes still another "meow." HUCK answers in kind.

By now the lights have come up to just enough illumination for the actors to be seen in ghostly outline. The effect should be one of total darkness.

HUCK: That you, Tom?
TOM (Creeping into the graveyard): Huckie?
HUCK: The same.

The two boys come together and shake hands fearfully. HUCK is carrying a dead cat. After looking around for a moment, the boys creep to a new grave. Just as they reach it, an owl hoots and wings beat against the darkness. The boys jump together and then hide behind a large tombstone (or a large tree, if such is available). Then they stalk back toward the open grave. The background of eerie sound has lessened by now.

TOM (As they approach the fresh grave): Huckie, do you reckon Hoss Williams knows we're here?
HUCK: Course he does. Leastways, his spirit does.
TOM (Staring at the fresh grave): Wish I'd said *Mister* Williams.
HUCK: You never meant no harm. Everybody called him *Hoss*.

There is a far-off sound of men's voices. As the boys talk, the murmur becomes louder.

TOM: Sh! Huckie, listen! D'you *hear* it?
HUCK: Yes! Oh, Tom, they're a-comin' after us!
TOM: Quick! We gotta hide!
HUCK: Come on! Behind these tombstones!

As the distant voices grow louder, the boys conceal themselves out of sight of anyone at the Williams grave, but in view of the audience. The concealment may be either tombstones or a large tree.

Just as the boys get settled, three men approach through the darkness. They are more shadows than people, but their names are MUFF POTTER, INJUN JOE, and DR. SAMUEL ROBINSON. They have a wheelbarrow, a lantern, a rope, and two shovels. MUFF is loudly drunk as they approach; INJUN JOE is also drunk but is sullen about it. ROBINSON is a slight, nervous man who is extremely tense but sober.

MUFF (Holding the lantern up to a tombstone): This ain't it. Where *is* Old Hoss?

JOE (Grabbing at MUFF): You fool! Hoss ain't *got* a stone yet.

MUFF (Drinking from a flask): Hee-hee, Hoss ain't got nothin' no more. Just you and me, Joe. Just you and me!

JOE (Trying to take the flask): Shut up! You're drunk!

MUFF (As JOE takes the flask, MUFF sits on a low tombstone): Would I be here now, if I was sober?

JOE (Taking a quick drink and heaving the now-empty flask away): If you *don't* sober up, you may be here permanent.

MUFF (Rising and staggering toward JOE): Aw, Joe, I'm all right. Just watch me—

ROBINSON (At the Williams grave): Here it is, men. Let's get to work.

JOE (Sitting on a tombstone): Who made *you* the boss?

ROBINSON: Who was dumb enough to hide the money in the coffin?

JOE (Rising): Watch who you're calling "dumb," Mr. Sawbones. Where else could I put it. The sheriff went through everythin' else.

ROBINSON: All right, all right. Just hurry!

JOE: Do it yourself, if you're so all-fired rushed.

ROBINSON: But the moon might come out.

MUFF (Drunkenly): Why don't you stop her, Mr. High-and-Mighty?

ROBINSON: Come on, Potter. Let's start digging. Won't you help, Joe?

JOE: All right, Doc. I'll dig for you.

———

MUFF and JOE start digging at the Williams grave. The new dirt is easy to shovel.

———

ROBINSON: Come on, don't take all night!

JOE: Muff, ain't it funny how *we* do the work and take the risks, and *he* gets the most money out of a job?

MUFF: How about that, Sawbones?

ROBINSON: *I'm* the one sets up the jobs. Besides, this gold is different from the robberies. We found it.

JOE: *Who* found it?

ROBINSON: It was my map showed where the French soldiers buried it.

MUFF (As he and JOE quit shoveling and try to lift the coffin): Whew! Old Hoss is more trouble dead than alive. Come on, Sawbones, give us a hand. Don't be so slow.

JOE: He ain't never been slow to take his cut.

ROBINSON (As he moves to help with the coffin): I know, I know. But now we've struck it rich!

MUFF: At last I'll have enough to drink!

ROBINSON: Hurry up and lift!

JOE: Stop givin' orders!

The three men wrestle the coffin out of the grave, set it on the ground, and open it. Quickly they start removing bags of gold coins, which they put in the wheelbarrow. When all the bags are out of the coffin, JOE steps aside and pulls out his knife. MUFF closes the coffin again, and ROBINSON seats himself momentarily on a nearby tombstone.

JOE (Fingering his knife): Notice anythin' funny about that coffin, Doc?
ROBINSON: What?
JOE: It's big enough for two. Hate to send Old Hoss off alone like that, in a box big enough for two.
ROBINSON: What do you mean?
JOE: I mean, bringin' Hoss into the gang was your idea. He's your partner, not ours.
MUFF (Drunkenly): You tell him, Joe!
ROBINSON: But he's gone, now. We got to stick together.
JOE: I'm for stickin', all right. Stickin' you in that coffin.
ROBINSON: But we're *partners*!
JOE: We wasn't *always* partners. Five years ago you drove me away from your father's kitchen one night, when I come to ask for somethin' to eat. When I swore to get even, your father had me jailed for a vagrant. And then you got in a tough scrape and had to use me and Muff to get you out. And you treatin' us like dirt all along. I ain't one to forget. I ain't got this Injun blood in me for nothin'!
ROBINSON: You try anything rough, I'll have you locked up *again*!
JOE: That burns it!

INJUN JOE, his knife held high, leaps on ROBINSON with a blood-curdling yell. Grabbing the wrist of the knife arm with one hand, ROBINSON hurls JOE over his shoulder to the ground. The jarring crash stuns JOE and knocks his knife out of his hand. ROBINSON is about to continue his attack when MUFF drunkenly crawls upon his back and attempts to pull him over. JOE comes to and, looking up, sees MUFF and ROBINSON struggling. Stealthily, JOE rises to his feet and creeps around the two wrestling men. By now, MUFF has his knife out and is trying to use it. ROBINSON, however, forces the knife out of MUFF's hand. The two men struggle away from the knife, and JOE quickly picks it up. Just then ROBINSON throws MUFF to the ground, grabs one of the shovels, and slams it into MUFF. At this point, as MUFF loses consciousness, JOE charges forward and, grabbing ROBINSON around the throat with one arm, plunges MUFF's knife into the doctor's breast. ROBINSON gasps and falls dead on top of MUFF. Then JOE places the knife in MUFF's hand, and sits nonchalantly on the coffin.

JOE: That score is settled—damn you!

After a few moments, MUFF wakes up. Moaning, he tries to extricate himself from under the dead body. Alternately staring at the knife and the body, MUFF begins to blubber.

———

MUFF: Joe, what happened?

JOE: It's a dirty business. What'd you do it for?

MUFF: Me! I never done it!

JOE: You was fightin' him after he knocked me out of it. Just as I was comin' to, you let him have it with the knife. You was crazy drunk.

MUFF: I thought I'd got sober. But I can't recollect anythin' after he hit you. Honest, Joe, *did* I do it?

JOE: Muff, we been pals a long time. I'd give anythin' if you *hadn't* done it. But just as he clipped you, you slammed the knife into him.

MUFF (Crawling to JOE): Oh, I didn't know what I was doin'! (MUFF is crying and blubbering as he pleads) Joe, please don't tell on me. Say you won't tell. Please!

JOE: You know I won't, Muff. You always been fair and square with me. I won't go back on you.

MUFF (Crying and kissing JOE's hand): Bless you, Joe. Bless you!

JOE (Lifting MUFF to his feet): Come on now, stop the blubberin'. (MUFF gets himself partially under control) That's it. You take off and head for Number Two, under the cross. Got that? Number Two, under the cross. I'll clean things up here. Move, now, and don't leave any tracks behind you. Git!

———

After wringing JOE's hand profusely, MUFF gallops off. JOE watches him a moment and then begins chuckling as he gathers up the equipment.

———

JOE: That takes care of the third fool. He forgot his knife, and it won't take Thatcher long to put two and two together. I'll just get this gold to Hideout Number Two. Then we'll see what Mr. Muff Potter says tomorrow when ever'body sees two corpses and one well-known knife.

———

Opening one of the bags, JOE fondles the gold and laughs weirdly for several moments. Then he goes off with the wheelbarrow and the lantern, but leaves the shovels and the rope. Once he is out of sight, TOM and HUCK creep out of their hiding place. Moving slowly and portentously, the boys peer into the grave and inspect ROBINSON's body. Suddenly there is a loud hoot from an owl. The boys jump up, stiffen, let out a moan, and run pell-mell out of the graveyard. The cemetery noises and/or music rise suddenly to a crescendo

Blackout

Scene Seven

The lights come up slowly to reveal the inside of a courtroom. A clerk is preparing two tables and a lectern for the trial, and people are entering gaily as if at a picnic. The townspeople are mostly in groups. One contains AUNT POLLY, SERENA HARPER, and WIDOW DOUGLAS. Another includes BECKY, KATHY AUSTIN, SUSY HARPER, and SALLY ROGERS—all schoolgirls. The boys are with their families, but they keep breaking away to roughhouse. Toward the end of the opening activity, PARRISH, the Prosecutor, and MCBRIDE, the Defense Counsel, enter and take seats at their respective tables. INJUN JOE enters and sits apart. All the people except INJUN JOE are talking, but only selected conversations become audible; the rest are pantomimed. HUCK and TOM enter together, quarreling. HUCK storms away from his friend and takes a seat. TOM hesitates a moment, then gravitates toward BECKY and her group.

POLLY (As her group is entering and getting seated): I tell you, Serena Harper, my Tom *did* swim over and write me a note.

SERENA: Maybe so, but I still say it was mean of those boys to run away and scare us like they did. I tanned my Joe, I surely did.

POLLY: I was so happy to have Tom back, all I could do was hug him. The main thing is they're *safe.*

WIDOW: With school out they just have too much time on their hands.

SERENA: That's so true. Seems like I'm after Joe all the time now.

POLLY: Boys will be boys, though.

WIDOW: We should be thankful they didn't drown.

SERENA: Are you going to let Tom and Sid go to the Thatcher picnic? Into that horrible cave and all?

POLLY: Reckon I'll have to. All the children are bein' invited.

SERENA: I told Glory Thatcher I'd let Joe and Susy go only if they kept that Huckleberry Finn away. He *is* a bad boy.

WIDOW: Now, Serena, there *are* no bad boys.

As the ladies take their seats, their conversation lapses into pantomime. Simultaneously, on top of the Widow's last speech, TOM comes up to BECKY.

TOM: Becky, I acted mighty mean the other day. I won't ever do it again as long as I live. Please make up with me.

BECKY: I'll thank you to keep to yourself, Mr. Thomas Sawyer.

Tossing her head, BECKY concentrates on her friends. TOM starts to walk away dejected, but almost runs into INJUN JOE. The Indian glares balefully at the boy, who quakes for a moment and then, visibly getting control of himself, saunters back in the direction of BECKY. She notices him, but pretends he is not there. TOM, shaken a third time, is about to leave when his attention is caught by the girls' conversation.

BECKY (As she sees TOM, but ignores him): Why, Kathy Austin, of *course* you can come to my picnic.

KATHY: Is everybody coming?

BECKY: Everybody except a certain boy.

SALLY: Oh, I know who you mean. It'll be such fun!

SUSY: Am I invited? And my brother, Joe?

BECKY: I said you're *all* invited. All the boys and girls are coming. Leastways, all that's friends to me—or want to be. Course, *some* people have other friends.

KATHY: Where'll we go?

BECKY: Across to the cave by boat. Then picnic in the cave all day. We'll have it soon as this awful trial is over.

SALLY: Oh, when will it *start*? My ma says it's a waste of time.

SUSY: Mine says that, too. He's guilty as sin, she says.

BECKY: Still, I can't help feeling sorry for him.

SUSY: My ma says hanging's too good for him.

BECKY: But he seems so pathetic, staring out of the jail.

SUSY: You ought to be ashamed of yourself, Becky Thatcher! A dirty old man like that!

BECKY: Pa says him and the doctor was fighting. Maybe it was—uh—self-defense.

KATHY: They say Injun Joe was a witness. I wouldn't want to get mixed up with *him*!

SUSY: *Both* of them are no good!

BECKY: Old Man Potter *is* dirty and all. But up till now he never *hurt* anyone.

SUSY: Oh, Becky, sometimes you *scare* me!

KATHY: Here they come!

———

There is a loud noise at the entrance to the courtroom. MUFF appears in the custody of the SHERIFF. The crowd goes wild as MUFF speaks to it. Meanwhile, BECKY and her friends have found seats near their parents. TOM, after a moment's hesitation, crosses to MCBRIDE and holds a whispered conversation with him.

———

MUFF (Over the CROWD remarks): Friends, I swear I didn't do it. Boys and girls, I swear I ain't never done nobody no harm. Didn't I mend your kites and show you where to fish? Didn't I mend your dollies?

CROWD (Interspersed with and punctuating MUFF's speeches): 1. Poor fellow! 2. Poor old man! 3. Dirty old man! 4. We ought to give a lesson to his kind! 5. Murderer! 6. Infernal impudence! 7. Why don't someone shut him up! 8. We ought to string him up! 9. Liar! 10. He ain't worth a trial!

MUFF (Over the CROWD remarks): It was the *drink*! Boys and girls, don't you *ever* get drunk! Drink'll ruin the best of us! (As he passes INJUN JOE) Oh, Joe, help me! You promised—

SHERIFF (Pulling MUFF to the Prisoner's Chair): Come on, Muff! And hush your face!

As the SHERIFF seats MUFF in the Prisoner's Chair and then crosses to stand in front of the Judge's Lectern, TOM finishes his chat with MCBRIDE and goes off by himself to a corner of the room. PARRISH and MCBRIDE confer briefly, then go to their respective tables. The jury files in and occupies its place. (*Note*: In arena staging, a section of the audience may become the "jury.") THATCHER appears in the doorway from which the jury has just entered. He stands there expectantly.

SHERIFF (When he sees the judge): All right, folks! Quiet! Let's have it quiet! (The noise gradually lessens) Everybody up, now! (All who are seated rise) Ready, Your Honor!

THATCHER (As he takes his place behind the Judge's Lectern): Be seated, please. (All sit) Now, then. The trial of Muff Potter for the murder of Dr. Samuel Robinson is now in session. Are both counsels ready? (PARRISH and MCBRIDE both nod) Mr. Clerk? (The CLERK nods). Very well, Mr. Parrish, as Attorney for the Prosecution, you may begin.

PARRISH (Rising): Thank you, Your Honor. If you agree, sir, Mr. McBride and I will dispense with the usual opening speeches. In this heat, we feel nothing will be gained by prolonging the trial one minute longer than necessary.

THATCHER (Glancing at MCBRIDE, who nods his assent): If both sides are in agreement, I will not stand in the way of brevity. Please proceed, Mr. Parrish.

PARRISH: Thank you, Your Honor. I call Sheriff Smithers.

SHERIFF (Crossing to the CLERK, who has risen with a Bible): Here, sir!

CLERK (To the SHERIFF): Place your left hand on the Bible, and raise your right hand. (The SHERIFF does so) Do you swear to tell the truth, the whole truth, and nothing but the truth, so help you God?

SHERIFF: I do.

CLERK: Be seated, please.

The SHERIFF seats himself in the Witness Chair. The CLERK returns to his table and takes up his pencil.

PARRISH: Sheriff, please tell us exactly what you found on the morning of June 18.

SHERIFF: I was called to the graveyard about eight in the mornin'. There I found the grave we'd just put Hoss Williams into the Saturday before had been opened. The coffin was out of the hole and the lid was off, but Hoss was still inside. Doc Robinson was lying on the ground in a pool of blood. Muff Potter's knife was stuck in him, and—

PARRISH (Taking a knife from the Clerk's Table): Is this the knife?

SHERIFF (Examining the knife): Yes, sir. Here's my mark.

PARRISH (Taking back the knife and showing it to the jury): How did you know this was *Muff Potter's* knife?

SHERIFF: I seen him use it many a time. Ever'body has.

PARRISH (Showing the knife to the audience): Your Honor, I enter Exhibit A, the knife found in the dead man and seen by the Sheriff many times in Muff Potter's possession.

THATCHER: Mr. Clerk, please enter the knife as Exhibit A.

PARRISH (Giving the knife to the CLERK): Please go on, Sheriff.

SHERIFF: Well, I got you and Mr. McBride there, and Injun Joe, to help me carry the body over to the undertaker's. That's when Muff Potter came up and started blubberin'. After we set down the body, I showed Muff the knife. He screamed, "It's no use!" and started to run away. When I collared him, he fell on the floor screamin', "Tell 'em, Joe! Tell 'em! It ain't no use!" Once we got Muff quiet, I asked Joe what he meant, and *he* said—

PARRISH: That's enough, Sheriff. Thank you. Your witness, Mr. McBride.

MCBRIDE: No questions.

There is a murmur in the courtroom as the SHERIFF looks to the judge for instructions.

THATCHER (Rapping softly with his gavel): Let's keep it quiet, please. You are excused, Sheriff Smithers.

PARRISH: Your Honor, I have several witnesses who will testify about the ownership of the knife. If Defense Counsel will stipulate as to who owns Exhibit A, we can save some more time.

THATCHER: Mr. McBride?

MCBRIDE (Rising): The Defense so stipulates, Your Honor.

THATCHER: Very well. (MCBRIDE sits) Proceed, Mr. Parrish.

PARRISH: Sarah Brown!

SARAH crosses slowly to the Clerk's Table. She savors every moment of the limelight.

CLERK (Rising and administering the oath more rapidly this time): Place your left hand on the Bible, and raise your right hand. (After some confusion, SARAH does so) Do you swear to tell the truth, the whole truth, and nothing but the truth, so help you, God?

SARAH (Dramatically): I *always* do, young man!

CLERK: Uh—yes, ma'm. Uh—be seated, please. (SARAH sits grandly in the Witness Chair, and the CLERK returns to his post)

PARRISH: State your name, please.

SARAH: Miss Sarah Brown!

PARRISH: Miss Brown, you live in the first house this side of the cemetery?

SARAH: Yes, sir. One step from the grave, you might say.

PARRISH (Speaking over the audience's laughter and the judge's gaveling): Please, Miss Brown. No levity. Just tell us what happened at your barn on the morning of June 18.

SARAH: Well, sir, at first light I went out to the barn to milk my cows— and there was more than cows in there. *What* do you think I found?

PARRISH: I am hoping you will tell us, Miss Brown.

SARAH: I'm aimin' to, young man, if you stop interruptin'. Layin' on the floor of my barn—disturbin' my cows—was *Muff Potter*. He was just comin' awake, and he was covered with blood from that sweet, young Dr. Robinson—

MCBRIDE: Objection! How did the witness *recognize* the blood?

THATCHER: Sustained!

PARRISH: I move to strike that portion of the testimony.

THATCHER: Mr. Clerk, strike the witness's last remark.

PARRISH: Please stick to the facts, Miss Brown.

SARAH: Ain't I tryin' to? Was you there, or was I?

PARRISH: Please continue, Miss Brown.

SARAH: Ain't much more. I yelled at Muff, he leaped up, gave a yell hisself, and run off. Don't know whose blood it was, but he left a heap of it in my barn.

PARRISH: Thank you, Miss Brown. Your witness, Mr. McBride.

MCBRIDE (Rising): No questions.

This time there is a louder murmur from the spectators. They seem angered by McBride's apparently weak defense.

THATCHER (Rapping with his gavel): Quiet in the court, please. Quiet! (The noise lessens) You may step down, Miss Brown.

SARAH rises grandly and virtually struts back to her seat. The spectators laugh loudly, and the judge pounds his gavel. After a few moments, all is quiet again.

PARRISH: I call Joseph Williams!

The spectators are struck dumb as INJUN JOE strides arrogantly to the Clerk's Table.

CLERK (Rising quickly and making his speech as fast as he can): Place your left hand on the Bible, and raise your right hand. (JOE merely gestures in both directions) Do you swear to tell the truth, the whole truth, and nothing but the truth, so help you—God?

JOE (Languidly): I do.

CLERK: Please—take your seat.

JOE lounges in the Witness Chair, takes out his knife, and cleans his nails. The CLERK stumbles to his post.

PARRISH: Please state your name and occupation.

JOE: Joseph Williams. Hunter and trapper.

PARRISH: Mr. Williams, will you please tell the jury what happened in the graveyard on the night of June 17?

JOE: I was down to the graveyard with Muff Potter and Doc Robinson. Muff, he was pretty drunk—was near dead drunk—and him and the Doc got to fightin'. They went thick and fast for a while, with Muff gettin' the worst of it. Then just as the Doc hauled off and slammed Muff with a shovel, Old Muff, he whipped out his knife—that knife on the table there—and run it into the Doc's breast. The blood shot out somethin' fierce, and they both collapsed on the ground, the Doc on top of Muff and Muff out cold. I waited till Muff woke up. Then I told him I thought it was a fair fight and I'd cover for him. He took off pretty fast. I started to clean ever'thin' up, but then I got scared and took off myself. The next mornin', Muff came back while we was movin' the body. I guess he just couldn't stay away. Muff, he broke down and told me I could spill ever'thin'. So I told the Sheriff just what I'm sayin' here. The Doc and Muff, they was both my friends. It was an awful thing to see.

PARRISH: You actually *saw* Muff Potter—the defendant, sitting over there —stab Dr. Robinson?

JOE: Yes, sir.

PARRISH: Was it self-defense?

JOE: They was fightin'.

PARRISH: Was the doctor trying to *kill* Muff Potter?

JOE: No, sir, I wouldn't say so. No, sir.

PARRISH: Your witness, Mr. McBride.

MCBRIDE: I have no questions for this—*witness*.

SPECTATORS (Exploding into noise): 1. He ain't even trying! 2. I bet that low-down Injun had somethin' to do with it! 3. Muff ain't got a chance! 4. He may be guilty, but he deserves better than this! 5. Coward! 6. That Injun's a killer! 7. Look at his eyes! 8. Poor old Muff! 9. I bet he's guilty as Muff is! 10. Hang'em both!

THATCHER (Pounding his gavel): Quiet! Quiet in this court! (The noise falls to a mutter) Silence, I say! (The spectators finally quiet down) One more outburst of this kind, and I will clear the courtroom! Mr. Williams, you may step down.

INJUN JOE, who has arrogantly eyed the crowd during its outburst, rises insolently and strides back to his seat. His baleful stare silences the last of the mutterers. In fact, it was his stare as much as the judge's gavel that caused the spectators to grow quiet.

THATCHER (After Joe is seated): Mr. McBride, do you intend to take any action in behalf of your client?

MCBRIDE (Rising): Yes, sir. When the time comes, I will present an adequate defense. So far I have little to quarrel with in the Prosecutor's case.

THATCHER: Very well. Please proceed, Mr. Parrish.

PARRISH: Your Honor, at this time I would like to read into the record the confession that Muff Potter signed for the Sheriff on the morning of June 18.

MCBRIDE (Standing up quickly): This time I *do* object.

THATCHER: On what grounds?

MCBRIDE: My client repudiates that confession. It was taken from him under duress, when he wasn't himself and when he had no lawyer to advise him.

PARRISH: But, Your Honor, Mr. McBride was present at the time his client confessed.

MCBRIDE: But I was not his *lawyer* at that time.

THATCHER: Objection sustained.

PARRISH (As MCBRIDE sits): Very well, Your Honor. May I address the jury?

THATCHER: If you have no further witnesses.

PARRISH: Thank you, Your Honor. Gentlemen of the jury, you all know the murdered man. You all know the accused. You all know the witnesses who have given testimony here today. You have heard your friends, the simple men and women of our village, testify under oath. Even though their word is above suspicion, they have sworn an oath to tell the absolute truth. You have heard them fasten not only the signs of this awful crime on the defendant, Muff Potter, but also the deed itself. And finally, you have seen that the Counsel for the Defense has been unable to challenge what these good, honest, simple men like yourselves have told us. Gentlemen, I am sure you can render no verdict other than guilty. The State rests.

As PARRISH has reiterated the points of his case, the spectators and the jury have nodded with increasing agreement. When he finishes, a sigh that is much like a cheer sweeps over the courtroom. PARRISH almost seems to be taking a bow as he returns to his seat.

THATCHER (After rapping lightly with his gavel): Mr. McBride, you may proceed.

MCBRIDE (Rising): Thank you, Your Honor. Gentlemen of the jury, in my refusal to question the witnesses today, I may have *seemed* to be convinced that my client did this awful deed while under the influence

of a blind and irresponsible delirium produced by drink. I can assure
you nothing is further from the truth. I call Thomas Sawyer!

———

Pandemonium breaks out in the courtroom. The judge must pound
his gavel vigorously to restore order. As quiet is returning, TOM crosses
slowly toward the Witness Chair. The clerk stands and waits for him.

———

CLERK (Almost inaudible in his surprise): Place your left hand on the
Bible, and raise your right hand. (TOM only halfheartedly gestures in
both directions) Do you swear to tell the truth, the whole truth, and
nothing but the truth, so help you God?
TOM (Croaking): I—do!
CLERK: Take the chair, then.

———

As the clerk returns to his post, TOM simply stands frozen. Finally,
MCBRIDE leads him to the Witness Chair and seats him. TOM is both
proud and frightened, and the impact of both emotions makes him shiver
uncontrollably.

———

MCBRIDE: Now, young man. Will you tell us your name, please?
TOM (Shaking and croaking): T—T—Thom—Thomas—uh—Thomas Sawyer!
MCBRIDE: Thomas Sawyer, where were you on the night of June 17, about
the hour of midnight?
TOM (Too low to be heard): In the graveyard.
MCBRIDE: Where, Thomas? Speak louder. Don't be afraid.
TOM (Shrieking): In the graveyard!
MCBRIDE: I see. In the graveyard. Were you anywhere near Horse Wil-
liam's grave?
TOM (Just barely audible): Yes, sir.
MCBRIDE: Please speak louder, Thomas. How *near* were you to Horse
Williams's grave?
TOM: Near as I am to you.
MCBRIDE: Were you hidden?
TOM: Yes, sir.
MCBRIDE: Where?
TOM: Behind those tombstones near the grave.
MCBRIDE: Was anyone with you?
TOM: Yes, sir. I went there with—
MCBRIDE: Wait! Don't say his name now. We will produce him at the
proper time. Did you carry anything with you?
TOM (After a pause): We had a—a—dead cat.
MCBRIDE (Topping the laughter of the spectators and the pounding of the
judge's gavel): We will produce the skeleton of that cat. Now, my
boy, please tell the court exactly what you saw in the graveyard on
the night of June 17, about the hour of midnight.
TOM (Slowly and hesitantly at first, then more fluently): I went there
to cure my warts with the dead cat. Afore I could get started with it,

I heard voices. Thinking it was demons, I hid behind the tombstones. The voices got louder and louder, and pretty soon I could make out three men. It was Muff Potter, Doctor Robinson and Injun Joe. They had a wheelbarrow, and some shovels and such like. They was talkin', but I couldn't make hide nor hair of what they meant. But I saw them dig out the grave and take out the coffin and open it. They fooled around the coffin some, and then the Doctor and Injun Joe begun to fight. Injun Joe said he was going to get even for the Doctor's father treatin' him so mean. The Doctor knocked Injun Joe to the ground. Muff—he was near out by this time—jumped on the Doctor, and they commenced to have a real showdown of it. Old Muff, he had his knife in his belt, but he didn't pull it out. Somehow it was shook loose and fell to the ground. Injun Joe picked up the knife and circled round and round the other two. Then the Doctor fetched the shovel round against Muff's head, and knocked him cold. Injun Joe, he jumped in beside the Doctor, grabbed him by the hair with one hand, and run the knife into his breast with the other. Then he threw the Doctor's body—

With a loud scream, INJUN JOE leaps to his feet. Pulling out his knife, he charges toward the Witness Chair.

JOE (While charging): You skulking whelp! I'll slit you from nose to tail! (The SHERIFF and PARRISH grapple with JOE, who struggles savagely) You and yours'll get worse than I gave the Doc! You'll hear from me, Tom Sawyer!

JOE hurls the SHERIFF and PARRISH away from him and into MCBRIDE, who is coming to help hold him. JOE tries again to reach TOM, but is stopped by a crowd of people who have blocked the way. Prominent among TOM's protectors are THATCHER, AUNT POLLY, and BECKY. With an unearthly scream, JOE heads for the window, slashing the air with his knife. Once at the window, he turns around to face his accusers. Waving and pointing his knife like a madman, he gives forth a blood-curdling Indian war-whoop that chills the souls of the people in the courtroom. Then, in the midst of his yell, he whirls and leaps through the window.

TOM leaps into view, and BECKY runs to him again and throws her arms about his neck.

The uproar swells to a crescendo.

Blackout

Scene Eight

The scene takes place at the village wharf, outside and inside Mc-Dougal's Cave, and at church. The time covered is two days—Saturday and Sunday. During the course of the scene, the village children gather for BECKY's picnic, go to the cave and have the picnic, explore the cave, and return to the village. While exploring the cave, TOM and BECKY become lost. The two children are discovered missing at church on Sunday morning, and a great search is carried out. Meanwhile, in the cave, TOM and BECKY confront INJUN JOE in his hideout. TOM emerges victorious from this final encounter with his enemy, and he and BECKY can at last rest in peace. Back at the village, the searchers are about to give up when word comes that the children have been found. TOM returns in triumph, not only with BECKY but also with the treasure, which he divides with HUCK. The scene ends happily as the villagers sing, "Praise God, From Whom All Blessings Flow!"

As the lights come up slowly, the children are seen milling around MCBRIDE and his wife, who are to serve as chaperones. The CAPTAIN of the steamboat is trying to get everyone aboard the boat. The boys and girls engage in games of tag, in rough-housing, and occasionally in hand-holding and kissing. For arena productions, the "boat" is offstage; in three-quarters arena or in proscenium productions, the boat may be either onstage or offstage.

All activities are in pantomime, except for squeals and laughter by the children and for the dialogue indicated below.

THATCHER (Approaching with BECKY and MRS. THATCHER): Ah, McBride! Ready for the big day?

MCBRIDE (As he and MRS. MCBRIDE nervously try to corral the children): Yes, sir! We'll be ready as soon as we get everyone together. (To some children) Here, now! Come along with you!

THATCHER: Well, now, I'm happy to see you have things under control.

MRS. THATCHER: Please don't keep the children out too late.

MCBRIDE: No, ma'm! We'll be home early, never fear.

MRS. MCBRIDE: Come along, girls. Ah, good morning, Judge Thatcher. Mrs. Thatcher. So nice to see you.

MRS. THATCHER: Good morning, Mrs. McBride. I see you have your hands full. Becky, you go along with Mrs. McBride. You don't want to hold up your own picnic.

BECKY: Yes, Mama.

MRS. THATCHER: If you're very late, dear, stay with one of the girls who lives near the wharf here.

BECKY: I'll stay with Susy Harper, Mama.

THATCHER: Have a good time, dear.

BECKY curtsies to her parents and the McBrides, and runs toward the boat.

BECKY: Susy Harper, have you seen Tom Sawyer?

MRS. THATCHER: Come along, Orin.

THATCHER: Very well, dear. Good day, McBride. Don't lose any of your charges along the way.

MCBRIDE: Good day, sir. I'll look after them.

The Thatchers leave and MCBRIDE continues gathering together groups of children and shooing them toward the boat.

CAPTAIN: Boat and crew are ready, sir!

MCBRIDE: Thank you, Captain. Hurry, children. We're about to sail. (To the landward) Last call for a boatride to the cave!

CAPTAIN: Hurry up there, me hearties!

The boat's whistle blows, and MCBRIDE and the CAPTAIN hurry themselves to the boat. TOM enters, pauses a moment, and then moves quickly toward the boat. HUCK enters.

HUCK (Catching up with TOM): Hey, Tom!

TOM: What is it, Huckleberry? I thought you was watchin' that tavern for Injun Joe and the gold.

HUCK: I said I would, and I will! But suppose that ain't what he meant by "Number Two"—the second room at the tavern—and by "under the cross," the Criss-Cross Tavern itself?

TOM: What else could he mean? You keep a watch today and tonight, and I'll spell you tomorrow.

HUCK: Don't worry, I will. But I still think you should've *told* about the gold.

TOM: Ain't it more fun to search it out?

HUCK: Not with Injun Joe lurkin' about waitin' to drown us!

TOM: But if we find it alone, it'll be *ours*. Wouldn't *that* be somethin'?

HUCK: Well, I'm pretty scared, but I'll give it all I got.

TOM: Now you're talkin', Huck! Don't you ever weaken!

The boat's whistle sounds, and HUCK shakes TOM's hand. The two boys stand thus for a moment, and then HUCK runs off. BECKY enters from the boat.

BECKY (As she enters): Tom! There you are! Ain't you comin'?

TOM (Looking after HUCK): Sure, Becky. So long, Huck!

BECKY (Coming up to TOM and taking his arm): I thought you'd never get here.

TOM (As they turn to leave): Would you have missed me?

BECKY: Oh, heaps! You were so *brave* in the courtroom!

TOM: Then we're engaged again?

BECKY: Forever and ever!

CAPTAIN (Appearing as the whistle sounds): Come aboard, you two!

If the boat is offstage, the CAPTAIN hurries the two children toward it. If the boat is onstage, the three climb aboard. The gangplank comes up behind them, the whistle blows, and the boat moves out into the river. Wherever the boat is imagined, the lights should come down slowly either to complete darkness or to very dim illumination. There should be steam hissing, bells ringing, and whistles blowing. The boat noises should take on a musical sound and rhythm, and should blend into the noise of children playing about the boat. The crossing is thus orchestrated in sound, and may take as long as is theatrically effective. (In the premiere production, which was done in three-fourths arena, MCBRIDE and the children went offstage and circled behind the audience while "boat music" was heard. The children screamed and yelled all the time the "boat trip" was being simulated. The trip took twenty to thirty seconds.)

Once the "other side of the river" is reached, the children should burst ashore as the lights come up to full illumination. Any number of games and activities may be started at once. Some children may even go off to explore. TOM and BECKY should remain constantly together, should join in various games, but should not go off alone at any time. (In the premiere production, MCBRIDE and the children entered from the opposite side of the arena from where they had exited. The picnic cloths were spread immediately, and then the children played for a while before settling down to eat their lunches.)

After the children have played for a while, the McBrides get them settled down to eat lunch. The eating may be pantomimed, or actual food may be used. During the lunch, much of the horseplay may be continued. Considerable exchange of delicacies may occur. Some of the children may play games while they eat.

Finally, at a high point in the excitement of eating lunch, someone remembers the cave.

TOM (Leaping up with BECKY): Who's ready for the cave?

The children shout their acquiescence, and there is much scurrying around to clear up the picnic mess, and to procure candles, twine, and other spelunking paraphernalia. Once everyone is ready, TOM and BECKY strike off into the cave. They are followed by the MCBRIDES and the rest of the group.

As the cave is entered, the lights come down slowly to minimum illumination. What is desired is an eerie glow broken by mysterious shadows. If the play is staged in arena, the actors leave the stage by one aisle and enter by another. For three-quarters arena or proscenium staging, the cave can be either platforms or an actual set piece. (In the premiere production, the audience sat on three sides of the regular proscenium stage, facing the orchestra pit and the auditorium. Permanent platforms filled the proscenium opening, with steps into the pit. For the cave scene, the actors entered the auditorium from the stage, then went into the pit. From there, they explored all parts of the platform.)

Sound effects can be helpful in achieving a "cave" effect. Eerie music and weird sounds can be broadcast, and the screams and squeals of the children as they "explore" the cave can establish the rifts, chasms, and labyrinths that Mark Twain calls for. (In the premiere production, the children were given the general situation, paths for each group to follow, and the times to arrive at certain points on the platform or in the pit. Given this context, the children were allowed to create the exploration scene themselves.)

At one point in the exploration, INJUN JOE is seen by the audience but not by the actors. He is skulking through the cave on the way to his hideout. When he speaks, all other sound should be either stopped or faint and far away. (In the premiere production, the children simply froze in position for his speech.)

JOE (After nearly being caught by a group of children): Damn them! I'd like to gather up the lot and send'em off to hell! Every last one of the tattlin', prattlin'—

INJUN JOE is interrupted by a sudden surge of noise when a group of squealing children come tumbling out of a passage and nearly discover him. He whirls about and runs off.

The children continue their fun and games, growing ever noisier. After a while the boat's bell and whistle can be heard far away. Gradually they override the cave noises, and the lights come up.

Simultaneously the children come storming out of the cave. MR. and MRS. MCBRIDE, both in a state of frantic exhaustion, are trying to collect all the children and their paraphernalia. The entire group returns to the "boat" the same way debarkation occurred at the beginning of the scene.

CAPTAIN (As the group exits from the cave): Ah, there, Mac and Mrs. Mac, it was a fine outing, wasn't it?

MCBRIDE (With great sarcasm): I don't know when I've had a better one!

CAPTAIN (Helping shepherd the children): Come aboard, now, me hearties!

As the picnickers come out of the cave and proceed toward the boat, the light of sunset fills the stage and then slowly changes to dusk and then to darkness. If an actual or simulated boat is used onstage, the running lights come into prominence as darkness occurs. This part of the scene may end now, or the river crossing may be simulated. If the latter approach is chosen, the boat pulls out slowly. Its noises seem strangely subdued, and even the children are content to sing quiet, sad songs. When the boat docks, the children separate into families and neighborhood groups, some still singing softly as they walk off into the night. The last sound is the CAPTAIN singing a river song as he leaves the boat. Throughout the crossing the lights come down slowly, in time with the singing and the rhythm of the scene, until there is a complete blackout.

(In the premiere production, the blackout occurred as soon as the MCBRIDES and the children had left the stage in the direction of the "boat." The next part of the scene began immediately.)

During the blackout, after several moments of absolute silence, the village church bells begin to chime—faintly at first, but with increasing loudness. The lights come up in time with the bells.

As soon as the stage is lit enough for actors to be seen, the villagers begin their entry into church. Everyone is behaving in a normal manner—except that the children are obviously tired. Various adults are panto-miming the usual conversations that precede a church service.

MRS. THATCHER (As she and THATCHER approach SERENA): Morning, Serena. Is my Becky going to sleep the day away?
SERENA: Your Becky?
MRS. THATCHER: I knew she'd be tired to death, but I did expect her to make church.
SERENA: Why, I haven't seen Becky since yesterday.
MRS. THATCHER: Didn't she stay with you last night? I told her she could.
SERENA: Why, no.
THATCHER: What's that? I wonder where she is. There's McBride. Ex-cuse me, ladies. I'll just run and ask him where the child is.

As THATCHER moves away toward MCBRIDE, POLLY joins SERENA and MRS. THATCHER. The judge tips his hat to POLLY, and she nods briefly.

POLLY: Good morning, ladies. Serena, I've got a boy that's turned up missing. Did he stay at your house last night?
SERENA: Why, no, Polly. I haven't seen him.
POLLY: I wonder where he could be. Slept out, I suppose, and now he's afraid to come to church. I declare, if I don't whip him ever so often—
SERENA: Joe, come here!
JOE HARPER (Coming to his mother): Yes'm?
SERENA: Have you seen Tom Sawyer this morning?
JOE: No, ma'm.
POLLY: When did you see him last?
JOE: Why, we all played together at the picnic, and then him and Becky Thatcher ran off into the cave, and—and—
MRS. THATCHER: My Becky! Did you see her, too, Joe?

JOE: Well, uh—uh—gosh, I can't really remember seein' her after we got in the cave.

MRS. THATCHER: In the cave! Oh, Orin, Orin—

THATCHER (From where he is talking with MCBRIDE): Yes, dear. I'm coming, my dear.

THATCHER leaves MCBRIDE, who runs quickly inside the church (or the belfry, if this part of the scene takes place inside the church). With his arms out comfortingly, THATCHER comes to his wife and embraces her. POLLY runs to another group to tell the news. Just then the church bells start to ring frantically, as if announcing the disaster.

THATCHER (As the bells sound a new note): There, there, my dear. Be calm, now. Mr. McBride thought he saw them on the boat coming back, but if Tom and Becky are still in the cave, we will find them. Now, now, mother.

THATCHER walks MRS. THATCHER to the church steps (or to the front of the sanctuary, if the scene is inside the church), sits her down on a portico (or in a pew), and mounts the porch (or the rostrum). He waves his arms for quiet. As he is doing so, MCBRIDE returns to stand beside him. The bells continue to peal.

THATCHER: Neighbors! Listen to me, friends! (Quiet ensues) It seems that Thomas Sawyer and my—my Becky have been lost in McDougal's Cave. (The crowd explodes into noise) Please be quiet, friends. Please! (The crowd quiets down) Now, as grieved as I am, I have not the slightest doubt we shall find them. Mr. McBride here will collect all the candles, ropes and ladders we need. He will select a crew of men to help him search the inner cave. (MCBRIDE moves to begin his assignment, gathering helpers as he goes) Take your men and equipment to the boat! (MCBRIDE and his crew move off toward the boat) Captain, you'll have to get up steam as fast as you can. Please hurry! (The CAPTAIN salutes briefly and hurries off) Mr. Parrish, I know you're exhausted from chasing Injun Joe at the Widow's last night, but could you organize the lines of communication between the searchers and the village? (PARRISH nods as MCBRIDE returns) Everything ready, McBride?

MCBRIDE: Yes, sir.

THATCHER: Be sure and assign the men to specific teams. No sense in duplicating our efforts.

MCBRIDE: Right, judge. But who knows the cave past the rooms we marked yesterday?

The crowd explodes into noise again, each individual questioning his neighbor. No one seems to know the cave well enough.

MUFF (Shouting above the crowd noises): Judge Thatcher! Judge Thatcher! I know more about that cave than anyone. Let me go.

PARRISH: Are you sober, Muff Potter?

MUFF: Sober enough to find the boys what saved me life, by God!

The crowd cheers at this. At the same time the CAPTAIN returns.

THATCHER (Signaling for quiet): Settle down, friends! (The noise abates
somewhat) All right, Potter, you go with Mr. McBride and the lead
group. Get a move on, now. Captain, is the boat ready?

CAPTAIN: Just about, sir! She'll have a full head of steam by the time
everyone's there.

THATCHER: Very well, Captain. You may proceed. (The CAPTAIN salutes
again and hurries off) Mr. McBride and Mr. Parrish, get your crews
moving. (MCBRIDE and PARRISH both exit) Ladies, you prepare sand-
wiches and other food. (The ladies gather their families and start
to exit) I will set up headquarters at the wharf. The Captain will
come back for food and drink. All right, everybody, let's go!

All the people disperse. The bell continues to ring as the lights come
down to blackout. The noise of the crowd, however, dies out with the light.

After a few moments of total blackness, the bells fade slowly as if
extinguished by the dark. In the darkness one may hear, faintly and
then louder and louder, the sounds of the cave. As these sounds establish themselves, candlelight may be seen flickering down a long, dark
passageway. The flickering grows brighter and throws long shadows. Then
TOM and BECKY come into view. As the scene fills with candlelight and
shadow, a large black cross can be seen on one rock wall of the cavern.
It is about twelve feet above the floor, and neither of the children notice
the marking.

TOM (As they come into view): This is where I heard the shout, Becky.
And look how the candle's fluttering. There's some kind of opening
up this way, I bet you.

BECKY (Sinking to the floor): Can't we rest some more? I'm worn out.

TOM: All right, we can stop here. (He sits beside BECKY) I just *know*
this was where I heard the shout.

BECKY: I just don't care anymore.

TOM (Rising and looking around the cavern): Halloo! (Echoes answer
him) Halloo! Anyone up there? (Again echoes redound)

BECKY (As the echoes die out): It ain't no use, Tom.

TOM (Standing under the cross and looking up): Halloo! (Echoes rise
and then fade away) Say, Becky, look up at that wall, would you?
(He points toward the cross) What do you see?

BECKY: Why, it looks like a cross to me. What's a cross doing in this cave?

TOM (Looking around suspiciously): You know, I bet it's—why, uh—it's—
I don't know. But it sure means that somebody's been here. If he *got*

here, we can get *out*! (Suddenly the candle burns to the bottom and goes out) Ouch! (Total darkness envelops the children) Derned old candle!

BECKY (Screaming): Tom, Tom, what'll we *do*?

TOM (Putting his arms around her): Never you mind. We'd 'a' had to put it out anyways so we could see the hole to the outside. Now it'll be easy to—

BECKY shrieks and points to a flickering light that suddenly appears below the edge of the precipice that lies under the cross. TOM starts toward the light, his face beaming. Just as he begins his shout of greeting, INJUN JOE vaults into view. TOM freezes in terror, and BECKY's shriek is choked off. JOE stands swaying on the edge of the precipice. He is obviously drunk, and he carries a torch. There is complete silence while the three contemplate each other for a moment.

JOE (After a moment, drunkenly): You! You blabbering whelp! I told you we'd settle up! (Slowly, elaborately, JOE pulls out his knife) I'm gonna cut your gizzard out! (Joe stalks drunkenly toward TOM, who backs away. This movement reveals BECKY cowering against the wall. JOE changes direction and thrusts his torch at the girl) Who's this? By God, it's Thatcher's girl! Well, ain't that sweet? I get two for the price of one! (JOE reaches out for BECKY)

BECKY (Screaming): Let me be, let me be!

Just as JOE is about to grab BECKY, TOM springs on his back. Thrashing about, JOE throws the boy off. Unable to control his whirling, however, JOE stumbles and falls to the floor. The torch flies into a corner, and BECKY crawls to it. There she cowers. Meanwhile, JOE staggers to his feet and stalks toward TOM. As JOE approaches the boy, the knife slashes back and forth in a crazy arc. TOM feints one way and then runs in another direction. Unfortunately, TOM stumbles to the floor and JOE is able to leap on him. JOE attempts simultaneously to stomp TOM and to slash him. TOM grabs the Indian's foot and tumbles him over. Then the boy scurries away several feet. When JOE rises, he sees BECKY and starts toward her. Once again TOM leaps on the Indian's back. JOE pulls the boy over his shoulder and hurls him in a corner, where he lies momentarily stunned. Then JOE begins to creep toward BECKY again. Just as he approaches her, cackling and shaking with glee as the girl cowers before him, TOM hurtles full tilt into the Indian's side. With a horrible scream that echoes and re-echoes as it dies away, JOE stumbles over the precipice.

TOM lies panting on the edge of the chasm while the Indian's scream dies out. Crumpled up, whimpering, BECKY is now lying in a dark corner. Slowly TOM regains his senses. As he rises to his feet, he investigates the edge of the chasm. Then, suddenly, he runs and gets the torch. Holding it before him, he carefully descends into the chasm. He and the light disappear from view, leaving only the flickering shadows. For a moment the glow is gone and total darkness comes once again. Just at this moment, BECKY regains possession of herself and looks up.

___

BECKY (Screaming): Tom, Tom, where are you? Tom!

___

As BECKY's scream echoes through the cavern, the glow appears once more.

___

TOM (From below the precipice): Down here, Becky!

BECKY (Running toward the sound of his voice): Tom! Where *are* you?

TOM (Coming up over the edge of the chasm): Down here, I said. (BECKY stops) Come on and see. (TOM takes her hand) It's a little room, Injun Joe's hideout, I guess. There's a ladder down to it, and ever'thin'. Plenty of food and water, and a place where we can sleep some.

BECKY: Oh, Tom, I couldn't. Not in *his* bed.

TOM: Sure you can. Injun Joe's long gone, and you're too tired to climb out anyway.

BECKY: Climb out?

TOM: Yes! There's another way out. I stuck my head around the corner and I could see light.

BECKY: Can't we go *right now*?

TOM: Heck, no! You'd never make it. We can rest, and eat some crackers and jerky. And get our fill of water. Come on, now!

BECKY (Starting down): Oh, Tom, I'm scared!

TOM: Ain't that just like a girl! Nothing can hurt you now, Becky.

BECKY: All right, Tom. If you stay with me, I won't be afeard.

TOM: Gee, ain't it great? Here you was lost, and about to be killed by the pirates, and I saved you, just like in all the books!

___

There is a sudden blackout. Very faintly in the distance can be heard the church bells. As the sound grows louder, the lights come up slowly. The bells peal sadly while the townspeople gather to mourn. All are there except DOBBIN, MUFF, and the CAPTAIN. Seated alone in a corner is HUCK FINN. THATCHER tries to comfort his grieving wife, and POLLY weeps in SERENA's arms. After everyone is settled, DOBBIN comes slowly to the platform. On the way he stops to whisper a few words to THATCHER, who nods his head. DOBBIN then shakes THATCHER's hand, and goes to the rostrum. The bells continue to peal in the background.

___

DOBBIN: Friends, this is a sad, sad day for all of us. How short the time seems since Rebecca and Thomas sat in this very church and distinguished themselves with their knowledge of the Good Book. Only three days ago, young Thomas bravely stood up in court, mastered his fear, and denounced that unholy rascal, Injun Joe. What many of you do not know is that only last night, while the merry little children were wending their way home, one who had been excluded from the picnic was distinguishing himself, also I refer to young Huckleberry Finn, against whom all of us have si ned. There he sits, mourning his beloved Thomas and Becky. Last night he bravely followed Injun Joe through the village when that dog was plotting to murder our sweet, beloved Widow Douglas. Young Huckleberry woke several of us and led us to the place where Injun Joe and his villainous cohorts were getting ready to enter the Widow's house. We drove the rascals away. And now, young Huckleberry sits alone, his best friends gone, a hero without anyone to care.

WIDOW (Rising and crossing to HUCK): Begging your pardon, Mr. Dobbin, but *I* care for the poor, motherless child. He saved me, and I intend to save him.

HUCK (Rising): Thank you, ma'm, but I—

WIDOW (Gathering HUCK to her bosom despite his protests, and taking him to her pew): Come, lad, you *shall* have a home!

DOBBIN: Bless you, Widow Douglas. Let no one in our village again be motherless! And now, friends, let us sing *Rock of Ages*. All together, now!

———

DOBBIN begins singing the hymn. As he moves his hands rhythmically, the entire group joins him. The hymn is sung with great sadness, slowly and sonorously. It is particularly important that the hymn be sung well. As the last notes of the first verse are sounded, a distant shot, then several in rapid succession, ring out. Almost at the same time, the steamboat whistles shrilly from the dock.

———

MUFF (From a distance, but clearly over the other sounds): Halloo! Halloo! Turn out! They're found, they're found!

———

As the sounds explode through the church, the people at first are stunned into complete silence. Then, jumping up excitedly, everyone starts laughing and cheering. THATCHER hugs his wife; POLLY hugs SID and MARY. At the height of the excitement, TOM, BECKY, and MUFF enter. The old man is exhausted, and he slumps to a convenient pew while the children go to their families.

———

DOBBIN (As the children and MUFF enter): Glory be to God!

CROWD (Not together): Glory be! Praise God! Amen! Amen!

———

Each of the two involved families engulfs its child, then passes him or her around the crowd for more hugging and kissing. MUFF has his hand pumped and his back slapped by the men. While pandemonium reigns, TOM manages to reach HUCK. The two boys talk excitedly as TOM, with many gestures, explains about the hideaway "under the cross" and about the gold. HUCK, as best he can, recounts the tale of INJUN JOE's attempted assassination of the WIDOW. Finally, DOBBIN speaks.

DOBBIN (Shouting): Friends! Friends, please! (The noise abates somewhat) Friends, this is indeed a time of wonderment. Now the little lost ones are back with us—(The crowd breaks into cheers again) Now, my friends—(The crowd quiets down again) Now, everything is perfect. Thomas and Rebecca are back in the arms of their beloved families, and—uh—Huckleberry Finn has proved he is a worthy member of society. Truly we see the signs of the Lord's grace, and these young people are especially blessed. Even young Huckleberry—homeless as he is—

WIDOW (Again capturing HUCK): Mr. Dobbin, I said before I was going to give this poor motherless child a home, and I *meant* it!

DOBBIN: Yes, of course, Widow, and we bless you for it.

WIDOW: And I intend to have him educated, too. If you won't do it, I'll send him to St. Louis.

DOBBIN: Why, I will be honored to have young Huckleberry in my school. With your kind offices at home and mine at school, he will become a shining example of the way the Lord's light shineth upon the earth.

CROWD (Not together): Amen!

WIDOW (Over the CROWD): And, listen everyone, when I can spare the money, I intend to set Huckleberry up in business. Times are tight for me right now, but by the time he finishes school—

DOBBIN: Maybe the rest of us in the village can help you. We—

TOM: Mr. Dobbin, Mr. Dobbin! Mrs. Douglas, ma'm! Listen, everyone! (The WIDOW and DOBBIN look blank, the CROWD mutters to itself, and TOM assumes the center position on the platform) It ain't necessary for you to help out Huck! He don't need nobody to help him in the world. Huck's *rich*! (The CROWD gasps at this, and is on the verge of laughter) Maybe you don't believe it, but Huck's got money. He's got *scads* of it! Hey, Muff, drag in that chest we brought back. (MUFF exits) Oh, you needn't smile. I reckon I can *show* you. (MUFF enters dragging a chest) Hurry up, Muff.

POLLY: Sid, what ails Tom? He—well, there ain't ever any makin' that boy out. I never—

TOM gets the chest open and dumps the sacks on a table. Then he opens one of the sacks and pours out a stream of gold coins. The CROWD gasps and cheers at this display of wealth.

TOM (Shouting over the CROWD): There, what did I tell you? It's twelve thousand dollars in gold coins. Injun Joe, Doc Robinson, and Muff Potter dug it up, and then Joe killed Doc and Hoss, who was in on it too, and tried to get Muff hanged so *he* could get it all. Joe hid the money in his hideaway in the cave. While he was tryin' to kill Becky and me, he fell in a hole what don't seem to have no bottom. I found the gold, and counted it while Becky was asleep. Me and Muff drug it back with us, only Muff, he says he don't want no more part of it. So half of it's mine, and half of it's Huckie's. You can bet we'll take care of old Muff, but nobody's got to pay for Huck to do nothin'. He can pay for himself! Huck and me, we're *rich!*

CROWD: 1. Well, I never! 2. Ain't never seen nothin' like it! 3. Well, if that don't beat the Dutch! 4. I never seen such luck! 5. They took care of Muff, and now he takes care of them! 6. Plucky little man! 7. Imagine, fightin' that Injun! 8. He saved her life! 9. Muff sure was lucky! 10. Wish I was them!

TOM (Topping the CROWD, which quiets down as he talks): So you see, ever'body. You can be proud of Huck, and you can be proud of Muff. They never let a friend down, and neither does—Tom Sawyer, The Black Avenger of the Spanish Main!

DOBBIN (Above the noise, as the CROWD starts to cheer): Come on, everyone! Let's hear *Old Hundred!* Sing! Put your *hearts* in it!

CROWD (As TOM, THATCHER, and MUFF count the money, and HUCK looks on, uncomfortable because the WIDOW is mothering him; all but HUCK singing):

> "Praise God, from whom all blessings flow;
> Praise Him, all creatures here below;
> Praise Him above, ye heavenly host;
> Praise Father, Son, and Holy Ghost.
> A-men!

Blackout

SUGGESTIONS FOR FURTHER READING

ALBRIGHT, H. D., WILLIAM P. HALSTEAD, and LEE MITCHELL. *Principles of Theatre Art.* 2nd ed. Boston: Houghton Mifflin Co., 1968.

BUSFIELD, ROGER M., JR. *The Playwright's Art.* New York: Harper and Brothers, 1958.

COLE, TOBY. *Playwrights on Playwriting.* New York: Hill and Wang, 1961.

GREBANIER, BERNARD. *Playwriting.* New York: Thomas Y. Crowell Co., 1961.

MATTHEWS, BRANDER (ed.). *Papers on Playmaking.* New York: Hill and Wang, 1957.

Chapter 6

Directors and Producers

During World War I, Marshall von Hindenburg led the Germans to a crushing defeat of their hereditary enemies, the Russians, in the Battle of Tannenberg. He was the hero of the hour. Then people began to whisper that the plan had been devised in every particular by Hindenburg's Chief of Staff, Major General Ludendorf. *He* became the hero of the German people. Finally word began to get around that the battle had in fact been devised *in toto* by a Captain Hauptmann of the Operations Section of the General Staff. *He* was the hero of Tannenberg.

After the war a lady asked Hindenburg who really had won the Battle of Tannenberg. He smiled and said simply: "Madam, I do not know who *won* the Battle of Tannenberg. I only know who would have *lost* it."

The emergence of the director as the man who is responsible for a failure, regardless of who produces a success, is a relatively modern phenomenon. Presumably someone like him must have existed in earlier times, but little notice was made. A playwright, an actor, a manager— whoever put up the money controlled the production.

To a considerable extent this is still true. During the nineteenth century, however, the notion developed that theatre is the work of many contributors who are under the direction of a single controlling artist. Something of a playwright, something of an actor, something of a designer—yet none of these completely—the director (in England, the producer; in France, the *régisseur*) makes the final decision about what will be done onstage. If it works, he goes unnoticed. If not, he is fired.

The Director's Characteristics

What kind of man is he, this Chief of Chiefs? First of all, he is an artist whose medium is *people*. He shapes the play through the art of others.

Because he manages the activities of many artists, the director must be an *administrator*. He must organize time, space, and people so that all are employed efficiently, happily, and to the full extent of their abilities. Though of course there are exceptions, most artists work best in situations without undue stress and confusion. If the creative situation is organized properly, the contributing artists seem to collaborate more easily and freely. Every necessary job should have a time and a place set aside for it. Moreover, the artists and the production staff should hold regular meetings at which the director may arbitrate many conflicting decisions. Often the director must plan the total theatrical effort and manage the business as well. And finally he must develop the dash and the polish—the *esprit*—that welds disparate talents and personalities into a working team and leads to a successful production.

Many times these functions are performed by someone other than the director. In the United States, there is the producer or the packager. University drama departments often assign these tasks to a director of theatre. In Europe, the manager handles administration; the producer makes the artistic contributions.

Nevertheless, the director of a production ought to be a good administrator. That is, he should have a talent for leadership, a desire for command, and a sense of responsibility. Many of the techniques involved in leadership can be learned. Any director would be improved for learning them.

Yet administration is not the heart of directing. Equally important, though not central, is a second quality every director should have. He ought to be a *scholar*—that is, a *critic-historian*. Since he must select, evaluate, and understand all the planes of meaning captured by a drama, he needs a frame of reference to use as a standard. The more he knows about esthetics and the history of drama and theatre, and indeed about the culture of the era from which the drama he is directing comes, the better director he will be. In fact, the more he knows about all fields of human endeavor, particularly the social sciences and philosophy, the more effective his directing will be. What he requires is a clear critical attitude that is based on solid knowledge. Such an attitude, and such knowledge, will not make him automatically a director, and certainly not a good one, but they will make him immeasurably a better one.

A third quality of good directors, particularly in the educational theatre, is that of *teacher*. Probably it is safe to say that when working with highly-trained and talented artists the director will learn as much as he teaches, but even here he must coach and coax (What else *is* teaching?) the best efforts out of his collaborators. In educational theatre, the director nearly always has to teach every member of the production his trade, and every actor his role. At the very least, he will have to teach the play or the period from which it comes.

This activity can be overdone, of course. I once had the dubious pleasure of working with a director who provided each member of the production an encyclopedia-sized notebook full of essays and comments. "This," he announced, "is the way we will do this play." So much time and energy were spent learning the notes that very little was left for the production itself. The result was a performance historically accurate and perfectly literate, but dead as an empty theatre. The teaching had interfered with, not aided the production.

On second thought, handing a class a sheaf of notes or reading from one's own book is not "teaching," either. That art has its own mystique. If a director has known one or two good teachers, he realizes how marvelous and how difficult their work is. All he can do is emulate them, and hope for the best, but not burden the actors and crews with irrelevancies. It is better to be inaccurate or anachronistic, but exciting, than the other way around.

Till now in this examination of the director's qualities, the focus has been on drudgery that can kill the creativity a director may possess. Yet command of drudgery is the craft behind any art. It can be foregone, but the art will suffer.

The director's fourth quality, some of which can be learned but most of which is inborn, is that of *inventor* or *creator*. Much of what happens on stage comes solely from the director. Sometimes this new material is as comprehensive as Joshua Logan's eventual co-authorship of *South Pacific* or Elia Kazan's new third act for *Cat on a Hot Tin Roof*. More often, the director just invents activities here and there for the actor, or creates a concept of the drama which helps interpret it.

Many people believe the director's *only* inventing for a drama should be that of an interpreter of someone else's creation. In this view, the playwright's words are sacred. Ordinarily the director strives mightily to reproduce the playwright's drama, the actor's impersonations, and the scenic designer's environment without alteration. What he is seeking, however, is the *truth* in the drama. Since he is the man who will "lose the battle," it seems unwarranted not to allow him complete freedom with the *means of revealing* that truth. ("Truth" in drama, remember, refers to "how a play means.") That is, a director is *not* the man who, in the words of many a directing textbook, "transfers a work of literature to the stage." Every theatre artist claims his royalty, his credits, and his praise—and the playwright gets the glory—and this is rightly so. But the "man who loses" can in the last analysis be responsible to nothing but his artistic conscience.

Proper realization of the dramatic action in all its ways of meaning is thus the only standard by which a director should be judged. In the production of *Mark Twain's Adventures of Tom Sawyer*, for example, the director invented the character of "Jackie." She was not in the novel or the original playscript as any sex, and certainly not as a tomboy. The playwright accepted the addition reluctantly. Yet the only fair judgment is that for an audience in 1968, the invention worked. The new character is now a permanent part of the playscript.

The ability to know what will work out of a number of more or less effective options is the primal quality that a director must have. This *faculty for knowing* usually cannot be explained. To one director it manifests itself as an itch in the seat of the pants, embarrassment for the people on stage, or an instantaneous and unconscious sliding down into a seat or a turning away of the eyes and closing of the ears. These are feelings when a grouping, a movement, a reading of a line, a piece of business, or a setting is *wrong*. When the work on stage is *right*, that knowledge comes instantly, without cerebration, predication, or even feeling.

This quality may well be inborn; it is the director's special talent. It is difficult to understand and describe. Probably it is the ability to react like the audience will react to everything on stage—particularly including the director's own contributions. Whether innate, or laid on moment by moment throughout the director's private and professional life, this "faculty for knowing" is the *sine qua non* of his existence.

All these characteristics—administrative ability, scholarliness, capability to teach, creativeness in choosing the drama's visual and aural analogues, and a faculty for knowing which analogues are best—exist in different quantities in different directors. Every director should have some of each. What is more important, however, is the way he applies his talents to the drama he is producing. He sets in motion and controls, but then is controlled by, a process leading to a successful performance. Let us seek first an overview of the process, and then the director's own peculiar artistic contributions.

The Directing Process

Let us employ the "imaginary you" again. Let us assume you have been chosen to direct three plays—*Mark Twain's The Adventures of Tom Sawyer,* which we have just studied from the playwright's point of view, *Othello,* and *Major Barbara*. Let us pretend you have plenty of warning and plenty of time to get ready, a situation that may never exist but ought to be the goal of every theatre group. The approach to directing we will thereby examine, remember, is only one of many possibilities. There are nine-and-sixty ways to direct a play, and every single one of them is right. What we will pretend, therefore, is a sample rather than a categorical imperative.

A play is an organized human action that seems to happen spontaneously in time and space. Spontaneity, the "illusion of the first time," *is* an important goal. But so are liveliness, precision, and ease of endeavor. As a rule, none of these goals can be reached if the preparation itself is "just a happening." Practice is needed, but not that alone, for practice makes permanent rather than perfect. The right kind of practice, done at the right time, is the way you achieve spontaneous, lively, precise, and effortless performances.

Probably you should think of this preparation as a three-stage process. The stages are pre-rehearsal, rehearsal, and performance. There are eight kinds of rehearsal: casting, reading, blocking, polishing, continuity, special, technical, and dress. As important as the activities themselves is the momentum and flow of events. Preparing a play is a carefully-controlled emotional surge to successful impersonation of the dramatic action. What happens is a controlled combustion that lights up the audience.

As we noted earlier, you need time to make the process work. How much time depends on your needs and on the specific situation—what the drama is, what the demands of the theatre or the season are, what your casting problems are. Mr. George E. Stewart and Miss Dorothy Pamelia, who in actuality did direct the version of *Tom Sawyer* you are working on, had a total of six weeks to do everything. The playscript was not even completed until after casting had to occur. On the other hand, they knew the novel well and they had excellent support from staff, cast, and technical crews. The director of *Othello* had one year for pre-rehearsal, plus some twenty years of studying Shakespeare in general and that drama in particular. The same director had three months to pre-rehearse *As You Like It*, and one month for *A Thousand Clowns*.

Many directors can work with even less time, and there is no rule to follow. No doubt you would like as much time as possible, but it is what you do with the time that counts. Pre-rehearsal consists of selecting the drama, analyzing the drama, cutting the drama, and perhaps revising the drama. You must immerse yourself in the dramatic construct, the characterization, the language, and the scenic environment. You must *become* the drama if you are to make it into a play.

This immersion should occur even before you select your drama. Let us say that you chose *Tom Sawyer* because your season of three children's plays needed a well-known author to help the box office and also because you felt that Twain's novel was ideal for an experiment in "revue dramaturgy." *Major Barbara* was picked to be the "modern comedy" in a season of classical and modern plays that dealt with "Dreams of Salvation." Sometimes you may simply be assigned a play to direct. Usually you have a choice. You should pick your drama not by its reputation, though often you may be forced into this kind of choice, but by the meaningfulness of its action for your audience, the demands of your season, and the capabilities of your producing group.

If you have the opportunity, you should select whole seasons rather than individual plays. The season should exhibit balance among types of plays, types of approaches, and types of dramatic action. Though some directors argue against the practice, you probably should build your season around a central theme or idea. Often this idea is external to the dramas themselves, as in a "Shakespeare Festival" or an "All-American Season," for example. The most saleable drama should head the season, and usually this means Shakespeare, a musical, or at least a "comedy." The next most appealing drama should end the season. If your season includes a work that will be relatively shocking to your audience, probably you should place it second or next-to-last so that your most appealing choices will help absorb the shock. An original play can occupy these two positions well for the same reason; the popular productions help the new one along. Many directors like to offer a new drama in the middle of the season, however, and perhaps place in the series is not all that important. Nor is there a magic number of productions to have. Five amply fill an academic season, and seven or ten take care of any type of repertory theatre. The rule in the commercial theatre, of course, is that each play is a new and unique event in the dramatic marketplace. Community and academic theatres, on the other hand, tend to work with seasons.

However you select your drama, or have it selected for you, the trick is to master it. If you have a choice, you must feel it or you must not direct it. Where there is no choice, you must do the best you can with it. The variance among directors is so great in this regard that absolutely no rule will fit. Once upon a time, for example, I attended a performance of *The Birds* (by Aristophanes, not Alfred Hitchcock) that still seems the funniest experience I have ever had in a theatre. Yet another director, one of the most creative and competent I have ever known, refused to do this play because he simply could not laugh at it. He could see no way to make it funny.

Let us say that puzzled though you may be with the playwright's technique in dramatizing *Tom Sawyer,* you find the script exciting and workable. Let us assume, also, that *Major Barbara* makes you laugh and you immediately see many ways to make it happen in a way that will cause the audience to laugh.

The second part of your pre-rehearsal involves analyzing the drama. This, too, everyone goes about in a manner different from everyone else. A method you may like is first to read the playscript as rapidly as you can three to five times. You simply relax and let the drama speak to you. At some point in these readings, though perhaps after they are finished, you should begin writing notes to yourself—in the margins of the script, in a journal, anywhere. Once you feel the drama in most of its particulars, you begin a more detailed analysis. Someone has said that directing a play consists of two moments of intense pleasure—when the drama first hits you and when the audience rewards you with applause— separated by countless moments of intense agony and unbearable drudgery. Undoubtedly this is a truism, though many moments of small pleasure occur when some part of the creative process first comes right.

Your analysis contains many such moments, of course, but the hard labor is what makes the play begin to take shape in your mind and spirit. In studying *Tom Sawyer* you discover the action seems to be the reenactment of "the American dream"—achieving money and fame through luck, pluck, and a gift for self-dramatization. The action is viewed tongue-in-cheek, with gentle satire the goal. (Shall we note in passing that in *Othello,* self-dramatization is "tragic"?)

Each of these actions—and their similarity is purely a coincidence—must be experienced first through plot and story and then through the other elements of drama. You quickly discover that *Tom Sawyer* is plotted as a collection of many stories which are supposed to flash in and out of the consciousness by means of associations projected by the audience.

It is the revelation that counts. You must examine each of these dramatic constructs to see what dramatic units inform it. As we noted in Chapter 1, these units may be classified by the actions of the characters in them, the symbol or image clusters, some combination of these, or the entrance or exit of an important character (French scene). Sometimes a unit may be only technical—there solely to serve such dramaturgic needs as exposition, transition, or character development. Within each unit you seek the purposes at work. You must accomplish all the dramaturgic purposes, and you must find ways to allow the purposes of the characters to reveal themselves. Often the interaction of character goals is the unit's central purpose.

Sub-units may occur at any time. They consist of the same possible articulating devices as the units themselves. The sub-unit, however, is particularly apt to be motivational. Many directors like to structure the production around such motivational units—that is, any series of moments that maintain the same motivational pattern. Each time a motive changes, a new unit occurs.[1]

You have discovered, let us say, that *Tom Sawyer* is not so much a collection of motives as a gathering of projected images. Some of the images exhibit conflicts and some do not. Some of the conflicts are motivational. No doubt you will try the motivational unit as a structuring device, but probably it will not work. Many times, character relationships and conflicts are the means of articulating the drama.

Another aspect of your analysis is your growing awareness of staging problems. We have already mentioned the problem of changing from scene to scene in *Tom Sawyer* and how a proscenium stage would provide the best answer except that it would eliminate the audience involvement an arena stage could bring to the production. The compromise is a three-quarters-arena, with platforms on one side and a rail between audience and actors. Besides serving as a fence and a chancel rail, this railing can be useful to your actors. They can sit on it, vault over it, whitewash it—whatever the scene calls for.

Between railing and audience you can place benches to serve as pews in church and seats in the courtroom. Along with a few chairs and tables, and a lectern, these benches are your only scenery. To aid the feeling of neutrality, you can have everything painted a plain brown.

If you choose the neutral arena, you will need to set and sustain the moods of the play with lighting, music, and sound effects. You may employ an eerie green light, for example, with "ghostly" music, sounds

---

1. In particular, see John E. Dietrich, *Play Direction* (Englewood Cliffs, N. J.: Prentice-Hall, Inc., 1953).

of dripping water, and weird echoes to make the cave scenes appear deep in the earth and the cave itself filled with tunnels, holes and escarpments. Blue light and tuneless music will help the graveyard scene, in which we have already noted the effect of large, white tombstones. Any scene using only a particular place on the stage can be illuminated with area lighting.

One of the problems that you may discover in your analysis is the necessity for cutting. As a general rule, you should be as true to the playwright's work as possible. If the play is too long, if a unit or a pattern of activity will not work for your audience, if lines are obscure in their meaning or seem offensive to your audience—these are times for judicious cutting. When you begin with a finished playscript, as with *Major Barbara*, the likelihood of severe editing is small. Copyright laws, of course, forbid rewriting without the playwright's permission. Performance contracts usually require the play to be produced "substantially" as it is printed in the script.

When you work with a completely new script, however, you may find that cutting is one of your major tasks. The dramatization of *Tom Sawyer* may arrive in as sprawling a state as the novel, unable to fit the playwright's own desire for a two-hour production. Moreover, since this is to be a children's play, you may decide that you want it to run no more than one and one-half hours. If you were an experienced director, you probably would seek first to restructure the drama to strengthen the storyline. It would take long conferences with the dramatist to establish that a "confusion of stories" had been woven into the play's structure, that Twain's satirical intent had to be realized, and that the filmic or stream-of-consciousness style should be stressed. Undoubtedly the playwright would welcome your editing, but would insist that you boil the drama down overall.

Another problem lies in the obligatory whitewashing scene. You would not work with it very long before you discovered that it appeared unplayable. Though full of human and critical interest, it may well seem overlong and undramatic. Your answer may be to pare it down to almost pure action, to allow it to go on for a limited number of children, and to invent a theatrical ending. You can reduce Ben's monologue about steamboats to two or three sentences, and you can remove the role of Jim. Then you can change one of the children into a tomboy and thus increase the variety of exchanges that can be portrayed. Finally, you can make the scene end with a quarrel between this new character—"Jackie"—and another child. The quarrel can result in her dumping the bucket of whitewash on her opponent's head. And that ends the scene.

You must perform this kind of gross but careful editing throughout. Once the largest part of it is accomplished, you can start removing passages of dialogue *within* scenes. If the playwright has included the dialogue about warts, for example, you may feel it can be removed except for the lines about the dead cat. These are necessary to set up the graveyard scene, but the other parts of the discussion about how to get rid of warts seem dated and obscure for today's audience. The Tom-Becky "love scenes," if presented in their entirety, can be edited in such a way that the relationship is merely suggested. Similarly, Tom's dialogue with the "new boy in town"—called "William Dayton" in the dramatization—can be reduced to about eight lines and the first stages of the fight. If the playwright has used more of the Tom-Aunt Polly incidents in the book than Scene III can legitimately project, you may want to keep only the jam incident and the inspection for evidence of Tom's having gone swimming. A brief passage referring to Tom's fight with William Dayton needs to be there, however, and you should be sure that Tom's escape from a whipping is included. This incident should prove popular with the children in your audiences.

If these cuts still do not bring the production within your time limit, you may also cut Tom and Mary's struggle over the scriptures and the blood-oath scene. The first is delightful enough, but the point it is making about "rote religion" is presented fully in the rest of the Sunday School scene. The blood oath is also very effective, but it merely amplifies the self-dramatization theme. Besides, the scene may interfere with your audience's believing Tom's change of heart in the courtroom scene that immediately follows.

The difference between cutting and revision is slight. In the first, portions of the drama are simply removed. In the second, nothing is cut out but the lines and the scenes are restructured and sometimes new lines are added. The cave scenes as the playwright proposed them may have had several separate moments when Tom and Becky were alone. Each of these moments, along with the frolicking of the other children, the fight with Injun Joe, and the mourning of the village until the triumphal discovery at the end, may have been a separate scene. No doubt you would seek to coalesce these events into a single scene (as in the playscript printed with Chapter 5). All but one of the Tom-Becky dialogues—the one in which they meet Injun Joe—can be eliminated. The picnic sequence can be staged to build toward this dramatic encounter. Then the scene can shift back to the church, relax, and build again to a climax—the discovery scene. Probably your single scene will need seven quick changes of locale.

At some stage in your pre-rehearsing you must begin planning both your administration of the production staff and your creative contributions. If the playwright is working with you, presumably you will confer with him at great length. The other artists—designer, costumer, and so forth—you need to bring into the process after you have an idea of how you want the play done but before you have completely made up your mind. Any approach to this collaboration that allows a unified development of the production is acceptable. Usually the number and type of artists, and the kind of people they are, will determine your administrative methods. Your own preferences must be considered as well. I like to depend heavily on the creative sensibilities and the artistic skills of my production staff. Another director may prefer to work every detail out himself before he consults any of the other artists.

Whatever your staff arrangements, they need to be established well before the time for casting. Half the battle in becoming a successful director is choosing a good play; the other half is choosing a good cast. But your organization of the artistic situation can help play and cast immeasurably.

Planning also involves choosing and recording your own artistic contributions. These we will examine in detail later; here we need only name them. Besides being responsible for the total production—for the entire experience of the audience—and you may apply your inventiveness to *any* phase of the production, you have particular responsibility for grouping the actors and the set pieces, movement of the actors, business performed by the actors, characterization, ensemble playing, interpretation of the language and other symbols, and the rhythm and tempo (the pacing) of the production. Some directors like to work all these out in detail before beginning rehearsals; others like to do everything while working with the actors. Some like to combine these two approaches, but my experience is that such a combination works least well of all.

At some point your pre-rehearsal activities begin to merge with rehearsal. This phase includes casting, reading the play, blocking, polishing, continuity, technical rehearsal, and dress rehearsal. These activities are generally arranged so that they occur in sequence and so that a momentum is set in motion. The high point of energy and concentration is your performances, and everything prior is channeled toward those moments with your audience. This is not to preclude any special rehearsal periods outside the main channel, but nothing can be allowed to interfere with the surge to performance.

Other than the drama you choose, nothing affects your production more than your casting. In the commercial theatre, plays are usually pre-cast, though tryouts are not uncommon. College and community theatres usually hold general tryouts for each production, for several productions at once, or for the entire season. If you have a permanent company of actors, for whom you select the dramas carefully, you may avoid having tryouts each time.

Whether your tryouts are open or selective, however, you should allot plenty of time to the process. Other things being equal, you keep casting until you have the right ensemble. Even when time is short, you should try for three to seven tryout periods. Each should last no longer than three hours. Prospective cast members can be asked to read the playscript without any preparation, or come with a scene or two ready for performance. Many directors like to have the actors present one or more short scenes from any play. One director I know of always asks the actors to recite nursery rhymes and sing common ditties like "Happy Birthday!"

Most directors who hold open tryouts allow the actors to read for any part. So long as the proceedings have a modicum of efficiency, this practice is valid. What is gained in feelings of free participation outweighs minor inconvenience. Another aspect of this problem is whether or not to require every person who wants to work on the production to read for a part. Many people want only to help out backstage, and perhaps it is unfair to force them to try out. On the other hand, unless you know each person's abilities you will not be able to select your cast from the widest range of possible choices.

Still another problem is peculiar to college and community theatres. At many places it is the rule that everyone tries out "for the production, not for a part." That is, if a person signifies his availability, he is presumed committed to any task the director may select. In the commercial theatre this practice is unnecessary. Everyone is a specialist, and there is strict separation between cast and crews. Large or semi-commercial college and community theatres may also follow this policy. But the usual non-commercial theatre gains from the total *esprit* of the group. Probably it is wiser for such an organization to enforce the "trying out for the production" rule. You need to make sure that everyone has a crack at any task he wants sometime during the season, however, or you will have wasted this helpful practice.

Casting principally involves the selection of an ensemble in which individuals are right for their roles but the most important thing is the way they fit together. Sometimes, as in *Death of a Salesman,* casting a technical person can be as important as casting the actors. The Miller play must have a superb lighting operator.

Be that as it may, you take your hopeful workers through a winnowing process. At the start of each tryout period, you should announce the performance dates, the rehearsal schedule, the policy about commitment to the production, and anything else important to the well-being of the cast. It is most crucial that every prospective member of the production be fully informed as to policy and procedures. Having everything written out for distribution is even more helpful than simply making announcements. You may also want to describe the drama, the characters, and the style of your production. Some directors find that a warming-up period of improvisations or theatre games helps the actors.

Your winnowing process contains the following stages. First, everyone reads for anything. Then you ask certain people to read for particular roles. Then you select tentative ensembles. Finally, you select a tentative cast with one person in each role and an understudy for each major role. At some schools, double-casting is practiced. It seems to me such a policy is acceptable only when a role is so strenuous that an inexperienced actor cannot play it two successive performances. Many roles in grand opera have this characteristic even for professional singers. The use of understudies, however, is highly recommended. The second actor in each role serves to protect the company from a sudden drop-out, and usually just the presence of a rival precludes withdrawals for any but emergency reasons. Moreover, a neophyte can learn much from observing the first cast going through its paces and from preparing the role somewhat on his own. This way your teaching function can pay double dividends.

As you choose your players, you look first for experience and talent (see Chapter 4); second for stage presence, creativity, and lack of inhibition; third for capacity to grow; fourth for suitability to your general conception of each *persona* in the drama; and finally, as we noted earlier, for balance among all the *personae*. At the tryouts for my production of *A Thousand Clowns,* for example, the best person for "Sandy" could not be cast because she was several inches taller than the best available "Murray."

As soon as possible after you have chosen a cast, a public announcement should be made. The usual method is to post the list on a callboard or a bulletin board, and require the actors to signify acceptance of their assignments by initialing beside their names. If time permits, it is sometimes helpful to notify each cast or crew member personally in writing. When this is done, you probably should require an acceptance in writing as well. Another helpful practice in college and community theatres is to announce technical crews as part of the cast list.

Whether you announce your technical staff along with the cast or not, you need to have one. There are many ways to organize such a staff. The one delineated in Figure 6.1 works for me.

All the positions in this ideal production staff may never be filled, of course, and you may vary your procedures from production to production. It is possible that designer, technical director, and business manager may be permanent staff or faculty, and only the other positions will change from play to play.

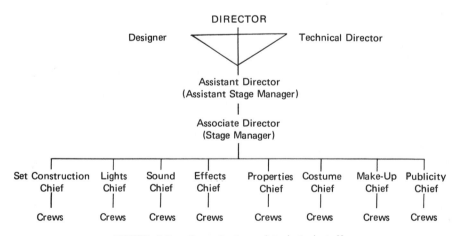

FIGURE 6.1.   Organization of technical staff.

What is more important than the particular method of organizing your staff is to realize that the members must work with you from first rehearsal onward, though in accordance with a schedule. Stage manager and assistant stage manager should be your assistant directors throughout the rehearsal period. In this capacity, they "hold book"—that is, they construct the production books from what happens at rehearsal and from what you give them from your prerehearsal period. Crew heads must also be consulted early in the rehearsal process. Give them their responsibility, their authority, and their assignments; then let them manage their crews. (This same rule applies to the business staff.) Your crews will literally make the play for you, and nothing can help you so much as skillful management of these hard-working and often unsung heroes.

Though you may have meetings with individual artists, crew heads, or crew members at any time, you should also schedule a series of regular production meetings. Both cast and crews should be present, and the meetings should be as brief as possible. A good time is thirty minutes prior to each Monday's rehearsal. At these meetings, problems and assignments can be ironed out. What is chiefly accomplished, however, is enhancement of *esprit*.

Once you have your cast and crews, or feel reasonably sure you can get them, you may proceed with your rehearsal schedule. It is important that whatever your favorite arrangement of the elements in the rehearsal period, you should prepare the schedule in writing, you should follow it constantly though not rigidly, and you should structure it carefully to fit your specific situation. A sample rehearsal schedule for *Major Barbara* appears below.

MAJOR BARBARA

Rehearsal/Performance Schedule

Day/Date	Time/Place	Activity/Call
Mon., Nov. 3	6:30 P.M., LA 106*	PRODUCTION MEETING (Entire cast and crew)
Mon., Nov. 3	7:00 P.M., LA 106	BLOCK Scenes 1-7 (pp. 1-16)
Tues., Nov. 4	7:00 P.M., LA 106	BLOCK Scenes 8-15 (pp. 16-25)
Wed., Nov. 5	7:00 P.M., LA 106	BLOCK Scenes 16-20 (pp. 26-40)
Thurs., Nov. 6	7:00 P.M., LA 106	BLOCK Scenes 21-31 (pp. 40-56)
Fri., Nov. 7	7:00 P.M., LA 106	BLOCK Scenes 32-48 (pp. 56-72)

*LA = Liberal Arts Building

Sat., Nov. 8	1:00 P.M., LA 106	RUN THROUGH BLOCKING, ACTS I-III (Entire Cast)
Mon., Nov. 10	6:30 P.M., LA 106	PRODUCTION MEETING (Entire cast and crew)
Mon., Nov. 10	7:00 P.M., LA 106	POLISH Scenes 1-6 (pp. 1-13)
Tues., Nov. 11	7:00 P.M., LA 106	POLISH Scenes 7-15 (pp. 13-25)
Wed., Nov. 12	7:00 P.M., LA 106	POLISH Scenes 16-18 (pp. 26-37)
Thurs., Nov. 13	7:00 P.M., LA 106	POLISH Scenes 19-23 (pp. 37-47)
Fri., Nov. 14	7:00 P.M., LA 106	POLISH Scenes 24-35 (pp. 48-61)
Sat., Nov. 15	1:00 P.M., LA 106	POLISH Scenes 36-48 (pp. 61-72)
Mon., Nov. 17	6:30 P.M., LA 106	PRODUCTION MEETING (Entire cast and crew)
Mon., Nov. 17	7:00 P.M., LA 106	POLISH ACT I (pp. 1-25)
Tues., Nov. 18	7:00 P.M., LA 106	POLISH ACT II (pp. 26-37)
Wed., Nov. 19	7:00 P.M., LA 106	POLISH ACT II (pp. 37-47)
Thurs., Nov. 20	7:00 P.M., LA 106	POLISH ACT III (pp. 48-72)
Fri., Nov. 21	7:00 P.M., LA 106	POLISH ACTS I-II (pp. 1-37)
Sat., Nov. 22	1:00 P.M., LA 106	POLISH ACT II-III (pp. 37-72)
Sun., Nov. 23	1:00 P.M., MAG*	CONTINUITY (Entire Cast)
Mon., Nov. 24	7:00 P.M., MAG	CONTINUITY (Entire Cast)
Wed., Nov. 26	7:00 P.M., MAG	CONTINUITY (Entire Cast)
Fri., Nov. 28	7:00 P.M., MAG	CONTINUITY (Entire Cast)
Sat., Nov. 29	1:00 P.M., MAG	CONTINUITY (Entire Cast)
Sun., Nov. 30	1:00 P.M., MAG	TECHNICAL RUNTHROUGH Costume Parade (Entire cast and crew)
Sun., Nov. 30	7:00 P.M.	TECHNICAL RUNTHROUGH Make-up Parade (Entire cast and crew)
Mon., Dec. 1	7:00 P.M. (CALL) 7:45 P.M. Cast Meeting) 8:00 P.M. (Rehearsal) MAG (Enter through rear)	DRESS REHEARSAL (Entire cast and crew)

---

*MAG = Magoffin Auditorium

Tues., Dec. 2	7:00 P.M. (Call) 7:45 P.M. (Cast Meeting) 8:00 P.M. (Rehearsal) MAG (Rear Door)	DRESS REHEARSAL (Entire cast and crew)
Wed., Dec. 3	7:00 P.M. (Call) 7:45 P.M. (Cast Meeting) 8:00 P.M. (Rehearsal) MAG (Rear Door) [COMPLIMENTARIES]	DRESS REHEARSAL (Entire cast and crew)
Thurs., Dec. 4	7:00 P.M. (Call) 7:45 P.M. (Cast Meeting) 8:00 P.M. (Performance) MAG (Rear Door)	PERFORMANCE (Entire cast and crew)
Fri., Dec. 5	7:00 P.M. (Call) 7:45 P.M. (Cast Meeting) 8:00 P.M. (Performance) MAG (Rear Door)	PERFORMANCE (Entire cast and crew)
Sat., Dec. 6	7:00 P.M. (Call) 7:45 P.M. (Cast Meeting) 8:00 P.M. (Performance) MAG (Rear Door)	PERFORMANCE (Entire cast and crew)
Sun., Dec. 7	1:30 P.M. (Call) 2:15 P.M. (Cast Meeting) 2:30 P.M. (Performance) MAG (Rear Door)	PERFORMANCE (Entire cast and crew)
Sun., Dec. 7	Approximately 4:30 P.M. MAG	STRIKE (Entire cast and crew)

The goal toward which your rehearsals surge is the performance. If you are having a long run, you should point toward the third or fourth performance as the highest plateau your cast will reach and maintain. If the total number of performances is four or less, you should aim for the last performance. It may seem strange to suggest that the peak should occur after opening night, when mothers and fathers, and critics, are present. The problem of critics will be examined in Chapter 9. Mothers and fathers will be no problem if you make your opening performance as near the peak as possible. For nonprofessionals, however, the habit of pointing toward the first performance tends to leave the remaining audiences—who also pay for their tickets—high and dry. Obviously the better the cast and the play, the better the director, the less likely you are to have this letdown. But you must devise any method you can to insure both high quality and evenness of performance throughout the run.

Successful performance really begins at your earliest contact with the drama. You, the director, must arrive at first rehearsal—indeed, at casting— with a full-fleshed vision of the final performance. The means of realizing that vision may well come from rehearsal, but you must *start* with a workable production concept.

Performances true to this concept, to repeat, are actually begun at your first rehearsal. Many directors believe this should be a readthrough of the entire play. Either the director can read to the cast or the actors can read their parts. (If the playwright is available, he may read and explain his manuscript.) Reading can be practiced as "detailed study," or you may combine analysis with a readthrough. The more complex or distant the play, the more helpful such reading and studying will be. The less well-trained the cast, on the other hand, the more likely it is that little will be accomplished until the actors are on their feet. Possibly you may want to combine reading with your initial blocking. That is, if you have worked out the details of your blocking in advance, you can explain it and have your actors copy down your instructions during the readthrough or the study of the drama.

Whatever your decision about reading and studying the drama with your cast, you probably should devote no more than three-to-five rehearsals to this technique. The second stage of rehearsing—or the first, if you begin with it—is *blocking*, a term which means the establishment of character positions and groups, movements from position to position, and the business of each character. The number of such rehearsals varies with each play and with each director. Probably the maximum is one to three rehearsal periods for each act. As a rule, gross blocking is best handled by dictating it rapidly the first time you try it, and then going over it one or two times to set it. Some directors, however, prefer to work out details of blocking as they go along. Others prefer to spend all the time on characterization and let the scenes more or less block themselves.

Whether to arrive at first blocking rehearsal with everything already planned, or to develop the blocking with the actors, seems to be simply a matter of preference. Certainly you should understand the entire drama before you begin rehearsals, but there is no inherent need for you to create the actual scenes until you have actors in harness. My own experience is that either of these extremes works, but that trying to combine them by writing down everything in advance and then trying to work with both your preconceptions and your actors simultaneously fails. Many directors, however, thrive on the combined approach. If you do prepare the blocking in advance, you should sit down with your cast and give them their instructions scene by scene. Then you should allow them to practice each scene's blocking until they know it well enough to proceed with more sophisticated rehearsals.

Once you have blocked your play, you then proceed to the polishing rehearsals. These periods of intense work—usually taken scene by scene or unit by unit—are the heart of your rehearsal period. You take the actors through the drama line by line, and you stop them over and over until each successive moment is polished nearly to perfection. Your actors may still be working with their scripts, though you should expect memorizing of lines to be finished about halfway through the polishing period. Rehearsing line by line tends to aid memorization.

No matter how many characters are in a dramatic unit, it is better to work with them one at a time than to try to view the unit as a whole. Simply work with the actor, or actors, until interpretation, grouping, movement, business, and body attitudes are nearly perfect. You can make any changes and improvements you want, but if at all possible you should avoid changing the blocking. That is, polish the drama all you need to but do not repeat earlier work if you can help it. Much of the actor's business is invented during the polishing rehearsals. It may help such invention if you attack each scene at random, but probably it is best if you have a plan—which can simply be "going from beginning to end." Yet you may want to do the climaxes first, then the openings, and then the middle of your scenes.

With such intense work there is bound to come a time when you reach a point of diminishing returns. Either you or your actors become restless, irritated, listless. When you believe you have polished a unit as much as is fruitful at a given rehearsal period, then move on to the next one after a short rest period. This moment you will have to recognize by experience.

Often much of your polishing can be accomplished by means of quiet talks with your actors, or with an individual. These periods of rapport serve to help the actor keep modifying his imaginary environment and thus to create his role. Coach-and-coax is the best way to proceed.

At the close of a given unit's work, it is wise to go over the unit one final time. This sets what you have done in the actor's consciousness. During this final run-through of the unit, you should let it proceed relatively free of interruptions.

Late in the period of polishing rehearsals, you may want to begin putting units together to make scenes, and scenes to make acts. But you continue the detailed work even with the larger segments of the play.

Once you believe your cast is ready for the change to larger units and more complete runthroughs, you may initiate a period of "continuities." You may do these first with a large segment, such as an act, or you may go immediately to a runthrough of the entire play. Whichever you choose, the idea is that your cast begins putting together the entire play and you become critic of your own work. Usually you should let the unit you are doing run without stopping for corrections. Then you hold a critique period at the end of the rehearsal or between acts. The only technical elements necessary for continuity rehearsals are those properties and costumes that may give your actors problems. You may not use the actual articles that will appear in performance, though this is not forbidden, but instead may work with rehearsal properties and costumes. Presumably, also, working parts of the scenery will be coming into the play as the continuities progress. Once again, special problems with the scenery need to be worked out as early as possible in the rehearsal period. Final scenery is not due until later in the period.

The number of continuities may vary, but full runthroughs should occupy at least five-to-seven rehearsal periods. You should feel no compunction about stopping a continuity if something is "all wrong" and a conference or starting over might help. But your aim should be to let the actors work together *on their own* with the play *as a whole*. Their concentration on this, their most difficult task, will be harmed if there are too many interruptions.

As your play begins to reveal its final shape, you need to bring in all the technical elements. The goal of the continuities, speaking practically, is to present the technical people with a production that is as good as it can be without them. You should schedule at least two or three technical rehearsals: one to establish the cues, one to set them, and one runthrough to familiarize everyone with the complete technical pattern. At a technical rehearsal other than a complete runthrough, you jump from cue to cue and ignore the material between them. Some directors even excuse the actors from these skeletal rehearsals. It is more important to remember that *all elements of the production should be working and complete by the first technical rehearsal.* At the time of the technical runthrough, moreover, you may want to schedule a costume and a make-up parade before the rehearsal starts. This is so you can see these elements under the lights.

Costumes and make-up become part of the production in dress rehearsals. There should be three to five of these, and each should be like a performance in all particulars. After each rehearsal, you may continue to offer suggestions about the polishing of details. It is too late to attempt radical changes, however, and what you want to accomplish is to make opening night simply an improved but little different "performance." Day by day your cast should get better, though often enough one of the dress rehearsals is so bad you wonder if you have wasted your time. It is not true in my experience, however, that "a bad dress rehearsal means a good opening performance."

The presence of an audience can do strange things to a cast, as everyone knows, and you may want to bring in a selected audience to your later dress rehearsals. This technique is particularly helpful with a comedy, because the timing of laughs is vital to success with this type of drama.

Once your play opens, it belongs to the actors, the technical crews, and the audience. You must give your people whatever type of encouragement they prefer, wish them well, turn them loose, and get out of the way. If you have done your job, they can do theirs.

The Director's Contributions

Out of your special talents and knowledge, by means of the artistic environment you have fashioned, you the director make a play. The whole production represents your contributions to the drama's success. Every decision is yours, if not always about means then certainly about ends. All the participating artists collaborate. *You* decide what the final product will be.

Yet there are special activities that are the particular province of the director. You must pattern the visual, aural, verbal, and personal stimuli. The visual stimuli include the scenic environment, and the grouping, the movement, and to some extent the business of the actors. You strive to make each of these express the action and all the planes of meaning in the drama—as well as character actions and interrelationships, and the mood or atmosphere which best expresses the drama.

The scenic environment we will discuss in some detail later. Suffice it to say now that you want the setting to be workable, striking, and a visual image of the drama as a whole.

Grouping refers to the placement of characters in a scene. When you are dealing with a proscenium stage, the term often used is "stage pictures." The play seems an infinite series of still pictures, like frames in a motion picture film. As we noted in Chapter 1, it is probably better to forget the idea of pictures, and think in terms of three-dimensional, sculptural effects. This is particularly true of arena staging, but also helpful with proscenium staging.

To get from one *grouping* to another, the actors use *movement*. Though it may seem they are simply going from one place to another, and such may be the case, the three-dimensional pattern their movement follows should be capable of expressing the meanings in the scene. If your audience sees the movement and nothing else, the scene should still work.

As an actor moves from place to place, or occupies a group, he may be performing innummerable activities with his body, with properties, and with the setting. This is *business,* and it should also express the total scene.

Usually grouping, movement, and business are so blended that one seems inseparable from the other. You may plan them together or separately, so long as each could carry the' scene if viewed alone. Each, that is, should express the dramatic action of the scene and suggest the central idea of the drama; reveal character actions, conflicts, and dominance in the scene and in the drama; and create the emotional impact of the play.

Let us take *Othello,* Act III, Scene iii, for an example. (Remember, this is only *one* understanding of this scene, and *one* method of staging it. What follows is an example rather than a mandate.) The intent of III, iii is to show the seduction of Othello. The Moor actually seduces himself, but the prime mover is Iago.

The scene opens with Cassio importuning Desdemona to intercede for him with Othello, and ends with what may be called a "Black Mass" in which Othello swears his devotion to revenge and to Iago, who "blesses" the new man of evil he has wrought. Along the way, Desdemona pleads with Othello. Distraught at his sudden rancor, she loses her handkerchief. Emilia picks it up and gives it to Iago.

Several grouping and movement ploys are obvious, and so is the business to accompany them. Desdemona and Cassio must be placed together so that, from a distance at least, intimacy is implied. Both can have business that requires them to touch, or Cassio perhaps to kiss her hand, and that further reinforces the impression that they are involved with each other. Othello and Iago are a second group, and if they move somewhat in tandem, their coming together at the end will be foreshadowed.

The positions of Othello and Desdemona, however, must show that they have not yet achieved the marital closeness necessary to forbid Othello's ever doubting her. Like their groupings, their movements must reinforce this feeling of separateness and unsureness in their relationship. At present, each simply needs the other; each merely serves the other. Each is a means, not an end, to the other.

The longest stretch of the scene involves the seduction. Othello should be grouped downstage of Iago, but close to him, to show the dominance of evil. On the other hand, Iago must be kept moving away from Othello, except for sudden darts toward him, so that the fact of Othello's seducing himself can be obvious. As the seduction progresses, Othello's movement should reveal an attempt to get away from Iago and to escape to Desdemona (where she has gone, that is). This visualizes the struggle between Iago and Desdemona for control of Othello. Increasingly Othello seems to move more and more like a puppet, and closer and closer to Iago.

At all times the Othello-Iago group should be distanced from the Desdemona-Cassio group. The greater the distance, the more credence Othello's misreading of the relationship will have. Since the Moor is wrong, however, his stage position should be weaker than Desdemona's. If you are using an arena stage, the concept of weak and strong areas does not apply. In proscenium and arena staging, the following layouts of stage space are traditional. The areas of a proscenium stage closest to the audience—DR, DC, DL—have more impact than upstage areas, unless upstage is raised in some way. In most groupings, the character upstage of another character is considered dominant, and if one of the *personae* is consistently upstage of another, the impression is that that character dominates the *persona* downstage.

Facing the audience, nearness to the audience, having all other characters look at one person—these techniques increase strength of a player or a playing area. As a rule, also, the brighter the lighting for a given area—relative to other areas—the stronger that area will be.

Another important factor—balance—is achieved by separating the Othello-Iago group from the Desdemona-Cassio group. All works of art exhibit a balance of tensions, and so should your stage groupings. The placement of the two groups in this scene from *Othello* balances the visual stimuli, the central conflict in the drama, and the opposing forces in the scene itself.

With the opening of the scene thus visualized, let us examine the ending. This is the point at which Othello swears fealty to Iago and the hatred he has fostered. No longer will the Moor serve Desdemona—love —for now he belongs to Iago—love-of-self. This moment is the ideational climax of the drama. It is also the emotional climax of the scene—toward

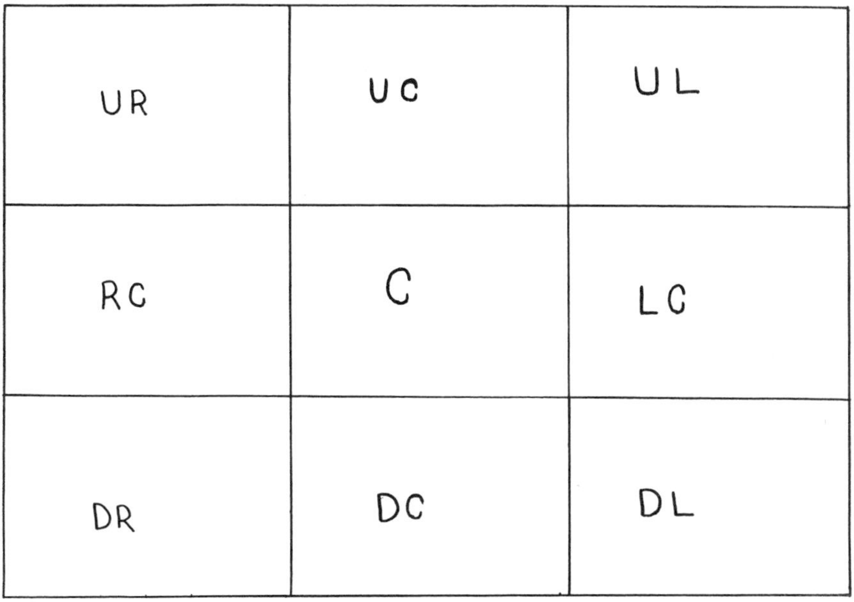

UR	UC	UL
RC	C	LC
DR	DC	DL

FIGURE 6.2. Acting areas for proscenium stage.

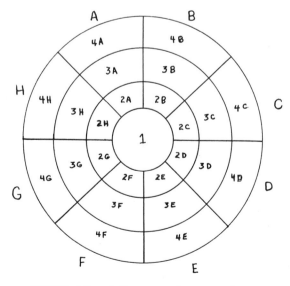

FIGURE 6.3. Acting areas for arena stage.

which all groupings have aimed and all movements have led—and the crisis is nearly overwhelming for the audience. Every director would have a different method of staging this climactic group, but probably each would seek to place it in as strong a position on the stage as possible. My preference would be for Down Right, but close to Center. With the rest of the stage relatively dark, Othello and Iago would be caught by a flickering bright light.

The image here would be that of a "Black Mass." The business of the actors would help throughout the scene as with Desdemona's handkerchief or Othello's puppet-like jerks, but nowhere so much as in the "Mass." Iago is the "priest," and Othello is the "worshipper." When they are through with their "ceremony," the audience is left with a feeling that absolute evil has prevailed.

These visual stimuli—groupings, movement, and business—you weave into patterns that express the drama in its entirety and, at the same time, create the dramatic action of each scene or unit. The test—and perhaps the impossible ideal—is whether each stimulus *alone* can make your audience feel and understand the total drama.

Your drama also presents aural stimuli—what your audience hears. To many directors, a drama is predominantly "sound," by which they mean "musical quality." More generally, however, the aural stimuli come from voice and speech, from music, from sound effects, and from silence. Voice and speech—the pitch, volume, duration, and quality of vocal sound—are usually the actor's responsibility. He gives you the vocal effects that fit his character *and* help achieve the total scene. Your contribution is to listen, and then to coach and coax him into the voice and speech that works best. There are no hard and fast rules about what is best. Typically loud volume, high pitch, slow rate, and deep quality are dominant over their opposites. But high pitch also means excitability; low pitch, calmness. Harshness or gutteral quality denotes vulgarity and comedy; rich or full quality means nobility and perhaps connotes tragedy. A fast tempo is typical of farce; a slow one more usual in tragedy. You have to decide in accordance with what seem to be the demands of each individual drama or scene. The voices and speeches can be as structured as music, though appearing totally spontaneous and conversational.

Music itself is usually part of a dramatic production, as we noted in Chapter 1. At one extreme is grand opera, which is totally musical; at the other is a play like *Tom Sawyer*, which as it came from the playwright demanded no music at all. Most dramas lie somewhere between the extremes. They have a song here and there—like "Yes, Sir, That's My Baby" in *A Thousand Clowns*. Or they use music as another actor or to set a mood, like *Death of a Salesman*. Even in *Tom Sawyer* we have noted how music is necessary to establish the cave scene. Many directors use music throughout every production—overture, accompaniment, *entre 'acte*, and so forth.

As a rule, music is useful chiefly for deepening the emotional effect of a scene or for establishing mood and atmosphere. A feeling of "joy" usually results from hearing music composed or performed in a major key. If "sadness" is the desired feeling, the music should be in a minor key. The chief thing is for the music not to intrude or call attention to itself, but it should communicate as much of the drama as it can.

The same holds true for sound effects. These are required mostly by actualistic productions, in which a given sound must represent a particular activity or event. The tendency often is to let the effects intrude on the rest of the drama in such a way that the audience begins worrying about the sound and forgets about the play. A drama that is actualistic, of course, must have its real sounds. But they need to be used first to get the drama across, and second to represent reality. Even in nonactualistic productions, sound effects can be helpful—as we noted in the graveyard scene of *Tom Sawyer*.

Finally, a drama gains much from its silences. To pause before a line or after a piece of business is often the best way to make it effective. Young actors, especially, seem unaware of the impact of silence. They hate to pause, except when failing to pick up a cue. Yet moments of no sound are extremely important to highlight the other effects.

The pause is particularly necessary when reading lines. Though the stimulus comes from the denotation and connotation of the words themselves, the context of silence in which they resound increases their impact. You must help your actors read their lines properly. If the language is well-done, it serves as a key to all other effects.

You may believe that all an actor needs to do is say his speeches in character and the rest will follow. It is more likely for the reverse to be true. Speak the speech as the author intended, and the drama may happen without any other assistance. This is particularly true of poetic drama. If you want to understand Othello, read his lines aloud.

Interpreting speeches in a drama involves treating the speech as an *action*; stressing key words or phrases; subordinating all other words or phrases; achieving both emotional and intellectual content while maintaining conversationality; and communicating the structure of the speech. In Chapter 4, we examined an approach to acting through the language of a drama. Each speech is an action toward a goal—a *doing*. You strive to get your actors to make the words and phrases *act* rather than *be*.

The place in a speech where the "action" occurs is the key word or phrase—or *thought group*—and the best method for highlighting this place is to subordinate (the usual term is "throw away") the rest of the speech. We have already mentioned the importance of pauses in line-reading. As an experiment, read the following sentence aloud: "The oak one day said to the elm, 'Bet I leaf the forest before you do.'" If you are like most people, you probably did not read the sentence correctly, which is as follows: "The oak/one day said to the elm, 'Bet I *leaf* the forest before you do.'" The pause after "oak" is almost always missed the first time through. What kind of an oak, we may ask, is an "oak one day"? Again, the emphasis on "leaf" is seldom made, thus causing the humor (low though it may be) to be missed. Most of the time "you" is made the key word, and the assertion of the oak thereby takes on the color of actuality rather than the nonsense it is intended to be.

Besides achieving the drama through words, the lines of a play directly reveal characterization. Helping your actors with characterization is one of your most important tasks. Portraying a character is a special form of visual, aural, and verbal stimuli. That is, the audience *sees* the actors stand in groups, move, and perform business; hears the speech, the music, the sound effects, and the silence; and *is moved* by the denotation and connotation of words and phrases, and the images they create. All these stimuli have meaning and impact of their own and as a result of their patterning. They are also the tools of characterization, which is the actor's *imagined dramatic action for a particular persona at a given instant in the drama.* You must help your actors imagine their actions, find means of portraying them, and fit them to the presentations of others—that is, the ensemble playing.

In short, what we have been asking you to do as director is pattern visual, aural, verbal, and personal stimuli. You seek ways to make each stimulus portray or suggest the dramatic construct, the character actions, the ideas and images, and the mood or atmosphere which make the drama what it uniquely *is.* Your patterning communicates dominance and subordination, comparisons and contrasts, conflicts, balance and proportion, tempo, progression, and rhythm. What your patterns achieve is *coherent unity.*

If you succeed in this endeavor, your play will succeed. When it does, all the artists will be praised. Particular kudos will go to the playwright and the actors. Rarely does an audience cry, "Director, Director!" Newspaper critics may praise every aspect of a production, but end by saying the direction was inadequate. At times like these, you can take heart in the fact that all the praiseworthy activities were selected or approved by you before they were released to the audience.

And if you really want to be a director, you must welcome the primal fact about dramatic production. No matter who makes the play succeed, there is only one person responsible for a failure. If you are the director, it is *you* who lose the war.

SUGGESTIONS FOR FURTHER READING

COLE, TOBY, and HELEN KRITCH CHINOY (eds.). *Directing the Play.* Indianapolis: Bobbs-Merrill, 1953.

DEAN, LEONARD F. (ed.). *A Casebook on Othello.* New York: Thomas Y. Crowell Co., 1961.

DIETRICH, JOHN E. *Play Direction.* New York: Prentice-Hall, Inc., 1953.

GALLAWAY, MARIAN. *The Director in the Theatre.* New York: The Macmillan Co., 1963.

JONES, MARGO. *Theatre-in-the-Round.* New York: Farrar & Rinehart, Inc., 1951.

WATKINS, RONALD. *On Producing Shakespeare.* New York: W. W. Norton & Co., 1951.

Chapter 7

Designers and Managers

"All the world's a stage," observed Jacques, "and all the men and women merely players." But is every stage a world and are all the players men and women?

As actor, playwright, and director—even historian and theatre architect—we have stressed the importance of a drama's scenic environment. Although this environment may exist principally in our imagination, the onstage world has a reality that goes far beyond what is merely actual. Our imagined *personae* carry out their dramatic actions in a particular place with particular artifacts. Scenes and machines may clarify, intensify, and localize the action of the drama.

Though director or dramatist may do it, usually a designer prepares what the audience sees and hears of the scenic environment. Often a technical director helps execute the designs. During rehearsals and performances your production should have a stage manager with an assistant. Working for them are a number of technical crews with their own crew chiefs. These are the unsung heroes who provide scenery, properties, costumes, lights, and sound or special effects. From their work comes a play's theatrical locale.

Let us assume that you have become designer/technical director for *As You Like It, Othello, Tom Sawyer,* and *Major Barbara.* You must prepare a scenic environment that frames and reinforces the sequence of events in each of these dramas. While the events are experienced in a time continuum, you may provide a constant scenic image of the drama as a whole. Or you may change the scene as frequently as the actors change position. At any rate, you must design the scenery, the stage lighting, the costumes and make-up, the stage properties, and the sound or special effects. And you must organize and manage the backstage operation that results in these technical contributions to the play's success.

The Scenery

All dramas require some kind of scenery or theatrical effects. Though many dramas may be presented in a single theatre that never changes decor, one part of the theatre is designed and constructed specifically for a particular drama. Let us first examine scene design procedures and then delineate the techniques required to give the designs physical reality.

If we survey the possibilities for designing the actor's space, we find two categories of style. A scenic environment may be either theatrical or actualistic. Though both styles have many variants, *theatrical scenery* attempts to provide only a symbol for the central idea, the dominant mood, or the metaphorical meaning seen in a drama. *Actors perform in front of, or against, the scenery.*

On the other hand, *actualistic scenery* pretends to be a more or less natural environment for the people in the drama. *The personae live in the place that is shown.*

Each drama is unique, and its scenery is peculiar to it alone. To some extent the playwright may demand both environment for his *personae* and symbolic reinforcement for their dramatic actions. Yet one approach or the other usually dominates the playwright or the director.

When you seek to design "environment," you first imagine an exact place where the *personae* live—an apartment, a cellar, a backyard, or what have you. Though you want to express all possible meanings in the drama, you strive primarily to create a milieu for the people whose lives are being dramatized. Using this total environment as a basis, you then design a representation of the milieu.

Terms from literary and art criticism have been used to describe various methods of portraying a drama's environment. Though the terms apply to the theatre only by analogy, they are helpful because no comparable theatrical terminology exists. The first style you may choose when you want to portray milieu is called *realism*. Without your design being apparent, you make every effort to create total detail with three-dimensional scenery and properties. Sometimes the term *naturalism* is used when the scenic details dominate the actors and the scenery focuses on the more visceral aspects of the environment or expresses the idea that man has no free will or choice in his life.

You may aim for a realistic or naturalistic setting and yet be selective about details. In such *selective* or *symbolic realism*, the picture onstage is not photographic. Each aspect of the scenery, each individual item onstage, is real enough, but it is selected only because it helps interpret the dramatic action. As a rule, no special symbolism is desired; the scenery does not intrude in the drama. Sometimes, however, a scenic unit or device is employed primarily as a symbol of something not shown. The rushing sound of the "Ellen N," for example, together with its whistle, may fit the locale of *A Streetcar Named Desire* accurately enough, but the sound effect's chief purpose is to stand for Blanche's desire to escape her fate.

Another form of symbolic realism is apparent when an entire location is represented by a single piece of scenery or furniture. A chair and a table, for example, represent a complete room.

Though more stage designs than not in the twentieth century are concerned mainly with capturing an environment, many of them avoid direct representation of a milieu. They attempt merely to suggest it. Actual scenery or properties may be used, but they are distorted. One such approach is called *impressionism*—the creation of visual and aural images as they are perceived at the moment of contact with the senses. Sensory data characteristically blur together without clear definition or reach the perceiver in fragments. When you design a set or a property in this style, you offer the spectator merely impressions of recognizable places or situations, rather than actual locations.

Another way to distort the environment is termed *expressionism*. Instead of portraying sensory data, your scenery shows the mind or the emotions of the playwright, a character in the play, or human beings in general. Dreams, the unconscious mind, and someone's stream of consciousness are objectified.

Often you may want to exaggerate a style of decoration—line, color, or both. A decorative motif appropriate to a historical period, a mode of painting, or a special quality like "spaciousness" is projected by means of enlargement or unusual treatment. This kind of scenery is called *stylization*—or *stylized realism*. The most important thing onstage is the conventionalized decoration. The environment is shown in heroic proportions or in striking colors.

Quite obviously, environmental settings and properties may also attempt various degrees of symbolic reinforcement. Your guide is the point at which you begin your design. If you think first of a milieu, which you then try to capture onstage in whatever manner seems suitable, you are seeking *actualism*. You want a scene in which people *actually live*.

You begin your approach to a *theatrical* setting, however, by conceiving first an idea, a mood, or a metaphorical image, and second the environmental means to express this abstraction. The term *theatricalism* may be applied to the scenery which results. Here, obviously, we have a problem with our terminology; all scenery and properties onstage in a theatre are "theatrical," even when actualism is the designer's goal. Yet there are plays in which the setting and other artifacts seek *only* a symbol experience. Playwright, director, actor, and designer wish in no way to confuse the stage with real life. Moreover, they consciously assert the unreality of the dramatic experience.

Although what we have here is as much a creative attitude as a distinct category of style, at least three methods for achieving theatricalism in this sense are discernible. The first—called *formalism*—employs nonrepresentational units such as platforms, arches, columns, draperies, and even the theatre building itself to create an effect of "neutral plasticity." A second type of theatricalism is called *wing-and-drop*. Here, the designer paints whatever he seeks to represent on pieces of canvas. These may be large or small, and may hang free or be stretched and fastened to wood or metal frames. Those hanging free are *drops*; those fastened to frames are *wings*. However the painted pieces are constructed, they can be put in position while the curtain is drawn, or placed and removed while the audience is watching.

A third method of theatricalizing a production is to build rough, uncovered frames, scaffolding, ramps, and steps—the whole without decoration of any kind. This approach—a skeleton without particular locale or a framework of some special place—is usually termed *constructivism*.

Whether you seek actualism or theatricalism, or some mode in between, you must limit your design to whatever is suited to the drama itself or to the style of production the director desires. Your scenery after all is just another actor—mute but not silent, visual but not obtrusive, and extremely important to a play's success.

Your scenery will work best if it is achieved through a controlled process of design and execution. This process aims primarily for the eyes of the audience—yours is mainly a spatial art—but your designs work through time as well. Not only does each performance exist as a series of visual effects, but also every play normally has a series of unique performances. Your design of the drama's playing-space thus achieves a cumulative effect through being ever-present. The sounds of your scenery work both directly and cumulatively on the ears of the audience.

Most directors will welcome your artistic contributions, even in areas of production normally assigned solely to the director. Once the general esthetic considerations have been dealt with, you and he must work out a floor plan. Nowhere in the design process is it more important to think of the setting as "another actor" than in the laying out of entrances and exits, levels and ramps, and stage pieces or furniture to be used by the actors. The plan should be drawn to scale and suitable for the stage on which the performance will take place.

When the drama is to occupy a proscenium stage, the floor plan should be followed in the design process by sketches of various scenes. You carefully paint and draw your sketches to scale and perspective. They add color, style, mood, and atmosphere to the spatial relationships indicated in the floor plan. The scale is that of the floor plan; walls and objects are drawn as they actually appear to the eyes of the audience. The lines of a setting are usually considered to have one, two, or three vanishing points; such perspective gives the impression of three dimensions. Though you are not trying to create a finished water-color, you should be as artistic as possible in your use of color, shade, and shadow.

Many directors will insist that sketches be followed by a scale model. Particularly when the staging is other than proscenium or the setting has many steps, ramps, or levels, the model will be necessary. Painting and drawing may not be as meticulous as in the sketches, but all scenic relationships should be clear. When the play is not intended for a proscenium stage, the model may serve as the "sketch."

Once you and the director have agreed on the plans, models, and sketches, you must prepare elevations and working drawings from which the technical director and his crews can build the settings. Even if you are your own technical director, you should still make drawings and elevations. An elevation is a drawing with no perspective, the object or wall being seen as if it were immediately in front of the eye. Working drawings are building plans from which scenery and properties are built. Both represent exactly what is expected as a finished product.

If the thing being constructed is overly complicated, you may have to prepare a cross-sectional view. The object appears as if it has been cut in two. Another technique is the orthographic projection, in which the exact shape of an object is shown through three drawings: the top (a plan), the front (the object), and the side (an elevation). Finally, some three-dimensional drawings may be necessary. For this an isometric projection is used. Principal lines, except diagonals, are measured, and up-and-down lines are either slanted or perpendicular. A plan is put on paper by means of a 30-60 degree triangle, which is drawn so that right angles are obtuse. The perpendiculars are the exact height of the object and extend from the corners of the plan. Details are drawn in, using the precise measurements of the object.

When you deal with plans, sketches, elevations, working drawings, and other practical matters, you must keep seven principles in mind:

1. The setting is a place rather than a picture. It is a three-dimensional framework for the actions of the characters.
2. The setting nevertheless must exhibit scale, proportion, balance, unity, and variety.
3. The scenery must interpret the drama by providing locale and atmosphere that "say" the dramatic action from the first moment of the play and continue to reinforce this impression as the drama unfolds.
4. The amount and tempo of the activity in the drama affect the setting.
5. The setting must conform to the place of performance.
6. The stage itself—particularly its depth—often determines the appearance of the setting.
7. Many dramas make special technical demands.

Carrying out these principles—solving the problems they indicate—may well be the responsibility of a *technical director*. Though he and the designer may be the same person, often one person designs a production and another builds it. But whoever handles the technical direction, he must be a jack-of-many-trades. He must build and paint scenery and accompanying pieces, set and adjust lights and sound, fashion properties, and supervise the work of crews backstage during the preparation of the drama. He must know carpentry, mechanics, painting, electricity, and black magic. He must also be a "leader" and to some extent a "designer." The people he leads are the technical crews, whose spirit and morale cannot make a bad production good but can certainly destroy a good or borderline effort. What the technical director designs are space, time, and human relationships.

Small wonder that in the commercial theatre each of these technical tasks is usually performed by a specialist, though often many specialists will work for one or more of the designers. In the educational or community theatre, however, one technical director usually does everything.

Let us assume for a few moments that you have become the technical director for a university theatre. All designs have been completed and the director is satisfied. You may have been part of the design process from the beginning, or you may start your work about the time of the first rehearsal. The first thing you may be asked to do is estimate costs. If they have been settled, you may have to purchase supplies. If you have been given a budget, you will have to stay within it. If you are responsible for the budget, you may have to prepare one before anything else can be accomplished. A typical budget for a single production might be as follows:

LUMBER	$135.00
PAINT	75.00
MUSLIN	75.00
STAGE HARDWARE	50.00
COSTUME MATERIALS	230.00
TOOLS (EMERGENCY REPLACEMENT)	50.00
LIGHTING	75.00
LABOR	180.00
OVERHEAD	25.00
TOTAL	$895.00

Your second task is to plan the construction period. Each job requires so many man-hours, the work time must be organized properly, and the construction ought to help the director rehearse. Moreover, when the production is part of a formal course or the workers are students, they must be utilized in such a way that systematic learning occurs. You must allow for teaching sessions that deal not only with the art and craft of each job but also with the basic skills (hammering, sawing, etc.). One technical schedule for a production appears below.

DAY/DATE	TIME/PLACE	ACTIVITY/CALL
Monday Nov. 3	6:30 P.M. LA-106*	Production Meeting/Entire Cast and Crew
Monday Nov. 3	7:00 P.M. LA-107	Technical Meeting to Set Deadlines/ Crew Chiefs

*LA = Liberal Arts Building

Tuesday- Friday, Nov. 4-7	1-5 P.M. Magoffin Auditorium (MAG)	Flat Construction/Set Crew and Workshop students
Monday Nov. 10	6:30 P.M. LA-106	Production Meeting/Entire Cast and Crew
Monday Nov. 10	7:00 P.M. LA-107	Technical Meeting to Discuss Problems; DEADLINE for Hand Properties not Requiring Construction/Crew Chiefs and Properties Crew
Tuesday- Friday Nov. 11-14	1-5 P.M. MAG	Construct Costumes, Sets, Properties/ Costume, Set, and Properties Crews, and Workshop Students
Monday Nov. 17	1-5 P.M. MAG-125	Publicity Meeting, DEADLINE for Stories and Poster Designs/ Publicity Crew
Monday Nov. 17	6:30 P.M. LA-106	Production Meeting/ Entire Cast and Crew
Tuesday- Friday Nov. 18-21	1-5 P.M. MAG	Construct Costumes, Sets, Properties, Posters/Costume, Set, Properties, Publicity Crews; Students
Saturday Nov. 22	9:00 A.M.- 5:00 P.M. MAG	Construct Set, Fit Costumes, Finish Properties, Distribute Posters/Entire Cast and Crew
Sunday Nov. 23	1-5 P.M. MAG	DEADLINE for Set and Properties, Program Copy; Construct Costumes/ Set, Properties, Costume, Publicity Crews
Monday Nov. 24	1-5 P.M. MAG	Place and Focus Lights, Prepare Sound and Special Effects/Light, Sound, Special Effects Crews
Monday Nov. 24	6:30 P.M. MAG	Production Meeting/Entire Cast and Crew
Tuesday- Wednesday Nov. 25-26	1-5 P.M. MAG	Finish Set, Properties, Costumes; Complete Lights, Sound, Special Effects; Prepare Make-up/Set, Properties, Costumes, Lights, Sound, Special Effects, Make-up Crews; Students
Thursday Nov. 27	ALL DAY	Thanksgiving Holiday
Friday Nov. 28	ALL DAY	Thanksgiving Holiday
Saturday Nov. 29	ALL DAY	Technical Runthrough, Costume Parade/Entire Cast and Crew
Sunday Nov. 30	ALL DAY	Technical Runthrough, Make-up Parade/Entire Cast and Crew

Day/Date	Time/Place	Activity/Call
Monday Dec. 1	8:00 P.M. MAG	Dress Rehearsal/Cast and Crew Report *by 7:00 P.M.*
Tuesday Dec. 2	8:00 P.M. MAG	Dress Rehearsal/ Cast and Crew Report *by 7:00 P.M.*
Wednesday Dec. 3	8:00 P.M. MAG	Preview Performance for Guests of Cast and Crew/Cast and Crew Report *by 7:00 P.M.*
Thursday- Saturday Dec. 4-6	8:00 P.M. MAG	Performance/Cast and Crew Report *by 7:00 P.M.*
Sunday Dec. 7	2:30 P.M. MAG	Performance/Cast and Crew Report *by 1:30 P.M.*
Monday- Saturday Dec. 8-13	8:00 P.M. MAG	Performance/Cast and Crew Report *by 7:00 P.M.*
Saturday Dec. 13	IMMEDIATELY AFTER PERFORMANCE MAG	STRIKE/ENTIRE CAST AND CREW

Third, if a shop is not already provided, you may have to set up one. An efficient shop is one which has the proper equipment, the right amount and kind of space, and an effective arrangement for both equipment and space. Few theatres are ideal in this respect, but the better ones consider the shop as important as the stage and the auditorium. The lay-out in Figure 7.1 may be considered a "typical ideal" shop for a theatre.

Given production designs, a budget, a schedule, and a shop, your fourth task is to purchase materials for the production. A good deal of money can be saved if you buy for an entire season, or for several productions at a time, but just as often as not the technical director has to buy for each production as it is prepared. You will need lumber; moldings; nails, screws, bolts, and tacks; covering materials; glues; stage hardware; *and* drapery materials for your sets. You will need costume materials for your costumes.

Fifth in the order of business—and about time, you may think—is the construction process itself. Here we will discuss scenery alone. Though any kind of carpentry may be used, theatrical settings are usually built with *flats*. These are wooden frames covered on one side (or sometimes on both sides) with muslin (or canvas) and paint. The drawing in Figure 7.2 is a flat seen from the rear (backstage), and each part is named.

Once the frame is constructed according to the diagram, the flat is turned over and muslin (or canvas) is attached to it. The procedure is to lay the frame on the floor (or on a table or sawhorses) and lay the covering material on the frame so that about four inches hang over each side and the ends. Then the material may be stapled to the wood with a staple gun. The material should sag in the middle about 3/4″. Then glue

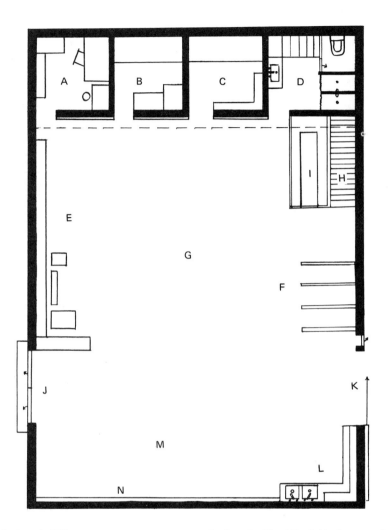

A. Designer's Office
B. Print Room
C. Properties Construction Room
D. Rest Room, with Lockers and Showers
E. Wood Storage Area, with Scrape Bin and Storage Space for Heavy Equipment Mounted on Lock Rollers
F. Flat Storage
G. Construction Area
H. Stairway to Balcony for Prepared Set-Piece Storage

I. Cage for Hand Tool, Hardware, and Supply Storage
J. Large Outside Doors to Truckbed and Loading Dock
K. Sliding Two-Story Door to Stage
L. Sinks and Paint Storage Area
M. Painting Area
N. Paint Rack

FIGURE 7.1. Floor plan of shop.

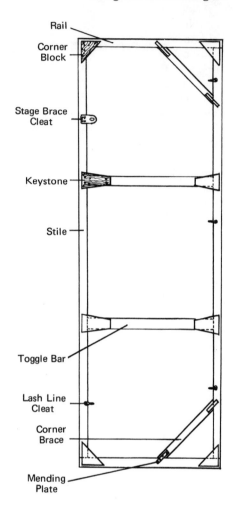

FIGURE 7.2. Standard flat (12' × 5').

is applied under the outer edges of the material, which is smoothed back over the wood. Once the glue dries, the muslin is trimmed 1/8" from the outer edges. Finally the entire flat is "sized" with a mixture of glue and water. This makes the covering material stiff and the flat wall-like.

When a flat is placed next to another one, the crack is covered with a strip of muslin about 5" wide. This strip is glued in place. Two or even three flats may be fastened together with hinges. The result is called a *book*, or a *two-fold* or a *three-fold*. The strip of muslin covering the cracks is called a *dutchman*.

Some flats contain doors, arches, or windows. Others serve as profiles or ground rows. The basic construction is the same in each instance as the drawing above indicates.

Not all sets call for flats. Dramas may require rocks, trees, columns, chimney pieces, or even automobiles. Both playwrights and directors, moreover, like to use steps and raised platforms. And often you may create the setting by arranging draperies. These may be plain or decorated, and they may be made of scrim—a thin gauze-like material that can be painted. It is opaque when lighted from the front, transparent when lighted from behind.

Once you have constructed the scenery, you must paint it. Painting scenery requires a knowledge of color, equipment, and procedures. Color is the result of the reflection of light from a surface, or the breaking of white light into various wave-lengths. Certain chemical pigments reflect certain wave-lengths and are perceived as colors. These colors may be said to have *hue* (the color itself), *intensity* (strength, or distance from gray), and *value* (degree of lightness or darkness). Primary colors are red, blue, and yellow; secondary colors (combinations of the primaries) are purple, green, and orange. The relationship among the colors is shown in Figure 7.3.

The use of color is highly complicated. Almost any color is apt to have almost any effect. Psychological reactions can be achieved, but not with certainty. Few will deny that colors can seem "warm"—red and yellow— or "cool"—green and blue. And once on the scenery, dark colors seem to approach the audience and thereby make the setting appear to decrease in size; colors like green and blue, on the other hand, seem to recede from the audience and somehow reduce the importance of the scenery.

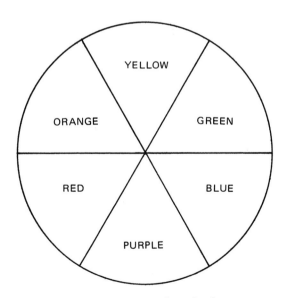

FIGURE 7.3. Color wheel.

You and your designer, it seems, are pretty much on your own when it comes to color. What works, works.

Preparing paint involves the use of pigment, carrier, and binder. Usually water carries and glue binds scene paint. Many scene painters prefer to mix pigment, water, and glue themselves—blended together in this order. Other painters mix the glue and water into *size water* first, then stir in the dry pigment. Three gallons of scene paint will cover about five hundred square feet. A noted scene designer offers the following suggestions about pigment mixing:

1. Because of the impurity of the pigment, colors lose intensity when they are combined.
2. White changes the intensity and value of a color, but does not change the hue.
3. Black paint will neutralize a color as well as darken it.
4. Black will give yellow pigment a slight greenish cast.
5. In order to *key* all colors to one dominant color, add a little of the key color to each portion of paint.
6. Glue and size water will darken a color slightly.
7. A color can be grayed by adding a little of its complement.
8. The painter can usually predict the color which will be produced by combining pigments next to one another on the wheel.[1]

Another method of scene painting involves the use of casein paint, which comes in cans already blended and must only be mixed half-and-half with water to be ready for use. Whether to use casein paint or to mix one's own is debatable. Each technical director should try both and then make a decision.

Whichever kind of paint is used for flats and set pieces, the actual painting goes through five stages: size coat, prime coat, ground coat, back painting, and texturing. The size coat is a mixture of size water and a little white pigment. Put on front and back, this coat covers the pores of the muslin, shrinks the material, and prepares it for later coats of paint. Often such sizing is done as soon as the flat has been constructed. The prime coat goes on next—a neutral shade that will serve as a base for the final coat of paint. This is called the ground coat. Care is taken with the job, since the audience will see it. Brush strokes are in various directions and without pattern.

Though back painting is not always necessary, many technical directors recommend the procedure. The back coat stops light-spill through the flats and gives the rear of the set a neat and trim appearance.

The front of the scenery is not left with only the ground coat. As a rule, texturing is required. The various methods of adding texture—and hence three dimensions—are indicated in Figure 7.4.

Painting cloth or draperies ordinarily requires analine dye. It is easy to work with, but it is permanent. Though it may be darkened after

---

1. Herbert Philippi, *Stagecraft and Scene Design* (Boston: Houghton Mifflin Co., 1953), pp. 121-122. Used by permission.

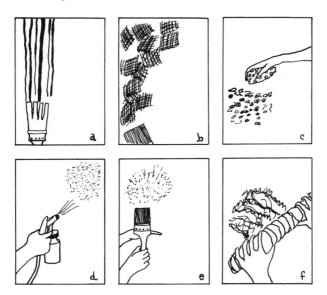

FIGURE 7.4. Methods of paint texturing.

application, it cannot be lightened. The translucent quality of dye makes it ideal for drops through which light must shine, as in scrim effects.

However constructed or painted, scenery is only as effective as its operation in performance. Flats may be lashed together and braced up with rope, nails, and special hardware such as the stage brace or the brace jack. Pictures of these bracing methods are shown in Figure 7.5.

Flats and other scenery can be moved by running, by footing, by floating, and by flying. To run a flat, you stand it on one end, grasp one edge with two hands well spread apart, and pull or push the flat along the floor. Footing means that one person stops the flat's edge with his foot while another person pushes the rest of the flat into the air. When a flat is floated, it is simply released so the air pressure will let it fall gently to the floor. Flying means attaching the scenery to a rigging system and raising it into the fly loft. Often scenery is placed on wagons or jacks, and rolled in and out (Figure 7.6). All these activities can take place in front of an audience, but normally they occur backstage with the curtain closed.

The Stage Lighting

Whether or not scenery is used in your production, the actors must be seen. If the production is outdoors in daylight, visibility is taken care of. But most productions are indoors or, if outside, at night. Hence the success of the drama rests to some extent with your lighting design and the

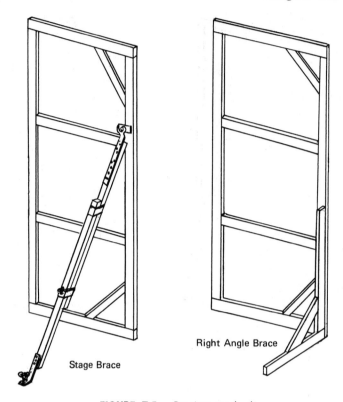

Stage Brace

Right Angle Brace

FIGURE 7.5. Bracing methods.

lighting technician. Moreover, the very appearance of your scenery will be affected by the kind, color, and intensity of the lights shining on it. And finally, the lighting can help immeasurably to unify and clarify the drama.

The art of lighting design and the technique of lighting require much more detailed study than we have space for. When designing the lighting, you work first of all for illumination. Then you attempt to shade and shadow the scenic environment so that everything seen becomes three-dimensional. This requires the simulation of natural light sources, lighting each area from at least two angles and with at least two different shades, and using light in tone with the type or style of drama. The concept of "lighting areas" must be noticed. The stage is divided into acting areas, and each has its own lighting. The separate angles from which the area is lighted, with warm or cool complementary colors from a particular side, aids the projection of three dimensions. The lights are focused on the actor's face, and the pools of light overlap so there are no dead spots. The best vertical angle from stage to lighting instrument is 45° but this is not always possible. Sometimes all that is available are

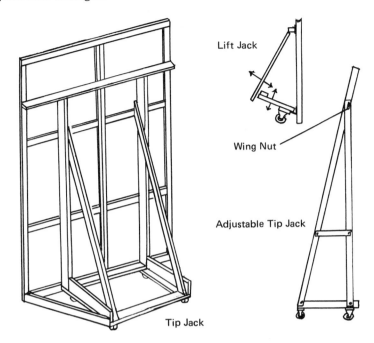

Lift Jack

Wing Nut

Adjustable Tip Jack

Tip Jack

FIGURE 7.6. Stage jacks.

lights directly above the stage and footlights. Although these positions may be used to help blend lighting areas, they are not so effective as positions in the ceiling of the auditorium for creating depth and dimension. Wherever the light source, there should be as little light-spill on the scenery as possible. If scenery is to be lighted, it should have its own lighting sources. Figure 7.7 shows a typical lighting design.

The instruments generally used for stage lighting are lamps, the ellipsoidal reflector spotlight, the Fresnel spotlight, the floodlight, and the border or strip lights (Figure 7.8).

Today all lighting operates by means of electricity. Electrical energy originates in an electromotive force (E.M.F.) and the pressure of this force is measured by a unit called the *volt*. The rate of flow of this energy, regardless of the pressure, is measured by the *ampere*. The power resulting from pressure and flow is counted by the *watt*—the current of one ampere as it moves under the pressure of one volt. The standard formula for this relationship is P (watts) = E (volts) $\times$ I (amperes). If two of these figures are known, the third can be determined. Since electrical circuits are rated in amperes, you must always know how many your lighting will require so you will not overload the circuit.

Electrical current flows only in a completed circuit. The flow may be in one direction (direct current, or D.C., which is seldom available) or in alternating directions (alternating current, or A.C., which is much more

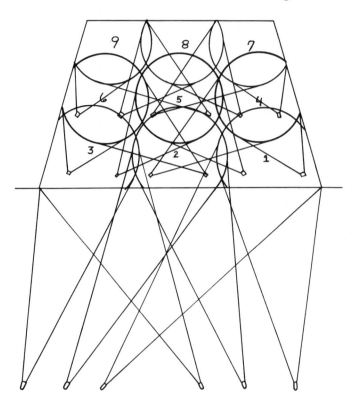

FIGURE 7.7. Typical lighting design.

common). Equipment designed for one type of current cannot be used with the other. Circuits normally are either in series or in parallel. Series circuits have one path for the current; parallel circuits, two paths. In a series circuit, each instrument is wired directly into the system; if one fails, all fail. Parallel circuits, on the other hand, have each instrument wired separately. One can be out, but the others will keep shining.

Another important formula to know when working with electricity is Ohm's Law, which deals with the resistance to electrical flow. Such resistance, always relevant to size, length, and composition of the circuit, is measured in *ohms*. The formula for this relationship is as follows:

$$\text{R (resistance in ohms)} = \frac{\text{E (electromotive force in volts)}}{\text{I (intensity of current in amperes)}}$$

The control of lighting generally requires a rheostat, which is a device through which electricity flows while meeting greater and greater resistance. As the resistance increases through movement of a contact, the

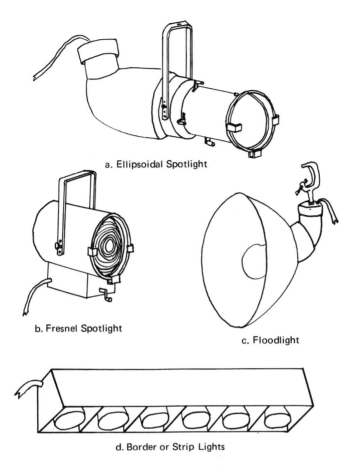

a. Ellipsoidal Spotlight

b. Fresnel Spotlight

c. Floodlight

d. Border or Strip Lights

FIGURE 7.8. Standard stage lighting equipment.

amount of wattage put out decreases. Thus the intensity of the illumination can effectively be changed at will. Some rheostats operate by means of an autotransformer—which dims the light by transforming voltage from higher to lower amounts. The most effective means of controlling light, according to many technical directors, is one which uses electronic tubes. The most common one is that developed by George Izenour. Regardless of the type, all systems for controlling stage lighting are called *dimmers*. Each circuit has it own dimmer, which may be controlled from any point in the theatre.

At that point there is usually a *light board,* through which all the circuits pass. Dials or levers control each circuit; moving them raises or lowers the illumination. Ordinarily the various changes in lighting can be pre-set in the control board. Then the given circuit is simply brought into action at the proper time. The Izenour systems characteristically allow considerable use of automatic arrangements.

Throughout our discussion of light, we have barely mentioned color. The light that comes from a lamp is white—that is, all the colors visible to the human eye are blended together. To make color in the white light visible, other than through the use of a prism, a colored medium must be placed in front of the light source. This medium—usually colored glass, colored gelatin, or lamp dip—subtracts one or more of the light primaries and transmits the others. A green gelatin, for example, absorbs everything but green. Light primaries, incidentally, are red, green, and blue; light secondaries are blue-green, purple, and yellow.

Lighting instruments, control boxes, and outlets generally are connected by cable that is heavily insulated. Some of the wiring or the cables may be concealed, but much of it is movable and can be changed. Different lengths or pieces of cable are joined by single or multiple *pin connectors,* or by *twist-lock connectors.* At each connection, the cable is tied in a simple overhand knot so the connectors cannot be pulled apart by accident.

One important lighting technique has been saved for last. This is the projection of scenic effects on a screen. Projectors may be without lens (the Linnebach projector) or with lens. The first is acceptable for projections that do not require detail and in which distortion will not harm the effect. For detail, an instrument with a lens must be used.

The Costumes and the Make-Up

If the setting is the place where the character lives or the actor performs, and the lighting allows the audience to see both, then the costumes and the make-up *are* both character and actor. A play done in arena style or on a bare stage may depend wholly on costumes and make-up for scenic effects, though lighting is almost always necessary.

While they may be considered separate parts of the production, costumes and make-up seek to accomplish the same goals. Hence they may be studied together. The goals are (1) to express the drama visually through line, shadow, and color; (2) to characterize the *personae*; (3) to emphasize or conceal; (4) to counteract the effect of stage lighting; (5) to complement the setting. Let us examine how costumes and then make-up achieve these goals.

Costumes are concerned principally with clothes worn by the actor. Questions always arise as to which are properties and which are costumes among items carried by an actor. Regardless of who makes an item, if it is worn by the actor, it is a costume; if it hangs on his body, unless it is a cape, it is a property.

Whatever the drama, you express it through silhouette, color, texture, accent, and aptness for character, actor, ensemble, and historical period. The silhouette may be fitted or draped, or some combination of these two. Sample silhouettes appear in Figure 7.9.

Greek

Bustle

Paniers

Empire

FIGURE 7.9. Sample silhouettes.

The color of a play's costumes must be coordinated with setting and lights. There should be chromatic unity, but each character should be color-keyed to his own dramatic action. Furthermore, his relationship with other *personae* should be expressed by the color. The overall effect should enhance the atmosphere of the drama—bright for comedy, somber for tragedy, and so forth.

Texture is equally as important as color in accomplishing these values. Bulky materials give an impression of heaviness; skimpy materials, the opposite. Density of the weave and the stiffness of the thread used for a material determine the appearance of rigidity or looseness. The tighter the weave and the stiffer the thread, the greater the rigidity. A similar effect lies in the surface characteristics of a material. Smoothness, sheen, and pattern tend to emphasize flimsiness; roughness, dullness, and lack of pattern stress heaviness.

Both color and texture are useful for accenting a costume, which may be accomplished simply by emphasizing some part of the actor's figure. If this part of the costume is in a special color or texture, the accent is even more effective.

The costume—regardless of its silhouette, color, texture, and accent— must fit the actor, the ensemble, and the historical period. (The period must fit the drama, if it is produced in a period other than that for which it was originally composed.) Fitting the actor involves three things: allowing him to be recognized, allowing him to move properly, and helping his characterization. All of these must complement the other *personae,* and the period of the costumes must exhibit unity, coherence, and a measure of accuracy.

Costumes, like clothes, should emphasize what is pleasing in an actor's physique or physiognomy and conceal or alter that which is displeasing. Fat actors may have to seem thin; skinny ones, fat. A face that recedes must be projected by the costume's silhouette and color. Unlike clothes, however, costumes must achieve their ends through movement and activity. Dramas calling for a great deal of activity generally require fitted costumes, for example, and dramas stressing verbal exchange are perhaps better suited to draped costumes or to those that are most pleasing while standing still, as on a mannequin. Footwear needs to enhance mobility and help the actor move as the drama requires.

The drama's lighting and setting, of course, make special demands on the costumes. Style, color, and period must fit the setting—serve as its extensions, as it were. Stage lighting must not be allowed to negate the color choices used in costuming, nor to change the effect of color and material. Lights tend to make cloth look skimpy, and if it has a high sheen, flimsy. Thus costumes need to use duller and heavier materials than clothes not designed for the stage.

Finally, the most important quality a costume can have is "playability." This is both the sum of all the other characteristics and a quality in its own right. A costume must work as the drama and the director need it to work. Quick changes, for example, may have to be facilitated. In *As You Like It,* women must be disguised as men; in *Othello,* the actors must fight vigorously with swords. In *Everyman,* the characters must achieve both realism and abstractness.

All these goals—expressing the drama visually, characterizing, emphasizing or concealing, counteracting the lights, complementing the scenery, and playability—are also assigned to make-up. By make-up we mean colored pastes and powders, hair, and various sprays applied to any portion of the actor's skin or hair but used principally on his face and hair.

The chief use for make-up is to counteract the effect of stage lighting. Faces tend to fade into blurs or blobs as the lights eliminate natural contours and bleach out skin color. So the actor first applies a base color to his skin. This color simply may increase visibility; or it may serve to project a character—e.g., a Negro or an oriental. Then to the base are added dark-colored pastes called liners, and various shades of rouge. These "lowlight colors" are applied to the face where creases, pouches, and shadows are needed (or already exist and need to be stressed). Where the face is meant to catch light are added light-colored pastes— or "highlights." The result should be a face that seems fully three-dimensional under stage lighting.

Where the audience is extremely close to the stage, make-up for the lights may not be necessary. But make-up for characterization is apt to be needed in any kind of theatre. The primary character trait suggested by make-up is age—particularly with student actors—and age should not mean only lines and wrinkles. The face must be manufactured "old" from the skin out, with highlighting and lowlighting to suggest the lessening of color and muscle tone that age brings. The differences in face ages are subtle rather than sharp, and so must be the making-up to project these differences. In arena staging, it might be better to cast for age than to rely on make-up. Another common method of suggesting age is to gray the hair. Again there must be subtlety, as if each hair follicle had its own shade of gray, and it is necessary to remember that "gray" is often a misnomer.

Make-up is especially useful when the actor must hide his age or stress some aspect of his face. The techniques that increase the appearance of age are reversed. Sunken areas are lightened, and the prominent cheekbones of age are not highlighted. Wrinkles and creases are removed by not lining them at all. Healthy, youthful colors are used. With make-up it is even possible to change the contours of the face.

Let us apply some of these ideas about costumes and make-up to our sample plays. The production of *As You Like It* from which the present playscript was taken set out to create the drama "in the mind's eye." Thus, the basis for all costumes was black tights and jerseys. For the girls, opera hose were substituted for tights. Color was achieved in boots or shoes, in cummerbunds or girdles, and in capes or shoulder decoration. Colors were keyed to character relationships, and Touchstone wore a jester's black-and-white jerkin. All the girls wore transparent skirts that were ankle-length. In casting, actors about thirty years old who had heavy, mature voices were used for the fathers; all other actors and actresses except the person playing Adam were around twenty years old. Only Adam had a problem with make-up, and the actor playing him had an especially thin and emaciated face, even though he was about eighteen. It was simple to make him look "old." The two dukes wore full beards, as did some of the courtiers in each camp. These last, however, had slight but stylized beards. All "youthful" characters were clean-shaven.

When Rosalind changed to a "boy," she fastened her normally long hair under a cap, replaced her slippers with boots, and covered her jersey with a red leather jerkin. She suggested "Ganymede," rather than becoming him.

The production of *Othello* that is part of Chapter 4 was costumed in the Italian Renaissance period. All males except Othello wore various shades of dark blue, dark green, and rich golden hues of the earth colors. Othello was in black and white. The three females wore long dresses of the period that were keyed in style to each other but differed in color. Desdemona wore pure white or very light blue, richly patterned; Emilia, orange-tinted earth colors, unpatterned; Bianca, bright red with black patterns in the cloth.

Cassio and the Duke were the only males who were clean-shaven. Elderly characters had flowing gray beards; others, pointed and stylized beards. Othello was played by a white man who was red-haired and red-bearded. His hair and beard were bleached, dyed black, and then frizzled, and his skin was dyed a dark mahogany. The new skin and hair colors, when added to his height of six-feet-five-inches and his athletic "Viking" frame, gave him an exceedingly noble appearance. When he "fell," it was physically as well as spiritually striking.

Desdemona, on the other hand, was made up pale and fragile. Her physical contrast with Othello thus emphasized the racial and cultural conflict.

Tom Sawyer was costumed to suggest the 1840's. All children went barefooted throughout the play, but the boys wore jackets and blouses with ties and the girls were otherwise replicas of their mothers. These "adults" had long dresses and bonnets, each with her own patterned cotton material. The adult men wore heavy wool trousers, long coats, boots, vests, and ties—except for Muff Potter, who dressed in rags, and Injun Joe, who wore buckskin and had a strip of cloth around his head. (We should note that Huckleberry Finn was dressed identically with Muff Potter in terms of rags.) Only Injun Joe and Muff Potter used make-up, the first to create an "Indian" and the other a dissipated "drunk." None of the adult men wore beards or sideburns, though Muff had several days' growth of hair on his face.

The Stage Properties

There were 875 separate properties used in a recent production of *A Thousand Clowns.* Each of them had a particular place on the set, except for those carried on by actors, and the properties crew was considerably larger than the cast. The crew chief and two different crew members set the stage before each of four performances. There were two important changes—when Murray's apartment was made to emulate an advertisement in the *Ladies Home Journal,* which took twenty minutes to accomplish, and when the apartment was messed up again. This second change took place during the ten-minute intermission between Acts II and III.

This production is no doubt an extreme that is seldom met, though dramas with long properties lists seem to be favorites of today's audiences (witness *You Can't Take It With You* or *Teahouse of the August Moon*).

What is it that a properties crew is responsible for? Technically, everything onstage is "scenic." The dividing line between scenery and properties is narrow and usually arbitrary with a given theatre group. One method of division is to say everything the actors carry is a "property," and everything attached to the set or located more or less permanently in the scene is "scenery." Another more arbitrary method is to call what the set crew handles "scenery" and what the properties crew handles "properties." A third way to differentiate between scenery and properties is to label everything that is not a structural part of a wall "properties." Thus, a rock, a chair, a candelabra hung on the wall, and an actor's sword are all properties.

Looked at in this way, properties come in three types: scene properties, trim properties, and hand properties. These categories are never arbitrary, but depend on the individual production or the practice of the group. Scene properties are those which are located on the floor of the setting, or on the furniture. These pieces could, in fact, serve as the setting. Trim properties are those items that are hung on the walls of the setting or that serve as decoration for the scenery. Hand properties are carried in the hand or on the person of the actor; here this category merges with costumes. The actor may get the properties backstage, or they may be onstage for his use. If it is handled by an actor, it is a hand property.

All properties must be designed to express the drama, to enhance characterization, to improve decor, to accent costumes, and to control audience reactions. There must be unity, coherence, and balance in the designing of properties, just as there are in all designs for a play. Size, color, type, style, and period of the properties must be carefully controlled toward a single impact on the audience. Every play is in some way expressed by its properties: the handkerchief in *Othello*; the dead cat and the chest full of gold in *Tom Sawyer*.

The Sound and the Special Effects

As the lights go down at the end of Scene 5 in *Tom Sawyer*, the sound of rushing wings is heard in the darkness. Eerie music fills the air. The audience *hears* the cemetery before it appears. A production of *As You Like It* may use voice-synchronization for the singing.

All these effects—plus whatever music is played before and during the drama—are part of the sound system for a given production. The music may be composed specifically for that play, or it may be taken from known works. There may be an orchestra or there may be records or tape. Sound effects may be performed by hand or played from record or tape. The closer to the drama the music and the sound are, the more effective they will be. That is, original materials are more effective than canned materials. If recordings of sound effects are used, there is always the problem of sounding artificial. Audiences are used to unmotivated music in a performance, but not sound, and neither should call attention to itself.

Every theatre should have a stereophonic sound system for both music and sound effects. More than likely tape is better than records. The total sound for a production can be cued into a tape, and then each portion played at the direction of the stage manager.

Not all special effects are aural. Rain and snow often must fall outside a window, for example, or characters must "fly" as in *Peter Pan*. In children's plays, especially, characters appear and disappear in a flash of light. All such effects must be used sparingly or they become tiresome and get in the way. But properly done, such spectacle can enhance a drama immeasurably.

The Backstage Operation

The technical crews for a production cannot make it good if it is bad, but they can easily destroy a good one. In the professional theatre, the backstage operation is set in motion by the producer. He simply hires the people which his contract with various craft unions forces him to hire. Presumably these workers are fully trained and, despite featherbedding and other such practices, competent at their specialties and devoted to doing the best possible job so long as union rules are enforced. No doubt *esprit* can develop, and the wise producer, director, or stage manager probably hires people he knows are competent and dependable and tries to establish a "production team" but such a result is not inherent in the professional theatre.

The non-professional theatre, whether in a community or on a college campus, usually strives for a different approach to production. "Being professional" is always stated as a goal for the technical crews, as for the actors, and by this is meant primarily the New York City theatres. (Whether this ideal is accurate perhaps no one can say. I have seen some very sloppy technical theatre in New York and Chicago at $8.80 per seat.) The usual means set forth to achieve this professionalism is the backstage crew system, organized by the director and operated by the stage manager. Reporting to the stage manager is a crew chief for each technical area—usually scenery, properties, lights, costumes and make-up, sound and special effects. Each crew chief has working for him a number of crew members who concentrate only on that particular specialty. Where necessary, of course, as when a massive scene change is required, all the crews may join together. It is better to assign each crew a particular responsibility and not intermix crew assignments on a single production.

The director, in consultation with the designer and the technical director (All three, or any two, may be a single person.), selects the production staff from among those who volunteer for it, those who have tried out for the production (including, if necessary, some who are in the cast), and those students assigned to the production as laboratory work for a drama course. We have already noted that this last group of workers must be treated primarily as students. Above all else, their assignments must reflect the learning process in the course for which they are receiving credit.

The principal technician to be selected is the stage manager. He will serve as assistant director, will make the production book, and will run the production backstage. As a rule, the most experienced person should hold this job. He should have been a crew member and a crew chief for every technical assignment. He should know something about acting and directing, and he should have served as assistant stage manager at least once and preferably several times. Finally, he should be a capable leader. This perhaps is the most important characteristic a stage manager can have. (Incidentally, "he" may mean either male or female; women have been the best stage managers I have worked with.)

The assistant stage manager should have the same qualifications as the stage manager, except for the experience running a major production. He will also make a production book, identical with that of the stage manager, and will function as a second assistant director. Backstage he may be given a number of special assignments or he may simply manage the side of the stage that is opposite the stage manager's position. Where the stage manager is, remember, is called the "Prompt Side"; the other side is "Opposite Prompt," or "O. P."

All the crews except the set construction crew, if it is separate from the scenery crew, work for the stage manager and the assistant stage manager during production. The set construction crew works for the technical director and the designer during the construction period. All the other crews report to the directors during this period, but serve the stage manager once technical rehearsals start. If there is a full-time costumer, costume designer, or seamstress, he or she normally is responsible to the designer and the director without interference from the crew chief.

Every director, producer, or director of theatre will work out his own scheme for a production or a season. The approach just described, however, is practical and effective. That is, the director is responsible for the entire production. The designer designs, the technical director executes everything except costumes, which are provided by a costumer, the crew chiefs carry out the technical director's instructions, and the crews work at their special assignments. If properly organized and led, such a scheme can achieve the spirited, competent unity-with-diversity that any well-run team exhibits. Each person is expected to do his job well, and to help when he can on other tasks. He cheerfully and willingly carries out instructions from crew chief or managers, or from another crew member who has more experience than he does. The leaders, on the other hand, do not have to throw their weight around because they know they command instant obedience. Since they have absolute power, they can lead rather than push. The hierarchy works because everybody works at it.

Naturally this is an ideal, but it is one that is met more often than it is missed. The wise director, designer, technical director, or stage manager does everything his skill and energy let him to achieve this ideal. The wise producer or director of theatre establishes a four-year (the number of years a given student is available) plan in which workers or students train themselves toward the ideal and each person progresses toward the highest level of management he feels equipped for. Ordinarily, in a college theatre, seniors will be your stage managers, juniors and perhaps sophomores your crew chiefs, and freshmen your crew members. There can be no set quota from each class, if only because there are never enough top-flight people to go around, but you should find some other way to reward competence and dependability than disarranging your hierarchy of responsibility.

Nor can even the ideal be so monolithic as this description makes it seem. Human activities are happily fluid when they are at their most enjoyable state, and creative activity is the most fluid of all. Yet almost everyone, artists included, works better in a really well-run organization.

Let us assume, therefore, that you have just such an organization for *Major Barbara.* Construction of sets, costumes, and properties is finished; lights, sound, and special effects are ready. Sketches of the three sets, the costume plot, and the properties plot appear below:

FIGURE 7.10. Stage sets for MAJOR BARBARA.

Costume Plot—Major Barbara

MORRISON ACT I, III
Black tailcoat
Gray-and-black striped
morning pants
Black shoes
Black socks
White stiff shirt
Black bow tie

ADOLPHUS CUSINS ACT I
Blue-and-white striped coat
Blue vest
White shirt
Blue bow tie
Blue slacks
Black socks
Black shoes

ACT II
Black Salvation Army jacket
and pants—red trim
Black Salvation Army short
cape—red trim
Black Salvation Army cap
Black shoes
Black socks

ACT III
Black formal suit
Gray shirt
Black cravat
Gold stick pin and links
Black shoes
Black socks
Gray overcoat
Gray hat

CHARLES LOMAX ACT I
Wine blazer—blue trim
Wine-and-blue plaid knickers
Off-white shirts
Wine bow tie
Brown shoes
Brown socks

ACT III
Dark-green suit
Green-and-gold striped vest
Pale-gold shirt

Brown shoes
Brown socks
Gold-brown overcoat
Dark-green neck scarf
Brown hat

SNOBBY PRICE ACT II
Dark-blue work pants
Faded blue work shirt
Dark-brown wool jacket
Dark-blue short stocking cap
Black socks
Brown work boots

PETER SHIRLEY ACT II
Old baggy brown suit
Faded blue work shirt
Green-and-brown striped
neck scarf
Dark-blue plaid shawl
Black socks
Heavy black shoes

BILTON ACT III
Blue overalls
Blue work shirt
Tan work apron
Brown boots
Black socks

STEPHEN UNDERSHAFT ACT I
Gray suit and vest
Black cravat
Black shoes
Black socks
Gray-and-white striped shirt

ACT III
Same as above—plus
Black gloves
Black overcoat
Black cane
Gray hat

ANDREW UNDERSHAFT ACT I
Dark-blue suit
Deep red vest
White shirt
Red-and-blue figured cravat
Black shoes

Black socks
Dark-blue overcoat
Dark-blue hat
Gold stick pin and links

ANDREW UNDERSHAFT ACT II
Black suit and vest
Black cravat
White shirt
Gold stick pin and links
Black shoes
Black socks
Black overcoat
Black hat

ACT III
Brown striped suit
Dark-brown vest
Tan shirt
Brown bow tie
Camel overcoat
Dark-brown hat
Brown shoes
Brown socks

BILL WALKER ACT II
Dark-green work pants
Green plain shirt
Tan turtleneck sweater
Black windbreaker
Green neck scarf
Black knit cap
Black socks
Black boots

RUMMY MITCHEN ACT II
Dark-green skirt
Red blouse
Brown sweater
Blue-green plaid shawl
Black head scarf
Black cotton stockings
Black heavy shoes

MRS. BAINES ACT II
Black Salvation Army jacket
and skirt—red trim
Black Salvation Army bonnet
Black Salvation Army
short cape

Black shoes
Black purse

JENNY HILL ACT II
Black Salvation Army dress—
red trim
Black Salvation Army bonnet
Black Salvation Army long
cape
Black cotton stockings
Black shoes

BARBARA UNDERSHAFT ACT I
Black Salvation Army jacket
and skirt—red trim
Black cotton stockings
Black shoes

ACT II
Same as above—plus
Black Salvation Army
long cape
Black Salvation Army bonnet

ACT III
Blue dress—rose trimmed
Rose coat
Rose-and-blue bonnet
Blue gloves
Blue shoes

SARAH UNDERSHAFT ACT I
Rose dress suit
White blouse
Black shoes

ACT III
Yellow-gold dress
Dark-green cape-coat
Green, black, yellow bonnet
Black shoes

LADY BRITOMART ACT I
Mauve morning dress
Black lace shawl
Black shoes

ACT III
Blue dress suit
Blue-and-green blouse
Green stole coat
Green-and-blue bonnet
Green shoes

Properties Plot—Major Barbara

ACT I LIBRARY

SET PROPERTIES
- 3 oblong gold-framed landscapes
- 2 matching oval gold-framed portraits
- 1 pair dark-blue velvet swag drapes for window seat
- 6 panels off-white lace curtains for window seat
- 2 matching old rose velvet Victorian high backed chairs
- 2 matching small Victorian writing tables
- 1 small dusty-blue velvet heart-backed Victorian side chair
- 1 medium-blue velvet Victorian settee
- 1 blue-and-rose figured Victorian captain's chair

HAND PROPERTIES PRE-SET
- 2 rose nib pens
- 2 gold inkwells
- 2 rose blotters
- 1 small gold table clock
- 1 gold bell button
- 45 assorted books—blues, browns, reds, greens
- 2 rose-and-blue figured glass table lamps

HAND PROPERTIES CARRY-ON
- 1 concertina

ACT II SALVATION ARMY YARD

SET PROPERTIES
- 1 wooden bench
- 2 wooden crates
- 1 wooden barrel
- 1 plank table
- 12 assorted weathered boards
- 1 banner on poles

HAND PROPERTIES PRE-SET
- 3 tin plates
- 3 tin mugs
- 1 loaf unsliced bread
- 1 pitcher of milk
- 1 pitcher of syrup

HAND PROPERTIES CARRY-ON
- 1 pencil
- 1 notebook
- 1 plaster bandage
- 1 drum
- 2 drumsticks

ACT III GUN MOUNT OVER-LOOKING MUNITIONS PLANT

SET PROPERTIES
- 3 straw dummies
- 1 cannon on wheels
- 1 large shell on track

HAND PROPERTIES PRE-SET
- 1 fur rug
- 1 fire bucket

HAND PROPERTIES CARRY-ON
- 4 open telegrams
- 1 small box of wooden matches
- 1 bouquet of wild flowers

From technical rehearsal through the last performance all necessary technical crew members are backstage or in various work areas helping the production succeed. The stage manager maintains a roll, and all cast and crew members must sign in at the proper time before each performance. Let us say check-in time is one hour prior to curtain, though this is different with every production. Production members should enter through the stagedoor, not through the lobby and the auditorium.

The scenery crew prepares the stage for performance. The set for the first act must be up and working. The floor must be swept and mopped.

The crew chief has all activities of his crew planned, duties written down, and the labor divided in the most efficient manner. Each crew member knows exactly what, how, and when he performs each duty. Practice has brought improvement until the director and the technical director are satisfied.

Once the scenery is ready, the crew chief reports to the stage manager. "Set ready," he says.

In the meantime, the properties crew has placed the properties for Act I. In view of the large number of properties, members of the scenery crew may help set up the initial scenes, may take full responsibility for trim properties, and may participate in the changes between acts. But the properties crew chief is the person responsible for the set-up. Properties are placed onstage or on a properties table in the appropriate wing, whichever is required. Actors pick up their offstage properties just before using them.

Once the set-up is complete, the crew chief reports to the stage manager. "Props ready," he says.

While the scenery and properties crews have been working, the light crew has run through every light cue or otherwise checked every instrument. All problems have been discovered and corrected.

When the crew chief reports that lights are "ready," the curtain is closed or lowered. Usually a member of the scenery crew pulls the curtain. When the curtain is down, the stage manager calls up the house manager on the intercom or the telephone (Some form of communication *must* exist.) and "releases the house." The production cannot start until the house manager "returns the house" to the stage manager.

Once the house manager has control of the house, he opens the lobby doors and lets the audience in. If there are ushers, they show the patrons to their seats. The patrons are given programs as they enter their row. Working for the house manager are the ushers, the ticket-taker, and the box office crew. This last crew should be locked in the box office with tickets and money for change. No one, including the house manager should enter the box office until that crew is finished with its job. When the box office has closed, the crew chief counts the money, makes up a report, locks up the tickets that remain, and turns everything over to the house manager. There should be a safe for money and unsold tickets.

Meanwhile, the backstage preparations continue. The sound crew has set up the tapes or the sound effects equipment—or the record player, if that is used. "Sound ready," states the crew chief.

The costumes crew will have placed all costumes in the dressing rooms. The crew chief and one or two crew members are on hand to help the actors get ready and to aid with any quick changes. When ready for all eventualities, the costumes crew chief reports: "Costumes ready." His crew may keep busy until curtain time, however, mending and helping the cast to dress.

Most of the time, unless there are special make-up problems, the actors put on their own make-up. During the technical rehearsals, at a "make-up parade," the director had approved the make-up. Presumably an actor can continue with the same amount and procedure. If not, one member of the costume crew can be assigned to check each actor's make-up.

When cast and crew are ready, the stage manager calls the house manager and says "We're ready backstage," or something similar. Probably the house manager does not return the house at this time (hopefully ten to fifteen minutes before curtain time).

There is no rule about the matter, but many directors like to hold a cast call about ten minutes before performance. Cast and crew gather, and the director may say a few words of encouragement. Sometimes there is a group prayer. Usually, however, the director simply tells the cast the show now belongs to them, and wishes them well. Whatever he feels, this is no time for a critique. Some directors believe a cast call is a waste of time.

Two minutes before curtain time, and the production should be *on time*, the house manager calls backstage. "The show is yours," he says to the stage manager, "Curtain time in two minutes."

The play begins.

SUGGESTIONS FOR FURTHER READING

APPIA, ADOLPHE. *Adolphe Appia: A Portfolio of Reproductions.* Zurich: Orell-Fussli, 1929.

BARTON, LUCY. *Historic Costume for the Stage.* Rev. ed. Boston: Walter H. Baker & Co., 1961.

CHENEY, SHELDON. *Stage Decoration.* New York: John Day Co., 1928.

CORSON, RICHARD. *Stage Make-up.* Rev. ed. New York: Appleton-Century-Crofts, 1949.

CRAIG, EDWARD GORDON. *Scene.* Oxford: Oxford University Press, 1923.

HUGHES, GLENN. *The Penthouse Theatre.* New York: Samuel French, 1942.

NELMS, HENNING. *Play Production.* New York: Barnes & Noble, 1950.

PHILIPPI, HERBERT. *Stagecraft and Scene Design.* Boston: Houghton Mifflin Co., 1953.

PARKER, W. OREN, and HARVEY K. SMITH. *Scene Design and Lighting.* New York: Holt, Rinehart and Winston, 1963.

SELDEN, SAMUEL, HUNTON D. SELLMAN, and HUBERT HEFFNER. *Stage Scenery and Lighting.* 3rd ed. New York: Appleton-Century-Crofts, 1959.

SIMONSON, LEE. *The Art of Scenic Design.* New York: Harper and Row, 1950.

Chapter 8

Children's Theatre and Creative Dramatics

If you would write your name among the stars, someone has said, write it in the hearts of children.[1] In this introduction to theatre, we have studied all drama as if it should be what is usually called "creative dramatics." That is, the spectator has been considered more an active participant than a passive though imaginative observer.

In the same manner, theatre has been examined as if it should be "children's theatre." Even at the risk of lacking sophistication when analyzing great dramas, we have tried to consider all drama and theatre a special kind of "game." The sample drama in the chapter on playwriting, for example, was a children's play adapted from a classic children's novel. Just as the Twain book was seen to be more adult than childlike, however, the greatest of dramas has the play of children at its heart.

The catch is that the play of children deals with very serious concerns—the unknown, one's true identity, the fear or the shame of failing, the strange feelings and thoughts that overwhelm and control us, and the "thousand natural shocks that flesh is heir to." These same problems, of course, are the subject-matter of great drama. Though the treatment may be more sophisticated, or the means of communication more subtle and complicated in *Othello* or in *Major Barbara* than in *Mark Twain's The*

1. The ideas in this chapter are derived from studies and productions at the American Children's Theatre Institute, of The University of Texas at El Paso. The institute met during each of four summers, 1967-70, for eight to twelve weeks to examine and develop principles governing "theatre for children." The participants were Professors Ralph B. Culp (Director), Jean Miculka, Albert C. Ronke, J. Henry Tucker, and Gifford Wingate; Technical Director Edward Houser; Graduate Assistants Joe Egoscue, John Justice, Alicia Muñoz, Ken Osman, Dorothy Pamelia, Patricia Resler, Sandra Rule, Joe Smith, and George E. Stewart; and several hundred college students, high school apprentices, and children of El Paso. The author is grateful for the contributions made by these artists and scholars. It is hoped the principles and practices that were jointly arrived at are presented accurately and with the dedication which characterized the institute.

Adventures of Tom Sawyer, the depth and complexity of the dramatic action varies only slightly from the adult plays to the children's play.

Yet if the relationship between *Tom Sawyer* and adults is well-noted, the opposite view is not so often observed. *Othello,* that is, works as well for children as for adults.

Children for Theatre

It is well-known that children love drama and theatre. The simplest play, the least pretext for dramatic impersonation, and almost any child is hooked. The theatre games which were described in Chapter 1 are more apparent in children at play than in any other situation. With no training and little experience, children intuitively create drama as they play. Given a formal drama, they are willing to surrender their real world completely for a while.

Yet perhaps it is more accurate to say the world of the play is just as real as any other world the child is forced into. It is adults who seek a distinction between the stage and life. They foster the idea that what appears in newspapers, in lessons at school, or in family discussions is more real than what happens to Othello or to Tom Sawyer. Unless forced to such a conclusion, children avoid this error. Their problem with reality is to find the onstage activities *more* real than their own lives.

As a rule, however, this problem is rare. More usual is full awareness that "play" is occurring no matter how vivid the onstage illusion. Along with awareness goes a special capability, indeed a predilection, to shift from offstage to onstage world with ease and clarity. The reverse change occurs just as easily, though perhaps not so swiftly.

The chief difference between children and adults in a theatre is this instant willingness to play. Another related and perhaps equally important difference is a distrust of words. As one child commented recently about *An Evening with Carl Sandburg,* "It's nothing but a lot of people talking." Nowhere in my experience has the theory that a play is an art of words—a system of performing speeches that develop a single, coherent, and complete action—been better refuted than in this child's indictment. Even Bernard Shaw, that most wordy of playwrights, would delightedly agree.

It is not that children cannot pay attention—observe a boy trying to take a toy apart. The truth is that children intuitively recognize the emptiness of talk and the all-pervading impact of action. Children are for theatre because it is action *in action,* and that is the only world children know.

This is not to say children reject words arbitrarily. Where the words are themselves action—in *As You Like It,* for example, where verbal felicity is central to the games of love being portrayed—children have no trouble. Fascination with Rosalind's actions makes even the most obscure of her words meaningful in a theatre for children, particularly when the play is staged so audience and actors are close together or are intermingled.

Here, we should quickly add, lies another important difference between children and adults in our theatre. We adults have been carefully taught that "theatre" means discomfort, separation from the action, and a museum-like presentation of pictures viewed from afar. Children without such training quite naturally rebel at thus being cut off from the action onstage. The so-called shortness of their attention span is more likely their rejection of this impossible viewing situation than their dissatisfaction with a dull or unsuitable play.

Children do not bring extensive knowledge to a play. Like the rest of us, they have only their short lives to join with any experience they undergo. Thus, much that adults may enjoy about a drama—the implications in the race issue in *Othello,* for example, or the satire of romance in *As You Like It*—may be overlooked by children in the audience.

What children know full well is the kaleidoscopic, topsy-turvy, and farcical nightmare that Othello must strive to find his way through. His failure is that of every child, just as Rosalind's mastery of a similar world is the constant dream of all children. Tom Sawyer strides determinedly along both avenues that deal with life in all its horror. He dips into nightmare but is saved each time, and he dreams his way to triumph over the adult world which the nightmares so closely resemble. Barbara, Undershaft, and Cusins may debate their status overmuch, but no child could miss their principal action—finding means to implement their dreams.

Such dreams often find expression in story. The love of a story no doubt has an effect on children's love of the theatre. Other than a concern for chronology, however, children are interested primarily in the immediate sensory and imaginative experience of a theatrical performance. The hot plotline holds them less than the immediate dramatic conflicts in a scene, and the conflicts less than the impersonation itself. Children like to be told stories in the form of drama. Storytelling, though, no matter how theatrical the performance may be, is no substitute for drama. This is to say the two media need not be confused. Among other things we noted in Chapter 1, drama is not narrative being given stage presentation. To insist that narrative in its turn is not drama would be laboring the obvious. Though one form may make use of techniques from the other, they are not interchangeable. Children know this better than adults. For a story they settle back to let the narrator work his will with them. At a drama, they lean forward to play their dreams themselves.

Another interesting thing about children and the theatre is that there are no "children's classics" unless the children make them so. When Walt Disney Productions or your hometown theatre group seeks an audience for children's theatre, the first choice is usually limited to "great children's works." That is, the producers look for something well-known to parents as a "children's" play or story. After all, parents bring the children to the show and what is more, buy the tickets. A children's classic may well be a work that parents think suitable for children. If such a classic is not available, the second choice ordinarily is something new but thought to have the qualities of "classic children's works"—simple characters, lots of children and animals, complicated but exceedingly sentimental stories, a cotton-candy outlook on life, a moral or some other sign of purity, and so forth. Such decision-making overlooks the terror at the heart of *The Adventures of Tom Sawyer, Peter Pan, Heidi*—to name but three admittedly classic works for children.

What leads children to return again and again to certain plays and stories—the chief factor that makes a work continue to live generation after generation—appears to vary somewhat with the age of the children involved. Though allowance must be made for individual, cultural, educational, social, and maturational differences, children today apparently come to the theatre in the following homogeneous maturation groups: 4-7, 8-11, 12-15, 16-18, for girls; 5-8, 9-12, 13-15, 16-18, for boys. Roughly grouped and named, with the sex differences indicated, these are preschool, primary, early adolescent and late adolescent children.

At all ages, the children's preference runs to two extremes of dramas and stories. The first, in which things happen to the protagonist, dominates the younger ages. The second, in which the protagonist makes things happen, is predominant in the later years. A definite change in preference from one type to the other seems to accompany maturation. Late adolescence is the peak of children's desire to command the world. Full adulthood, they believe, means total independence, complete rightness in all things, and essentially godlike powers of strength and life. Dramas and stories symbolizing these natural desires for control obviously have great popularity—take, for example, *Tarzan of the Apes.*

At the same time, the feeling of helplessness that characterizes early childhood remains deep beneath the surface of adolescent behavior. Some observers believe, in fact, that the braggadocio of adolescents is merely a cover-up for that fear. Be that as it may, the drama or story in which things happen to the protagonist—for example, *Huckleberry Finn*—continues to hold a measure of popularity.

In the primary and early adolescent years (7-12, approximately, and 12-15), the two types of dramatic fare merge in their positions of importance as the children's power to dominate their environment seems to grow. *Cinderella* (to whom things happen) vies with *Robin Hood* (who makes things happen). Comedy, in which the protagonist triumphs in the end, outdraws tragedy. *Othello* performed as a farce-tragedy, however, blends the two kinds of world the adolescent recognizes. He can identify both with Iago, who manipulates the environment, and Othello, who is destroyed by it. *As You Like It,* which consists mostly of Rosalind commanding the world she lives in, appeals more to later adolescence.

More factors operate in children's preferences than the relative success of the protagonist. As children mature through the stages indicated above, certain other tastes develop. Verbal dexterity and word-play increase in importance during early adolescence, then lose a measure of their impact (language used for its own sake, remember, not words that perfectly express actions). Stories increase in importance continuously through to adulthood, and onward if the popularity of melodrama is any criterion. That is, as children mature they more and more seek a matrix of cause-and-effect in the dramas they prefer. This urge is so strong that only with great reluctance, if at all, can the most mature adult live successfully in a world in which all is relative.

The thrill with impersonation continues unabated, but the ability to enter the world of the imagination freely and instantaneously seems to atrophy as children grow older. Perhaps this is concomitant with the powerful urge to command the "real" world. In early years, apparently because real and unreal are merged in children's minds, magic has little appeal. In primary and early adolescent years, however, magical acts become thrilling manifestations of power. Greater sophistication may dampen this particular enthusiasm in the adolescent, but the Faustus legend and plays dramatize its continued existence well into adulthood.

Escape fare also becomes increasingly important from the primary ages onward. As children come to realize the immensity of their daily task (to dominate the world), they require means of imaginatively getting away from the grind.

Another area of importance to children participating in theatre or reading a story is an increasing demand for realism. The closer the surface of the onstage world comes to approximating the surface of the world children know (and need we mention that in today's world of television children seem to know more than ever before about surfaces), the more children will like the drama. This is not to say children prefer actualistic to theatrical dramas, but to assert that the forms probably should not be mixed. Children appear quite willing to suspend the actual surface world they know, if other values inhere in the dramatic work. Anything actualistic, however, must be totally so or suffer rejection.

Escapism combines with realism most obviously in plays and stories of adventure or romance. Indeed, a strong desire for surface actuality may well be an important means of escape. The focus of such a drama lies on thrills and spills, on strange and wonderful events, and the theatrical artist must concentrate on giving the production a patina of reality. The usual method—as in *The Adventures of Tom Sawyer*—is to show exact details of every situation or to replicate certain activities with technical precision. Tom and his friends speak the dialects of the Middle Mississippi Valley, Twain tells us in his "Author's Note," regardless of the fancifulness of their actions.

Not that children cannot enjoy realms of fancy. Characteristically children will accept almost any construct, *personae*, language, and environment that allows them to get on with the play. Their sense of probability is bounded only by the attitude, "let's pretend." If Iago *says* he will perform villainous deeds, that is enough; he is a villain.

This relaxed sense of probability is nowhere more evident than in children's well-observed love of animal *personae*—a love shared, strangely enough, with many adults. In Chapter 1, we discussed the human tendency to project human characteristics on nonhuman objects and creatures. Children seem almost to demand animal-humans in plays and stories. Aside from the need to project, this insistence on animals probably results from four related factors. First, animals are more familiar to children than people. To find them talking, thinking, behaving as humans as they go about their natural actions makes more sense than struggling with the impossibly complicated behavior of adults. Second, since children realize that animals are not in fact human beings, whatever dramatic actions they undergo receive an extra dollop of esthetic distance. In this way the terror at the heart of most dramatic actions becomes manageable. Third, the animals are definitely "inferior" to the children, who can feel "superior" and hence triumphant with little trouble. Puss-in-Boots is just a pussycat after all.

Finally, somewhat in contradiction with the inferiority-superiority pattern just mentioned, children as well as adults seek a utopia among animal societies. These always exhibit greater wisdom than human societies. They seem places where we can escape the "ills we have," where law and order rule and problems are solved easily and neatly. The need for such a place is well-established in philosophical and religious treatises. We have already mentioned the employment of this theme in *As You Like It*. Perhaps the seeming simplicity, perhaps the lack of competing evidence about animal societies, leads children to desire if not to prefer animal stories and characters. Kipling's "Law of the Jungle," Milne's well-ordered though gently satirical "Hundred-Acre Wood," Aristophanes' sharply satirical "Cloud Cuckoo Land" are but three examples of the superiority of animals to human beings.

Animal or human, the characters in children's drama must always seem to be "people like us." No one is more overwhelmed with this desire than a child. Franco Zeffirelli's motion picture version of *Romeo and Juliet* is a recent case in point. Countless adolescent and primary spectators discovered not Shaksepeare's "star-crossed lovers," but themselves. As a result of conscious directorial choice (not to mention, perhaps, the playwright's intent), the youthfulness of the lovers, their struggle with the adult world, their destruction by its malignancy, their essential purity—these favorite themes of adolescence were stressed in many ways. No damage was done to the original, either. We have already noted a similar reaction to *As You Like It*. An "absurd" production of *Othello*—described in Chapter 4—was the most popular "high school classic" of recent years with the students themselves.

Theatre for Children

Undoubtedly it should be easier to say what plays ought to be given for children of any age than to find out precisely why children come to the theatre (when they have freedom of choice) or what they experience when they get there. Since at present the liveliest branch of theatre (if not the only live one) is that devoted to the entertainment of children, producers must be doing the right things. That reliable indicator, the turnstile, supports this conclusion with an overpowering cacophony of bell-ringing. To paraphrase our opening sentence in this chapter, if you want to write your name on checks that do not bounce, write and produce plays for children.

Not that this is wrong or that answers to the questions "Why?" and "What is going on here?" must be discovered before anyone produces children's plays. One of the few precepts insisted upon in this book is that there ought to be a minimum of prescriptions for artistic or audience behavior in a theatre. The success of children's theatre and the vagueness of our knowledge about it should in no way interfere with our attempts to provide theatre for children.

These attempts should operate according to stringent educational and esthetic principles, rather than simply as a maneuver to sell tickets. It goes without saying that children's plays make money. The question must always be *to what end?* or *for what value?*

First of all, the distinction between adult theatre and children's theatre needs to be erased. That is, theatre is theatre. It may be good or bad esthetically, successful or unsuccessful, but what is acceptable for adults is also acceptable for children. If this principle seems a two-edged sword, reducing sophistication on the one hand, polluting innocence on the other, it need not be. The classics of world drama are equally impactful on a five-year-old or a fifty-year-old, though each no doubt views the performance differently and finds his own values there. Is not the action of *Othello,* for example, a familiar pattern in the life of almost any child? Who is more insistent that his own world-picture is the only right one than a child? Who "thinks men honest that but seem to be so" more often than a child? Who suffers from manipulation by people he trusts more completely than a child?

But, as is commonly asked, what of ribaldry? Is it proper to expose children to the foul-mouthed Touchstone, for instance, or the *double entendre* of *The Moon Is Blue?* The answer must be, listen to any children's group when unobserved. Foul language and bawdiness are second nature to healthy children. Whether they should be or not is beside the point. Drama deals with men *as they are,* not as one might wish them to be. Besides, as St. Paul observed, "unto the pure all things *are* pure: but unto them that are defiled and unbelieving *is* nothing pure; but even their mind and conscience is defiled." No one, except perhaps certain entrepreneurs, advocates salaciousness in any kind of drama. Yet more harm comes from dishonesty than from vulgarity, particularly when dealing with children.

A more important question focuses on the advisability of exposing children to the world's serious problems. When a loved one dies, for example, should children be given or protected from the knowledge? Must *children* know evil, sorrow, fear, bewilderment, and all the other horrors of human existence? The answer here is, they know already. What they need is a means of dealing with these concomitants of man's life on earth. The sooner they learn how to cope with the world they have been thrust into, the better will they be able to protect themselves. It is not hard knocks from life that harm the psyches of children, but hard knocks among strangers without explanation and without means of amelioration ready at hand. Plays that show children the world as they know it are children's plays, regardless of their aim.

Principle Number One, therefore, is that *nearly all good plays are children's plays.*

A second principle develops from the first. *Children ought to experience plays of all kinds regularly, unattended by adults, and uncoached in either their choices or their behavior.* "Regularly" ought to mean at least once a week at a formal theatre and daily in more relaxed esthetic circumstances (in a classroom, for example, or a recreation center). "Unattended" means the children should involve themselves in the play because it captures and holds them rather than because some teacher or parent is crying, "Pay attention!" The relativity of "uncoached" is obvious. If we can get children to the theatre without forcing them and without insisting on what they must find in the drama or what they must get from the experience, that freedom should be encouraged. If children must be taken to the theatre because otherwise they would have no way of knowing about it, that is all right. The point is, the theatre should be provided the way parks and playthings are provided: left in the children's way until they find it.

This is certainly not to forbid adult participation in theatre with the children. The more the merrier, so long as the dramatic event occurs easily and freely. Nor does this principle eliminate discussion of the values inherent in a play, provided the children desire the inquiry.

Principle Number Three is that *children's theatre should educate as well as enlighten its spectators.* It is quite obvious that learning can and ought to occur in the theatre. The delicate balance is to allow education that is inherent in the play without attempting to sell products, foster creeds, or satisfy other ulterior motives. Commercial television seems particularly abhorrent in this regard. Yet this is not to insist on "a moral" in every children's play—only truth without fakery. The distinction lies between *Tom Sawyer,* or *The Jungle Books,* for example, and *Pollyanna.*

The educational and the entertainment goals are best reached through a conscious attempt to communicate on a preschool, a primary, an early adolescent, and a late adolescent level or plane simultaneously—Principle Four. *Tom Sawyer* does, Kipling does, indeed most of the fine plays and stories do. This principle aims not at "something for everyone," but at discovering and portraying a human action so truthfully and so completely that the audience's comprehension of it is not dependent on sophistication.

The only change from age-group to age-group is that more can be gotten from the play by the older groups. What is communicated to the younger children, however, is sufficient to hold them enthralled.

Enthrallment is not only a result of appeal or truth-value. An important fifth principle is that involving the length of any children's play. *Regardless of other factors, theatre for children ought to run short, not long.* Absolute precision in this matter is impossible. A rule-of-thumb pattern of running times, one that seems apt in my experience, would be:

PRE-SCHOOL: thirty minutes to forty-five minutes;
PRIMARY: forty-five minutes to seventy-five minutes;
EARLY ADOLESCENT: seventy-five minutes to ninety minutes;
LATE ADOLESCENT: ninety minutes to one hundred thirty-five minutes.

These times are figured without intermission. Division of the play into acts has very little effect on the total span of attention available to the performance. What is affected, however, is the recall of the audience from the world of the lobby to the world of the play. Such recall is very nearly impossible with the younger children, fairly futile even with the older ones.

Principle Six focuses on the coolness of the dramatic medium. Children react to plays in terms of each separate incident. What holds them most strongly is the relationship of characters or activities foremost in their perceptual field. *Storyless, episodic productions held together by the force of continuing characters or by a central image or idea have the greatest impact in a theatre.* This is particularly true for the younger age-groups.

No contradiction is intended by Principle Seven, that *the desire for a story—so obvious in human beings—is best met in a play through dramatization of stories well-known to the audience.* The necessary matrix of cause-and-effect then becomes subordinated to the immediate episode or "bit." We should not confuse story as narration of causes and their effects with mere chronology. Even where no causation is established, concern for what happens next in a sequence of events is usually overwhelming. The point, however, is that an audience of children—in particular, but of adults also—lives each event as it happens and wonders about the future rather than the past. Nor are we violating the need for the playwright's tool called "foreshadowing." Our examination of the attention process in Chapter 1 quite clearly indicated the human predilection for seeing only what is already known.

The importance of children's direct participation in the drama cannot be stressed too much. Too often children are forced to view plays from far away, across vast distances. Such an experience is better than no theatre at all, but not by much. It is considerably more effective to perform children's plays for small groups (100 to 300), with the actors in close proximity to the audience. Perhaps the ideal staging is arena, three-quarters arena, or thrust, but the main thing is closeness of play and children. Having audience and performance on the same level, so long as viewing is not hampered, is an important part of this closeness. The aim is to encourage the spectators to participate. During a recent production of *Huckleberry Finn,* for example, when the Duke and the King were on their knees counting the money they had just discovered, several children from the audience in the small room crawled into the acting group and helped with the counting. The production of *Tom Sawyer* which was described in Chapter 5 made a special effort to cause such direct involvement. *Other things being equal,* asserts Principle Eight *this involvement is the ultimate goal of children's theatre.*

The question must always be "involvement in what?" Given the assumption that all good plays are children's plays, what distinction can be made among them or laid to theatre artists making new plays for children? Principle Nine states that *the production of plays for children ought to be guided by the following strictures:*

1. *The central action, idea, or image of the play, its treatment or development, and the attitude of the players toward it must be scrupulously honest and straightforward.*
2. *The world of the play must be recognizable as the world of the children in the audience, though no limit need be set on the range of probabilities and there is no requirement for "realism" in the dramatic or scenic environment.*
3. *The emphasis of the production should lie on physical realization, not verbal development, of the dramatic actions.*
4. *Insofar as esthetic integrity permits, a children's play should provide means for the child to control the make-believe world, to determine himself where "belief" and "suspension of belief" meet, and to maintain or cease playing at will.*
5. *Where possible, the play should dramatize a decision-making situation from the lives of the children in the audience, provide viable data about the working-out of problems and solutions inherent in the children's comprehension and acceptance of the world they live in, and enlarge or extend the children's capacities for "playing the role of the other."*

The final principle to be described is that relating to a special problem that besets children's theatre the world over. This problem is best termed "exploitation." Parents, teachers, and even the children themselves often view participation in the theatre as a stepping-stone to some goal outside the immediate theatrical experience. If the children are in the play, runs this view, they are learning to be actors and actresses, technicians and artists, but not as an end in itself. They hope to become "professionals." If the children are in the audience, they are encouraged to idolize the performers and to look for hints that will help develop their own skills of theatrical expression. Often it is difficult to gain the support of parents, and hence the participation of their children, without promulgation of this star syndrome. Though teachers usually seek to avoid this exploitation of children and parents, it takes a brave person to turn away participants and audiences, or to challenge the "associations for childhood education" that seek to bring "culture" to children, and the classes in drama, dance, expression, and what have you so eagerly sought by parents and by entrepreneurs of the arts. In an affluent society, only the children are hurt when children's theatre masks as education.

Principle Number Ten, therefore, states that *children's theatre must have no other aims than the joyous coming together of children and drama, and, where the performers themselves are children, the involvement of these children in theatre art for its own sake.*

Creative Dramatics

If children are natural dramatists, actors, directors, and scenic artists—and if participation in drama and theatre is its own *raison d'être*—then the more use of drama in schools, churches, clinics, and other educational or therapeutic institutions the better. Judging by the membership in organizations like the Children's Theatre Conference of the American Educational Theatre Association, a new predilection for the use of playlets in the public schools, and an emphasis on role-playing and other dramatic games in psychotherapy, something like creative dramatics may be taking its rightful place in our educational system.

What, however, do we mean by *creative dramatics*? A consensus definition would be that

> "creative dramatics" is unstructured, informal use of drama and theatre, including creative songs and rhythms, dramatic play, informal portrayal of incidents, experiences, and stories, pantomime and puppetry, *and* playwriting and play production through improvisation, *for the purpose of* developing a child's sense of play and mimesis, providing outlets for his views of the world, encouraging the playing of the role of the other, working out problems, and learning subject matter through dramatization of its components, *without the presence of an audience of any kind except the participants in the dramatic activities.*

To demonstrate what this definition means in practice, let us cite two rather lengthy examples. The first takes place in an ordinary third grade classroom. The teacher has much to accomplish in a given day, week, or semester. Undoubtedly she will want to stage short plays from time to time. They are fun for the children, and they seem well-suited to the celebration of certain holidays. At no other time and for no other reason will she employ drama in her classroom.

When she thinks of drama, moreover, she immediately thinks of words arranged on a page in the form of dialogue. Since the words have to be spoken by someone, she next thinks of "characters." They have to be dressed, and so costumes are necessary. The teacher's considerable experience with storytelling makes her insist that the play ought to tell a story. Better yet, the play should tell a "classic" story.

Beyond these four thoughts—written dialogue, characters, costumes, and storytelling—the teacher probably will not go, except she may add other technical elements if they are available. When the play is ready, she may invite parents to see it, show it to the P.T.A., or perform it for other classes.

Of course she may do none of these things. Without question the children who participate will have fun. Even those who watch will catch a measure of excitement. Depending on what the play is, the children may acquire a number of things: some insights about play production, a few myths about the holiday being celebrated in drama, how to yearn for applause, acceptable ways to show off, the idea that drama is something separate from daily experiences and can be enjoyed only through a great deal of special activity, and perhaps greater sociability.

To parallel this first example, let us consider another classroom. The children are in the third grade, and the teacher has many things to teach and do in a given day. Unlike her colleague, however, this teacher believes and is trained in creative dramatics. (She also has the cooperation of her principal, her superintendent, and her school board.)

As you may guess, the second teacher approaches all the subjects she must teach, all the therapeutic functions she must perform, in the spirit of the dramatist whose goal is to lead the children into varied methods of impersonating ideas and experience. She wants them so deeply involved in *life,* regardless of the data to be comprehended at a given moment, that the wonder of it catches them by the throat. She knows that theatre lies at the heart of childhood. Pretending, imitating, playacting, pantomiming—these are daily adventures for children. They grow by experimenting with life, by becoming for a moment anything they can imagine, and that is *everything.* Given the chance, boys and girls happily become their own actors, dramatists, directors, and designers. A lesson that is made into a play is "child's play" to learn—and remember ever after.

Good teachers have always kept games at the heart of the learning process. Along with word games for reading, number games for mathematics, and so forth, the teacher in our example employs as many games as she can that portray "life." Where possible, she turns ideas and information completely over to the children. She lets them respond freely to the materials. The children organize them, revise them, and then dramatize them and present them to others. The ideas, the knowledge, and the total experience become free-ranging plays that allow the children to take on the human aspects of the subject-matter. Non-readers scurry to read-up on the things they need to know in order to play their parts. Shy children find themselves suddenly outgoing because they forget their self-consciousness in the rigors of playing the role of the other. At no time is there an audience other than the children who are performing the plays.

What this teacher strives mightily to avoid also is any idea that she is doing "dramatics." The occasional playscript in a supplementary reader may be ignored or it may be used if it fits in with the other drama and theatre activities. The teacher may let the children perform certain classics, or let some touring players perform them for the children, but she never force-feeds the children. And she never seeks to make money from classroom drama and theatre. Nor does she associate interclass or interpersonal rivalries, that reward winners and punish losers, with the dramas her children perform.

Undoubtedly both these examples overstate the case. No teacher avoids any activity that will help her pupils learn, though she may regret the time and labor necessary to give her proficiency enough in drama and theatre to employ them with the same ease and freedom that she uses pencils, paper, and chalk. Nor will creative dramatics save the world, or revitalize the schools. All philosophies and techniques of education succeed only if the individual teacher makes them work. So it is with drama and theatre.

Creative drama will assist the teacher and enhance the lives of the pupils only if used properly. The relationship with literature seems obvious. What more effective way is there to tell a story than to act it out? To teach stories and the values they contain seems a natural goal of drama and theatre. Instead of narrating the story, play it; act it out, impersonating everything—including inanimate objects.

Literature of any kind, however, even folk tales and original story-telling, is often a blind alley when it comes to creative dramatics. Theatre and drama are subordinated to story; creativity, to performing the story effectively. The free-wheeling scattering of ideas and images, of actions and reactions, that should characterize creative drama is often blocked by the structure of the story and by the necessity to make the play conform to it. Telling a story—well-known or not—is certainly an important phase of creative dramatics, but it is neither the goal nor the chief tool.

Creative dramatics is a process that can exist for itself or provide a means of transferring knowledge from teacher to children. The knowledge can be from any field. As a general rule, the process goes through the following stages:

1. Rhythm activities and exercises to develop unselfconscious freedom of expressive movement and to condition the bodies of the children.
2. Vocal activities and exercises to develop free and easy use of voice and articulation.
3. Singing, dancing, choral speaking and reading.
4. Sense-developing exercises and activities both to create awareness of sensory impressions and to find ways of remembering, acting-out, and communicating the sensory perceptions.
5. Concentration and relaxation exercises to train the children in methods of commanding their senses, their imaginations, and their communication of what they feel and envision.
6. Individual and group impersonation of observed situations, including the animals, people, and inanimate objects.

7. Pantomime.
8. Improvisations, both in pantomime and in dialogue.
9. Playmaking: informal theatre without an audience, usually based on well-known stories.
10. Play production: formal theatre with an audience, usually based on well-known stories.

Looked at overall, this process is normally designed to accomplish five objectives. These are (1) development of creativity and esthetic attitudes and skills, (2) promulgation of creative thinking, (3) encouragement and improvement of sociability, (4) training of skills needed for communication, and (5) inculcation of moral, spiritual, and cultural values. Some practitioners of creative dramatics would add a sixth objective, the presentation of basic data—along with the development of the skills needed to use it—from a number of specified fields.

Throughout the process, however it is used, the emphasis lies on freedom, informality, lack of structure, and avoidance of "performing for an audience." The heart of the matter is improvisation and role-playing solely for the values they may have for the participants, never for the creation of an art-object. Individual self-expression and growth are the primary goals.

SUGGESTIONS FOR FURTHER READING

ALLSTROM, ELIZABETH. *Let's Play a Story.* New York: Friendship Press, 1957.

ANDREWS, GLADYS. *Creative Rhythmic Movement for Children.* Englewood Cliffs, N. J.: Prentice-Hall, 1954.

BATCHELDER, MARJORIE H., and VIRGINIA L. COMER. *Puppets and Plays: A Creative Approach.* New York: Harper and Row, 1956.

BRUFORD, ROSE. *Teaching Mime.* London: Methuen & Co., 1958.

CROSSCUP, RICHARD. *Children and Dramatics.* New York: Charles Scribner's Sons, 1966.

DAVIS, JED, and MARY ANN WATKINS. *Children's Theatre: Play Production for the Child Audience.* New York: Harper and Row, 1960.

McCASLIN, NELLIE. *Creative Dramatics in the Classroom.* New York: David McKay, 1968.

SIKS, GERALDINE B. *Creative Dramatics: An Art for Children.* New York: Harper & Row, 1958.

————. *Children's Theatre and Creative Dramatics: Principles and Practices.* Seattle: University of Washington Press, 1961.

SLADE, PETER. *Child Drama.* London: University of London Press, 1954.

STONE, L. JOSEPH, and JOSEPH CHURCH. *Childhood and Adolescence: A Psychology of the Growing Person.* 2nd ed. New York: Random House, 1968.

WARD, WINIFRED. *Playmaking with Children.* New York: Appleton-Century-Crofts, 1957.

————. *Theatre for Children.* Anchorage, Ky.: The Anchorage Press, 1958.

Chapter 9

Reviewers and Critics

The censure of the judicious (and presumably the praise), says Hamlet to the Players, must overweigh a whole theatre of others. Throughout our introduction to theatre, though we have tried from time to time to play the artist at work, we have continually asserted the importance of the audience. By this we have meant the entire crowd of spectators. The dreams of Everyman are the stuff that plays are made on.

The time has come, however, to consider a special kind of spectator. From the beginning of theatre as we know it, reviewers and critics have proffered analyses and suggestions about what drama is or should be. If these judicious patrons have often seemed comparable to the man who watches a drowning swimmer struggle to safety and then offers to help, their observations have many times served to enlighten both artists and audiences.

The purpose of criticism is generally two-fold. First the critic must discern how a work of art achieves its effects. Then he must evaluate the success or failure of the art-work by some viable standard.

Either of these tasks may involve many errors. The chief ones are *pre*-scribing rather than *de*scribing how an art-work means (as when stating that Shakespeare must be performed only in the manner favored by the Elizabethans) and using standards of judgment that are arbitrary, inflexible, or entirely personal.

Another problem for the drama and theatre critic is to avoid judging the play as an artist. He should not ask, that is, how would *I* act, direct, or design this drama? If he does, the chances are he will not see the drama clearly enough to judge it.

For the critic who must evaluate plays by groups other than professional, a special problem exists: that of establishing a context of standards. Quite obviously, a high school play cannot be judged in the same manner as the latest Broadway success. Yet it is not, as some people insist, unfair to criticize the amateur. The technique is to judge him against the best of his league, not against even the worst of a presumably higher league.

Finally, the critic must avoid simply reviewing the play. The conditions of professional criticism today are such that usually either a deadline comes up much too soon to allow a proper critique to be prepared or a person untrained and perhaps unsuited to drama and theatre criticism is assigned to review the play.

The successful critic avoids these problems and develops a taste for the most successful practice of theatre art. Every art has a critical methodology to be followed, however, and experience of reputable criticism is as important to the training of a critic as experience of the art-works themselves. Let us examine a few of the more influential critics of drama and theatre, and then establish a set of principles to guide our own criticism.

The Great Critics

The writing of criticism is an art that many attempt but few achieve. No doubt there are men with a talent for it; perhaps much of it can be learned. The great critics, however, are not those who write criticism well, but those who have influenced the art they criticized. Here we must distinguish three kinds of "critics"—the historian, the esthetician, and the analyst. The first furnishes a report of what happened in the past, the second formulates or discovers the principles governing an art, and the third evaluates past or present activity. With regard to theatre, the analyst works only in the present. Insofar as drama alone can be evaluated outside the theatre, the analyst studies both past and present. The historian may formulate principles and evaluate art-works, but such is not his main purpose. The esthetician may also evaluate past or present works, but to do so is not inherent in his task. One man may attempt all three approaches—and many do—but few men succeed equally in each area.

The critics who have counted historically in the theatre far outnumber those whose ideas have had permanent influence. Each historical period has had its important critics, but the works of only a few of them have gained permanence.

HISTORY OF CRITICS

In the Greek period, there were two chief critics of theatre: Plato and Aristotle. At first glance they seem counterposed to each other. Both men worked from the same premise, however, for they were both concerned about the moral and philosophical usefulness of theatre. Plato found that drama (he used the term "poetry") was harmful to the welfare of the state. Drama imitated the material world, which was itself a poor imitation of the ideal world, and furthermore, stirred up the emotions of the populace falsely. Therefore, drama was to be banned from the Republic.

Aristotle's answer was that drama imitated not the material substance but its "soul"—that is, its forming idea. Furthermore, the arousing of emotions was healthy, not harmful, because such emotions were then purged from the spectator and he became healthier. Aristotle provided a "scientific" analysis of the tragedy he knew (and in a lost treatise, some authorities believe, an analysis of comedy).[1]

Plato's attack on drama (poetry) was thoroughly detailed in a clear and overwhelming argument. Anyone who wants to attack the theatre can find plenty of ammunition there. A critic who rejects an art-form, however, is not our primary concern. The idea that drama and theatre ought to have a socially useful purpose dominates criticism through the ages. A few, like Plato, simply reject the art. Most critics follow Aristotle in accepting the need for utility and in finding goals that suffice. Almost no one has accepted the idea that drama has no purpose, that it is a fact of life neither useful nor harmful, just there.

The chief goal assigned to drama is that it teaches and delights (or the reverse). This view followed that of Horace, in *Ars Poetica*, though what Horace actually said was "either to be of profit (beneficial) or to please."

The influence of Horace on later critics was considerable. Along with Aristotle's *De Poetica*, which was largely misread, Horace's works were credited with insistence on the unities of time, place, and action; the absolute separation of tragedy from comedy; the presentation of "types" rather than particular persons or actions; the need for tragedy to be in verse; and verisimilitude.

The neo-classical critics of the Renaissance, and their successors in the 17th and 18th centuries, established these principles as rules that must be obeyed by every dramatist. The ideal was set forth or amplified by Julius Caesar Scaliger (*Poetics*, 1561), Antonio Sebastian Minturno (*L'Arte Poetica*, 1564), Lodovico Castelvetro (*Poetics*, 1570), Sir Philip Sidney (*An Apologie for Poetrie*, 1583), Ben Jonson (*Timber: or, Discoveries*, 1641), Nicholas Boileau-Despréaux (*L'Art Poétique*, 1674), and John Dryden (*An Essay of Dramatic Poesy*, 1668).

The neoclassical ideal was dominant in drama criticism from about 1550 to the latter half of the 18th century. The reaction began with Gotthold Ephraim Lessing's *Hamburgische Dramaturgie* (1769), which argued that the neoclassicists were not reading Aristotle right and that a dramatist's only goal was to affect his audience. If he accomplished that, his devotion to rules was immaterial. The peak of revolt against neoclassicism, however, came with Victor Hugo's series of prefaces to his dramas. The most important was *Preface to Cromwell* (1827). Between Lessing and

---

1. See Lane Cooper, *Aristotle on the Art of Poetry* (Ithaca, N. Y.: Cornell University Press), *passim*.

Hugo, August Wilhelm Schlegel published *Lectures on Dramatic Art and Literature* (1809-11).

The romantic critics insisted that mood, atmosphere, and emotion were everything, plot and story were nothing; the unities of time and place were unimportant; the individual character, particularly the lowly, the exotic, the adventuresome person, was a fitter subject than the general type and particularly the highborn; didacticism was unacceptable; reason was to be replaced by emotion; God was in every phenomena, but was more easily discoverable in "natural, unspoiled, primitive" people and situations; and man was essentially body and soul, with the spirit striving always toward an ideal that transcended the material or the corporeal. For the romanticist, drama had to be episodic, rambling, and disorganized—focused on strivings of noble and individualistic characters who "bucked the system." Each drama was highly subjective. The plays of Shakespeare seemed closest to the romantic ideal for drama; Gothic tales, Medieval romances, and tales of revolution were the perfect subjects for dramatization. The logical result of romantic theory were Goethe's *Faust*, Hugo's *The Hunchback of Notre Dame* (a novel) and *Hernani*, Büchner's *Danton's Death*, and the melodramas of Kotzebue.

New treatments of romantic ideas—such as the "well-made play" and thesis dramas—only underscored the basic outlook. Even attempts at realism were romantic drama in disguise. The new importance of science, however, and particularly the "scientific outlook," epitomized perhaps by Charles Darwin's *The Origin of Species* and *The Descent of Man*, led eventually to new theorizing about the nature and intent of drama. In France, works of comparable influence were Auguste Comte's *Positive Philosophy* and *Positive Polity*.

Though a number of dramatists began to apply the principles of science to their dramaturgy in the middle and late nineteenth century—notably Henrik Ibsen, August Strindberg, Gerhart Hauptmann, Henri Becque—and though theatre groups rose to foster realism and naturalism—for example, André Antoine's *Théâtre Libre* in Paris, the *Freie Bühne* led by the critic Otto Brahm in Germany, and the English group called the Independent Theatre and led by J. G. Grein—the chief theorist of realism and naturalism was Émile Zola. In the *Preface to Thérèse Raquin* 1873), *Naturalism in the Theatre* (1881), and *The Experimental Novel* (1881), Zola expounded the view that drama must become scientific. What should be seen onstage was the "inevitable laws of heredity and environment," actual or seemingly actual case studies, and in fact, not art but life. One of Zola's disciples, Jean Jullien, coined the phrase "slice of life" to describe what the naturalist drama should achieve. Unfortunately, naturalism was attached to the revelation of social ills and to the dramatization of the dregs of society. The concept of eliminating dramatic effects, of simply viewing "life" through a fourth wall, was the vital core of the new theory. For a while, romanticism was banished from the theatre—or at least from the new theatres.

We have already noted that modern drama and theatre can be studied as a series of movements in reaction to naturalistic theories. Though such an approach seems patently inaccurate, we can observe that modern drama seems eclectic in its approach to the theory as well as the practice of dramaturgy. All theories of the past have been sorted out, dusted off, and reworked to justify whatever mode of drama a given playwright prefers. Without attempting to discover sources and theorists, let us quickly define the terms most often used to describe the types of drama enjoyed in the twentieth century:

1. *Neoromanticism*—the return to glorious heroes, historical tales, and striving for ideals with cloak and sword; chief practitioner: Edmond Rostand, with *Cyrano de Bergerac* (1897).
2. *Symbolism*—the idea that everything onstage is not "real" but a symbol, legend, or myth *standing for* ultimate, spiritual, or higher "truth" or "reality"; chief practitioners: Maurice Maeterlinck, with *Pélleas et Mélisande* (1892); Gerhart Hauptmann, with *The Sunken Bell* (1896); Hugo von Hofmannsthall, with *Everyman* (1912).
3. *Expressionism*—the drama is actually the unconscious mind of the play-wright, or sometimes a character in the drama, or perhaps a dream; structure approximates that of free association; characters, sequence of events, language are distorted; chief practitioners: August Strindberg, with *The Ghost Sonata* (1907); Georg Kaiser, with *From Morn to Midnight* (1916); Ernst Toller, with *Transfiguration* (1918) and *Man and the Masses* (1921).
4. *Selective Realism/Naturalism*—the same basic idea as realism and naturalism, except that the playwright selects what is to appear onstage according to an artistic plan; most popular playwrights of the twentieth century are part of this movement; a typical example: Eugene O'Neill, with *Desire Under the Elms* (1924).
5. *Surrealism*—the drama should reject ordinary logic and form a mode of expression all its own, the aim being presentation of pure thought from the subconscious mind; chief advocates: Tristan Tzara, in Switzerland; Guillaume Apollinaire, with *The Breasts of Tiresias* (1903 and 1917); André Breton; Jean Cocteau, with *Orpheus* (1926).

The critics and the playwrights who advanced these "isms" were concerned essentially with modifying the illusion witnessed by the spectator. What was altered was the *staging* of the drama. Other approaches to a modern esthetic for drama and theatre sought to eliminate the separation between the drama and the spectator. A collective term that was often used—and was contrasted with "illusionism" and "realism"—was "theatricalism." That is, the audience and the drama were joined consciously in a theatre that both not only were aware of but attempted to emphasize. "We are engaged in theatre," was the first and foremost statement while the drama was going on. Storyline and language were placed on a par with the other elements of theatre, and all were merged ritualistically in a kind of "total theatre."

The men who advocated this removal of the separation between stage and spectator were chiefly Bertolt Brecht, Antonin Artaud, and the dramatists of the "theatre of the absurd." Brecht believed that the theatre should encourage the audience to participate critically in the drama without illusion of any sort. He recommended *verfremdungseffekt*, or alienation of performance and spectator from the "reality" of the theatrical events, so "contemplation" may occur. There was to be no unified production, only commentary by each and every theatrical element—including the audience. *The Threepenny Opera* (1928), *Mother Courage and Her Children* (1937), and *Galileo* (1938-39) were examples of Brecht's theory given artistic expression.

Artaud and the "absurdists" sought to avoid even the attempt at argument that characterized Brecht. For them, "true theatre" was pre-logical, nonverbal, and incantatory. Magic and myth, in Artaud's view, or the theatrical elements "as theatre," to sum up the absurdists' position, were to represent the true, internal conflicts experienced by the spectator and the deepseated sources of existence and awareness. Where Artaud hoped for theatre to expel the conflicts so that "theatrical communion" may occur among the spectators, the absurdists—Samuel Beckett, with *Waiting for Godot* (1953), Eugène Ionesco, with *The Bald Soprano* (1949), and Jean Genet, with *The Balcony* (1956)—seemed content just to create the absurdity of human existence onstage and in the heart of the spectator. The chief forerunner of these works was Alfred Jarry's *Ubu Roi* (1896), which showed the animal nature of man by filling the theatre with consciously puppet-like characters in a scene like a child's nightmare—a collection of pure symbols that burlesqued their referents.

The Poetics of Drama and Theatre

Our separation of the great critics from their ideas of theatre has obviously been artificial. In the twentieth century, critic and dramatist have often been one person whose dramas have offered in themselves the poetics for a new approach to theatre. Yet taking our sub-title from the central work of drama and theatre criticism—Aristotle's *De Poetica*—we may profitably (and briefly) sketch an esthetic for theatre as it has been formalized by certain critics through the ages. Some of these were also dramatists, some of the esthetic ideas were presented only in dramas, and many of the critics were not cited as "great" in the previous section. Theorists ever fall below artist and critic.

The *Poetics* of Aristotle, however, represented both theorist and critic (as well as historian, but we will ignore that contribution) working at their peak. Though Aristotle was writing primarily about tragedy, his delineation of it applied to all drama. It is this contribution from *De Poetica* that we are interested in here.

What then *was* a drama in Aristotle's view? If you have read Chapter 1 closely, you have already comprehended the Aristotelian approach to drama. The essential element was a human experience in the form of action or process—in Aristotle's terms, "an action." What appeared onstage was an "imitation" of that action. By this Aristotle meant that the universal mode of the action, which was presupposed in the particular manifestation of it, was expressed by the representation onstage. Since this was characteristic of all the arts, what distinguished drama and theatre was the fact that they *showed human experience in process.* Drama was an imitation of an action *by means of action rather than narrative, painting, or sculpture.*

Our analysis of drama and theatre in Chapter 1 was based on that of Aristotle. The elements of drama he established were plot, character, language, thought, rhythm, and spectacle. No subsequent critic offered anything better with which to develop a theory of drama and theatre. There is no intent in this remark to insist with the critics of the Renaissance, and of the 17th and 18th centuries, that all dramas must slavishly follow Aristotle (or Horace, whom we have already dealt with). Yet subsequent estheticians largely applied the techniques and the ideas revealed in *De Poetica.*

The plotting of a drama received a major share of attention. Aristotle stated merely that a drama must be of a certain magnitude— that is, only long enough to be witnessed in a given period of time— and must have a beginning, middle, and end. Moreover, a tragedy showed a character moving from good to bad fortune. (Presumably a comedy would show movement from good to bad to good fortune.)

Later critics focused on the means of movement from one state to another. A majority of observers agreed with Ferdinand Brunetiére, who wrote in *La loi du théâtre* (1894) that the basic element in a dramatic plot was a struggle of wills. Someone wanted to do something, and someone (or some thing) blocked the achievement of the goal. The subsequent ploys and counterploys *were* the drama, said Brunetiére.

Other critics took exception to this insistence on conflict. William Archer, for example, wrote in *Playmaking* that a drama should be plotted as a series of crises. Conflict *might or might not* figure in the crisis or its causes at a given instance. All that was necessary was that the crisis be shown onstage. Another critic, William T. Price, stated in *The Analysis of Play Construction and Dramatic Principle* (1908) that a drama should be plotted as a three-premise syllogism—which he called the "proposition." The first premise asserted the *conditions* of the dramatic action; the second, the *causes* of the action; the third, the *result* of the action. The third premise was phrased as a "problem." Taking *Othello* as an example (Price used *Romeo and Juliet*), the proposition would be stated as follows: "Othello, a middle-aged, black, 'barbarian' soldier who has spent his life in military camp and in battle, takes up residence at the court of Venice and marries Desdemona, the romantic young daughter of a Venetian nobleman. One of Othello's lieutenants, Iago, conspires to destroy Othello any way he can. Is it possible for Othello to overcome the results of Iago's intriguing and achieve success and happiness in his new life?"

Still other critics sought to shift the central concern from plot to character, or character and dialogue. That is, a drama consisted of characters telling a story by means of dialogue but in a form suitable for theatrical representation. Nineteenth-century criticism of Shakespeare, for example, was fond of studying only his "characters." Typical of this view was A. C. Bradley, in *Shakespearean Tragedy* (1904), who found that the heart of Shakespeare's dramas was "character issuing in action." Extended treatments of Shakespeare's language, of course, whether considering it dialogue or poetry, are the rule rather than the exception. Caroline Spurgeon's *Shakespeare's Imagery, and What It Tells Us* (1935) is a good example of a critic separating language from the rest of the drama.

Aristotle's other three elements of drama—thought, rhythm, and spectacle—have not stirred up so much critical comment as the three we have just examined. Of major importance to critics, however, has been the nature of tragedy and comedy. Aristotle himself distinguished tragedy as the form of drama that dealt with persons better than average, whose fate caused the audience to feel pity and fear. Comedy focused on people worse than average. Aristotle did not explore the effects of comedy, however, other than to imply that it was different from that of tragedy.

Until the twentieth century, the distinction between the two *genres* was generally considered measurable and fairly rigid. Two recent collections of essays—*Tragedy: Vision and Form* and *Comedy: Meaning and Form* (both 1965)—contain a wide range of papers dealing with tragedy and comedy, and with melodrama and farce, from a number of different points of view. These are simply recent examples of an ancient critical phenomenon—the desire to create categories of drama and theatre and then study drama in terms of them.

Finally, in the *De Poetica*, there was the celebrated statement about the effects of tragedy: that it arouses pity and fear so as to cause a catharsis of these emotions. Later writers on comedy sought to prove that it, too, caused a catharsis of emotions—though no one could say for sure what they were. The principle at the heart of such studies as Sigmund Freud's *Wit and the Unconscious* or John Gassner's "Catharsis and the Modern Theatre" was that drama must have some socially acceptable effect. A more pertinent subject might have been "what brings the audience to the theatre"—a point we explored in Chapter 1.

Drama and Theatre Criticism

As you finish this introduction to theatre, as you attempt to criticize drama and theatre, your chief conclusion may be that it is impossible. Study of any art requires contemplation over a long period of time. The quintessential attribute of drama and theatre is that they are ephemeral. You do not have time to contemplate what you are experiencing. Indeed, if you try to contemplate while experiencing drama in a theatre, you may miss experiencing it at all. The drama that *allows* you to contemplate it may not be succeeding.

Another important attribute of drama and theatre is the number of artistic elements that contribute to the effect of a play. At a given moment, assuming evaluation is even possible, can you simultaneously study plot, character, and all the rest? Probably the correct answer is "no."

Nor is it correct to arrive at the theatre with your critical faculties set to an ideal and then simply observe whether the drama you are watching measures up. Even Aristotle fell into this trap, for he judged all plays by *Oedipus Tyrannus*. We have noticed how the neoclassicists judged drama by their interpretation of Aristotle and Horace.

Given these problems, then, how should we go about criticizing drama and theatre? The following principles have been extrapolated from the writings of many critics and from many years of evaluating plays onstage and in the classroom.

First, drama can legitimately be criticized only when it is played before an audience. If the audience the play is being produced for is not actually present, as at a dress rehearsal, the critic must imagine that audience and respond accordingly. Such imagining, however, is part of "directing," and does not properly belong to "criticism." Above all, the play must be criticized onstage, not in the critic's head. If this is true, though, what about the playscript as literature? Can we evaluate that alone? The answer is "Yes, but." Anything created by man can be criticized by man, but evaluating a playscript is not drama and theatre criticism. It is either analysis for possible productions—a directorial function again—or a truncated kind of literary study. We may examine the literary values of any play, but such an examination is like using the plays of your college football team that are chalked on a board as the source for an evaluation of next Saturday's game the Friday before. When reading a drama, you may discover the way the playwright seems to want his elements of theatre to work. These elements *at work* can be studied only through the live production.

Second, when functioning as a critic, you should strive to know the drama in advance. You should be familiar with the dramatic construct, the characterization, the language, and in a very general way, the scenic environment. At the very least, you should know the drama's action or central idea, and the way the playwright has treated it—that is tragically, comically and so forth.

Third, you should expect the production to communicate to its audience. All art is communication, and a play first of all must move the spectators emotionally and intellectually. Since you cannot fully analyze the audience, you can only guess that silence, laughter, or applause mean "communication" and coughing, rustling programs, or restless movements indicate "failure to communicate." Whatever else happens or fails to happen at a play, a continuum of impact between production and audience is basic.

Fourth, you must look at the elements of the production as they immediately affect the audience. The chief element is acting. Here you must keep character and actor separate. The fascination of Othello is one thing, the art and skill of James Earl Jones, or Laurence Olivier, quite another. You must ask if this creature before you *is* Othello. Assuming the *persona* does move before you, then you must ask how the actor projected him to you. The primary ingredient of such projection is the actor's seeing truly what the dramatic actions of Othello are at each moment in the play and finding true means of realizing these actions. The means will vary to the extent actors vary one from another. Sometimes you will see the action carried out so truly it seems incandescent. Other times there will be breaks in the truth of the playing. The windows of this truth are the actor's body and voice. They must accurately imitate the human manifestations of the action being portrayed at a given moment. Such manifestations do not have to be real or natural, but only probable in the theatrical context. In fact, they may well be carefully selected, crafted, and theatrically heightened. The chief sign of acceptability is a sense of control, of concentration, and of power in reserve. The action and the means of realizing it seem at one and the same time full-powered and without strain. Voice and body do not call attention to themselves.

More than the leading actor must be evaluated. Along with each player's performance considered solo, you must be aware of the interaction among the company of players. Here you are judging the director's peculiar contributions as well. Grouping, movement, and business are controlled if not invented by the director. He shares with the actor the responsibility for the polish and theatrical effectiveness of the ensemble playing.

Wherever the individual and the group playing get their effectiveness, their goal is the revelation of characters in action, the projection of the drama's language, and delineation of the play's central idea in all its planes of meaning. You should expect the playing to illuminate these meanings without calling attention to itself in the act of revelation (except, of course, in productions attempting Bertolt Brecht's "alienation effect").

The philosophical ideas in the drama—Aristotle's "thought"—are also revealed through actions and language. Once you recognize an idea— Brabantio's "Look to her, Moor, if thou hast eyes to see. She has deceived her father, and may thee."—you may judge it on its own merits and on its participation in the drama.

The scenic environment always merits your attention. Sets, lights, properties, costumes, make-up, music, and sound or special effects—all contribute to the illumination of the central idea or action. Often one or the other may detract from the total communication.

And finally, you may want to evaluate the playwright's plotting of his elements and effects. Aristotle called plot the most important of the elements of drama. Study of the finest and the poorest dramas of history bears him out. You must not confuse plot with story, narrative, or chronology, as we have noted several times in this book. Plot as the organic scheme controlling the selection and arrangement of incidents, *personae*, theatrical elements, and effects, however, *does* lie at the heart of every play. How the play controls its unique self throughout the performance may be judged as you watch, but more usually this judgment comes after the performance is over.

All in all, as you evaluate the elements of a play, you are examining "*how* the play means." Through the "how," you may arrive at "*what* the play (or the playwright) means." All the art of criticism requires, however, is your description of *how*.

Fifth, you must develop standards of excellence to guide your judgment. The only way to do this is to experience as many well-performed plays as possible. After many evaluations, you may come to approximate what is "best of breed." Since each drama, and each production of it, are new adventures, you must strive to keep your standards open. You cannot bend an artist to a critical theory. You can only ask that he do well whatever he has set out to do. Your job is to encourage him by responding on the highest possible level to what he has tried to accomplish and by asking him to achieve the impossible—but on his own terms. If you are truly judicious, he can only thank you for your help.

SUGGESTIONS FOR FURTHER READING

CLARK, BARRETT H. *European Theories of the Drama.* Rev. ed. New York: Crown Publishers, 1947.

COOPER, LANE. *Aristotle on the Art of Poetry.* Rev. ed. Ithaca, N. Y.: Cornell University Press, 1947.

CORRIGAN, ROBERT W. (ed.). *Comedy: Meaning and Form.* San Francisco: Chandler Publishing Co., 1965.

————. *Tragedy: Vision and Form.* San Francisco: Chandler Publishing Co., 1965.

GASSNER, JOHN, and RALPH G. ALLEN. *Theatre and Drama in the Making.* Boston: Houghton Mifflin Co., 1964.

SMITH, JAMES HARRY, and EDD WINFIELD PARKS (eds.). *The Great Critics: An Anthology of Literary Criticism.* 3rd ed. New York: W. W. Norton & Co., 1951.

The curtain is closed, the lights are out, the costumes are hung in the closets, the make-up is washed away, and the actors have vanished like insubstantial dreams. Only the dreams were *ours*, for they are the stuff theatre is made on. Without the projected images from our lives, there can be no drama. Without the artistic effort put forth by actor, playwright, director, designer, and a host of technicians, our drama cannot be enacted.

Your study of this wondrous process, it is hoped, has been a labor of love. You may or may not go on to become one of the artists or technicians whose work we have examined so closely. It is enough if you now approach the theatre and its drama with finer understanding and if you now make imaginary puissance with greater ease.

As you pay attention to, identify with, project upon, rationalize by means of, impersonate through, and imitate with the help of the activities onstage, you now should match your awe with understanding. There before you stands a dramatic construct of action, purpose, situation, and perhaps story—all plotted carefully to allow your dreams a run for their money. There, moreover, are people like you to carry out your every whim, and to express what is in your heart with words and music, with images and rhythms, you yourself might never think of in a million years. And all this will happen not only in your mind's eye, but also in a physical environment that is both nowhere and everywhere your soul has reached "when reaching out of sight."

It has happened since time out of mind, this gathering of audience and actors. Whatever excites the fancy in the 1970's—nudity, eroticism, homosexuality, violence—one thing is certain: it has been there ten eons before. The golden tapestry of theatre contains all possible answers to the necessary questions about how a play means. The Greek and Roman amphitheatres, the *commedia* troupes, the pageant wagons and the *autos,* the "wooden O," the well-framed scenes and machines of the Renaissance that are still with us—these showed man at his most vulgar moments, and his most sublime.

That today we have no idea of a theatre at the heart of our community is a truism. To some extent there is no community for the theatre to mirror. The question must always be asked, however, if the development of the picture-frame stage with its drama seen from afar could not have caused as well as reflected the splintering of Western culture into separate and ignorant armies with no sense of the community-at-large. Which came first, that is, a theatre without concern for the group audience or the fragmented photoflashes in the darkness that characterize both drama and culture in the West since 1650 or thereabouts? The constant attempts by actors to break out of the frame, to rejoin the audience, seem a blind creative urge to re-establish what is gone forever—a communal histrionic experience.

That motion pictures and television have usurped this function says nothing. They are the ultimate in picture-frame theatre, and they are no theatre at all. Attempts to break the frame in the theatre itself—corresponding with theatricalization—ultimately must fail unless the audience can be returned to full participation. Until this occurs, drama cannot truly participate in human affairs.

Through the ages, the history of theatre tells us, people made drama by their delight with histrionic events. Given a situation in which this activity was second nature, the great dramatists performed their magic. The theatre was there in all its glory, and the drama followed. The cutting-off of the modern dramatist from the heartland of his endeavor has been artistic tragedy. The dramatists whose works rank with those of the masters, in fact, have had such a source even though in miniature—the Bergen theatre for Ibsen, the Provincetown Playhouse for O'Neill, to name but two examples.

The first step to success in playmaking is the discovery of an audience. The second is the development of a theatre. Such ill-fated recent experiments as the Living Theatre, various failing regional theatres, and festivals like those at Stratford, Ontario and Connecticut, are on the right track. So are the university theatres, if they seek to mirror the world of their students. Yet such a mirror must show not *The College Widow* or *Babes in Arms*, but the living library of theatre—five thousand years of civilization and striving in all the tragic and the comic gambits man is capable of.

The mirror contains principally the actor—a poor player who forces the drama into being with the strength and focus of his imagination, and the intensity of his presence. If he is both mountebank and player, he is also the high priest of playing.

Who would help him in his work? Is there any reward to make a man create for the insubstantial pageant called theatre? Many have tried, more have failed than have met with success, but even the best are at the mercy of theatre's changing, shifting moment of light. That moment comes and goes, with each day's production, and to stand still is death.

In the twentieth century, the director has assumed responsibility for the ephemeral theatre. He alone patterns the visual, aural, and verbal imagery that controls the audience's experience. He makes the play, that is, though he has plenty of help. Men there are to take the glory of winning—designers of all kinds, technicians of every stripe—but only the director can lose. He is an artist whose medium is people, and he is an artist because he dares to fail. If the audience rejects his effort to make a play, if reviewers and critics malign him, he has no place to go.

Criticizing drama and theatre, however, is no easy work. The play exists once, and is no more. Today the job is even rougher. Theatre for the most part has no audience with a common heritage, no community to reflect, and hence the critic has no frame of reference. As if to strike in all directions as the nameless dark approaches, playwrights, directors, and actors—even designers and technicians—are seeking creativity in precedence-shattering, in rule-breaking, in scurrying to be new. The loud, the naked, the nude, the licentious—also the arcane and the trivial—play has always sought a place in the theatrical marketplace. That men and women, particularly ·in a puritan culture, will chase after any vestige of sex in the theatre was well-known long before *Oh! Calcutta!* On the other hand, that a romantic upbringing leads to a desire for bathetic melodrama was proved before the arrival of *The Sound of Music.*

The critic needs to foster a community with the idea of theatre at its heart. All practitioners of theatre, in fact, need to go forth in search of an audience. Playing anywhere they can find a crowd willing to provide imaginary puissance, theatre artists must remember the spectator is more than just a paying customer who is entertained. He should be the living source of the drama. Whatever the vehicle onstage, the actors and the drama must portray the dreams of their audiences. The portrayal may be sad or funny—perhaps ought to be hard and unequivocal—so long as it allows the spectator to find his essential identity in the drama and—usually—so long as there is no attempt to teach, to preach, or to enhance the culture.

Nowhere in our present culture are the chances for such a theatre of the community better than in the strange and wonderful world of children's theatre and creative dramatics. This is not to say the banal and the ugly cannot thrive here as well as elsewhere. Yet if anyone is willing to deck the players with his own visions, to find his life through playing, it is a child. The most exciting fact about *Hair* or *Your Own Thing,* for example, is not their loudness or their vulgarity, but their closeness to the magical world of children's theatre. They are creative dramatics raised to the ultimate.

The trick for those who would foster dramatic art is not to find an audience, but to enter and portray the spectator's dreams. There the theatre artist will discover audiences a-plenty.

Absurd, Theatre of the. Various plays that represent mankind and the universe as illogical, senseless, futile, and meaningless; usually structured and performed so as to be wildly funny.

Act. To perform; a performance; the interval between the parts of a play (Elizabethan); one of the parts of a play.

Act Curtain. A curtain which separates the audience from the stage and which is directly upstage from the fire curtain.

Acting Area. That part of the stage which is visible to the audience when the curtain is open.

Action. The physical activity of the actors; the motive of a character; the speeches of the characters; an incident or episode in the drama; the central experience which is portrayed onstage.

Actor. A performer in a play, male or female, but principally male.

Actress. A performer in a play, female.

Ad-lib. To improvise words, gestures, movements, or activity not provided for in the playscript and, usually, not previously rehearsed.

Admiral's Men. Theatrical company in Elizabethan England, principal rival of Shakespeare's company (Lord Chamberlain's Men, King's Men).

Alienation Effect. In the drama theory of Bertolt Brecht, the idea that the activities onstage should work to destroy any illusion the audience may have, prevent emotional involvement, and cause detached thought about the ideas being examined in the play (*Verfremdungseffekt*).

Allegory. A drama or narrative in which the characters and sometimes the scenery represent moral qualities, general concepts, or other abstractions, which are made concrete in order to communicate a moral.

Alternating Current. Electrical current that changes its direction at regular intervals.

Anticlimax. The lines or incidents in a drama become less important as the play goes on.

Apron. The part of the stage that extends beyond the proscenium arch toward the audience; sometimes called the *forestage*.

Arena Stage. In Britain, a stage with a back wall and the audience on three sides; in the United States, a stage completely surrounded by the audience.

Asbestos Curtain. In the proscenium theatre, a curtain that can be lowered to protect the audience if there is a fire onstage or backstage.

Aside. A speech, usually brief, which is directed by a character to the audience but which by convention is unheard by other characters onstage.

Atmosphere. See *mood.*

Audience. The spectators at a performance of a play.

Auditorium. The part of a theatre in which the spectators sit or stand while attending a performance.

Audition. The activity wherein a prospective performer tries out for a role.

Auto Sacramental. Spanish religious drama, played both inside and outside the churches.

Backdrop. A screen or curtain that hangs behind the performers; usually painted as an interior or exterior scene. Also called *backcloth* and *backscene.*

Backing. A masking piece placed behind doors and windows to eliminate the view of the backstage area.

Backstage. That part of the stagehouse which the audience ordinarily does not see during a performance. Side areas backstage are called wings.

Batten. A strip of wood or a metal pipe used to stiffen the bottom or the top of a cloth, or to hang lights or scenery from; battens usually hang over and around the stage.

Beat. A unit in a play, usually the same as *motivational unit*; the length of pauses between speeches or actions; a method of counting the tempo of a scene.

Blocking. The planning of groups, movements, business of actors within a setting.

Book. The playscript, particularly the copy which has the director's or the stage manager's instructions and notes; two flats hinged together; the libretto of a musical show.

Border. A horizontal masking piece for the space above a set.

Borderlights. Overhead lights, usually in strips, with reflectors but no lenses.

Bourgeois Drama. A serious play about middle-class life.

Box. Compartment at the sides of the auditorium above the level of the stage, with four to six chairs.

Box Office. The place in a theatre where tickets are sold.

Box Set. A setting with three walls (sometimes two), with the proscenium opening being the fourth wall.

Braggart Soldier. In comedy, a stock figure of the vain, boastful, cowardly soldier; also called *miles gloriosus* and *capitano.*

Brightness. The lightness or darkness of a color.

Burlesque. A comic imitation of a mannerism or a minor flaw; a variety show, particularly one with bawdy humor and a strip-tease.

Business. Actions taken by the actor to delineate his character or to secure an effect; includes gestures and body attitudes, and often properties, but is distinct from movement about the stage.

Cast. The performers in a play.

Catastrophe. In the drama theory of Gustav Freytag, the resolution of the plot. Also called *denouement.*

Catharsis. In Aristotelian theory, a purgation of audience emotions similar to those portrayed onstage; e.g., pity and terror in tragedy.

Cellar. The space below the stage floor. See *trap.*

Character. The personage in a drama; such a figure's personality or behavior patterns.

Character Actor. An actor who plays roles that are types or that are considerably different from his own personality.

Choregus. The wealthy citizen of fifth-century Athens who paid for the work of one playwright and one chorus in the City Dionysia.

Chorus. A group of performers who speak, dance, or sing an introduction to, and comment upon, the actions in a drama; usually performs as a group; may be a single person (called *choral character or raisonneur*); often serves to represent and guide the reactions of the audience.

Chronicle Play. A drama which depicts historical events in chronological sequence.

Climax. In the drama theory of Gustav Freytag, the moment of highest tension in the plot of a drama; sometimes a turning-point in the action.

Comedy. A type of drama in which the human experience being portrayed may range from high seriousness to no consequence; playwright, performers, and audience are relatively detached; events usually lead to happiness or well-being; *personae* tend to be types or stereotypes, and particularly stock characters; effects depend on exaggerated activities, sudden changes of direction, fast pacing, or a spirit of joy and good feeling; *and/or* the audience is principally amused, entertained, or diverted into relaxed laughter. Comedies may be termed Aristophanic, satiric, domestic, sentimental, romantic, of manners or wit, of humours, or of character. A tragic series of events may be treated in a comic manner, but the reverse seems unlikely if not impossible.

Commedia dell'Arte. A popular, improvisational, professional comic drama in Italy between the Middle Ages and the eighteenth century, with stock characters from daily life.

Commedia Erudita. In the same period as the *commedia dell'arte,* the theatre of classic plays or their imitations.

Complication. In the drama theory of Gustav Freytag, the moment in a play when the protagonist is opposed.

Confidant. A character whose purpose is to listen while a central character confides his state of mind, his plans, or a history and background of the dramatic action. The feminine is *confidante.*

Conflict. A type of plotting in which the protagonist is opposed in some way.

Convention. An agreed-upon device which is unrealistic but helpful in furthering a play's action; usually developed through long usage.

Costume. What the actors wear when performing their roles.

Cue. A written or spoken signal, in the play or in the stage manager's book, to which actor or crew member is required to respond in a particular way.

Curtain. A drapery that conceals the stage, or some part of it, from the audience.

Cycle Plays. In the Middle Ages, plays dealing with a history of the world or with an event based on the Bible or religious tradition.

Cyclorama. A C-shaped cloth or plaster drop at the rear of the stage, made without seams, upon which lights are shown, giving an illusion of infinite depth. Also called *cyc* and *sky-dome.*

Deus ex Machina. The device of having a "god" arrive and resolve the action of a drama; now applied to any solution to the plot complications that seems contrived or unmotivated.

Denouement. In the drama theory of Gustav Freytag, the moment when the plot of a drama is resolved.

Development. In the drama theory of Gustav Freytag, the moments in a drama when the plot moves toward the climax, after initial exposition.

Dialogue. Words exchanged between characters in a play.

Diction. The selection and management of words, particularly the vocabulary, or the kind and style of imagery in a drama; the verbal language.

Dimmer. An electrical apparatus for graduated control of lighting.

Dionysus. Greek god of wine, the phallus, growth, and irrationality, at whose festivals dramas were performed.

Director. The artist who controls and unifies all the contributing elements in a play. In England, the *producer*; in Europe, the *régisseur*.

Discovery. In Aristotelian theory, a scene in which recognition of something previously unknown occurs; in ordinary stage parlance, to reveal an actor or a scene by opening or raising a curtain.

Dithyramb. A narrative or lyric poem spoken or sung by a chorus at Dionysian festivals in Ancient Greece.

Domestic Tragedy. A tragic drama dealing with a private citizen rather than a person of high rank.

Doubling. The playing of more than one character in a given play by a single actor.

Downstage. In a proscenium theatre, that part of the stage nearest the audience but still within the proscenium opening; that part of any playing area nearest the audience. Positions are *down left, down center,* and *down right* (when facing the audience). See *upstage.*

Drama. A serious but non-tragic playscript; also called *drame.*

Dress Rehearsal. A rehearsal at which performance conditions exist; usually toward the end of the rehearsal period.

Drop. An unframed cloth unit that hangs from a batten and may be painted.

Dumb Show. A scene of action without words.

Ekkyklema. In the Greek theatre, a wagon that brought people or objects onstage, probably through doors in the *skene.*

Epic Theatre. In the theories of Bertolt Brecht and Erwin Piscator, the idea that drama should be narrative and cause detachment rather than involvement, and didactic rather than esthetic; hence, plays and techniques embodying this idea.

Epilogue. A concluding address to a play.

Episode. In Greek drama, the action between the choral odes; hence, the incidents in a drama.

Esthetic Distance. The idea that a spectator is, or should be, detached from a work of art he is viewing. Also called *distancing* and *psychical distance.*

Expressionism. A type of drama in which subjective feelings are portrayed, rather than objective actions.

Falling Action. In the drama theory of Gustav Freytag, the moments in a play after it is clear how the plot must go.

Farce. A type of drama in which ludicrous situations or ridiculous activities, stock characters, a rapid-fire series of events, witty repartee, and sudden reversals are not only dominant throughout or carried to their extremes, but also their own reasons for being; virtue or innocence triumphs; *and* events turn on fortuitous circumstances, sly machinations, or both.

Flies. The space above the stage.

Floodlight. Any lamp having a wide-angle beam with a soft edge.

Flying. Raising and lowering scenery or actors over the stage; also moving an actor horizontally through the air.

Foil. A character who is compared with another, or who shows different aspects of another's personality.

Foreshadowing. Words or actions that suggest what is to come in the action of a drama.

Greenroom. A room where actors rest while waiting to go onstage.

Gridiron. Framework of beams above the stage. Also called the *grid*.

Ground Plan. Drawing of the set, with all acting areas, set pieces, furniture, and levels indicated. Also called a *floor plan*.

Hamartia. In Aristotelian theory, a flaw, error, shortcoming, or misstep that causes the tragic hero to be doomed.

Hero. The central character in a play, male. A female central character is a *heroine*.

Heroic Drama. A play in rhymed couplets, in which a noble hero is in conflict with love and honor, and wins both.

Hubris. In Greek drama, overweening arrogance that led to a tragic character's downfall.

Imagery. A series of single images, or the patterns of images, created in the consciousness of the spectator by the words and phrases in a drama that characters and chorus speak; may involve any of the senses, and characteristically are vivid and particularized. Often referred to as *figurative language*—i.e., similes, metaphors, and the like. Frequently the imagery in a drama consists of "image clusters" or recurrent groups of metaphors. See *diction*.

Improvisation. The invention of characterization, business, action, and dialogue by the actors, without using a prepared script.

Ingenue. An innocent young woman in a play; hence, the actress who plays it.

Irony. A condition in which affairs are different from what the characters in a drama suppose, with the audience usually having greater knowledge than the characters; may be comic or tragic.

Lazzo. A piece of business regularly used by an actor in the *commedia dell'-arte*. Plural: *lazzi*.

Lead. The principle role in a play.

Living Newspaper. A theatrical performance that dramatizes a social problem, using mixed-media; invented by the Federal Theatre Project in 1935; similar to *epic theatre*.

Lobby. The place in a theatre where the spectators lounge before the performance or between the acts.

Melodrama. A type of drama in which a sensational situation is the main item of interest; virtue triumphs after a series of thrilling mishaps; characterized by extensive spectacle.

Mise en Scène. The physical staging of a play.

Mood. The emotional state created, usually indirectly, by the theatrical elements of a play or by the play as a whole. Also called, from the standpoint of the staging alone, *atmosphere*.

Motif. A frequently recurring character, incident, idea, or image in a drama; sometimes called *theme* (q.v.).

Motivational Unit. In dramatic structure, a unit defined by a change in the motivation of the dominant person in the unit.

Myth. An image, idea, or story that organizes and gives meaning to facts of life; usually a projection of personal and cultural needs and attitudes.

Naturalism. A drama in which people and events are presented with scientific accuracy to "real life" and in proliferating and seemingly unmotivated detail; the attempt is made to show psychological reality, particularly as it is affected by heredity and environment—which are seen to determine man's fate; also a movement in modern drama with the same point of view.

Objective. A character's goal in a unit, a scene, or an entire play. Sometimes referred to, respectively, as *superobjective, spine, through line of action* of the unit, scene, or play.

Obligatory Scene. A scene which the audience foresees and hence desires. Also called *scène à faire* (in the theory of Francisque Sarcey).

Pace. The sense of speed at which a drama moves in performance. Also called *pacing* and *tempo*.

Parados. In the Greek theatre, the place where the chorus entered; hence, the opening song of the chorus.

Part. A character in a play; the character's lines or action. Also called *role*.

Periaktos. A three-sided prism, with scenes painted on each side, which pivoted so the scenes could revolve. Plural: *periaktoi*.

Peripeteia. A moment when the action of a play reverses and turns out the opposite from what was expected; may be tragic or comic. Also called peripety.

Play. The joining of audience and actors in the performance of a dramatic action, usually in a theatre and controlled by a playscript.

Plot. The whole structure of the drama, in particular the order of what happens; sometimes the purpose governing the selection and arrangement of incidents; in common parlance, the story or the sequence of events, sometimes causally linked.

Properties. Objects used by the actors during a performance, except for costumes and the settings. Also called *props*.

Protagonist. In Greek theatre, the first actor; now the central character (or characters) in a drama. Often opposed by the *antagonist*.

Rake. The slope of a stage floor or the angling of a set at greater than right angles.

Realism. A drama that attempts to reproduce life on the stage; hence, a movement advocating this style.

Recognition. The moment in a scene or play when a character discovers something he had not known before. Also called *discovery* and *disclosure*.

Revenge Play. A drama in which an otherwise good man sets out to revenge atrocities committed against his family.

Reversal. A moment in a play when the action changes direction from that in which it has seemed to be heading. Also called *peripeteia* and *peripety*.

Rhythm. Recurrence or repetition, usually in a pattern, of words, pauses, ideas, images, or themes.

Scenario. An outline of a plot or a description of a play; used particularly by the *commedia dell'arte*.

Scene. A unit of a play, shorter than an act, and usually determined by the entrance and exit of a major character or a change of locale, or both; sometimes delineated by a change in motivation.

Scrim. A gauze-like fabric that is transparent when lighted from behind, opaque when lighted from the front.

Script. The book or text of a play. Also termed *playscript.*

Sides. A set of papers containing one actor's lines, cues, etc.

Sight Lines. Imaginary lines of vision from any seat to any part of the stage.

Soliloquy. A set speech in which a character talks to himself when he is alone in front of an audience; sometimes he talks directly to the audience.

Spotlight. A lamp with both a reflector and a lens, giving a hard-edged light.

Subtext. The interaction of characters in a given scene.

Tableau. Static scene using live figures.

Theatre in the Round. Arena staging.

Theatre of Cruelty. That using dramas with direct audience involvement, usually for purposes of shock and violence; intended to reflect the cruelty of existence.

Theme. Often the term used to describe an abstract concept which is said to inform the dramatic construct, the character relationships, the language, and the scenic environment of a nondidactic drama. Sometimes used synonymously with *thesis* (q.v.). Frequently employed in the same way as *motif* (q.v.).

Thesis. The proposition or doctrine which a didactic drama is designed to persuade its audience to accept. See *allegory* and *theme.*

Thrust Stage. A stage with audience on three sides, usually sticking out from a proscenium but sometimes lacking a proscenium.

Timing. Performing at the right instant whatever words and actions are called for in the performance.

Tragedy. A type of drama in which the human experience being portrayed is always of high seriousness; playwright, performers, and audience are relatively involved or concerned; events usually turn out catastrophically for the protagonist and often for his family or community as well; the protagonist and other *personae* are more apt than in a comedy to be unique persons with relatively complex motivations; effects depend on activities undergone seriously, a turn of events that is the reverse of what was originally expected but is seen at the last to have been somehow fated or predetermined, stately pacing, or a spirit of doom, hopelessness, terror, or extreme sadness; *and/or* the audience is principally moved to pity, awe, terror, or a similar reaction. In some views, enlightenment of the audience must also occur. Tragedies may also depend on *hubris* (prideful arrogance); *hamartia* (flaw, error, or misstep); excessive or wanton destruction, particularly of the innocent; conflict with universal laws; or *all of these.* Often the "tragic character" learns from his downfall.

Trap. A place beneath the stage floor, from which actors or scenery may enter the playing area; the hole in the stage floor leading to such an area. See *cellar.*

Try-Out. See *audition.*

Upstage. In a proscenium theatre, that part of the stage farthest from the audience but still within the proscenium frame and in full view of the audience; that part of any playing area farthest from the audience. Positions are *up left, up center,* and *up right* (when facing the audience).

Well-made Play. A term used to describe plays with a carefully constructed pattern of opening situation, inciting incident, development or complication, build to a climax, and denouement; used derogatorily. Also called *pièce bien faite*.

Wing. A two-dimensional scenic piece that is placed upright facing the audience, usually but not always on the side of the stage in a proscenium theatre, and on which scenes are painted.

Zanni. In the *commedia dell'arte*, the comic servant.

Absurd, theatre of the, vii, 129, 422
Accent (of costumes and make-up), 388, 390
Acharnians (Aristophanes), 119
Act curtain, 179
Acting, 425
Action, 8, 10, 285-286, 419, 422-423, 425
Actions, as part of the craft of acting, 186
Active infinitive, as part of the craft of acting, 187
Actor, 5, 184-189, 426
Actors and Acting
    Classical Greece and Rome, 131-133
    England, 1650-1750, 135-136
    Europe and America, 1750-1850, 135-136
    France and Italy, 1500-1750, 135-136
    Italian Renaissance, 135
    Middle Ages, 133-135
    Modern Drama, 1850-present, 136-138
    Spain and England, 1200-1650, 135
Actors, in Greek Playhouses, 103
Actualism, (actualistic setting, scenery, or style), 169, 372
Actuality, surface, demand for in plays for children, 407
Addison, Joseph, 126
Administration, of a production, 355
Admission charges, in Elizabethan and Jacobean England, 108
Adult theatre and children's theatre, distinctions between, 409
Adventure, in plays for children, 407
Adventures of Tom Sawyer, The (Twain), 285-299, 351-353, 403, 406-407, 410
Aeschylus, 117
Agamemnon (Aeschylus), 118

Agamemnon (Seneca), 121
Agonothetes, 133
Ah, Wilderness! (O'Neill), 131
Ajax (Sophocles), 118
Alarcón, Juan Ruiz, 124
Albee, Edward, 12-13
Albright, H. Darkes, viii
Alcestis (Euripides), 118
Alchemist, The (Jonson), 123
Alienation effect (Verfremdungseffekt), 422, 426
All for Love (Dryden), 126
Alliteration, 296
Ampere, 385
Amphitryon (Plautus), 120
Andria (Terence), 120
Andromache (Euripides), 119
Andromaque (Racine), 125
Analysis, of a drama, 352
Analysis of Play Construction and Dramatic Principle, The (Price), 423
Analyst, critic as, 418
Angle perspective, 134
Animal *personae,* in plays for children, 408
Antagonist, 290
Anthesteria, 98
Antigone (Sophocles), 118
Antistrophe (Strophe), 119
Antithesis, 296
Antoine, Andre, 420
Apollinaire, Guillaume, 421
Apologie for Poetrie, An (Sidney), 419
Appia, Adolph, 137
Apron (forestage), 115-116, 175, 180
Aptness of costumes and make-up, 388, 390-400
Archer, William, 423
Arches, construction of, 360

Architettura (Serlio), 111
Arena staging, 117, 166-168, 181
Argumentation, in the dramatic construct, 10
Argument, drama as, 130
Aristophanes, 95, 117-118, 408
Aristotelian tragedy, 2
Aristotle, viii, 7, 14, 96, 418-419, 422-423, 425-426
Aristotle on the Art of Poetry (Cooper), 7n
Arms and the Man (Shaw), 130
Ars Poetica (Horace), 419
Artaud, Antonin, 421-422
Artists of Dionysus, 133
Artists of theatre, 5
L'Arte Poetica (Minturno), 419
L'Art Poetique (Boileau), 419
Asbestos curtain, 178, 179
Aside, 295
Assistant stage manager, 359, 395
Assonance, 296
As You Like It (Shakespeare), 9, 13, 14, 15-91, 290, 351, 371, 391, 394, 404-406, 408
Athens (Fifth Century), 97-98
Atmosphere scene, in the plot of a drama, 287
Attention, process of, 3-4
    in arena staging, 166-168
    in panoramic staging, 171-175
    in proscenium staging, 168-171
    in the ideal theatre, 181-182
    in the standard theatre, 175-181
Attitude, drama and changes in, 94-95
Attitudes, frames of reference, and needs, in the process of attention, 4
Attitudinal pattern, of a drama, 96
Audience, 2, 425
    as collaborator in a play, 3-8
    as crowd, 167
    as part of actor's effect, 183-184
    as participant in actor's effects, 135
    concentration on play, 168
    Elizabethan and Jacobean, 101
    in Greek playhouses, 103
    in the standard theatre, 175-178
    participation in plays for children, 411
    size and closeness, at performances for children, 411-412
    size in Elizabethan and Jacobean England, 108-109
    staging, 117
Audiences yesterday and today, 97-103
Auditorium, shapes of, in the standard theatre, 177
Augier, Émile, 129
Auleum, in Roman playhouses, 105

Aural images or symbols, 8
Aural language, 295-296
Aural stimuli, patterning by a director, 365, 368-369
Autonomy, of *dramatis personae*, 11
Autos sacramentales, 109
Auto transformer, 387
Awareness and existence, as elements of theatre, 422

Bacchae (Euripides), 119
Bacchides (Plautus), 120
Backdrop, 111
Backpainting, 382
Backstage area, 179
Backstage operation, 371, 394-402
Balcony, The (Genet), 422
Bald Soprano, The (Ionesco), 422
Ballad opera, 127
Barefoot in the Park (Simon), 2
Bartholomew Fair (Jonson), 123
Batten(s), 151, 155
Bawdiness, in plays for children, 309
Beatles, the, 3
Beaumont, Francis, 123
Beaux' Stratagem, The (Farquhar), 126
Beckett, Samuel, 131, 422
Becque, Henri, 420
Beggar's Opera, The (Gay), 127
Beginning, middle, end, in plotting drama, 423
Behavior patterns, human as elements in a play, 3, 11
Bejaget (Racine), 125
Belasco, David, 134
Believability, of *dramatis personae*, 12
Believing, as part of the craft of acting, 188-189
Berenice (Racine), 125
Bewilderment, in plays for children, 410
Bibiena Family, 134-135
Bicycle Thief, The, 184
Binder, in scene painting, 382
Birds, The (Aristophanes), 98, 119, 352
Blackfriars Theatre, 109
Blank verse, 122
Blocking rehearsal, 351, 362
Boileau-Despreaux, Nicholas, 419
Book of flats, 380
Borders, overhead, in Italian Theatres, 114
Boucicault, Dion, 129
Box set, 136
Boy Friend, The (Wilson), 170
Boys' companies, in Elizabethan and Jacobean England, 109, 122
Brace jack, 383
Bracing (scenery), 383
Bradley, A. C., 424
Braggart Warrior, The (Plautus), 120

Brahm, Otto, 420
Brand (Ibsen), 129-130
Breasts of Tiresias, The (Apollinaire), 421
Brecht, Bertolt, 130, 131, 421-422, 426
Breton, Andre, 421
Bridge scene, in the plot of a drama, 287
Britannicus (Racine), 125
Brothers, The (Terence), 120
Brunetiere, Ferdinand, 423
Buchner, Georg, 128, 420
Budget, of a production, 376
Burbage, Richard, 135
Burlador de Seville, El (Molina), 124
Burlesques, 127
Business, actor's, 356, 365-368
Business manager, 358
Butcher, S. H., 91

Cafetorium, 181
Calderon de la Barca, Pedro, 124
Camerata of Florence, 121
Camille (Dumas *fils*), 129
Candida (Shaw), 130
Capa y espada (cape and sword), 124
Caplan, Harry, viii
Captives, The (Plautus), 120
Carbon arc lamp, 137
Carrier, in scene painting, 382
Carros, 109
Carthaginian, The (Plautus), 120
Casein paint, 382
Casina (Plautus), 120
Casket, The (Plautus), 120
Castelvetro, Lodovico, 419
Casting rehearsal, 351, 356-358
Castro, Guillen de, 124
Catharsis, 2
"Catharsis and the Modern Theatre" (Gassner), 424
Catiline (Jonson), 123
Cato (Addison), 127
Central idea, in a drama, 2, 9, 13, 425-426
Central image or idea, in plays for children, 411
Cervantes, Miguel de, 124
Change or growth in *dramatis personae*, 291
Chapman, George, 123
Character development scene, in the plot of a drama, 287
Characterization, 356, 368, 370
Character(s), in a drama, 5, 10-13, 186-189, 290, 292, 423-426
Children for theatre, 404-408
Children of Heracles (Euripides), 118-119
"Children of the Revels of the Queen," 109

Children's classes, 405-406
Children's plays, 410
Children's theatre, 12, 403
China
    audiences in, 102
    playhouses in, 117
Choice, willful, in the theatrical experience, 4
Choosing a season, 351-352
Choosing the director's artistic contributions, 356
Choral character, 11-12, 287
Choral scene, in the plot of a drama, 287
Choregus, 132
Chorus, 11, 287
    Greek, 132
    in Greek playhouses, 103
Chronicle play, 122
Chronology, in plays for children, 411
Church, the, and drama, 99-100
Churches, as playhouses for Medieval drama, 106
Cid, Le (Corneille), 124-125
Cinderella, 406
Cinna (Corneille), 125
Circus, the, compared with the theatrical experience, 7-8
City Dionysia, 98
Classical Greece and Rome
    audiences in, 98-99
    dramatists and dramas in, 117-121
    playhouses in, 103-105
Classics for children, 405-406
Climax, in the plot of a drama, 287, 288
Clouds (Aristophanes), 119
Cocteau, Jean, 421
Collective focusing of attention, in the theatrical experience, 4
Collier, Jeremy, 126
Color
    costumes, 388, 390
    paint, 381-382
Comedy, 98, 111, 126, 419, 423-424
Comedy: Meaning and Form (Corrigan, ed.), 424
Comedy of Asses, The (Plautus), 120
Comedy of Calisto and Melibea, The (Rojas), 123
Comfort, of audience in the standard theatre, 176-178
Comic Negro, 129
Comic opera, 127
Commanding image, in the dramatic construct, 9, 13
Command of the real world, in plays for children, 407
Commedia, 121, 124-125, 133
Commedia all'improviso, 100
Commedia a soggetto, 100
Commedia dell'arte, 100, 110

Commedia dell'arte, Othello as, 190-191
Commedia erudita, 100
Communication, drama as, 425
Comparison, in a drama, 288
Complex plot, 289
Complication, in the plot of a drama, 288
Compound plot, 289
Comte, Auguste, 420
Concentration, as a factor in acting, 375, 379
Cone, Clinton, viii
Confidant(e), 125
Conflict, 11, 288-289, 422
Conflict *vs* impersonation, in plays for children, 405
Congreve, William, 126
Conquest of Granada, The (Dryden), 126
Conscious Lovers, The (Steele), 126
Consistency, in *dramatis personae,* 251
Constant Couple, The (Farquhar), 126
Constructivism (scenery), 374
Continental seating, 176-177
Continuing characters, in plays for children, 411
Continuity rehearsal (runthrough), 351, 363-364
Continuum of impact, 425
Contour curtain, 179
Contrast, in drama, 11, 288
Control boards, 175, 180
Conventions, theatrical, 131
Cool (warm) colors, 384
Coolness of dramatic medium, in plays for children, 411
Cooper, Lane, viii, 7n, 419n
Copyright, 353
Corneille, Pierre, 124-125
Corrales, 107, 109-110
Costumes, 371, 388-392, 426
Costumes crew, 401
Cothurnus, 132
Counterweight system, 175-179
Country Wife, The (Wycherley), 126
Craft of acting, the, 186-189
Craig, Edward Gordon, 137
Creative dramatics, 184, 403, 413-416
Crew chiefs (heads), 359, 394-402
Crisis, in the plot of a drama, 287, 423
Criticism, 417-418, 424-427
Critics, 418-422
Cross-section drawing, 375
Crowd
        as part of the actor's effects, 183
        in the theatrical experience, 4-5
Cruelty, theatre of, vii
Cueva, Juan de la, 124
Cultural differences, in children's preferences, 406
Curculio (Plautus), 120
Cutting a drama, 354-355

Cyclops (Euripides), 119
Cyclorama, 175, 180
Cyrano de Bergerac (Rostand), 421

Dafne, 131
Danton's Death (Buchner), 128, 420
Dark Ages (Europe), Theatre in, 99-100
Darwin, Charles, 420
Data, in the process of attention, 4
Davenant, William, 126
Dead End (Kingsley), 134
De Architectura (Vitruvius), 111
Death of a Salesman (Miller), 357, 368
Declamatory acting, 136
Dekker, Thomas, 123
Denouement, in the plot of a drama, 287
De Poetica (Aristotle), 419, 422-423, 424
Descent of Man, The (Darwin), 420
Design, 374-375
Designer, 358, 371
Desire for story, in plays for children, 411
Desire Under the Elms (O'Neill), 131, 421
Devil's Disciple, The (Shaw), 130
Dialogue, 13, 295-296, 423-424
Dianoia, 96
Diction, 204
Dilemma, 197
Dimmers, 387
Dionysus, dramatic contests at festivals of, 98
Direct conflict, 289
Directing, 425
Directing process, 350-364
Director, 137-138
        as administrator, 348
        as faculty for knowing, 350
        as inventor or creator, 349
        as scholar (critic, historian), 348
        as teacher, 348-349
Directors and producers
        Classical Greece and Rome, 131-133
        England, 1650-1750, 135-136
        Europe and America, 1750-1850, 135-136
        France and Italy, 1500-1750, 135-136
        Italian Renaissance, 135
        Middle Ages, 133-135
        Modern Theatre, 1850-present, 136-138
        Spain and England, 1200-1650, 135
Direct participation, in plays for children, 411
Dished floor, in the standard theatre, 177-178
Dishonesty, in plays for children, 409
Dissatisfaction with poor theatres, as clue to children's inattention, 405

Distancing, process of, 4, 7
  in arena staging, 166-168
  in panoramic staging, 171-175
  in proscenium staging, 168-171
  in the ideal theatre, 181-182
  in the standard theatre, 175-181
Dithyrambic chorus, 93
Doctor in Spite of Himself, The
  (Molière), 125
Door flat, 380
Double casting, 357
Double entendre, in plays for children,
  409
Downer, Alan, viii-ix
Drama, 5
  and audience stereotypes, 95-97
  and ideas, 94-97
  and theatre criticism, 424-427
  and theatre, poetics of, 422-424
  as "form and fashion," 94
  as imitation, 418-419
  definition of, 422
  in the American Revolution, 94
Dramatic actions and the actor, 426
Dramatic construct, 3, 8-10, 13, 285-
  290, 425
Dramatic contests at Festivals of Diony-
  sus in Athens, 98
Dramatic effect, poetry of, 13
Dramatic environment, 3, 14-15
Dramatic situation, in the dramatic con-
  struct, 10
Dramatic suspense, 290
Dramatis persona, relationship with the
  actor, 186-189
Dramatis personae, 3, 10-13, 193, 195,
  198-202, 204
Dramatists and their dramas, 117-131
Dramatized myths and theatre, 93
Draperies, painting on, 382-383
Dreams, implementation of, in plays, 405
Dress rehearsal, 351, 363, 425
Dressing rooms, 175, 181
Drop, 374
Drummond, Thomas, 136-137
Dryden, John, 126, 419
Due Regola della Prospettiva Pratica, Le,
  iii
Dumas, Alexandre, *fils*, 129
Dutchman, 380
Dyeing, 382-383

Ease of impersonation and role-playing,
  for children, 404
Ecclesiazusae (Aristophanes), 119-120
Eclecticism, 129, 137
Editing a drama, 354-355
Education, in plays for children, 410
Educational theatre, 138
Edward II (Marlowe), 122
Eighteenth century critics, 423

Ekkyklema, 132
Electra (Euripides), 119
Electra (Sophocles), 118
Electricity, 385-386
Electromotive force, 385
Elements of production, 425-426
Elevations, 375
Elizabeth I, 97
Ellipsoidal reflector spotlight, 385, 387
Elizabethan and Jacobean England,
  audiences in, 100-101
Elizabethan public theatres, 107-109
Emilia Galotti (Lessing), 128
Emotional climax, 288, 366, 368
Emotions, as part of the craft of acting,
  186
Encina, Juan del, 123
Endgame (Beckett), 96
Energy, from the process of attention in
  the theatrical experience, 4-5
England, 1688-1750, audiences in, 101
England, 1200-1750
  dramatists and their dramas in,
    122-123, 125-127
  playhouses in, 107-109, 115-116
England and Spain, audiences in, 26-27
Enlightenment, in plays for children, 410
Ensemble acting, 136, 356
Entremése (interlude), 124
Environment
  and heredity, laws of, 420
  dramatic, 3, 14-15
  scenery as, 372
  scenic, 8
Epic theatre, 130
Epidaurus, theatre at, 105
Epidicus (Plautus), 120
Episkenion, in Hellenistic playhouses, 105
Episode, in plotting a drama, 287
Episodes
  in Greek drama, 119
  in the dramatic construct, 8-9
Episodic presentation, in plays for chil-
  dren, 411
Eretria, theatre at, 105
Escape dramas, as plays for children,
  407
Essay on Dramatic Poesy, An (Dryden),
  419
Esthetician, critic as, 418
Etherege, George, 126
Ethical motivation, 291
Ethical sub-stratum, of a drama, 96
Eumenides (Aeschylus), 118
Eunuch (Terence), 120
Euripides, 117, 118-119
Europe and America, 1750-1850
  audiences in, 101-102
  dramatists and their drama in, 127-
    129
  playhouses in, 116

Evening with Carl Sandburg, An, 404
Everyman, 10, 95-96, 100, 138-162
Everyman (Hofsmannsthall), 421
Every Man in His Humour (Jonson),
    123
Evil, in plays for children, 410
Existence and awareness, as elements of
    theatre, 422
Existential drama, 129
Experience of plays by children, regular,
    410
Experimental Novel, The (Zola), 420
Exploitation of children by children's
    theatre, 412-413
Exposition scene, in the plot of a drama,
    287
Expressionism, 120, 373, 421
Expression of a drama, 14, 186-187
External manifestation of a character, as
    part of the craft of acting, 187

Fabula atellana, 121
Fact of life, drama as, 419
Failure to communicate in drama, 425
Fair Penitent, The (Rowe), 126
Fairy-tale drama, 122
Fancifulness, in plays for children, 407
Farce, tragic, 2
Farquhar, George, 126
Faust, I and II (Goethe), 128, 420
Faustian hero, 122
Fear, in plays for children, 400
Fergusson, Francis, viii
Ferrex and Porrex, or Gorbuduc (Sack-
    ville and Norton), 122
Fielding, Henry, 127
Fifth-century Athens, audiences in, 98
Fin de Partie, Le, (Beckett), 96
Fire laws for theatres, 177-178
Flame-proofing, 178
Flats, construction of, 378-380
Fletcher, John, 123
Flexible theatre, 116-117, 176
Floating flats, 383
Floodlight, 385, 387
Floor arrangement, in the standard
    theatre, 177-178
Floor (ground) plan, 374
Flying scenery, 383
Fly loft (fly area, flies), 175, 179
Focused setting, 172
Focusing of attention, in the theatrical
    experience, 4
Footing, 383
Forced perspective, 114
Ford, John, 123
Foreshadowing, in plays for children, 411
Forestage (apron), 115-116, 175, 180
Formal drama, 98
Formalism (of scenery), 373

Formal setting, 169, 172
Forming idea of a drama, 419
Fortune, the, 107
Foul language, in plays for children, 409
"Fourth wall," 136, 420
Frames of reference, needs, and attitudes,
    in the process of attention, 4
France and Italy, 1500-1750
    audiences in, 100-101
    dramatists and their dramas in,
        124-125
    playhouses in, 107-115
Freie Bühne, 420
French neo-classical tragedy, 125
French scene, 353
Fresnel spotlight, 385, 387
Freud, Sigmund, 424
Frogs (Aristophanes), 119
From Morn to Midnight (Kaiser), 421
Fuente Ovejuna (Lope de Vega), 124
*Funny Thing Happened on the Way to
    the Forum, A,* 170

Galileo (Brecht), 422
Game, theatre as a, 2-3, 98, 181, 404
Gammer Gurton's Needle (Mr. S.), 122
Gassner, John, 424
Gay, John, 127
Genet, Jean, 131, 422
Gestural language, 13
Gestural symbols, 294-295
Ghost Sonata, The (Strindberg), 130, 421
Given circumstances of a drama, as part
    of the craft of acting, 188
Goethe, Johann Wolfgang von, 127-128,
    135-136, 138
Gothic tales, 420
Goetz von Berlichingen (Goethe), 128
Grand drape, 179
Great critics, the, 418-424
Great God Brown, The (O'Neill), 131
Greece, Fifth-century
    audiences in, 98
    dramatists and their dramas in,
        117-120
    playhouses in, 103-104
    playmaking in, 131-132
Greene, Robert, 122
Greenroom, 175, 181
Grein, J. G., 420
Gridiron (of a theatre), 175, 179
Gropius, Walter, 117
Ground cloth, 170
Ground (floor) plan, 374
Ground row (profile), 380
Grouping, 356, 365-368, 426
Growth or change in *dramatis personae,*
    291
Grumbler, The, 120
Gymnatorium, 181

Hair (Ragni, Rado, and MacDermot), vii, 190
Hamburgische Dramaturgie (Lessing), 419-420
Hamlet (Shakespeare), 15, 290
Hand properties, 393
Happenings, vii, 131
Hartke, The Reverend Gilbert V., O. P., viii
Haunted House, The (Plautus), 120
Hauptmann, Gerhart, 420-421
Headblock, 179
Hearing, in the standard theatre, 177-178
Hebbel, Friedrich, 128-129
Hecuba (Euripides), 119
Heidi (Spyri), 406
Helen (Euripides), 119
Hellenistic theatre, 99, 104-105
Henri IV (Pirandello), 130
Heracles (Euripides), 119
Hercules on Oeta (Seneca), 131
Heredity and environment, laws of, 420
Hernani (Hugo), 129, 420
Heroic drama, 126
Heywood, Thomas, 123
Hippolytus (Euripides), 118
Historian, critic as, 418
Historical accuracy in dramatic productions, 136
Historical *vs.* topical approach to theatre history, 93-94
History of critics, 418-422
Histrionic capability, as a characteristic of an actor, 185
Histrionic urge, as a characteristic of an actor, 184
Hitchcock, Alfred, 352
Hofmannsthall, Hugo von, 421
Homogeneous maturation groups, in children, 406
Hôpital de la Trinité, 110
Horace (Quintus Horatius Flaccus), 419, 423
Horace (Corneille), 125
Horatio Alger hero, 129
Hôtel de Bourgogne, 110
Hot plotline, in plays for children, 405
House manager, 401-402
How a play means, criticism of, 427
Huckleberry Finn (Twain), 168, 412
Hue (of a color), 381
Hugo, Victor, 129, 419-420
Humours, comedy of, 123
Human behavior patterns, as an element in a play, 11
Hunchback of Notre Dame, The (Hugo), 420
"Hundred-Acre Wood," 408

Ibsen, Henrik, 129-130, 138, 420
Idea, central, in the dramatic construct, 9

Idea of a theatre, 93
Ideal playhouse, 181-182
Ideas in a drama, 96, 426
Ideational climax, 288, 366, 368
Identification, process of, 4, 6
    in arena staging, 166-168
    in panoramic staging, 171-175
    in proscenium staging, 168-171
    in the ideal theatre, 181-182
    in the standard theatre, 175-181
Iffland, August Wilhelm, 127-128
Ignoble redskin, 129
Illumination (as goal of lighting), 384
Illusionism, 421
Illusion of ideal beauty, 136
Illusion of reality, 136
Image of the world, theatre as, 2
Imagery, 13, 295-297
Imaginary Invalid, The (Molière), 125
Imaginary puissance, 2
Imagination, as a characteristic of an actor, 185
Imitation of action, drama as, 422-423
Imitation, process of, 4, 7
    in arena staging, 166-168
    in panoramic staging, 171-175
    in proscenium staging, 168-171
    in the ideal theatre, 191-192
    in the standard theatre, 175-191
Immediate sensory and imaginative experience, in plays for children, 405
Impact of action, for children, 404
Impersonation, process of, 4-6
    in arena staging, 166-168
    in panoramic staging, 171-175
    in proscenium staging, 168-171
    in the ideal theatre, 181-182
    in the standard theatre, 175-181
Impersonation *vs.* conflict, in plays for children, 405
Impressionism (as a characteristic of scenery), 373
Incantatory, theatre as, 421
Incidents
    in plotting a drama, 287
    in the dramatic construct, 8
Inciting incident, 287-288
Independent Theatre, 420
India, audiences in, 102
Individual differences in children's preferences, 406
Individual, in the theatrical experience, 4
Informal drama, 98, 413, 415-416
Inner below, 108, 190
Inner goals of a character, as part of the craft of acting, 187
Inner thoughts, as the language of a drama, 295
Intellectual sub-stratum of a drama, 96
Intensity (of lighting), 381

Intensity of concentration, as part of the craft of acting, 189
Intention, as part of the craft of acting, 186
Interaction among players, in dramatic criticism, 426
Interludes, 122
Internal conflicts of the spectator, as an element of theatre, 422
Intermezzo (intermezzi), 121-122
Interpretation
    in the dramatic construct, 9
    of language, 356, 368-370
    of the expression of a drama, 186-187
Involvement in a drama, 7, 166, 412
Ion (Euripides), 119
Ionesco, Eugene, 131, 422
Iphigenia in Aulis (Euripides), 119
Iphigenia in Tauris (Euripides), 119
Iphigénie (Racine), 125
Irving, Henry, 137
Isometric projection, 375
Italianate stage (staging), 126, 135
Italian Renaissance
    audiences in, 100-101
    dramatists and their dramas in, 121-122
    playhouses in, 110-111
Italy, 1500-1750, playhouses in, 111-115
Izenour, George, 387

Jacobean audience, 101
Jacobean public theatres, 107-109
James I, 97
Japan
    audiences in, 102-103
    playhouses in, 117
Jarry, Alfred, 422
Johnson, Samuel, x, 3
Jones, Inigo, 115-116
Jones, James Earl, 426
Jonson, Ben, 122-123, 419
Jullien, Jean, 420
Jungle Books, The (Kipling), 410
Juvarra, Filippo, 135

Kabuki, 102-103
Kaiser, Georg, 421
Kathakali, 102
Kemble, John Philip, 136
Key word, in interpretation of language in a drama, 369
Killing of Sister George, The (Marcus), 96
King Lear (Shakespeare), 96
King, Richard Corey, ix
Kingsley, Sidney, 134
Kipling, Rudyard, 408
Knights (Aristophanes), 119

Knowledge brought to a play by children, 405
Kommos, 119-120
Kotzebue, August Friedrich von, 127-128, 420
Kyd, Thomas, 122

Lamps (for lighting instruments), 385, 387
"Land of Counterpane, The" (Stevenson), 6-7
Language, 3, 13-14, 285, 294-298, 421, 423, 425-426
Lashing (of scenery), 383
Latin comedy, 121
Laugh-In, vii, 190
"Law of the Jungle," 408
Lazzo (lazzi), 121
Lenaia, 98
Length of plays for children, 411
Leonce and Lena (Buchner), 128
Lessing, Gotthold Ephraim, 127-128, 419-420
liaison, 125
Libation Bearers (Aeschylus), 118
Licensing Act of 1737, 127
Life and vitality of *dramatis personae*, 292
Life in action, in the dramatic construct, 8
Life Is a Dream (Calderón), 124
Life, theatre as, viii
Light board, 387-388
Light crew, 401
Lighting, 137, 371, 383-388
Lighting control board, 175-180
Lights, in dramatic criticism, 426
Lillo, George, 127
Limelight, 137
Limitations of Science, The (Sullivan), 6n
Linnebach projector, 388
Liturgical drama, 122
Loading facilities, 175, 180-181
Lobby area, 175
Loi du Théâtre, Le (Brunetiére), 423
London Merchant, The (Lillo), 127
Long Day's Journey into Night, A (O'Neill), 131
Love for Love (Congreve), 126
Lyly, John, 122
Lyon, Milton, viii
Lysistrata (Aristophanes), 119

Machiavellian hero, 122
Mad Hercules, The (Seneca), 121
Maeterlinck, Maurice, 421
Magic, as an element of theatre, 407, 422
Magic circle, in acting, 183
Magnitude of drama, 423
Maid of Orleans, The (Schiller), 128

Major Barbara (Shaw), 10, 95, 130, 168, 290-292, 350-352, 354, 359-361, 371, 396-400, 403
Make-up, 371, 391, 426
Make-up crew, 402
Man and Superman (Shaw), 130
Man and the Masses (Toller), 421
Man of Mode, The (Etherege), 126
Mansion, 106-107, 110, 134
Manual for Constructing Theatrical Scenes and Machines (Sabbatini), 114
Maria Magdalena (Hebbel), 128-129
Mark Twain's The Adventures of Tom Sawyer (Culp), 14, 288, 299-345, 350-354, 368, 371, 392-393, 403-404, 412
Marlowe, Christopher, 14, 122
Marriage á La Mode (Dryden), 126
Marston, John, 123
Marx Brothers movie, as analog for *Othello*, 190
Mary Stuart (Schiller), 128
Masks of the drama, 11, 131-133
Massinger, Philip, 123
Mastery of the world, in plays for children, 405
Matrix of cause and effect, 288, 407, 411
Maturation, effect of, on children's preferences in drama, 406-408
McCalmon, George A., viii
Meaning, in the process of attention, 4
Mechane, 132
Medea (Euripides), 118
Medea (Seneca), 121
Medieval romances, 420
Melancholia, Elizabethan idea of, 2
Melodrama, popularity of, among adolescents and adults, 407
Menaechmi, The (Plautus), 120
Menander, 95, 120
Merchant, The (Plautus), 120
Metaphor, theatre as, 2
Middle Ages
    audiences in, 99-100
    dramatists and their dramas in, 121
    playhouses in, 106-107
Middleton, Thomas, 123
Miles, Nell, viii
Milieu, scenery as, 372
Milne, A. A., 408
Mimes in Greece, 98
Mimesis, as part of the craft of acting, 189
Minturno, Antonio Sebastian, 419
Minna von Barnhelm (Lessing), 128
Mirror up to nature, in the dramatic construct, 9
Misanthrope, The (Moliere), 125

Miser, The (Moliere), 125
Miss Julie (Strindberg), 130
Miss Sara Sampson (Lessing), 128
Mithridate (Racine), 125
Mixed media, vii
Mixing pigment, 382
Modern Theatre, 1850-Present
    audiences in, 28
    dramatists and their dramas in, 129-131
    playhouses in, 116-117
Moliere (Jean-Baptiste Poquelin), vii, 97, 125, 138
Molina, Tirso de, 124
Momentum in directing a play, 351, 356, 369
Montfleury (Zacharie Jacob), 135
Moon Is Blue, The (Herbert), 409
Morality plays, 121
Mostel, Zero, 170
Mother Courage and Her Children (Brecht), 130, 422
Mother-in-Law (Terence), 120
Motivation in drama, 11, 201
Mountebank, as opposed to player, 186
Mourning Becomes Electra (O'Neill), 131
Movement in directing, 356, 365-368
Movements,
    in dramatic criticism, 426
    in modern drama, 421
Multiple staging, 172
Music in a drama, 14, 268-269, 426
Mystery plays, 121
Myth as an element of theatre, 19, 98, 421

Naharro, Bartolomé de Torres, 423
Narrational plot, 288
Narrative, relation to drama, 423
Narrative suspense, 290
Narrative *vs.* drama, in plays for children, 405
Narrator, 287
Nathan the Wise (Lessing), 128
Natural light simulation, 384
Naturalism, 129, 372, 420-421
Naturalism in the Theatre (Zola), 420
Needs, attitudes, and frames of reference, in the process of attention, 4
Neo-classicism, 127-128
    critics, 419
    ideals of drama, 125
    tragedy, 125-126
Neoromanticism, 421
Noble redskin, 129
Noh, 102
Nonverbal, theatre as, 422
Norton, Thomas, 122

Obligatory scene, 354
Odes, in Greek drama, 119
Oedipus (Seneca), 121
Oedipus at Colonnus (Sophocles), 118
Oedipus Tyrannus (*Oedipus Rex, Oedipus the King*), 2, 96, 98, 118, 174, 425
Oh! Calcutta!, vii
Ohm's Law, 386
Old Greek Comedy, 98
Olivier, Laurence, 426
O'Neill, Eugene, 130-131, 421
Onkos, 132
Opening, in the plot of a drama, 287
Opera, 121-122
Opposite prompt (O. P.), 180
Oral language, 13, 296
Orchestra, 103, 105
Orchestra pit, 175, 180
Oresteia (Aeschylus), 94, 118
Orestes (Euripides), 119
Oriental Theatre, 1400-1950
  audiences in, 102-103
  playhouses in, 117
Origin of Species, The (Darwin), 420
Orpheus (Cocteau), 421
Orthographic projection, 375
Othello, The Tragedy of (Shakespeare), 2-3, 7-8, 10, 12-15, 95, 173, 188, 190-283, 290, 292, 350-352, 365, 371, 391-393, 403-405, 407-408, 423
Otway, Thomas, 126
Outlook, scientific, 420
Overhead borders in Italian theatres, 114

Pacing (tempo), 356
Pageant wagons, 133
Painting scenery, process of, 381-383
Palladio, Andrea, 114, 116
Pamelia, Dorothy, 299, 351
Panoramic staging, 172-175
Panoramic theatre, 181
Parabasis, 120
Parados, (*paradoi*), 103, 119
Paraskenion (*paraskenia*), 105
Parigi, Giulio, 116
Participation by audience, in plays for children, 411
Participation, theatre of, vii
Pastoral drama, 111, 122
Patio, 110
Patterning visual, aural, verbal, and personal stimuli, 365
Patterns of imagery, 13
Pause, as a tool of the director, 369
Peace (Aristophanes), 119
Peer Gynt (Ibsen), 129-131
Pélleas et Mélisande (Maeterlinck), 421
People in a drama, 290

"People like us," as a factor in plays for children, 408
People worse than average, in comedy, 424
Perception, in the process of attention, 4
Performance, 6
Performance time
  in Elizabethan and Jacobean England, 109
  in Golden Age Spain, 110
Periaktos (*periaktoi*), 111, 132-133
Periods of theatre, 97
Persecution and Assassination of Jean-Paul Marat as Performed by the Inmates of the Asylum of Charenton Under the Direction of the Marquis de Sade, The (Weiss), vii, 131
Persians (Aeschylus), 118
Persian, The (Plautus), 120
Persona, 10-13, 291, 426
Persons better than average, in tragedy, 424
Perspective painting, in Italian theatres, 111, 114
Perspective scenery, 134-135, 165, 374
Persuasion through drama, 94-97
Peter Pan (Barrie), 394, 406
Phaedra (Seneca), 121
Phèdre (Racine), 125
Philoctetes (Sophocles), 118
Phoenician Women (Euripides), 119
Phoenician Women, The (Seneca), 121
Phoenix, the, 109
Phormio (Terence), 120
"Photoflashes in the darkness," theatre as, 97
Physical actions, as part of the craft of acting, 187
Pictorial language, 13
Picture-frame stage, 117, 135
Pigment, 382
Pin connector, 388
Pinakes, 132
Pinrail, 175, 179-180
Pirandello, Luigi, 130-131
Piranesi, Gian Battista, 135
Pity and fear, in tragedy, 424
Place, 106
Place, unity of, 419
Plain Dealer, The (Wycherley), 126
Platforms, 381
Plato as critic, 418-419
Plautus, 95, 99, 120-121
Plays for children, strictures about, 412
Play, the, 6
Playacting, 5
Player, as opposed to mountebank, 186
Players, company of, 2
Playhouses then and now, 103-117

Playmaking (Archer), 423
Playmaking through the ages, 131-138
Playscript as literature, 425
Playwrights and playwriting, 5, 121, 285-299
Plot, 10, 285, 287-290, 423
Plotline, in plays for children, 405
Plotting, criticism of, 426-427
Plutus (Aristophanes), 120
Poetics (Aristotle), viii, 7, 14, 422
Poetics (Castelvetro), 419
Poetics (Scaliger), 419
Poetics of drama and theatre, 422-424
Poetry, 13, 295
Poetry of the theatre, 13-14
Polishing rehearsal, 351, 362-363
Pollyanna (Porter), 410
Poquelin, Jean-Baptiste (Molière), vii, 125, 138
Positive Philosophy (Comte), 420
Positive Polity (Comte), 420
Pot of Gold (Plautus), 120
Preconceptions, in the process of attention, 4
Preface to Cromwell (Hugo), 419-420
Preface to Tèrèse Raquin (Zola), 420
Preference for theatre, children's, 404-408
Preferences in drama, children's, 406-408
Pre-logical, theatre as, 422
Pre-rehearsal, 351-356
Presence, as a characteristic of an actor, 185
Presentational acting, 135
Price, William T., 423
Primary colors (light), 388
Primary colors (pigment), 381
Primitive rituals and theatre, 93
Principles governing theatre for children, 410-413
Principles of design, 375
Private theatres in Elizabethan and Jacobean England, 109
Prizes in Athens for tragedy and comedy, 98
Probability, sense of, in plays for children, 408
Problems of criticism, 417-418
Process in action, as drama, 422-423
Producer, 347
Production, 6
Production budget, 476
Production, live, importance to criticism, 425
Production staff, 355-356, 358-359, 395
Production team, 394
Profile (ground row), 380
Progression of incidents, 289
Projection, as a characteristic of an actor, 185
Projection of scenery, 117, 388

Projection, process of, 4, 6
  in arena staging, 166-168
  in panoramic staging, 171-175
  in proscenium staging, 168-171
  in the ideal theatre, 181-182
  in the standard theatre, 175-181
Prologue, in Greek drama, 119-120
Prometheus Bound (Aeschylus), 118
Prompt side, 170
Propaganda in drama, 94-97
Properties, 371, 392
Properties crew, 401
Properties, in dramatic criticism, 426
Proposition, in drama, 423
Proscenium arch and opening, 175, 179
Proscenium arch in Italian theatres, 114
Proscenium staging, 168-171
Proscenium theatre, 181
Prose, 295
Proskenion (*proskenia*), 105
Protagonist, 290
Protagonist makes things happen, as a type of children's play, 406
Pseudolus (Plautus), 120
Psychological motivation, 291
Psychological processes, in theatre games, 3
Psychological reality (unreality) of *dramatis personae,* 11
Public theatres in Italy, 114-115
Purchasing for a production, 378
Purge of emotions, as an attribute of drama, 419
Purpose
  as part of the craft of acting, 186
  in the dramatic construct, 9
  of criticism, 417

Racine, Jean, 97, 125
Raissoneur, 11, 287
Raked floor, in the standard theatre, 177-178
Ralph Roister Doister (Udall), 122
Rationale, in the dramatic construct, 9
Rationalization, process of, 4, 6
  in arena staging, 166-168
  in panoramic staging, 171-175
  in proscenium staging, 168-171
  in the ideal theatre, 181-182
  in the standard theatre, 175-181
Reading rehearsal, 351, 362
Realism, 11, 129-130, 372, 407, 420
Realism, selective, 421
Reality of onstage world, for children, 404
Recognition scene, 287
Recruiting Officer, The (Farquhar), 126
Régisseur, 347
Rehearsal, 351
Rehearsal room, 175, 181

Relaxation, as part of the craft of acting, 189

Renaissance,
  audiences in, 100-101
  critics in, 423

Renderings (sketches), 374-375

Renshaw, Edyth, viii

Representational acting, 135

Restoration comedy, 126

Revelation of character traits, 291

Reversal, 289

Revision, 355

Revolution, tales of, 420

Revolving stages, 180

Revue plot, 288

Rheostat, 386-387

Rhetoric (Aristotle), viii

Rhythm in drama, 14, 296, 356, 424

Ribaldry, in plays for children, 409

Rigging loft (fly loft, fly area, flies), 175, 179

Rip Van Winkle character, 129

Rising action, in the plot of a drama, 388

Robertson, Willy, viii

Robin Hood, 406

Role-playing, 5, 184

Romance, in plays for children, 407

Romanticism, 127, 420
  critics, 420
  drama, 128-129, 420

Rome
  audiences in, 99
  dramatists and their dramas in, 120-121
  playhouses in, 105

Romeo and Juliet (Shakespeare), 423

Rooney, Mickey, 170

Rope (Plautus), 120

Rostand, Edmond, 421

Rowe, Nicholas, 126

Rowley, William, 123

Rueda, Lope de, 123-124

Running scenery, 383

Rural Dionysia, 98

Sabbatini, Nicola, 114, 116

Sackville, Thomas, 122

Safety in the standard theatre, 178

Sainete (short farce), 124

Saint Joan (Shaw), 130

Salisbury Court Theatre, 109

San Cassiano Theatre, 115

Sardou, Victorien, 129

Saxe-Meinengen, Duchy of, 136-138

Scaenae frons, 105, 133

Scale model, 374-375

Scaliger, Julius Caesar, 419

Scamozzi, Vincenzo, 114, 116

Scene changes in Italian theatres, 114

Scene dock, 175, 170

Scenehouse, 103

Scene, in plotting a drama, 287

Scenery and scenic practices, 14-15, 371-383
  Classical Greece and Rome, 131-133
  England, 1650-1750, 135-136
  Europe and America, 1750-1850, 135-136
  France and Italy, 1500-1750, 135-136
  Italian Renaissance, 135
  Middle Ages, 133-135
  Modern Theatre, 1850-Present, 136-138
  Spain and England, 1200-1650, 135

Scenery as actor, 374

Scenery crew, 400-401

Scenic environment, 8, 285, 298, 425-426

Schiller, Friedrich, 127-128

School for Wives, The (Molière), 125

Science, as important to drama, 420

Scribe, Eugène, 129

Scrim, 381

Season, choosing a, 351-352

Seating arrangements in the standard theatre, 176-177

Secondary colors (light), 388

Secondary colors (pigment), 381

Second Shepherd's Play, The, 100

Sejanus (Jonson), 123

Selective realism/naturalism, 372-373, 421

Self-Tormentor (Terence), 120

Seneca, Lucius Anneaus, 99, 120-122

Sense of probability, in plays for children, 408

Sentimental comedy and tragedy, 123, 126-127

Separation of tragedy from comedy, 419

Sequential conflict, 289

Serious problems, in plays for children, 409-410

Serlio, Sebastiano, 111, 116, 134

Set pieces (rocks, trees, columns, chimneys, etc.), 381

Set (scene) properties, 393

Sets, in dramatic criticism, 426

Set speech, 295

Seven Against Thebes (Aeschylus), 118

Seventeenth century critics, 423

Shade (lighting), 384

Shadow (lighting), 384

Shadwell, Thomas, 126

Shakespeare, William, vii, 2, 14, 122, 138, 420, 424

Shakepearean Tragedy (Bradley), 424

Shakespearean tragedy, *Othello* as, 190-191

Shakespeare's Imagery, and What It Tells Us (Spurgeon), 424
Shaw, George Bernard, 14, 96, 130-131, 138
Sheave, 179
Sheepwell, The (Lope de Vega), 124
Shirley, James, 123
Shop in a theatre, 175, 180, 378
Short View of the Immorality and Profaneness of the English Stage, A (Collier), 126
Sidney, Sir Philip, 419
Siege of Rhodes, The, 126
Sight lines, in the standard theatre, 177-178
Silence, as a tool of the director, 369
Silhouette, 388-389
Simple plot, 288-289
Simultaneous communication to all age groups, in plays for children, 410-411
Simultaneous setting, 172
Simultaneous staging, 106
Siparium, 105
Situation, in the dramatic construct, 10, 285, 290
Six Characters in Search of an Author (Pirandello), 130
Sizing flats, 380, 382
Skene, 103, 105
Sketches (renderings), 374-375
Sky dome (cyclorama), 175, 180
Slice of life, 420
Social differences in children's preferences, 406
Socially-useful purpose as an attribute of drama, 429
Soliloquy, 304
Sophocles, vii, 117, 179
Sorrow, in plays for children, 410
Sound control board, 175, 180
Sound effects, 369, 371, 393, 426
Spain, 1500-1700
    dramatists and their dramas in, 123-124
    playhouses in, 109-110
Spain and England, 1200-1650
    audiences in, 100-101
    dramatists and their dramas in, 122-124
    playhouses in, 107-110
Spain, Golden Age, 97
Spanish Tragedy, The (Kyd), 122
Special effects, 371, 393, 426
Spectacle, 15, 134, 423-424
Spectator and illusion, 421
Speech as action, 369
Spine of a drama, as part of the craft of acting, 186

Spoken thoughts, as the language of a drama, 295
Spurgeon, Caroline, 424
Staatliches Bauhaus, 117
Stadium slope, 178
Stage brace, 383
Stage floor, 175, 178-180
Stagehouse in Roman theatres, 105, 178-180
Stage in Hellenistic playhouses, 105
Stage manager, 180, 359, 395-402
Stage presence, as a characteristic of an actor, 185
Stageworthiness of *dramatis personae,* 291-292
Staging, 421
Standards of excellence in dramatic criticism, 427
Standard theatre, the, 175-181
Stasima, 119
Steele, Richard, 126
Step units, 381
Stereotypes as *dramatis personae,* 11, 12
Stereotypes of the audience, drama and, 95-97
Stevenson, Robert Louis, 6
Stewart, George E., 299, 351
Stichus (Plautus), 120
Stock character, 11-12, 121
Story, in dramas, 9, 285, 288-290, 405, 407, 411
Storyless presentation, in plays for children, 411
Storyline, 421
Storytelling, as drama, 423-424
Strange Interlude (O'Neill), 131
Streetcar Named Desire, A (Williams), 290, 372
Strindberg, August, 130-131, 420-421
Strophe (antistrophe), 119
Sturm und Drang ("Storm and Stress"), 128
Stylization of scenery, 373
Stylized realism (scenery), 373
Sullivan, J. W. N., 6n
Sunken Bell, The (Hauptmann), 421
Suppliants (Aeschylus), 118
Suppliants (Euripides), 119
Surface actuality in plays for children, 407
Surrealism, 421
Suspense, 289
Syllogism, 423
Symbolic realism or naturalism, of scenery, 372-373
Symbolic reinforcement, scenery as, 372-373
Symbol system, 13
Symbol, theatre as, viii
Symbolism, 421

Tableau curtain, 179
Tamburlaine I and II (Marlowe), 122
Tartuffe (Moliere), 125
Tarzan of the Apes (Burroughs), 406
Teach and delight, as goals of drama, 419
Teahouse of the August Moon (Patrick), 393
Teaser curtain strips (teaser curtains), 175, 179
Teatro cuerpo (theatre of corpse), 124
Teatro Farnese, 114
Teatro Olimpico, 114
Teatro ruido (theatre of noise), 124
Technical crews, 394-402
Technical direction, 375-402
Technical director, 358
Technical rehearsal, 351, 364
Technical schedule, 376-378
Technical units, in the plot of a drama, 287
Tempest, The (Shadwell), 126
Tempo (pacing), 356
Terence (Publius Terentius Afer), 107, 120-121
Texture of costumes and make-up, 388, 390
Texturing paint, 382-383
Theatre as "form and pressure," 98
Theatre as game, 181
Theatre, drama and, criticism, 424-427
Theatre experience, elements in, 3
Theatre for children, 408-413
Theatre '48 (Dallas, Texas), 166
Theatre games, 3, 98, 404
Theatre Libre, 420
Theatre of the absurd, 131, 422
Theatres of the world, 97-141
Theatre, the standard, 175-181
Theatrical communion, 422
Theatrical realism, 131, 134
Theatrical scenery, 372-373
Theatrical setting, 169
"Theatrum," 107
Thesis dramas, 129-130, 420
Thesmophoriazusae (Aristophanes), 119
Thespis, vii
Things happen to the protagonist, as a type of children's play, 406
Thought group, 369
Thought in drama, 296, 423-424
Thousand Clowns, A (Gardner), 292, 351, 358, 393
Threefold of flats, 380
Threepenny Opera, The (Brecht), 422
Thrills and spills, in plays for children, 407
Through line of action, as part of the craft of acting, 186
Thrust stage, 116-117

Thyestes (Seneca), 121
Thymele, 103
Thyromata, 105
Timber: or, Discoveries (Jonson), 419
Time, as a factor in *Othello*, 191
Time, unity of, 419
Timeworthiness of *dramatis personae*, 292
Toller, Ernst, 421
Tom Thumb, or the Tragedy of Tragedies (Fielding), 127
Topical *vs.* historical approach to theatre history, 93-94
Tormentor curtain strips (tormentor curtains), 175, 179
Total theatre, 131, 134, 421
Tourneur, Cyril, 123
Trachiniae (Sophocles), 118
Tragedy, 2, 98-99, 111, 419, 423-424
Tragedy of Jane Shore, The (Rowe), 126
Tragedy: Vision and Form (Corrigan, ed), 424
Tragical History of Doctor Faustus, The (Marlowe), 122
Tragic farce, 2, 190
Trained instrument, as a characteristic of an actor, 185
Transfiguration (Toller), 421
Transition scene, in the plot of a drama, 287
Trapdoors (traps), 175, 180
Treatment, playwright's, 425
Trim properties, 393
Trinummus (Plautus), 120
Trojan Women, The (Euripides), 94, 119
Trojan Women, The (Seneca), 121
Truculentus (Plautus), 120
Twist-lock connector, 388
Twofold of flats, 380
Types, as necessary to drama, 419
Tzara, Tristan, 421

Ubu Roi (Jarry), 422
Udall, Nicholas, 122
Understudies, 357-358
Unities of time, place, action, 419
Units, in the plot of a drama
Universal, the, in drama, 423
Unreality of *dramatis personae*, 11
Utopia, as a factor in plays for children, 408

Value (color), 381
Value system, in a drama, 96
Vega Carpia, Lope Félix de, 124
Venice Preserv'd (Otway), 126
Verbal dexterity and word play, children's preference for, 406-407
Verbal images or symbols, 8
Verbal language, 13

Verbal stimuli, 365, 369-370
Verbal symbols, 294-295
Verfremdungseffekt, 422
Verisimilitude, as necessary for drama, 419
Verse, as necessary for tragedy, 419
Vidularia (Plautus), 120
Village farces in Greece, 98, 121
Vincente, Gil, 123
Visual images or symbols, 8
Visual stimuli, patterning by a director, 365-368
Vitruvius, 111, 141
Vocal symbols, 294-295
Volpone (Jonson), 123
Volt, 385
Vulgarity, in plays for children, 409

Wagner, Richard, 137
Wagons for Medieval drama, 107
Wagons, stage, 180, 383
Waiting for Godot (Beckett), 12, 96, 422
Wallis, J. M., ix
Warm (cool) colors, 384
Wasps (Aristophanes), 119
Watt, 385
Way of the World, The (Congreve), 126
Webster, John, 123
Weimar Theatre, 128, 135-136, 138
Weiss, David, ix
Weiss, Peter, 131
Well-known stories, in plays for children, 411
Well-made play, 129, 420

Western hero, 129
What a play means, criticism of, 427
Whitefriars Theatre, 109
Wilhelm Tell (Schiller), 128
Willful choice, in the theatrical experience, 4
Willful focusing of attention, in the theatrical experience, 5
Willingness to play, children's, 404
Wills, struggle of, in drama, 423
Window flat, 380
Wing-and-drop scenery, 373-374
Wing scenery, 374
Wings, 111, 114
Wisecracking city boy, 129
Wit and the Unconscious (Freud), 424
"Wooden O, Shakespeare's," 135
Word play and verbal dexterity, children's preference for, 406-407
Words as action, appeal to children, 404-405
Workability of *dramatis personae*, 12
Working drawings, 375
World as nightmare to children, 405
World Theatres, 97-138
Would-Be Gentleman, The (Moliére), 125
Woyzeck (Buchner), 128
Wycherley, William, 126

Yankee character, 129
"Yes, Sir, That's My Baby," 368
You Can't Take It With You (Kaufman and Hart), 393

Zola, Émile, 420